ECONOMIC POLICY IN THEORY AND PRACTICE

Also by Assaf Razin

A THEORY OF INTERNATIONAL TRADE UNDER UNCERTAINTY (*with Elhanan Helpman*)

Also by Assaf Razin and Efraim Sadka

HOUSEHOLD AND ECONOMY: Welfare Economics of Endogenous Fertility (*with Marc Nerlove*)

Economic Policy in Theory and Practice

Edited by

Assaf Razin
Professor of Economics
Tel Aviv University

and

Efraim Sadka
Professor of Economics
Tel Aviv University

MACMILLAN
PRESS

First published 1987

Published by
THE MACMILLAN PRESS LTD
Houndmills, Basingstoke, Hampshire RG21 2XS
and London
Companies and representatives
throughout the world

Printed in Hong Kong

British Library Cataloguing in Publication Data
Economic policy in theory and practice:
essays in memory of Abba P. Lerner.
1. Economic policy
I. Razin, Assaf II. Sadka, Efrain
III. Lerner, Abba P.
330.9 HD87
ISBN 0–333–39259–0

Dedicated to the memory of
ABBA P. LERNER

Contents

Preface

Economic policy has been and will be a focus of interest for economists, in academia, in government, and in the private sector. In May 1984, the Pinhas Sapir Center for Development at Tel Aviv University sponsored a conference on economic policy in theory and practice in memory of Abba P. Lerner (1903–82). Abba Lerner had been deeply concerned with the development of economic theory and the formulation of economic policy in light of the theory. This volume contains the proceedings of this conference.

This conference is the third in a series of international conferences of the Pinhas Sapir Center for Development.[1] The centre is concerned with all aspects of development. Pinhas Sapir, Israel's seventh Minister of Trade and Industry (1955–63) and third Minister of Finance (1963–74), had been deeply concerned about development in Israel and contributed greatly to it.

The book puts together fourteen papers presented at the Pinhas Sapir Conference in memory of Abba Lerner, held at Tel Aviv University in May 1984. The papers cover a wide range of issues related to economic policy: public debt, budget deficits and inflation, world debt problems, resource allocation and taxation, efficiency of various forms of market organisation, and a positive theory of the state. The contributors of the papers are: Alan Auerbach, Eitan Berglas, Willem Buiter, Rudiger Dornbusch, Ronald Findlay, Stanley Fischer, Jacob Frenkel, David Fresko, Sanford Grossman, Oliver Hart, Zvi Hercowitz, Daniel Kovenock, Anne O. Krueger, Franco Modigliani, David Pines, Assaf Razin, Michael Rothschild, Efraim Sadka, Thomas Sargent, Neil Wallace, Yoram Weiss, Robert Willig and John Wilson.

We would like to thank Mali Nudel and Rina Elman of the Sapir Center who ran the office and co-ordinated the conference activities.

Note

1. The first conference, held in June 1979, was: 'Development in an Inflationary World'. The proceedings were published in M. June Flanders and Assaf Razin (eds), *Development in an Inflationary World* (Academic Press: New York, 1981). The second conference, held in

December 1980, was: 'Social Policy Evaluation: Health, Education and Welfare'. The proceedings were published in: (1) Elhanan Helpman, Assaf Razin and Efraim Sadka (eds), *Social Policy Evaluation: An Economic Perspective* (Academic Press: New York, 1983). (2) Shimon Spiro and Ephraim Yuchtman-Yaar (eds), *Evaluating the Welfare State: Social and Political Perspectives* (Academic Press: New York, 1983).

List of the Participants

Alan Auerbach, Department of Economics, University of Pennsylvania, USA

Haim Ben-Shahar, Department of Economics, Tel Aviv University, Israel

Eitan Berglas, Department of Economics, Tel Aviv University, Israel

Avishay Braverman, The World Bank, Washington, DC, USA

Dagobert Brito, Department of Economics, Rice University, USA

Michael Bruno, Department of Economics, The Hebrew University, Israel

Willem Buiter, London School of Economics and Political Science, London, UK

Alex Cukierman, Department of Economics, Tel Aviv University, Israel

Rudiger Dornbusch, Department of Economics, Massachusetts Institute of Technology, USA

Zvi Eckstein, Department of Economics, Tel Aviv University, Israel

Rafael Eldor, Department of Economics, Tel Aviv University, Israel

Ronald Findlay, Department of Economics, Columbia University, New York, USA

Stanley Fischer, Department of Economics, Massachusetts Institute of Technology, USA

June Flanders, Department of Economics, Tel Aviv University, Israel

Jacob A. Frenkel, Department of Economics, University of Chicago, USA

David Fresko, Department of Economics, Tel Aviv University, Israel

Sanford Grossman, Department of Economics, Princeton University, USA

Oliver Hart, Department of Economics, Massachusetts Institute of Technology, USA

Zvi Hercowitz, Department of Economics, Tel Aviv University, Israel

Dan Kovenock, Department of Economics, Purdue University, USA

Anne O. Krueger, The World Bank, Washington, DC, USA

Franco Modigliani, Department of Economics, Massachusetts Institute of Technology, USA

David Pines, Department of Economics, Tel Aviv University, Israel

Assaf Razin, Department of Economics, Tel Aviv University, Israel

Michael Rothschild, Department of Economics, University of California at San Diego, USA

Efraim Sadka, Department of Economics, Tel Aviv University, Israel

Thomas Sargent, Department of Economics, University of Minnesota, USA

Abba Schwartz, Department of Economics, Tel Aviv University, Israel

Eytan Sheshinski, Department of Economics, The Hebrew University, Israel

Yair Tauman, Faculty of Management, Tel Aviv University, Israel

Neil Wallace, Department of Economics, University of Minnesota, USA

Yoram Weiss, Department of Economics, Tel Aviv University, Israel

Robert Willig, Department of Economics, Princeton University, USA

Charles Wilson, Department of Economics, New York University, USA

John Wilson, Department of Economics, Indiana University, USA

On Abba Lerner

Haim Ben-Shahar

Abba Lerner ranks with the great economists of the twentieth century. His comprehensive contributions to modern economics in a variety of fields were so basic that they seem to have become a common economic knowledge which has lost the identification of their origin.

It was Lerner who introduced the concept of 'functional finance', and who first raised the dilemma between high unemployment and price stability. It was Lerner who brought up the basic differentiation between demand inflation and administrative inflation and who introduced the idea that monopoly position is a relative concept that can be measured by the relative difference between price and marginal cost. It was Lerner who laid the foundations for the modern theory of capital, and in the field of international economics left us the first proof of the rules on complete equalisation of factor prices by free trade in products. And it was Lerner who first showed that import and export duties had exactly equal influence. Lerner was apparently also the first to look for the factors and conditions required for an optimum currency area. A detailed and comprehensive account of Lerner's works was recently reviewed by Tibor Schitovsky in 'Lerner's Contributions to Economics', *Journal of Economic Literature* (Dec. 1984) pp. 1547–71.

Lerner's major preoccupation, however, was an heroic attempt to merge economic theory with social objectives, on which he expanded in his most famous book, *The Economics of Control*, that was based on the theory which he developed together with Oscar Lange on market pricing in socialist economies. This was also connected to the Lerner and Hotelling condition that marginal cost pricing is a universal welfare maximising rule. In this respect, Lerner developed the concept of economic efficiency to its ultimate ideal, as a pure and abstract idea, which, through the price mechanism in the market, serves as a most valuable instrument to achieve the social aims of a modern society.

On this notion Lerner prophesied that the capitalist and socialist systems would eventually draw close to each other by the 'gravitation' of economic efficiency. Socialism, which relies on inefficient government intervention, will slowly gravitate towards a greater efficiency by gradually introducing the market mechanism; while the capitalistic system which relies too heavily on uncontrolled market mechanism with its accompanied inefficiency and lack of social goals will gradually gravitate towards that amount of optimal intervention that improves efficiency and helps to achieve social goals with minimum damage to efficiency.

Lerner identified himself with the social aims of socialism, not with its methods and means. He defined these social aims as democracy, freedom of the individual, a just distribution of income, and full employment as a result of optimal use of economic resources. His dream of a better society also guided him in his scientific work, motivating him often to leave aside his theoretical studies, in which he had displayed unusual creativity and originality for the sake of applied economics and policy recommendations. In this way Lerner paid a personal price for his social idealism.

Throughout his life Lerner used analytical logic equally in his theoretical and his applied studies. As one who shrank from the 'establishment' and distanced himself from 'power', he refused to compromise with the restrictions that these imposed on the social and political behaviour of society. For this reason, Lerner's policy recommendations, while standing the test of logic, seem sometimes to float in a political vacuum disregarding bureaucratic and human nature constraints. This is why many of his recommendations were not accepted for implementation, despite their logical soundness.

I first met Abba when he came to Israel in the 1960s, at the onset of an economic recession which was initiated by the government and resulted in unemployment that became uncontrollable. Lerner, while justifying government economic intervention which improved the efficiency of the market mechanism and raised the level of social welfare, found it difficult to understand how this intervention could be used to create unemployment and reduce economic welfare. He therefore decided to publish a book on *Efficient Economy and Its Application in Israel*, on which I had the privilege to work with him.

That was Lerner's second visit to Israel. His first visit, which lasted nearly four years, was in the early 1950s. He was the most important economist then in newly born Israel and the whole country, its government and its 'establishment' was open to him. He could have chosen any activity and position that he wished, but neither the 'establishment' nor the remuneration it offered interested him.

In the mid-1960s he was invited to join the newly created Tel Aviv

University in order to establish the Faculty of Social Sciences. He served as the Faculty's first Dean for one year, when he resigned. Again this was to avoid becoming part of the 'establishment's' authority and power, and to enable him to return to private life.

Abba Lerner was faithful to his principles and beliefs throughout his life. His relationship to society was based on deeply held values, and not on superficial form, style or organisational ties. His private life, although focused on economics, was versatile. He loved art, and possessed the spark of an artist, expressing his artistry in the creation of fabulous 'mobiles', highly imaginative in concept and precise in execution.

To a considerable extent these 'mobiles' expressed the economic world as he saw it, as they hang in space, as if in a vacuum, seen as complex shapes, somehow continuously moving, then arranging themselves in balanced patterns, moving again and returning to balance, repeating the process continuously. They hang in space as though divorced from the world; the threads that bind them together almost invisible. Is not this the form in which Abba Lerner perceived the economic world, with its pure ideal economic efficiency? Is not this the world which Abba tried to improve by presenting so many recommendations and suggestions for better economic and social policies?

Abba Lerner resembled those poets and composers whose works were so natural and spontaneous that during their own lifetime they have become folklore which passes from generation to generation, not recognising that they were the creation of one ingenious human being.

University in order to establish the Faculty of Social Sciences and served as the Faculty's first Dean for one day, when he resigned. Again this was to avoid becoming part of the establishment, its authority and power, and to enable him to return to private life.

Abba Lerner was faithful to his principles and beliefs throughout his life. His relationship to society was based on deeply-held principles and not on superficial form, style or organisational uses. His private life, although focused on economics, was versatile. He loved art and possessed the spark of an artist, expressing his artistry in the creation of fabulous 'mobiles' highly imaginative in concept and precise in execution.

To a considerable extent these mobiles expressed the economic world as he saw it, as they hung in space, as if on a weightless thread, complex shapes, somehow continuously moving, they rearranged themselves in balanced patterns, moving again and returning to balance, repeating the process continuously. They hang suspended as though divorced from the world, the threads that bind them together almost invisible. Is not this the form in which Abba Lerner perceived the economic world, with its pure ideal economic efficiency? Is not this the world which Abba tried to improve by presenting so many recommendations and suggestions for better economic and social policies.

Abba Lerner resembled those poets and composers whose works were so natural and spontaneous that during their own lifetime they have become folklore which passes from generation to generation, not acknowledging that they were the creation of one specific human being.

Biographical Sketch and Publications

Abba P. Lerner (1903–82)

BSc (Econ), 1932, PhD (Econ), 1943, London, England.
Born Russia, 1903, to England, 1906; to US 1937; Naturalised US 1949.

Experiences

Cap Machinist, Hebrew School teacher, Business–London, England, 1919–29

Student – London School of Economics, 1929–34, Cambridge and Manchester, 1934–5

Assistant Lecturer – London School of Economics, 1935–7

Lecturer in Economics – Columbia University, Fall, 1939–40

Assistant Professor – University of Kansas City, 1940–42

Associate Professor – New School for Social Research, New York, 1942–6

Professor of Economics – New School for Social Research, 1946–7, Roosevelt University, Chicago, 1947–59, Michigan State University, 1959–65, UC Berkeley, 1965–71, Florida State State University, 1978–82

Distinguished Professor of Economics–Queens College, CUNY, 1971–8

Visiting Professor

UC Berkeley, Spring, 1938, 1958–9, Summer 1960, 1962 and 1973; University of Virginia, Spring 1940; Amherst College, Fall 1942–3; Roosevelt College, Spring, Summer 1947; New School for Social Research, Summer, 1948 and 1950; The Hebrew University, Jerusalem 1954–6; Columbia University, New York, Spring Summer 1957; Johns Hopkins University 1957–8; Michigan State University, Summer 1958 and 1959; University of Hawaii, Summer 1965; University of Tel Aviv 1965–6, FSU, Winter and Spring 1976, 1977.

Consultant

Rand Corporation, Summer 1949
Economic Commission for Europe, Geneva, Fall, 1950–51.
Economic Advisory Staff, Jersulem, Israel, 1953–5.
Institute for Mediterranean Affairs, NY, 1958–9.

Adviser

The Treasury, Government of Israel and the Bank of Israel, 1955–6.

Distinctions

Director's First Year Essay Prize, 1930; Tooke Scholarship, 1930; Hugh Lewis Essay Prize, 1932 (bracketed); Gonner Prize, 1932 (first place in Economics in BSc. Econ.); Gladstone Memorial Prize, 1932 (first place in BSc. Econ.); London School of Economics Research Fellowship, 1932–4; Leon Fellowship of the University of London, 1934–5; Rockefeller Fellowship in US, 1938–9; Fellow, Econometric Scoiety, 1950–, Fellow, Center for Advanced Study in the Behavioral Sciences, Stanford, 1960–1; Vice-President Am. Econ. Ass., 1963; Regent Lecturer, UC Santa Barbara, 1964; Distinguished Fellow, Am. Econ. Ass., 1966; Honorary Fellow, London School of Economics, 1970–, Fellow, American Academy of Arts and Sciences, 1971–; Pres. University Centers for National Alternatives, 1973–; Member, National Academy of Sciences, 1974–, BSc (Honorary) Northwestern University, 1978.

Publications

A. Books

The Economics of Control (Macmillan: New York, 1944); *The Economics of Employment* (McGraw-Hill; New York, 1951); *Essays in Economic Analysis* (Macmillan; London, 1953); *Everybody's Business* (MSU Press, 1962; Harper Torchbooks, NY, 1964); *Kalkala Ye'ilah* (Economic Efficiency) (with Ben Shahar) (Amikam; Tel Aviv, 1969); *Flation* (Quadrangle, NY, 1972; Penguin, NY, 1973); *The Economics of Efficiency and Growth* (with Ben Shahar) (Ballinger; Cambridge Mass., 1975); *Illuf Hasoreret* (The Taming of the Shrew – playful Hebrew title for translation of *Flation*) (Tel Aviv; Am Oved, 1976); *MAP: A Market Anti-Inflation Plan* (with David Colander) (Harcourt Brace Jovanovich: New York, 1980).

B. Articles

'The Diagrammatical Representation of Cost Conditions in International Trade', *Economica*, August 1932.

'The Diagrammatical Representation of Elasticity of Demand', *The Review of Economic Studies*, October 1933.

'The Diagrammatical Representation of Elasticity of Substitution', *The Review of Economic Studies*, October 1933.

'A note on the Elasticity of Substitution', *The Review of Economic Studies*, February 1934.

'The Concept of Monopoly and the Measurement of Monopoly Power' *The Review of Economic Studies*, June 1934.

'The Concept of Arc Elasticity of Demand', *The Review of Economic Studies*, June 1934.

'The Diagrammatical Representation of Demand Conditions in International Trade', *Economic*, August 1934.

'Economic Theory and Socialist Economy', *The Review of Economic Studies*, October 1934.

'Economic Theory and Socialist Economy' ('Rejoinder to Dobb), *The Review of Economic Studies*, February 1935.

'A Note on the Theory of Price Index Numbers', *The Review of Economic Studies*, October 1935.

'Further Notes on Index Numbers' IV A Reply, *The Review of Economic Studies*, February 1936.

'The Symmetry of the Elasticity of Substitution', *The Review of Economic Studies*, February 1936.

'The Symmetry between Import and Export Taxes', *Economica*, August 1936.

'Mr. Keynes' 'General Theory of Employment, Interest and Money', *International Labour Review*, October 1936.

'A Note on Socialist Economics', *The Review of Economic Studies*, October 1936.

'Capital, Investment and Interest', Proceedings of the Manchester Statistical Society, 1936–37.

'Some Notes on Duopoly and Spatial Competition', *The Journal of Political Economy*, April 1937 (with H. W. Singer).

'Statics and Dynamics in Socialist Economies', *Economic Journal*, June 1937.

'International Trade and Transfer', *Econometrica*, October 1937.

'A Rejoinder to Professor Cassel', *International Labour Review*, November 1937.

'Savings Equals Investment', *Quarterly Journal of Economics*, February 1938.

'An Undialectical Account of Dialectics', *Science and Society*, Spring 1938.

'Alternative Formulations of the Theory of Interest', *The Economic Journal*, June 1938.

'Theory and Practice on Socialist Economics', *The Review of Economic Studies*, October 1938.

'The Relation of Wage Policies and Price Policies', *American Economic Review*, Supplement, March 1939.

'Equilibrium and Dynamic Concepts in the Theory of Employment', *Econometrica*, April 1939.

'Budgetary Principles', *Cowles Commission Conference* (Report), July 1939.

'Saving and Investment, Definitions, Assumptions, Objectives', *Quarterly Journal of Economics*, August 1939.

'From Vulgar Political Economy to Vulgar Marxism', *Journal of Political Economy*, August 1939.

'Ex Ante Analysis and Wage Theory', *Economica*, November 1939.

'Professor Hicks' Dynamics', *Quarterly Journal of Economics*, February 1940.

'Vulgar Marxism', a further note, *Journal of Political Economy*, April 1940.

'Some Swedish Stepping Stones in Economic Theory', *Canadian Journal of Economics and Political Science*, November 1940.

'Peace and Finance', *University Review* (Kansas City), Spring 1941.

'Full Employment and Total Democracy', *Social Change*, May 1941.

'The Economic Steering Wheel', *University Review* (Kansis City), June 1941.

'Design for a Streamlined War Economy' (written 1942), Mimeo by Rand, February 1949.

'Democratic Perspective', *University Review* (Kansas City), September 1942.

'Functional Finance and the Federal Debt', *Social Research*, February 1943.

'Economic Liberalism in the Postwar World', *Postwar Economic Problems*, March 1943.

'User Cost and Prime User Cost', *American Economic Review*, March 1943.

'The American Way of Business', with Oscar Lange, National Education Association, 1944.

'Interest Theory – Supply and Demand for Loans or Supply and Demand for Cash', *Review of Economic Statistics*, May 1944.

'Bimettalism', 'Coinage', 'Economics', 'Money', *American Peoples Encyclopedia*, 1945.

'Government Spending, Public Debt, and Postwar Taxation', *International Postwar Problems*, January 1945.

'Marxism and Economics' – Sweezy and Robinson, *Journal of Political Economy*, March 1945.

'Planning and Freedom', *International Postwar Problems*, July 1945.

'Full Employment and the Atomic Bomb', *Commonsense*, October 1945.

'Money', *Encyclopaedia Britannica*, 1946.

'An Integrated Full Employment Policy', *International Postwar Problems*, January 1946.

'Monetary Policy and Fiscal Policy', *Review of Economic Statistics*, May 1946.

'The Problem of Full Employment – Discussion', *American Economic Review Supplement*, May 1946.

'How to Keep the Peace', *Bulletin of the Atomic Scientists*, September 1946.

'Investment, Economic Aspects', *Encyclopaedia Britannica*, 1946.

'Geometrical Comparison of Elasticities', *American Economic Review*, March 1947.

'The President Addresses the World', *Bulletin of the Atomic Scientists*, April–May 1947.

'Money as a Creature of the State', *American Economic Review*, May 1947.

'Foreign Economic Relations of the United States', *Saving American Capitalism*, 1948.

'The Burden of the National Debt', *Income, Employment and Public Debt. Essays in Honor of Alvin H. Hansen*, 1948.

'Rising Prices' (in symposium, 'Ten Economists on the Inflation'), *The Review of Economics and Statistics*, February 1948.

'An Economist Comments on Daniel and Squires, "Freedom Demands Responsibility"', *Bulletin of the Atomic Scientists*, October 1948.

'Does Control of Atomic Energy Involve a Controlled Economy?', *Bulletin of the Atomic Scientists*, January 1949.

'A Note Suggested by Samuelson's "Market Mechanism and Maximization"' (On Minimum Cost Diet), Mimeo by RAND as LPC_2 (Linear Programming Conference), June 16, 1949.

'The Myth of the Parasitic Middleman' (originally in Yiddish, *Yivo Bletter*, January 1947, Journal of the Yiddish Scientific Institute), *Commentary*, July 1949.

'The Inflationary Process' 1. Some Theoretical Aspects, *The Review of Economics and Statistics, August 1949*.

The Replacement Problem (Project Rand), D(L)–642, Copy no. 17, 1 September, 1949.

Notes on the Price Mechanism (Project Rand), D(L)–663, Copy no. 12, October 13, 1949.

'When Should Wages be Increased?', *Studies in Business Economics*, No. 23, The Conference Board, January 1950.

'Wage Policy in Full Employment', in Report of the Varese Meeting of the Econometric Society, 6–8 September, 1950. *Econometrica*, 1951.

'Fighting Inflation', *The Review of Economics and Statistics*, August 1951.

'Factor Prices and International Trade', *Economica*, February 1952.

'The Essential Properties of Interest and Money', *The Quarterly Journal of Economics*, May 1952.

'Discussion – Professor Hart's criticisms of Mr. Brill's paper', *Econometrics*, July 1952.

Comments on Hirschleifer's 'War Damage Insurance', Project Rand, D(L)–1345, Copy no.. 12, 28 July, 1952.

War Damage Insurance, Project Rand, 30 August, 1952.

'Reply to review by W. S. Woytinsky', 'Economics of Employment', *Industrial and Labor Relations Review*, October 1952.

'On the Marginal Product of Capital and the Marginal Efficiency of Investment', *Journal of Political Economy*, February 1953.

'Should We Break our Biggest Monopoly', *Bulletin of the Atomic Scientists*, May 1953.

'Discussion on Social Choice Functions', *Econometrica*, September 1953.

'Stabilization and Economic Independence', *Rivon L'kalkalah*, August 1954.

'Inflation – Will it Wreck the Israel Economy in 1956?', mimeo to Prime Minister of Israel, November 1955.

'Should Wages Rise or Fall?', *Here and Now* – Israel's weekly of News and Comment, No. 36, 7 December, 1955.

'Letter to Israel', Mimeo, August 1956.

'Review of Joan Robinson's *The Accumulation of Capital*', *American Economic Review*, September 1957.

'The Backward-Leaning Approach to Controls' Review of J. Meade's The Theory of International Economic Policy, Vol. II, in Trade and Welfare and Mathematical Supplement of *The Journal of Political Economy*, October 1957.

'The Histadrut and the Israel Economy', *Midstream*, October 1957.

'Immigration, Capital Formation and Inflationary Pressure', *The Economics of International Migration*, 1958.

'Halting the Current Recession – A Proposal for dealing with "Sellers" Inflation', *Commentary*, February 1958.

'Inflationary Depression and the Regulation of Administered Prices', Joint Economic Committee, Conference on Economic Stability and Growth, 31 March, 1958.

'Inflationary Depression', Summary Opening Statement for Joint Economic Committee, 15 May, 1958.

'Planning for Israel's Solvency', *Midstream*, Summer 1958.

The Problem of the Palestine Arab Refugees, Report of a Panel of the Institute of Mediterranean Affairs, 10 September, 1958.

'Testimony of Abba P. Lerner before the Committee on Foreign Relations of the U.S. on the Subject of Foreign Aid', 22 May 1959.

'Statement to Joint Economic Committee of the Senate for the Study of Employment, Growth and Price Levels', 24 September, 1959.

'Consumption-Loan Interest and Money', *Journal of Political Economy*, October 1959.

'A Rejoinder', *Journal of Political Economy*, October 1959.

'On Generalizing the General Theory', *The American Economic Review*, March 1960.

Review of Henry Hazlitt's 'The failure of the "New Economics"', *The Review of Economics and Statistics*, May 1960.

'Problems of Achieving and Maintaining a Stable Price Level', *Proceedings of the A.G.A.*, May 1960.

'Economics and the Control of Man – The Case of the Economist', *American Scholar*, Summer 1960.

'Meta Economics ', *Study of Soviet Economy: Its Place in American Education* (First given as a Panel Speech at Conference at Indiana University, 3–4 February, 1961.

'The Burden of Debt', *Review of Economics and Statistics*, May 1961.

'Discussion of Harry Johnson on "Keynes after 25 years"', *American Economic Review* (Papers and Proceedings), May 1961.

'A Note on the Rate of Interest and the Value of Assets', *Economic Journal*, September 1961.

'Administered Depression', Mimeo, Center for Democratic Studies, 28 November, 1961.

'Depression Administrada', *Revista de Economica Latinoamericana*, December 1961.

'Automation', Center for Democratic Studies, 1 December, 1961.

'Macro-economics and Micro-economics', Paper read August 1960 at International Congress for Logic, Methodology and Philosophy of Science, *Logic, Methodology and Philosophy of Science: Proceedings of the 1960 International Congress, 1962.*

'Consumer's Surplus', *Encyclopaedia Britannica*, 1962.

Collective Bargaining, Center for Study of Democratic Institutions, 7 March, 1962.

Review of Milton Friedman's 'A Program for Monetary Stability', *Journal of the American Statistical Association*, March 1962.

'The Wasted Billions', *Encounter*, March 1962 (Review article on Graham Hutton, *Inflation and Society*.)

'A Program for Monetary Stability (Part II)', Conference on Saving and Residential Financing US S & L League, 10–11 May, 1962, also discussion of 'Part I'.

'Own Rates and the Liquidity Trap', *Economic Journal*, June 1962.

'The Problems of Rising Prices', Review, *Journal of Political Economy*, August 1962.

'A Macro-Analytical Approach to the Space Effort, prepared for the Committee on Space Effort and Society, August 1962.

'Money in a Theory of Finance', Review of Gurley and Shaw in *JASA*, September 1962.

'The Analysis of Demand', *American Economic Review*, September 1962.

'The Death of the Class Struggle', *The Strategy of Deception*, 1963.

'Sellers' Inflation and Administered Depression', *Administered Prices: A Compendium on Public Policy*, subcommittee on Antitrust and Monopoly of US Senate, 1963.

'Comments on Modigliani and Johnson, *Debt, Exchange Rates, Inflation vs. Employment', Review of Economic Statistics, February 1963.*

'Consumer's Surplus and Micro-Macro', *Journal of Political Economy*, February 1963.

'Financial Institutions and Monetary Policy', *American Economic Review*, May 1963.

'Review of Milton Friedman's *Capitalism and Freedom*', *American Economic Review*, June 1963.

'Keynesian Economics in the Sixties', *Keynes' General Theory–Reports of Three Decades*, 1964.

Testimony before House Banking and Currency Committee, *The Federal Reserve After 50 Years*, 11 March, 1964 (hearing).

'Let's Get Rid of Our Cross of Gold', *Challenge*, April 1964.

'The Cross of Gold', *Washington Post*, April 1964.

'Nuclear Symmetry as a Framework for Coexistence', *Social Research*, Summer 1964.

'Our Declining National Debt–Is it too Small?', *Banking*, November 1964.

'On Some Recent Developments in Capital Theory', *American Economic Review*, May 1965.

'Professor Samuelson on Theory and Realism: Comment', *American Economic Review*, December 1965.

'Conflicting Principles of Public Utility Price Regulations', *Journal of Law and Economics*, June 1966.

'Employment Theory and Employment Policy', Ely Lecture, AEA, 27 December, 1966, *American Economic Review*, May 1967.

'The Big Powers and Economic Development in the Middle East, *The Big Powers and Present Crisis in the Middle East*, 1968.

Discussion on 'Political and Economic Development in the Middle East', *The Middle East in the Contemporary World*, 9–10 December, 1967, *American Professors for Peace in the Middle East*, 1968.

'Micro-economic Theory', *Perspectives in Economics*, 1968.

'The Economist's Can Opener', *Western Economic Journal*, March 1968.

'Capital', *International Encyclopaedia of the Social Sciences*, May 1968.

'The Death of the Gold Standard', Lecture at Miss. State U., *New Leader*, June 1968.

'On Instrumental Analysis', *Economic Means and Social Ends*, 1969.

'Black Studies: The Universities in Moral Crisis', *The Humanist*, May/June 1969. (Includes 'Some Anonymous Thoughts on Some "Black" Proposals'), mimeo, February 1969.

'Discussion vs. Confrontation', in *University and Unrest*, A Condensation of the Seattle Statement, June 1969.

'The Enemy Within', on student and faculty unrest, *Measure*, September 1969, grew out of manifesto for CCAC, June 1969.

'Innovation and Public Enterprise East and West', Discussions at AEA–ACE Panel at AEA meeting, 30 December, 1969.

'Some Thoughts on Landauer's *Theory of National Economic Planning*'. Essays in Socialism and Planning in Honor of Carl Landauer, 1970.

'Consumer's Surplus and Micro-Macro: A Discussion. A Reply'. *JPE*, 78 (1): January–February 1970.

'Consumer's Surplus and Micro-Macro: A Discussion. Methodological Epilogue'. *JPE* 78 (1): January–February 1970.

'The "International Money" Myth and Foreign Exchange Policies', originally Bernhard Moses Memorial Lecture, 19 February, 1970.

'Distributional Equality and Aggregate Utility – Reply'. *American Economic Review*, June 1970.

'Depression and Inflation in the 70's', *Rivon L'kalkalah*, 1971.

'Three Kinds of Inflation', Lecture delivered to the University seminar on the Political Economy of War and Peace, Columbia University, October 28, 1971.

'The Ivory Tower', *The Humanist*, March 1971 (extract from Commencement speech, Eco-Berkeley, June 1970).

Letter to Editor, *Measure*, March 1971 on Capaldi – Social Science.

'Social Scientist Has No Special Right', *Freedom at Issue*, July/August 1971.

'The 1971 Report of the President's Council of Economic Advisors: Priorities and Efficiency', *American Economic Review*, September 1971.

'Keynesian Theory and Keynesian Policy: Some Deeper Level Assumptions', Paper presented to the Southern Economic Association meeting in Miami, 5 November, 1971.

A note on 'Understanding the Marxian Notion of Exploitation', *Journal of Economic Literature*, March 1972.

'The Economics and Politics of Consumer Sovereignty', *American Economic Review*, May 1972.

Letter 'On Dr. Burns' Blueprint for a New Monetary System', *New York Times*, 28 May, 1972.

'Group Think', *Freedom at Issue*, July–August 1972.

'Pollution Abatement Subsidies', *American Economic Review*, December 1972.

'Wage–Price Policy: The Theoretical Issues', Paper to the Conference Board, February 1973.

'The Deformation of Affirmative Action', *Midstream*, April 1973.

'The Challenge of Full Employment with Price Stability "Income Policies"', Report of Conference at University of British Columbia, April 1973.

Letter 'The Energy Crisis: What a Surtax on Oil Would Do', *New York Times*, 28 November, 1973.

'Money, Debt, and Wealth', in *Econometrics and Economic Theory, Essays in Honor of Jan Timbergen* (Macmillan: London, 1974).

'Market Power and the Wage-Price Problem' – one of *Two Lectures*, University of British Columbia, 1974.

'Price Flexibility and the International Money Market' – Essay Four in *Understanding Economics, Essays in Public Policy* (ed.) Yung-Bing Chen (Little Brown, 1974).

'Wage-Price Controls II: Appraisal of U.S. Wage and Price Control Program – A View from Academe' (Lecture in ASA-AEA Symposium at the Allied Social Sciences Meetings, San Francisco, 28 December, 1973) *American Statistical Association Journal*, 1974.

'Reflection on the Agonies of the University', in *The Idea of a Modern University* (ed.) Sidney Hook and others (Prometheus Books: Buffalo, 1974).

Letter *On Oil Price Policies and OPEC New York Times*, 31 January, 1974.

'From the Treatise on Money to the General Theory', *Journal of Economic Literature*, March 1974.

'Intraregional and International Trade'. Lecture given at the 4th World Congress of the International Economic Association, Budapest, 19–24 August, 1974.

'Priorities and Pollution'. *American Economic Review*, September 1974.

'If the Cost of Living Allowance is Not Paid, Conditions Could Get Worse' (in Hebrew). Article in *Maariv* (largest circulation, daily in Israel). 7 September, 1974.

Letter on *'Inflation Policy'*. *New York Times*, September 1974.

'Marxian Value, Surplus Value, and Surplus' (in Hebrew), in *Rivon L'kalkalah* (Economic Quarterly). Tel Aviv, December 1974.

Letter *'Don't Bleed the Economy'*. *New York Times*, 19 December, 1974.

'Three Kinds of Inflation', in *Policy Formation in an Open Economy* (ed.) Mundell and van Snellenberg (University of Waterloo, 1974) pp. 153–70.

'On the Ingredients of a full employment Act'. Lecture at a workshop,

Hunter College New York City, 14–15 February, 1975 (in preparations for a conference on 'Committing the Nation to Full Employment').

'Groupism or How "Affirmative Action" Caught the Disease it Was Fighting', Testimony before the Office of Federal Contract Compliance of the Department of Labor in *Phoenix*, A Queen's College Student paper, 10/21/75.

'Stagflation', *Intermountain Economic Review* (Fall 1975) pp. 1–7.

Letter *'Of City Aid in an Upside-Down Economy', New York Times*, 20 November, 1975.

'Wages, Profits and Marginal Analysis in *Inflation, Trade and Taxes* (ed.) Belsley *et al.* (Ohio UP, 1975) pp. 23–8.

Review of 'John Maynard Keynes' by Hyman Minsky, *Challenge*, May–June 1976, pp. 69–70.

'A Reluctant Keynesian', *Intermountain Economic Review*, vol. VII, no. 2 (Fall 1976) pp. 55–60.

'The Transmissions of Inflations from Country to Country', in *Geographical Aspects of Inflationary Process, Part One* (ed.) Peter B. Corbin, for American Geographical Society, 1976, Redgrave, pp. 47–50.

'Marginal Cost Pricing in the 1930's', *American Economic Association*, Feb. 1977, pp. 235–9.

'Environment – Externalizing the Internalities?' *American Economic Review* March 1977, pp. 176–8.

Introduction

This volume contains a variety of papers on economic policy in theory and practice. They deal with a wide range of aspects of economic policy: public debt, government budget and inflation, the world debt problems, resource allocation and taxation, efficiency of various forms of market organisation, and issues in political economy.

Modigliani returns to the old issue, which is still at the heart of macro policy-making, of the economics of public deficits. He deals conceptually with three questions. First, do deficits contribute to the creation of aggregate demand, and thereby induce a positive effect on output and investment; or do they, instead, crowd out investment, or consumption, or both?

Second, are deficits a source of inflation through their direct effect on demand or via a policy-induced dependence between larger deficits and more expansionary monetary policy. Third, to the extent that crowding out occurs, what is it: consumption, investment or both?

Dealing with the first question, which was at the core of the debate between the Keynesian and the classical view, the paper reminds us that the answer depends on whether or not the economy operates at a full capacity. There must be enough slack in the economy and sufficiently accommodative monetary policy, to permit the expansion of output, in order to prevent significant crowding out.

Dealing with the second question *Modigliani* maintains that for countries with a reasonably well-developed financial system deficits need not be a source of money creation, and thus, deficits should not be considered a major source of inflation. The recent association between reported deficits and inflation, he argues, is to be found in 'inverse causation'. That is, high inflation raises nominal interest rates. Thus, reported deficits which are not inflation-corrected tend to rise with inflation. In addition, stagflation contributed to the decrease in tax revenues and thereby to the deficit.

The analysis of the third question which is the main focus of the paper, is done by a number of empirical tests. For the US *Modigliani* finds that there is little evidence that private wealth (inclusive of public debt) has responded to public debt. Thus, the Ricardian proposition, which suggests that the regression coefficient of private wealth on public debt should be one, is rejected by this test. The next empirical analysis tests, with post-war data for the US and Italy, whether consumption responds to public debt. The estimated effect of debt on consumption is found to be even greater than that of the other components of private wealth, and here again the tax neutrality hypothesis is rejected by the test. These tests together with supplemental cross-country evidence are rather unfavourable to the strict Ricardian proposition.

Frenkel and *Razin* reconsider the celebrated topic of the international transmission of the effects of fiscal expenditures and budget deficits. This time the analysis is done in a micro-based framework which includes individuals with the possibility of finite horizon, through lifetime uncertainty. This uncertainty results in an equilibrium in which private and social rates of discount differ. The difference between the two discount rates, which enables the departure from the Ricardian propositions, permits a meaningful analysis of the effects of public debt.

Frenkel and *Razin* show that current deficits are transmitted negatively to the rest of the world: they result in a higher world interest rate and in declining foreign consumption. An expected future deficit is also negatively transmitted internationally but its effect on the world (spot) rate of interest depends on whether the country, which is introducing this deficit, runs a surplus or a deficit in the current account of its balance of payments. The economic channel works through the world interest rate. Budget deficits which are viewed as net wealth by the current generations change the world demand for current and future goods and the term structure of interest rates should adjust accordingly. Public debt, which has been generated from cumulative budgetary deficits, raises also the long-run interest rate while the effect on foreign consumption is not unambiguous.

The analysis of government spending makes the distinction between temporary and permanent budgetary changes. A transitory rise in the domestic government spending raises interest rates and lowers foreign consumption. In contrast, the effect of a permanent rise in government spending on the world interest rate depends on whether the country, whose budget changes, runs a current account deficit or surplus.

The paper also analyses changes in the terms of trade, in addition to interest rates, as a channel for the international transmission of fiscal policies. *Frenkel* and *Razin* show that the impact of government spending depends on a comparison among (a) domestic and foreign spending propensities, (b) domestic and foreign saving propensities, and (c) domestic and foreign patterns of government spending.

Buiter also analyses the international impact of government budget deficits in an analytical framework very similar to that which is used by *Frenkel* and *Razin*. He, however, allows for the process of investment, which responds to rates of interest, and which changes the paths of outputs. Any policy change that raises the world rate of interest lowers the long-run capital stock at home and abroad. Thus a higher public debt, generated from a sequence of budget deficits, is associated with a long-run fall in world output. The only way to avoid the detrimental effect of the higher world interest rate, which results from the short-run expansionary fiscal policy in a foreign country is for the home country to engage in short-run contractionary fiscal policies.

The paper by *Zvi Hercowitz* and *Efraim Sadka* deals with the question of financing the government's budget, when the use of the well known inflation tax on domestic money holdings is impeded by the existence of a substitute to domestic money in the form of foreign money. They employ a framework in which the demand for moneys is generated from inventory theoretic considerations. Both kinds of money can serve as a store of value but only domestic money can serve as a medium of exchange. *Hercowitz* and *Sadka* assume that the foreign money has a stable real value while the real value of the domestic money, of course, depreciates at the rate of inflation. There is no natural cost of converting foreign money to domestic money. Thus, if no man-made restrictions on such conversions are imposed, then, with any positive inflation rate, individuals would hold only foreign money and convert it to domestic money just before making real transactions. This would *practically* eliminate the demand for domestic money and make the foreign money the medium of exchange. In this case the government would have no revenue from inflation. Imagine, however, that the government can prevent the foreign money from being a perfect substitute to the domestic money as a medium of exchange. For instance, government regulations can require that conversion from one kind of money to another be carried out through commercial banks, involving non-trivial waste of real resource in the form of paper-work, waiting time and use of physical capital. (The case of Israel is a good example.)

The magnitude of these restrictions, which are by themselves a deadweight loss but induce an increase in the revenue from the inflation tax, is one of the policy variables. The inflation tax and an income tax are the other policy variables. *Hercowitz* and *Sadka* first examine the effects of these policy variables on the frequency of financial transactions (i.e. conversions from one kind of money to another), the demand for consumption, the supply of labour and individual welfare. They then optimise with respect to these policy variables, subject to the government's budget constraint. *Hercowitz* and *Sadka* conclude that the government should not use the inflation tax because its use can be made possible only by incurring a deadweight loss inherent in the necessary accompanying restrictions on financial conversions. This solution can be seen as corresponding to either the adoption of a stable-valued foreign currency for domestic use – the dollarisation scheme considered by the Israeli treasury in 1983 – or to a fixed exchange rate against such a currency, coupled with a completely passive monetary policy.

Sargent and *Wallace* return to the economic and econometric issues concerning hyperinflations. The standard model of hyperinflation has two stationary equilibria, which enable the government to raise the required amount of revenue from the printing of money, induce the public to hold the amount of money outstanding, and maintain the inflation rate constant. Around the low inflation equilibrium the inflation revenue increases with the rate of inflation while the rate of inflation at the second equilibrium exceeds the seignorage-maximising inflation rate.

Embodying the simple framework in a stochastic process for money creation and prices result in a multidimensional continuum of equilibria. In many of these equilibria, there is a spurious indicator, or 'sunspot' variable, that affect money and prices even though it fails to influence the fundamental variables (the demand for money and the governments' budget constraint).

They are able to construct an econometric procedure for this model which permits an estimation of the behavioural parameters that describe portfolio balance and the government budget constraint, and also the 'nuisance parameters' that serve to randomly select one from the continuum of equilibria. One important property that could be imposed on their model is that inflation Granger causes money creation while money creation fails to cause inflation. This was found to be an important characteristic of the hyperinflationary episode. *Sargent* and *Wallace* also show that if the monetary authority selects a unique contingency plan for money creation, based on the parameters of the model (including the stochastic parameters) then the equilibrium is unique. This illustrates the importance of the specification of agents' behaviour (private or government) in order to ensure the uniqueness of equilibria.

This highly innovative approach has the potential of explaining some important time-series characteristics of hyperinflations that previous models failed to explain; such as the tendency for real balances to fall and inflation to rise during hyperinflation.

Dornbusch and *Fischer* review the world debt problem, especially that of Latin America. The framework within which they discuss debt history and proposed solutions is in terms of debt accumulation equation with the debt–export ratio serving as measure of the debt burden. The evolution of the current debt–export ratio is governed by the debt–export ratio of the preceding period, the world real interest rate, the rate of growth in export prices, the growth rate of exports, and the non-interest current account. To assess the role of external factors and domestic policies they perform a counterfactual exercise by asking what part of the debt increase would have occurred if the debtor countries had pursued policies that ensured zero non-interest current account. They find that external circumstances – which they assume to be interest rates and export growth – cannot by themselves account for the severe debt problems over 1970–83 period. The experience of several Latin American countries points to the interaction of domestic policy which led to an over-exposure in terms of the external debt.

Dornbusch and *Fischer* discuss a variety of proposals which have been offered for the solution of the debt problem but they focus on proposals for an interest rate cap. This comes in two variants: (a) a concessional cap which places a ceiling and forgive any excess of market interest rates over this ceiling indefinitely – the concessional cap; (b) a cap which sets a ceiling on the interest rate but, rather than forgive the excess of market interest rates over the ceiling, it adds the difference to the principal of the debt – the liquidity cap. They argue against the first variant (at an interest rate cap of 7 per cent) because it would amount to an almost certain bankruptcy of some major banks and thus it is unreasonable to assume that the banks would accept such a proposal. Based on their discussion of the adjustment efforts in the debtor countries and the economic outlook for the next years, *Dornbusch* and *Fischer* maintain that the liquidity cap offers little attraction from the debtor point of view. It is primarily a proposal to make the creditor cartel more operational but would require unrealistic and inequitable adjustment efforts on the part of the debtor countries. *Dornbusch* and *Fischer*'s proposal is intermediate between the concessionary-cap and the liquidity-cap proposals. They recommend a 9–10 per cent ceiling on interest rates and that only during a three-year grace period the excess of market rate and the ceiling be forgiven. They maintain that the scheme should not be implemented unconditionally. It should be rationed to those countries genuinely in need and undergoing appropriate domestic adjustment.

They caution that this proposal of limited debt relief is based on the assumption that current high interest rates are transitory. If this assumption is incorrect debtor countries will have to take a significantly different view of their debt problems.

Krueger assesses the world debt problem in an analytical perspective which identifies real world deviations from a well-functioning, and efficient, international credit market. First, domestic savings and investments, which determine capital flows, may be inappropriate owing to an interaction between the public sector budget and private spending decisions. Specifically, debt servicing problems may arise from public sector deficits financed by borrowing abroad. Second, there are circumstances where a realistic tax structure can recapture additional income stream from an investment that is financed by international borrowing. Third, there could be difficulties in transforming domestic currency in foreign exchange.

Fourth, large shifts, during a short adjustment period in macroeconomic variables, entail high economic, as well as social and political costs. Also, to the extent that the portfolio of capital inflow is unbalanced towards debt (lacking equity capital which can share in risk), and especially short-term debt, the likelihood of debt-servicing difficulties increases.

In assessing the causes of the debt problem *Krueger* reviews Enders–Mattione calculations of overall adjustment (or disadjustment) to external shocks in some Latin American debtors. For this group of countries the internal causes of crisis predominates over the external causes. *Krueger* observes that external shocks, inappropriate domestic economic policies, and the shift in the optimal level of borrowing all contributed to the debt problem, but the relative importance of each component differed vastly among countries.

Some inferential evidence on the extreme adjustment that took place recently is presented in terms of the 'real transfer'. This concept, net borrowing less interest payments, reflects the additional resources that were available for domestic utilisation over and above domestic production. *Krueger* observes that these transfers fell sharply in the early 1980s. The shifts in the non-interest current account relative to real income in developing countries implied staggering adjustments in the domestic economy. But from the viewpoint of policymakers in developing countries there will be high costs entailed in failing to adjust further should the real interest rate remain high.

The paper by *Ronald Findlay* and *John Wilson* is an attempt to provide a general equilibrium type theory of the state. Their view of the state as an institution is intrinsically both 'productive' and potentially 'predatory' in character and they try to capture this dual character. They construct a simple general equilibrium model which includes behavioural hypotheses about the agents exercising the power of the state to tax and spend. The allocation of resources between the public and private sectors is determined endogenously in this model.

Findlay and *Wilson* first study the optimal allocation in their model which is defined as the allocation which maximises national income. Labour employed by the state is taken away from the private sector, thus reducing the output of the private sector. But, on the other hand, the product of the state is a good not a bad in that it raises the productivity of the private sector itself through the provision of the indisposable framework of law and order without which the enforcement of contracts and so on would be impossible. Thus, an optimal balance between private and public employment can be found and this defines an optimal allocation of resources.

Next, they turn to study the behaviour of a purely self-interested 'Leviathan'. However, for the most part, this Leviathan is restricted to its ability to change existing tax *rates*. *Findlay* and *Wilson* claim that even the absolute monarchs of early modern Europe could not raise tax rates without the consent of some representative assemblies, nor are modern dictators less constrained by fears of riots and revolts. As for the objective function of this self-interested Leviathan, they consider two major alternatives.

As a first case, *Findlay* and *Wilson* consider an absolute ruler (a King of earlier times or a contemporary dictator). The ruler acts so as to maximise the 'surplus' defined as the excess of tax revenues over government expenditure. In their model government expenditure increases national income and consequently tax revenues (for given tax rates). Thus, a well defined maximum surplus exists. They show that the ruler will employ less government workers than the socially optimal level and national output will not be at a maximum. Nevertheless, it is still usually the case that the citizens are better-off than with no government at all.

A second alternative is to assume that government expenditure expands to absorb all the revenue available to finance it. For high enough (exogenously given) tax rates, this results in over-employment in the public sector and less than maximal national income. This kind of bureaucratic Leviathan has the advantage, from the citizens' point of view, that there exist tax rates which induce the Leviathan to employ the socially optimal number of workers and produce a maximum level of national income.

The paper by *Daniel Kovenock* and *Michael Rothschild* examines the difference between the effective tax rate on capital gains and the statutory tax rate and, in particular, the effect of uncertainty on this difference. A capital gains tax is usually levied on a realisation rather than accrual basis.[1] By postponing realisation one can postpone the payment of the capital gains tax (the lock-in effect). This is the reason why the effective tax rate on capital gains is thought by most economists to be lower than the statutory law. Indeed, this is true in a world of no uncertainty. *Kovenock* and *Rothschild* follow the traditional definition of the effective rate of capital gains taxation: it is the rate of accrual taxation, λ, which would ensure equality between the after-tax profits on an investment subject to the statutory capital gains tax rate on a realisation basis and the after-tax profits on the same investment taxed on an accrual basis at rate λ. They show that the effective rate falls substantially below the statutory rate as the length of time the investment is held increases.

The main point of *Kovenock* and *Rothschild* is that the effective rate of capital gains tax is much higher than is commonly believed if we introduce uncertainty. With uncertainty, diversification plays an important role. In order to postpone paying the capital gains tax, one has to follow the rule: 'sell losers and hold winners'. But such a rule may be opposite to the investor's desire to diversify his portfolio. Thus, tax avoidance has a price in terms of giving up the privilege to optimally manage a portfolio over time. This price should be calculated as part of the effective rate of taxation. *Kovenock* and *Rothschild* define the effective rate of taxation under uncertainty as that rate of accrual taxation, λ, which makes an investor indifferent between holding a fixed (over time) portfolio which is taxed at the statutory rate on a realisation basis and holding a continually managed portfolio which is taxed at accrual rate λ. They calculate the effective rates of taxation for various parameter values and show the rates to be substantially higher than in the certainty case. In fact, they even present examples where the effective rates are higher than the statutory rate.[2]

The paper by *Eitan Berglas*, *David Fresko* and *David Pines* considers the issue of common versus separate facilities (roads or lanes within roads) for two modes of transportation, private cars and buses, in congested urban areas, under either a first-best or second-best regime. A first-best regime prevails when the Pigouvian congestion tolls on these modes can be levied. A second-best regime prevails when a congestion toll on cars cannot be levied, so that only buses are subjected to a Pigouvian congestion toll. The two modes of transportation may differ from each other in two features reflected in the congestion function commonly used in the literature: the effect of a passenger trip on congestion and the effect of congestion on cost.

Suppose there is no cost to separation of facilities, i.e. building two roads of equal sizes cost exactly as much as building one road of a double size. In this case the society can always do at least as well with separate facilities as with a common facility, even if the two modes of transportation do not differ in the two features mentioned above. If they do differ, then segregation is most likely to emerge as the optimal policy. This result holds both under first-best and second-best regimes. *Berglas*, *Fresko* and *Pines* go on to compare the optimal level of congestion in a common facility with the optimal levels of congestion in two separate facilities. This comparison is again done under both first-best and second-best regimes. Finally, they consider the question whether in the second-best regime, when only buses can be subjected to a congestion toll, this toll must be positive or negative. On the one hand, since buses cause congestion we would like to impose a positive congestion toll. But, on the other hand, buses may cause less congestion per passenger trip than private cars, so that we may want to divert passengers from cars to buses by subsidising bus rides. With a common facility, no clear cut result about the sign of the optimal congestion toll on buses can be obtained. With separate facilities, *Berglas*, *Fresko* and *Pines* show that the toll should be positive under quite plausible assumptions.

A survey of corporate taxation in the US is provided in *Alan Auerbach*'s paper. The revenue from the corporate tax has declined steadily since the early 1950s from 5.4 per cent of GNP to merely 1.3 per cent of GNP in 1983. This decline is due primarily to changes in the tax base (e.g. accelerated depreciation, investment tax credit, 'safe harbour' leasing etc.), since there has been little movement in the statutory corporate tax rate during that period. *Auerbach* points out that the decline in the corporate tax collections does not necessarily indicate a corresponding reduction in the distortions caused by the corporate tax (with respect to the overall level of investment, asset choice, financial policy etc.).

Auerbach presents estimates of the effective marginal tax rates faced by individual investments in each year. He then aggregates these rates by industry and also obtains the overall effective tax rate on corporate investment. *Auerbach* defines the effective corporate tax rate as that rate of tax on the corporation's *true economic* income which would present the same incentive to invest as the existing tax laws (with their various provisions for depreciation, investment tax credit etc.). The overall effective tax rate shows a declining trend from the early 1950s to the early 1980s. But what is most important is how much, in any given year, the effective tax rates vary across investments. (The widest gap is between general industrial equipment and industrial buildings.)

These many effective tax rates cause distortions *within* the corporate sector. Assuming that each industry has a production function which is Cobb–Douglas in each type of capital used and labour, *Auerbach* calculates a measure of the welfare cost of the differential capital taxation. This measure is an answer to the following question: given the vector of outputs being produced by the corporate sector, how much of the existing capital stock could be disposed of with no change in production, if the remaining capital were allocated optimally. *Auerbach* finds that the welfare cost of differential capital taxation increased over time and reached over 5 billion dollars in 1981, despite the fall in the effective marginal tax rates.

Auerbach then goes on to examine the effects of the asymmetric tax treatment of gains and losses and of inflation on the effective marginal tax rates. He maintains that it appears difficult to measure with any degree of certainty these effects.

Auerbach concludes with a sort of warning. Although the corporate tax revenue has declined to a very low level and abolition of this tax has its appeal, such a move would be an ineffective way of stimulating investment and, in addition, would amount to forgiving the implicit debt owed the government in deferred taxes (for instance, because of accelerated depreciation), currently in excess of 20 per cent of the fixed capital stock.

The paper by *Yoram Weiss* employs an overlapping generation model to study union behaviour. He first considers a union dominated by the existing members of the union (the old generation): they can control the amount of training required from new entrants (the young generation) and impose entry fees on them. These new entrants will control the union in the next period and they will then set the amount of required training of new entrants and will impose entry fees. Weiss shows that all the rent that a union can extract accrues to the first generation. All other generations enjoy no rent.

The main question that Weiss considers is whether the training standards set by the union are above the competitive (efficient) level, reflecting an attempt to discourage entry. He points out that when entry fees are unlimited (except to the effect that a potential new entrant cannot be forced to join the union if he can do better by not doing so) then they can adequately serve as an entry barrier and therefore there is no reason to deviate from the competitive level of training. *Weiss* shows that in the long-run (that is, in the steady-state) the training standards set by the union conform with the competitive (efficient) standards. In the short run, however, overtraining will be required.

Next, *Weiss* allows for the participation of the young workers in the union's decision making. Each period, senior members and potential entrants agree on a binding contract which determines the training standards, the entry fees etc. He shows that if the bargaining over the share of the young in total rents can be characterised by the Nash bargaining model, then the young will opt for longer training periods in order to enhance their future bargaining position.

Finally, *Weiss* imposes some limitations on the use of entry fees. Specifically, explicit entry fees are no longer allowed. Instead, the training process serves also as an implicit entry fee: during the training period, junior workers work for the senior workers, receiving an apprenticeship wage which may be set below their marginal value product. As the apprenticeship wage cannot be negative, the size of the implicit entry fee (the difference between the marginal value product and the apprenticeship wage) is thus limited. In this case, the gain to the senior workers (from the implicit entry fees) depends on the duration of training period and there is therefore an incentive to require a longer training period. Indeed, *Weiss* shows that the steady-state level of training will be above the competitive (efficient) level.

The paper by *Robert Willig* examines the conventional wisdom that movements in the market away from monopoly towards competition are doubly advantageous to social welfare in that they decrease deadweight losses in the product market while, at the same time, eliminating wasted resources and unnecessary costs internal to the firm (x-inefficiency). Specifically, *Willig* is concerned with the question of x-inefficiency.

He constructs a model with a principal–agent relationship between the owner and the manager of the firm. Information is asymmetric: some variables, including the manager's effort, are observable by the manager only. The firm has some monopoly power: it faces a downward sloping demand curve for its product. *Willig* describes the equilibrium in this model. It results in excessive levels of cost. He then addresses the following question: Does added competitive pressure on the firm in the product market reduce x-inefficiency and thereby make a contribution to social welfare over and above the reduction in deadweight loss in the firm's supply of output?

The answer depends on the form this added pressure takes. *Willig* shows that a pivotal change in the demand curve around the original equilibrium point in a direction of increased elasticity does reduce x-inefficiency. Such a change results also in greater compensation paid to the manager. On the other hand, a radial contraction of the demand curve for the firm's product raises x-inefficiency and reduces managerial compensation. Typically, increased competition will both shrink demand and render it more elastic. Then, there are two opposing forces on x-inefficiency and the balance can swing either way.

The paper by *Sanford Grossman* and *Oliver Hart* presents a theory of vertical integration of firms. They define a firm to consist of those assets which it owns or over which it has control. They do not distinguish between ownership and control and virtually define ownership as the power to exercise control. *Grossman* and *Hart* consider an upstream and downstream production process, with the upstream firm being the seller, and the downstream firm being the buyer. They assume that it is extremely costly to write a contract which specifies unambiguously the payments and actions of all parties in every observable state of nature. It is further assumed that vertical integration in itself does not change the cost of writing down a particular contractual provision. What it does change is who has control over those provisions not included in the contract.

Grossman and *Hart* consider two general types of missing provisions. Perhaps the more interesting one is where it is too costly to write a contract which specifies how the quantity (assumed zero or one) and the price of the product, must vary with the state of nature. The state of nature determines the cost (to the seller) and the benefits (to the buyer) of the product. They consider three possibilities: separate integration (i.e. non-integration), integration where the buyer owns the seller, and integration where the seller owns the buyer. With no integration, the product will be delivered from the seller to the buyer if and only if it is in the interest of both parties to do so. With integration, the owner has the right to determine whether the transaction will take place. *Grossman* and *Hart* establish conditions under which non-integration is optimal, conditions for buyer control to be optimal, and conditions for seller control to be optimal.

Finally, *Grossman* and *Hart* consider a second type of missing provisions where some dimension of the quality of the product is unspecified in the initial contract. The owner has the ability to choose this aspect of quality *ex post* to extract the surplus from the non-owner. They show that this distorts the non-owner's benefits from *ex-ante* investments and reliance expenditures.

Notes

1. Israel, however, is an exception. During the period 1982–4 capital gains accruing to corporations were taxed on an accrual basis.
2. It should be mentioned, however, that this surprising result need not be accepted by all economists, since it follows from some quite strong, perhaps implausible, assumptions which lead to the *Kovenock* and *Rothschild* definition of the effective capital gains tax rate in the case of uncertainty.

Part One
The Economics of Public Debt

1 The Economics of Public Deficits[1]

Franco Modigliani

INTRODUCTION

There are three basic issues connected with the economic consequences of the flow of deficits and the resulting stock of public debt.

1. Does the deficit contribute to the creation of aggregate demand and thus to output (with or without effect on prices), or does it, instead, crowd out other components, leaving the total unchanged? This issue is reviewed in Section I.

2. Are deficits *the* major, or at least *a* major source of inflation, either through the effect on demand and/or through the way they are financed? This is the question that is examined in Section II.

3. In so far as the crowding out occurs, what is crowded out, consumption or national saving and investment? And who bears the burden (the cost) of the resources absorbed by government purchases under alternative ways of financing them? The answers to these questions, in turn, are essential for an understanding of the intergenerational effect of expenditure and financing, and the choice of tax versus debt financing. Section III confronts these questions at the theoretical level, while Section IV brings to bear a variety of empirical evidence.

I SHORT RUN EFFECTS OF DEFICITS: INCREASED OUTPUT VERSUS CROWDING OUT, PARTICULARLY OF INVESTMENT

This is an old issue which was at the core of the debate between the Keynesian and the classical view, but deserves a brief review to allow for the role of monetary policy. One must distinguish several possibilities.

Slack and Accommodating Monetary Policy – The Pure Keynesian Multiplier Case

According to the standard Keynesian analysis, a rise in deficit not only does not crowd out investment but, instead, it increases – or crowds in – output by the additional demand directly produced by the fiscal action, amplified by the multiplier. The extent and composition of the increase depends on the source of change in deficit and can be inferred from the standard national income identity and aggregate demand equation:

$$Y = C + I + G; \qquad C = c(Y - T); \qquad Def = G - T \tag{1}$$

where Y, C, I, G, Def, and T are respectively income produced, consumption, investment, government expenditure, deficit and taxes net of transfers. Consumption is assumed, conventionally, to depend on disposable income, thus abstracting from the Barro-type hypothesis, discussed later, that it might also be affected, directly, by government consumption. From these relations, one can infer that a rise in Def due entirely to a reduction, ΔT, in taxes, 'crowds in' consumption and output by $(c/1-c)\Delta Def$ (a direct effect of $c\Delta T$, magnified by the multiplier $(1/(1-c))$). If Def rises because of a rise in G, T constant, then to the above effect one must add the rise in output needed to meet the government demand, ΔG. This result is the standard investment multiplier:

$$\left(1 + \frac{c}{1-c}\right) \Delta Def = \left(\frac{1}{1-c}\right) \Delta Def$$

Finally, if the rise in G is accompanied by an equal rise in T, leaving Def unchanged, then the consumption effect is cut off and what is left is only the direct effect of 1 (balanced budget multiplier). In addition, there can be a rise of investment through accelerator effects, increasing the impact on output.

But these results are subject to some important qualifications. First, they represent short-run effects – i.e., while the slack persists. In the long run, there may still be crowding out effects, as discussed below. Second, for those results to hold, even in the short run, two crucial conditions must be satisfied: there must be enough slack in the economy for the additional demand to be satisfied without pressure on prices, and, even when there is enough slack, there must be an accommodating monetary policy that permits the expansion of output, with stable prices, without putting pressure on interest rates and credit market.

Slack and Non-accommodating Monetary Policy – the Intermediate Case

Suppose there is adequate slack in the economy, but monetary policy is not fully accommodating in the sense of providing enough liquidity to keep interest rates and credit markets from tightening in the face of a rise in output such as would correspond to the fiscal action and the multiplier. Then the rise in interest rates will crowd out investment, reducing demand directly, and through the multiplier and thus enforcing the containment of Y. The extent of the crowding out will depend on monetary policy as well as the type of fiscal expansion. Specifically, from (1) one can derive:

$$\Delta I = (1-c)\Delta \bar{Y} - \Delta G + c\Delta T \qquad (2)$$

It is seen that a rise in deficit due to G, T constant, will crowd out Investment, dollar per dollar, less, however, $(1-c)\Delta\bar{Y}$, the rise in saving due to the rise in income $\Delta\bar{Y}$ allowed by Central Bank policy. But, as long as monetary policy is not fully accommodating, and thus the rise in income is constrained to fall short of the full multiplier response, the rise in saving must be insufficient to prevent crowding out from occurring. In the limiting case where income is prevented from rising at all, the additional deficit crowds out I fully, as government absorption replaces investment, while consumption remains constant.

If the deficit rises through a fall in taxes, then I gets crowded out by a rise in consumption. But, the crowding out is less than dollar per dollar. In the first place, consumption rises, and investment is reduced, only by $c\mathrm{d}T$, while $(1-c)$ of the tax cut is saved, reducing the crowding out effect of the rise in deficit. In addition, to the extent that monetary policy allows Y to rise, the resulting rise in saving reduces the crowding out further, though again not to the point of eliminating it.

Finally, if G rises with a balanced budget, and hence with an equal rise in T, most of G is accommodated by a fall in consumption by $c\mathrm{d}G$, due to the higher taxes, while the crowding out of investment is limited to the fall in saving, $(1-c)\Delta G$, less, again, the rise in saving resulting from the rise in income and saving.

It appears therefore that, as long as the money supply is not accommodating enough to permit the rise of income by the full multiplier, an expansionary fiscal policy – i.e. a rise in deficit or even a rise in expenditure covered by taxes – will create some crowding out of private investment, even if there is excess capacity and wasting resources.

Note that when monetary policy forces a *de facto* crowding out in the presence of idle capacity, this may be due to errors in the design or execution of policy, but it may also be due, as was the case recently, to a target Y below feasible full employment, in order to help the winding down of inflation.

No Slack: the Classical Case

When there is no slack, the effect of deficit can be inferred from (2) above by putting $dY=0$: the deficit will necessarily crowd out investment, dollar for dollar, when due to G, and by $(1-c)$ dollar per dollar when due to tax reduction. This conclusion holds as long as consumption does not directly respond to expenditure, for given taxes. The implication of that assumption, as well as its empirical relevance, are taken up in Sections III and IV below.

It must be recognised that even when the fiscal expansion occurs in an economy at full employment, if the money supply is unchanged, there will tend to be some upward pressure on prices and some temporary rise in output. To this extent, the crowding out may be less than indicated above, but only transiently. Similarly, the inflation should also be transient, resulting in a higher price level but not in an inflationary process (see Section II below).

II DEFICITS AS THE CAUSE OF INFLATION

The 'Conventional Wisdom'

The view that budget deficits cause inflation, or, in the extreme view, that they are its main cause, is a popular one. Apparently it has its origin in the view that when the government spends more than it collects, it pays for the differences by the 'printing press', and that the printing of money is inflationary. This perception is reinforced by memories of major war deficits, being accompanied by monetary expansions, and by major inflationary episodes. There is also a strand of Keynesian origin that holds that deficits can cause inflation by increasing demand. Most recently these views have been reinforced by the experience of the 1970s after the oil crisis. In many, indeed most, countries there were fairly severe bouts of inflation, accompanied by significant deficits or, at the very least, appreciable deterioration in the government account.

This view that deficits cause inflation was at the core of the Reagan economic platform through the early part of his administration. In fact, he suggested that deficits were the cause of the widespread stagflation of the time, as the inflation produced economic turmoil, which, in turn, led to unemployment.

Deficits and Money Creation

The basic fallacy in the argument is the proposition that government deficits have to be financed by creation of money. This is patently false in economies with a reasonably well developed financial system. There, the government does not create money and pays for deficits by issuing appropriate non-money IOU's. Money is created, instead, by the Central Bank when it buys government debt or other assets, or by the banking system buying assets with monetary liabilities, within limits set by Central Bank.

The task of the Central Bank is to stabilise output and prices through its control of M. Hence, there is no reason why it should expand or contract money and credit according to the size of deficit. The only limited exception is when a deficit accompanies a cyclical slack, either through built-in stabilisers or through *ad hoc* budget policy. In this case, the growing deficit (surplus) should be accompanied by an appropriately expansionary (contractionary) monetary policy. But, in these circumstances, there should be no cause for inflation.

There are, however, some special circumstances in which the deficit is accompanied, more or less unavoidably, by monetary expansion, and thus inflation. One is the case of major war, referred to earlier. In such cases, the government may need to acquire more resources than can be secured through taxation and absorption of government liabilities on the part of the public, both voluntary and compulsory –

account being taken of the disincentive effects of taxation and forced saving. In that case, the government may have to fill the gap by selling part of the debt to the Central Bank and the banking system, who pay by creating money for the government to spend.

A second case is that of primitive financial structure when there are no mechanisms for the government to sell its debt to the public (or private banks). It must therefore sell it to Central Banks, expanding the money stock. This mechanism seems to be important in some Latin American type inflation.

A third circumstance in which deficits might lead to inflation is the one described by Sargent and Wallace (1981) in which, essentially, the debt grows so large that the interest cannot be paid by tapping current private saving. Hence, at least a part of the deficit has to be paid by money creation (or, equivalently, through the inflation tax). But this extreme case would seem to be of very limited empirical relevance.

One fourth and final mechanism arises from the circumstance described earlier about the impact of deficit under conditions of near full employment. The crowding out of investment may not occur promptly unless interest rates are allowed to rise through a stable (or in fact appropriately reduced) money supply. However, the Central Bank might endeavour to prevent interest rates from rising, either by mistake or because of subservience to a Government that does not wish to see an unpopular rise in interest. This policy tends to lead to an expanding M and continuing inflation, as long as it persists. Here the expansion of M and accompanying inflation might be directly associated to the deficit. Yet what feeds the inflation is not printing of money to finance the deficit, as in the naive version, but the endeavour to hold the line on interest rates, in the face of the more expansionary fiscal policy. Indeed, in this case, the growth of money is related to a more expansionary fiscal policy, regardless of whether such a policy leads to a deficit or merely to a smaller surplus. Little is known as to whether this particular mechanism of inflation is empirically important. But, at least for the United States, empirical studies do not generally seem to find that it is (see, e.g., Blinder (1983), and the references cited therein).

Can Deficits Explain the Recent Inflation?

If the recent inflation were due to the deficits that developed more or less simultaneously, it would have to be through one of the four mechanisms examined above. Yet the first three are clearly inapplicable in the relevant period, at least for the developed countries. As for the last mechanism, whatever one's assessment about its empirical relevance in general, one can rule out the possibility that the recent inflation was due to it for one quite compelling reason, namely that there were no significant 'true' deficits through most of the period. This statement is fully consistent with the above-mentioned observation of rising deficits reported in most countries, because the reported deficit represents the growth in *nominal* deficit. To measure the deficit correctly, one must calculate the change in the real debt; that change is equal to the nominal deficit less the loss of purchasing power of the outstanding debt, GD, in the course of the year, due to the inflation, $\dot{P}$, i.e., less $\dot{P}GD$. This is equivalent to saying that the true interest actually paid and received on the government debt should be computed as $RD - \dot{P}D = rD$, when the first term in the left side is the actual interest paid, and $r = R - \dot{P}$ is the real rate. The correction term $\dot{P}D$, can be quite large when inflation gets high. It is therefore not surprising that, once corrected for inflation, in general, the deficits as a percentage of income do not appear to have risen significantly over the recent period, and may even have declined in some cases.

Thus, Cukierman and Mortensen (1983) in a study of five major Common Market countries found that, according to official statistics, in all countries but one (France), there were substantial reported deficits by the end of the 1970s, and they were generally strikingly larger than a decade earlier. However, once the official figures are corrected for inflation, they find that the deficit increased significantly for only one country, Belgium, where inflation was not particularly serious, and very moderately for Germany, a low inflation country. For the remaining high inflation countries, the deficit has been steady or has even declined as in France and Italy, while in the UK there were mostly surpluses, though declining in the course of the 1970s.

An alternative way of minimising the effect of the inflation bias in the official statistics is to look at the behaviour of the ratio of government debt to nominal GNP, which provides a good measure of whether there has actually been an increase in the burden of the debt. Siegel and Protopapadakis (1984) have studied the behaviour of this ratio in recent years for seven major industrial countries, including in the debt the entire public sector. They find that since the early 1970s this ratio has risen appreciably only in three countries, Germany, Japan and Italy, of which the first two had relatively moderate inflation and also had very low debt at the beginning. For the remaining countries, including high inflation ones, like the UK and France, but also the US and Switzerland, the ratio has been roughly constant.

What Accounts for the Recent Association Between Reported Deficits and Inflation?

We suggest that a major, if not *the* major answer is to be found in 'inverse causation': it was the relatively high and widespread rate of inflation (generated primarily by the successive oil shocks – see below) that caused a rise in nominal deficit, and not vice versa. Inflation contributed to nominal deficits both by increasing outlays and by decreasing revenues.

Outlays rose for two reasons. First, the inflation tended to be reflected in higher nominal interest rates (as suggested by Fisher's law), and hence interest expenses. This effect can be quite substantial. Thus, if we suppose a debt income ratio of 30 per cent, (not far from the average for OECD countries), and a real rate of 3 per cent, then a rise in inflation from zero to 10 per cent will increase the interest bill more than fourfold, from 0.09 to 3.9 per cent of income. Second, the effort at stopping and reducing the inflation through a non-accommodating monetary policy resulted, at least for a time, in a fall in employment and output, which in turn reduced revenues and increased expenditure for transfers, such as unemployment compensation. This is the standard cyclical reaction of the budget in the presence of automatic stabilizers. The only partial offset to these mechanisms has tended to come through the so-called 'bracket creep' – the effect of inflation of pushing tax payers with an unchanged real income into higher tax brackets, thus raising real taxes and revenues. But, the magnitude of this effect, which in any event depends on specific tax institutions, was frequently reduced by adjustments of the brackets, whether automatic or discretionary.

Of course, the budget deficit could have been controlled by raising taxes, but this course was not followed on a significant scale, either because governments knew that the increase of the deficit was partly fictitious and partly the result of built-in stabilisers, or because they were disinclined to raise taxes in an already depressed economy.

But if inflation was not caused by deficits but rather caused them, then what caused inflation? As already indicated, the major cause in the 1970s and early 1980s were supply shocks, basically oil shocks. They sparked a wage price spiral, made possible by partial monetary accommodation. But the accommodation was, or at any rate, eventually became, sufficiently limited to generate substantial cyclical unemployment and thus stagflation.

We conclude therefore that deficits can be the cause of inflation only under rather special circumstances. These circumstances were, in particular, not present during the widespread inflationary episodes of the 1970s. Those episodes were, instead, largely the results of huge supply shocks, which produced stagflation and hence government deficit.

III WHAT IS CROWDED OUT BY DEFICITS AND DEBT – AND WHAT DIFFERENCE DOES IT MAKE?

A Review of the Traditional Debate

The classic issue relating to the public deficit is generally posed as: are there any costs in using deficit financing in place of taxes? What are they? Who bears them? What is implied with respect to using it? Going back in the centuries, one finds a variety of sharply contradictory major views, with countless variants.

1. There is, first, the timeless view held by the concerned man of the street that the public deficits are essentially like a family's debt. They are a burden on the family's future by 'mortgaging' future resources for the payment of interests and the repayment of principal. It was last heard with great vigour by Keynesian supporters of the New Deal deficit spending and during the battle over the Kennedy tax cut, in the early 1960s.

2. There is next the sophisticated rebuttal of that view set forth by 'economists' since a couple of centuries ago, arguing that the analogy with private debt is false because we owe it to ourselves: the future generations pay the interest and principle, but future generations get it. It is but a transfer; disposable income is unaffected. This argument is reinforced by the proposition that the deficit cannot be a burden on future generations because we cannot consume their resources of the future which have not yet been produced. It also follows from this reasoning that an exception must be made for public debt contracted outside the family, i.e., abroad; that, and only that, will impose a future burden, analogous to private debt.

3. Next comes the yet more sophisticated rebuttal of the sophisticated rebuttal, also going back a long time, according to which the man in the street is pretty much right after all, even if, largely, for the wrong reason. This view rests on three basic considerations.

(a) Deficit financing is a burden on future generations to the advantage of the current generation because it reduces the tax burden of the current generation, allowing it to consume more, and the larger consumption crowds out investment, as saving is diverted from financing investment to financing the government deficit.

(b) It is through this crowding out process that the current generation can, in effect, succeed in consuming more at the expense of a reduction in the future availability of means of production and thus, finally, of future output.

(c) The interest on the debt is not a transfer: in the absence of deficit, the payment received by holders of the claim would have come *not* from taxing others but from the additional output made possible by the investment; thus, the higher taxes paid are, indeed, a measure of the output lost and of the burden borne by the future.

(d) The intergenerational effects of Deficit financing in (a) and (b) hold independently of whether the government borrows domestically or abroad. In the latter case, there need not be a crowding out of domestic capital formation or stock of capital. However, that capital will not produce income for the domestic population but, instead, for the foreign lender. This conclusion holds well if the government borrows domestically, but the higher domestic interest rates attract foreign capital, which is tapped by the private sector. This is, broadly speaking, the mechanism that has prevailed in the course of the current US deficits binge.

Some variant of this crowding out effect represents the prevailing (but not uncontrasted) view at present.

Crowding Out in an LCH Framework

Basic formulation

The above argument runs in terms of flows – the deficit crowds out investment. It suffers from failure to demonstrate that the initial loss of investment will not be made up later. This issue can be investigated by carrying out the analysis in terms of stocks – where one can also, usefully, bring to bear the Life Cycle Hypothesis (LCH) framework.

One can start from the identity that non-human net wealth (net worth), W, held by the private sector and representing the aggregate market value of net asset of individual households, is the sum of two components: (i) the market value of tangible assets and equity claims to tangible assets, K, and, (ii) the market value of all Government Debt, GD. Thus, $W = K + GD$. It follows that $K = W - GD$, so that an increase in GD must reduce K by an equal amount, *provided only the aggregate amount of wealth the private sector wishes to hold is not significantly influenced by the size of the public debt*. This condition is referred to hereafter as 'Wealth Independent of National Debt', or WIND. A sufficient condition for WIND is that private saving is not affected by the extent of government deficit current or past. But this is, at least to a first approximation, what is implied by the LCH where accumulation in relation to income is controlled by retirement and other hump saving requirements which can be fulfilled by any existing asset. (Some reasons why WIND may not hold exactly are considered below.)

Under WIND then, the government debt displaces, or crowds out, an amount of private capital, ΔK, equal to the market value of debt held by the public – that is, the relation between flows holds equally between stocks. The (annual) burden of the debt can then be measured as the income lost because of the debt. That is equal to the amount of capital crowded out, ΔK, times the productivity of capital; the former is $\Delta K = -GD$, and the latter can be approximated by (no less) than r. Thus, to a first approximation, the (annual) burden of the debt is rGD, or the interest service. In terms of flows, the current deficit reduces capital formation by $\Delta I = Def$, and the loss of investment leads to a permanent reduction in the capital stock, which makes future generations poorer, by $rDef$.

Some qualifications and limitations

The above formulation helps to call attention to a number of limitations of the proposition (cf. Modigliani, 1961).

(i) To the extent that the government debt is offset by government capital, KG, whose real return is commensurate with the private return, r, then the loss of income, rGD, is compensated by the higher income, rGK. To that extent, there is no net burden on future generations (though there may still be redistribution within generations). Thus, the burden is more precisely $r(GD - GK)$, or, the service on the so-called deadweight debt. In flow terms what matters is the deadweight deficit. Needless to say, the task of measuring net government investments, including (net) expenditures producing future flows of income, is a formidable one. The National Income Account measures are but a rough approximation.

(ii) The rate paid by the Government on *GD* is likely to be a substantial underestimate of the true productivity of Capital. The main reason is profit taxes, introducing a wedge between productivity and the market rate, *r*. In other words, when the government issues debt, it must not only collect *rD*, but, in addition, it loses the tax revenue on the income generated by the displaced project. Another reason is that the government may grant special privileges and/or impose constraints with respect to holding its debt: for instance, require financial institutions to hold debt at low interest rates, or grant tax exemptions. Thus, the interest bill tends to underestimate the true burden.

(iii) A third reason why *r* may differ from the marginal productivity of capital is the risk premium required by the market, which causes a wedge between the riskless rate *r* and the (expected) return on risky capital – though a very good case can be made that this correction of *r* is unwarranted.

(iv) The crowding out is accompanied by, indeed occurs through, a rise in *r*. But this may cause *GD* to affect the optimum life path of accumulation and thus, indirectly, aggregate wealth. Unfortunately, it is impossible to say in what direction, though available information suggests the effect is unlikely to be large.

(v) The stock of tangible capital consists of two components: reproducible tangible capital, *RTW*, and non-reproducible, tangible *NRTW* – like land and other natural resources. Since we can take the latter as fixed in quantity, what is relevant is the effect of *GD* on *RTW*. Now the market value of *NRTW* can be expected to depend inversely on *r*. Thus, as *GD* rises, raising *r*, the value of *NRTW* will tend to decline: if *W* is unaffected, then a rise in *G* will actually reduce *RTW* by less than one-for-one. The importance of the 'offset' mechanism depends on the size of *NRTW* relative to *W* and *GD* (for the US, in recent years, *NRTW* (basically private land) is estimated at about 20 per cent of private net worth (cf. Board of Governors of the Federal Reserve System, 1981)).

(vi) There is finally one potentially important mechanism through which *G* or *Def* could affect *W* and hence modify the one-for-one crowding out. At the time the *Def* occurs, the future generations that suffer from the reduction in *K*, or future payment of *rDef*, consist of all those living beyond the time of the crowding out. Obviously, that includes members of the current generations, as long as they survive. This has two implications: (i) part of the burden of the deficit falls on the current generation – basically the present value (*PV*) of the taxes to pay the interest, which will be levied on the current generation. Still, because of mortality (finite life), the taxes paid by the current generation must be a declining fraction of the taxes collected to pay interest in successive years. Therefore, the *PV* of those taxes must, necessarily, be less than the taxes the current generation has saved itself through the deficit; (ii) the deficit may have some transitory effects on the accumulation and the stock of privately held wealth, to the extent that the private sector is a highly rational calculator and a smoother of consumption.

To see this, suppose *Def* arises from a rise in *G*, tax (and net of tax income) remaining constant, and it is expected to continue indefinitely, or at least for a while. Then, the debt must rise in time, and the rational consumer will anticipate paying rising taxes to cover the interest bill: *t* years later total interest will have grown to *rtDef*. The cost to the representative household is the *PV* of the stream, adjusted for mortality. If he is a consumption smoother he will cut the consumption over his remaining *T* years of life, by an annuity whose *PV* is the *PV* of the loss. Because *C* is, thus, reduced by a step, while net of tax income falls gradually as the debt grows, the current generation might be expected to respond to the deficit by saving more for a number of years, which grows with the length of the remaining life (*T*). In the limiting case where *T* is infinite, and only in that case, the cut in *C* and rise in *S* is, initially, precisely equal to *Def* and remains such thereafter. Accordingly, the government debt has the effect of increasing wealth by an equal amount thereby failing to cause crowding out of private capital. But this result occurs only with inifite life. When life is finite, the wealth will rise, but the rise is less than the debt – and is transitory. Thus, there will be some initial crowding out of *K*. How much depends on both the average length of life and on the rate of discount, both as shown by Sterling (1984). For reasonable values of these parameters the difference between the growth in wealth and debt is substantial. And the effect on wealth is transitory in the sense that, if and when the debt stops growing, eventually the crowding out will become complete.

Similarly, suppose the *Def* is due to a *one time* cut in taxes. A rational smoothing consumer would increase consumption less than the cut in taxes in order to avoid the need to reduce *C* later, to meet the rising taxes. Instead, he would determine the extent of maintainable rise in C by taking the difference between the tax rebate and the PV of new taxes, and spreading it into an annuity of T years. With T finite, the result is again some temporary saving and a temporary bulge in W partly offsetting *Def* and *GD*.

The same general approach and conclusion holds if the cut in taxes relative to government expenditure is *permanent* and *rGD* rises over time: consumption will rise by a step, but less than the cut in taxes, initially producing saving, which eventually, as the taxes levied grow larger, turn to dissaving, completing the crowding out.

Non-crowding-out in the Barro Hypothesis

Barro's hypothesis

Quite recently, the issue of who bears the burden of deficit financed government expenditure has been reopened by a school arguing that the view that the man in the street is right, is, after all, really wrong: there are no intergenerational effects, or shifting of the burden to the future, resulting from debt as such. This argument is today commonly associated with the name of Barro (1974), though it was first set forth – and rejected – by Ricardo (Sraffa, 1962, p. 887) two centuries ago.

The basic contention of this new line is that there is a burden on the current, and possibly future, generations when the government uses resources for current consumption (as distinguished from investment yielding a social return, comparable to that of private investment); but that the way the acquisition of resources is financed – taxes or deficit – is of no consequence to anyone. Taxes and deficit are equivalent (tax neutrality).

Though at first surprising, this conclusion is really a straightforward implication of the perfect rationality, perfect markets, *LCH*, for the limiting case of life approaching infinity. As was just shown, in that limiting case, the deficit arising, e.g., from a reduction in taxes, results in an equal rise in W, or additional S, matching *Def* and leaving I and K unchanged.

The most obvious objection to the Barro model is that life *is* finite, and that this circumstance is sufficient to establish the intergenerational effects of deficits.

However, Barro has demonstrated that infinite life is sufficient (under perfection of markets and rationality) but not necessary to establish the tax neutrality proposition. Finite life can lead to the same implications, if one supposes that, through the bequest mechanism, the members of the current generation allocate optimally their resources over the current generation and their heirs; the allocation being optimal in the sense that any other allocation within the feasible set would make the *current* generation worse off. It is then obvious that, if the government rebates taxes, thus financing a part of G by deficit, and if the current generation increased its consumption accordingly, leaving its bequests unchanged, it would accept a redistribution of resources away from the initial allocation, in its favour and against future generations. But the initial allocation is still available since the fiscal reshuffling does not change the budget constraint. In fact, that allocation can be easily secured by not consuming the rebate and using it to buy the debt. This incremental investment in government securities is first used to pay the new tax, as long as the initial agents survive, and then left as a bequest to be used by the heirs to pay their new taxes, without changing consumption. And this course will actually be followed since, by assumption, the initial allocation was optimal.

This imaginative reasoning relies on a large number of explicit and implicit assumptions, whose failure will invalidate his conclusions, at least in part.

Shortcomings within Barro's bequests framework

Let us for a moment grant Barro his assumption that every household is bent on making optimal allocations of his resources over the family tree. His conclusions will still fail to the extent that:

(i) Significant *market imperfections*, plus uncertainty, create liquidity constraints and make government borrowing cheaper than private. To this extent, government surplus and deficits may be an effective device to reshuffle consumption over time;

(ii) Not all agents are *super rational* in the sense of being able to figure out precisely the implications of the government's fiscal actions and how to remedy them; in particular, they may suffer from myopia about effects of deficit on future generations.

(iii) *A tax rebate* accompanied by later taxes is *not readily predictable* nor is it *neutral* in terms of distributional effects between different *stirpe* (lineage), as is implied by relying on 'the representative household'. Such a failure is especially evident with progressive taxes which make it essentially impossible to foresee what share of the burden will fall on one's heir. But even under the simplifying assumption that all pay the same per capita tax at any given date, it is obvious that the deficit will enrich *stirpes* with no, or less than average, children (and descendants) and impoverishes those with many descendants.

One might think that Barro's proposition could still be salvaged in the aggregate; for while those who are better off will increase their consumption, those worse off will reduce theirs; and why should the two effects not cancel? But in fact that is most unlikely: the increase in consumption of those with less children, who are made better off, will tend to exceed the decline of those who cut back. This can be illustrated in the convenient case in which the change in resources is allocated evenly over the current and next generation. One can then write an expression for the change in C of the current generation which shows that the change in consumption as a function of the number of children is convex from above. It follows that, if with two children per family, ΔC is zero, if the same children are redistributed, creating some childless families and some numerous families, the former will increase their C more than the large families will reduce theirs.

(iv) *Bequests are constrained to be non-negative*. With existing institutions, an individual's ability to secure the optimal allocation between generations is constrained by the fact that he cannot enforce a *negative* transfer. Suppose the optimal solution calls for that – and it may well be a common event, given that, these days, our children, on the average, are substantially richer than we are. Then, the non-negativity constraint prevents enforcement, and we end with a corner solution of no bequests, where the person's welfare would be increased if he could arrange to transfer resources from future generations to himself. If then taxes are raised, expenditure constant, unconstrained households would choose to reduce their bequests; but with the bequest already at zero, they have no choice but to reduce consumption, raising national saving and investment. Conversely, when taxes are reduced (or fail to rise to meet higher expenditure), this provides an opportunity to improve allocation by raising current consumption through the transfer of resources from the future. In short, non-negativity may lead even Barro type agents to behave as though they had no concern for their heirs, destroying tax neutrality.

But, if this is so, why do we not observe more deficit financing? One may suspect that, under normal conditions, people will be bound by a self-imposed constraint, calling for them not to go out of their way to encroach on their children. But deficits might be relied upon (and seem to be) in cases when exogenous circumstances make the current generation poorer than surrounding ones, e.g., major war.

Critique of bequest framework

(i) *How important are bequests?* For the Barro hypothesis to be empirically relevant it would have to be the case that all households generally plan to, and actually do, leave substantial bequests to their heirs. Yet there is a good deal of evidence that inheritance accounts for a relatively small fraction of private wealth, though this proposition is, at present, rather controversial.

Before the development of the LCH, it was widely understood that the major reason for saving was to leave bequests, and that, accordingly, the existing stock of wealth was, primarily, the result of transfers from earlier generations. The LCH, or more generally hump saving, provided an alternative explanation for the origin of wealth; in particular, it was shown (cf. Modigliani and Brumberg, 1979) that, relying on some stylised assumptions about the length of life and retirement, the LCH could account, all by itself, for the amount of wealth, relative to income, held by the private sector in the United States (and in other countries as well when data became available).

Clearly, bequests and major gifts also contribute to wealth: just how large a share is an interesting empirical issue. A number of empirical studies, many carried out in the mid-1960s and reviewed in Modigliani (1984), arrived at several interesting conclusions: (i) a remarkably small fraction of households say that they save for the purpose of leaving bequests, even among relatively well-to-do families, while the overwhelming proportion give reasons consistent with hump saving; (ii) from the answers to a question asked by several surveys about what fraction of the respondent wealth was received by inheritance, one arrives at an estimate of the overall share of inherited wealth (excluding intramarital transfers) of 15–20 per cent; (iii) estimating this share from the annual flow of bequests derived from a variety of sources (survey, probate statistics, wealth of deceased), one arrives at a broadly similar figure – but ranging up to 25 per cent; (iv) estimates for Great Britain, the only other country for which some information seems available, suggests a share comparable to the United States, if anything a little lower.

These estimates have recently been subjected to a number of

criticisms, in particular by Kotlikoff and Summers (1981). These authors endeavour to estimate directly the share of life cycle wealth, from which they derive the share of transfer wealth as a residual. Their basic procedure is to calculate the LC wealth held by each age (and sex) group by capitalising and cumulating the difference between an estimate of labour income and of consumption, at each earlier age. They find that the share of life cycle wealth in total wealth is quite low, probably as low as 15 per cent, implying that the share of wealth received by transfer could be put at 85 per cent. It has been shown by Modigliani (1984) that the huge difference between this estimate and that of around 20–25 per cent, arrived at by directly measuring bequests and major gifts, can be accounted for by three specific factors, rather than by that to which K & S hint, namely huge unreported flows of *intra vivos* transfers.

One cause of discrepancy arises from a conceptual error, which affects their estimates and is, numerically, quite sizeable; it concerns the treatment of consumers' durables which were, in effect, regarded as consumption instead of an investment. A second source arises from their way of measuring LC saving and wealth which is at odds with, and greatly understates, what is usually meant by LC saving (wealth). There are two major discrepancies. The first is their definition of income which is quite different from the standard one in that it excludes one part of property income, namely the part that represents the return on transfers received plus accumulated interest thereon (but includes the return on wealth transferred, plus accumulation thereon!): This definition implies that the return on inherited wealth is not income but a further inheritance. It, clearly, results in a substantial understatement of LC income and hence saving and wealth, while correspondingly overestimating the flow of transfers and the stock of transferred wealth.

The second difference originates in their decision to depart from the standard practice of taking the household as the basic decision unit and holder of wealth and to rely, instead, on individual males and females to which they have to assign (labour) income and consumption by an elaborate imputation procedure. With this formulation they cannot rely on household formation as an objective criterion for deciding whether a person has entered the life cycle accumulation process. They, thus, decide, quite arbitrarily, that the criterion is eighteen years of age, regardless of whether the person is self-supporting or is, instead, primarily supported by another household and thus part of *its* consumption. Those aged eighteen and over, not yet working, are thus assigned appropriate positive consumption and a *zero* labour income. This results in large, negative, LC savings at the beginning of life, that cumulate into a large, *negative*, LC wealth until the person begins working.

When one makes allowance for these errors and conceptual differences, one finds that one can account pretty closely for the entire difference between the 85 per cent transfer of wealth claimed by K & S and the estimate of 20–25 per cent for the share of wealth actually received by inheritance and major bequests.

We may thus conclude that according to presently available evidence, the process of bequests and other transfers is not of a dimension sufficient to support the intergenerational links implied by the Barro hypothesis.

(ii) *Non-Barro motivated bequests.* The estimate of 20–25 per cent for the share of wealth received through transfers is likely to overstate appreciably the importance of bequests that might respond to the motivation postulated by Barro. As examples of alternative motivations, one might suggest a utility function whose arguments are life consumption and bequests, independently of the utility or endowment of one's heirs. An even more important motivation is uncertainty of life together with limited annuity markets. A third and very different mechanism has been suggested by Bernheim *et al.* (1985).

IV SOME EMPIRICAL TESTS OF CROWDING OUT

Criticism of Barro's hypothesis suggests that his no-crowding out theorem is likely to have limited emirical relevance at best. However, there should be no need to speculate on this issue since the proposition is in principle testable. This section presents a number of such tests.

It has been shown that the controversy about crowding out can be reduced to the following: whether, and to what extent, the amount of wealth held at any point depends on the stock of government debt, properly measured. Equivalently, in terms of flows, the issue is whether the private sector's saving depends on the (properly measured) deficit of the government. The LCH model suggests that there should be some dependence, but modest and partly transient. The Barro (and partly the US Treasury (1983)) tax neutrality hypothesis, in its pure form implies, instead, that the effect should be dollar for dollar, and permanent: each dollar of public debt would increase wealth by a dollar – or each dollar of deficit should increase saving by a dollar, except possibly for some short run slippage.

These contrasting hypotheses can, in principle, be tested, and a number of such are reported in the rest of this section.

Tests Based on Stocks – US 1900–83

A number of tests, focusing on the stock aspect, were carried out for the US nearly twenty years ago, well before Barro's hypothesis (see Modigliani, 1966). The test relies on the LCH hypothesis of accumulation which implies that, with a relatively stable rate of growth, and in the absence of government debt, private net worth, W, should be proportional to (permanent) disposable income, $D\hat{Y}$, up to stochastic disturbances. Allowing for debt, the test equation can be formulated as:

$$\hat{W} = aD\hat{Y} + bGD \qquad 0 < b < < 1 \tag{3}$$

where $\hat{W}$ is the equilibrium wealth (which now includes the public debt), $D\hat{Y}$ anticipated permanent private disposable income, and b should be unity for Barro and positive but relatively small under the standard view. For testing purposes $\hat{W}$ was replaced by $W+e$, e being an error term, and W an estimate of private net worth based on Goldsmith's information. $D\hat{Y}$ was approximated by an estimate of private income after net taxes, and GD by an estimate of net public sector debt. To minimise the problem of heteroscedasticity, the equation was estimated in ratio form, scaled by Y, for the years then available, 1900 to 1955. The estimate of a came to 4.7, very much in line with the implications of simple life cycle models, while that of b is essentially zero (slightly negative) with a standard error of 0.1 (the standard error of 0.22 given in the original article is incorrect). If one adds the post-war years, and replaces the estimates for the years 1946 to 1958 by later estimates, the results are strikingly similar: a is 4.6, and b is slightly negative with a standard error of 0.16.

These results, however, suffer from one serious shortcoming, which passed unnoticed at the time of writing because of the then state of the arts, namely that the residuals are highly serially correlated, as evidenced by a DW statistic of 0.66 for the first period, and 0.55 for the entire period. Such a high serial correlation is, of course, very much to be expected: for when any shock (e.g., a boom in the stock market) pushes the wealth income ratio away from its equilibrium value, it will take considerable time before saving (and capital gains) gradually restore the equilibrium. This consideration suggests reformulating the hypothesis in stock adjustment form:

$$\Delta W = \gamma[\hat{W} - W(-1)]$$

Substituting for $\hat{W}$ from (1) yields:

$$\Delta W = \alpha \hat{D} Y + \beta D - \gamma W(-1) \qquad \alpha = a\gamma,\ \beta = b\gamma \qquad (4)$$

This equation was estimated using $W(-1)$ as the scale factor. (Some estimates were also done with Y as the deflator, but the results were always quite close.) Another desirable improvement would be to measure permanent income, $\hat{Y}$, by consumption, rather than current income. Unfortunately, an estimate of consumption (as distinguished from consumer expenditure) is available only for the post-war period.

A summary of results is provided in Table 1.1. For each period and subperiod we give two estimates. The first is based on (4) above, while the second is obtained from an equation in which we have added to (4) the percentage change in an index of the stock market. The reason is that, in the short run, such changes can be taken as largely exogenous to the process of accumulation and yet account for a substantial fraction of the short run movements in wealth. By controlling for this important but erratic source of capital gains, we are able to analyse more effectively the determinants of other sources of accumulation and, in particular, saving.

It appears from the table that the gradual adjustment hypothesis is well supported by the evidence. Indeed, the speed of adjustment is rather low, mostly between 20 and 30 per cent per year, and falls further to the 10–20 per cent range, when one controls for those swings in wealth that are associated with the stock market. Understandably, the estimated speed does become larger when the target wealth is related to the more stable measure of permanent income, represented by consumption, a formulation which, as expected, also leads to a closer fit (cf. col (5) of rows 5 to 8). The estimate of the equilibrium wealth–income ratio (a in col (3)) is quite stable, especially when the stock market variable is included: 5.7 for the entire 80-year period (row 2), versus 5.8 for the original period (row 4)

Table 1.1 Tests of crowding out – for the US stock from 1900–1980*

		(1)	(2)	(3)	(4)	(5)
		β	γ	*a*	*b*	*SE*
1. 1900–50	$\hat{y}=y$	−0.01	0.20	5.3	−0.05	0.058
		0.1	0.05			
2. Same + Stock Market	(*SM*)	−0.06	0.12	5.7	−0.5	0.042
		0.08	0.04			
3. 1900–58	$\hat{y}=y$	−0.07	0.21	5.5	−0.3	0.063
		0.13	0.06			
4. Same	+ *SM*	−0.07	0.12	5.8	−0.62	0.047
		0.1	0.05			
5. 1947–80	$\hat{y}=y$	0.02	0.27	4.7	0.06	0.045
		0.14	0.14			
6. Same	+ *SM*	−0.12	0.16	5.4	−0.8	0.03
		0.1	0.09			
7. 1948–80	$\hat{y}=dCon$	0.17	0.35	5.1	0.5	0.039
		0.14	0.16			
8. Same	+ *SM*	−0.06	0.27	5.7	−0.2	0.028
		0.11	0.11			
9. Replace Gov. Debt by Eisner's Net Worth	+ *SM*	0.06	0.27	5.4	0.22	0.028
		0.09	0.11			

*The entries below the parameter estimates are standard errors.

and 5.4 for the post-war period (row 6). These figures are somewhat higher than the observed mean of the ratio, but this is to be expected in a growing system, in the presence of a rather slow adjustment.

From the point of view of testing Barro versus the standard view, the crucial parameter is, of course, the coefficient of debt, *b*, and the associated estimate of β. It is seen that in the equations without the stock market, *b* is sometimes positive and sometimes negative, but always insignificant and negligibly small, except possibly for the post-war period regression in which permanent income was approximated by consumption (row 7). However, when the stock market variable is added (with a substantial reduction in the standard error), then the *b* coefficient is found to be uniformly negative, though still insignificantly different from zero. This applies also to the equation of row 9, where the net government debt has been replaced by a variable which, as indicated earlier, is theoretically more appropriate, namely an estimate of the 'dead weight debt' or difference between the debt and the capital held by the government (see Eisner and Pieper, 1984). Actually, in row 9 we use the government net worth, which is the negative of deadweight debt; accordingly, for Barro this coefficient should be close to -1. Instead, the estimate is positive, though, again, not significant.

The conclusion from this battery of tests seems unequivocal: using the LCH, it is possible to account rather closely for the behaviour of wealth in the United States over nearly a century, but there is no evidence that accumulated wealth grows or declines significantly in response to movements in the national debt, or in government net worth.

Tests Based on Saving Flows

Operational formulation

The Barro and the standard hypothesis also have different, testable implications for the determinants of consumption (and hence saving). According to the traditional view, private consumption, C, responds to: (i) long term expectations of before tax income, $\hat{Y}$, less, (ii) the taxes (net of transfers including interest) expected to be levied against that income (both measured as rates per unit of time); and (iii) private net worth, W, consisting of the market value of tangible assets plus net claims on the public sector (plus, in an open economy, net claims on the rest of the world). Thus:

$$C = c(\hat{Y} - \hat{T}) + \mathrm{d}W \tag{5}$$

According to Barro, instead, taxes, as such, have no effect on consumption, and the same is true of that component of private net worth which consists of claims in the public sector. What influences consumption, instead, is the current (and anticipated) government purchase of goods and services for consumption, $\hat{GC}$, which results in a loss of resources available to the private sector, no matter how they are financed. Again, this hypothesis can be formulated operationally as:

$$C = c(\hat{Y} - \hat{GC}) + \mathrm{d}(W - GD) \tag{6}$$

Clearly, these hypotheses are not mutually exclusive. Certainly the LCH version of the standard view suggests that, within modest limits, some of the people some of the time might behave in a way consistent with (6). Conversely, we have seen that, even if one accepts Barro's assumption of super-rational behaviour and concern for heirs, there might still be a non-negligible response to taxes and government debt. For test purposes, then, we can formulate a general hypothesis by taking a linear combination of (5) and (6) with positive weights, w_1 and w_2, adding up to one:

$$\begin{aligned} C &= c[w_1(\hat{Y}-\hat{T})+w_2(\hat{Y}-\hat{G}C)]+\mathrm{d}[w_1 W+w_2(W-GD)] \qquad (7)\\ &= c(\hat{Y}-\hat{T})+\mathrm{d}W-cw_2(\hat{G}C-\hat{T})-\mathrm{d}w_2 GD \end{aligned}$$

Thus, if we regress C on the four right-hand side variables of (7), the coefficient of the first variable – 'disposable income' – provides an estimate of the marginal propensity to consume, c, that of the third – the government deficit – divided by c, yields an estimate of the weight w_2; it is seen that if Barro's limiting hypothesis held exactly, or $w_2=1$, then, for given disposable income, a dollar of deficit would reduce C by c (or increase private saving by c). The second and the last coefficient measures, respectively, the propensity to consume with respect to wealth, and the same multiplied by w_2.

From (7) we can infer the following expression for the national saving function:

$$S=Y-C-GC=s(\hat{Y}-\hat{T})-(1-cw_2)\,(\hat{G}C-\hat{T})-\mathrm{d}W+\mathrm{d}w_2 GD$$

$$=sD\hat{Y}-(1-cw_2)(\hat{D}ef)-\mathrm{d}W+\mathrm{d}w_2 GD+TDY-TDef$$

Here, $D\hat{Y}$ and $\hat{D}ef$ are 'permanent' disposable income, and government deficit respectively, while $TDY=(Y-T)-(\hat{Y}-\hat{T})$ is transitory disposable income and $TDef$ the transitory budget deficit. Thus, under the standard hypothesis ($w_2=0$) for given disposable income, a permanent deficit reduces national saving (and national investment in a closed economy) by a dollar per dollar, whereas for the extreme Barro hypothesis the reduction is only $(1-c)=s$ dollars per dollar.

Equation (7) embodies the basic test with which we are concerned, namely how closely consumption (and saving) behaviour can be accounted for by this hypothesis, and how large is w_2: relatively close to zero as called for by the LCH, or close to unity, as implied by Barro's model?

There are, however, some auxiliary issues, revolving around the deficit and its measurement which we also propose to test. The most serious one concerns the measurement of T which we have defined as taxes net of all transfers, including the interest on the national debt. the national income accounts of the US (and other countries as well) measure that interest as the amount actually paid by the government, say RGD, where R is the nominal interest rate, without making any allowance for the fact that inflation, $\dot{P}$, erodes the purchasing power of the debt by the rate of inflation or by $\dot{P}GD$. As noted earlier, when account is taken of this loss, the income effectively earned by the holders, as well as the effective cost to the government becomes:

$$RGD - \dot{P}GD = rGD$$

where $r = R - \dot{P}$ is the so-called effective 'real rate of interest'. We shall accordingly measure T as $T^* - \dot{P}GD$, where T^* is net taxes, as reported in the government budget and National Income Accounts; note that T appears both in the calculation of net of tax income and of the deficit.

This procedure, however, raises another issue, namely the possibility that the private sector may suffer from some inflation illusion (as the public sector budget seem to suffer) and actually base its consumption, at least partially, on nominal rather than real interest. We can test this hypothesis by adding to (7) a term $f\dot{P}GD$. If there were complete money illusion, f would be equal to the coefficient of the interest variable, which is implicitly constrained to equal $c(1-w_2)$. Less than full illusion would imply a lower value.

There remains one further problem. By calculating T as described above, we are implicitly assuming that rational consumers respond to the current real return on debt, r. In reality, we should expect them to respond to the 'permanent' return, say $\hat{r}$ (both with respect to income and with respect to the perceived deficit in Barro's formulation). Now, in periods of high and volatile inflation, the *ex post* real rate, r, is likely to be a very poor approximation to $\hat{r}$. Unfortunately, $\hat{r}$ is unobservable and difficult to measure. Yet, in view of the experience of the post-war period, which constitutes our sample, we propose as a reasonable approximation, to treat $\hat{r}$ as constant, say $\bar{r}$. This suggests adding to (7) one further term of the form $g(r-\bar{r})GD$. Noting that $\bar{r}GD$ is a constant, (7) finally reduces to:

$$C = cDY + \mathrm{d}W - cw_2 Def - (\mathrm{d}w_2 + g\bar{r})GD + f\dot{P}GD + grGD \tag{8}$$

The coefficient g should be negative, if, in forming expectation about the future real return on government debt, the market gives relatively more weight to $\bar{r}$ and little weight to the current rate r; in the limit it could be as small as $-c(1-w_2)$. However, these inferences are uncertain because, at least according to LCH, the coefficient of property income, given wealth, could be quite different from that of labour income and hence from c (cf. Modigliani, 1975). However, whatever the value of g, to test money illusion, the coefficient f should be compared with $c(1-w_2)+g$, which measures the total effect of government interest income.

Equation (8) – or as close an approximation to it as was permitted by the availability of data – was used to test the alternative hypothesis, with three distinct sets of data as follows:

(i) Quarterly data for the US for the period from 1952 to 1983. The US was chosen because of its obvious importance as well as because of the availability – and presumably quality – of the data.

(ii) Time series of annual data for Italy, from 1952 to 1982. Italy provides an unusually interesting case because of the extreme variations that have characterised many of the crucial variables. Thus, the debt income ratio ranged from a low of less than 40 per cent up to 71 per cent, and inflation has also been quite variable reaching at times close to 20 per cent. As a result, variables such as the ratio of government interest payments to nominal income have been as low as just over 1 per cent up to very nearly 10 per cent. Unfortunately, only annual data are available at this time and some of the series, such as private wealth, could only be estimated in a somewhat crude way.

(iii) A sample covering some 33 countries for five selected years in the interval between 1960 and 1980. The sample covers all the countries included in the *UN Yearbook of National Account Statistics* for which the required data were available for a sufficient number of years (at least three).

United States

Several tests of the Barro tax neutrality propositions, based on the effects of fiscal variables on consumption, have been carried out for the US (and Canada) besides those reported below. However, none has used the specifications of equation (8) which we regard as the warranted ones. Several of the previous tests, especially those using specifications closer to ours, have reported results which, like ours, tend to reject the Barro hypothesis. These include Yawitz and Meyer

(1976), Barro (1978), Tanner (1979), Seater (1982), Carmichael and Hawtrey (1981) and Feldstein (1982). A few others, however, have reached opposite conclusions, some on the basis of very inadequate specification, e.g., Tanner (1970), and Kochin (1974). The one puzzling case is that of Kormendi (1983) whose specifications are, at first sight, not so terribly different from our own and yet reports diametrically opposite results in almost all respects. That case will be discussed in a forthcoming note. A few other papers reach essentially inconclusive results.

Table 1.2 reports the results of a test of equation (8) for the US in the post-war period. The first row shows the standard consumption function including only net-of-tax income and wealth. Expected income was approximated by a first degree polynomial distributed lag including the current and 19 lagged quarters. (A few tests were made allowing for separating disposable income into before-tax income and net taxes, and allowing the coefficients of these two components in the distributed lag to be different – cf. Modigliani and Steindel (1977). Since the coefficients of the two variables turned out to have a fairly similar shape, and no other estimates seem to be appreciably different, these results are not reported here.) There was strong evidence that lagged value of wealth contributed significantly to the explanation of consumption and, accordingly, all tests include a first order polynomial distributed lag including four quarters. The residuals exhibited high serial correlation (see column (8)), and, therefore, all the results reported are based on the autoregressive transformation.

The only slight surprise in the first row is the relatively high value of the income and low value of the wealth coefficients, both of which appear to be the result of the autoregressive correction. The second row tests Barro's tax neutrality proposition by adding two fiscal variables, the national debt and the annual deficit. The estimated coefficient of debt is positive – that is, *larger* than that of other wealth. This result rejects the Barro hypothesis according to which the contribution of Debt should be smaller – around zero – implying a negative coefficient in col (4) of the magnitude of that of wealth; it is, instead, consistent with the LCH. At the same time it must be acknowledged that, in view of the larger standard error, this conclusion cannot be regarded as very robust. The coefficient of Deficit is negative, as expected under either Barro or LCH; but the implied value of w_2 – a measure of the empirical relevance of the Barro hypothesis – is close to zero, and with a relatively small error of estimate – on this score, the rejection of Barro is quite robust.

Table 1.2 US flow tests, 1952–82, quarterly

ID no.	*Const.*	*Income*	*Wealth*	*National Debt*	*Deficit*	*Inflation loss*	*Govt. interest*	ρ	*SE*
1	−0.21	0.91	0.022					0.82	0.0110
	0.04	0.03	0.008						
2	−0.30	0.92	0.022	0.047	−0.002			0.83	0.0110
	0.09	0.03	0.008	0.042	0.029				
3	−0.30	0.93	0.020	0.046	−0.022	−0.45		0.83	0.0111
	−0.09	0.034	0.008	0.043	0.032	0.43			
4	−0.20	0.91	0.019	0.011	−0.021	0.47	0.51	0.83	0.0992
	0.11	0.03	0.008	0.046	0.032	0.33	0.32		
5	−0.22	0.92	0.022		−0.014	−0.47		0.83	0.0111
	0.04	0.03	0.008		0.031	0.51			
6	−0.17	0.90	0.019		−0.019	0.51	0.56	0.82	0.0109
	0.05	0.03	0.008		0.031	0.29	0.28		

The next row, 3, tests the inflation illusion hypothesis and appears to reject it, as the estimate of the coefficient of col (6) is actually negative, though the difference from zero is not very significant. Row 4 probes further into inflation illusion by dropping the maintained hypothesis that government interest has the same effect on consumption as any other income (on top of the effect of debt as part of net worth). As pointed out, the effect could be larger or smaller, and it is the total effect that is relevant in assessing the coefficient of inflation. Accordingly, in row 4 we add the government interest (which is already included in net taxes and thus in income and deficit). The effect of this addition turns out to be rather unexpected. From column (7) it appears that the estimated effect of government interest on consumption is positive rather than negative, and fairly large. It implies an overall effect in the order of 1.4 dollars of additional consumption per dollar of government real interest. What is even more puzzling is that the estimates of col (6) imply an appreciable inflation illusion effect. The point estimates suggest that the public treats about one-third of the compensation for the inflation loss (0.47/1.4) as though it were true income. The other difference in row 4 is that the coefficient of debt becomes smaller, but it still remains positive.

Because the three variables, Debt, Interest and Inflation (*GD*, *PGD* and *rGD*) all involve the variable, *GD*, they might suffer from multicollinearity problems which could contribute to the surprising results of row 4. Accordingly, in rows 5 and 6, we drop the insignificant variable *GD*. But this turns out to throw little light on the puzzle. In row 5, which includes only inflation, the results are very close to row 3; in particular, inflation has a very similar negative coefficient. But, when interest is added back in row 6, its coefficient, as well as that of inflation, are even a bit larger and more significant than in row 4.

One puzzling aspect of these results is why inflation appears to have little, or even negative, effect before interest appears in the equation, and then turns around so strongly. One possible clue may be provided by a very strong negative correlation between the inflation and real interest variables (-0.87), reflecting in part the effect of unanticipated inflation. Suppose that real interest truly has an appreciably stronger effect on consumption than other sources of income, but that its effect is forced to be the same as other income, as in rows 3 and 5. Then a high inflation will, on the average, be accompanied by a low real rate, which will make for a lower consumption than accounted for by those equations. As a result, the error term will be negatively correlated with inflation which would make for a negative, or at least a downward biased, inflation coefficient. Under this interpretation, the negative values of rows 3 and 5 would reflect downward bias, while the positive ones of rows 4 and 6 could be relatively unbiased.

A second question is whether the very high estimate of the effect of government interest on consumption should be believed or, instead, be attributed to some type of bias. We shall postpone facing this issue until we have examined the outcome of remaining tests.

Italy

A set of results for Italy is reported in Table 1.3. They are taken from a forthcoming joint paper by the author together with Marco Pagano and Tullio Jappelli (1984). The tests in Table 1.3 are laid out pretty much along the same lines as in Table 1.2, and the results are, in many ways, surprisingly similar, though in Table 1.3 we can provide only results for annual observations.

The basic consumption function of Row 1 is based only on *current* income and taxes, since, in contrast to the US, there was no indication of any significant role for lagged values of the variables. The other major differences with the US are: (i) the much lower propensity to consume, 0.6 versus 0.9, offset by an appreciably higher wealth coefficient. (The differences may be partly spurious because of the constant terms appearing in each equation with opposite signs, accounting for somewhat less than 1 per cent of mean consumption of the US but nearly 5 per cent for Italy. These constants should really be zero, and the non-zero estimate may reflect some missing variables which could bias the estimate of *c* and *d*; (ii) the appreciably poorer fit – the error is about 3 per cent of the mean as against just over one-half of 1 per cent. These differences suggest that the hypothesis is not as effective in explaining consumption behaviour in Italy as it is for the US, but it is hard to say how much of the difference might be traced to the quality of the data.

Row 2 tests the role of the fiscal variables with results qualitatively similar to the US. The coefficient of Debt is again positive, though a bit smaller; that of Deficit is negative, as expected, but substantially higher. Still it implies a value of w_2 which is only 30 per cent as high as that hypothesised by Barro.

Row 3 tests inflation illusion by adding an estimate of the inflation loss on the national debt; its coefficient should be between zero (no money illusion) and a positive value, possibly as high as the coeffi-

Table 1.3 Italy. Consumption function and fiscal variables – 1952–82 annual. Dependent variable: aggregate consumer expenditure

		Coefficient of								
ID no.	*Method of estimation*	*Const.*	*YD NI-Tax*	*Wealth*	*National debt*	*Deficit*	*Govt. interest*	*Inflation loss*	ρ	*SE*
1	AR	0.040	0.60	0.045					0.67	0.79–0.02
		0.012	0.032	0.006						
2	AR	0.037	0.59	0.046	0.029	−0.22			0.69	0.79–0.02
		0.012	0.032	0.007	0.043	0.071				
3	AR	0.043	0.61	0.040	0.007	−0.18		0.19	0.68	0.80–0.02
		0.019	0.022	0.013	0.070	0.12		0.48		
4	AR	0.041	0.60	0.042	0.026	−0.16	−0.11	0.06	0.68	0.82–0.02
		0.014	0.031	0.005	0.030	0.13	0.33	0.6		
5	AR	0.042	0.61	0.040		−0.16	−0.05	0.20	0.69	0.84–0.02
		0.016	0.033	0.012		0.13	0.23	0.30		
6	INS	0.043	0.59	0.043	0.044	−0.092	−0.22	−0.01	0.70	0.83–0.02
		0.021	0.063	0.017	0.096	0.15	0.36	1.0		
7	INS	0.041	0.63	0.036		−0.16	−0.05	0.25	0.65	0.80–0.02
		0.016	0.035	0.013		0.16	0.19	0.31		

cient of government interest, which is $c(1-w_2)$, or around 0.4, in the present case. The point estimate turns out to lie just about midway between the two polar cases. At the same time it is seen that the estimate has a large standard error and that the variable does not contribute significantly to explaining consumption.

The next row, 4, probes further into inflation illusion by adding the (real) government interest, *rGD*. The result is far more reasonable than for the US, as the coefficient of interest is slightly negative. Surprisingly, the inflation coefficients also falls near zero. The other coefficients do not change appreciably. Dropping the insignificant, and possibly collinear debt variable, makes the interest coefficient yet closer to zero, while raising again the inflation estimate to 0.20.

The final two rows present an alternative set of estimates of the coefficients of the previous two rows, 4 and 5, using an instrumental variable approach to minimise the danger of simultaneity bias that could affect, in particular, the income and the deficit coefficients. It is seen that these estimates are generally close to those of the corresponding rows 4 and 5. In 5, the coefficient of debt is a bit higher and that of interest noticeably lower, but both are rather insignificant, and so is inflation. Row 7 is just about the same as 5 – except for a little large inflation effect, still, however, lower than its standard error.

To summarise, the Italian evidence agrees with that for the US in decidedly rejecting the implications of tax neutrality – the coefficient of debt is generally positive and higher than that of other wealth, and the effect of deficit, though larger than for the US, is still much smaller than required by Barro's hypothesis. The large effect of government interest is not supported by the Italian evidence, and as for inflation illusion, the hypothesis fails to receive a strong backing because of high standards errors, presumably reflecting collinearity.[2]

Evidence from a cross-section of countries

Table 1.4 reports the results of some cross-country tests carried out in a forthcoming joint paper by Modigliani, Mason and Sterling (1984). A test based on a cross-section of countries is appealing for two main reasons. First, one would expect to find more variations across countries, than for a single country over time, in variables such as the Government debt–income ratio, the deficit rate, and the rate of inflation, which are crucial for testing the two sets of hypotheses with which we are concerned. Second, by taking as the unit of observation for each country an average of several years, one can come close to measuring long run effects, thus eliminating the additional large variations in the saving or consumption–income ratio, that come from short run cyclical and other disturbances. Furthermore, an average of past values is likely to provide a better measure of long run expectations, which should govern behaviour.

However, the cross-section approach also involves some costs and difficult trade-offs. The trade-off is between the sample size and the quality of the data. Obviously, one would prefer a sample as large and diversified as possible. But this preference conflicts with the requirement that the data for each country be, as nearly as possible, comparable conceptually, of high quality, and available for a span of time long enough to permit the desired averaging.

To ensure the comparability, we limited the sample to those countries whose national income accounts are included in the *UN Yearbook of National Income Statistics* and which also report in the *UN Demographic Yearbook*. Table 1.4(a) gives a list of the 33 countries which satisfied this criterion, as well as the time span criterion discussed further below.

The 'cost' of cross-sectional tests is twofold. In the first place, our basic hypothesis (8) calls for two variables that are not part of the National Accounts framework, namely Wealth and Government Debt. Unfortunately, estimates of Wealth are available only for a handful of countries, and, frequently, only for selected years. Information on National Debt, appropriately measured (net, domestic, privately held), is also very limited. Accordingly, these two variables had to be dropped from the test.

The second 'cost' of the cross-sectional approach is that, especially in the absence of wealth information, one cannot presuppose a stable marginal (and average) propensity to consume, c, for different countries, as is the case for different years for a single country. Indeed, there are wide variations in the private saving rates across countries, ranging from near zero, or even negative, to over 20 per cent in a few cases. Hence, in a cross-section, one has not only to model the (expected) income flow which determines consumption, as in Tables 1.2 and 1.3, but also what accounts for the variation of c. The research that has been done on this issue points to two major forces responsible for cross-country differences, namely: (i) the rate of growth of income, and (ii) demographic composition in terms of the share of the non-working age population.

With these considerations in mind, we propose to rely on the following cross-sectional variant of equation (8):

Table 1.4(a) Countries and years included in cross-section sample

Country	*1960*	*1965*	*1970*	*1975*	*1980*
Algeria			×	×	×
Australia	×	×	×	×	×
Austria	×	×	×	×	×
Belgium	×	×	×	×	×
Canada	×	×	×	×	×
Denmark	×	×	×	×	×
Finland	×	×	×	×	×
France	×	×	×	×	×
Germany	×	×	×	×	×
Greece	×	×	×	×	×
India	×	×	×	×	×
Ireland	×	×	×	×	×
Italy	×	×	×	×	×
Japan	×	×	×	×	×
Korea, Republic of	×	×	×	×	×
Madagascar		×	×	×	
Netherlands	×	×	×	×	×
Norway	×	×	×	×	×
Papua New Guinea	×	×	×	×	×
Peru	×	×	×	×	×
Portugal	×	×	×	×	×
Spain	×	×	×	×	×
Sudan		×	×	×	
Sweden	×	×	×	×	×
Switzerland	×	×	×	×	×
Taiwan			×	×	×
Thailand	×	×	×	×	×
Tunisia	×	×	×	×	×
United Kingdom	×	×	×	×	×
United States	×	×	×	×	×
Venezuela	×	×	×	×	×
Zambia		×	×	×	×

$$C=[c_0+c_1g+c_2gd][(NY-T)+a_1(G-T)+a_2\dot{P}D+a_3RD \qquad (9)$$

The first square brackets replaces c in equation (8) with a function of g, the rate of growth of permanent income, and d a measure of the effects of demographic factors, summarised by the 'dependency ratio' or ratio of population under 15 to population over 15. This variable is multiplied by g, on the general ground that the effect of growth is multiplicative; with zero growth, saving should be zero (or, $c=1$).

The second bracket models the effect of the expected income flow, net of taxes. As in (8), it includes income measured by National (NY), less direct taxes, the deficit, the inflation loss, and the interest bill. However, it omits the two stock variables, Debt and Net Worth, which are not available.

For each country, the data for each variable in the second square bracket were obtained from the *UN Yearbook* for as many of the five years 1960, 1965, 1970, 1975, and 1980 as were available. For each country, 'decadal' observations were computed when possible by averaging three consecutive observations, spanning a ten-year interval. As shown in Table 1.4(a), some of the required annual observations are missing at the beginning or at the end. In such cases, the country is included in the sample, provided at least three consecutive data points were available, but the number of observations for that country was cut down to two (e.g., Turkey) or one (e.g., Taiwan). For this reason, and also because of other occasional missing data, the total number of observations used in the regression is reduced to 80 (compared with a potential maximum of 99).

As for the variables in the first bracket, g (the growth rate of permanent income), is measured by the percentage growth of (real) consumption between the two end points of each decade. The dependency ratio, d (a very slowly changing variable), is calculated from the *UN Demographic Yearbook* for the single year 1970. Finally, in the regression, all the national income data for each included year were scaled by national income (before averaging), thus avoiding both the problem of converting them in equivalent real units and the problem of heteroscedasticity produced by the large variability, across countries of variables like real income or consumption, whether aggregate or per capita.

Some problems are encountered in measuring government interest, rGD, and the inflation loss, $\dot{P}GD$. The *nominal* interest, RGD, can be obtained from the National Income data. However, lacking information on the net government debt, GD, we are unable to obtain a direct measure of either $\dot{P}GD$ or the *real* interest, rGD. Accordingly, in computing taxes net of transfers less government interest, we subtract the nominal interest (RGD) rather than the appropriate rGD. As for the inflation loss, we have endeavoured to arrive at a rough estimate by relying on information on the rate of inflation and on *nominal* interest. To this end, we first note the identity for each country, j, and decade, t,:

$$(\dot{P}GD)_{jt} = \frac{(RGD)_{jt}}{r_{jt}\dot{P}_{jt}} \dot{P}_{jt} \tag{10}$$

which follows from the definition of the real rate. We next make the rather heroic assumption that the difference in the ten-year average real rate across countries, and 'decades', is sufficiently small so that r_{jt} can be approximated by a constant $\bar{r}$. We have tried to estimate $\bar{r}$ by scanning over values from 0 to 0.07 to find the value minimising the residual variance, for several of the equations reported in Table 1.4(b). It was found that in some form of the equation the error variance decreased slightly as $\bar{r}$ rose, while in others it declined slightly, but in every case it was quite insensitive to the value assigned to $\bar{r}$. It was therefore decided that one could save computations and the multiplication of variants of the test, by assigning to r a reasonable value, which was finally chosen to be 3 per cent. Replacing this value for r_{jt} in (10) yields the estimate of $(PGD)_{jt}$ which was used in all relevant tests of Table 1.4(b). It should be recognised that, as long as we use the nominal interest in computing net taxes, if the private sector has no, or limited, inflation illusion, the equation could be misspecified, unless it includes the variable *PGD*, which, in principle, can provide an offset to *RGD*.

The outcome of the tests is summarised in Table 1.4(b). The first row reports the results of estimating the scaled version of equation (9) reproduced at the top of the table. The two variables designed to

Table 1.4(b) Cross-section of 33 countries, 1960–80

Hypothesis tested:

$$\frac{C}{NY}=\left[\ c_0+c_1g+c_2d\ \right]\left[1-\frac{T}{NY}+a_1\left(\frac{G-T}{NY}\right)+a_2\frac{PGD}{NY}+a_3\frac{RGD}{NY}\right]$$

Specification

Weighting	*Taxes* (*T*)	c_0	c_1	c_2	a_1	a_2	a_3
Unweighted	*NT–RD*	0.88	−1.56	1.46	0.27	0.17	
		0.019	0.42	0.46	0.12	0.54	
Unweighted	*NT*	0.88	−1.57	1.49	−0.27		0.78
		0.019	0.33	0.42	0.12		0.32
Unweighted	*NT*	0.88	−1.64	1.58	−0.24	−1.82	2.24
		0.19	0.43	0.49	0.13	2.19	1.61
Weighted	*NT–RD*	0.89	−2.48	2.85	−0.22	0.64	
		0.12	0.30	0.53	0.18	0.52	
Weighted	*NT*	0.89	−2.54	2.88	−0.24		1.19
		0.012	0.31	0.52	0.17		0.31
Weighted	*NT*	0.88	−2.68	3.28	−0.15	−5.6	5.47
		0.012	0.29	0.52	0.17	2.7	1.52

account for propensity to consume, c, namely, growth, g, and dependency ratio, d, are both quite significant, with t-ratios above 3. Assigning to the dependency ratio a typical value of one-third, the effect of income growth, g, is just over one, implying that an increase of one percentage point in the consumption–income ratio and hence to an equal rise in the saving rate; similarly, for a growth rate of 5 per cent, roughly the mean for the sample, a rise of 0.10 in the dependency ratio decrease the saving rate by about two-thirds of one percentage point.

Proceeding to the test of fiscal policy, the estimated coefficient of deficit, a_1, is negative, as expected, and fairly significant; however, its size is only about one-fourth as large as predicted by the Barro hypothesis, whereas it is quite consistent with LCH. Finally, the effect of inflation, a_2, is rather close to zero; however, because we are subtracting from net taxes the *nominal* interest, in the absence of inflation illusion, the coefficient of $\dot{P}D$ should have been equal to $(1-a_1)$, or -0.73. The estimate of 0.17 is some 0.9 higher, supporting the hypothesis even though the standard error is large.

In the estimate of row 1, all the observations are weighted equally. But since the countries in the sample vary greatly in size, a good case can be made for appropriately weighting the observations. Several weighting schemes have been proposed and used in this type of analysis; one scheme that has been used repeatedly is to weight the observations in proportion to the square root of population. (Cf. Houthakker, 1965; Modigliani, 1961.)

The results of the weighted regression are given in the last three rows, each of which matches the specifications of each of the first three rows. They are broadly similar to the corresponding unweighted ones but do present some interesting differences. First, the estimated effect of growth on the saving rate is appreciably higher; e.g., in row 4, for a dependency ratio of one-third it comes to $1\frac{1}{2}$ percentage points per one percentage point change in g, which agrees more closely with some earlier results (cf. Modigliani, 1961; Modigliani and Sterling, 1983). Similarly, the effect of d is also larger: at a 5 per cent growth, a rise in dependency by 0.10, decreases saving by nearly $1\frac{1}{2}$ percentage points. The estimated effect of deficit is marginally lower and less significant. With respect to inflation effects, row 4 shows a rather surprisingly large coefficient, a_2, even allowing for a large standard error; indeed, even with inflation illusion, the coefficient should not exceed zero.

Once again one may wonder whether this result might be related to having constrained the interest coefficient to be the same as that of other components of income. To throw light on this question in rows 2 and 5, we have taken the nominal interest, *RGD*, out of net taxes and added it as a separate variable. In row 2, the estimate of the interest coefficient a_3, (0.78), turns out quite close to the constrained value $(1+a_1)$, or 0.73, while the weighted regression, 5, is somewhat high, but not significantly so, when allowing for the standard error.

The last step in our test is again to enter both interest and inflation. Here we should again expect little change in the estimate of a_3, while a_2 should be between zero (full illusion) and $-a_3$. Unfortunately, the result of this specification is, again, disconcerting. In the first place, not unlike the case of the US, the coefficient of interest rises to a surprising extent. In equation (5), it is threefold larger than in (4), and it is quite significant. At the same time, the inflation coefficient turns quite negative; it approaches $-a_3$ in (5). In (8), the rise of a_3 is even more conspicuous and alarming, and so is that of a_2. As a result, the 'no illusion' hypothesis, $a_2 = -a_3$, could clearly not be rejected.

We conclude that the results of the international cross-section confirm the role of income growth and dependency as major determinants of the consumption (or saving) income ratio; they also confirm that deficits tend to reduce consumption and encourage saving, but to a relatively modest extent, which is consistent with the LCH but amounts to only one-sixth to one-fifth of the full Barro effect. Finally, the results with respect to inflation illusion are largely inconclusive. As long as the coefficient of interest is forced to be equal to that of all other pre-tax income, the evidence, notably from the more reliable weighted regression, suggests a rather strong inflation illusion effect, though subject to a non-negligible error. However, when we drop that constraint, the coefficient of interest rate becomes large, while the inflation illusion effect largely vanishes. It is entirely possible that this inconclusiveness reflects the rather crude approximation to inflation on which we were forced to rely.

CONCLUSIONS

This chapter is concerned with analysing the impact of government expenditure and tax policies on the stock of capital in the economy and, thereby, on future generations. The issue is examined both in the presence of economic slack and when resources are fully utilised, a condition that may be associated with the long run.

It is argued that the conventional Keynesian multiplier, according to which an increase in deficits – or an increase in expenditure matched by an equal rise in taxes – will not 'crowd out' investment but will instead 'crowd in' output, requires for its validity not only enough economic slack but also a suitable monetary policy. Crowding out of investment will occur despite the slack, if monetary policy fails to accommodate fully the expansion of output that would be called for by the multiplier.

Concerning the long-run effects, various theories are reviewed and, in particular: (i) the currently prevailing one, according to which a dollar of National Debt displaces, permanently, a dollar of private tangible capital – or close to a dollar in the Life Cycle version – and, (ii) the newly fashionable one that claims, instead, that deficits cause an equal permanent increase in private wealth with the result that the path of private capital is unaffected and tax policy is 'neutral'.

The differential observable implications of the two theories are brought out and made the basis of a number of empirical tests. A test based on US data finds that, for a period of nearly a century, there is absolutely no evidence that private wealth has responded to the size of the national debt. The other test, based on post-war data for the US and Italy, pursues two central implications of tax neutrality: (1) that the government *debt*, unlike other private wealth, does not affect consumption, and (2) that, given after-tax income, government *deficit* displaces consumption by a roughly equal amount. The evidence rejects squarely these implications of tax neutrality; the estimated effect of debt on consumption is even greater than that of other wealth, and the effect of deficit, though of the right sign, is much too small to come even near to support tax neutrality. These results are, instead, fully consistent with the LCH version and very large tax effects. One final test was based on a cross-section of 33 countries. Though this test could not provide information on the effect of the debt, because of lack of data, it does fully confirm the modest magnitude of the effect of deficit.

The tests also provided the opportunity for investigating the distinct, but related, question of inflation illusion; given that consumption responds to taxes less government interest, does it seem to respond to the real interest, as it should? Or does the private sector suffer from inflation illusion so that consumption responds, at least in part, to nominal interest? The results of the tests show some evidence of inflation illusion, but far from conclusive, as the estimates for each sample are sensitive to small changes in specifications, and they further vary across samples in an apparently unsystematic fashion.

Notes

1. I wish to express my appreciation to Arlie Sterling who provided valuable advice and assistance, in particular for the US and cross-section tests reported below, and to Marco Pagano and James Poterba for reading the manuscript and making helpful suggestions.
2. A recent paper of Lecaldano *et al.* (1984) has explored similar issues. The results, though hard to compare because of differences in the period covered, in data, in frequency (they use quarterly data versus annual), and in emphasis, appear to be broadly consistent with ours, both with respect to the fiscal variables and to inflation illusion. Some of their tests suggest a more pronounced inflation illusion.

REFERENCES

Barro, R. (1974). 'Are Government Bonds Net Wealth?', *Journal of Political Economy*, vol. 82, no. 6.

Barro, R. (1978). *The Impact of Social Security on Private Savings – Evidence from U.S. Time Series*. American Enterprise Institute, Washington, DC.

Bernheim, B., Shleifer, A. and Summers, L. (1985). 'The Strategic Bequest Motive', *Journal of Political Economy*, 93, no. 6 (December), pp. 1045–76.

Blinder, A. S. (1983). 'On the Monetization of Debt', in *The Economic Consequences of Government Deficits*, Laurence H. Meyer (ed.) (Boston: Kluwer-Nijhoff Publishing).

Board of Governors of the Federal Reserve System (1981). Flow of Funds Section, Division of Quarterly Statics, *Balance Sheets of the U.S. Economy 1945–1980*, October.

Carmichael, J. and K. Hawtrey (1981). 'Social Security, Government Finance, and Savings', *Economic Record*, vol. 57, no. 159, pp. 332–43.

Cukierman, A. and J. Mortensen (1983). 'Monetary Assets and Inflation Induced Distortions of the National Accounts – Conceptual Issues and Corrections of Sectoral Income Flows in 5 EEC Countries', Commission of the European Communities – Directorate General for Economic and Financial Affairs.

Eisner, R. and Paul Pieper (1984). 'A New View of the Federal Debt and Budget Deficits', *American Economic Review*, vol. 74, no. 1, pp. 11–29.

Feldstein, M. A. (1982). 'Government Deficits and Aggregate Demand', *Journal of Monetary Economics*, 9.

Houthakker, H. W. (1965). 'On Some Determinants of Saving in Developed and Underdeveloped Countries', in E. A. G. Robinson (ed.), *Problems of Economic Development* (London: Macmillan) ch. 10.

Kochin, L. (1974). 'Are Future Taxes Discounted by Consumers', *Journal of Money, Credit and Banking*, 6 (August) pp. 385–94.

Kormendi, R. (1983). 'Government Debt, Government Spending and Private Sector Behaviour', *American Economic Review*, vol. 75, no. 5 (December) pp. 994–1010.

Kotlikoff, L. T. and L. H. Summers (1981). 'The Role of Intergenerational Transfers in Aggregate Capital Accumulation', *Journal of Political Economy*, vol. 89, no. 3.

Lecaldano, E., S. La Terza, G. Marotta and R. S. Masera (1984). 'Consumo, Risparmio e Fasso di Interesse: la Correzione per l'Inflazione', in *Moneta ed Economia Nazionale* (Cassa di Risparmio di Torino).

Leff, N. H. (1969). 'Dependency Rates and Savings Rate', *American Economic Review*, LIX (December) 886–95.

Modigliani, F. (1961). 'Long-Run Implications of Alternative Fiscal Policies and the Burden of the National Debt', *Economic Journal*, vol. 71 (December).

Modigliani, F. (1966). 'The Life Cycle Hypothesis of Saving, the Demand for Wealth, and the Supply of Capital', *Social Research*, 33 (Summer) pp. 160–217.

Modigliani, F. (1975). 'The Life Cycle Hypothesis of Saving Twenty Years Later', in M. Parkin (ed.), *Contemporary Economic Issues* (Manchester University Press).

Modigliani, F. (1983). 'Government Deficits, Inflation and Future Generations', in D. W. Conlkin and T. J. Courchene (eds), *Deficits: How Big and How Bad*, Ontario Economic Council Special Research Project.

Modigliani, F. (1984). 'Measuring the Contribution of Intergenerational Transfers to Total Wealth.' *Proceedings of Conference on Modeling the Accumulation and Distribution of Personal Wealth, Paris, France*, September 1984, forthcoming.

Modigliani, F. and R. Brumberg (1980). 'Utility Analysis and Aggregate Consumption Functions: An Attempt at Integration', in Andrew Abel (ed.), *The Collected Papers of Franco Modigliani: The Life Cycle Hypothesis of Saving*, vol. 2 (Cambridge, MA, The MIT Press).

Modigliani, F. and C. Steindel (1977). 'Is a Tax Rebate an Effective Tool for Stabilization Policy', *Brookings Papers on Economic Activity*, 1.

Modigliani, F. and A. Sterling (1983). 'Determinants of Private Saving with Special Reference to the Role of Social Security-Cross Country Tests', in F. Modigliani and R. Hemming (eds), *The Determinants of National Saving and Wealth*, London: Macmillan Press, pp. 24–55.

Modigliani, F., Tullio Jappelli and Marco Pagano (1985). 'The Impact of Fiscal Policy on National Saving: the Italian Case', *Banca Nationale del Lavoro Quarterly Review*, no. 153, June 1985, pp. 91–126.

Modigliani, F., A. Mason and A. G. Sterling (1984). 'Effects of Fiscal Policy on Saving: Evidence from an International Cross-Section', unpublished manuscript, MIT, Sloan School.

Sargent, T. and N. Wallace (1981). 'Some Unpleasant Monetarist Arithmetic', *Federal Reserve Bank of Minneapolis Quarterly Review*, vol. 5 (Fall).

Seater, J. J. (1982). 'Are Future Taxes Discounted', *Journal of Money, Credit, and Banking*, vol. 14, no. 3 (August) pp. 376–89.

Siegel, J. J. and A. Protopadakis (1983). 'An Overview of Trends in Government Debt and National Income in Seven Industrialized Countries'. Presented at the Conference on Economic Policy and National Accounting in Inflationary Conditions, Dorga, Italy.

Sraffa, P. (ed.) (1962). *The Works and Correspondence of David Ricardo*, Vol. IV, *Pamphlets and Papers, 1815–1823* (Cambridge).

Sterling, A. G. (1984). *Public Debt and Private Wealth: The Role of Anticipated Taxes*, Doctoral dissertation, Dept. of Applied Economics, MIT, preliminary.

Tanner, J. E. (1970). 'Empirical Evidence on the Short-Run Real Balance Effect in Canada', *Journal of Money, Credit, and Banking*, vol. 2 (November) pp. 473–85.

Tanner, J. E. (1979). 'An Empirical Investigation of Tax Discounting', *Journal of Money, Credit, and Banking*, vol. 11, no. 2 (May) pp. 214–18.

Tobin, J. and W. Buiter (1980). 'Fiscal and Monetary Policies, Capital Formation, and Economic Activity', in G. M. von Furstenberg (ed.), *The Government and Capital Formation* (Cambridge, MA: Ballinger).

US Treasury Department (1983). 'Government Deficit Spending and its Effects on Prices of Financial Assets', Office of the Assistant Secretary for Economic Policy, May.

Yawitz, J. B. and L. H. Meyer (1976). 'An Empirical Investigation of the Extent of Tax Discounting', *Journal of Money, Credit, and Banking*, vol. 8 (May) pp. 247–54.

Comments on Franco Modigliani, 'The Economics of Public Deficits' by Michael Bruno

The paper deals with three major issues. The first is the possible association, or lack thereof, of the deficit with inflation. The second deals with crowding out theory, and the third with the empirical testing of Barro's tax neutrality hypothesis. In terms of emphasis and coverage most of the paper is concerned with the last issue. Here the author assembles an impressive array of empirical evidence based on US and Italian time series as well as a cross-country regression to show that crowding out has been consistent with his own life cycle hypothesis (LCH), but not with the extreme form of non-crowding out proposed by Barro. I find this major part of the paper very interesting and quite convincing, but, as is often unfortunate for a discussant, I had little to argue with. I will therefore confine my comments to some aspects of the preceding discussion which are linked to the broader title of this paper and some of which are more relevant to a non-US context.

In his discussion of the short-term macroeconomic effects of government deficits Modigliani appeals to a standard Keynesian framework. He discusses one Keynesian unemployment situation in which the deficit crowds in both output and investment, providing monetary policy is accommodating. If the latter is not the case investment may be crowded out even if there is slack. There is the third full employment situation in Modigliani's analysis in which crowding out by a deficit will be complete. In the context of the 1970s this analysis seems to me incomplete unless one adds another intermediate possibility in which labour is unemployed but output and investment are constrained from rising in the short-run, but prices will, because of real wage rigidity. This was probably never the case in the US but may have been common to some European countries in the context of the supply shocks of the last decade.

This point also has some relevance to the other issue discussed in the first part of the paper, namely the argument that deficits did not cause the inflation of the 1970s and if anything, there was reverse causality. It is probably generally true that real deficits (inflation corrected) did not increase for most industrial countries during the period as a whole, and that the underlying cause of inflation lay elsewhere. At the same time the size of budgets and their finance did play an important role in the stagflation process. One key example is the attempt in several European economies to avoid potential deficits caused by earlier increases in expenditure on social services, by appending to payroll taxes and thus further enhancing already high and rigid real labour costs.

This brings me to another European angle of US budget deficits and their crowding out effects. Large US deficits, coupled with monetary restraint, were expansionary and probably inflationary in the domestic economy. By raising dollar interest rates, however, they certainly contributed not only to the crowding out of European investment (in favour of capital flows into the US) but helped to devalue their currencies and thus increase costs of imports in Europe. Thus stagflation may for a time, at least (at the turn of the 1980s) have been exported from the US to Europe.

My final points have to do with the controversial role of government deficits in Israel's inflationary process. Our deficit has been notoriously high for more than a decade (on the order of 10–15 per cent of GNp) yet the jumps in the inflation rate took place with no systematic change in the relative size of deficits. Following Franco Modigliani's argument one might be led to add this observation as a further proof that deficits do not cause inflation. In the Israeli context, at least, such a statement would seem quite mistaken. Unlike the Latin American example that is mentioned in the paper, Israel's financial structure is far from primitive. The public debt, which is indexed, has simply grown so large relative to GNP, that the government is no longer able to extend it any further. It has also resorted to a pegged real interest policy thus paralysing monetary policy and help turn it into a fully accommodating monetary system. It is an extreme case, indeed, but one that is not devoid of empirical relevance. Another point often made is the fact that in Israel the deficit mainly crowds out exports and feeds directly into the balance of payments deficit. The most popular policy measures that have been adopted to tackle this dual deficit are a cut in consumption subsidies and devaluations (or import duties). During the last decade such measures have usually caused jumps in the inflation rate. The mechanism by which the deficit affects the inflationary process may not be of the conventional textbook variety, but it has certainly been dominant.

Finally, let me state again that all of these comments are only minor additions to a small part of this paper whose main and very important contribution lies in the analysis and testing of the neutrality hypothesis.

Comments on Franco Modigliani, 'The Economics of Public Deficits' by Alex Cukierman

Public deficits raise three fundamental questions.

(a) What is the effect of deficits on output and employment?
(b) What is their effect on inflation?
(c) To the extent that deficits crowd private production out does the burden of the consequent decrease in resources fall mostly on consumption or on investment?

Those questions which go to the heart of macro policymaking have been and still are the subject of heated debate among economists. This paper reviews the various approaches taken to answer those questions and then turns to the data in order to establish whether deficits crowd out consumption or mostly investment. This is done by testing the contrasting implications of the Life Cycle Hypothesis (LCH) and of the Neo-Ricardian Hypothesis (NRH) for the effects of deficits and government debt on consumption and total private wealth. The first three sections try to answer respectively the three questions above at a general level. The fourth section plunges into a detailed empirical investigation of the third question. My remarks are organised in the same order.

The paper reminds us that the answer to the first question depends on whether the economy operates at full capacity or not. In the first case an increase in deficits caused by an increase in government consumption crowds either investment or consumption or both out. In the second it increases output, consumption and investment through the multiplier and the accelerator. I have two observations. First, application of this distinction to actual economies in order to predict whether an increase in the deficit will increase or decrease the resources of the private sector is not a simple matter because our measurement of 'full capacity' is based to a substantial extent on institutional conventions and subjective evaluations. Second, even when the economy is at full capacity a bond financed increase in government expenditures may have an effect on output. By decreasing total resources available for private uses the government induces individuals to work and produce more in order to (at least) partly compensate for the decrease in private resources. The magnitude of this effect depends importantly on whether the increase in government expenditures is perceived as being permanent or as being temporary.

The ultimate conclusion reached in the paper about the effects of deficits on inflation is that there is no necessary connection unless there is a policy induced dependence between larger deficits and more expansionary monetary policies. Modigliani then provides an interesting explanation of the recently observed positive association between deficits and inflation that relies on reverse causality in particular inflation induced errors in the measurement of the real rate paid on the public debt. I tend to agree with this explanation for the particular episode and countries under consideration. But I am not convinced that deficits are not inflationary in countries like Israel that are characterised by relatively thin private capital markets. In such countries the ratio of governmental deficits to private savings is so high that any attempt to finance most or all of the deficit by tapping private capital markets leads to very strong pressures on real rates. More precisely those economies operate in a range of the supply curve of funds to government that is highly inelastic. In such countries the pressures on the policymaker to monetise the deficit are much stronger than in the US and some Western European countries. I believe it is no accident that the Federal Reserve enjoys a relatively high degree of independence while in countries that are characterised by a relatively inelastic supply of funds, decisions about monetisation are left to the central government. Governments of countries with thin capital markets and large deficits are obviously reluctant to give away their monopoly on money creation because of their restricted ability to borrow. As a consequence the link between deficits, monetary expansion and inflation is more direct and potent than in countries with elastic demands for governmental obligations.

With full capacity utilisation deficits crowd out consumption or investment depending on the extent to which government debt is perceived as net wealth. Under the NRH individuals are fully aware of the future tax liabilities created by debt financed deficits so they save an amount equal to the present value of this liability in order to maintain their future consumption. As a result deficits crowd out current consumption. By contrast the conventional view (including the LCH) implies that an increase in debt financed deficits leads to an increase in interest rates and consumption and to crowding out of investment. Section III presents a variety of arguments against the NRH some of which seem rather compelling. One of the arguments is based on the observation that, as an empirical matter, bequests represent no more than 25 per cent of total wealth. Although this argument seems intuitively appealing I am not aware of an analytical framework that relates the fraction of bequests generated wealth to the validity of the NRH. If individuals heavily discount the utility of their heirs, bequests may be small even if individuals subtract the full present value of future taxes from the family wealth. To put it differently; Is there a minimum ratio of bequest generated wealth to total wealth above which any such ratio is consistent with the NRH? It seems that a meaningful answer to this question can be obtained only after controlling for the effects of other factors like the rate of growth and the degree of time preference.

On the other hand I would like to add to the already long list of arguments that invalidate the NRH the possibility of avoiding future taxes through emigration. A substitution of current for future taxes increases current disposable income as well as future tax liabilities. But the latter can be avoided by leaving the country before the tax liability 'becomes due'. The intention to do that at some point in the future causes an increase in the wealth and the current consumption of those who have such an intention. This observation also implies that in a world with high labour mobility large deficits stimulate emigration. Obviously those who intend to stay will have to bear a higher share of future taxes. To the extent that they anticipate correctly the size of the induced emigration they will experience a decrease in wealth equal in size to the increase in wealth felt by those who intend to leave. In this case the NRH still holds provided there are no distribution effects. But such conditions of perfect foresight are not very likely to hold in reality particularly in view of the fact that intentions are hard to pinpoint firmly before they are implemented.

Section IV confronts the LCH and the NRH with data from various countries. For the US both stock and flow tests are performed. For other countries only flow tests are tried. The stock test is based on a regression of total wealth (inclusive of the public debt) on disposable permanent income and on the public debt. Under the NRH the coefficient of the public debt should be 1 and much smaller under the standard view. On this criterion the test strongly rejects the NRH in the US and yields support for the standard view. This contrasts with results obtained by Plosser[1] for the US. Plosser investigates whether large real stocks of debt are associated with higher real interest rates as implied by the standard view and finds no evidence to sustain such a relationship. If nothing else those results suggest that attempts at testing the standard against the neo-Ricardian view – are sensitive to the type of implications and data used to discriminate between the two. A test which would focus simultaneously on the implications for both real rates and the effect of public debt on private wealth seems to be a logical next step.

The LCH implies that consumption depends on permanent disposable income and on private wealth including the public debt. The NRH implies that consumption depends on permanent income net of permanent government consumption and on private wealth excluding government's debt. The flow tests focus on those differences. Two important empirical innovations are incorporated in some of those tests. First, the public debt net of governmentally owned capital is used instead of the gross public debt. Second, taxes are adjusted for the inflation tax on governmental debt. The equation that is ultimately estimated also includes a term designed to test for possible inflation illusion with respect to the inflation component of the debt as well as a term that depends on the difference between the actual and the permanent real rates of interest. The results tend to reject the NRH. The evidence on inflation illusion is mixed. I have several remarks.

First, if we abstract from the term $(r-\bar{r})$ the NRH implies that the coefficient of wealth inclusive of public debt should be equal in absolute value to the coefficient of the public debt (see equation (7)). In spite of the fact that eyeballing suggests that this condition is violated it might be instructive to test it explicitly. Second, the inflation illusion term that is equal to actual inflation multiplied by the public debt may be capturing (particularly during the 1970s) the effect of forecast errors on consumption. When inflation is unusually high individuals normally underestimate inflation and overestimate the real return on government debt. This induces them (under the standard view) to consume more thus creating a positive link between inflation and consumption. Third, under the NRH inflation should have no effect on consumption even if individuals are subject to inflation illusion since they are indifferent between current and future taxes. Hence the inflation illusion term should appear in equation (5) but not in equation (6). This implies that in equation (8) the inflation illusion term should be multiplied by the weight w_1.

Overall the evidence of the paper is rather unfavourable to the NRH. On the other hand, the work of Plosser[1] that focuses on the relationship between deficits and interest rates is unfavourable to the view that government debt is net wealth. Reconciliation of those different findings is a task that still lies ahead.

Note

1. Plosser, C. 'The Effects of Government Financing Decisions on Asset Returns', *Journal of Monetary Economics*, vol. 9 (May 1982) pp. 325–52.

2 The International Transmission of Fiscal Expenditures and Budget Deficits in the World Economy[1]

Jacob A. Frenkel and Assaf Razin

I INTRODUCTION

This paper deals with the international transmission of the effects of fiscal expenditures and budget deficits. One of the major sources of recent friction between Europeans and Americans has been the interpretation of the economic implications of US budget deficits. Theorists and policymakers on both sides of the Atlantic have differed in the analysis of the role of budget deficits in affecting key macroeconomic aggregates. Specifically, some have argued that large budget deficits are responsible for the recently observed high real rates of interest while others have claimed that budget deficits cannot be blamed for these real rates. The latter group claimed that theory does not predict a clear-cut relation between budget deficits and rates of interest and that the empirical record itself is very weak.

The increased integration of the world economy has resulted in increased concern in each country over policy measures taken in the rest of the world. A major topic of recent analysis concerns the impact of government spending and budget deficits on key macroeconomic aggregates. The complex pattern of the economic linkages within the interdependent world economy resulted in a variety of models of the international transmission mechanisms (for surveys see Fair (1979) and Mussa (1979)). These models include those that highlight the implications of foreign trade multipliers (e.g., LINK models which build on a Keynesian structure) as well as those that highlight the role of the terms of trade along the lines of the elasticity approach to the balance of payments. In addition, some analyses have examined whether disturbances can be transmitted negatively to the rest of the world. For example, Laursen and Metzler (1950) showed that in a model without capital flows, domestic autonomous government expenditures which raise domestic output, lower the level of output abroad; i.e. domestic spendings are transmitted negatively to the rest of the world. Parallel to these developments there were examinations of the transmission mechanism along the lines of the Mundell–Fleming models (see Mundell (1968) and Fleming (1962)), where it was shown that an expansionary monetary policy is transmitted negatively to the rest of the world whereas fiscal policy is transmitted positively. More recently modelling of exchange-rate dynamics focused on the role of expectations and relied on the real rate of interest as a key factor in the transmission mechanism (see Dornbusch (1976) and Frenkel and Rodriguez (1982)).

The question of the effects of budget deficits on rates of interest, on consumption, and on the nature of the real equilibrium, has been the subject of analysis in both closed and open economy contexts. Much of the traditional analysis demonstrating that budget deficits exert real effects have built on the presumption that government bonds constitute net wealth to individual asset-holders. The key issue of debate has been whether asset-holders take full account of the prospective tax liabilities that are associated with the need to service the debt created by current deficits. Recent research on the effects of fiscal policies has embodied the Ricardian proposition according to which individuals take full account of future tax liabilities and, therefore, as long as government spending remains unchanged, the path of taxes and thereby the path of budget deficits do not affect the real equilibrium of the system. (For expositions see Bailey (1962) and Barro (1974).)

As is well known there are several ways by which a 'fully rational' model can incorporate the feature that budget deficits influence the nature of the real equilibrium. For example, models which allow for distortionary taxes (e.g. Barro (1979), Kydland and Prescott (1980), Lucas and Stokey (1983), and Razin and Svensson (1983)), price rigidities or incomplete markets for intergenerational risk sharing (e.g. Stiglitz (1983)), capital controls (e.g. Greenwood and Kimbrough (1984)), or individuals with finite horizons (e.g. Samuelson (1958) and Diamond (1965)), will all yield the result that fiscal deficits matter.

In this paper we develop a model that is suitable for the analysis of

(i) the linkage between fiscal policies and rates of interest, and (ii) the international transmission mechanism of fiscal policies. The key characteristics of our model are: (i) a fully integrated world capital market; (ii) full rationality of all economic agents whose decisions are based on self-fulfilling expectations and are subjected to temporal and intertemporal budget constraints, and (iii) government behaviour that is constrained by an intertemporal solvency requirement. The model is of a general equilibrium nature, and the various economies have access to, and are governed by, world markets. These markets determine both temporal prices (commodity terms of trade) and intertemporal prices (rates of interest).

In order to deal with the role of budget deficits in effecting world rates of interest, consumption and international indebtedness, and to study the resulting nature of the international trransmission mechanism, our model includes individuals with the possibility of finite horizons. We adopt the formulation developed in Blanchard (1985) according to which the finiteness of the horizon is introduced through the assumption that at each point in time, individuals, who are assumed to have no bequest motive, face a given probability of death. The uncertainty concerning the length of life results in an equilibrium in which private and social rates of discount differ. This difference between discount rates (which is responsible for the departure from the Ricardian proposition on the irrelevancy of budget deficits), permits a meaningful analysis of the impact of budget deficits.

Section II presents the key features of the model and Section III characterises the properties of equilibrium in the two-country world economy. In Section IV we analyse the effects of a current budget deficit that is brought about through a reduction in the home-country's taxes. It is shown that a current budget deficit raises the rate of interest. In addition, the budget deficit raises the value of domestic wealth and lowers the value of foreign wealth. Thus, the deficit is transmitted negatively to the rest of the world. Similar qualitative results apply to the analysis of the effects of expected future budget deficits. As shown in Section V, an expected future deficit also raises domestic wealth and lowers foreign wealth but its impact on the current period's rate of interest is ambiguous as it depends on whether the country introducing the budgetary deficit runs a surplus or a deficit in the current account of its balance of payments. In Section VI we apply the model to an analysis of the steady-state consequences of budget deficits.

In Sections VII and VIII we turn to examine the impact of changes in the level of government spending. In order to separate the analysis of the level of fiscal spending from the analysis of budget deficits, we focus on the implications of a balanced-budget change in government spending. It is shown that a transitory rise in government spending raises interest rates and lowers domestic and foreign wealth. On the other hand, an expected future rise in government spending lowers interest rates and reduces the value of domestic wealth and consumption, while it raises the value of foreign wealth and consumption. We then analyse the effect of a permanent rise in government spending. It is shown that its impact on the rate of interest depends on whether the domestic economy is a net saver or dissaver in the world economy or, equivalently, whether it has a current account surplus or deficit. If the home country runs a current account surplus then a rise in government spending raises world interest rates and lowers domestic and foreign wealth and consumption. On the other hand if the home country runs a current account deficit then a permanent balanced-budget rise in government spending lowers interest rates and domestic wealth and raises foreign wealth. We thus show the critical importance of specifying the details of fiscal policy in terms of the level and timing of government spending and taxes.

In Sections IX and X we generalise the model to a multi-commodity world. The extended model is then applied to examine the effects of government spending on the intertemporal terms of trade (as measured by the rates of interest) and on the temporal terms of trade (as measured by the relative price of importables in terms of exportables). We show that the impact of government spending as well as the dynamics of debt accumulation depend on a comparison among (i) domestic and foreign patterns of private sector spending, (ii) domestic and foreign private sectors' saving propensities, and (iii) domestic and foreign patterns of government spending. These comparisons generate a multitude of 'transfer problem criteria' that are familiar from the theory of transfers in international trade (see Mussa, 1969). Finally, Section XI contains concluding remarks followed by six appendices that provide technical material underlying some of the statements made in the text.

II THE MODEL

The model has two economies consisting of consumers and governments. The path of output in each economy is assumed given. Individuals are assumed to face a given probability of death which is independent of age. We denote the probability of survival between two consecutive periods by γ. Because of uncertain lifetime all loans require in addition to regular interest payments a purchase of life insurance as in Yarri (1965) and Blanchard (1985). In case of death, the estate is transferred to the life insurance company which, in turn, guarantees to cover outstanding debts. It is assumed that there are a large number of individuals and, therefore, competition among insurance companies implies that the percentage insurance premium equals the probability of death. The present-value factor, which is composed of one-period rates of interest compounded from period zero up to period t, is denoted by α_t and, therefore, α_{t-1}/α_t equals one plus the market rate of interest in period $t-1$. Analogously, γ^{t-1}/γ^t equals one plus the life insurance premium. It follows that the *effective* interest rate faced by individuals is $(\gamma^{t-1}/\gamma^t)(\alpha_{t-1}/\alpha_t)-1$. This is the effective cost of borrowing relevant for individual decision making.

Under the assumptions that the utility function is logarithmic and that the subjective discount factor, δ, is constant, it can be shown[2] that the aggregate consumption function (which is derived from individuals' maximisation of expected utility) is

$$c_t=(1-\gamma\delta)W_t \tag{1}$$

where W_t denotes aggregate wealth. Aggregate wealth in turn equals the difference between human wealth, H_t, and private debt B_{pt}. The value of human wealth is the discounted sum of disposable income, Y_t, which is computed by using the *effective* rates of interest.

Government spending can be financed by taxes or by debt issue. The requirement that over time government spending must obey the intertemporal solvency constraint can be expressed as

$$\sum_{v=0}^{\infty} \alpha_v(T_v-G_v)=B_{g0} \tag{2}$$

where T_v, G_v denotes taxes and government spending in period v and where B_{g0} denotes the value of government debt at $t=0$. Equation (2) states that the value of government debt must equal the sums of the present values of current and future budget surpluses. The sum of private debt, B_p, and government debt, B_g, equals the value of the economy's external debt, B.

The behavioural equations for the foreign economy can be derived in a similar way and, in what follows, we denote variables pertaining to the foreign economy by an asterisk (*).

III WORLD EQUILIBRIUM

In this section we analyse the determination of the equilibrium path of world rates of interest in the two-country world economy. We will assume that world capital markets are fully integrated and, therefore, that individuals and governments in both countries face the same *market* rates of interest. This feature provides for the key channel through which policies undertaken in one country impact on economic conditions in the rest of the world. The structure of the model embodies the assumptions that the behaviour of individuals is rational, that it is based upon self-fulfilling expectations, and that governments and individuals are constrained by intertemporal budget constraints. These assumptions imply that economic policies have an impact on the entire path of interest rates and, thereby, on the paths of the key economic variables relevant for current and future generations in both countries.

World equilibrium requires that in each period the given supply of world output equals the demand. To facilitate the exposition we start by dividing the horizon into two periods: the present, which is denoted by $t=0$, and the future ($t=1, 2, \ldots$), and we suppose that outputs, government spending and taxes do not vary across future periods ($t=1, 2, \ldots$). This procedure of time-aggregation is modified in Section V below. In aggregating the future into a composite single period we need to compute the present values of the various flows. For that purpose we define an *average*-interest factor

$$R=\frac{1}{(1+\mathrm{r})}$$

where r denotes the rate of interest. This average-interest factor represents the entire path of the rates of interest that actually do change over time. For further reference R may be termed a 'constancy equivalent' interest factor.

The equality between world demands and world output in period $t=0$ is written as

$$(1-\gamma\delta)W_0+(1-\gamma\delta^*)W_0^*=(Y_0-G_0)+(Y_0^*-G_0^*). \tag{3}$$

where the left-hand side of equation (3) describes the sum of domestic and foreign private sectors' consumption and the right-hand side describes the sum of domestic and foreign outputs (Y_0 and Y_0^*) net of governments' spending.[3] For expositional simplicity we have also assumed in equation (3) that $\gamma=\gamma^*$. Two additional equilibrium conditions specify the initial values of domestic and foreign wealth:

$$W_0=(Y_0-T_0)+\frac{\gamma P}{1-\gamma R}(Y-T)+B_{g0}-B_0. \tag{4}$$

$$W_0^*=(Y_0^*-T_0^*)+\frac{\gamma R}{1-\gamma R}(Y^*-T^*)+B_{g0}^*+B_0. \tag{5}$$

In equations (4)–(5) the term $\gamma R/(1-\gamma R)$ denotes the present value of an annuity evaluated by using the effective constancy equivalent interest factor. Equation (5) embodies the requirement that the sum of the balance of external indebtedness of both countries must be zero and, therefore, the foreign country's external debt is $-B_0$. It is noteworthy that by Walras' Law we have excluded from the equilibrium conditions the equation stating that the sum of the present values of world outputs net of government spending in the future equals the corresponding sum of world demand.

The system of equations (3)–(5) can be solved for the values of W_0 and W_0^* and R for any given value of the parameters. The solutions obtained for the initial values of wealth W_0 and W_0^*, are the same as those which may be obtained from the complete system for which the values of the rates of interest within the future may vary. The use of the constancy-equivalent interest factor simplifies the analysis considerably, and it provides complete information about the impact of policies on the precise *current* values of all key variables including wealth, consumption, and debt accumulation, as well as on the average value of the rate of interest.

IV THE IMPACT OF BUDGET DEFICITS

In this section we analyse the impacts of budget deficits on world rates of interest and on the levels of domestic and foreign wealth and consumption. The analysis of the effects of budget deficits on the levels of foreign wealth and consumption serves to clarify the nature of the international transmission mechanism of fiscal policies. In order to focus on the impact of deficits rather than the impact of government spending, we assume that changes in budget deficits are brought about through changes in taxes for a given path of government spending. Since government spending remains unchanged, solvency requires that current changes in taxes be accompanied by offsetting changes in future taxes. The present values of these tax changes must be equal to each other. Thus, starting with an initial balanced budget, a change in current taxes, $\mathrm{d}T_0$, must be related to the future change, $\mathrm{d}T$, according to

$$\mathrm{d}T_0 = -\frac{R}{1-R}\mathrm{d}T. \tag{6}$$

In equation (6) the term $R/(1-R)$ equals $1/r$, which is the annuity value of a unit tax change.

Throughout the analysis in this section we assume that the foreign government follows a balanced-budget policy. This assumption ensures that changes in world rates of interest which result from domestic fiscal deficits, do not impact on the solvency of the foreign government and, therefore, do not necessitate secondary changes in foreign fiscal policies.

Using equations (3)–(5) the impacts of changes in domestic taxes on R, W_0, and W_0^* (evaluated around an initial balanced budget) are:

$$\frac{\mathrm{d}R}{\mathrm{d}T_0} = \frac{(1-\gamma)}{\Delta}\frac{(1-R)}{R}\frac{(1-\gamma\delta)}{(1-\gamma R)} > 0 \tag{7}$$

$$\frac{\mathrm{d}W_0}{\mathrm{d}T_0} = -\frac{(1-\gamma)}{\Delta}\frac{(1-\gamma\delta^*)}{R(1-R)(1-\gamma R)}[\theta(Y-G)+\omega(Y^*-G^*)] < 0 \tag{8}$$

$$\frac{\mathrm{d}W_0^*}{\mathrm{d}T_0} = \frac{(1-\gamma)}{\Delta}\frac{(1-\gamma\delta)}{R(1-R)(1-\gamma R)}[\theta(Y-G)+\omega(Y^*-G^*)] > 0 \tag{9}$$

where, as shown in the Appendix Section II, Δ, θ, and ω are positive.

Equation (7) shows that a budget deficit arising from a reduction in domestic taxes lowers R thus and raises the value of the world interest rate. The economic interpretation of this result is as follows. From equation (4) we note that, at the prevailing rate of interest, the fall in current taxes (which is accompanied by a corresponding rise in future taxes according to equation (6)), raises the value of domestic wealth by $(1-\gamma)(1-R)/R(1-\gamma R)$ and, thereby, raises spending by the value of the marginal propensity to spend, $1-\gamma\delta$, times the change in wealth. The resulting excess demand for current goods raises their relative price in terms of future goods, and thus raises the world interest rate. As shown in the Appendix Section II, $(1/\Delta)$ serves to translate excess demands for current goods into equilibrating changes in the rate of interest.

Equations (8)–(9) show that the domestic budget deficit raises the equilibrium value of domestic wealth, W_0, and lowers the corresponding value of foreign wealth, W_0^*. Thus, domestic budget deficits are transmitted *negatively* to the rest of the world. The international transmission mechanism is effected through the rate of interest. The rise in the world interest rate lowers the value of foreign wealth and mitigates the initial rise in the value of domestic wealth. These changes in wealth raise domestic spending, lower foreign spending and worsen the domestic current account of the balance of payments.

As may be seen from equations (7)–(9), when the probability of survival, γ, is unity budget deficits do not alter interest rates and wealth. In that case the model yields the familiar Ricardian proposition according to which the timing of taxes and thereby the timing of deficits do not influence the real equilibrium of the system as long as the path of government spending remains intact. In the general case, however, with $\gamma < 1$, budget deficits exert real effects.

The explanation for these results can be given as follows. If the probability of survival, γ, is unity, then the rise in future taxes which is equal in present value to the reduction in current taxes leaves wealth unchanged. On the other hand, the same change in the pattern of taxes raises wealth if each individual knows that there is a positive probability that he will not survive to pay these higher future taxes. Under such circumstances, therefore, the current reduction in taxes constitutes net wealth. Equivalently, the explanation can be stated in terms of the difference between the market and the effective interest factors. While the government solvency requirement implies that changes in current taxes must be made up for by $R/(1-R)$ times the offsetting change in future taxes, individuals discount these future taxes by $\gamma R/(1-\gamma R)$. therefore, as long as $\gamma < 1$, the current budget deficit raises wealth. Yet another interpretation may be given in terms of a 'transfer problem criterion' familiar from the theory of international transfers. Accordingly, the budget deficit exerts real effects because it redistributes wealth from those who have not yet been born, and whose marginal propensity to consume current goods is obviously zero, to those who are currently alive, and whose marginal propensity to consume current goods is positive. The clear presumption concerning the effects of an international transfer on relative prices in the presence of non-traded goods.

V THE IMPACT OF FUTURE BUDGET DEFICITS

The previous analysis of the impact of budget deficits was conducted within a framework which consolidated the *entire* future into a single period. Consequently, in order to ensure solvency, a current budget deficit had to imply a corresponding rise in future taxes. This procedure of time-aggregation did not permit an analysis of the impact of *future* budget deficits which are not accompanied by current changes in taxes. In order to examine the effects of future deficits we modify in this section the aggregation of the periods. Specifically, we divide the future into two parts – the *near* future and the *distant* future. As before, the distant future is represented by a consolidation of the entire period subsequent to that of the near future into a single period. In what follows a subscript 1 designates variables pertaining to the near future and, finally, variables which appear without a time subscript pertain to the distant future.

Consider an expected change in taxes occurring in the near future. Without changes in present taxes government solvency requires that such a change must be accompanied by further offsetting changes in the distant future. Thus, solvency requires that

$$\mathrm{d}T_1 = -\frac{R_1}{1-R_1}\mathrm{d}T \qquad (6')$$

where R_1 is constancy-equivalent interest factor in the distant future; i.e., it is the average one-period interest factor linking the near future with the distant future. In order to compute the effects of such future policies we note that the equilibrium system consists of the following requirements: (i) world output in the present period must be demanded (analogously to equation (3)), (ii) world output in the near future must be demanded, (iii) the equilibrium values of domestic and foreign wealth consist of the sums of the present values of disposable incomes in the present, the near future and the distant future, adjusted for the initial debt (analogously to equations (4)–(5)). This equilibrium system is described in the Appendix Section III.

The impacts of the near-future budget deficit on domestic and foreign wealth are:

$$\frac{dW_0}{dT_1} = -(1-\gamma)\frac{(Y_1 - G_1 + Y_1^* - G_1^*)}{\gamma(1-\gamma\delta)J} < 0 \tag{10}$$

$$\frac{dW_0^*}{dT_1} = (1-\gamma)\frac{(Y_1 - G_1 + Y_0^* - G_1^*)}{\gamma(1-\gamma\delta^*)J} > 0, \tag{11}$$

where

$$J = \frac{(Y-G)(Y_1 - G_1 + Y_1^* - G_1^*)(1-\gamma R_1)}{\gamma_2 R_1 R_0} \times \left(\frac{1}{(1-\gamma\delta)(Y-G)} + \frac{1}{(1-\gamma\delta^*)(Y^*-G^*)}\right) > 0.$$

As seen, analogously to the analysis of the effects of current budget deficits, future deficits (that are brought about through a reduction in taxes) also raise the equilibrium value of domestic wealth, W_0, and lower the corresponding value of foreign wealth W_0^*. Thus, domestic *future* budget deficits are also transmitted *negatively* to the rest of the world. As before, these changes in wealth do not occur when $\gamma = 1$.

The impact of the future budget deficit on the current and future one-period interest factors, R_0 and R_1, respectively, are:

$$\frac{dR_0}{dT_1} = \frac{(1-\gamma)(\delta^* - \delta)}{J} \tag{12}$$

$$\frac{dR_1}{dT_1} = \frac{(1-\gamma)(1-\gamma R_1)(Y-G)[(1-\gamma R_1)(Y-G) + \nu(Y^* - G^*)]}{R_1 R_0 \gamma^3 (1-\gamma\delta^*)(Y^* - G^*)J} > 0 \tag{13}$$

where

$$\nu = 1 - \gamma R_1 + (\delta - \delta^*)\gamma^2(1-\gamma\delta^*)) > 0.$$

Equation (12) shows that the effect of a future budget deficit on the current one-period rate of interest depends on the relation between the domestic and the foreign saving propensities, and, therefore, one may not argue that a future budget deficit *per se* raises short term interest rates. If $\delta < \delta^*$ the future budget deficit lowers R_0 and raises the current one-period rate of interest and conversely if $\delta > \delta^*$. Equation (13) shows that a future budget deficit raises the future rate of interest.

The interpretation of these results is as follows. The future budget deficit creates an excess demand for goods in the near future (i.e., in the period in which the deficit occurs). In order to eliminate this excess demand the future rate of interest must rise according to equation (13). In interpreting the impact of the future deficit on the current short-term interest rate, we note that in the present period no government action takes place and, therefore, the change in the current rate of interest results only from changes in world savings which, in turn, stem from changes in domestic and foreign wealth. At the prevailing short term interest rate foreign wealth falls because of the rise in the future rate of interest while the rise in domestic wealth consequent on the future budget deficit is mitigated by the rise in the future rate of interest. These changes in wealth lower the foreign demand for current goods and raise the domestic demand for these goods. World demand for current goods rises or falls depending on the difference between the two spending propensities. Therefore, in order to restore world equilibrium with zero savings the current one-period interest rate must fall if $\delta > \delta^*$ and must rise if $\delta < \delta^*$. Again, when $\gamma = 1$ the future deficit does not alter the rate of interest.

Our analysis of the effects of budget deficits on the values of domestic and foreign wealth has demonstrated that the international transmission of the deficit must always be negative independent of whether the budget deficit occurs in the present or in the future. On the other hand we have shown that the impact of a future budget deficit on the current short-term rate of interest depends on whether the country which introduces the budgetary changes runs a surplus or a deficit in its international current account, i.e., if its saving propensity exceeds or falls short of the foreign saving propensity. Since it was shown in equations (10)–(11) that the directions of the changes in wealth do not depend on the direction of the changes in the current short-term rates of interest and since the link between foreign wealth and domestic budget deficits operates only through world capital markets, it follows that a future deficit must raise the overall 'appropriate average' of short and long term rates of interest. In the special case with $\delta = \delta^*$ a future budget deficit does not alter the short term interest rate and is reflected only in higher long-term rates; it thus steepens the yield curve. Again, the Ricardian proposition reemerges and these changes vanish when $\gamma = 1$.

VI LONG-RUN EQUILIBRIUM

In this section we analyse the long-run effects of budget deficits on the *steady state* levels of domestic and foreign wealth and on world rates of interest.

The steady-state value of domestic wealth is[4]

$$W = (1-\gamma)\frac{R(Y-T)}{(1-\gamma R)(R-\gamma\delta)}. \tag{14}$$

Analogously, the steady-state value of foreign wealth is:

$$W^* = (1-\gamma^*)\frac{R(Y^*-T^*)}{(1-\gamma^* R)(R-\gamma^*\delta^*)}. \tag{15}$$

World equilibrium requires that the sum of domestic and foreign consumption equals the level of world output net of governments' spending. Using the steady-state value of wealth in the consumption function (1) along with the analogous expressions for the foreign country yields equation (16) as the condition for world equilibrium:

$$(1-\gamma\delta)\frac{(1-\gamma)(Y-T)R}{(1-\gamma R)(R-\gamma\delta)} + (1-\gamma^*\delta^*)\frac{(1-\gamma^*)(Y^*-T^*)R}{(1-\gamma^* R)(R-\gamma^*\delta^*)} = Q + Q^* \tag{16}$$

where $Q = Y - G$ and $Q^* = Y^* - G^*$ denote the levels of domestic and foreign outputs net of government absorption. Equilibrium also requires that both governments be solvent, and thus that in each country the value of government debt equal the sum of the present values of current and future budget surpluses[5]

$$(T-G) = (1-R)B_g \tag{17}$$

$$(T^*-G^*) = (1-R)B_g^*. \tag{18}$$

For given values of government debt, B_g and B_g^* (which reflect past budget deficits) and for given values of government spending, G and G^*, the system (16)–(18) can be used to obtain the solutions for the equilibrium steady-state values of world interest factor, R, and of domestic and foreign taxes, T and T^*. Positive steady-state consumption in both countries requires that the equilibrium value of R must be larger than $\gamma\delta$ *and* $\gamma^*\delta^*$. For exogenously given values of the parameters the existence of such a steady-state is not guaranteed. If this steady-state does not exist, then when $\gamma\delta > \gamma^*\delta^*$ the wealth of the foreign country approaches zero while the home country saves until it owns the entire wealth of the world, and vice versa. Finally, it is relevant to note that when $\gamma = \gamma^* = 1$ steady-state equilibrium with positive levels of consumption in both countries requires that $\delta = \delta^*$. In that case the equilibrium value of R equals the common value of the discount factors.

We now examine the effects of past cumulative budget deficits on the long run values of the rate of interest and wealth. A higher cumulative value of past budget deficits in the home country is reflected in a higher steady-state value of government debt, B_g. By differentiating equations (16)–(18) it is shown in the Appendix Section III that

$$\frac{dR}{dB_g} < 0. \tag{19}$$

Thus, a rise in the steady-state value of domestic government debt raises the steady-state rate of interest (i.e. it lowers the interest factor). It follows therefore that past (cumulative) budget deficits also tend to raise world rates of interest.

The effect of a rise in the steady-state value of domestic government debt on the steady-state value of foreign wealth is specified in equation (20):

$$\text{sign}\frac{dW^*}{dB_g} = \text{sign}[\delta^*(1-\gamma R) - R^2(R-\gamma^*\delta^*)]. \tag{20}$$

Thus the direction of the transmission of past domestic budget deficits on the steady-state value of foreign wealth may be positive or negative depending on the relative magnitudes of the parameters. Specifically, if R falls short of δ^* (but still exceeds $\gamma^*\delta^*$ so that the steady state exists), higher cumulative domestic budget deficits *raise* the steady-state value of foreign wealth. In view of equation (20) it is of interest to note that even though current and future budget deficits must lower the current value of foreign wealth (as shown in Sections IV and V), the long run effects of the cumulative past deficits on the (steady-state) value of foreign wealth are still ambiguous. Finally, we also show in the Appendix Section III that the effect of a higher value of B_g on the domestic value of steady-state wealth contains, in addition to the interest-rate effect discussed above, also a direct negative effect associated with the rise in steady-state taxes necessary to service the debt.[6]

VII GOVERNMENT SPENDING, INTEREST RATES AND TRANSMISSION

The previous sections analysed the effects of budget deficits on the equilibrium of the system. In that analysis changes in the deficit were brought about through changes in taxes while holding government spending intact. In the present section we analyse the effects of changes in the level of government spending. In order to focus on the level of fiscal spending rather than on the consequent changes in deficits, we suppose that all changes in government spending are accompanied by corresponding changes in taxes so as to yield balanced budgets. In what follows we return to the time-aggregation of Sections III and IV where we divided the periods into two, the present and the consolidated future. We also distinguish between transitory and permanent changes. Transitory changes alter only current spending by $\mathrm{d}G_0$ whereas permanent changes also alter future spending by $\mathrm{d}G$.

Using equations (3)–(5) with the aid of the Appendix Section II, the impact of a transitory balanced-budget change in domestic fiscal spending on the interest factor is:

$$\frac{\mathrm{d}R}{\mathrm{d}G_0} = -\frac{\gamma\delta(1-R)}{\Delta R} < 0. \tag{21}$$

Equation (21) shows that a *transitory* rise in government spending lowers R and, therefore, raises the interest rate. This change in the interest rate is necessary in order to eliminate the excess demand for current goods consequent on the rise in government spending. This balanced-budget rise in government spending results in an excess demand for current goods because the rise in taxes lowers wealth by an amount equal to the rise in government spending and, since the private sector's marginal spending propensity is smaller than unity, private expenditure is reduced by only a fraction of the rise in government spending.

The rise in the rate of interest lowers both domestic and foreign wealth and, thereby, results in a reduction of domestic and foreign consumption. Thus, the current transitory balanced-budget rise in domestic fiscal spending is paid for in part by the foreign country.

The same argument applies to the analysis of the effect of an expected future change in government spending. Formally, using equations (3)–(5) we obtain

$$\frac{dR}{dG}=\frac{\gamma(1-R)(1-\gamma\delta)}{\Delta(1-\gamma R)}>0. \tag{22}$$

As seen in equation (22) a *future* balanced-budget rise in government spending raises R (namely, it lowers the rate of interest). The fall in the rate of interest is necessary since, at the prevailing rate of interest, the expected rise in future taxes lowers wealth and reduces consumption demand and, thereby, results in an excess supply of current output. This excess supply is eliminated by the fall in the rate of interest which raises foreign wealth and which mitigates the initial fall in domestic wealth.

The results in equations (21)–(22) provide the ingredients necessary for the analysis of the effects of a permanent balanced-budget rise in government spending. In the case $dG_0=dG=d\bar{G}$, and the impact of this fiscal expansion on the rate of interest can be obtained by adding the expressions in equations (21)–(22). It follows, therefore, that

$$\frac{dR}{dG}=\frac{\gamma(1-R)}{\Delta R(1-\gamma R)}(R-\delta). \tag{23}$$

Thus, the effects of a *permanent* rise in government spending on the rate of interest depends on whether the interest factor, R, exceeds or falls short of the discount factor, δ. The interpretation of this result can be given in terms of the effect of fiscal spending on the excess demand for current goods or, equivalently, in terms of its effect on world savings. As a result of the permanent rise in fiscal spending, at the prevailing interest rate, both the supply of output net of government absorption, as well as the demand for consumption, are reduced by the same proportion. Therefore, the excess supply of current goods or, alternatively, the level of savings, also changes by the same proportion. If the initial level of domestic savings was negative, then the rise in fiscal spending raises the value of savings (by making it less negative) and, thereby, induces a fall in the relative price of present goods, that is, a fall in the rate of interest. On the other hand, if the initial value of domestic savings was positive, the permanent rise in government spending lowers domestic savings and results in a higher rate of interest. These results are analogous to those obtained for the effect of a future budget deficit on the current one-period rate of interest. The link between this explanation and the expression in equation (23) is completed by noting that if $R > \delta$ the initial value of the home country's savings is negative and the economy runs a current account deficit, whereas the opposite holds if $R < \delta$.

The change in the rate of interest alters the values of domestic and foreign wealth and consumption. If the rate of interest rises, then foreign wealth falls and if the rate of interest falls foreign wealth rises. As is obvious, the permanent rise in domestic fiscal spending lowers domestic wealth; the fall in wealth occurring at the initial rate of interest is reinforced or mitigated depending on whether the equilibrium rate of interest rises or falls.

VIII GOVERNMENT SPENDING AND INTEREST RATES: A FURTHER ELABORATION

The previous analysis employed the constancy-equivalent interest factor in order to collapse the entire future into a single period. This procedure permitted a complete specification of the impact of policies on the current values of the key variables. However, it did not permit a detailed examination of the impact of policies on the paths of the various variables *within* the consolidated future. Since the central channel of the transmission mechanism operates through the rates of interest, it is instructive to analyse in further detail the impact of government spending on the entire path of these rates. For that purpose we need to return to the complete disaggregated system. Since the qualitative results in equations (21)–(23) of the impact of government spending do not depend on whether γ is smaller than or equal to unity, we assume henceforth that $\gamma = \gamma^* = 1$. The complete system is described in the Appendix Section IV, where the precise solution for the entire path of the present value factors, α, is given in equation (IV–6). We turn to an analysis of the role of the timing of government spending on the path of the rates of interest and we distinguish between transitory and permanent changes in fiscal spending.[7] Suppose that a *transitory* change is expected to occur in period s in the *future*. The impact of a future transitory change in government spending on the path of the present-value factors is obtained by differentiating equation (IV–6) with respect to Q_s for $t=s\neq 0$ and for $t\neq s\neq 0$. These changes in the present-value factors can be translated into corresponding changes in rates of interest by recalling that $at=[(1+r_0)(1+r_1)\ldots(1+r_t)]^{-1}$. Specifically, when the paths of outputs are stationary the effect of a transitory reduction in future government spending on the rates of interest prevailing in the adjacent period $s-1$, i.e. on r_{s-1} (where $r_{s-1}=(\alpha_{s-1}/\alpha_s-1)$) is

$$\frac{dr_{s-1}}{dQ_s}=\frac{(1-\delta^*)\alpha_{s-1}}{\bar{Q}\alpha_s\Delta_1} \times\left[\frac{\alpha_s}{\alpha_{s-1}}\lambda(\delta^{s-1}-\delta^{*s-1})+\frac{1-\delta^{*s}}{1-\delta^*}+\lambda\frac{\delta^{*s}}{1-\delta^*}+\frac{\lambda^*\delta^s}{1-\delta}\right]>0. \tag{24}$$

An analogous expression pertains to dr_s/dQ_s.[8] The effect of the transitory future reduction in government spending on interest rates prevailing in all other periods $t-1$ (excluding $t=1$, $t=s$, $t=s+1$) depends on the relation between the saving propensities. Thus,

$$\frac{dr_{t-1}}{dQ_s}=\frac{\alpha_s\lambda(1-\delta^*)}{\bar{Q}a_t^2\Delta_1}\delta^{t-1}\delta^{*t-1}(\delta^*-\delta). \tag{25}$$

The results reported in equations (24)–(25) specify the effects of future changes in government spending on the various rates of interest. Figure 2.1 illustrates the effect of a transitory future reduction in government spending occurring in period $s=4$ on the pattern of current and future short (one-period) interest rates for the case $\delta>\delta^*$. In that figure the solid curve (for which $\lambda=\lambda^*=0.5$) describes the initial pattern of interest rates, and the dashed curve describes the pattern corresponding to a situation with an expected future transitory fall in fiscal spending. As is seen, the expected transitory reduction in future government spending tilts the entire term structure of interest rates.

We turn now to examine the effect of a *permanent* fall in domestic fiscal spending (i.e., a permanent rise in net output) on the rates of interest. This effect is best illustrated for the case in which outputs are stationary. Differentiating equation (IV–6) yields:

$$\frac{dr_{t-1}}{dQ}=\frac{\lambda^*\delta^{*t-1}\delta^t(1-\delta)(1-\delta^*)}{\alpha_t^2\bar{Q}}(\delta^*-\delta). \tag{26}$$

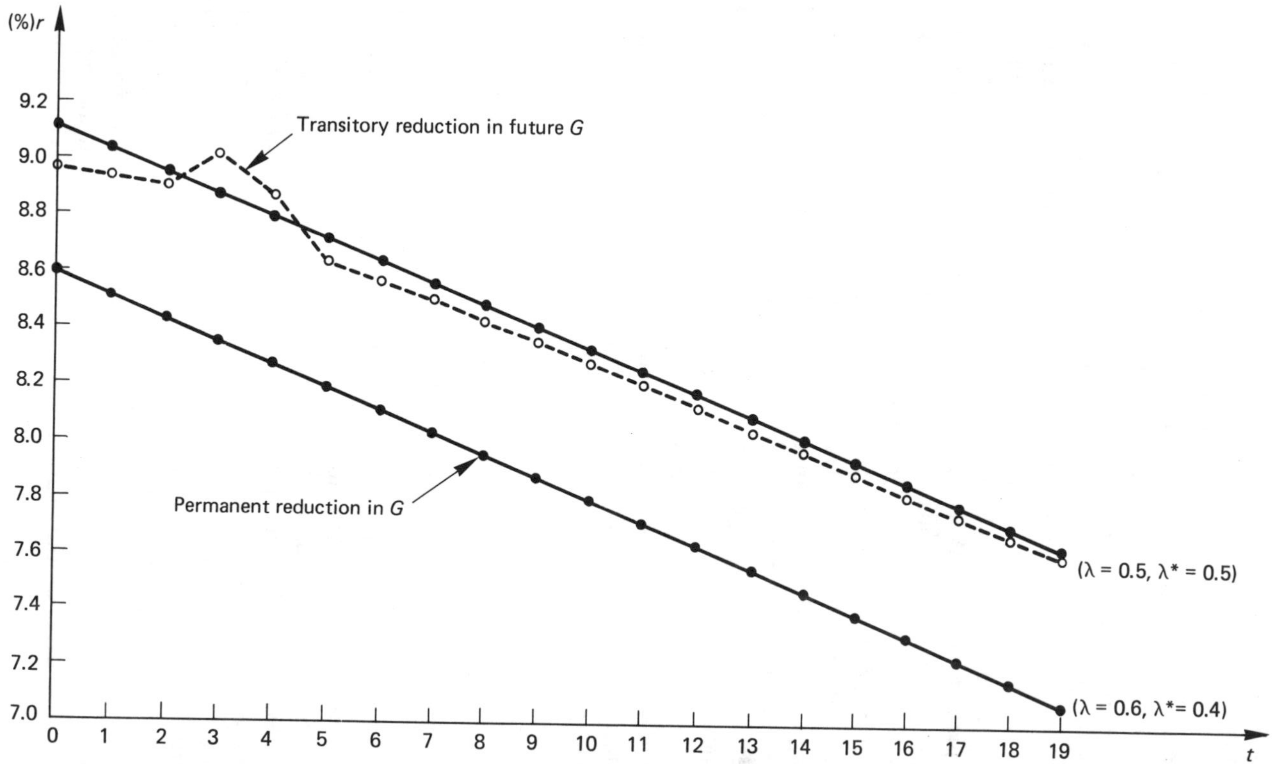

Figure 2.1 The effects of permanent and transitory reduction in government spending on interest rates when $\delta > \delta^*$ ($\delta = 0.95$, $\delta^* = 0.90$).

In terms of Figure 2.1, the solid schedules illustrate the effect of a permanent change in government spending (as parameterised by the values of λ and λ^*) for the case in which $\delta > \delta^*$. As seen, with $\delta > \delta^*$, a permanent fall in domestic government spending (i.e. a rise in λ and a fall in λ^*), lowers the entire structure of interest rates. This qualitative result is reversed if $\delta < \delta^*$.

The interpretation of this result can be given in terms of the effect of the change in government spending on world savings at the prevailing rates of interest. The rise in net domestic output changes current domestic savings by $[dQ_0 - (1-\delta)dW_0]$. In the stationary case, with the prevailing rates of interest, the percentage change in domestic output, $dQ_0/Q_0 = \mu$, equals the percentage change in domestic wealth dW_0/W_0. In that case the incipient change in domestic savings is $\mu[Q_0 - (1-\delta)W_0]$, where the term in the brackets measures the initial value of domestic savings. Clearly, at the prevailing rates of interest, foreign savings do not change. As is evident, the initial value of domestic savings is positive if the domestic marginal propensity to save exceeds the foreign propensity, i.e. if $\delta > \delta^*$ (in that case equilibrium requires that initially foreign savings were negative). Conversely, if $\delta < \delta^*$, domestic savings were negative. Thus, the permanent fall in domestic fiscal spending (the rise in Q), raises world savings and induces a fall in the rates of interest if $\delta > \delta^*$, and vice versa.

IX THE MODEL WITH VARIABLE TERMS OF TRADE

The analysis in the previous sections was confined to a world with a single composite commodity. In that world the only relevant price was that of consumption in different periods, i.e., the rate of interest. In this section we extend the model to allow for two different commodities. Therefore, in addition to the intertemporal terms of trade, the extended model also incorporates the role of the more conventional terms of trade, i.e., the relative price of importables in terms of exportables. The two-good world contains additional channels of interdependence that were not present in the one-good world. Since the relative prices of goods reflect the pattern of spending in both countries, the analysis of fiscal policies needs to specify the spending patterns of the government. In general it will be seen that the impact of policies depends on relations between various behavioural propensities. Specifically, the key factors determining the outcomes of policies are differences among the spending patterns and the saving propensities of four groups: foreign and domestic private sectors as well as foreign and domestic governments. These differences govern the evolution of relative prices and rates of interest following fiscal changes. In order to highlight the key economic factors that affect the equilibrium we abstract in this section from issues concerning the timing of government spending. We thus assume that all changes are permanent and that the paths of outputs (net of government spending) are stationary. We also continue to assume that $\gamma=\gamma^*=1$.

Let the home country exportable good be denoted by x and its importable good by m. To simplify the analysis assume that each country is completely specialised in production. Thus, good x is only produced in the home country at the level X and good m is only produced in the foreign country at the level M. Consumers on the other hand are assumed to consume both goods but, since tastes may differ across countries, consumption patterns may differ. More formally, the expanded menu of goods is now incorporated into the utility function by noting that c_t is a composite good which is defined as a Cobb–Douglas function of its components, i.e., $\log c_t=\beta \log c_{xt}+(1-\beta) \log c_{mt}-\gamma$.[9] Private spending is $z_t=c_{xt}+p_t c_{mt}$, measured in units of good x. Government spending also falls on both goods; G_x denotes government spending on x and G_m denotes government spending on m. Intertemporal utility maximisation yields the spending function $z_t=(1-\delta)W_t$. The temporal utility maximisation yields the demand functions $c_{xt}=\beta z_t$ and $c_{mt}=(1-\beta)(z_t)/p_t$. It is relevant to emphasise that δ measures the marginal propensity to save out of *wealth* whereas β measures the marginal propensity to consume good x out of *spending*. The foreign country is modelled in an analogous fashion.

In order to facilitate the analysis of comparative statics we define henceforth x as domestic product net of the home country's government spending on domestic product, and m as the foreign product net of the foreign country's government spending on its product. Thus, $x=X-G_x$ and $m=M-G_m^*$.

The equilibrium conditions are outlined in the Appendix Section V. In addition to the previous requirements, equilibrium now also requires that the world market for *each* good clear. The solution of the system for the equilibrium values of W_0^*, W_0 and p_0 is given in equations (27)–(29):[10]

$$W_0^* = \frac{(x-G_x^*)[-\beta(xm-G_m G_x^*)+m(x-G_x^*)+\beta(1-\delta)(m-G_m)B]}{(x-G_x^*)[\beta^*(1-\delta^*)m-\beta(1-\delta)G_m]+\beta\beta^*(mx-G_x^* G_m)(\delta^*-\delta)} \tag{27}$$

$$W_0 = \frac{(x-G_x^*)[\beta^*(xm-G_m G_x^*)-G_m(x-G_x^*)-\beta^*(1-\delta^*)(m-G_m)B]}{(x-G_x^*)[\beta^*(1-\delta^*)m-\beta(1-\delta)G_m]+\beta\beta^*(mx-G_x^* G_m)(\delta^*-\delta)} \tag{28}$$

$$p_0 = \frac{(1-\beta)(x-G_x^*)+(1-\delta^*)(\beta-\beta^*)W_0^*}{\beta(m-G_m)}. \tag{29}$$

The explicit solution for p_0 can be obtained by substituting (27) for W_0^* into (29).[11]

The equilibrium solutions of the present-value factors, in terms of goods x and m are given by equations (30)–(31):

$$p_t = \delta^t + \frac{(1-\delta^*)[(1-\beta)x+(1-\beta)\beta B](\delta^{*t}-\delta^t)}{x[1-(1-\beta)\delta^*-\beta\delta]} \tag{30}$$

$$\alpha_t p_t = \frac{(1-\beta)x[\beta^*(1-\delta)\delta^t+(1-\beta^*)\times(1-\delta^*)\delta^{*t}]+(1-\delta^*)(1-\delta)[\beta(1-\beta^*)(\delta^{*t}-\beta^*(1-\beta)\delta^t)]B}{\beta^* m[1-(1-\beta)\delta^*-\beta\delta]} \tag{31}$$

X GOVERNMENT SPENDING, THE TERMS OF TRADE, INTEREST RATES AND TRANSMISSION

In this section we analyse the effects of fiscal spending on domestic and foreign real wealth and on the rates of interest. In general it will be seen that the key factors determining the outcomes of government spending are differences among the spending patterns and the saving propensities of four groups: foreign and domestic private sectors as well as foreign and domestic governments. These differences govern the evolution of relative prices and rates of interest following fiscal changes.

Since real consumption levels are proportional to real wealth, we examine the nature of the transmission mechanism by focusing on the impact of fiscal spending on real consumption levels. Recalling that the values of real consumption at home and abroad are

$$c_t = (1-\delta)W_t/p_t^{1-\beta} \quad \text{and} \quad c_t^* = (1-\delta^*)W_t^*/p_t^{1-\beta^*},$$

it can be shown from equations (27)–(29) that the logarithmic derivatives of real consumption with respect to changes in government spending on domestic goods, G_x, and on foreign goods, G_m, evaluated around an initial equilibrium with zero government spending and zero initial debt are:

$$\frac{\mathrm{d}\log c_0^*}{\mathrm{d}G_x} = -\frac{\beta^*}{x} < 0 \tag{32}$$

$$\frac{\mathrm{d}\log c_0^*}{\mathrm{d}G_m} = \frac{1}{m}\left[\frac{\beta(1-\delta)}{\beta^* K} - (1-\beta^*)\frac{1+JS}{1+J}\right] \tag{33}$$

$$\frac{\mathrm{d}\log c_0}{\mathrm{d}G_x} = -\frac{\beta}{x} < 0 \tag{34}$$

$$\frac{\mathrm{d}\log c_0}{\mathrm{d}G_m} = \frac{1}{m}\left[\frac{\beta(1-\delta) - K}{\beta^* K} - (1-\beta)\frac{1+JS}{1+J}\right] \tag{35}$$

where

$$K = 1-(1-\beta)\delta^* - \beta\delta > 0$$

$$J = \frac{(\beta-\beta^*)(1-\delta^*)}{\beta^* K}$$

$$S = \frac{\beta(1-\delta)\beta^*(1-\delta^*) - \beta\beta^*(\delta^*-\delta)}{\beta^* K}$$

As may be seen, a rise in fiscal spending on *domestic* goods lowers the values of real consumption at home and abroad. The reduction in foreign consumption thus 'finances' part of the increased government spending. The extent of the reduction in the values of real consumption of the private sectors in both countries is proportional to β^* and β – the importance of that good in private sectors' budgets. The precise effects of a rise in government spending on *foreign* goods depends on the magnitudes of the various propensities as may be seen from equations (33) and (35).

In order to highlight the role of the government's spending propensities we define the government spending function G as:

$$G=G_x+pG_m \tag{36}$$

and we assume that the government spending propensities are β_G on good x, and $(1-\beta_G)$ on good m. Thus, $G_x=\beta_G G$ and $pG_m=(1-\beta_G)G$, which implies that, formally, G_m becomes a function of G_x; $G_m=G_m(G_x)$. It follows that around an initial equilibrium with zero government spending:

$$\mathrm{d}G_m=\frac{\varphi}{p}\mathrm{d}G_x \tag{37}$$

where $\varphi=(1-\beta_G/\beta_G$. Using this specification of government spending we note that

$$\frac{\mathrm{d}\log c_0^*}{\partial G}=\frac{\partial \log c_0^*}{\partial G_x}+\varphi\frac{\partial \log c_0^*}{p\partial G_m}. \tag{38}$$

To obtain insights into the economic factors which are at play, we now turn to examine some special cases. These cases correspond to specific assumptions concerning the marginal propensities. Assume first that the domestic and foreign marginal saving propensities are the same, i.e. $\delta=\delta^*$. Using equations (32)–(33) and the specification of government spending which is embodied in (38) along with the solution for p_0 we obtain:

$$\frac{\mathrm{d}\log c_0^*}{\mathrm{d}G}=\frac{\beta^*}{\beta_G\beta(1-\beta)x}[\beta(\beta-\beta_G)+2(1-\beta^*)(1-\beta_G)(\beta-\beta^*)]. \tag{39}$$

Thus, when $\delta=\delta^*$ the effect of domestic fiscal spending on foreign real consumption depends on differences among the patterns of spending of domestic private and public sectors, $\beta-\beta_G$, as well as between domestic and foreign private sectors, $\beta-\beta^*$. The economic interpretation of this result is as follows. When $\delta=\delta^*$ we know from equation (30) that in both countries the interest rate equals the subjective discount rate. Therefore, in each country savings are zero. In that case, neither the rates of interest, nor the total level of world spending are altered in response to government spending since the government, like the private sectors, is a zero saver. It follows that the potential effects of fiscal policies can only operate through changes in relative prices. In conformity with the standard analysis of economic transfers, such changes can occur only if the spending patterns differ among private and public sectors.

To demonstrate the role of the spending patterns consider the following special cases:

(i) When *all* spending patterns are identical, i.e. when $\beta = \beta^* = \beta_G$, we note from equation (39) that d log $c_0^*/\mathrm{d}G = 0$. Thus, in this case only the domestic private sector is crowded out and the effects of fiscal policy are not transmitted internationally. In that case aggregate behaviour in the various markets is not affected by the fiscal policy and, therefore, there are no changes in relative prices.

(ii) When only the spending patterns of the domestic and foreign *private* sector are identical, i.e. when $\beta = \beta^*$, we note from equation (30) that the direction of the change in foreign real consumption following a rise in domestic fiscal spending depends only on the difference between β and β_G. If $\beta > \beta_G$, a rise in government spending creates an excess supply of good x and an excess demand for good m at the initial relative price. Equilibrium is restored through a rise in p, the relative price of good m. This rise in p raises the real value of foreign wealth and, thereby, raises real consumption. In the extreme case for which $\beta_G = 1$, i.e. when government spending falls entirely on good x, foreign real consumption must fall (as was already shown in equation (32)). At the other extreme, when $\beta_G = 0$, i.e. when government spending falls entirely on good m (the case which corresponds to equation (33)), the value of foreign real consumption must rise.

The effect of the rise in government spending on the home country's real consumption must always be negative independent of the patterns of government spending. Thus, in conformity with the traditional results of economic transfers, the secondary gain that might occur through an improvement of the terms of trade cannot offset the primary loss which, in the present case, is the tax levied to finance government spending.

The preceding analysis was confined to the case in which $\delta = \delta^*$ so that each country's income equalled its spending. In that case the international transmission of government spending operated entirely through changes in the relative price of goods without any impact on the rates of interest. We turn now to examine the case in which the saving propensities differ, i.e. $\delta \neq \delta^*$. In order to isolate the effects of differences between private and public spending patterns we will assume that $\beta = \beta^*$. Analogously to the previous derivation it can be shown that if

$$(1-\delta)-(1-\beta)[1-(1-\beta)\delta^*-\beta]>0$$

then

$$\text{sign}\frac{\mathrm{d}\log c_0^*}{\mathrm{d}G} = \text{sign}\left\{\frac{(1-\beta_G}{\beta_G} - \frac{(1-\beta)[1-(1-\beta)\delta^*-\beta\delta]}{(1-\delta)-(1-\beta)[1-(1-\beta)\delta^*-\beta]}\right\}, \tag{39'}$$

and vice versa. Thus, the sign in (39) depends on the relation between the spending patterns of the private sectors and the government, as well as on the relationship between the saving propensities. In the special case for which $\beta = \beta_G$, equation (39) becomes

$$\text{sign}\frac{\mathrm{d}\log c_0^*}{\mathrm{d}G} = \text{sign}\,(\delta^*-\delta). \tag{39''}$$

In that case, with $\beta = \beta^* = \beta_G$, the patterns of world spending on goods are independent of fiscal policies, and the two goods can be aggregated into a composite commodity as in Section VII. In that case the key factor determining the effect of fiscal spending on foreign wealth and, thereby, real consumption is the relation between δ^* and δ. Analogously to the analysis of the one commodity world, the interpretation of this result is in terms of the effect of government spending on the rate of interest. If $\delta^* > \delta$, the foreign country saves part of its income whereas the domestic economy dissaves; thus the domestic country's marginal propensity to save out of *income* is negative. In that case, a rise in the home country's government spending amounts to transferring income from a dissaver (the home country's private sector) to a zero saver (the government) and, thereby, creating (at the prevailing rates of interest) excess world savings. To restore equilibrium the rates of interest must fall. The fall in the rates of interest raises foreign wealth and real consumption. The opposite occurs when $\delta^* < \delta$. The effect of government spending on the home country's real consumption is always negative and the analysis is analogous to that of the one-commodity world. As usual, the secondary gain arising from a fall in the rate of interest (that occurs when

$\delta^* > \delta$) cannot outweigh the primary loss from the tax that is levied to finance government spending.

One of the central mechanisms governing the international transmission mechanism operates through the real rates of interest. In what follows we elaborate on the effects of government spending on the real rates of interest. The example underlying equation (39″) assumes that the patterns of spending are identical among domestic and foreign governments and private sectors. The equality between β and β^* implies that the real rates of interest are equal across countries. The additional assumption that $\beta = \beta_G$ implies that the effects of changes in fiscal spending on the real rates of interest depend only on the differences between the domestic and the foreign saving propensities. The example underlying equation (39′), assumes that $\beta_G \neq \beta = \beta^*$. In that case real rates of interest are equal across the world but the impact of government spending on the real rates of interest depends not only on the relation between the two countries saving propensities, but also on the relation between β and β_G. In the general case for which all spending patterns differ, real rates of interest differ across countries and the effect of government spending on these rates is more complex.

To illustrate, consider the special case in which government spending falls entirely on the domestically produced good, i.e. $\beta_G = 1$. The effects of government spending on the real rates of interest can be computed from the effects of government spending on the present value factors measured in terms of the consumption baskets. The domestic and foreign real present-value factors are $\alpha_t p_t^{1-\beta}$ and $\alpha_t p_t^{1-\beta^*}$, respectively. It can be shown that

$$\frac{\mathrm{d}\log(\alpha_t p_t^{1-\beta})}{\mathrm{d}\log x} = -(1-\beta) < 0, \tag{40}$$

and

$$\frac{\mathrm{d}\log(\alpha_t p_t^{1-\beta^*})}{\mathrm{d}\log x} = -(1-\beta^*) < 0. \tag{40'}$$

Thus, a reduction in government spending G_x (i.e., a rise in x) lowers the real present-value factors in both countries and raises the corresponding real rates of interest. In contrast with the case of equality among private and public spending patterns (in which the direction of changes in real rates of interest depended on the relation between saving propensities), here these propensities play no role. In the present case with $\beta_G = 1$, domestic and foreign real rates of interest move in the same direction. The extent of their response to government spending depends on the relative share of the good which is not consumed by the government (good m) in private sectors' spending.

In the intermediate case for which government spending falls on both goods but the relative share β_G exceeds the corresponding shares of the private sectors, β and β^*, the effect of government spending on the real rates of interst reflects the influence of both spending patterns and savings propensities. For example, if $\delta^* > \delta$ a reduction in government spending lowers world savings (as demonstrated for the one-commodity world) and necessitates a higher rate of interest; this reinforces the effects embodied in equations (40)–(40′). On the other hand, if $\delta > \delta^*$, the reduction in government spending raises world savings. Its impact on the real rates of interest tends to mitigate and may even reverse the effects operating via equations (40)–(40′).

XI CONCLUDING REMARKS

In this paper we analysed the effects of budget deficits and government spending, on world interest rates, and wealth. We examined in detail the nature of the international transmission mechanism. The model that was used embodied the assumptions that world capital markets are fully integrated and that individuals behave rationally on the basis of self-fulfilling expectations. Economic behaviour of individuals and governments was assumed to be governed by temporal and intertemporal budget constraints. In order to capture the effects of budget deficits on world equilibrium, we assumed that the probability of survival is less than unity and, therefore, individuals behave as if their horizons were finite. The formulation assured that the model was not subject to the Ricardian proposition according to which budget deficits do not matter. Our analysis demonstrated that the dependence of world rates of interest, wealth, and consumption, on fiscal policies is highly sensitive to the detailed specification of the policies in terms of the level and the time path of government spending and taxes.

The departure from the Ricardian proposition in this paper stems from the difference between the *effective* interest-factor that individuals use in discounting future taxes and the corresponding *market* interest-factor that governs governments' behaviour. In the present analysis the specific reason responsible for the difference between the two interest factors was that individuals were assumed to be mortal while governments were implicitly assumed to be immortal. In general, of course, the probability that governments and their commitments survive indefinitely is also less than unity. Under such circumstances the impact of budget deficits is governed by the relation between the survival probabilities of individuals and governments. It is relevant to note that while the formulation in this paper has focused on the survival probability as the reason for the departure from the Ricardian proposition, the key argument need not hinge on this specific formulation. In general, independent of the reasons for the differences between effective and market interest factors, such differences imply that, within the present framework, budget deficits exert real effects on the world economy.

The examination of the effects of government spending showed that the impact of fiscal expenditures can be analysed by reference to a multitude of 'transfer problem criteria', which are familiar from the theory of international economic transfers. In the present case the impact of policies depended on relations among the spending propensities of domestic and foreign private sectors and governments as well as on the difference between domestic and foreign saving propensities. Our analysis drew a distinction between permanent and transitory policies as well as between current policies and expected future policies.

The analysis of the impact of government spending on real rates of interest revealed that even when capital markets are highly integrated, real rates of interest may differ if spending patterns differ across countries. With such differences in spending patterns, fiscal policies exert different quantitative effects on real rates of interest in the various countries. An implication of this analysis is that in the presence of non-traded goods, fiscal policies may also exert different qualitative effects on real rates of interest in different countries since, depending on the nature of the transmission mechanism and on the patterns of government and private sectors' spending, the relative prices on non-traded goods, and thereby the price indices, might be negatively correlated between countries (see Dornbusch, 1983).

Our analysis is subject to several limitations which stem from some of the simplifying assumptions. We assumed that the output levels were given exogenously. An extension would allow for a process of investment which responds to rates of interest and which changes the paths of outputs (see, for example, Buiter, 1984). Such an extension would modify the pattern of the current account and debt accumulation (see, for example, Sachs, 1981). The endogeneity of output could also be introduced through the incorporation of some Keynesian features such as price rigidities. Under such circumstances government spending would alter the level of economic activity and would be transmitted internationally through mechanisms similar to those of the foreign-trade multipliers.

An additional extension would modify the utility function so as to generate a saving function possessing life-cycle characteristics, specifically, the possibility that savings respond negatively to the rate of interest would influence the impact of budget deficits on interest rates.

Throughout the analysis in this paper we assumed that the foreign government followed a balanced-budget policy. This assumption was adopted in order to ensure that changes in world rates of interest which result from domestic fiscal policies do not impact on the solvency of the foreign government. If the foreign government does not follow a balanced-budget policy, then interest-rate changes would necessitate secondary changes in foreign spending or taxes in order to restore solvency. An extension of the analysis would relax the foreign balanced-budget assumption and would allow for the necessary adjustment of foreign fiscal management. A more major extension would recognise that the interdependencies among the various open economies provide incentives for strategic behaviour by individual countries. With such incentives, countries would attempt to exploit monopoly power in goods and capital markets and to extract maximum seigniorage from debt issue (see, for example, Hamada, 1984). The analysis would then determine the optimal pattern of government spending along with the optimal trade-cum-capital-flows tax structure as implied by the optimal tariff literature. Such a strategic behaviour could then be incorporated into a more elaborate game-theoretic framework. Further, the interdependencies and the strategic behaviour could result in inefficient outcomes from a global perspective that may call for harmonisation of fiscal policies. In such an extended framework, government spending and the timing of taxes would become endogenous variables that are determined in the context of world equilibrium.

APPENDIX

I The Formal Model

Let the utility function at period t of an individual who was born in period s be:

$$u=\sum_{v=t}^{\infty} \delta^{v-t} \log c_{sv} \tag{I-1}$$

where δ denotes the subjective discount factor and where c_{sv} denotes the rate of consumption in period v of an individual born in period s. The probability, as of period t, that the individual will be alive in period v (and enjoy the utility level $\log c_{sv}$) is γ^{v-t}. Therefore, expected utility is:

$$E_t\sum_{v=t}^{\infty} \delta^{v-t} \log c_{sv}=\sum_{v=t}^{\infty} (\gamma\delta)^{v-t} \log c_{sv}. \tag{I-2}$$

The budget constraint in period $t-1$ for an individual born in period s is:

$$b_{st}=\frac{\gamma^{t-1}\alpha_{t-1}}{\gamma^t\alpha_t}(b_{st-1}+c_{st-1}-\tilde{y}_{t-1}) \tag{I-3}$$

where b_{st} denotes the value of debt at the end of period t (which resulted from decisions made in period $t-1$), and $\tilde{y}_{t-1}$ denotes disposable income which is assumed to be the same across all individuals regardless of age. The solvency requirement is

$$\lim_{t\to\infty} \gamma^t\alpha_t b_{st}=0. \tag{I-4}$$

Consolidation of the periodical budget constraints together with the solvency requirement yields:

$$\sum_{v=t}^{\infty} \frac{\gamma^v\alpha_v}{\gamma^t\alpha_t}c_{sv}=\sum_{v=t}^{\infty} \frac{\gamma^v\alpha_v}{\gamma^t\alpha_t}\tilde{y}_v-b_{st}=w_{st} \tag{I-5}$$

where w_{st} denotes wealth.

Maximisation of (I-2) subject to the consolidated budget constraint (I-5) yields:

$$c_{sv} = (1 - \gamma\delta)\frac{\delta^v \alpha_t}{\delta^t \alpha_v} w_{st} \tag{I-6}$$

where c_{sv} denotes planned consumption for period v of an individual born in period s and who makes his plan in period t.

Population is normalised so that every cohort born in period s starts with one individual. Due to death, its size in period t becomes γ^{t-s}. The equality between the probability of survival of a given cohort and its frequency relative to its initial size stems from the law of large numbers. Since at each period t there are γ^{t-s} members of each cohort, the (constant) aggregate size of population is:

$$\sum_{s=-\infty}^{t} \gamma^{t-s} = \frac{1}{1-\gamma},$$

and, therefore, aggregate disposable income is $y_v = 1/(1-\gamma)/\tilde{y}_v$.

Aggregate consumption in period t is the sum of consumption of individuals from all cohorts. Since consumption of the s cohort is $\gamma^{t-s} c_{st}$, aggregate consumption, c_t, is

$$c_t = \sum_{s=-\infty}^{t} \gamma^{t-s} c_{st}. \tag{I-7}$$

Using the individual consumption function (I-6) (for $v = t$) and the definition of wealth from equation (I-5) yields

$$c_t = (1 - \gamma\delta)(H_t - B_{pt}) = (1 - \gamma\delta) W_t \tag{I-8}$$

where

$$H_t = \sum_{v=t}^{\infty} \frac{\gamma^v \alpha_v}{\gamma^t} y_v \tag{I-9a}$$

and

$$B_{pt} = \sum_{s=-\infty}^{t} = -\infty \frac{\gamma^t}{\gamma^s} b_{st}. \tag{I-9b}$$

Lagging equation (I-9a) by one period yields an analogous expression for H_{t-1} which, together with equation (I-9a), yields:

$$H_t = \frac{\gamma^{t-1}\alpha_{t-1}}{\gamma^t \alpha_t}(H_{t-1} - y_{t-1}). \tag{I-10}$$

The evolution of aggregate private debt, B_{pt}, can be obtained by substituting equation (I-3) into the definition of debt in equation (I-9b) along with the definitions of lagged aggregate consumption, income and debt:

$$B_{pt} = \frac{\alpha_{t-1}}{\alpha_t}(B_{pt-1} + c_{t-1} - y_{t-1}). \tag{I-11}$$

Using the aggregate consumption function from equation (I-8), together with the law of motion of human wealth from equation (I-10), and iterating yields:

$$B_{pt} = \frac{(\gamma\delta)^t}{\alpha_t}\ (B_{p0} - H_0) - (1-\gamma)\sum_{v=1}^{t-1}(\gamma\delta)^{-v}\alpha_v H_v \quad + H_t \tag{I-12}$$

where H_v is defined by equation (I-9a) and where B_{p0} is the initially given level of debt. The path of total wealth W_t can be obtained by subtracting equation (I-12) from H_t:

$$W_t = \frac{1}{\alpha_t}\left[\ (\gamma\delta)^t W_0 + (1-\gamma)\sum_{v=1}^{t}(\gamma\delta)^{t-v}\alpha_v H_v\ \right]. \tag{I-13}$$

Government solvency requirement is:

$$\sum_{v=t}^{\infty}\frac{\alpha_v}{\alpha_t}(T_v - G_v) = B_{gt} \tag{I-14}$$

where T_v, G_v denote taxes and government spending in period v and where B_{gt} denotes the value of government debt in period t.

Equation (I-14) implies that government debt in period t is:

$$B_{gt} = \frac{\alpha_{t-1}}{\alpha_t}(B_{gt-1} + G_{t-1} - T_{t-1}). \tag{I-15}$$

The sum of private debt, B_p, and government debt B_g equals the value of the economy's external debt, B. Thus, by adding equations (I-11) and (I-15) we obtain:

$$B_t = \frac{\alpha_{t-1}}{\alpha_t}[B_{t-1} + (c_{t-1} + G_{t-1}) - T_{t-1}] \tag{I-16}$$

where $Y_{t-1} = y_{t-1} + T_{t-1}$ is gross domestic product.

World equilibrium requires that in each period the given supply of world output equal world demand. Equilibrium in period $t = 0$ requires that world private spending equal world output net of world government's spending:

$$(1-\gamma\delta)(H_0 + B_{g0} - B_0) + (1-\gamma^*\delta^*)(H_0^* + B_{g0}^* + B_0) = \bar{Y} - G_0 - G_0^*. \tag{I-17}$$

In equation (I-17) the left-hand side describes the sum of domestic and foreign consumption where domestic consumption reflects equation (I-8) and where foreign variables are indicated by an asterisk (*); $\bar{Y}$ denotes world output, and we have substituted B_0 for $-B_0^*$.

For all future periods ($t > 0$), the equilibrium condition can be written as:

$$\begin{aligned}(1-\gamma\delta)\ &[(\gamma\delta)^t(H_0 + B_{g0} - B_0) + (1-\gamma)\sum_{v=1}^{t}(\gamma\delta)^{t-v}\alpha_v H_v] \\ &+ (1-\gamma^*\delta^*)\ [(\gamma^*\delta^*)^t(H_0^* + B_{g0}^* + B_0) \\ &+ (1\gamma^*)\sum_{v=1}^{t}(\gamma^*\delta^*)^{t-v}\alpha_v H_v^*] = \alpha_t(\bar{Y}_t - G_t^*).\end{aligned} \tag{I-18}$$

The next set of conditions states that the values of human wealth in each period must equal the sum of the present values of disposable incomes. Thus, for period $t = 0$, this requirement is:

$$H_0 = \sum_{v=0}^{\infty} \gamma^v \alpha_v (Y_v - T_v), \tag{I-19}$$

$$H_0^* = \sum_{v=0}^{\infty} \gamma^{*v} \alpha_v (Y_v^* - T_v^*), \tag{I-20}$$

and for all other period ($t > 0$):

$$\alpha_t H_t = \frac{1}{\gamma^t}\sum_{v=t}^{\infty} \gamma^v \alpha_v (Y_v - T_v) \tag{I-21}$$

$$\alpha_t H_t^* = \frac{1}{\gamma^{*t}}\sum_{v=t}^{\infty} \gamma^{*v} \alpha_v (Y_v^* - T_v^*). \tag{I-22}$$

The system is closed by the requirements that both governments be intertemporally solvent. Using equation (I-14) and its foreign-country analogue, we obtain:

$$\sum_{t=0}^{\infty} \alpha_t (T_t - G_t) = B_{go} \tag{I-23}$$

$$\sum_{t=0}^{\infty} \alpha_t (T^*_t - G^*_t) = B^*_{g0}. \tag{I-24}$$

For any given initial values of the external debt, governments' debt and the paths of governments' spending, the system of equations (I-17)–(I-24) solves for the initial period's values of H_0 and H^*_0 as well as for α_t, $\alpha_t H_t$ and $\alpha_t H^*_t$ for all other periods (t>0). In addition, the system also solves for the sum of the present values of taxes in each country. Finally, it is relevant to note that by Walras' Law one of the equations (I-17)–(I-22) can be excluded.

II The Impact of Current Budget Deficits

In this section we derive the formal solution to the impact of current budget deficits on R, W_0 and W^*_0. Differentiating equations (3)–(5) of the text (under the assumption that $\gamma = \gamma^*$) yields:

$$\begin{bmatrix} 1-\gamma\delta & 1-\gamma\delta^* & 0 \\ 1 & 0 & \dfrac{-\gamma(Y-G)}{(1-\gamma R)^2} \\ 0 & 1 & \dfrac{-\gamma(Y^*-G^*)}{(1-\gamma R)^2} \end{bmatrix} \begin{bmatrix} \mathrm{d}W_0 \\ \mathrm{d}W^*_0 \\ \mathrm{d}R \end{bmatrix} = \begin{bmatrix} 0 \\ -1 \\ -1 \end{bmatrix} \frac{1-\gamma}{1-\gamma R} \mathrm{d}T_0$$

The determinant of the matrix is denoted by $-\Delta$. The value of Δ is:

$$\Delta = \frac{(1-\gamma\delta^*)}{R(1-R)} [\psi(Y-G) + \omega(Y^* - G^*)] > 0$$

where

$$\omega = \frac{(1-\gamma R)^2 - (1-\gamma)(1-\gamma R^2)}{(1-\gamma R)^2} > 0$$

$$\psi=\gamma\frac{(1-\gamma R^2)-(1-R)^2\gamma(\delta-\delta^*)}{(1-\gamma R)^2}>0.$$

The solutions of the system are given in equations (7)–(9) in the text where

$$\theta=\frac{(1-\gamma R)^2-\gamma(1-R)^2-(1-\gamma)(1-\gamma R^2)}{(1-R)^2}>0.$$

III The Impact of Future Budget Deficits and Steady-State Equilibrium

In Part A of this section we derive the formal solutions to the impact of future budget deficits on world rates of interest (short-term and long-term) and on W_0 and W^*_0, for the case in which $\gamma=\gamma^*$. In Part B we examine the impact of cumulative budget deficits on the steady-state values of interest rates and wealth.

A. The equilibrium conditions are

$$(1-\gamma\delta)W_0+(1-\gamma\delta^*)W^*_0=(Y_0-G_0)+(Y^*_0-G^*_0) \tag{III-1}$$

$$(1-\gamma\delta)[\gamma\delta W_0+(1-\gamma)R_0H_1]+(1-\gamma\delta^*)[\gamma\delta^*W^*_0 +(1-\gamma)R_0H^*_1]=R_0[(Y_1-G_1)+(Y^*_1-G^*_1)]. \tag{III-2}$$

$$W_0=(Y_0-T_0)+R_0\gamma(Y_1-T_1)+R_0\frac{\gamma R_1}{1-\gamma R_1}(Y-T)+B_{g0}-B_0 \tag{III-3}$$

$$W^*_0=(Y^*_0-T^*_0)+R_0\gamma(Y^*_1-T^*_1)+R_0\frac{\gamma R_1}{1-\gamma R_1}(Y^*-T^*)+B^*_{g0}+B_0 \tag{III-4}$$

where

$$H_1=(Y_1-T_1)+\frac{R_1}{1-\gamma R_1}(Y-T)$$

and

$$H^*_1=(Y^*_1-T^*_1)+\frac{R_1}{1-\gamma R}(Y^*-T^*).$$

Equations (III-1) and (III-2) specify the world goods market clearing conditions for the present and for the near future periods; and equations (III-3) and (III-4) define the values of domestic and foreign wealth in the present period, where H_1 and H_1^* denote the values of human capital in the near future as evaluated at $t=1$. Differentiating this system with respect to future tax changes and evaluating the solutions around the point of balanced budgets and the stationary future (i.e., $Y_1=Y$, $T_1=T=G_1=G$ and $Y_1^*=Y^*$, $T_1^*=T^*=G_1^*=G^*$), we obtain equations (10)–(13) in the text.

B. The steady-state equilibrium conditions are shown by equations (16)–(18) in the text. Differentiating these equations around an initial equilibrium with $B_g=B_0^*=0$, $Q=Q^*$, $\gamma=\gamma^*$ yields

$$\frac{dR}{dB_g}=R(1-R)(1-\gamma\delta)(1-\gamma R)(R-\gamma\delta)(R-\gamma\delta^*)^2/$$
$$Q\{(R-\gamma\delta)(R-\gamma\delta^*)[(1-\gamma\delta)(R-\gamma\delta^*)+(1-\gamma\delta^*)$$
$$\times(R-\gamma\delta)]-R[(1-\gamma\delta)(R-\gamma\delta^*)^2+(1-\gamma\delta^*)(R-\gamma\delta)^2]\}<0. \tag{III-5}$$

In order to compute the effect of B_g on the steady–state value of foreign wealth, we first note that $dW^*/dB_g=(dW^*/dR)(dR/dB_g)$ and since, from (III-5), $dR/dB_g<0$, we only need to determine the effects of R on W^*. Differentiating equation (15) in the text yields

$$\frac{dW^*}{dR}=(1-\gamma)Q^*\frac{\gamma R^2(R-\gamma\delta^*)-\gamma\delta^*(1-\gamma R)}{(1-\gamma R)^2(R-\gamma\delta^*)^2}\gtrless 0. \tag{III-6}$$

As is seen the transmission of domestic past deficits to the steady-state value of foreign wealth may be positive or negative. For example, if $R<\delta^*$ (but still $R>\gamma\delta^*$ so as to ensure the steady-state) $dW^*/dR<0$ and, therefore, $dW^*/dB_g>0$ and the transmission of past budget deficits to foreign wealth is positive.

The effect of B_g on the steady-state value of domestic wealth is

$$\frac{dW}{dB_g}=\frac{\partial W}{\partial R}\frac{dR}{dB_g}+\frac{\partial W}{\partial B_g}. \tag{III-7}$$

Differentiating equation (14) in the text yields

$$\frac{dW}{dB_g}=(1-\gamma)\left\{Q\frac{\gamma R^2(R-\gamma\delta)-\gamma\delta(1-\gamma R)}{(1-\gamma R)^2(R-\gamma\delta)^2}\frac{dR}{dB_g}-\frac{(1-R)R}{(1-\gamma R)(R-\gamma\delta)}\right\} \tag{III-8}$$

The second term on the right-hand side of equation (III-8) does not have a counterpart in the expression for dW^*/dB_g; this negative term represents the direct effect of B_g on domestic wealth which operates through the necessary rise in steady-state tax collections. A sufficient condition for a decline in domestic steady-state wealth consequent on a rise in B_g is that $\gamma R^2(R-\gamma\delta)\rangle\gamma\delta(1-\gamma R)$.

IV The Solution of the Complete System with $\gamma=1$

In this section we examine the properties of the model for the special case in which the probability of survival is unity. In that case, with $\gamma=1$, the market interest factor equals the effective interest factor, and the equilibrium conditions are:

$$(1-\delta)W_0+(1-\delta^*)W_0^*=\bar{Q}_0 \tag{IV-1}$$

$$(1-\delta)\delta^t W_0+(1-\delta^*)\delta^{*t}W_0^*=\alpha_t\bar{Q}_t \tag{IV-2}$$

$$W_0=\sum_{t=0}^{\infty}\alpha_t Q_t-B_0 \tag{IV-3}$$

where

$$W_0=H_0+B_{g0}-B_0,\ W_0^*=H_0^*+B_{g0}^*+B_0$$

$$Q_t=Y_t-G_t \quad \text{and} \quad \bar{Q}_t=(Y_t-G_t)+(Y_t^*-G_t^*).$$

Equation (IV-1) describes the requirement that current world demand equal current world output net of governments' spending, and equation (IV-2) describes the corresponding requirement for $t=1, 2, \ldots$. Equation (IV-3) defines the equilibrium value of domestic wealth. This specification substitutes government spending, G_t, for taxes, T_t, by using the government solvency requirement. The solution of this system is

$$W_0=\frac{[\bar{Q}_0\Sigma_{t=0}^{\infty}\delta^{*t}\lambda_t-B_0]}{(1-\delta)\Delta_1} \tag{IV-4}$$

$$W_0^* = \frac{\bar{Q}_0 \Sigma_{t=0}^{\infty} \delta^t \lambda_t^* + B_0}{(1-\delta^*)\,\Delta_1} \tag{IV-5}$$

$$\alpha_t = \frac{\{\bar{Q}_0[\delta^{*t} \Sigma_{\tau=0}^{\infty} \delta^{\tau} \lambda_{\tau}^* + \delta^t \Sigma_{\tau=0}^{\infty}\, \delta^{*\tau} \lambda_{\tau}] + (\delta^{*t} - \delta^t)\, B_0\}}{\bar{y}_t \Delta_1} \tag{IV-6}$$

where $\Delta_1 = \Sigma_{t=0}^{\infty}\, \delta^{*t} \lambda_t + \Sigma_{t=0}^{\infty} \delta^t \lambda_t^* > 0$, and where λ_t^* denotes the share of foreign product net of government spending, i.e. $\lambda_t^* = Q_t^* / \bar{Q}_t$ and, λ_t denotes the corresponding share of the home country, i.e. $\lambda_t = (Q_t / \bar{Q}_t) = 1 - \lambda_t^*$.

As is evident by inspection of equations (IV-4)–(IV-6), the system conforms with the Ricardian proposition. Thus, since in present case we assume that $\gamma = 1$, it follows that as long as the paths of government spending (which govern the paths of Q and Q^*) are given, the time patterns of taxes and government debt issues are irrelevant for the determination of world equilibrium.

V The Two-Commodity System

The equilibrium conditions for the system can be obtained as follows: equilibrium requires that the world market for *each* good clear. Using the demand functions, the equilibrium conditions for both goods are:

$$\beta(1-\delta)\frac{\delta^t}{\alpha_t} W_0 + \beta^*(1-\delta^*)\frac{\delta^{*t}}{\alpha_t} W_0^* = x_t - G_{xt}^* \tag{V-1}$$

$$(1-\beta)\,(1-\delta)\frac{\delta^t}{\alpha_t p_t} W_0 + (1-\beta^*)\,(1-\beta^*)\frac{\delta^{*t}}{\alpha_t p_t} W_0^* = m_t - G_{mt}. \tag{V-2}$$

In period 0, $\alpha_0 = 1$ and, therefore, the market clearing conditions for $t = 0$ become:

$$\beta(1-\delta) W_0 + \beta^*(1-\delta^*) W_0^* = x_0 - G_{x0}^* \tag{V-3}$$

$$(1-\beta)\,(1-\delta)\frac{W_0}{p_0} + (1-\beta^*)(1-\delta^*)\frac{W_0^*}{p_0} = m_0 - G_{m0} \tag{V-4}$$

where the values of wealth are

$$W_0 = x \sum_{t=0}^{\infty} \alpha_t - G_m \sum_{t=0}^{\infty} \alpha_t p_t - B \tag{V-5}$$

$$W_0^* = m\sum_{t=0}^{\infty} \alpha_t p_t - G_x^* \sum_{t=0}^{\infty} \alpha_t + B. \tag{V-6}$$

By Walras' Law we may ignore one of the equations in the system. Substituting (V-5)–(V-6) into (V-3)–(V-4) yields:

$$\beta(1-\delta)[x\sum_{t=0}^{\infty} \alpha_t - G_m^* \sum_{t=0}^{\infty} \alpha_t p_t - B] +$$
$$\beta^*(1-\delta^*)[m\sum_{t=0}^{\infty} \alpha_t p_t - G_x^* \sum_{t=0}^{\infty} \alpha_t + B] = x - G_x^* \tag{V-7}$$

$$(1-\beta)(1-\delta)[x\sum_{t=0}^{\infty} \alpha_t - G_m \sum_{t=0}^{\infty} \alpha_t p_t - B]$$
$$+(1-\beta^*)(1-\delta^*)[m\sum_{t=0}^{\infty} \acute{\alpha}_t p_t - G_x^* \sum_{t=0}^{\infty} \alpha_t + B] = p_0(m - G_m). \tag{V-8}$$

We then multiply both sides of (V-1) by α_t, sum both sides over all t (from 0 to ∞) and substitute (V-5) and (V-6) for W_0 and W_0^*. The resulting equation is then:

$$\beta\left[\, x\sum_{t=0}^{\infty} \alpha_t - G_m \sum_{t=0}^{\infty} \alpha_t p_t - B \,\right] + \beta^*\left[\, m\sum_{t=0}^{\infty} \alpha_t p_t - G_x^* \sum_{t=0}^{\infty} \alpha_t + B \,\right]$$
$$= (x - G_*^*) \sum_{t=0}^{\infty} \alpha_t. \tag{V-9}$$

Equations (V-7), (V-8) and (V-9) constitute the relevant system. The economic interpretations is as follows: Equations (V-7) and (V-8) describe the equilibrium in the markets for the two goods in period 0. It is evident that this is a rational expectations equilibrium since the demand functions are based on the fully expected realisation of future values of rates of interest and prices. Equation (V-9) requires that the sum of the present values of world demand for good x equal the corresponding sum of world supply. As may be noted we have used Walras' Law to ignore the analogous requirement for good m.

This system is used to solve for the three unknowns: The sum of the present value factors in terms of good x–$\Sigma_{t=0}^{\infty}\alpha_t$; the sum of the present value factors in terms of good m–$\Sigma_{t=0}^{\infty}\alpha_t p_t$; and the relative price of good m in terms of x in the first period – p_0. These solutions can then be used in (V-5) and (V-6) to obtain the values of W_0 and W_0^*. These are the solutions that are reported in equations (27)–(29) in the text.

VI Effects of Fiscal Spending in the Two-Commodity System[12]

In this part of the appendix we derive the effects of fiscal policies on the real values of domestic and foreign consumptions as well as on real rates of interest. These results are computed around an initial equilibrium with zero debt and zero government spending. From equations (27) in the text we obtain

$$\frac{dW_0^*}{dx}=\frac{1-\beta}{\beta^* D} \qquad \text{(VI-1)}$$

$$\frac{dW_0^*}{dG_m}=\frac{x}{m}\frac{\beta(1-\beta)(1-\delta)}{\beta^{*2}D^2}. \qquad \text{(VI-2)}$$

From (V-3) in Section V and from (VI-1) and (VI-2) we obtain

$$\frac{dW_0}{dx}=\frac{1}{D} \qquad \text{(VI-3)}$$

$$\frac{dW_0}{dG_m}=\frac{x[\beta(1-\delta)-D]}{\beta^* m D^2}. \qquad \text{(VI-4)}$$

Differentiating equation (29) in the text with respect to x and using (VI-1) yields

$$\frac{dp_0}{dx}=\frac{(1-\beta)-(1-\delta^*)(\beta-\beta^*)(1-\beta)/\beta^* D}{\beta m}. \qquad \text{(VI-5)}$$

From equations (27)–(29) in the text we obtain

$$W_0^*=\frac{(1-\beta)x}{\beta^* D}, \qquad \text{(VI-6a)}$$

$$W_0=\frac{x}{D} \qquad \text{(VI-6b)}$$

where $D=1-(1-\beta)\delta^*-\beta\delta>0$. To convert (VI-5) into a logarithmic derivative we first substitute (VI-6a) for W_0^* into equation (29) in the text to obtain:

$$p_0=\frac{(1-\beta)x}{\beta m}\left[1+\frac{(1-\delta^*)(\beta-\beta^*)}{\beta^* D}\right]; \tag{VI-7}$$

and dividing (VI–5) by (VI–7) yields

$$\frac{\mathrm{d}\ \log\ p_0}{\mathrm{d}x}=\frac{1}{x}. \tag{VI-8}$$

Multiplying (VI-8) by $(1-\beta^*)$ and subtracting from the logarithmic derivative of W_0^* with respect to x (obtained from (VI-1) and (VI-6a)) we get $\mathrm{d}\log c_0^*/\mathrm{d}x$ which is equation (32) in the text, with a minus sign (since $\mathrm{d}x=-\mathrm{d}G\mathrm{x}$).

Analogously, dividing (VI − 3) by (VI-6b) yields the logarithmic derivative of W_0 with respect to x, from which we subtract the product of $(1-\beta)$ and (VI-7), to obtain $\mathrm{d}\log c_0/\mathrm{d}x$ which is equation (34) in the text (with a minus sign).

To compute the effects of changes in G_m on real consumption we first note that from (29) and (VI-2):

$$\frac{\mathrm{d}p_0}{\mathrm{d}G_m}=\frac{(1-\beta)}{\beta}\frac{x}{m^2}\left\{1+\frac{(\beta-\beta^*)(1-\delta^*)}{\beta^{*2}D^2}\right. \\ \left.[\beta(1-\delta)-\beta^*(1-\delta^*)-\beta\beta^*(\delta^*-\delta)]\right\} \tag{VI-9}$$

and dividing by (VI-8) yields

$$\frac{\mathrm{d}\ \log\ p_0}{\mathrm{d}G_M}=\frac{1}{m}\frac{1+JS}{1+J} \tag{VI-10}$$

where J and S are defined in equation (35) in the text. Multiplying (VI-10) by $(1-\beta^*)$ and subtracting from the ratio of (VI-2) and (VI-6a) yields equation (33) in the text.

Analogously, dividing (VI-4) by (VI-3) and subtracting the product of $(1-\beta)$ and (VI-10) yields equation (35) in the text.

In computing the effects of domestic permanent fiscal spending on domestic and foreign real rates of interest we focus on the case in which government spending falls entirely on good x, i.e. the case for which $\beta_G=1$.

Equation (V–1) in Section V (around an initial equilibrium with zero government spending and initial debt) implies that

$$\alpha_t = 1/x[\beta(1-\delta)\delta^t W_0 + \beta^*(1-\delta^*)\delta^{*t} W_0^*]. \qquad \text{(VI-11)}$$

and its logarithmic derivative is:

$$\frac{\mathrm{d}\log\alpha_t}{\mathrm{d}x} = \theta\frac{\mathrm{d}\log W_0}{\mathrm{d}x} + (1-\theta)\frac{\mathrm{d}\log W_0^*}{\mathrm{d}x} - \frac{1}{x} \qquad \text{(VI-12)}$$

where, using (VI-5a)–(VI-6b)

$$\theta = \frac{\beta(1-\delta)\delta^t}{\beta(1-\delta)\delta^t + (1-\beta)(1-\delta^*)\delta^{*t}}.$$

Using (VI-3) and (VI-6b) for d log $W_0/\mathrm{d}x$, and using (VI-1) and (VI-6a) for d log $W_0^*/\mathrm{d}x$, we obtain

$$\frac{\mathrm{d}\log\alpha_t}{\mathrm{d}x} = 0. \qquad \text{(VI-13)}$$

Analogously, from equation (V–2) in Section V we obtain:

$$\frac{\mathrm{d}\log p_t}{\mathrm{d}x} = \tilde{\theta}\frac{\mathrm{d}\log W_0}{\mathrm{d}x} + (1-\tilde{\theta})\frac{\mathrm{d}\log W_0^*}{\mathrm{d}x} - \frac{\mathrm{d}\log\alpha_t}{\mathrm{d}x}. \qquad \text{(VI-14)}$$

where

$$\tilde{\theta} = \frac{\beta^*(1-\delta)\delta^t}{\beta^*(1-\delta)\delta^t + (1-\beta^*)(1-\delta^*)\delta^{*t}}$$

Using (VI-3) and (VI-6b) for d log $W_0/\mathrm{d}x$, and using (VI-1) and (VI-6a) for d log $W_0^*/\mathrm{d}x$, we obtain after substituting (VI-13):

$$\frac{\mathrm{d}\log p_t}{\mathrm{d}x} = \frac{1}{x}. \qquad \text{(VI-15)}$$

As may be observed by comparing (VI-15) with (VI-8), the effect of x on the initial price p_0 is the same as its effect on the entire path of prices, p_t. This result reflects the finding in (VI-13) where it was shown that the change of x does not alter the entire path of interest rates.

Finally, differentiating logarithmically the real present-value factors, $(\alpha_t p_t^{1-\beta})$ and $(\alpha_t p_t^{1-\beta^*})$ with respect to x, and using (VI-13) and (VI-15), yields equations (40)–(40′) in the text.

Notes

1. Parts of this paper were written during the Fall of 1983 while J. A. Frenkel was a Fellow at the Sackler Institute for Advanced Studies at Tel-Aviv University, Israel, and during the winter of 1984 while A. Razin was a visiting Professor at the Woodrow Wilson School of International Affairs, Princeton University. The final draft was prepared during the summer of 1984 while both authors participated in the Summer Institute of the NBER. We are indebted to these institutions as well as to Itzhak Gilboa for assistance in the computations. In revising the paper we have benefited from useful comments by J. Aizenman, G. Calvo, A. Dixit, R. Dornbusch, E. Helpman, R. E. Lucas, Jr., F. Modigliani, M. Mussa, M. Obstfeld, T. J. Sargent and L. Svensson. The research reported here is part of the NBER's research programme in International Studies and Economic Fluctuations. Any opinions are those of the authors and not of the National Bureau of Economic Research.
2. The complete model and the various derivations are outlined in Appendix I which draws on Frenkel and Razin (1986).
3. In this formulation government spending reduces the resources available for private sector consumption without yielding utility services. The interaction between public and private goods in the utility function is a separate issue, with which we do not deal in the present paper. It is relevant to note, however, that none of our results are altered by the introduction of 'useful' government as a *separable* argument in the utility function.
4. In order to compute the long-run values of wealth we use equations (I-10) and (I-13) of the Appendix, we first substitute R^v for α_v (where $R=1/(1+r)$ is the constant steady-state interest factor), and $(Y-T)$ for (Y_t-T_t); then we take the limit of W_t as $t\rightarrow\infty$. To ensure a finite value of long-run wealth we assume that $R>\gamma\delta$ since if $R<\gamma\delta$, wealth is unbounded. As is evident from equation (14) if $\gamma=1$ then, if $R>\delta$ wealth shrinks to zero.
5. Formally, equation (17) is obtained by substituting B_G for B_{gt} and $(T-G)$ for (T_v-G_v) in equation (I-14) in the Appendix: an analogous procedure underlies the derivation of equation (18).
6. While it seems likely that a higher value of domestic government debt lowers the steady-state value of domestic wealth, we were unable to formally rule out the opposite outcome.
7. The subsequent analysis draws on Frenkel and Razin (1985a).
8. Recall that Q is defined as the value of output net of government spending; thus, a reduction in government spending is equivalent to a rise in Q.
9. The constant term $\gamma=\beta\log\beta+(1-\beta)\log(1-\beta)$ is chosen so as to simplify, without loss of generality, the subsequent expressions of real consumption.
10. This specification assumes that B is denominated in units of good x. This assumption concerning the indexation of debt may be material when there are unexpected changes in the terms of trade. In our subsequent analysis we assume that the initial value of B is zero and, thereby, the

specification of the units of B does not alter our results. In general, however, such changes may provide for an additional channel through which government spending impacts on the real equilibrium.

11. To gain insight into the determinants of p_0 we note that the equilibrium price must equate one country's trade balance surplus with the other's trade deficit or equivalently, the equilibrium price must ensure that the value of *world* spending on goods equal the value of *world* output. Thus, the equilibrium price p_0 must satisfy $[(1-\delta)W_0+G_x+P_0G_m]-X=p_0M-[(1-\delta^*)W_0^*+G_x^*+p_0G_m^*]$ where the left-hand side measures the home country's trade balance deficit and the right-hand side measures the foreign country's trade balance surplus. To ensure that the market for *each* good clears we use the market clearing condition for good x in period $t=0$ and substitute for W_0 into the trade-balance condition. The solution for p_0 yields equation (29).
12. This Appendix is drawn on Frenkel and Razin (1985b).

REFERENCES

Bailey, M. J. (1962) *National Income and the Price Level* (New York: McGraw-Hill).

Barro, R. J. (1974) 'Are Government Bonds Net Wealth?' *Journal of Political Economy*, vol. 82, no. 6 (Nov./Dec.) pp. 1095–1117.

Barro, R. (1979) 'On the Determination of the Public Debt', *Journal of Political Economy*, vol. 87, no. 5, Part 1 (Oct.) pp. 940–71.

Buiter, W. H. (1984) 'Fiscal Policy in Open Interdependent Economies', National Bureau of Economic Research Working Paper Series, No. 1429, August 1984.

Blanchard, O. J. (1985) "Debt, Deficits and Finite Horizons', *Journal of Political Economy*, 93, No. 2 (April) pp. 223–47.

Diamond, P. A. (1965) 'National Debt in a Neoclassical Growth Model', *American Economic Review*, vol. 60, no. 5 (Dec.) pp. 1126–50.

Dornbusch, R. (1976) 'Expectations and Exchange Rate Dynamics', *Journal of Political Economy*, vol. 84, no. 6 (Dec.) pp. 1161–76.

Dornbusch, R. (1983) 'Real Interest Rates, Home Goods, and Optimal External Borrowing', *Journal of Political Economy*, vol. 91, no. 1 (Feb.) pp. 141–53.

Fair, R. C. (1979) 'On Modeling the Economic Linkages Among Countries', in Dornbusch, Rudiger and Frenkel, Jacob A. (eds), *International Economic Policy: Theory and Evidence* (Baltimore: Johns Hopkins University Press).

Fleming, J. M. (1962) 'Domestic Financial Policies Under Fixed and Floating Exchange Rates', *International Monetary Fund Staff Papers*, vol. 6 (Nov.) pp. 369–79.

Frenkel, J. A. and A. Razin (1986) 'Fiscal Policies in the World Economy', *Journal of Political Economy*, 94, no. 3, June.

Frenkel, J. A. and A. Razin (1985a) 'Government Spending, Debt and

International Economic Interdependence', *Economic Journal*, vol. 94 (Sept. 1985) pp. 619–36.

Frenkel, J. A. and A. Razin (1985b) 'Fiscal Expenditures and International Economic Interdependence', in Buiter, Willem and Marston, Richard C. (eds) *International Economic Policy Coordination* (Cambridge: Cambridge University Press, 1985) pp. 37–73. This is a revision of the paper entitled 'Fiscal Policies, Debt and International Economic Interdependence', National Burea of Economic Research, Working Paper Series, No. 1266, January 1984.

Frenkel, J. A. and C. A. Rodriguez (1982) 'Exchange Rate Dynamics and the Overshooting Hypothesis', *International Monetary Fund Staff Papers*, vol. 29, no. 1 (Mar.) pp. 1–30.

Greenwood, J. and K. P. Kimbrough (1984) 'Capital Controls and the International Transmission of Fiscal Policy', Centre for the Study of International Economic Relations, University of Western Ontario, Working Paper No. 8432, July 1984.

Hamada, K. (1984) 'Strategic Aspects of International Fiscal Interdependence', unpublished manuscript, Tokyo University.

Kydland, F. E. and E. C. Prescott (1980) 'A Competitive Theory of Fluctuations and the Feasibility and Desirability of Stabilization Policy', in Fischer, Stanley (ed.), *Rational Expectations and Economic Policy* (Chicago: University of Chicago Press).

Laursen, S. and L. A. Metzler (1950) 'Flexible Exchange Rates and the Theory of Employment', *Review of Economics and Statistics*, vol. 32 (Nov.) pp. 281–99.

Lucas, R. E. Jr. and N. L. Stokey (1983) 'Optimal Fiscal and Monetary Policy in an Economy Without Capital', *Journal of Monetary Economics*, vol. 12, no. 1 (July) pp. 55–93.

Mundell, R. A. (1968) *International Economics* (New York: Macmillan).

Mussa, M. (1969) 'Three Times and Transfer Problem Plus David Hume', unpublished manuscript, University of Chicago.

Mussa, M. (1979) 'Macroeconomic Interdependence and the Exchange Rate Regime', in Dornbusch, Rudiger and Frenkel, Jacob, A. (eds), *International Economic Policy: Theory and Evidence* (Baltimore: Johns Hopkins University Press).

Razin, A. and L. E. O. Svensson (1983) 'The Current Account and the Optimal Government Debt', *Journal of International Money and Finance*, vol. 2, no. 3 (Aug.) pp. 215–24.

Sachs, J. D. (1981) 'The Current Account and Macroeconomic Adjustment in the 1970s', *Brooking Papers on Economic Activity*, no. 1, pp. 201–18.

Samuelson, P. A. (1958) 'An Exact Consumption Loan Model of Interest With or Without the Social Contrivance of Money', *Journal of Political Economy*, vol. 66, no. 3 (Aug.) pp. 467–82.

Stiglitz, J. E. (1983) 'On the Relevance or Irrelevance of Public Financial Policy: Indexation, Price Rigidities, and Optimal Monetary Policy', in R. Dornbusch and M. H. Simonsen (eds), *Inflation, Debt and Indexation*, MIT Press, Cambridge.

Yaari, M. E. (1965) 'Uncertain Lifetime, Life Insurance and the Theory of the Consumer', *Review of Economic Studies*, vol. 32, no. 2 (April) pp. 137–50.

Comments on J. A. Frenkel and A. Razin, 'Budget Deficits and Rates of Interest in the World Economy' by Franco Modigliani

The paper of Frenkel and Razin (F & R) is rich in valuable qualities: it deals with a timely issue, it is ingenious in the choice of framework and brilliant in the way it is manipulated, it is clearly and rigorously written, without being bogged down in tedious mathematics, and it leads to a number of definite conclusions, some conforming and satisfying one's intuition and some definitely less obvious or even surprising. For all of these qualities, the authors deserve to be warmly congratulated.

But, despite these numerous virtues, I feel that the paper suffers from a number of limitations, which cast serious doubts on the relevance and empirical validity of some of its results. These limitations arise from two main features of the paper: (i) the authors rely exclusively on Blanchard's framework for describing consumption and saving behaviour in the economy; (ii) they assume away the existence of a stock of physical capital – representing both a means of production and a 'store of value' – and the related flow of investment – except for a brief reference to investment as a 'possible extension'.

My main complaint is not so much that they have chosen this particular simplifying framework, but rather that they failed to give any indications that dropping these simplifications could change their results in certain directions, or even that it could change them at all. In addition, their second failure is particularly disappointing since, in my view, the really interesting issue related to fiscal policies and public deficits is not their effect on interest rates, but rather their impact on the stock of capital and thereby on future generations. In what follows, I propose to spell out these objections and offer some speculation of the extent to which a less (unreasonably) restrictive set of assumptions could change conclusions.

The approach developed by Olivier Blanchard, which forms the basis for the generalisation of F & R, is unquestionably a highly ingenious one, which permits studying the implications of finite life without the stifling format of the overlapping generations model or the frequently unwieldy algebra of a full scale life cycle (LC) model; I have referred to the overlapping generations model as the poor man's life cycle model; but, Blanchard's formula must be acknowledged at least as middle class!

That model implies that, in the absence of a Barro type bequest motive, taxes are not neutral, just like the standard LC model. This is because life, though stochastic, has a finite expectation that plays a role similar to that of the length of life in deterministic LC models. None the less, the version of the model used by F & R makes some very restrictive assumptions, and in particular an additive, logarithmic utility function. This assumption, coupled with the assumption that earning is independent of age (which, of course, rules out retirement and accumulation to finance it), and that life expectancy implies that consumption is proportional to total wealth (human plus non-human), with a proportionality factor independent of the interest rate. And, since wealth – at least the human component – is, clearly, a decreasing function of the rate of market discount, consumption itself turns out to be a decreasing function of the interest rate.

It is well known that there is nothing in the postulate of rational behaviour that implies such a relation. The elasticity of consumption with respect to the interest rate can have either sign, in principle. Furthermore, a positive sign is particularly plausible if the main purpose of accumulation is to provide for retirement consumption on a scale similar to active consumption. It is also well known that the empirical evidence on the interest elasticity of consumption is contradictory, to say the least.

Yet, F & R ignore altogether the possibility of a positive response of consumption to interest rates, and its implications. To be sure, such a response might create problems of instability, in the absence of a stock of capital. But, this consideration does not seem to justify ignoring the problem; on the contrary, if the authors had faced it, they might have appreciated more fully the importance of allowing for the physical capital.

To see the implications of a non-conventional interest effect on consumption, consider the case of a reduction in taxes, expenditure constant, in one of the countries. This creates, in that country, a higher consumption demand, through the higher disposable income, and hence an excess demand that requires a decline in consumption, for given disposable income. In F & R, this occurs through a *rise in interest rate* which also *lowers wealth and consumption* in both countries. But, if the elasticity of consumption with respect to interest rates is positive, then what is required to eliminate the excess demand is a *fall* in interest rate, which will reduce consumption in both countries, though it would *raise wealth in both countries*. (It is, however, unclear why one should be interested in changes in wealth *per se*, when such movements are exclusively the result of changes in discounting and not of variations in physical capital.)

Similarly, in the case of a tax financed, permanent, rise in the government expenditure, if the country has positive saving, there is, initially, a current excess demand for commodity, because consumption falls less than the rise in taxes and, hence, in expenditure. If the interest elasticity of consumption is positive, the equilibrium interest rate will *be lower*, which will lower consumption both domestically and abroad, even though foreign wealth will rise (though domestic wealth will, presumably, still fall, though the permanent reduction is disposable income).

Consider, next, the likely implications of allowing for the existence of physical capital. A first important consequence is that a *positive* interest elasticity of consumption need not be inconsistent with stability, provided total private demand, which now consists of consumption and investment, has a *negative* elasticity. If this condition holds, then a reduction in taxes, expenditure constant, should increase domestic consumption and the interest rate, and crowd out investment, independently of the sign of the response of consumption to interest rates. It should also increase domestic wealth (as the higher disposable income effect outweighs the effect of a higher discount factor) while decreasing foreign wealth. All of these responses are qualitatively the same as in F & R. However, foreign consumption need not necessarily fall; it may rise, instead, if $\mathrm{d}c/\mathrm{d}r$ is sufficiently positive, though foreign investment must decline enough to reduce total private foreign absorption, and increase foreign lending. It is also apparent that a positive response of consumption to interest rates will make for a higher equilibrium interest rate and more crowding out of total investment.

The existence of a capital stock has implications also for the case of a tax financed increase in government expenditure. Indeed, under the usual assumption of decreasing return to capital, it must be presumed that, in equilibrium, R cannot exceed δ, or, more generally, that saving cannot be negative (at least as long as population and productivity are not declining) though the country may still be borrowing to finance investment. It then follows that, even in the case of a *permanent* rise in expenditure and taxes, consumption cannot fall more than the rise in expenditure. But this means, in turn, that the interest rate must rise, or, at any rate cannot fall, which disposes of the major counter-intuitive result of F & R. So, even in this balanced budget case, there will be non-negative crowding out of investment and domestic consumption, and declines in domestic and foreign wealth, while the foreign consumption response remains uncertain. At the same time, the fraction of expenditure that will be accommodated by crowding investment will depend on the initial saving rate and presumably be small, going to zero in the limiting case of zero saving.

It can be seen from these illustrations that once the analysis is generalised to allow for a stock of capital goods and the possibility of a positive response of consumption to interest rates, then one finds that, a rise in a deficit, expenditure constant, will always imply crowding out of investment, accompanied by a redistribution from later generations to the current. (To be sure, some redistribution occurs also without capital, as the current generation increases its later consumption through the interest it earns, which is financed from taxes levied partly on the younger – but the redistribution should be on a much smaller scale.) If consumption rises with the interest rate, then the crowding out will be larger. These conclusions hold as well for tax-financed expenditure. However, in this case, at least when the rise in expenditure and taxes is not purely transitory, the crowding out of investment will, generally, be small and may even dwindle to nothing.

In closing, let me express the hope that F & R will be inclined to generalise their analysis along the lines suggested above, and that, in so doing, they will not find serious holes in my conjectures.

3 Fiscal Policy in Open, Interdependent Economies

Willem Buiter

I INTRODUCTION

The paper studies fiscal policy in the open economy. It proceeds from the very small country, which is a price taker in the world financial market and in the markets for imports and exports, via the semi-small country, which has some market power in the market for its exportable, to the interdependent two-country case. To keep the analysis tractable, a very simple production structure is assumed: each country consumes both domestic and foreign output but is wholly specialised in the production of its exportable. So as to be able to analyse 'crowding out' issues in the short run and the long run, firms in each country can engage in capital formation. Only domestic output can be transformed into domestic capital, and the investment process is subject to strictly convex internal costs of adjustment. There is no money in the model, but international portfolio lending and borrowing can occur in an integrated global financial market. There is no direct foreign investment. Rational point expectations and certainty equivalence are assumed throughout, so all stores of value are perfect substitutes in private portfolios. As cyclical, Keynesian issues are not the focus of this paper, full employment is assumed throughout.

The fiscal policy issue that is our primary concern is the choice of borrowing versus tax financing of a given programme of public spending on goods and services ('exhaustive spending'). The model can of course be used equally well for the analysis of alternative spending-cum-financing policies. So as not to get side-tracked into issues of excess burdens and deadweight losses, all taxes are assumed to be lump-sum. From the government's budget constraint, or rather from its 'present value budget constraint', or solvency constraint, it then follows that our concern is with the consequences for private saving and capital formation of intertemporal redistributions of the tax burden. This means that, given the perfect financial markets that are assumed in the model, the analysis could stop right here if we specified households either as infinite-lived or as endowed with operative intertemporal gift and bequest motives (see e.g. Frenkel and Razin, 1984a). To get a non-trivial analysis of the central issue of financial policy one therefore either has to adopt the overlapping generations framework without gift and bequest motives (see e.g. Buiter, 1981) or the 'uncertain lifetime' approach first developed by Yaari (1965) and applied to macroeconomic issues of fiscal policy in open and closed economies by Blanchard (1983a, b). The overlapping generations approach has the major drawback that its most popular variant, the two-period life cycle model, has a unit period of about 38 years. This makes it a suitable vehicle, at most, for the study of the Kondratieff cycle. To obtain a more interesting periodisation a high price is paid in the form of higher order difference equation systems and difficult aggregation problems. The Yaari–Blanchard approach, adopted in the present paper, captures the essential notion of finite private decision horizons while preserving lower-order dynamics and easy aggregation. There is a price to be paid of course: the instantaneous probability of death is assumed to be independent of age and consequently there are no characteristic life-cycle patterns of saving and wealth.[1]

This paper investigates the consequences of domestic and foreign governments' taxation-borrowing mixes for saving and capital formation in the two countries and for the interest rate and the real exchange rate. Qualitative, analytical methods are relied on as much as possible, but a large part of the dynamic analysis can only be performed using numerical simulation algorithms.

Section II presents the model. The very small country case is studied in Section III, followed by the semi-small country case in Section IV. The two-country model is put through its paces in Section V.

II THE MODEL

The paper studies the effects of fiscal policy in a dynamic, two-country, two-good rational expectations model. Each country is completely specialised in the production of its exportable. Fixed domestic capital formation takes the form of accumulation of domestic output only (subject to internal costs of adjustments). Each country's labour market clears and the world markets for the two traded commodities are in competitive equilibrium. There is a single, integrated, global financial market in which a bond denominated in terms of home country output is traded.

The derivation of the behavioural equations of the model is given in Blanchard (1983b). Consumer behaviour follow's Yaari's (1965) uncertain lifetime approach, as applied to an aggregated macroeconomic model by Blanchard (1983a, b). Investment behaviour is governed by a Tobin's q type relationship based on increasing and strictly convex internal costs of adjustment.

The equations governing the two-country model are:

$$q(s) = (\theta + \lambda)(w(s) + h(s)) \qquad \theta, \lambda > 0 \tag{1}$$

or

$$\dot{q}(s) = (r(s) - \theta)q(s) - (\theta + \lambda)\lambda w(s) \tag{1'}$$

$$\dot{w}(s) = r(s)w(s) + j(K(s)) - \tau(s) - q(s) \tag{2}$$

$$\dot{h}(s) = \tau(s) - j(K(s)) + (r(s) + \lambda)h(s) \tag{3}$$

or

$$h(s) = \int_s^\infty (j(K(t)) - \tau(t)) \exp[-\int_s^t (r(u) + \lambda)\mathrm{d}u]\mathrm{d}t \tag{3'}$$

$$c_x(s) = \alpha q(s) \qquad 0 \leqslant \alpha \leqslant 1 \tag{4}$$

$$c_y(s) = (1 - \alpha)\frac{q(s)}{\pi(s)} \tag{5}$$

$$\dot{K}(s) = (\psi(s) - 1)\zeta^{-1}K(s) \qquad \zeta > 0 \tag{6}$$

$$\frac{\dot{\psi}(s)}{\psi(s)} = r(s) - \frac{f'(K(s))}{\psi(s)} - \frac{1}{2\psi(s)}\zeta \left(\frac{\dot{K}(s)}{K(s)}\right)^2 \tag{7}$$

$$\dot{b}^G(s) = g_x(s) + \pi(s)g_y(s) + r(s)b^G(s) - \tau(s) \tag{8}$$

$$q^*(s) = (\theta^* + \lambda^*)(w^*(s) + h^*(s)) \qquad \theta^*, \lambda^* > 0 \tag{9}$$

or

$$\dot{q}^*(s) = \left(r(s) - \frac{\dot{\pi}(s)}{\pi(s)} - \theta^* \right) q^*(s) - (\theta^* + \lambda^*)\lambda^* w^*(s) \tag{9'}$$

$$\dot{w}^*(s) = \left(r(s) - \frac{\dot{\pi}(s)}{\pi(s)} \right) w^*(s) + j^*(K^*(s)) - \tau^*(s) - q^*(s) \tag{10}$$

$$\dot{h}^*(s) = \tau^*(s) - j^*(K^*(s)) + \left(r(s) - \frac{\dot{\pi}(s)}{\pi(s)} + \lambda^* \right) h^*(s) \tag{11}$$

or

$$h^*(s) = \int_s^\infty (j^*(K^*(t)) - \tau^*(t)) \exp\left[-\int_s^t (r(u) - \frac{\dot{\pi}(u)}{\pi(u)} + \lambda^*) \mathrm{d}u \right] \mathrm{d}t \tag{11'}$$

$$c_x^*(s) = \alpha^* \pi(s) q^*(s) \qquad 0 \leqslant \alpha^* \leqslant 1 \tag{12}$$

$$c_y^*(s) = (1 - \alpha^*) q^*(s) \tag{13}$$

$$\dot{K}^*(s) = (\psi^*(s) - 1)\zeta^{*-1} K^*(s) \tag{14}$$

$$\frac{\dot{\psi}^*(s)}{\psi^*(s)} = r(s) - \frac{\dot{\pi}(s)}{\pi(s)} - \frac{f^{*\prime}(K^*(s))}{\psi^*(s)} - \frac{\frac{1}{2}\zeta^*}{\psi^*(s)} \left(\frac{\dot{K}(s)}{K^*(s)} \right)^2 \tag{15}$$

$$\dot{b}^{*G}(s) = g_x^*(s) + \pi(s) g_y^*(s) + r(s) b^{*G}(s) - \pi(s)\tau^*(s) \tag{16}$$

$$f^*(K^*(s)) = c_y(s) + g_y(s) + \dot{K}^*(s) + c_y^*(s) + g_y^*(s) + \frac{1}{2}\zeta^* \frac{(\dot{K}^*(s))^2}{K^*(s)} \tag{17}$$

$$f(K(s)) = c_x(s) + g_x(s) + \dot{K}(s) + c_x^*(s) + g^*{}_x(s) + \frac{1}{2}\zeta \frac{\dot{K}(s)^2}{K(s)} \tag{18}$$

$$F(s) = w(s) - \psi(s)K(s) - b^G(s) \tag{19}$$

These nineteen equations determine the behaviour over time of q, q^*, w, w^*, h, h^*, K, K^*, c_x, c_x^*, c_y, c_y^*, ψ, ψ^*, b^G, b^{*G}, r, π and F given the values of the fiscal instrument, τ, τ^*, g_x, g_x^*, g_y and g_y^*.

Equations (1) to (8) describe the domestic economy. Aggregate consumption, q (measured in terms of domestic output), is a constant linear function of total (human h plus non-human w) wealth (equation 1). The constant of proportionality is the sum of the pure rate of time preference, θ and the constant (i.e. age-independent) instantaneous probability of death, λ. The familiar infinite-lived consumer world with its debt-neutrality properties is the special case of our model when $\lambda=0$. The rate of change of aggregate private non-human capital $\dot{w}$, equals private disposable income minus private consumption. Disposable income is labour income $y \equiv j(.)$, plus interest income rw minus taxes τ. Private financial wealth consists of private holdings of domestic government bonds, b^G, of claims on the rest of the world, F, and of claims on the domestic capital stock, K. All assets are perfect substitutes in private portfolios, so their expected rates of return are equalised. All bonds, whether issued by domestic or foreign private or public agents are denominated in terms of domestic output (good x) and are of the fixed market value, variable interest rate variety. $r(s)$ is the instantaneous own rate of interest on these bonds. Labour income y is the product of the wage rate and the exogenous labour supply, which is fully employed. Choice of units sets employment equal to unity. The production function is linear homogeneous in capital, K, and labour, is strictly concave and satisfies the Inada conditions. Output (and output per worker) u is therefore given by $u=f(K), f'>0$, $f''<0, f(0)=0, \lim_{K\to 0} f'(K)=+\infty, \lim_{K\to\infty} f'(K)=0$. Under competitive market-clearing conditions, the wage rate (and labour income) is given by $j(K)=f(K)-Kf'(K)$ with $j'=-Kf''>0$. Equation (3) or (3′) expresses human capital h as the present discounted value of future after-tax labour income. Note that the discount rate equals the market rate of interest, r, plus the instantaneous probability of death, λ. $h(s)$ is the human capital of those currently alive. They do not expect to be around forever even though a population of constant size is around forever.

The instantaneous utility of current consumption function is Cobb–Douglas in the consumption of the domestic good c_x and consumption of the foreign good c_y. The constant share of consumption of domestic output in total consumption spending (q) is α. The relative price of foreign goods in terms of domestic goods (i.e. the reciprocal of the terms of trade) is denoted by π.

Each country is completely specialised in the production of its own exportable. Households and governments consume both domestic and foreign goods. Capital accumulation in each country only involves that country's own output. Investment is subject to quadratic internal adjustment costs. Depreciation is ignored. Because both the production function and the cost-of-adjustment function are assumed to be linear homogeneous, the shadow price of domestic capital ('Tobin's marginal q'), also equals the value of a unit of existing, installed capital in terms of current output, ψ. In equation (6) ζ is the cost-of-adjustment parameter. Equation (7) is the familiar condition that value of the marginal product of capital (corrected for adjustment costs) equals the cost of capital, i.e. the sum of the interest rate and the expected proportional rate of change of ψ. The government budget constraint is given in (8). g_x denotes government spending on domestic consumption goods and g_y government spending on imports.

Equations (9), (9′), (10), (11), (11′), (12), (13), (14) and (16) are self-explanatory foreign counterparts of domestic behavioural relationships. q^*, w^* and h^* are measured in terms of foreign output.

Equation (15) is the foreign cost-of-capital equation with the assumption of a perfectly integrated set of financial markets substituted in. The (costs-of-adjustment corrected) value of the marginal product of foreign capital (in terms of foreign output) equals the domestic interest rate *minus* the expected proportional rate of change of the relative price of foreign goods *minus* the expected proportional rate of change of ψ^*.

There are three economy-wide market equilibrium conditions: market-clearing for foreign output (17), for domestic output (17′) and for financial claims. Because of Walras' Law, the financial market equilibrium condition will be dropped from explicit consideration. Equation (19) defines net domestic claims on the rest of the world F. Its rate of change equals the domestic current account surplus, i.e.

$$\dot{F}(s)=f(K(s))+r(s)F(s)-\left(q(s)+g_x(s)+\pi(s)g_y(s)+\dot{K}(s)+\frac{1}{2}\zeta\frac{\dot{K}(s)^2}{K(s)}\right) \tag{19′}$$

Note that (17) and (18) imply the following loanable funds type flow equilibrium condition:

$$\begin{aligned}&r(s)(w(s)+\pi(s)w^*(s))+j(K(s))+j^*(K^*(s))\\&\quad\times\pi(s)-\tau(s)-\tau^*(s)\pi(s)-q(s)-\pi(s)q^*(s)\\&=\psi(s)\dot{K}(s)+\pi(s)\psi^*(s)\dot{K}^*(s)+\dot{b}^G(s)+\dot{b}^*(s)^G+K(s)\dot{\psi}(s)\\&\quad+K^*(s)\pi(s)\dot{\psi}^*(s)+K^*(s)\psi^*(s)\dot{\pi}(s)\end{aligned} \tag{18′}$$

Its stock equilibrium counterpart is

$$w(s)+\pi(s)w^*(s)=\psi(s)K(s)+\pi(s)\psi^*(s)K^*(s)+b^G(s)+b^{*G}(s). \tag{18″}$$

In the derivation of the optimal household consumption programme use has been made of the household 'present value budget constraint' or 'solvency constraint'.

$$\int_s^\infty \bar{q}(t,v)\exp[-\int_s^v(r(u)+\lambda)\mathrm{d}u]\mathrm{d}v=\bar{w}(t,s)+\int_s^\infty[\bar{j}(t,v)-\bar{\tau}(t,v)]$$
$$\exp[-\int_s^v(r(u)+\lambda)\mathrm{d}u]\mathrm{d}v-\lim_{l\to\infty}\bar{w}(t,l)\exp[-\int_s^l(r(u)+\lambda)\mathrm{d}u] \tag{20}$$

($\bar{q}(t, v)$ denotes consumption at time v by a household born at time t and similarly for $\bar{w}(t, v)$, $\bar{j}(t, v)$ and $\bar{\tau}(t, v)$). The conventional transversality condition is:

$$\lim_{l\to\infty}(\bar{w}t,l)\exp[-\int_s^l(r(u)+\lambda)\mathrm{d}u]=0 \tag{20'}$$

The operational meaning of this is that the present value of future household debt must ultimately go to zero. It precludes household Ponzi games. Equally important is the public sector's 'present value budget constraint' or 'solvency constraint'

$$\int_s^\infty[g_x(t)+\pi(t)g_y(t)]\exp[-\int_s^t r(u)\mathrm{d}u]\mathrm{d}t=\int_s^\infty\tau(t)\exp[-\int_s^t r(u)\text{-}$$
$$\mathrm{d}u]\mathrm{d}t-b^G(t)+\lim_{l\to\infty}b^G(l)\exp[-\int_s^i r(u)\mathrm{d}u] \tag{21}$$

The terminal condition we impose here,

$$\lim_{l\to\infty}b^G(l)\exp[-\int_s^l r(u)\mathrm{d}u]=0$$

rules out Ponzi games for the public sector: the present value of future spending programmes and the servicing of the existing stock of debt must be equal to the present value of future taxes. The condition that it is not feasible to service debt through further borrowing indefinitely is of course only plausible if the real interest rate exceeds the natural (long run) proportional rate of growth of real economic activity. Note that while existing households discount future taxes at a rate $r+\lambda$, the government, which knows it will tax both existing and yet-to-be born households, discounts future taxes at a rate r.

III THE VERY SMALL OPEN ECONOMY

The very small open economy treats both the interest rate and the terms of trade as parametric. The behaviour of the household sector is given by

$$\dot{q} = (r - \theta)q - (\theta + \lambda)\lambda w$$

$$\dot{w} = rw + j(K) - \tau - q$$

The remaining dynamics can be summarised by:

$$\dot{K} = \left(\frac{\psi - 1}{\zeta}\right)K$$

$$r = \frac{f'(K)}{\psi} + \frac{\dot{\psi}}{\psi} + \frac{1}{2}\frac{\zeta}{\psi}\left(\frac{\dot{K}}{K}\right)^2$$

and

$$\dot{F} = f(K) + rF - \left(q + \dot{K} + g_x + \pi g_y + \frac{1}{2}\zeta\frac{\dot{K}^2}{K}\right)$$

Under the assumption of exogenous factor income, this model is studied in Blanchard (1983b). Since the capital stock dynamics is a function only of the exogenous rate of interest, r, we can analyse the behaviour of q, w and F in response to any shocks other than interest rate changes, while treating K as exogenous. Indeed, by considering an initial position of stationary equilibrium, with $\dot{K} = \dot{\psi} = 0$ (and $\psi = 1$), K can be treated as constant throughout. Furthermore, the (q, w) subsystem is self-contained and $\dot{F}$ is determined recursively given q and w. The state-space representation of the system (with $\dot{K} = 0$) is given in (22).

$$\begin{bmatrix} \dot{q} \\ \dot{w} \\ \dot{F} \end{bmatrix} = \begin{bmatrix} (r - \theta & -(\theta+\lambda)\lambda & 0 \\ -1 & r & 0 \\ -1 & 0 & r \end{bmatrix} \begin{bmatrix} q \\ w \\ F \end{bmatrix} + \begin{bmatrix} 0 \\ j(K) - \tau \\ f(K) - (g_x + \pi g_y) \end{bmatrix} \quad (22)$$

The (q, w) subsystem has two characteristic roots, $r - (\theta + \lambda)$ and $r + \lambda$. It will be saddle-point stable if $-\lambda < r < \theta + \lambda$. q is non-predetermined and, with ψ exogenous, w is predetermined. We assume this condition to be satisfied. In addition we assume $r > 0$. The third root (the one governing F) is r.

The steady-state conditions for the private economy are, for $\lambda > 0$:

$$w = \frac{-(r-\theta)}{r^2 - \theta(r+\lambda) - \lambda^2}(y-\tau) = \frac{-(r-\theta)}{[r-(\theta+\lambda)][r+\lambda]}(y-\tau) \tag{23}$$

$$q = \frac{-(\theta+\lambda)\lambda}{r^2 - \theta(r+\lambda) - \lambda^2}(y-\tau) = \frac{-(\theta+\lambda)\lambda}{[r-(\theta+\lambda)](r+\lambda)}(y-\tau) \tag{24}$$

The case of the infinite-lived consumer ($\lambda = 0$) yields no meaningful solution unless $r = \theta$. We shall not consider it any further here.

The 'saddlepoint' condition implies that the denominator of (23) and (24) is negative.

Even if the private economy settles down to a stationary equilibrium, the equation of motion for the current account could, apparently, exhibit perpetual deficits or surpluses. Indeed, the root governing the predetermined variable F in (22) is $r > 0$, implying explosive behaviour. This unfortunate feature of many small open economy models with a perfect international capital market is, however, ruled out by the government's present value budget constraint (PVBC) given in (21) and the no-Ponzi game transversality condition given in (21′). We can therefore only consider budgetary and financial strategies which are consistent with bounded values of government debt. Consider any set of strategies which has the property that the stock of public sector debt converges, possibly asymptotically, to a finite stationary value. In steady-state equilibrium such strategies, are, from the government budget constraint in (8) characterised by

$$g_x + g_y + rb^G = \tau \tag{25}$$

with $\dot{b}^G = 0$.

Note that with (25), a stationary equilibrium for w implies a stationary equilibrium for F. Consider alternative stationary equilibria with identical constant values for exhaustive public spending g_x and g_y but different values of taxes τ and public debt b^G. Across such steady states a lower value of taxes will be associated with higher private consumption and lower public debt. Private non-human wealth will be higher (lower) when steady-state taxes are lower, according as to the interest rate is above (below) the pure rate of time preference. All this holds for a constant level of exhaustive public spending.

$$\frac{dq}{d\tau}=\frac{(\theta+\lambda)\lambda}{r^2-\theta(r+\lambda)-\lambda^2}<0$$

$$\frac{db^G}{d\tau}=\frac{1}{r}>0$$

$$\frac{dw}{d\tau}=\frac{(r-\theta)}{r^2-\theta(r+\lambda)-\lambda^2}\lesseqgtr 0 \qquad \text{if } r\gtreqless\theta$$

$$\frac{dF}{d\tau}=\frac{r-\theta}{r^2-\theta(r+\lambda)-\lambda^2}-\frac{1}{r}\leqslant 0 \qquad \text{if } r\geqslant\theta$$

For example if $r=\theta$, public debt displaces foreign assets one-for-one in private portfolios across steady states. Note that when private agents have infinite horizons ($\lambda=0$) changes in τ and b^G have no effect (short run or long run) on consumption or net foreign assets if exhaustive public spending is constant.[2]

Note that we cannot use (25) by itself to analyse the 'real time' consequence of a change in τ with g_x and g_y constant. b^G is predetermined at a point in time. Except through default, a government cannot engineer a finite, discrete change in b^G at a point in time; real-time changes in b^G have the dimension of $\dot{b}^G$, i.e. b^G is a continuous function of time. What we must do in order to be able to use (25) to derive the 'real time' long-run effects of a change in τ is to specify rules for spending, taxation and borrowing that are consistent with convergence to a steady-state equilibrium for b^G and with unchanged values of g_x and g_y across steady states.

Ideally, such rules would reflect the optimising behaviour of governments. In this paper only *ad hoc* rules that are likely to satisfy the government's solvency constraint are considered.

A fairly general stabilising rule for taxes is given in equations (26) and (27) for the home country and the foreign country respectively:

$$\tau=\tau_1+\mu_\tau\dot{b}^G+\nu_\tau b^G \tag{26}$$

$$\tau^*=\tau_1^*+\mu_\tau^*\frac{\dot{b}^{*G}}{\pi}+\nu_\tau^*\frac{b^{*G}}{\pi} \tag{27}$$

Thus taxes have a lump-sum component but also respond either to the deficit and/or to the size of the debt.

The behaviour of domestic and foreign public debt under these rules is given by:

$$\dot{b}^G = \left(\frac{r-\nu_\tau}{1+\mu_\tau}\right) b^G + \frac{1}{1+\mu_\tau}(g-\tau_1) \tag{28}$$

$$\dot{b}^{*G} = \left(\frac{r-\nu^*_\tau}{1+\mu^*_\tau}\right) b^{*G} + \frac{1}{1+\mu^*_\tau}\pi(g^*-\tau^*_1) \tag{29}$$

where

$$g \equiv g_x + \pi g_y \tag{30a}$$

and

$$g^* \equiv \frac{g^*_x}{\pi} + g^*_y \tag{30b}$$

Total taxes under this rule evolve according to

$$\tau = \frac{1}{1+\mu_\tau}\tau_1 + \frac{\mu_\tau}{1+\mu_\tau} g + \left(\frac{r\mu_\tau + \nu_\tau}{1+\mu_\tau}\right) b^G \tag{31}$$

$$\tau^* = \frac{1}{1+\mu^*_\tau}\tau^*_1 + \frac{\mu^*_\tau}{1+\mu^*_\tau} g^* + \left(\frac{r\mu^*_\tau + \nu^*_\tau}{1+\mu^*_\tau}\right) \frac{b^{*G}}{\pi} \tag{32}$$

Any rule with $(r-\nu_\tau)/(1+\mu_\tau) < 0$ satisfies home country government's solvency requirement. In most of the examples considered below we assume $\nu_\tau = \nu^*_\tau = 0$ in which case the solvency condition becomes μ_τ, $\mu^*_\tau < -1$.

The main fiscal experiment will be a change in τ_1 or τ^*_1. With $\nu_\tau = \nu^*_\tau = 0$, this change in the lump-sum component of the tax bill also equals the steady-state change in total tax receipts.

Note, however, from (31) and (28) that a long-run, steady-state tax increase is 'achieved' by a short-run tax cut which results in an initial budget deficit. Indeed, the authorities run a net cumulative budget deficit during the adjustment process towards the new long-run equilibrium. With a given spending programme on goods and services, the higher long-run taxes will be exactly sufficient to service the higher volume of public debt.

If we wish to use (22) to analyse the short-run and long-run consequences of a constant, exogenous change in taxes, the government's present value budget constraint (PVBC) can only be satisfied if we assume that public spending $(g_x + \pi g_y)$ is adjusted to maintain solvency.

By analogy with (26) and (27) we could specify potentially stabilising public spending rules that make spending responsive to the level and/or rate of change of public debt, e.g.

$$g = g_1 + \mu_g \dot{b}^G + \nu_g b^G \tag{30}$$

$$g^* = g_1^* + \mu_g^* \frac{\dot{b}^{*G}}{\pi} + \nu_b^* \frac{b^{*G}}{\pi} \tag{31}$$

The behaviour of domestic and foreign public debt under these rules is given by

$$\dot{b}^G = \left(\frac{r + \nu_g - \nu_\tau}{1 - \mu_g + \mu_\tau} \right) b^G + \frac{1}{1 - \mu_g + \mu_\tau} (g_1 - \tau_1) \tag{32}$$

$$\dot{b}^{*G} = \frac{(r + \nu_g^* - \nu_\tau^*)}{1 - \mu_g^* + \mu_\tau^*} b^{*G} + \frac{1}{1 - \mu_g^* + \mu_\tau^*} \pi (g_1^* - \tau_1^*) \tag{33}$$

Even with exogenous taxes $(\nu_\tau = \nu_\tau^* = \mu_\tau = \mu_\tau^* = 0)$ the spending rule parameters can be chosen in such a way as to make (32) and (33) convergent processes. For illustrative purposes, consider the case of exogenous taxes and $\nu_g = 0$. A convergent debt process requires $\mu_g > 1$ since

$$\dot{b}^G = \frac{r}{1 - \mu_g} b^G + \frac{1}{1 - \mu_g} (g_1 - \tau_1) \tag{34}$$

The behaviour of the (q, w) system with exogenous taxes and endogenous spending (equation (30) with $\nu_g = 0$ and equation (34)) is illustrated in Figure 3.1 for the case $r = \theta$. The unique convergent saddlepath SS' in q–w space is upward-sloping.

Starting from E_0, an unanticipated, immediate permanent tax cut moves the q, w system immediately to its new stationary equilibrium value at E_1. The unexpected announcement at t_0 of an immediate temporary tax cut, to be ended at $t_1 > t_0$ causes consumption to increase immediately to some intermediate position E_{01}, between E_0

and E_1. From there the system moves gradually along a divergent trajectory drawn with reference to the E_1 equilibrium, until at t_1 it arrives at E_{12} on SS' from where it converges asymptotically to E_0. Between t_0 and t_1 part of the tax cut is saved. Dissaving takes place from t_1 onwards.

Since $F \equiv W - K - b^G$ and $\dot{K} = 0$, the current account surplus is given by $\dot{F} = \dot{w} - \dot{b}^G$.

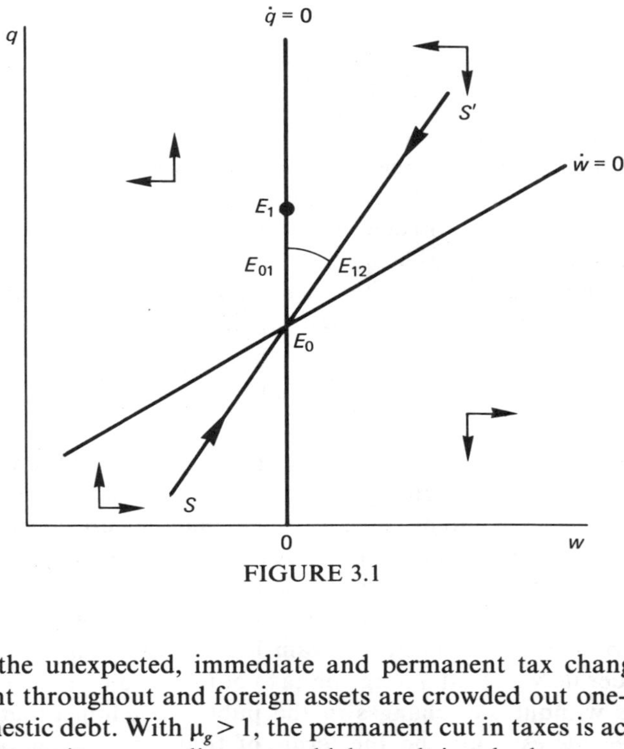

FIGURE 3.1

For the unexpected, immediate and permanent tax change, w is constant throughout and foreign assets are crowded out one-for-one by domestic debt. With $\mu_g > 1$, the permanent cut in taxes is accompanied by transitory spending cuts which result in a budget surplus and a current account surplus. The government obtains the means to finance the permanent tax cut by reducing its debt in the short run. As public spending converges back to its original value, the public sector PVBC exhibits matching reductions in a liability, b^G and in an asset – the present value of future taxes.

In general, with exogenous taxes and endogenous spending given by (30) with $\nu_g = 0$ (and therefore by (34)), the behaviour of q, w and F is governed by:

$$\begin{bmatrix} \dot{q} \\ \dot{w} \\ \dot{F} \end{bmatrix} = \begin{bmatrix} r-\theta & -(\theta+\lambda)\lambda & 0 \\ -1 & r & 0 \\ -1 & \dfrac{-r\mu_g}{1-\mu_g} & \dfrac{r}{1-\mu_g} \end{bmatrix} \begin{bmatrix} q \\ w \\ F \end{bmatrix} + \begin{bmatrix} 0 \\ j(K)-\tau_1 \\ f(K)+\dfrac{r\mu_g}{1-\mu_g}K-\dfrac{1}{1-\mu_g}g_1+\dfrac{\mu_g}{1-\mu_g}\tau_1 \end{bmatrix} \tag{35}$$

The characteristic roots are $r-(\theta+\lambda)$, $r+\lambda$ and $r/(1-\mu_g)$. With $-\lambda<r<\theta+\lambda$ and $\mu_g>1$ there will be two stable and one unstable characteristic roots and the system will have the desired saddlepoint configuration for two predetermined variables (w and F) and one non-predetermined variable, q.

With a temporary tax cut there is no change in the long run values of q, w, F and b^G. On impact, however, since

$$g=\frac{1}{1-\mu_g}g_1+\frac{\mu_g r}{1-\mu_g}b^G-\frac{\mu_g}{1-\mu_g}\tau_1 \quad \text{and} \quad \mu_g>1,$$

spending is cut by more than taxes and the home country runs a current account surplus. In Figure 3.1, between E_{01} and E_{12} the private sector saves. There is no private investment and the public sector has a budget surplus. When the tax cut is reversed at t_1, spending is raised by more and the government runs a budget deficit. The private sector also dissaves from E_{12} to E_0 in Figure 3.1 and the economy as a whole has a current account deficit that vanishes asymptotically.

Consider now instead a long-run tax cut financed by short-run tax increases without any changes in the public spending programme. Since the interest rate and the terms of trade are exogenous, this policy leaves the present value of the future tax programme (discounted at r) unchanged and merely redistributes taxes over time and between generations. Under this rule the equations of motion are given by:

$$\begin{bmatrix} \dot{q} \\ \dot{w} \\ \dot{F} \end{bmatrix} = \begin{bmatrix} (r-\theta) & -(\theta+\lambda)\lambda & 0 \\ -1 & \dfrac{r}{1+\mu_\tau} & \dfrac{r\mu_\tau}{1+\mu_\tau} \\ -1 & 0 & r \end{bmatrix} \begin{bmatrix} q \\ w \\ F \end{bmatrix}$$

$$+\begin{bmatrix} 0 \\ j(K)+\frac{r\mu_\tau}{1+\mu_\tau}K-\frac{1}{1+\mu_\tau}\tau_1-\frac{\mu_\tau}{1+\mu_\tau}g \\ f(K)-g \end{bmatrix} \tag{36}$$

The three characteristic roots of the system are $r-(\theta+\lambda)$, $r+\lambda$, and $r/1+\mu_\tau$. The first two are the same ones that governed the q–w subsystem in (35) when taxes were exogenous. The third comes from the government debt equation

$$\dot{b}^G=\frac{r}{1+\mu_\tau}b^G+\frac{1}{1+\mu_\tau}(g-\tau_1).$$

With $-\lambda<r<\theta+\lambda$ and $\mu_\tau<-1$, there will be two stable roots and one unstable root and the system will again have the proper saddle-point configuration.

What happens on impact to aggregate consumption in response to a long run tax cut (τ_1 down) financed through a short-run tax increase, depends entirely on what happens to human capital h. From equation (3′) we see that, with K given, the effect on human capital depends only on the effect on the present value of future taxes discounted at $r+\lambda$. Let

$$T(s)\equiv\int_s^\infty \tau(t)\exp[-\int_s^t (r(u)+\lambda)\mathrm{d}u]\,\mathrm{d}t$$

It is easily checked that

$$\frac{\mathrm{d}T(s)}{\mathrm{d}\tau_1}=\frac{1}{r+\lambda}-\frac{1}{r+\lambda\frac{(1+\mu_\tau)}{\mu_\tau}}$$

this confirms the intuition that with infinite-lived households ($\lambda=0$) and perfect capital markets, redistribution of taxes over time has no real effects. However, with finite lives ($\lambda>0$) and $\mu_\tau<-1$, $\mathrm{d}t(s)/(\mathrm{d}\tau_1)<0$: raising taxes in the long run and lowering them in the short run so as to keep their present value dicounted at r constant, lowers their present value discounted at $r+\lambda$.

Thus a policy of cutting taxes in the long run and financing this by raising taxes in the short run, will lower human capital and lower private consumption in the short run, even though it will raise both in the long run.

Changes in the Terms of Trade

It is apparent from equation (22) that changes in the terms of trade, π^{-1}, have no effect, short-run or long-run, on the behaviour of aggregate private consumption q and private sector non-human wealth w. Furthermore, except in so far as public spending on goods and services $g_x + \pi g_y$ is a function of π, the current account is independent of the terms of trade in the short-run and in the long-run. This is the powerful simplifying effect of our choice of utility function. A more general analysis of the Harberger–Laursen–Metzler effect can be found in Svensson and Razin (1983) and Bean (1984).

Changes in the Interest rate

In a steady state, $r = r(K)$ or $K = k(r)$ $k' < 0$. The long-run effects of a change in the world interest rate on private consumption and non-human wealth are in general ambiguous, as shown in (37a, b), where we use the fact that $j'k' = -K$.

$$\frac{dq}{dr} = \frac{qr + (w\text{-}K)(\theta + \lambda)\lambda}{-[r^2 - \theta(r+\lambda) - \lambda^2]} \tag{37a}$$

$$\frac{dw}{dr} = \frac{(r\text{-}\theta)(w\text{-}K) + q}{-[r^2 - \theta(r+\lambda) - \lambda^2]} \tag{37b}$$

If $r = \theta$, then $dw/(dr) > 0$ but dq/dr is still ambiguous, as it equals $(\theta + \lambda)[rh - \lambda K]/-[r^2 - \theta(r+\lambda) - \lambda]$.

In a neighbourhood of the steady-state equilibrium $K = K_0$, $\psi = 1$, the behaviour of K and ψ can be linearly approximated by (38).

$$\begin{bmatrix} \dot{K} \\ \dot{\psi} \end{bmatrix} = \begin{bmatrix} 0 & \dfrac{K_0}{\zeta} \\ -f''(K_0) & r_0 \end{bmatrix} \begin{bmatrix} K - K_0 \\ \psi - 1 \end{bmatrix} + \begin{bmatrix} 0 \\ r - r_0 \end{bmatrix} \tag{38}$$

This yields the familiar saddlepoint equilibrium shown in Figure 3.2.

The (K, ψ) dynamics is entirely self-contained, but feeds into the q, w dynamics as shown in (39) for the case where public spending adjusts to satisfy the government's PVBC.

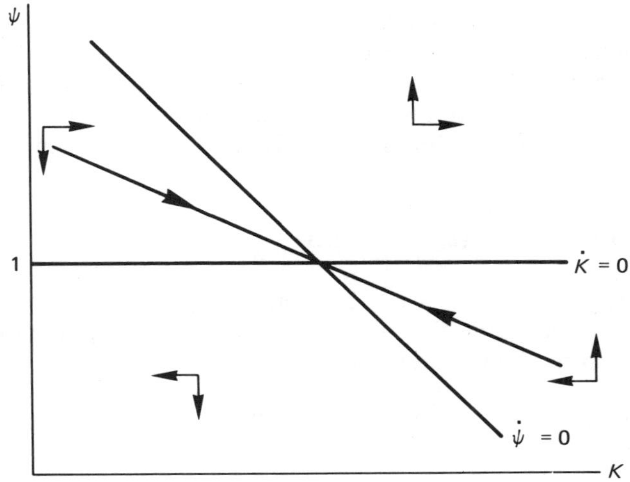

FIGURE 3.2

$$\begin{bmatrix} \dot{K} \\ \dot{\psi} \\ \dot{q} \\ \dot{w} \end{bmatrix} = \begin{bmatrix} 0 & \frac{K_0}{\zeta} & 0 & 0 \\ -f''(K_0) & r_0 & 0 & 0 \\ 0 & 0 & -(r_0-\theta) & -(\theta\lambda)\lambda \\ j'(K_0) & 0 & -1 & r_0 \end{bmatrix} \begin{bmatrix} K-K_0 \\ \psi-1 \\ q-q_0 \\ w-w_0 \end{bmatrix} + \begin{bmatrix} 0 \\ r-r_0 \\ q_0(r-r_0) \\ w_0(r-r_0) \end{bmatrix} \quad (39)$$

We saw that when K is treated as constant, the (q, w) subsystem is saddlepoint-stable under mild restrictions. It will therefore have a (locally) well-behaved solution when K is governed by an exogenous process provided K does not 'explode too fast' (see Buiter, 1984).

Since K in turn will be (locally) well-behaved provided only that r does not explode too fast, the system given in (39) will be a saddlepoint equilibrium with two stable and two unstable characteristic roots. ψ and q are non-predetermined, the boundary condition for K takes the form of an initial condition and w is subject to the simple linear restriction that at $t=t_0$, say

$$w(t_0)=w(t_0^-)+(\psi(t_0)-\psi(t_0^-))K(t_0) \tag{42}$$

where $x(t_0^-)=\lim_{\Delta\to 0/\Delta>0} x(t_0-\Delta)$. While $w(t_0^-)$ is predetermined (inherited from the past), discontinuous jumps in ψ in response to 'news' at t_0 can cause discontinuous jumps in $w(t_0)$.

The four roots are $\frac{1}{2}(r_0 \pm \sqrt{(r_0^2-(4K_0/\zeta)/f''(K_0))}$, $r_0-(\theta+\lambda)$ and $r_0+\lambda$.

IV THE SEMI-SMALL OPEN ECONOMY

The semi-small open economy is a price taker in world financial markets but has some influence on the world price of its exportable. Price-taking behaviour in the world capital market is specified as the home country taking $r^* \equiv r-(\dot{\pi}/\pi)$ as given. Through the endogeneity of π therefore, the domestic interest rate, r, becomes endogenous, at any rate in the short run. The terms of trade are endogenised through the domestic output equilibrium condition

$$f(K)=\alpha q+g_x+\left(\frac{\psi-1}{\zeta}\right)K+\alpha^*\pi q^*+g_x^*+\frac{1}{2}(\psi-1)^2\frac{K}{\zeta}$$

We also assume that g_x is independent of π and that $(\alpha^*\pi q^*+g_x^*)\pi^{-1}$ is independent of π, i.e. that $(\alpha^*\pi q^*+g_x^*)\pi^{-1}=M^{-1}$, say, which permits us to solve for π as

$$\pi=\left[f(K)-\alpha q-g_x+\frac{(1-\psi)K}{\zeta}-\frac{1}{2}(\psi-1)^2\frac{K}{\zeta}\right]M \tag{43}$$

This has the sensible property that an increase in world demand for the home good *ceteris paribus* raises its relative price (lowers π). Note that this representation makes π a function of domestic demand for domestic output but not of domestic demand for foreign output.[3]

The long-run comparative statics of q, w, K and ψ are the same as those of the very small open economy, since in long-run equilibrium $r=r^*=f'(K)$ and q is independent of π. If in addition total government spending, measured in domestic output ($g \equiv g_x + \pi g_y$) is independent of π, the long-run comparative statics of b^G and F are also the same as in the very small open economy.

The long-run effects of fiscal policy changes and changes in the world rate of interest on π all follow straightforwardly from the unit elastic foreign demand for domestic output function. The steady-state version of (43), given in (44), yields the following long-run comparative static results:

$$\pi = [f(K) - \alpha q - g_x]M \tag{44}$$

$$\frac{d\pi}{d\tau} = -M\alpha\frac{(\theta+\lambda)\lambda}{\Omega} > 0 \tag{45a}$$

$$\frac{d\pi}{dg_x} = -M < 0 \tag{45b}$$

$$\frac{d\pi}{dg_y} = 0 \tag{45c}$$

$$\frac{d\pi}{dr^*} = \frac{Mf'}{f''} + \frac{M\alpha}{\Omega}[qr + (w-K)(\theta+\lambda)\lambda] < 0^4 \tag{45d}$$

where

$$\Omega \equiv r^2 - \theta(r+\lambda) - \lambda^2 \langle 0 \tag{45e}$$

Dynamic Response of the Semi-small Open Economy

The essential dynamics of the semi-small open economy are described by the following six equations:

$$\dot{K} = (\psi - 1)\zeta^{-1}K$$

$$\dot{\psi} = \psi r - f'(K) - \frac{1}{2}\zeta\left(\frac{\dot{K}}{K}\right)^2$$

$$\dot{q} = (r - \theta)q - (\theta + \lambda)\lambda w$$

$$\dot{w} = rw + j(K) - \tau - q$$

$$r = r^* + \frac{\dot{\pi}}{\pi}$$

$$\pi = \left(f(K) - q - g_x - \dot{K} - \frac{1}{2}\zeta\frac{\dot{K}^2}{K}\right)M$$

Having solved for the behaviour of K, ψ, q, w, r and π, we can then solve for the behaviour of public debt and net external assets from

$$\dot{b}^G = g_x + \pi g_y + rb^G - \tau$$

and

$$\dot{F} = f(K) + rF - \left(q + \dot{K} + g_x + \pi g_y + \frac{1}{2}\zeta\frac{\dot{K}^2}{K}\right)$$

A Long-run Tax Cut Financed by a Temporary Spending Cut

Consider first the consequences of a permanent cut in the exogenous level of taxes, τ, under the strongly stabilising public spending rule given by (30) with $\nu_g = 0$, i.e.

$$g = g_1 + \mu_g \dot{b}^G \qquad \mu_g > 1$$

which implies

$$\dot{b}^G = \frac{r}{1 - \mu_g} b^G + \frac{1}{1 - \mu_g}(g_1 - \tau)$$

In order to simplify the analysis further, it is also assumed that all variations in public spending take the form of variations in public spending on imports, i.e. g_x is held constant throughout.

We eliminate r from the system through the real interest equalisation condition and obtain $\dot{\pi}/\pi$ by logarithmic differentiation of the relative price equation. In a neighbourhood of the stationary equilibrium $[K_0, \psi_0, q_0, w_0]$ corresponding to $[r_0^*, \tau_0$ and $g_{x_0}]$ we can represent the behaviour of K, ψ, q and w by:

$$\begin{bmatrix} \dot{K} \\ \dot{\psi} \\ \dot{q} \\ \dot{w} \end{bmatrix} = \begin{bmatrix} 0 & \frac{K_0}{\zeta} & 0 & 0 \\ \frac{-f''\zeta(\pi + M\alpha q_0)}{\Lambda} & r^* & \frac{-\zeta M\alpha(r^*-\theta)}{\Lambda} & \frac{\zeta M\alpha(\theta+\lambda)\lambda}{\Lambda} \\ \frac{q_0 MK_0 f''}{\Lambda} & 0 & \frac{(\pi\zeta + MK_0)(r^*-\theta)}{\Lambda} & \frac{-(\pi\zeta+MK_0)(\theta+\lambda)\lambda}{\Lambda} \\ g' + \frac{w_0 MK_0 f''}{\Lambda} & 0 & -\left[1 + \frac{w_0\zeta M\alpha(r^*-\theta)}{\Lambda}\right] & r^* + \frac{w_0\zeta M\alpha(\theta+\lambda)\lambda}{\Lambda} \end{bmatrix}$$

$$\times \begin{bmatrix} (K-K_0) \\ (\psi - 1) \\ (q-q_0) \\ (w-w_0) \end{bmatrix} + \begin{bmatrix} 0 & 0 & 0 \\ \frac{\pi_0\zeta}{\Lambda} & 0 & \frac{-\zeta M}{\Lambda} \\ q_0\frac{\pi_0\zeta}{\Lambda} & 0 & \frac{-q_0\zeta M}{\Lambda} \\ w_0\frac{\pi_0\zeta}{\Lambda} & -1 & \frac{-w_0\zeta M}{\Lambda} \end{bmatrix} \begin{bmatrix} r^* - r_0^* \\ (\tau - \tau_0) \\ \dot{g}_x \end{bmatrix} \tag{46a}$$

$$\Lambda = \pi_0\zeta + M\alpha q_0\zeta + MK_0 \tag{46b}$$

and

$$\pi - \pi_0 \approx Mf'(K_0)(K-K_0) - M\alpha(q-q_0) - MK_0\zeta^{-1}(\psi - 1) - M(g_x - g_{x_0}) \tag{46c}$$

$$\frac{\dot{\pi}}{\pi} \approx \frac{MK_0 f''(K_0)}{\Lambda}(K-K_0) + \frac{M\alpha(\theta+\lambda)\lambda\zeta}{\Lambda}(w-w_0) - \frac{M\alpha\zeta(r^*-\theta)}{\Lambda}(q-q_0) - \frac{(M\alpha q_0\zeta + MK_0)}{\Lambda}(r^* - r_0^*) - \frac{\zeta M}{\Lambda}\dot{g}_x \tag{46d}$$

The characteristic equation of the state matrix in (46a) does not appear to factorise in any convenient manner. Experimentation with a range of plausible numerical values did, however, consistently yield the right kind of saddlepoint configuration with two stable and two unstable characteristic roots. The following results of simulations involving a world interest rate increase and a tax cut for two distinct numerical versions of the model illustrate its general properties.[5] For the first version of the model, $\alpha=0.6$, $\theta=0.03$, $\zeta^{-1}=0.031$[6] and $\lambda=0.03$. The production function is Cobb–Douglas with $f(K)=K^{\beta}$ and $\beta=0.25$ in both versions of the model.

In version I, $r^*=\theta=0.03$. This means that the steady-state value for w equals zero. We also assume that the initial value of taxes, τ_0, is 25 per cent of initial labour income, that g_{x_0} is 15 per cent of initial labour income, that $\pi_0 g_{y_0}$ is 5 per cent of labour income and that $M=0.8968$. The initial steady state value of the relative price of foreign goods, π_0, is then equal to unity. The initial steady-state equilibrium is furthermore characterised by $K_0=16.90$; $f(K_0)=2.03$; $j(K_0)=1.52$; $\psi_0=1$, $b_0^G=2.54$ and $F_0=19.43$.

The characteristic roots of the linearised system (given in (46a)) are all real and given by $(-0.02284;\ -0.01226;\ 0.03696;\ 0.05841)$. Because the stable roots are so small, convergence to the steady state tends to be slow. The root governing b^G is $r^*/1-\mu_g$. We assume $\mu_g=2$, so the public debt converges with a mean lag of 33.3 periods when $r^*=0.03$. The consequences of a permanent tax cut financed by a temporary cut in spending are as follows. The long-run effect is to boost domestic private consumption, because human wealth increases, and to lower the relative price of foreign goods, π. K, w, ψ and r are unchanged in the long run; since $r^*=\theta$, public debt decreases and net foreign assets increase by equal amounts.

If the tax cut is not only permanent but also unanticipated, the full long-run adjustment of all endogenous variables other than b^G and F takes place immediately, i.e. π falls instantaneously to clear the market for the domestic good at the higher level of domestic consumption demand and nothing else changes.

An anticipated future permanent tax cut also causes an immediate, discrete upward move in aggregate consumption, q, at the date that the unexpected announcement of the future tax cut occurs. After the initial jump, q is still slightly below its new steady state level and continues to rise towards it. It is the effect of future tax cuts on current human capital that causes this response. The relative price of foreign output falls discretely on impact, but by less than the long-run decline: it 'undershoots' its long-run equilibrium value. Since π continues to fall after the initial drop, the interest rate declines on impact and stays below the world level throughout the adjustment process. ψ increases on impact and capital begins to accumulate. This process, however, is reversed in due course as ψ falls below unity and the capital stock returns to its initial value. At the announcement date, w increases because of the increase in ψ. Saving, however, is very negative initially, as consumption is raised before the tax cuts come through. w becomes negative, reaches a minimum at the date the tax cut comes through and then returns to zero.

With the unanticipated tax cut, b^G declines and F rises throughout the adjustment process (with $\dot{b}^G = -\dot{F}$). In the case of the anticipated future tax cut, F falls until the tax cut is actually implemented and rises thereafter. b^G rises until the tax cut occurs and declines thereafter. It is no longer the case that $\dot{F} + \dot{b}^G = 0$ at each instant.

An unexpected permanent increase in the world real interest rate r^* lowers K in the long run, raises w and q and lowers π. F increases and b^G falls. The impact effect on w, q and π with K predetermined, is the exact opposite. ψ falls discretely, reducing wealth (w becomes negative). Consumption falls because both w and h are lower. With private domestic consumption and investment demand down, but output still predetermined, π rises. In the long run, of course, π falls, so $\dot{\pi}/\pi$ becomes negative immediately following the initial increase in π. The positive effect of the increase in r^* on r is not, however, offset completely by the (anticipated) decline in π and r rises on impact. Savings are positive and w increases steadily after the initial capital loss. Capital decumulates steadily.

The second version has $r^*_0 = 0.05$, $\theta = 0.04$, $\lambda = 0.03$, $\zeta^{-1} = 0.031$, $\beta = 0.25$, $M = 1.3155511$, $\alpha = 0.6$ and as before, $\tau_0 = 0.25$, $j(K_0)$, $g_{x_0} = 0.15\ j(K_0))$ and $\pi_0 g_{y_0} = 0.05\ j(K_0)$. This implies that $K_0 = 8.55$, $b^G = 1.28\ (= j(K_0))$ and $F_0 = -3.82$. The four characteristic roots of the K, w, q, ψ subsystem are (-0.01558, -0.01115, 0.05820 and 0.07853). The root governing b^G (with $\mu_g = 2$) is -0.05.

A permanent tax cut raises q and w in the long run, leaves K unaffected and lowers π. F increases by more than b^G decreases. If the tax cut is unexpected, ψ increases on impact, thus raising w. Consumption jumps up discretely and continues to rise gradually thereafter. w, after the initial capital gain, rises smoothly. The capital stock increases initially, as ψ exceeds unity, but then falls back to its original value. π drops sharply on impact (because none of the public spending cuts fall on demand for domestic output) and then declines gradually to its new steady-state value, i.e. it undershoots on impact. The interest rate falls on impact and rises gradually back to its original value.

An anticipated future tax cut (of the same magnitude), leads to a smaller discrete increase in q at the announcement date. π also declines by less on impact and its subsequent rate of decline is initially smaller numerically than under the immediate tax cut, but becomes larger subsequently. ψ rises by more on impact. Dissaving takes place between the announcement date and the implementation date. Once the tax cut is in effect saving becomes positive again.

A permanent increase in r^* has the long-run effect of lowering K, b^G and π and raising w, F and q. Again the impact effects on w, q and π are in the opposite direction. The analysis is qualitatively very similar to the case where $r^* = \theta$.

A Long-run Tax Cut Financed by a Temporary Tax Increase

We now treat both $g \equiv g_x + \pi g_y$ and g_x as parametric and have taxes determined by (26) with $\nu_\tau = 0$, i.e. by

$$\tau = \tau_1 + \mu_\tau \dot{b}^G \qquad \mu_\tau < -1$$

and, therefore,

$$\dot{b}^G = \frac{r}{1+\mu_\tau} b^G + \frac{1}{1+\mu_\tau}(g - \tau_1).$$

Note that a change in τ_1 in the semi-small open economy model, unlike in the very small open economy model, does not merely involve the redistribution over time of a given present discounted value of future taxes; while the spending programme is given, the interest rate is endogenous in the semi-small open economy outside the steady state.[7]

The values of the parameters for both numerical versions are the same as with the 'spending endogenous' policy except that now $\mu_g = 0$ and $\mu_\tau = -2$. The long-run effects of changes in τ_1 (and in r^*) are the same under the 'tax endogenous' policy as under the spending endogenous policy. The transitional dynamics are, however, very different.[8]

Both in version 1 ($r^* = \theta = 0.03$) and in version 2

($r^*=0.05>\theta=0.04$) an unexpected, immediate reduction in τ_1 lowers consumption in the short run. The reason is that total taxes τ are actually increased initially by so much that human capital declines. ψ (and therefore w) and π increase on impact.

After the initial capital gain, dissaving takes place. This is ultimately reversed with w going back to the original steady state value of zero in version 1 ($r^*=\theta$) and rising beyond it in version 2 ($r^*>\theta$). Capital accumulates for a while and then reverts to its original level. The initial decline in consumption is reversed as human wealth increasingly reflects the long-run tax cuts and non-human wealth recovers. Government debt is retired continuously, even after total tax receipts have become less than in the initial equilibrium. This reflects the budgetary effects of lower debt service payments. The current account is in surplus throughout.

The unexpected announcement of a future cut in τ_1 has a qualitatively smaller impact effect on ψ, w, q and π, although the direction is unchanged.

After the initial capital gain at the 'announcement date', non-human wealth, w, continues to accumulate until the moment τ_1 is actually cut. The sharp increase in total taxes at the 'implementation date' starts a process of dissaving which is in due course reversed again as the long-run tax cut comes through. There still is a current account surplus and a public sector budget surplus throughout, although the latter is very small until τ_1 is actually cut (and τ increased).

V THE TWO-COUNTRY MODEL

Stationary Equilibrium

In a long-run stationary equilibrium the exogenous variables are constant and all state variables have become stationary. The crucial steady-state conditions are:

$$\psi=\psi^*=1 \tag{47}$$

$$r=f'(K)=f^{*\prime}(K^*) \tag{48}$$

$$h=\frac{j(K)-\tau}{r+\lambda} \tag{49}$$

$$h^* = \frac{(j^*(K^*) - \tau^*)}{r + \lambda^*} \tag{50}$$

$$w = \frac{(\theta - r)}{[r - (\theta + \lambda)](r + \lambda)}(j(K) - \tau) \tag{51}$$

$$w^* = \frac{(\theta^* - r)}{(r - (\theta^* + \lambda^*))(r + \lambda^*)}(j^*(K^*) - \tau^*) \tag{52}$$

$$q = \frac{-(\theta + \lambda)\lambda}{(r - (\theta + \lambda))(r + \lambda)}(j(K) - \tau) \tag{53}$$

$$q^* = \frac{-(\theta^* + \lambda^*)\lambda^*}{(r(\theta^* + \lambda^*))(r + \lambda^*)}(j^*(K^*) - \tau) \tag{54}$$

$$f(K) = \alpha q + g_x + \alpha^* \pi q^* + g^*_x \tag{55}$$

$$f^*(K^*) = (1 - \alpha)\frac{q}{\pi} + g_y + (1 - \alpha^*) q^* + g^*_y \tag{56}$$ [9]

$$b^G = \frac{\tau - (g_x + \pi g_y)}{r}$$ (Domestic government balanced budget condition) (57)

$$b^{*G} = \frac{\pi\ (\tau^* - (g^*_x/\pi + g^*_y))}{r}$$ (Foreign government balanced budget condition) (58)

$$F = \frac{q + g_x + \pi g_y - f(K)}{r}$$ (Current account balance condition) (59)

It is informative to solve the domestic output market equilibrium condition (55) and the foreign output market equilibrium condition (56) for the two 'fundamental' long-run endogenous variables r and π.

The analysis can be simplified somewhat by specifying public spending analogously with private consumption in the following sense:

$$g_x + \pi g_y = g \qquad \text{where } g \text{ is independent of } \pi. \tag{60a}$$

$$g_x = \frac{\beta^x}{\beta^x + \beta^y} g \qquad \beta^x, \beta^y \geqslant 0 \tag{60b}$$

$$g_y = \left(\frac{\beta^y}{\beta^x+\beta^y}\right)\frac{g}{\pi} \tag{60c}$$

$$\frac{g^*_x}{\pi}+g^*_y=g^* \qquad \text{where } g^* \text{ is independent of } \pi \tag{61a}$$

$$g^*_x = \left(\frac{\beta^{*x}}{\beta^{*x}+\beta^{*y}}\right)\pi g^* \qquad \beta^{*x},\ \beta^{*y}\geqslant 0 \tag{61b}$$

$$g^*_y=\frac{\beta^{*y}}{\beta^{*y}+\beta^{*y}}g^* \tag{61c}$$

Noting from (48) that $K=k(r)$, $k'=\frac{1}{f''}<0$ and $K^*=k^*(r)$, $k^{*\prime}=\frac{1}{f^{*\prime\prime}}<0$ we get

$$f(k(r))=\frac{-\alpha(\theta+\lambda)\lambda}{(r-(\theta+\lambda))\,(r+\lambda)}(j(k(r))-\tau)+\frac{\beta^x}{\beta^x+\beta^y}g$$
$$-\frac{\alpha^*(\theta^*+\lambda^*)\lambda^*}{(r-(\theta^*+\lambda^*))\,(r+\lambda^*)}\pi(j^*(k^*(r)-\tau^*)+\frac{\beta^{*x}}{\beta^{*x}+\beta^{*y}}\pi g^* \qquad (yy)$$

(62)

$$f^*(k^*(r))=\frac{(1-\alpha)(\theta+\lambda)\lambda}{(r-(\theta+\lambda))(r+\lambda)}\frac{(j(k(r)))-\tau)}{\pi}+\left(\frac{\beta^y}{\beta^x+\beta^y}\right)\frac{g}{\pi}$$
$$-\frac{(1-\alpha^*)(\theta^*+\lambda^*)\lambda^*}{(r-(\theta^*+\lambda^*))(r+\lambda^*)}(j^*(k^*(r))-\tau^*)+\frac{\beta^{*y}}{\beta^{*x}+\beta^{*y}}g^* \qquad (y^*y^*)$$

(63)

The linearised yy locus is given by:

$$\left[rk'+\frac{\alpha[qr+(\theta+\lambda)\lambda(w-K)]}{\Omega}+\alpha^*\pi\frac{[q^*r+(\theta^*+\lambda^*)\lambda^*)\lambda^*(w^*-K^*)]}{\Omega^*}\right]\mathrm{d}r$$
$$-\left[\alpha^*q^*+\frac{\beta^{*y}}{\beta^{*y}+\beta^{*y}}g^*\right]\mathrm{d}\pi$$
$$=\frac{\alpha(\theta+\lambda)\lambda}{\Omega}\mathrm{d}\tau+\frac{\alpha^*(\theta^*+\lambda^*)\lambda^*\pi}{\Omega^*}\mathrm{d}\tau^*$$
$$+\frac{\beta^x}{\beta^x+\beta^y}\mathrm{d}g+\pi\frac{\beta^{*x}}{\beta^{*x}+\beta^{*y}}\mathrm{d}g^* \qquad (yy)$$

(64)

The linearised y^*y^* locus is given by:

$$\left\{rk^{*\prime}+\frac{(1-\alpha)}{\Omega}\frac{[qr+(\theta+\lambda)\lambda(w-K)]}{\pi}\right.$$

$$\left.+\frac{(1-\alpha^*)}{\Omega^*}\left[q^*r+(\theta^*+\lambda^*)\lambda^*(w^*-K^*)\right]\right\}\mathrm{d}r$$

$$+\left\{(1-\alpha)\frac{q}{\pi^2}+\left(\frac{\beta^y}{\beta^x+\beta^y}\right)\frac{g}{\pi^2}\right\}\mathrm{d}\pi$$

$$=\frac{(1-\alpha)(\theta+\lambda)\lambda}{\Omega\pi}\,\mathrm{d}\tau+\frac{(1-\alpha^*)(\theta^*+\lambda^*)\lambda^*}{\Omega^*}\,\mathrm{d}\tau^*$$

$$+\left(\frac{\beta^y}{\beta^x+\beta^y}\right)\frac{1}{\pi}\mathrm{d}g+\frac{\beta^{*y}}{\beta^{*x}+\beta^{*y}}\mathrm{d}g^* \qquad (y^*y^*) \tag{65}$$

where

$$\Omega=r^2-\theta(r+\lambda)-\lambda^2<0 \tag{66a}$$

$$\Omega^*=r^2-\theta^*(r+\lambda^*)-\lambda^{*2}<0 \tag{66b}$$

Under very mild restrictions, the yy locus is downward-sloping and the y^*y^* locus upward-sloping as drawn in Figure 3.3. Note that in this case, if a stationary equilibrium exists, it will be unique.

The long-run comparative static effects of changes in public spending and taxation, at home and abroad, on r and π are summarised in equations (67(a)–(i)).

$$\frac{\mathrm{d}r}{\mathrm{d}\tau}=\frac{\left[\alpha(1-\alpha)q+\alpha^*(1-\alpha)\pi g^*+\alpha\frac{\beta^y}{\beta^x+\beta^y}g+\frac{(1-\alpha)\beta^{*x}}{\beta^{*x}+\beta^{*y}}\pi g^*\right]\frac{(\theta+\lambda)\lambda}{\Omega\pi^2}}{\Delta}>0 \tag{67a}$$

$$\frac{\mathrm{d}\pi}{\mathrm{d}\tau}=\frac{\frac{(\theta+\lambda)\lambda}{\Omega\Omega^*}[q^*r+(\theta^*+\lambda^*)\lambda^*(w^*-K^*)](\alpha^*-\alpha)+\frac{r(\theta+\lambda)\lambda}{\Omega}\left[\frac{(1-\alpha)k'}{\pi}-\alpha k^{*\prime}\right]}{\Delta} \tag{67b}$$

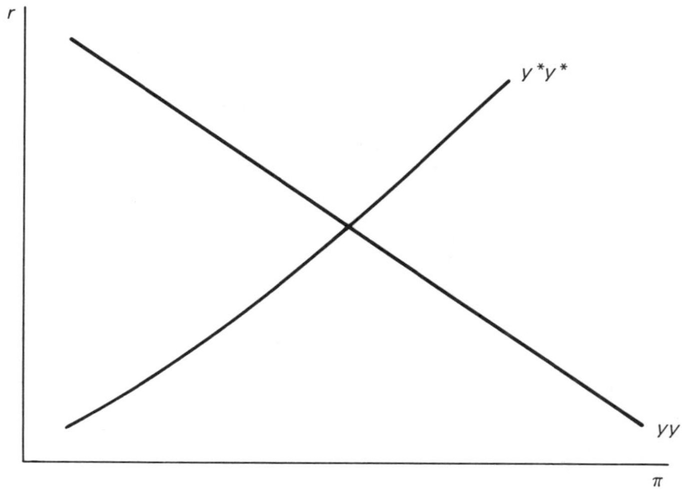

FIGURE 3.3

$$\frac{\mathrm{d}r}{\mathrm{d}\tau^*}=\frac{\left[\alpha^*(1-\alpha)q+\alpha^*(1-\alpha^*)\pi q^*+\alpha^*\frac{\beta^y}{\beta^x+\beta^y}g+(1-\alpha^*)\frac{\beta^{*x}}{\beta^{*x}+\beta^{*y}}\pi g^*\right]\frac{(\theta^*+\lambda^*)\lambda^*}{\Omega^*\pi}}{\Delta}>0 \quad (67c)$$

$$\frac{\mathrm{d}\pi}{\mathrm{d}\tau^*}=\frac{\frac{(\theta^*+\lambda^*)\lambda^*}{\Omega\Omega^*}[qr+(\theta+\lambda)\lambda(w-K)](\alpha-\alpha^*)+\frac{r(\theta^*+\lambda^*)\lambda^*}{\Omega^*}[(1-\alpha^*)k'-\alpha^*k^{*\prime}\pi]}{\Delta} \quad (67d)$$

$$\frac{\mathrm{d}r}{\mathrm{d}g}=\frac{\frac{\beta^x}{\beta^x+\beta^y}\left[\frac{(1-\alpha)q}{\pi^2}+\left(\frac{\beta^y}{\beta^x+\beta^y}\right)\frac{g}{\pi^2}\right]+\left(\frac{\beta^y}{\beta^x+\beta^y}\right)\frac{1}{\pi}\left[\alpha^*q^*+\frac{\beta^{*x}}{\beta^{*x}+\beta^{*y}}g^*\right]}{\Delta}<0 \quad (67e)$$

$$\frac{d\pi}{dg}=\frac{\left[\frac{qr+(\theta+\lambda)\lambda(w-K)}{\Omega\pi}\right]\left[\alpha-\left(\frac{\beta^x}{\beta^x+\beta^y}\right)\right]+\left[\frac{q^*r+(\theta^*+\lambda^*)\lambda^*(w^*-K^*)}{\Omega^*}\right]\left[\alpha^*-\left(\frac{\beta^x}{\beta^x+\beta^y}\right)\right]}{\Delta}+\frac{r\left[\frac{k'}{\pi}\left(1-(\frac{\beta^x}{\beta^x+\beta^y})\right)-k^{*\prime}\left(\frac{\beta^x}{\beta^x+\beta^y}\right)\right]}{\Delta} \tag{67f}$$

$$\frac{dr}{dg^*}=\frac{\frac{\beta^{*x}}{\beta^{*x}+\beta^{*y}}\left[\frac{(1-\alpha)q}{\pi}+\frac{\beta^y}{\beta^x+\beta^y}\frac{g}{\pi}\right]+\frac{\beta^{*y}}{\beta^{*x}+\beta^{*y}}\left[\alpha^*q^*+\frac{\beta^{*x}}{\beta^{*x}+\beta^{*y}}g^*\right]}{\Delta}<0 \tag{67g}$$

$$\frac{d\pi}{dg^*}=\frac{\left[\frac{qr+(\theta+\lambda)\lambda(w-K)}{\Omega}\right]\left[\alpha-\left(\frac{\beta^{*x}}{\beta^{*x}+\beta^{*y}}\right)\right]+\pi\left[\frac{q^*r+(\theta^*+\lambda^*)\lambda^*(w^*-K^*)}{\Omega^*}\right]\left[\alpha^*-\left(\frac{\beta^{*x}}{\beta^{*x}+\beta^{*y}}\right)\right]}{\Delta}+\frac{r\left[k'\left(1-\frac{\beta^{*x}}{\beta^{*x}+\beta^{*y}}\right)-k^{*\prime}\pi\frac{\beta^{*x}}{\beta^{*x}+\beta^{*y}}\right]}{\Delta} \tag{67h}$$

$$\Delta\equiv\left\{rk'+\alpha\frac{[qr+(\theta+\lambda)\lambda(w-K)]}{\Omega}+\alpha^*\pi\frac{[q^*r+(\theta^*+\lambda^*)\lambda^*(w^*-K^*)]}{\Omega^*}\right\}\left[\frac{(1-\alpha)}{\pi^2}\quad q+\left(\frac{\beta^y}{\beta^x+\beta^y}\right)\frac{g}{\pi^2}\right]$$
$$+\left\{rk^{*\prime}+\frac{(1-\alpha)\,[qr+(\theta+\lambda)\lambda(w-K)]}{\pi\Omega}+\frac{(1-\alpha^*)}{\Omega^*}(q^*r+(\theta^*+\lambda^*)\lambda^*(w^*-K^*))\right\}\left[\frac{\alpha^*q^*}{\pi}+\frac{\beta^{*x}}{\beta^{*x}+\beta^{*y}}g^*\right]$$
$$<0$$

The effect of lower taxes and higher public spending (domestic or foreign) is to lower the long-run world interest rate. This is only a paradox until one remembers that lower taxes or higher spending are, across steady states, associated with lower public debt (see (57) and (58)). Of course the process of adjustment towards such a lower debt steady state will involve transitorily higher taxes and/or lower public spending to achieve the surpluses necessary for retiring the debt. The association of higher spending with lower interest rates is present regardless of the composition of the spending increase between domestic and foreign output.

The effect of tax cuts on the terms of trade in the long run can be explained in terms of a familiar transfer problem criterion plus a correction for supply adjustments. For example from (67b), ignoring supply-side adjustments ($k' = k^{*\prime} = 0$), a domestic tax cut will raise the relative price of domestic output ($d\pi/(d\tau) > 0$) if $\alpha > \alpha^*$, i.e. if the marginal (and average) propensity to consume domestic output is greater at home than abroad. Lower taxes also are associated with lower interest rates, higher capital–labour ratios and higher output. If there is no bias in domestic private consumption towards home goods $\left(\alpha = \frac{1}{2}\right)$ and if technologies are similar in the sense that $k' = k^{*\prime}$, the output adjustment term vanishes. If there is a bias towards home goods $\left(\alpha > \frac{1}{2}\right)$ and if k' and $k^{*\prime}$ are similar, then the supply effect reinforces the transfer effect and $d\pi/(d\tau) > 0$ *a fortiori*. By exactly analogous reasoning, given supply, $d\pi/d\tau^* > 0$ if $\alpha^* > \alpha$ or $1 - \alpha^* < 1 - \alpha$. A cut in foreign taxes will raise the relative price of foreign goods if foreigners allocate a larger fraction of their total consumption spending to foreign goods than do domestic residents. Again the same kind of supply-side effect that was discussed for a domestic tax cut must be allowed for. We shall not consider it any further here or below when the effects of spending increases on π are discussed.

An increase in domestic public spending raises the relative price of domestic output ($d\pi/(dg) < 0$) if the domestic public sector's marginal propensity to spend on domestic output ($\beta^y/\beta^x + \beta^y$) exceeds a weighted average of the domestic and foreign private marginal propensities to spend on domestic output, i.e. if (ignoring supply effects)

$$\frac{\beta^x}{\beta^x+\beta^y} > \frac{[qr+(\theta+\lambda)\lambda(w-K)]\Omega^*}{[qr+(\theta+\lambda)\lambda(w-K)]+\pi[q^*r+(\theta^*+\lambda^*)\lambda^*(w^*-K^*)]\Omega\Omega^{*-1}}\alpha$$

$$+\frac{+\pi[q^*r+(\theta^*+\lambda^*)\lambda^*(w^*-K^*)]}{\Omega^*\Omega^{-1}[qr+(\theta+\lambda)\lambda(w-K)]+\pi[q^*r+(\theta^*+\lambda^*)\lambda^*(w^*-K^*)]}\alpha^*$$

Similarly, an increase in foreign public spending will raise the relative price of foreign output ($d\pi/(dg^*)>0$) if the foreign public sector's marginal propensity to spend on foreign output $(1-(\beta^{*x})/\beta^{*x}+\beta^{*y})$ exceeds a weighted average of domestic foreign private marginal propensities to spend on foreign output $1-\alpha$ and $1-\alpha^*$. The exact condition can be obtained from (67h).

In terms of Figure 3.3, a domestic tax increase or spending cut shifts yy up and to the right while y^*y^* shifts up and to the left. A foreign tax increase or spending cut shifts yy and y^*y^* in the same directions.

Having derived the steady-state effects on π and r, the remaining long-run comparative statics is straightforward. Any policy change that raises r lowers the capital stock at home and abroad. Lower long-run domestic taxes are associated with a lower long-run stock of domestic public debt, with a lower global interest rate and a higher capital stock in both countries. Domestic human capital is higher and consumption is almost certain to increase. Foreign human capital (measured in foreign output) is also increased because of the lower r and higher K^*; the lower interest rate is likely to reduce foreign non-human wealth and foreign consumption in the long run.

With τ^* and g^* given, a lower world interest rate still requires, at a given value of π, a larger long-run stock of foreign public debt (assuming $b^{*G}>0$ initially). This could be reversed by a decline in π.

Finally, there is the effect of domestic and foreign fiscal policy on the long run value of F.

From equation (59) it is easily checked that, in response to a change in some exogenous variable z, F changes as follows:

$$\frac{dF}{dz}=-\frac{1}{r}\left[F+\frac{rq+(\theta+\lambda)\lambda(w-K)}{\Omega}+f'k'\right]\frac{dr}{dz}+\frac{1}{r}\frac{(\theta+\lambda)\lambda}{\Omega}\frac{d\tau}{dz}+\frac{1}{r}\frac{dg}{dz} \tag{68}$$

At a given interest rate, a higher steady state level of public spending must be associated with a larger stock of claims on the rest of the model, in order to finance the increase in the excess of domestic absorption over domestic income. Since increased public spending is associated in the long run with a lower interest rate, and thus a larger domestic capital stock and domestic output level, this indirect effect will tend to lower F. The reduction in private consumption likely to be associated with a lower value of r will also tend to lower F. Finally, a lower value of r will *ceteris paribus* worsen (improve) the current account through the debt service (foreign investment income) component rF if the country is a net creditor with $F>0$ (a net debtor with $F<0$). Thus *ceteris paribus* a positive (negative) value of F will tend to make $\mathrm{d}F/\mathrm{d}g$ positive (negative) through the net foreign interest component. With minor and obvious changes, the argument about the effect of an increase in g on F also applies to a cut in τ. It is also easily seen that an increase in g^* will tend to have the opposite effect on F of an increase in g and that a cut in τ^* will tend to have the opposite effect on F of a cut in τ. It seems plausible that the 'direct' effect of an increase in g or a cut in τ of raising F in the long run will outweigh the indirect effects through production, private consumption and net foreign investment income. Our numerical examples do indeed all have this property, although it is not implied by all parameter values consistent with saddlepoint stability.

Dynamic Adjustment

The linearised structural form of the two-country model is straightforward. The production functions in the two countries are assumed to be Cobb–Douglas with competitive capital shares β and β^* respectively. To calculate the initial stationary equilibrium we must assign values to β, β^*, ζ, ζ^*, θ, θ^*, λ, λ^*, α, α^*, $\beta^x/\beta^x+\beta^y$, $\beta^{*x}/\beta^{*x}+\beta^{*y}$, g, g^*, τ_1 and τ_1^*. A full characterization of the dynamic behaviour also requires values for μ_τ and μ_τ^*. There are eight linearly independent state variables in the linearised state-space representation of the model. A convenient choice of state variables is b^G, b^{*G}, K, K^*, w, h, h^* and ψ. For a (locally) unique convergent saddlepoint equilibrium solution to exist we therefore require five stable and three unstable characteristic roots in the state matrix.

The One-commodity Case

First consider the special case of the model where the relative price of foreign goods, π, is constant throughout in response to tax changes.

This requires not only that the private domestic propensity to spend on domestic output equals the foreign private propensity to spend on domestic output ($\alpha=\alpha^*$) but also that the supply responses to the interest rate changes induced by the fiscal policy have no further effect on π (see equations (67b) and (67d)). This extension of the familiar transfer criterion for a change in the terms of trade is of course unnecessary when output is exogenous ($k'=k^{*\prime}=0$).

The numerical details of the first simulation are given in Table 3.1. The two countries are identical (with $\alpha=\alpha^*=0.5$) and the initial long-run equilibrium is one with $F=0$.

Table 3.1 One-good economy; zero external debt of home country

Parameter values

$\beta=\beta^*=0.25$; $\zeta^{-1}=\zeta^{*-1}=0.031$; $\lambda=\lambda^*=0.03$; $\theta=\theta^*=0.035$;

$\alpha=\alpha^*=0.5$: $\dfrac{\beta^x}{\beta^x+\beta^y}=\dfrac{\beta^{*x}}{\beta^{*x}+\beta^{*y}}=0{,}5$; $\tau_{1,0}=\tau^*_{1,0}=0.3\,206\,205$;

$g_0=g^*_0=0.1\,469\,511$; $\mu_\tau=\mu^*_\tau=-2$.

Key initial equilibrium values

$r_0=0.05$; $\pi_0=1$; $F_0=0$.

Characteristic roots

-0.05326; -0.05; -0.01543; -0.01539; -0.015; 0.06539; 0.07628; 0.08

The policy experiment is an increase in τ_1. Because of our tax function this policy experiment amounts to a short-run tax cut followed by (and indeed necessitating) a long-run tax increase through its effect on the stock of outstanding public debt.

Figure 3.4 shows the dynamic response of the key variables in the two countries.

The long-run response to the increase in τ_1 is a larger stock of domestic public debt, a small reduction in the foreign stock of public debt; equal reductions in the domestic and foreign capital stocks; a small increase in domestic private non-human wealth; a larger increase in foreign non-human wealth; a large reduction in domestic human capital and a smaller reduction in foreign human capital. The interest rate goes up, domestic consumption falls and foreign consumption rises. The net foreign asset position of the home country becomes negative as domestic government debt crowds out domestic net foreign assets as well as domestic and foreign real capital. π is, of

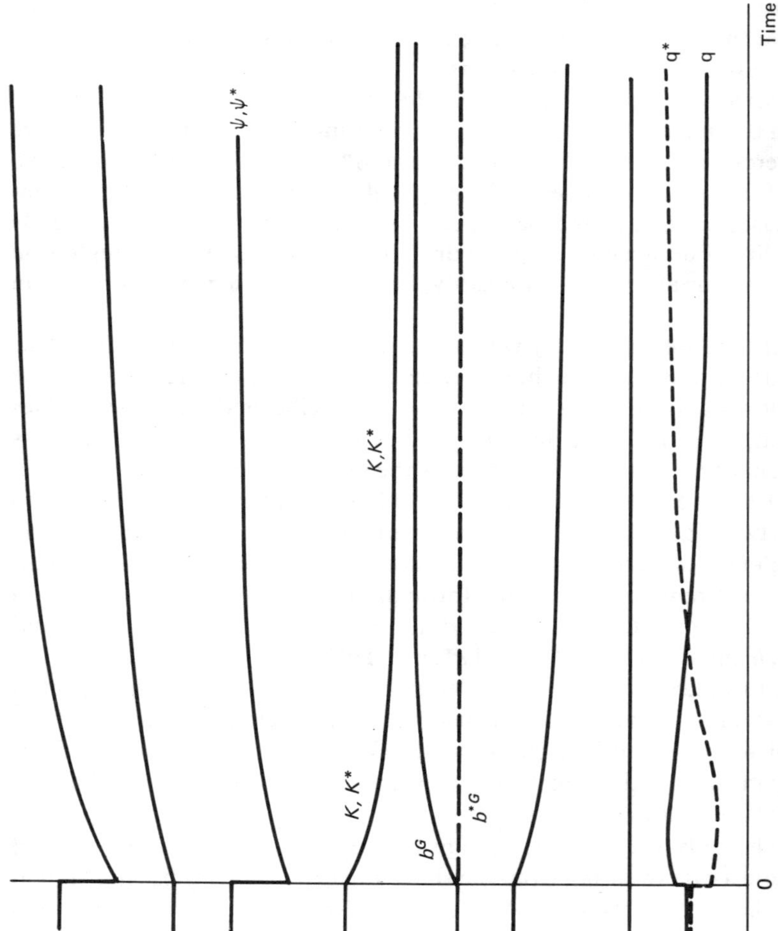

FIGURE 3.4

course, unaffected in the long run as in the short run. The system exhibits (local) saddlepoint stability.

The dynamic response to an unexpected, immediate (at $t=0$) and permanent increase in τ_1 as follows.

In the short run, taxes are cut by about the same amount they will be raised in the long run. The tax cut is reversed gradually and becomes an increase from period 14 on. The stock markets (ψ and ψ^*) fall on impact in both countries, reflecting higher anticipated future interest rates. The behaviour of ψ and ψ^* and of K and K^* is identical. The interest rate rises only gradually. Domestic consumption increases on impact, reaches a peak soon after and then begins a steady decline. Foreign consumption drops on impact, reaches a trough soon afterwards and increases steadily thereafter to its higher new long-run level.

If the foreign country were to raise τ_1^* at the same time and by the same amount as the home country raises τ_1, the results are the following. In the long run, all 'country-specific' endogenous variables change by the same amount in each country. F of course remains unchanged. b^G and b^{*G} increase by the same amount and the change in $b^G + b^{*G}$ is exactly twice that when only τ_1 was increased. K and K^* fall by twice as much while r increases twice as much. Consumption declines in both countries, as does human capital. The current account remains in balance throughout the adjustment process. In fact, all domestic and foreign variables (b^G and b^{*G}, K and K^*, w and w^*, h and h^*, ψ and ψ^*, q and q^*, τ and τ^*) move in the same way. The long-run tax increase is preceded in both countries by an initial cut in total taxes which boosts consumption and creates budget deficits which only vanish asymptotically. The joint move towards fiscal expansion in the short run creates a steeper decline in the two countries' stock markets.

The only way for the foreign country to avoid the higher world interest rate resulting from the short-run expansionary fiscal action in the home country, is for the former to engage in short-run contractionary fiscal action. Consider, for example, a policy response by the foreign country which consists of a reduction in τ_1^* (and therefore a short-run increase in τ^*) equal in magnitude to the increase in τ_1. The result is no change in r, ψ, ψ^*, K and K^* in the short run or in the long run. All other country-specific endogenous variables change by opposite amounts in the long-run and during the adjustment process. The home country runs budget deficits and current account deficits throughout while the foreign country runs budget surpluses and current account surpluses. In the long run w and h are down (and w^*

and h^* are up by equal amounts). Consumption falls at home in the long run and declines abroad. The short term response is in the opposite direction.

These results are not affected qualitatively by changing parameter values in such a way that the initial stationary equilibrium is one in which the home country is a net creditor ($F_0 > 0$) or a net debtor ($F_0 < 0$). For example consider $g_0 = 0.1939$ and $g_0^* = 0.10$ while keeping the other parameter values the same as those given in Table 3.1. This 'shifting' of public spending towards the home country lowers the initial long-run value of b_0^G to 2.534, raises that of b_0^{*G} to 4.412 but leaves r_0 and π_0 unchanged. The home country becomes a net creditor with $F = 0.939$. The characteristic roots are virtually the same as in the case where $F_0 = 0$ (specifically, the saddlepoint equilibrium configuration with five stable and three unstable roots persists) and even quantitatively the short-run and long-run response of the system is not much affected. Shifting public spending the other way, towards the foreign country, with $g_0 = 0.10$, $g_0^* = 0.1939$ and $b_0^G = 4.412$, $b_0^{*G} = 2.543$ and $F_0 = -0.9\,390\,213$ again does not yield a picture that is significantly different from that shown in Figure 3.4.

The Two-commodity Case

We now introduce a bias in private spending towards a country's own good, i.e. $\alpha > \alpha^*$. The first numerical example, specified fully in Table 3.2(a), again has $F_0 = 0$. The adjustment process following an unanticipated permanent increase in τ_1 is shown in Figure 3.5. The long-run effect of an increase in τ_1 on most endogenous variables is qualitatively the same as in the one-good case. One exception is that b^{*G} shows a small increase rather than a small decline. The reason for this, as can be seen from equation (58), is the long-run increase in π. The long-run reduction in home (consumption) demand worsens the home country's terms of trade since the share of domestic consumption spending falling on domestic output is higher than the share of foreign consumption spending allocated to domestic output ($\alpha > \alpha^*$).

Because π now varies over time, there is a certain amount of 'decoupling' between domestic and foreign capital formation during the adjustment process. The short-run domestic tax cut outweighs the long-run tax increase, so h and q increase on impact. With q^* falling, the terms of trade improve in the short run. After the initial discontinuous drop in π, however, π rises smoothly throughout the adjust-

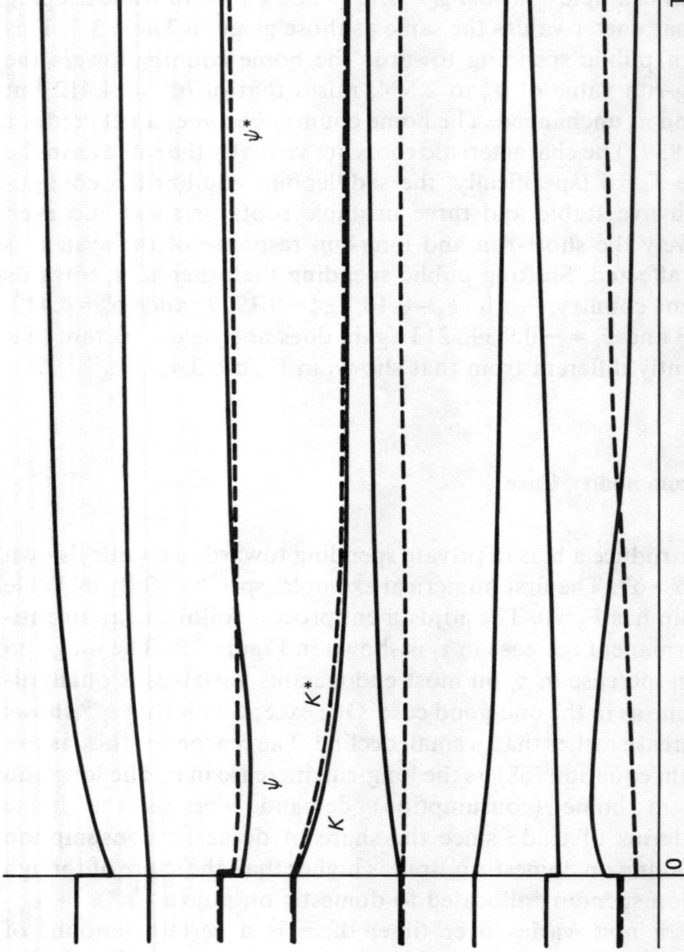

FIGURE 3.5

Table 3.2 Two-good economy

(a) Home country has zero net external debt ($F_0=0$).

Parameter values:

$\beta=\beta^*=0.25;\ \zeta^{-1}=\zeta^{*-1}=0.031;\ \lambda=\lambda^*=0.03;\ \theta=\theta^*=0.035;$

$\alpha=1-\alpha^*=0.7;\ \frac{\beta^x}{\beta^x+\beta^y}=1-\frac{\beta^{*x}}{\beta^{*x}+\beta^{*y}}=0.7;\ \tau_{1,0}=\tau^*_{1,0}=0.3\,206\,205;$

$g_0=g^*_0=0.1\,469\,511;\ \mu_\tau=\mu^*_\tau=-2$

Key initial equilibrium values

$r_0=0.05;\ \pi_0=1;\ F_0=0$

Characteristic roots

$-0.05326;\ -0.04861;\ -0.01545;\ -0.01505;\ -0.01068;\ 0.06101;\ 0.07628;\ 0.07834$

(b) Home country is external debtor ($F_0<0$)

Parameter values

$\beta=\beta^*=0.25;\ \zeta^{-1}=\zeta^{*-1}=0.031;\ \lambda=\lambda^*=0.03;\ \theta=0.04;\ \theta^*=0.035;$

$\alpha=1-\alpha^*=0.6;\ \frac{\beta^x}{\beta^x+\beta^y}=0.75;\ \frac{\beta^{*x}}{\beta^{*x}+\beta^{*y}}=0.3624;$

$\tau_{1,0}=\tau^*_{1,0}=0.3\,206\,205;\ g_0=0.2\,885\,585;\ g^*_0=0.3\,059\,254;\ \mu_\tau=\mu^*_\tau=-2$

Key initial equilibrium values

$r_0=0.05;\ \pi_0=1;\ F_0=-3.1795$

Characteristic roots

$-0.05059;\ -0.04992;\ -0.01605;\ -0.01533;\ -0.01470;\ 0.06334;\ 0.07763;\ 0.07937$

(c) Home country is external creditor ($F_0>0$)

Parameter values

$\beta=\beta^*=0.25;\ \zeta^{-1}=\zeta^{*-1}=0.031;\ \lambda=\lambda^*=0.03;\ \theta=0.035;\ \theta^*=0.04;$

$\alpha=1-\alpha^*=0.6;\ \frac{\beta^x}{\beta^x+\beta^y}=0.6\,375\,548;\ 1-\frac{\beta^{*x}}{\beta^{*x}+\beta^{*y}}=0.75;$

$\tau_{1,0}=\tau^*_{1,0}=0.3\,206\,205;\ g_0=0.3\,059\,254;\ g^*_0=0.2\,885\,585\ \mu_\tau=\mu^*_\tau=-2$

Key initial equilibrium values

$r_0=0.05;\ \pi_0=1;\ F_0=3.1795$

Characteristic roots

$-0.05039;\ -0.04981;\ -0.02130;\ -0.01562;\ -0.01520;\ 0.06320;\ 0.07766;\ 0.07942$

ment process. This rise in π is anticipated. Since $r^* = r - \dot{\pi}/\pi$ is the interest rate governing ψ^*, the foreign stock market falls by less initially than the domestic one and domestic capital decumulates more swiftly than foreign capital.

A simultaneous, equal increase in τ_1 and τ_1^* has exactly the same effect as it has in the one-good version of the model since π remains constant throughout. While this stabilises the real exchange rate relative to a unilateral increase in τ_1, it reinforces the effect on the interest rate.

A policy of reducing τ_1^* by the same amount as the increase in τ_1 does indeed stabilise the interest rate (r) but reinforces the swings in π which falls by more in the short run and rises by more in the long run. To prevent both π and r from changing, two fiscal instruments (e.g. τ^* and g^*) must be used.

Even when the terms of trade are endogenous, the sign of the initial external net worth position of the two countries does not appear to have crucial implications for the qualitative stability or saddlepoint properties of the model. Table 3.2 shows how the desired saddlepoint configuration is present when F_0 is negative (Table 3.2(b)) and when F_0 is positive (Table 3.2(c)). Qualitatively, the long-run and short-run responses of the endogenous variables in the net external creditor and the net external debtor cases are similar to each other and to the zero net external debt case.

CONCLUSION

The purpose of this paper has been to study certain aspects of public debt and deficits in the open economy using a model in which private sector behavioural relationships have been derived explicitly from optimising behaviour. The public sector's present value budget constraint or solvency constraint, together with the assumption that the real interest rate exceeds the rate of growth, was shown to tie together current tax cuts and future tax increases.[10] In a two-country setting such a policy would raise the interest rate in an integrated global capital market, crowd out private capital at home and abroad and worsen a country's external net worth position. If in addition private spending shows a preference, at the margin, for domestic output over foreign output, then the policy would improve the terms of trade in the short run but cause them to worsen in the long run.

The analysis brings out the central role of the interest rate in transmitting disturbances between countries when capital markets are highly integrated. While there always exist paths (or contingent rules) for the domestic fiscal policy instrument that can neutralise any incipient shocks to the path of interest rates originating from abroad, such 'stabilising' policy actions inevitably involve costs. Even if lump-sum taxes are used, intertemporal (and therefore intergenerational) redistribution of the tax burden is inevitable. If lump-sum taxes are not available, dead-weight losses and excess burdens will be imposed. Varying the public spending programme involves distortions in the intertemporal allocation of public consumption. If public sector capital formation (not considered in this paper) is varied yet other costs are incurred. Taxing international capital flows may be an interesting second-best policy.

The finite private decision horizon (or the excess of the effective private discount rate over the government's discount rate) permits a non-trivial analysis of one of the central current issues of financial policy: the consequences for private saving and capital formation of varying the time pattern of taxation and borrowing.

Several possible extensions of the model come to mind. The first is to add money to the asset menu. To do this properly would be a major task, but the *ad hoc* inclusion of domestic money as an argument in the direct utility function may be a useful first step. If non-interest-bearing government fiat money is added to the instantaneous utility function in logarithmic form ($+\gamma \ln m$, where m is the nominal money stock deflated by the Cobb–Douglas price index, p, appropriate to the utility function) the extension is trivial.

Money demand is given by $m = [\lambda/r + (\dot{p}/p)]\, q$ and is unit elastic with respect to the nominal interest rate $r + \dot{p}/p$. If all non-money assets are index-linked, money is a veil. Super-neutrality prevails in the short run as in the long run and in response to any kind of monetary shock. Real interest rates are unaffected by monetary policy. The real seigniorage the authorities can extract through monetary expansion is independent of the rate of growth of nominal money and of the rate of inflation. The terms of trade are independent of the behaviour of the nominal exchange rate.

If nominally denominated interest-bearing public debt exists in addition to money, unanticipated monetary policy changes which cause discontinuous jumps in the general price level can inflict capital losses or gains on the holders of these nominal assets. A non-unitary interest elasticity of demand for real money balances permits the consideration of seigniorage issues.

A second important issue is the *de facto* non-existence of lump-sum taxation. Barro (1979) analysed the problem of the optimal intertemporal pattern of distortionary taxation and (under very strong conditions) derived a version of the 'uniform tax rate over time' result for an economy in which 'first-order debt neutrality' held. It would be rather more relevant to study this problem in a world which does not have this strong first order debt neutrality property, such as the Yaari–Blanchard model or the overlapping generations model without operative intergenerational gifts and bequests.

A further desirable extension would be to relax the unattractive, highly restrictive perfect capital market assumption which permits private agents, once allowance is made for their finite expected lifetimes, to borrow on the same terms as the government.

Fourth, labour market disequilibrium could be added as a feature to the model. The simplest approach simply posits different combinations and degrees of nominal and real wage rigidity. The obvious starting point here is the work of Sachs (1983).

Finally, the model is inhabited by well-informed, rationally anticipating and optimising private agents and rather mechanically acting governments. Clearly, government behaviour should be endogenised in a more satisfactory manner. The interaction between the two national governments could be strategic in nature. Recent developments in differential game theory and its applications to economics hold considerable promise (see e.g. Miller and Salmon, 1983).

The Yaari–Blanchard model, as developed in this paper would seem to be a flexible vehicle for the analysis of a wide range of interesting issues in international economics.

Notes

1. After completing an earlier version of this paper I became aware of two other applications of the Yaari–Blanchard consumption model to the analysis of fiscal policy in a two-country setting. The first, by Alberto Giovannini (1984) has the same behavioural equations as the model of the present paper, except for the investment functions which are specified without internal or external costs of adjustment. Since only steady-state analysis is conducted, this is not a serious flaw. The second by Frenkel and Razin (1984b) does a dynamic analysis but has no capital formation (i.e. exogenous output) and only considers the one commodity case.
2. $r=\theta$ must be assumed when $\lambda=0$.

3. We must of course assume that

$$f-\alpha q-g_x+\frac{(1+\psi)K}{\zeta}-\frac{1}{2}(\psi-1)^2\frac{K}{\zeta}>0$$

for π to be positive.
4. We assume $\mathrm{d}q/\mathrm{d}r \geqslant 0$.
5. These simulations made use of the algorithm 'saddlepoint' of Austin and Buiter (1982).
6. The value of ζ was taken from Summers (1981).
7. In the two-country model interest rates are endogenous both in the short run and in the long run.
8. The two versions can be summarised as follows:

Version 1
$r^*=\theta=0.03$; $\lambda=0.03$: $\zeta^{-1}=0.031$; $\beta=0.25$; $M=0.897$; $\alpha=0.6$; $\tau_0=0.380$; $g_{x_0}=0.228$; $\pi_0 g_{y_0}=0.076$; $K_0=16.895$; $b_0^G=2.534$; $F_0=-19.429$; $\mu_\tau=-2$.

Characteristic roots of K, b^G, w, ψ, q system: -0.03268; -0.02159; -0.01216; 0.03662; 0.05746.

Version 2
$r_0^*=0.05$; $\theta=0.04$; $\lambda=0.03$; $\zeta^{-1}=0.031$; $\beta=0.25$; $M=1.3\,155\,511$; $\alpha=0.6$; $\tau_0=0.321$; $g_{x_0}=0.192$; $\pi_0 g_{y_0}=0.064$; $K_0=8.550$; $b_0^G=1.282$; $F_0=-3.821$; $\mu_\tau=-2$.

Characteristic roots of K, b^G, w, ψ, q system: $=0.05\,094$; $-0.01\,563$; $-0.01\,105$; $0.05\,781$; $0.07\,800$.

9. Equations (55) and (56) imply that $r(w+w^*)+j(K)+\pi j^*(K^*)-\tau-\pi\tau^*-q-\pi q^*=0$. This in turn implies that $w+\pi w^*=K+\pi K^*+b^G+b^{*G}$.
10. This is the same point as was emphasised in the context of a monetary economy by Sargent and Wallace (1981).

REFERENCES

Austin, G. and W. H. Buiter (1982) 'Saddlepoint: a Programme for Solving Continuous Time Linear Rational Expectations Models', SSRC LSE Econometrics Programme, Discussion Paper A. 37, November.

Barro, R. J. (1979) 'On the Determination of the Public Debt', *Journal of Political Economy*, 87 (October) pp. 940–71.

Bean, C. R. (1984) 'The Terms of Trade, Labour Supply and the Current Account', Centre for Labour Economics Discussion Paper No. 190, March.

Blanchard, O. J. (1983a) 'Current and Anticipated Deficits, Interest Rates and Economic Activity', unpublished, July.

Blanchard, O. J. (1983b) 'Debt, Deficits and Finite Horizons', unpublished November.

Buiter, W. H. (1981) 'Time Preference and International Lending and Borrowing in an Overlapping Generations Model', *Journal of Political Economy*, 89 (August) pp. 769–97.

Frenkel, J. and A. Razin (1984a) 'Fiscal Policies, Debt and International Economic Interdependence', unpublished, January.

Frenkel, Jacob A. and Assaf Razin (1984b) 'Budget Deficits and Rates of Interest in the World Economy', April 1984 mimeo.

Giovannini, Alberto (1984) 'Fiscal Policy, the Capital Stock and the Exchange Rate', unpublished, Columbia University.

Miller, M. H. and M. Salmon (1983) 'Dynamic Games and the Time Inconsistency of Optimal Policies in Open Economies', University of Warwick, mimeo, June.

Sachs, J. (1983) 'Energy and Growth under Flexible Exchange Rates: a Simulation Study', in J. S. Bhandari and B. H. Putnam (eds), *Economic Interdependence and Flexible Exchange Rates*, pp. 191–220.

Sargent, T. J. and N. Wallace (1981) 'Some Unpleasant Monetarist Arithmetic', *Federal Reserve Bank of Minneapolis Quarterly Bulletin*.

Summers, L. H. (1981) 'Taxation and Corporate Investment: A *q*-Theory Approach', *Brookings Papers on Economic Activity*, 1, pp. 67–127.

Svensson, L. E. O. and A. Razin (1983). 'The Terms of Trade and the Current Account: The Laursen–Harberger–Metzler Effect', *Journal of Political Economy*, 1, pp. 97–125.

Yaari, M. E. (1965) 'Uncertain Lifetime, Life Insurance and the Theory of the Consumer', *Review of Economic Studies*, 32 (April) pp. 137–50.

Part Two
The Government Budget and Inflation

4 On Optimal Currency Substitution Policy and Public Finance

Zvi Hercowitz and Efraim Sadka

I INTRODUCTION

One of the means of raising revenue available to a government is the inflation tax on domestic money balances. The demand for these balances and the revenue from inflation depend, among other things, on the tax rate itself and on the degree of substitutability between domestic money and alternative assets, which are referred to in the paper as foreign exchange. (However, the discussion can be interpreted as involving money substitutes in general.)

The approach adopted in the paper is the following. The physical or technological differences between the two monies are only with respect to characteristics such as the colour or the size of the bills, which cannot explain less-than-perfect substitutability. It is the domestic government that may create imperfect substitution by imposing barriers or regulations on the use of foreign exchange. Only by these means can the government tax domestic money at a rate higher than the inflation rates in other countries. Given this link between restrictions on foreign exchange and the revenue from inflation, there is room for determining the socially optimal severity of these restrictions.

Phelps (1973) and later Siegel (1978), Helpman and Sadka (1979) and Drazen (1979) studied the optimal determination of the inflation tax from a public finance point of view. In this framework, where all taxes are distortionary and there is an exogenous revenue to be collected, the inflation tax is determined along with the other taxes so as to minimise the total deadweight losses from taxation. A common feature of the aforementioned works is the assumption of an exogenous degree of substitutability between domestic money and alternative assets. Using a similar optimal taxation approach, this paper extends this literature by assuming an endogenous substitutability between domestic money and alternative assets and focusing on the restrictions on money substitutes as a policy variable.

The discussion here is also related to Fischer's (1982) in which he addressed the consequences for public finance and welfare, of using a foreign currency instead of a domestic one. The present framework pursues these considerations by treating the two extremes that Fischer considers as the possible corner solutions of a problem in which the two assets may in principle coexist. The issue addressed here is also related, in spirit, to Bryant and Wallace's (1980) discussion of restrictions on the denomination size of money substitutes.

To study the effects of the restrictions on money substitutes at the micro level, we use here a framework in which the demand for monies is generated from inventory theoretic considerations, as in Baumol (1952), Tobin (1956), Barro (1970), Feige and Parkin (1971), Grossman and Policano (1975), and more recently, Jovanovic (1982).[1] There is a legal restriction that only domestic money can be used in transactions. Also, the cost of converting domestic to foreign money and vice versa involves a lump-sum cost. However, this cost is not given by nature, but imposed by government regulations. Hence, there is an attempt here to explain endogenously the size of the financial transaction costs.

From the private point of view, the critical difference between domestic and foreign currency is that the real value of the former depreciates at the rate of inflation while the second is assumed to maintain its real value. Since there is no natural cost of converting foreign exchange to domestic money, if no man-made restrictions on such conversions are imposed, then, with any positive inflation rate, the individuals would hold only foreign exchange and convert it to domestic money just before transacting. This would practically eliminate the demand for domestic money and make the foreign exchange the medium of exchange. In this case the government would have no revenue from inflation. However, regulation can prevent this from happening. For instance, imagine the government requiring all these transactions to be carried out through commercial banks, involving non-trivial waste of real resources in the form of paper-work, waiting time and use of physical capital (the case of Israel, which motivated this paper, is a good example). Clearly, a preferred way to impose this cost would be to levy a tax on foreign exchange transactions. However, we prefer to address a more realistic problem, in which for some reason or another (perhaps, prohibitive collection costs) such a tax is not used.

The paper is organised as follows. Section II presents the analytical framework. The behaviour of the representative individual and firm is analysed in Section II (a). Section II (b) addresses the general equilibrium and the public finance considerations. To obtain a closed form solution for the individual's decision variables we adopt in Section III a specific utility function. In Section IV we derive the results about optimal public finance and foreign exchange restrictions under a general utility function. Section V contains concluding remarks.

II THE MODEL: A GENERAL ANALYTICAL FRAMEWORK

(a) The Private Sector

Consider a competitive economy consisting of a continuum of identical, infinitely lived individuals who consume an aggregate non-storable consumption good (c), and provide labour services (L). There is also a continuum of identical firms producing under constant returns to scale: a unit of labour produces $\bar{w}$ units of consumption. Therefore, the competitive nominal wage rate $w(t)$ will be equal to $\bar{w}p(t)$, where $p(t)$ is the price of the aggregate good.

The individuals can hold two financial assets. One is a fiat money issued by the government. This is a nominal asset whose real value depreciates with inflation. The other asset has a fixed real value but bears no real interest. This could be, for instance, a currency of a stable-price foreign country, a foreign exchange denominated bank deposit, an indexed bond (bearing no real interest), etc. The two assets serve as stores of value but only the first one (domestic money) can be used as a legal medium of exchange. The second one, which cannot be used as a medium of exchange is referred to from now on as foreign exchange.

Our analysis is confined to a steady state. The representative individual receives his salary once every T units of time in domestic money. The length T of this period is considered exogenously given by institutional arrangements.[2] Also, we assume no discounting of utility over time. Therefore, all these payment periods are identical and hence it suffices to analyse what happens within one such period, say the period starting at time zero and ending at time T.

The objective of the individual is to maximise utility $U(c(\cdot), L(\cdot))$

from the streams of consumption, $c(\cdot)$, and labour services, $L(\cdot)$, over the period $[0, T]$. The function U has the form

$$U(c(\cdot), L(\cdot)) = \int_0^T u(c(t), L(t))\mathrm{d}t, \tag{1}$$

where u is interpreted as the instantaneous utility function ($u_1 > 0$ and $u_2 < 0$). Notice that the individual will in general choose $c(\cdot)$ and $L(\cdot)$ which vary over time. This makes the model extremely difficult to deal with without adding any significant insight into the nature of the problem at hand.[3] For this reason, we simplify the optimisation problem by constraining $c(\cdot)$ and $L(\cdot)$ to be constant over time.[4] Then the objective of the individual becomes that of maximising $u(c, L)$.

We define the beginning of the payment period (henceforth T-period) as the date in which the individual receives his salary. Given the steady state assumption, it does not matter whether this compensation corresponds to the labour services supplied during the preceding T-period or for those to be supplied during the T-period just started. The nominal after-tax salary is

$$(1-\beta)w(0)\int_0^T L(t)\mathrm{d}t = (1-\beta)\bar{w}LT, \tag{2}$$

where β is a proportional income tax rate and $p(0)$ is normalised to unity. If the individual does not perform any financial transaction at $t=0$, (2) will remain his stock of domestic money. However, he can also convert part or all of it into foreign exchange. In what follows we analyse the simultaneous determination of the optimal portfolio and labour-consumption choice.

The type of government regulation of foreign exchange described in the introduction is modelled as follows. Each conversion of domestic money to foreign exchange and vice versa involves the cost of b units of the aggregate good. The size of b is determined by the government, but for the individual it is given. Because of this cost, conversions will not be performed continuously. Denote thus the time lapse between two of these transactions by τ. This means that an individual makes T/τ such conversions during a T-period. We abstract from the difficulty that arises from T/τ not being in general an integer.

Let us now examine what happens within a τ-period, defined as the time lapse between two conversions. Since all these periods will be identical at the individual's optimum, consider a τ-period starting at 0 and ending at τ. Given the assumption that consumption is non-storable, consumption at each t must be purchased at the same t. The total nominal cost of these purchases in domestic money is $c\int_0^\tau p(t)\mathrm{d}t$.

Therefore this amount of domestic money has to be held at time 0. For the sake of simplicity, and denoting the instantaneous inflation rate by Π, the price level $p(t)$ is linearly approximated *within a τ-period* by $p(t) \doteqdot 1+\Pi t$ (instead of $p(t)=e^{\Pi t}$, recalling that $p(0)$ was normalised to unity).[5] Therefore, the individual needs the amount

$$c\int_0^\tau p(t)\mathrm{d}t \doteqdot c\tau(1+\Pi\tau/2)$$

of domestic money at time 0. Since by the very definition of a τ-period one financial transaction is made in each τ-period, the individual also incurs a real cost of b. Recall from (2) that the salary received at time 0 is $(1-\beta)\bar{w}LT$. This salary must suffice for T/τ τ-periods, so that each τ-period is allocated a real amount of $(1-\beta)\bar{w}LT/(T/\tau)=(1-\beta)\bar{w}L\tau$. Thus, the individual budget constraint is

$$c\tau(1+\Pi\tau/2)+b \leqslant (1-\beta)\bar{w}L\tau,$$

which, upon division by τ, becomes

$$c(1+\Pi\tau/2)+b/\tau \leqq (1-\beta)\bar{w}L. \tag{3}$$

Equation (3) has a simple interpretation. It implies that the real cost of c to the individual (namely, $1+\Pi\tau/2$) is greater than the (social) production cost which is one, whenever Π and τ are positive. This difference in the cost is due to the depreciation of the domestic money balances that the individual chooses to hold between a financial transaction and the purchases of c. The average length of time between these two kinds of transactions is $\tau/2$. Since the instantaneous inflation rate is Π, the individual loses on average $\Pi\tau/2$ per unit of consumption. An alternative, more standard interpretation of the price of c can be obtained by considering the average real balances of domestic money that the individual holds. These average real balances are approximated by $(c\tau+0)/2=c\tau/2$. Since Π is the instantaneous depreciation rate of domestic money, the expression $\Pi c\tau/2$ represents the corresponding inflation tax per unit of time.

Notice that in this framework the price of c is determined by the individual: by choosing a lower τ he can bring down the price closer to the social cost which is unity; but in this way the frequency of the financial transactions increases, implying higher transaction costs per unit of time (b/τ). By choosing the optimal τ, the individual simultaneously chooses the privately optimal price of c and the financial transaction costs per unit of time. The individual's problem is thus to choose τ, along with c and L, so as to maximise $u(c, L)$, subject to the budget constraint (3). This yields an indirect utility function $v(\beta, \Pi, b)$, a consumption demand function $c(\beta, \Pi, b)$, a labour supply function $L(\beta, \Pi, b)$, and an optimal length of the τ-period, $\tau(\beta, \Pi, b)$. These functions imply the individual's demand for real balances of domestic money, which on average during a τ-period is

$$c(\beta, \Pi, b)\tau(\beta, \Pi, b)/2.$$

As already mentioned, there is a continuum number (nT) of individuals. The payment day of salaries is uniformly distributed across individuals, so that at each t there is an equal number (n) of individuals receiving their salaries.

Consider now a representative firm. We assume that the payment day of salaries is uniformly distributed across the workers of each firm, so that at each t, there is an equal number of the firm's workers who receive their salaries at this t. We also assume that the buyers are uniformly distributed across firms at each t. Therefore, the inflow and outflow of money of the firm are constant over time and, by the constant-returns-to-scale assumption, they are equal to each other: the gross wage bill is equal to the sales revenue. This set-up of the model has the important implication that the firm's demand for money is zero. It enables us to concentrate our attention on the household demand for money which comprises the total demand for money in this economy.

(b) General Equilibrium and Public Finance

Consider now the government budget constraint. It demands a fixed amount of real resources equivalent to G units of the consumption good per person per unit of time. This expenditure is financed by the revenue from wage taxation and by printing new money. At each t, there are n individuals receiving each a gross nominal salary of $w(t)TL$. Thus, the government's tax revenues at t are $\beta nw(t)TL$ which amounts to $\beta w(t)L$ per capita. Denoting the nominal per capita supply of money at t by $M(t)$, then the government's per capita revenue from printing money at t is $\dot{M}(t)$, where a dot stands for differentiation with respect to time. Thus, the government faces the following budget constraint at each t:

$$p(t)G \leqq \beta w(t)L + \dot{M}(t).$$

Dividing through by $p(t)$ yields (recalling that $w(t) = \bar{w}p(t)$):

$$G \leqq \beta \bar{w} L + \dot{M}(t)/p(t).$$

Since at a steady-state the real per capita supply of money $m \equiv M(t)/p(t)$ is constant, it follows that $\dot{M}(t)/p(t) = \Pi m$ and hence the government budget constraint at each t can be written as

$$G \leqslant \beta \bar{w} L + \Pi m. \tag{4}$$

The resource constraint of the economy (or, equivalently, the commodity market equilibrium condition) is given in per capita terms by

$$c(\beta, \Pi, b) + G + b/\tau(\beta, \Pi, b) \leqslant \bar{w}L(\beta, \Pi, b). \tag{5}$$

The term b/τ on the left-hand side of (5) represents the real cost of the foreign exchange restrictions. Since there are nT individuals, each making one transaction in foreign exchange every τ units of time, it follows that there are nT/τ individuals making such a transaction at each point of time. The total cost per unit of time is bnT/τ and the per capita cost is thus b/τ.

Consider now the equilibrium condition for the demand and supply of domestic money. The per capita real supply was denoted by m. As discussed above, the individual holds an average balance of $c\tau/2$. This average is for a given individual over a τ-period. But notice that in our model, averaging over time for a given individual is the same as averaging over individuals at a given point in time. Hence, $c\tau/2$ is also the per capita real balance of domestic money. Thus, the equilibrium condition for domestic money is

$$m = c(\beta, \Pi, b)\tau(\beta, \Pi, b)/2. \tag{6}$$

Finally, notice that when the individual determines c, τ and L, he implicitly decides on his holding of foreign exchange. By the same reasoning used above, the average holding of foreign exchange by an individual over time equals the average across individuals at each point in time. Hence, the per capita holdings of foreign exchange is constant over time, and is equal, in the steady state, to the per capita stock of foreign exchange that was accumulated in the indefinite past. Thus, the foreign exchange market is in equilibrium. Put differently, the real rate of exchange was determined once and for all in the indefinite past so as to equilibrate the market for foreign exchange.

The government's objective is to maximise the individual's welfare. It determines the tax rate, the money growth rate and the foreign exchange regulations. It has to abide by its budget constraint and to take into account the individual behaviour, as described above. Formally, the government chooses β, Π, b and m so as to maximise the individual's indirect utility function $v(\beta, \Pi, b)$, subject to its budget constraint (4) and the equilibrium conditions (5) and (6). By Walras' Law, one of the latter two equilibrium conditions is redundant. The reader can easily verify that, for instance, (4), (6) and the individual budget constraint (3) imply (5), so that (5) may be deleted.[6] Also, m can be substituted from (6) into (4). Thus, the government's optimisation problem is reduced to: choose β, Π and b so as to solve the problem.

$$\max v(\beta, \Pi, b) \tag{7}$$

subject to:

$$G \leq \beta \bar{w} L(\beta, \Pi, b) + \Pi c(\beta, \Pi, b)\tau(\beta, \Pi, b)/2. \tag{8}$$

Instead of proceeding to the general solution of this optimisation problem, we first adopt in the next section a specific form of the utility function to study the individual response to the government's policy variables (β, Π and b); and use numerical simulation methods in Section IV to obtain some insight into the government's optimisation problem. These numerical results lead us to conjecture some general analytical conclusions about the desirability of various government financing tools. Finally, we prove these conjectures.

III INDIVIDUAL BEHAVIOUR: A SPECIFIC UTILITY FUNCTION

In this section we adopt a Cobb–Douglas utility function in order to be able to study the individual choice of c, L and τ. Specifically, consider the utility function

$$u(c, L)=c^{\alpha}(H-L)^{1-\alpha}, \qquad 0<\alpha<1, \tag{9}$$

where H is the total available leisure per unit of time. With this utility function we are able to obtain explicit solutions for the individual's choice of c, L and τ as functions of the government's policy variables β, Π and b.

The budget constraint (3) can be rewritten as

$$c(1+\Pi\tau/2)+(1-\beta)\bar{w}(H-L)\leqq(1-\beta)\bar{w}H-b/\tau.$$

Then, for a given τ, we can interpret $(1-\beta)\bar{w}H-b/\tau$ as the individual's net full-income, and $1+\Pi\tau/2$ and $1(-\beta)\bar{w}$ as the prices for the commodities c and $(H-L)$, respectively. Thus, for a given τ, the choices of c and $(H-L)$ are given by the standard Cobb–Douglas demand expressions:

$$c=\frac{\alpha[(1-\beta)\bar{w}H-b/\tau]}{1+\Pi\tau/2}$$

$$H-L=\frac{(1-\alpha)[(1-\beta)\bar{w}H-b/\tau]}{(1-\beta)\bar{w}}=(1-\alpha)\left[H-\frac{b}{(1-\beta)\bar{w}\tau}\right]. \tag{10}$$

Substituting (10) into the utility function (9) yields the expression

$$\alpha^{\alpha}(1-\alpha)^{1-\alpha}[1+\Pi\tau/2]^{-\alpha}[(1-\beta)\bar{w}]^{-(1-\alpha)}[(1-\beta)\bar{w}H-b/\tau], \tag{11}$$

in which τ is the only remaining choice variable. By maximising now (11) with respect to τ, we find the individual's choice of the financial transactions period:

$$\tau(\beta, \Pi, b)=\frac{(1+\alpha)b}{2\alpha(1-\beta)\bar{w}H}+\left[\frac{(1+\alpha)^2b^2}{4\alpha^2(1-\beta)^2\bar{w}^2H^2}+\frac{2b}{\alpha\Pi(1-\beta)\bar{w}H}\right]^{\frac{1}{2}} \tag{12}$$

The choices of c and L, namely the functions $c(\beta, \Pi, b)$ and $L(\beta, \Pi, b)$, respectively, are then obtained by substituting the expression for τ in (12) into (10).

From (12) it is straightforward to obtain standard results in the inventory-theoretic approach to the demand for money that:

$$\frac{\partial\tau}{\partial\beta}>0, \quad \frac{\partial\tau}{\partial\Pi}<0 \quad \text{and} \quad \frac{\partial\tau}{\partial b}>0. \tag{13}$$

Thus, a rise in the net wage (i.e. a fall in β) lowers τ. Intuitively, as the individual has a higher net income, the stream of consumption rises and with it the need to hold more domestic money; therefore, the individual's exposure to the inflation tax increases which induces him to accelerate the frequency of conversion of foreign exchange.[7] Similarly, a rise in Π also lowers the length of the holding time of domestic money, while an increase in the cost of converting foreign exchange (b) increases it.

By multiplying (12) by Π, we can see that $\partial(\Pi\tau)/\partial\Pi>0$. Thus, it follows from (10) that $\partial c/\partial\Pi<0$ (recall from (13) that $\partial\tau/\partial\Pi<0$). That is, a higher inflation reduces consumption. Also, by dividing (12) by b, we can see that $\partial(\tau/b)/\partial b<0$, so that $\partial(b/\tau)/\partial b>0$. Hence, $\partial c/\partial b<0$, i.e. an increase in the financial transaction cost lowers consumption. The effect of a change in the tax rate β on c is indeterminate.

Since $\partial\tau/\partial\Pi<0$, it follows from (10) that $\partial L/\partial\Pi>0$, i.e. a higher inflation rate induces more labour supply. By multiplying (12) by $1-\beta$, we can see that $\partial[\tau(1-\beta)]/\partial(1-\beta)>0$. Thus, $\partial L/\partial(1-\beta)<0$. This is quite a surprising result, as it implies a backward-bending labour supply curve. We have already seen that $\partial(b/\tau)/\partial b>0$ and hence it follows from (12) that $\partial L/\partial b>0$: a higher financial transaction cost induces more labour supply.

We also observe that all the three policy variables (β, Π and b) reduce the individual utility. This follows from the envelope theorem which implies that

$$\frac{\partial v}{\partial\beta}=-\theta\bar{w}L, \quad \frac{\partial v}{\partial\Pi}=-\theta c\tau/2 \quad \text{and} \quad \frac{\partial v}{\partial b}=-\frac{\theta}{\tau},$$

where $\theta>0$ is the marginal utility of income (i.e. the Lagrangian multiplier associated with the individual's constrained optimisation problem of maximising $u(C, L)$, subject to the budget constraint (3)).

Finally, the length of the τ-period depends on the structure of preferences over the real variables – consumption and leisure. This is seen immediately from (12) where the right-hand side depends on α which is a parameter in the utility function; furthermore, the formula itself for τ will change if we employ a utility function different from the Cobb–Douglas.

IV OPTIMAL FINANCING OF THE BUDGET: THE DESIRABILITY OF INFLATION

The numerical simulation of the government optimisation problem (7)–(8) is performed using the utility function (9). For this purpose, we assume that H is equal to 24 hours per day and that $\alpha = \frac{1}{3}$ which means that roughly $(1\frac{1}{3}) \times 24 = 16$ hours per day are consumed as leisure time. The value of $\bar{w}$ employed is approximately the average wage in Israel during the fiscal year 1980/81, IS 25 per hour (1 dollar = IS 6). Among other things, we wanted to see how the various government control variables – β, Π and b – vary with the size of budget – G. For this reason, we considered various levels of G ranging from IS 40 to IS 100 per person per day, i.e. from approximately 20 per cent to 50 per cent of the national income.

The numerical results are depicted in Table 4.1. This table shows that inflationary finance is never optimal. We always get $b = \Pi = 0$ and wage taxation as the only source of revenues. As the size of the government's budget (G) increases, β rises, L stays constant and c falls a shekel for a shekel of G. This means that the resources needed for the government are provided by lowering consumption rather than by increasing work effort.[8] Notice that with $\Pi = b = 0$, τ is indeterminate and irrelevant – τ enters the equations of the model, (3) and (8), only through the product $\Pi\tau$ or the quotient b/τ which are both zero. When $\Pi = b = 0$, both the private sector and the government are indifferent between the use of domestic or foreign currency. The government does not tax nor regulate the transactions sector of the economy. The budget is satisfied by taxing labour only. This solution can be seen as corresponding to either the adoption of a stable-valued foreign currency for domestic use – the dollarisation scheme considered by the Israeli treasury in 1983 – or to a fixed exchange rate

Table 4.1

G	C	L	β	Π	b
40	160	8	0.2	0	0
60	140	8	0.3	0	0
80	120	8	0.4	0	0
100	100	8	0.5	0	0

against such a currency, coupled with a completely passive monetary policy.

The question naturally arises whether this result about the inefficiency of inflationary finance, which we observed for the Cobb–Douglas utility function and certain parameter values, is a more general result. The answer is in the affirmative under quite reasonable assumptions. The feature of the analysis – which seems fairly general – that is primarily responsible for this result is the type of money demand function generated by the model. As indicated by equation (6), money demand is proportional to consumption (in general, it could be some other economic activity variable). This proportionality holds for any transaction frequency and, in particular, for the optimal one. Because of this link, a tax on money holdings amounts to an implicit tax on consumption.[9] This is reflected in the private budget constraint (3), where the term $1+\Pi\tau/2$ multiplies c. Aside from some wealth effects (see below), the distortionary effects of the inflation tax on the relative price and the revenue collected by the government are the same as those under an appropriate explicit tax rate. However, the inflation tax is accompanied by a waste of resources in transaction costs. This waste directly reduces welfare, but in our second-best world it may have some desirable indirect effect: The loss of income induces more labour supply – assuming that leisure is a normal good. As the labour supply increases, so do wage tax revenues; this in turn allows the government to lower the wage tax rate and thereby improve welfare.

However, as we see below, the condition for the indirect effect to dominate is highly implausible and therefore we can rule out inflationary finance under quite weak assumptions.

To formalise this result, let us compare welfare in two situations. One in which there is no inflation ($b^*=\Pi^*=0$) and all revenues are raised by a wage tax, i.e. $\beta=\beta^*$, such that $\beta^*\bar{w}L=G$. The other is an inflationary finance case characterised by $b=\tilde{b}>0$, $\Pi=\tilde{\Pi}>0$ and $\beta=\bar{\beta}$.

Consider first the inflationary finance case. Given $\bar{\beta}$, $\tilde{\Pi}$, $\tilde{b}$ and $\tilde{\tau}=\tau(\bar{\beta}, \tilde{\Pi}, \tilde{b})$, the consumer budget constraint can be written as

$$c(1+\tilde{\Pi}\tilde{\tau}/2)+\tilde{b}/\tilde{\tau}\leqq(1-\bar{\beta})\bar{w}L.$$

Putting $\tilde{\gamma}\equiv 1+\tilde{\Pi}\tilde{\tau}/2$, and dividing by $\tilde{\gamma}$, this constraint is transformed to

$$c\leqq(1-\bar{\beta})\bar{w}L-\tilde{b}/\tilde{\tau}\tilde{\gamma}, \tag{3'}$$

where $1-\tilde{\beta}=(1-\hat{\beta})/\tilde{\gamma}$, and $\tilde{\beta}$ can be interpreted as the inflation adjusted tax rate. The consumer welfare is then $V((1-\tilde{\beta})\bar{w}, \ -\tilde{b}/\tilde{\tau}\tilde{\gamma})$, where V is the standard indirect utility function which depends on the net wage $(1-\tilde{\beta})\bar{w}$ and the 'non-wage income' $-\tilde{b}/\tilde{\tau}\tilde{\gamma}$. By subtracting (3′) from the resource constraints (5), we can write the government's budget constraint (8) as

$$G+\tilde{b}(\tilde{\gamma}-1)/\tilde{\tau}\tilde{\gamma}\leqq\tilde{\beta}\bar{w}L \tag{8′}$$

The point to be made from (3′) and (8′) is that the inflationary case can be interpreted as follows: There is a wage tax at the rate $\tilde{\beta}$ and a lump sum tax of $\tilde{b}/\tilde{\tau}\tilde{\gamma}$. The proceeds from this lump sum tax are destroyed, as they do not appear as a source of revenue to the government. Moreover, the government incurs an extra cost of $\tilde{b}(\tilde{\gamma}-1)/\tilde{\tau}\tilde{\gamma}$ (recall that $\tilde{\gamma}>1$), equalling the difference between the transaction cost $\tilde{b}/\tilde{\tau}$ and the lump-sum tax $\tilde{b}/\tilde{\tau}\tilde{\gamma}$.

Consider now the case without inflationary finance, i.e., $b^*=\Pi^*=0$. In this case the individual budget constraint (3) and the government budget constraint (8) can be written as:

$$c\leqq(1-\beta^*)\bar{w}L=(1-\beta^*)\bar{w}L-b^*/\tilde{\tau}\tilde{\gamma}. \tag{3″}$$

$$G+b^*(\tilde{\gamma}-1)/\tilde{\tau}\tilde{\gamma}\leqq\beta^*\bar{w}L. \tag{8″}$$

In this case – unlike the inflationary finance case – notice that the term $b^*(\tilde{\gamma}-1)/\tilde{\tau}\tilde{\gamma}$ is equal to zero, so that the government does not incur any extra cost.

We want then to find when

$$V((1-\beta^*)\bar{w}, \quad -b^*/\tilde{\tau}\tilde{\gamma})>V((1-\tilde{\beta})\bar{w}, \quad -\tilde{b}/\tilde{\tau}\tilde{\gamma}). \tag{14}$$

In other words, we ask when an increase in lump-sum taxation from $b^*/\tilde{\tau}\tilde{\gamma}=0$ to $\tilde{b}/\tilde{\tau}\tilde{\gamma}>0$, coupled with a change in the wage tax rate from β^* to $\tilde{\beta}$ reduces welfare.

To proceed further we have to find the relationship between b and β as implied by the government's budget constraint. For this purpose, write the latter constraint as

$$G+b(\tilde{\gamma}-1)/\tilde{\tau}\tilde{\gamma}\leqslant\beta\bar{w}L((1-\beta)\bar{w}, \quad -b/\tilde{\tau}\tilde{\gamma})$$

and employ total differentiation to get:

$$\frac{d\beta}{db} = \frac{\beta\bar{w}L_2/\tilde{\tau}\tilde{\gamma} + (\tilde{\gamma}-1)/\tilde{\tau}\tilde{\gamma}}{\bar{w}L - \beta\bar{w}^2L_1}, \tag{15}$$

where L_i is the partial derivative of $L = L((1-\tilde{\beta})\bar{w}, -\tilde{b}\tilde{\tau}/\tilde{\gamma})$ with the respect to its ith argument, $i = 1,2$.

Clearly, (14) holds if

$$\frac{dV}{db} < 0 \tag{16}$$

everywhere between $b = b^*$ and $b = \tilde{b}$, when (15) is taken into consideration. Employing Roy's identity, we find that

$$\frac{dV}{db} = -V_1\bar{w}\frac{d\beta}{db} - \frac{V_2}{\tilde{\tau}\tilde{\gamma}} = -V_2\left(\bar{w}L\frac{d\beta}{db} + \frac{1}{\tilde{\tau}\tilde{\gamma}}\right), \tag{17}$$

where V_i is the partial derivative of V with respect to its ith argument, $i = 1, 2$. Since V_2 is positive, it follows from (17) that (16) holds if:

$$\bar{w}L\frac{d\beta}{db} + \frac{1}{\tilde{\tau}\tilde{\gamma}} > 0. \tag{18}$$

Substituting (15) into (18) yields

$$\frac{\beta\bar{w}^2LL_2 + \bar{w}L(\tilde{\gamma}-1) + \bar{w}L - \beta\bar{w}^2L_1}{\bar{w}L - \beta\bar{w}^2L_1} > 0. \tag{19}$$

We assume that $\partial(\beta\bar{w}L)/\partial\beta = \bar{w}L - \beta\bar{w}^2L_1 > 0$ for all values of β in the relevant range, i.e., we assume that all relevant tax rates correspond to the upward sloping part of the 'Laffer curve'. (The case in which it is violated is mentioned below in the concluding section.) Employing the Hicks–Slutsky equation $L_1^c = L_1 - LL_2$, where L_1^c is the compensated wage derivative of L, (19) becomes:

$$-\beta\bar{w}^2L_1^c + \tilde{\gamma}\bar{w}L > 0. \tag{20}$$

Since $\tilde{\gamma} > 1$, it follows that (20) holds if $-\beta\bar{w}^2L_1^c + \bar{w}L > 0$. The latter condition can be written in two alternative formulations:

$$\sigma < (1-\beta)/\beta, \tag{21a}$$

or

$$(\beta\bar{w})(\beta\bar{w})L_1^c/2<\beta\bar{w}L/2, \tag{21b}$$

where $\sigma\equiv L_1^c\bar{w}(1-\beta)/L$ is the compensated wage elasticity of the labour supply.

Inequality (21) is a sufficient condition for ruling out inflationary finance. It always holds at low tax rates for then $(1-\beta)/\beta\rightarrow+\infty$. Thus, inflationary finance is never desirable under a 'small' government. More generally, inflationary finance is not desirable whenever the excess burden of wage taxation is not extremely high. This can be seen either from (21a) or from (21b). In (21a), a low compensated elasticity (σ) and/or a low marginal tax rate (β) are indicators of low excess burden. In (21b), the term $(\beta\bar{w})(\beta\bar{w})L_1^c/2$ is approximately the excess burden (Harberger's triangle) of wage taxation.[10] Thus, (21b) holds whenever the excess burden does not exceed one-half of the tax revenues.

CONCLUDING REMARKS

The question addressed in this paper is whether it is socially desirable that the government imposes restrictions on foreign exchange in order to make possible the taxation of domestic money by inflation. Under some reasonable assumptions, the answer obtained is negative. As discussed in the previous section, the basic reasoning behind this result is that inflation works as an indirect tax on the economic activity affecting money demand – consumption, in the present case. A financing scheme that replaces the inflationary tax for a higher direct taxation of that activity or a closely related one – as income in the present case – saves transaction costs associated with inflation and hence it is likely to be optimal.

The simplicity of this result has to do with the uniform flow of consumption resulting from the particular form of utility functions adopted. In a more general case, consumption during the transaction period would vary. Under inflation the individual would tend to concentrate consumption purchases after a financial transaction. An additional, intertemporal, distortion of inflation would then be present. For this reason, one can conjecture that in the general case inflationary finance is likely to be even less desirable.

In order to put the main result of this paper in an appropriate perspective, we want to discuss here some additional considerations that can potentially make the case for inflationary finance stronger. Consider a set-up in which the demand for money depends on total private income, but only part of it is generated in activities reported to the tax authority. In this case, inflation works as an indirect tax on total income, while the direct income tax applies practically to only a part of it. The substitution of the inflation tax for a higher explicit income tax may be undesirable in this set-up, because then one type of activity – that unreported – goes completely untaxed. This is likely to aggravate the non-optimality of the relative tax burdens of the reported and unreported activities.

Also, the present discussion assumed no tax-collection costs. This assumption is clearly appropriate with respect to the inflation tax because it is collected simply by printing more money under negligible costs. With regard to the income tax, this assumption is more of an approximation. Consider, for example, an underdeveloped type of economy in which the accounting practices and the administrative apparatus necessary to enforce an efficient income taxation are not well developed. In this case the government may face increasing tax collection costs that could generate an interior solution involving inflationary finance. However, it seems to us that this type of consideration may not be important in more modern economies.

Another case for inflationary finance can be made when the assumption that the optimal tax rate β^* corresponds to the upward sloping part of the Laffer curve is violated. Namely, government spending can be increased to a point where the maximum amount of revenue that can be raised by income taxation is less than government spending. Then, if there is no other tax available, inflation has to be activated. This result was not obtained in Section IV (see Table 4.1) because under the Cobb–Douglas utility function revenue from the income tax is always increasing – of course, for rates lower than 100 per cent. In this respect, recall that throughout this paper government spending was assumed exogenously given. If G is made endogenous, the marginal benefit from it would be compared with the marginal distortion of taxation. When only inflationary finance can increase total revenue, its heavier welfare cost will make a level of G beyond the maximum revenue from the income tax less likely to be desirable.

ACKNOWLEDGEMENTS

We wish to thank our colleagues Eitan Berglas and Allan Drazen with whom we had some useful conversations.

Financial support from the Horowitz Institute for Developing Countries is gratefully acknowledged.

Notes

1. Feige and Parkin (1971) and Jovanovic (1982) also addressed normative issues related to inflation. The fundamental difference between our approach and theirs is that in our model the revenues from printing money (the inflation tax) are used, together with other distortionary sources of revenues to finance government consumption, whereas in theirs the proceeds from inflation are returned to the consumer in a lump sum. In our opinion, the practical relevance of discussing the optimal inflation rate is questionable when one ignores the government's need to raise revenues.
2. In principle, the analysis could be extended to incorporate an endogenous payments period, as in Barro (1970). However, for the present purposes we do not see any possible additional insights that would be obtained in such an extension.
3. See also Barro (1970):

   > as inflation intensifies, employees are ... motivated to concentrate expenditures closer to payment times in order to reduce money holdings and incur smaller losses from inflation. However, a preliminary model of this behaviour suggests that the general relationship between average money holdings and the rate of inflation is not materially altered by a consideration of this motive.

4. The constancy of $c(\cdot)$ and $L(\cdot)$ may be obtained by assuming that (1) takes the special form

   $$U(c(\cdot), L(\cdot)) = u(\min\{c(t)/0 \leqslant t \leqslant T\}, \max\{L(t)/0 \leqslant t \leqslant T\}). \tag{1a}$$

5. This approximation amounts to calculating a simple inflation rate *within* a τ-period instead of a compounded rate. Given that realistic values of τ are relatively small, this approximation, which is a common practice in the inventory-theoretic approach to money demand, seems quite reasonable.
6. Strictly speaking, since the indidivual budget constraint (3) and the money market equilibrium condition (6) were obtained by some approximations, then Walras Law does not have to hold in general. However, in our case Walras Law does hold because we simply chose the approximations in (3) and (6) in such a way as to maintain Walras Law. The reader

can in a straightforward way verify that Walras Law will, of course, hold when (3) and (6) are replaced by their exact forms, namely

$$c(e^{\Pi\tau}-1)/\Pi\tau+\beta/\tau\leqq(1-\beta)\bar{w}L$$

and

$$m=\frac{1}{\tau}c\int_0^\tau\left(\int_t^\tau e^{\Pi(s-t)}ds\right)dt,$$

respectively.

7. This result hinges upon our assumption that the transaction cost b is not in leisure time and therefore it does not rise with the net wage.
8. Given that $b=\Pi=0$, this result follows from the assumption of Cobb–Douglas preferences which yield a perfectly inelastic labour supply.
9. Notice that we do not have a consumption tax, but a wage tax can achieve a similar effect as a consumption tax, and the same one when $b=0$.
10. The approximation is exact when L_1^c is constant.

REFERENCES

Barro, R. J. (1970) 'Inflation, the Payments Period, and the Demand for Money', *Journal of Political Economy*, vol. 78, pp. 1228–63.

Baumol, W. J. (1952) 'The Transactions Demand for Cash: An Inventory Theoretic Approach', *Quarterly Journal of Economics*, vol. 66, pp. 545–66.

Bryant, J. and N. Wallace (1980) 'A Suggestion for Further Simplifying the Theory of Money', Federal Reserve Bank of Minneapolis, Staff Report 62.

Drazen, A. (1979) 'The Optimal Rate of Inflation Revisited', *Journal of Monetary Economics*, vol. 5, pp. 231–48.

Feige, E. L. and M. Parkin (1971) 'The Optimal Quantity of Money, Bonds, Commodity Inventories and Capital', *American Economic Review*, vol. 61, pp. 335–49.

Fischer, S. (1982). 'Seigniorage and the Case for a National Money', *Journal of Political Economy*, vol. 90, pp. 295–313.

Grossman, H. I. and A. J. Policano (1975) 'Money Balances, Commodity Inventories, and Inflationary Expectations', *Journal of Political Economy*, vol. 83, pp. 1093–112.

Helpman, E. and E. Sadka (1979) 'Optimal Financing of the Government's Budget: Taxes, Bonds, or Money', *American Economic Review*, vol. 69, pp. 152–60.

Jovanovic, B. (1982) 'Inflation and Welfare in the Steady State', *Journal of Political Economy*, vol. 90, pp. 561–77.

Phelps, E. S. (1973) 'Inflation in the Theory of Public Finance', *Swedish Journal of Economics*, vol. 75, pp. 67–82.

Siegel, J. (1978) 'Notes on the Optimal Taxation and the Optimal Rate of Inflation', *Journal of Monetary Economics*, vol. 4, pp. 297–305.

Tobin, J. (1956) 'The Interest Elasticity of the Transactions Demand for Cash', *Review of Economics and Statistics*, vol. 38, pp. 241–7.

Comments on Zvi Hercowitz and Efraim Sadka Optimal Currency Substitution Policy and Public Finance by Jacob Frenkel

Recent experience in various countries has demonstrated that a heavy reliance on inflationary finance provides strong incentives for the emergence of currency substitution. This substitution arises as asset holders attempt to protect themselves from the inflation tax by substituting foreign currencies for the depreciating domestic currency. Faced with the erosion of their inflationary-tax base many governments have imposed various foreign exchange controls in order to raise the cost and slow down the process of currency substitution.

In their paper 'On Optimal Currency Substitution Policy and Public Finance' Zvi Hercowitz and Efraim Sadka deal with one of the key questions raised by the process of inflationary finance. They provide an analytical framework for the determination of optimal policies concerning the rates of income tax, inflation and currency substitution. Their model provides a very useful blend of theorising along the lines of macroeconomics and public finance. Their paper is clear and thorough and the analysis represents a useful addition to this important body of knowledge. One of the central messages of the analysis is that governments should refrain from imposing restrictions on foreign exchange and that they should also refrain from using inflation tax as means of public finance. Rather, in the framework developed by Hercowitz and Sadka, government spending should be financed only by an income tax. In order to put this important proposition in perspective and to discuss its generality my comments focus on the key factor responsible for this result.

Hercowitz and Sadka assume that the cost of income tax collection is zero and that the inflation tax is accompanied by a waste of resources associated with the cost of transactions. Using a Cobb–Douglas utility function and simulating for the optimal values of the income tax rate, (β), the inflation rate (Π) and the (resource) cost of conversions between domestic and foreign currencies (b), they show (in Table 4.1) that at the optimum $b=\Pi=0$ and the entire budget is financed through income tax. Thus, Hercowitz and Sadka show that, at the optimum, both the government and the private sector are indifferent between the use of foreign and domestic currencies. It is relevant to note, however, that once this optimum obtains then as long as the rate of inflation is zero, the maximised level of utility does not depend on the cost of conversion, b. If, for example, the authorities prohibited any substitution of foreign for domestic currency (by setting $b=\infty$) then as long as $\Pi=0$ the level of utility would still reach the same maximum value as it reached with $b=0$. In what follows, in order to obtain insights into the role of the cost of fiscal management, suppose that this maximum level of utility was achieved with $b=\infty$. How much of the government budget should be financed by income tax and how much by inflation tax?

Consider the Cobb–Douglas utility function.

$$U=\alpha \ln c+(1-\alpha) \ln (H-L) \tag{1}$$

where c denotes that rate of consumption, H denotes the (fixed) number of hours available and L denotes labour supply. Thus, $H-L$ measures the amount of leisure. The private sector's budget constraint is

$$c=(1-\beta)wL-\Pi m \tag{2}$$

where β denotes the income tax rate, w denotes the wage rate, and m denotes real balances. Following Hercowitz and Sadka let the demand for money be proportional to disposable income according to

$$m=(1-\beta)wL. \tag{3}$$

Using (3) in (2) yields the consumption function (2)

$$c=(1-\beta)(1-\Pi)wL. \tag{2'}$$

Substituting (2′) into (1) and maximising utility with respect to L yields equation (4) as the supply of labour:

$$L=\alpha H \tag{4}$$

Substituting (2′) and (4) into (1) yields

$$u^*=A+\alpha \ln (1-\beta)(1-\Pi) \tag{1'}$$

where A denotes a constant

$$A=\alpha \ln w+\alpha \ln \alpha+(1-\alpha) \ln (1-\alpha)+\ln H.$$

In (1′) the asterisk (*) indicates that the utility function incorporates the optimal values of consumption and leisure.

The exogenously given level of government spending G can be financed by income tax, βwL, and by inflation tax, Πm. Thus, using equation (3), the relative share, g, of government spending in wage income ($w\alpha H$) is:

$$g=\frac{G}{w\alpha H}=1-(1-\beta)(1-\Pi), \tag{5}$$

and the optimisation problem amounts to a maximisation of u^* in (1′) with respect to Π and β subject to the government budget constraint (5).

As is evident in this case there is perfect substitution between using income tax or inflation tax to finance the budget. Formally, inspection of (1′) and (5) reveals that in this case the two taxes are symmetric as they appear only as the product $[(1-\beta)(1-\Pi)]$. Thus, as long as the value of this product is given, that is, as long as the budget constraint is satisfied, the level of welfare is independent of the distribution of revenue between income tax and inflation tax. This case of complete symmetry between the two financing sources serves as the benchmark for the subsequent analysis of alternative assumptions on the cost of tax collections. Departures from this benchmark case provide insight into the Hercowitz–Sadka theorem.

Consider the situation in which there is resource cost of income tax collections. Let the cost be proportional to the amount collected. In that case government revenue from income taxes would be $\theta\beta wL$ instead of βwL (where $0<\theta<1$), and its budget constraint becomes $G=\theta\beta wL+\Pi m$. Thus, the relative share, g, becomes

$$g=\theta+(1-\beta)(\Pi-\theta). \tag{5}$$

In order to obtain the optimal values of Π and β we note that the maximisation of u^* with respect to Π and β subject to the government budget constraint (5′) is equivalent to the maximisation of

$$\tilde{u}^*=(1-\beta)(1-\Pi) \tag{6}$$

subject to the constraint that

$$\frac{g-\theta}{\Pi-\theta}=1-\beta,$$

or, equivalently

$$\max \tilde{u}^* = \frac{g-\theta}{\Pi-\theta}(1-\Pi). \tag{6'}$$

As is evident, if $\Pi = 0$ the level of utility is:

$$\tilde{u}^*\big|_{\Pi=0} = 1 - \frac{g}{\theta}$$

whereas if $\beta = 0$, $g = \Pi$ and the level of utility is

$$\tilde{u}^*\big|_{\beta=0} = 1 - g.$$

Thus, a comparison between the utility levels with $\pi = 0$ and $\beta = 0$ shows that, in the present case with $0 < \theta < 1$, the level of utility obtained when there is only inflationary finance and no income tax exceeds the corresponding level obtained when there is only income tax without inflationary finance. Therefore, in this case optimal policies result in a heavy reliance on the inflation tax as the means for government finance.

The difference between this prescription and that of Hercowitz and Sadka stems from the assumption that income tax collections involve resource cost. This cost results in a departure from the symmetric benchmark case towards the extreme in which the entire budget is financed through inflation. In contrast, Hercowitz and Sadka's formulation departs from the symmetric benchmark case in the opposite direction. By assuming that income tax collection is costless while the entire resource cost stems from conversions between domestic and foreign currencies they generate the other extreme outcome in which the entire budget is financed through income tax.

In general, it stands to reason that, when all the means of finance involve resource cost, the optimum outcome will be neither of the two extremes. Rather, the outcome is likely to be an interior one in which both income tax and inflation tax are used as means of government finance; the details of the solution depend on the specification of the relative cost of finance. Hercowitz and Sadka, of course, recognise that the assumption that income tax collection is costless is very important in yielding their proposition but they believe that these costs are relatively insignificant in modern economies. They may well be right. The purpose of this discussion, however, was to highlight the point that the direction of the departures from the neutral-symmetric benchmark case is determined, by and large, by the specific formulation of the relative costs of alternative sources of government revenue.

In conclusion it is worthwhile reiterating the opening remarks. This paper approaches the analysis of inflationary finance in just the right way. Viewing the problem of the inflation tax as a problem of public finance, the authors provided a very relevant and useful integration of elements from macroeconomic theory and public finance theory. Such an integration yields a natural and a convenient framework for the analysis of these important issues.

Note

1. I am indebted to Joshua Aizenmann for useful discussions.

5 Inflation and the Government Budget Constraint

Thomas Sargent and Neil Wallace

I INTRODUCTION

In Sargent and Wallace (1973), we created a rational expectations model of the bivariate inflation-money creation process by solving the 'inverse optimal predictor problem' for Cagan's (1956) adaptive expectations scheme. Our model was constructed by working backwards and finding a bivariate process for inflation and money creation that implied both that Cagan's portfolio balance equation held and that adaptive expectations were rational.[1] That model is 'successful' in several ways. First, the model explains the pattern of Granger causality in Cagan's data, in which inflation Granger causes money creation, but not vice versa. Second, a version of the model predicts the pattern of correlations across countries between Cagan's estimates of λ and α (see Sargent and Wallace, 1973). Third, the model predicts that the residuals in the regression equation fit by Cagan will be random walks, which explains the very high serial correlation that Cagan actually encountered (see Sargent, 1977). Fourth, the model predicts a pattern of results obtained by Rodney Jacobs (1975) when he reversed the direction of regression in Cagan's equation (see Sargent, 1976).

Against these 'successes', the Sargent–Wallace model suffers some notable 'failures'. First, the model implies that both inflation and real balances will behave like processes with the highest autoregressive root being unity, so that while both may drift, they would not be expected to move systematically in one direction over time. However, for six out of the seven hyperinflations studied by Cagan, there is a noticeable tendency for real balances to fall and inflation to rise during the course of the hyperinflation. Figure 5.1(a)–(g) graph the

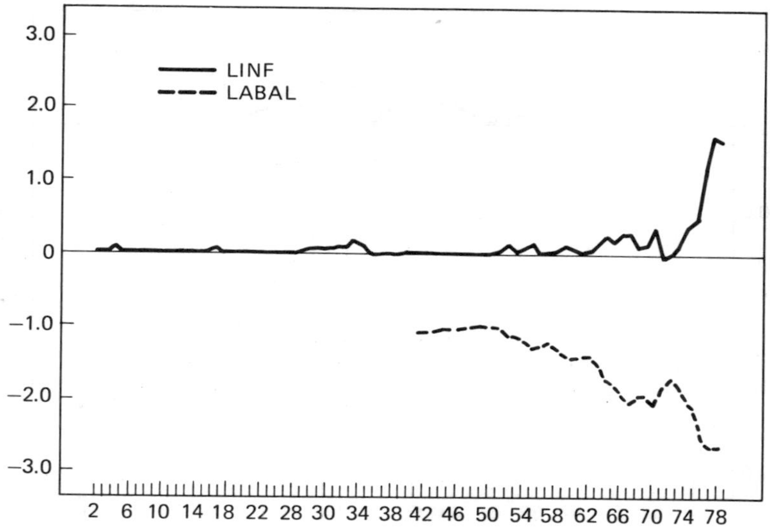

FIGURE 5.1a *German hyperinflation: log real balances, log P_t/P_{t-1} [inflation: 1917* VI–1923 II; real balances: 1920 IX–*1923* II*]*.

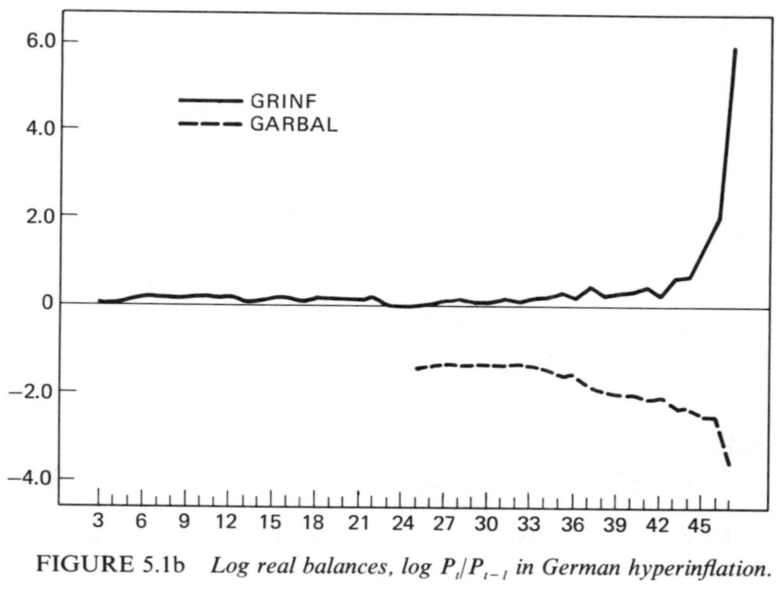

FIGURE 5.1b *Log real balances, log P_t/P_{t-1} in German hyperinflation.*

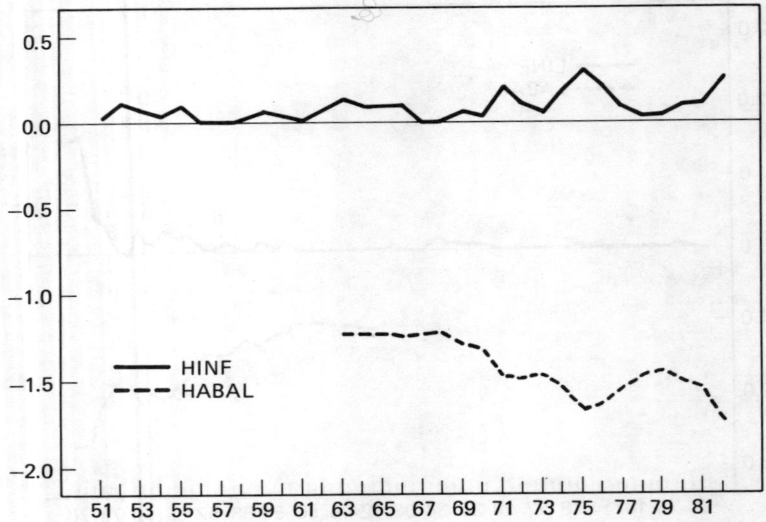

FIGURE 5.1c *Log real balances, log P_t/P_{t-1} in first Hungarian hyperinflation.*

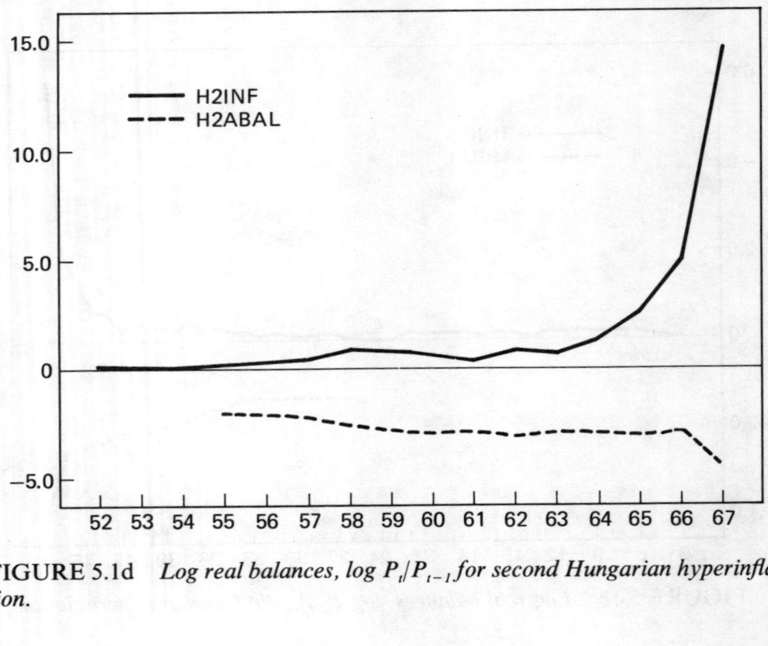

FIGURE 5.1d *Log real balances, log P_t/P_{t-1} for second Hungarian hyperinflation.*

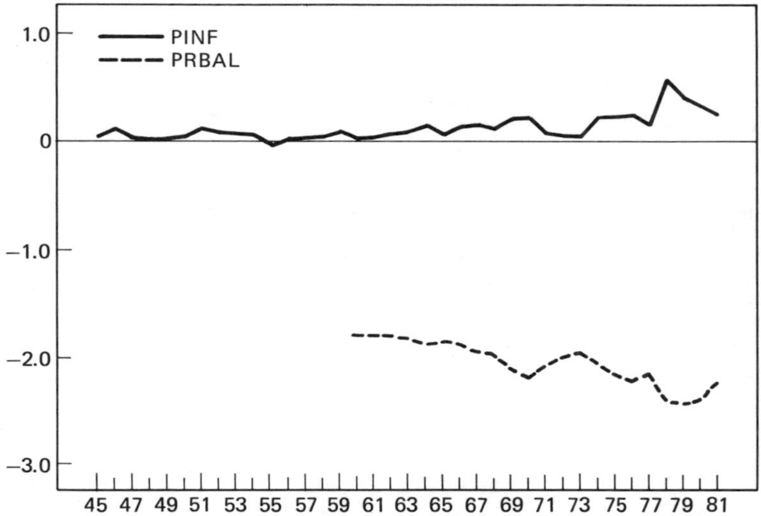

FIGURE 5.1e *Log real balances, and log P_t/P_{t-1} for Polish hyperinflation.*

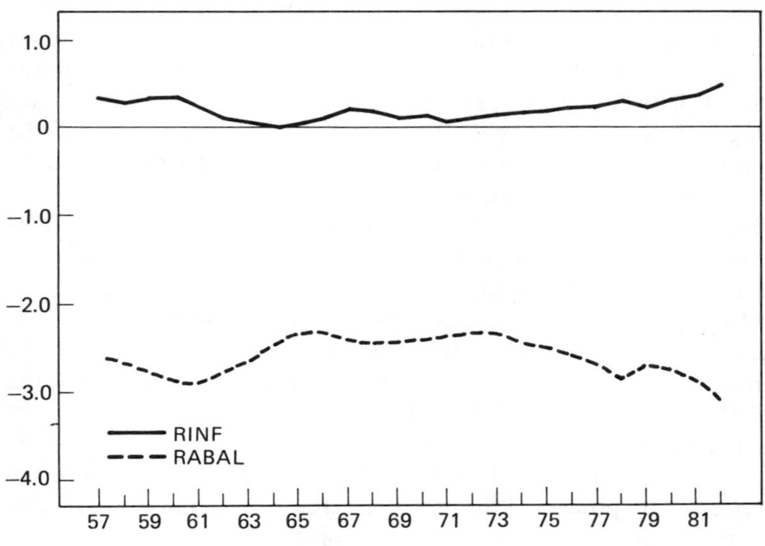

FIGURE 5.1f *Log real balances, and log P_t/P_{t-1} for Russian hyperinflation.*

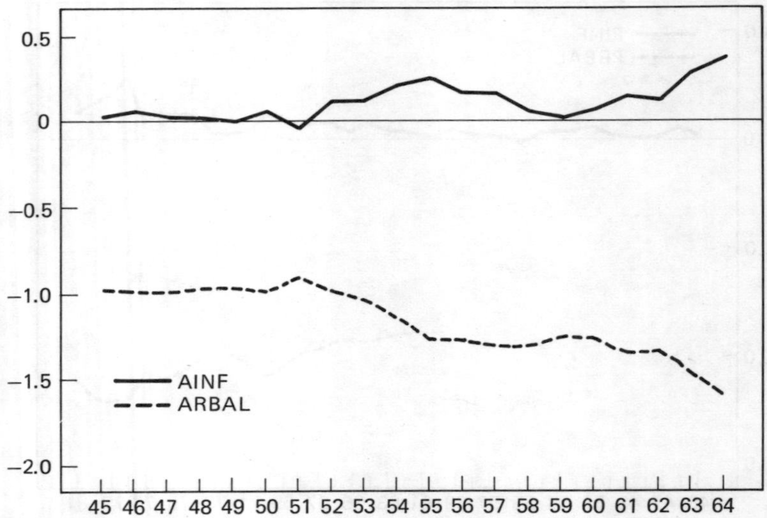

FIGURE 5.1g *Log real balances, and log P_t/P_{t-1} for Austrian hyperinflation.*

data. The apparent exception to this general tendency is Russia. The original Sargent–Wallace model does not explain this general pattern.

Second, there is a long-standing claim, which Cagan's estimates in his Figure 9 support, that the hyperinflations eventually proceeded at rates of inflation that exceeded the seignorage-maximising stationary average inflation rates. (Again, Russia seems to be an exception to the general pattern in Cagan's table.) Our original model does not shed any light on this phenomenon.

Third, the model is weak in terms of economic motivation because it posits a stochastic process for money creation that was discovered on the statistical grounds that it solved the inverse optimal predictor problem. We argued informally that the extensive feedback from inflation to money creation embodied in this stochastic process might be interpreted as reflecting a feedback from prices through the government's budget constraints that would arise if the government were to attempt to finance a constant deficit through money creation. This heuristic argument is insufficient to permit interpreting the money creation process of the model in terms of economic parameters appearing in the government's budget constraint.

This paper describes a model that is designed to account for the two anomalous patterns in the data. The model explicitly incorporates a version of the government's budget constraint and consists of two linear expectational stochastic difference equations. The first equation is a linear version of Cagan's portfolio balance equation under rational expectations and summarises behaviour of the public. The second equation is the government's budget constraint with a particular and convenient parameterisation of the part of the real government deficit that the government chooses to finance by creating base money. An equilibrium of the model is a solution of these two equations. The model possesses what Stanley Fischer (1983) has aptly dubbed a 'slippery side of the Laffer curve'. This feature of the model is the key in giving it the potential to account for the two aforementioned puzzles in the data. Equilibria of the model potentially possess two autoregressive roots, one larger than the other and each larger than unity, which correspond to the two stationary average gross inflation rates that would finance the average real government deficit. That there are two such stationary inflation rates (or tax rates on currency) that finance the deficit is a reflection of the Laffer curve. In time series generated by this model, the higher root will normally come to dominate as time passes. Along such paths, real balances gradually fall and inflation gradually rises on average. Furthermore, the inflation rate usually ends up exceeding the seignorage-maximising rate of inflation.

In constructing and using our model, a number of technical issues had to be confronted. These issues are of interest in their own right, since they occur in a variety of other contexts. Among the issues encountered are the following ones: (a) uniqueness issues involving the connection between, on the one hand, the dimensionality of the equilibria that can be represented as depending on square summable linear combinations of current and lagged values of innovations to 'fundamental' forcing variables; and, on the other hand, the dimensionality of additional solutions depending on 'spurious indicators' (or sunspots); (b) the proper estimation of a model in which there are restrictions across the parameters of initial conditions, the exponentially growing coefficients on trend terms, and the remaining parameters in moving averages of white noises; (c) proper econometric identification and estimation of a model in which a 'spurious indicator' may be impinging on the solution; (d) delineation of the econometric information and operating rules for the government that would be required in order to rule out or to correct non-optimalities associated with 'spurious indicator' equilibria.

The present paper confronts the preceding issues, and deduces the restrictions that our model places on time series data. A planned sequel to this paper will contain estimates of the model from time series drawn from various hyperinflationary episodes.

II THE MODEL

Our model is a stochastic version of the non-random one that we analysed in our earlier paper (Sargent and Wallace, 1981). It is useful briefly to begin by reviewing that model, which consisted of the two equations

$$p(t=\lambda p(t+1)+\gamma h(t) \tag{0a}$$

$$h(t)=\frac{1}{1+n}h(t-1)+\xi p(t) \tag{0b}$$

where $0<\lambda<1$, $\gamma>0$, and where $p(t)$ is the price level at t, $h(t)$ is per capita nominal balances at t, ξ is the constant real government deficit per capita that must be financed by printing new base money, and n is the rate of growth of the economy, assumed constant. It is assumed that

$$0<\xi<\frac{\lambda}{\gamma}\left[\frac{1}{1+n}+\frac{1}{\lambda}-2\sqrt{1/(1+n)\lambda}\right]\equiv\xi \max,$$

where ξ max is the maximal constant deficit which it is feasible to finance through seignorage. Equation (0a) is a linear version of Cagan's portfolio balance equation, while (0b) is the government's budget constraint. The system is imagined to run over the period $t\geqslant 1$, and to be subject to a single initial condition for $h(0)$. There is no initial condition for the price level $p(1)$, it being the job of the model to determine a price path for $p(t)$, $t\geqslant 1$. Letting $\pi(t+1)=p(t+1)/p(t)$, Sargent and Wallace showed that (0a) and (0b) imply the difference equation

$$\pi(t+1)=\varphi-(1/(1+n)\lambda)/\pi(t)$$

where $\varphi\equiv(\lambda^{-1}+(1+n)^{-1}-\xi\gamma/\lambda)$.

The preceding equation is graphed in Figure 5.2, which is taken from Sargent and Wallace (1981). Evidently, there are two stationary points π_1 and π_2 that satisfy $(1+n)^{-1}<\pi_1<\pi_2<\lambda^{-1}$. These stationary points correspond to two alternative stationary levels of the gross inflation rate $p(t+1)/p(t)$ that satisfy portfolio balance and that finance a constant per capita real deficit of ξ. Alternatively, direct calculations on (0) show that the solution is

$$\begin{bmatrix} p(t) \\ h(t) \end{bmatrix} = \begin{pmatrix} \dfrac{\gamma J_1}{1-\lambda\pi_1} \\ J_1 \end{pmatrix} \pi_1^t + \begin{pmatrix} \dfrac{\gamma J_2}{1-\lambda\pi_2} \\ J_2 \end{pmatrix} \pi_2^t$$

where J_1 and J_2 are chosen to satisfy the initial condition for $h(0)$. The absence of an initial condition for $p(1)$ means that there is a variety of choices of (J_1, J_2) pairs that work, each implying a different value for $p(1)$ but satisfying the initial condition for $h(0)$. Evidently, unless $J_2=0$ (which corresponds to a choice of $p(1)$ that starts the system at π_1 in Figure 5.2), the gross inflation rate converges to π_2 as $t\rightarrow\infty$. Figure 5.2 and the preceding equation both embody the 'slippery side

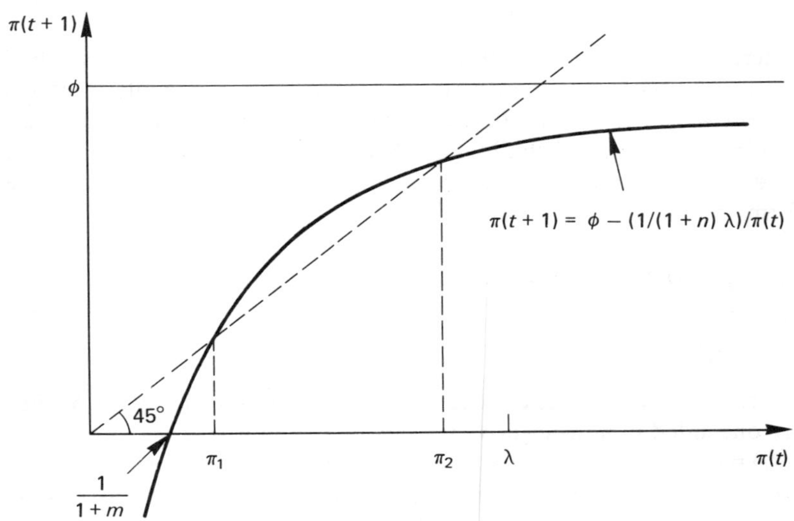

FIGURE 5.2

of the Laffer curve'. There is a continuum of equilibria, indexed by either J_2 or the initial inflation rate $\pi(0)$ or the initial price level $p(1)$. All of the equilibria but one slide towards the higher of the two sustained gross inflation rates π_1 and π_2 that will finance the deficit. Along all of these 'slippery' paths, the inflation rate increases over time, while real balances fall. Also, along these paths, the inflation rate eventually exceeds the revenue-maximising rate. It is these features of these paths that seem potentially to give a version of our model the ability to match the anomalous facts cited at the beginning of this paper.

Our concern now is to study how such non-uniqueness surfaces in a stochastic version of the model. Our reasons for studying a stochastic version of the model are, first, that we want an econometrically implementable version of the model; and second, that presence of imperfect foresight by itself creates the possibility of additional equilibria that are random.

We now study the system

$$p(t)=\lambda E_t p(t+1)+\gamma h(t)+u(t) \tag{1a}$$

$$h(t)=\frac{1}{1+n}h(t-1)+\xi p(t)+\varepsilon(t), \tag{1b}$$

where $0<\gamma<1$, $\gamma>0$, $n\geqslant 0$, $\theta\geqslant 0$, and where $(u(t), \varepsilon(t)$ is a stochastic process with means of zero. We shall begin our analysis of the system at $t=1$. As a normalisation, we shall assume that $(u(s), \varepsilon(s))=0$ for $s\leqslant 0$, and shall take $h(0)$ as an initial condition. For $t\geqslant 1$, we assume that $(u(t), \varepsilon(t))$ has a moving average representation of the form

$$\begin{pmatrix} u(t) \\ \varepsilon(t) \end{pmatrix} = \begin{bmatrix} a_{11}(L) & 0 & 0 \\ 0 & a_{22}(L) & 0 \end{bmatrix} \begin{bmatrix} w_1(t) \\ w_2(t) \\ w_3(t) \end{bmatrix}, \tag{2}$$

where $a_{11}(L)$ and $a_{22}(L)$ are each polynomials in the lag operator that are one-sided in non-negative powers of L, and $w_1(t)=u(t)-E_{t-1}u(t)$, $w_2(t)=\varepsilon(t)-E_{t-1}\varepsilon(t)$. These last equalities imply that $w_1(t)$ is a white noise that is fundamental for $u(t)$ and that $w_2(t)$ is a white noise that is fundamental for $\varepsilon(t)$. In (2), $w_3(t)$ is a serially uncorrelated random process of mean zero that is uncorrelated at all leads and lags with $w_1(s)$ and $w_2(s)$. In particular, we assume that

$$Ew(t)w(t-s)^T = \begin{pmatrix} \sigma_{11}(t) & \sigma_{12}(t) & 0 \\ \sigma_{12}(t) & \sigma_{22}(t) & 0 \\ 0 & 0 & \sigma_{33}(t) \end{pmatrix} \text{for } s=0$$

$$= \begin{pmatrix} 0 & 0 & 0 \\ 0 & 0 & 0 \\ 0 & 0 & 0 \end{pmatrix} \text{for } s \neq 0, \qquad (3)$$

where $w(t)^T = (w_1(t),\ w_2(t),\ w_3(t))^T$. For purposes of estimation, we would impose more structure on $Ew(t)w(t)^T$. In particular, we might eventually assume a version of

$$Ew(t)w(t)^T = \mu^t V \qquad (4)$$

where μ is a positive scalar, and V a positive semidefinite (3×3) matrix with a pattern of zeros conforming with (3).

In (2), $w_3(t)$ plays the role of a 'spurious' indicator that will be permitted to influence the solution for $(p(t),\ h(t))$, but which has no influence on the 'fundamentals' $u(t)$ and $\varepsilon(t)$, the disturbances to portfolio balance and the nominal deficit, respectively.[2] The agents in the model are supposed at time t to see $\{w_1(s),\ w_2(s),\ w_3(s),\ s=1,\ \ldots,\ t;\ p(1),\ h(0)\}$. Equivalently, the agents see $\{u(s),\ \varepsilon(s),\ w_3(s),\ s=1,\ \ldots,\ t;\ p(1),\ h(0)\}$. The econometrician will be imagined to possess a record of $\{p(t),\ h(t),\ t=1,\ \ldots,\ T\}$, from which he tries to estimate the structure.

The entire class of solutions of the pair of stochastic difference equations (1) can be represented in the form

$$\begin{aligned} p(t) &= d(L)w(t) + \pi_1^t F_1 + \pi_2^t F_2 \\ h(t) &= g(L)w(t) + \pi_1^t J_1 + \pi_2^t J_2, \quad t \geq 1 \end{aligned} \qquad (5)$$

where $d(L)$ and $g(L)$ are each particular 1×3 polynomials in non-negative powers of L; F_1, F_2, J_1, and J_2 are particular random variables that represent the initial conditions; and π_1 and π_2 are the same stationary inflation rates mentioned in the introduction. The J_j's are related to the initial condition for $h(0)$ as follows:

$$h(0) = J_1 + J_2. \qquad (6)$$

The parameters F_1 and F_2 can be thought of as determining an initial price level $p(0) = F_1 + F_2$, which is regarded not as an initial condition given to the analyst, but as a random variable representing one dimension of the continuum of possible equilibrium stochastic processes.

To be a solution, $d(L)$ and $g(L)$ must satisfy a set of restrictions as must also F_1 and J_1, and F_2 and J_2. Given our assumption that at t, agents see $\{w_1(s), w_2(s), w_3(s), s=1, \ldots, t; p(1), h(0)\}$, Wiener–Kolmogorov prediction formulas for moving averages in terms of the $w(t)$'s hold for agents' expectations. Cross-equation restrictions in (5) can be derived by assuming (5) to be correct, then applying the Wiener–Kolmogorov prediction theory to (5), substituting the results into (1) and solving for the restrictions.[3] After many computations, this process leads to the following concrete version of (5)

$$\begin{bmatrix} p(t) \\ h(t) \end{bmatrix} = \frac{-\lambda^{-1}L}{(1-\pi_1 L)(1-\pi_2 L)} \times \begin{bmatrix} (1-\frac{1}{1+n}L)(a_{11}(L)-\lambda d_{01}L^{-1}), & -(1-\frac{1}{1+n}L)\lambda d_{02}L^{-1}+\gamma a_{22}(L), & -\lambda d_{03}L^{-1}(1-\frac{1}{1+n}L) \\ \xi(a_{11}(L)-\lambda d_{01}L^{-1}), & -\xi\lambda d_{02}L^{-1}+a_{22}(L)(1-\lambda L^{-1}), & -\xi\lambda d_{03}L^{-1} \end{bmatrix} \begin{bmatrix} w_1(t) \\ w_2(t) \\ w_3(t) \end{bmatrix}$$

$$+\pi_1^t \begin{pmatrix} \dfrac{\gamma J_1}{1-\lambda\pi_1} \\ J_1 \end{pmatrix} + \pi_2^t \begin{pmatrix} \dfrac{\gamma J_2}{1-\lambda\pi_2} \\ J_2 \end{pmatrix}. \tag{7}$$

In (7), $(d_{01}, d_{02}, d_{03}) = d_0$, the vector of coefficients on L^0 in $d(L)$. The parameters π_1 and π_2 are reciprocals of the zeros of the characteristic polynomial of the deterministic part of system (1). That is, (π_1, π_2) satisfy

$$\left[1-\left(\frac{1}{\lambda}+\frac{1}{1+n}-\frac{\gamma\xi}{\lambda}\right)L+\frac{1}{(1+n)\lambda}L^2\right]=(1-\pi_1 L)(1-\pi_2 L),$$

and are given by

$$\pi_1, \pi_2 = \left[(\lambda^{-1}+(1+n)^{-1}-\xi\gamma/\lambda) \pm\sqrt{\left(\left(\lambda^{-1}+(1+n)^{-1}-\frac{\xi\gamma}{\lambda}\right)^2-4/(1+n)\lambda\right)}\right]/2. \tag{8}$$

This formula implies that when

$$0<\xi<\xi_{max}\equiv\frac{\lambda}{\gamma}\left[\frac{1}{1+n}+\frac{1}{\lambda}-2\sqrt{\left(\frac{1}{\lambda(1+n)}\right)}\right],$$

$(1+n)^{-1}<\pi_1<\pi_2<\lambda^{-1}$; that when $\xi=0, \pi_1=(1+n)^{-1}, \pi_2=\lambda^{-1}$; and that when $\xi=\xi_{max}$, $\pi_1=\pi_2=\sqrt{((1+n)^{-1}\lambda^{-1})}$. Here ξ_{max} is the maximal value for the real deficit that is feasible.

Equation (7) represents the entire class of solutions of the stochastic difference equations (1) and (2), so far as their second moments are concerned. Equation (7) represents a solution of (1) and (2) for *any* values of the parameters d_{01}, d_{02}, d_{03}, J_1, and J_2. There is thus a multidimensional continuum of solutions to (1) and (3), a continuum that is conveniently indexed by the list of parameters $(d_{01}, d_{02}, d_{03}, J_2)$. In indexing things in this way, we are regarding the setting of J_1 as reflecting a 'choice of units': note that variations in J_1 affect the entire time paths of $p(t)$ and $h(t)$ proportionately.

From the form of solution (7), it is evident that in general the $(p(t), h(t))$ process becomes of mean exponential order π_2. Components of mean exponential order π_2 are 'activated' in two ways. First, if $J_2\neq 0$, then the final term, which is a constant times π_2^t, occurs in the solution. Second, the presence of $(1-\pi_2 L)$ in the denominators of the polynomials operating on each component of $(w_1(t), w_2(t), w_3(t))$ implies that in general non-zero values of the random variables $w_1(t)$, $w_2(t)$, $w_3(t)$ will cause $(p(t), h(t))$ to become of mean exponential order π_2.

Notice that in general the spurious indicator $w_3(t)$ occurs in the solution for $(p(t), h(t))$ so long as $d_{03}\neq 0$, and that it gives rise to a component of mean exponential order π_2. The moving average in $w_3(t)$ appears in the solution despite the fact that it influences neither of the 'fundamentals' $u(t)$ or $\varepsilon(t)$. In connection with this spurious indicator, there is a technical question about how we measure the extent of the multiplicity of solutions that is introduced by the freedom to make solutions depend on spurious indicators. As the reader can verify, moving averages in any number of 'spurious' white noises $w_4(t)$, $w_5(t)$, ..., can be added to the solution (7), so long as the moving average polynomials on each such white noise are proportional to those on $w_3(t)$; e.g., the polynomials on $w_4(t)$ must be given by

$$\frac{-\lambda^{-1}L}{(1-\pi_1 L)(1-\pi_2 L)}\qquad\begin{bmatrix}-\lambda d_{04}L^{-1}\left(1-\dfrac{1}{1+n}L\right)\\ -\xi\lambda d_{04}L^{-1}\end{bmatrix}$$

This means that given a particular $w_3(t)$ process, so far as sample paths are concerned, an indefinite number of additional solutions can be generated by adding moving averages in additional spurious indicators. However, each of these additional solutions will have population second moments that can be completely represented by equation (7) with $Ew_3(t)^2 = \sigma_{33}(t)$ chosen appropriately. This means that so far as concerns their second moments, all of these additional solutions are observationally equivalent with the solution that we have represented in (7). In this sense, the possibility of adding spurious indicators adds a one-dimensional multiplicity of solutions.[4]

For simplicity, we now focus on the special case in which $a_{11}(L) = 1$, $a_{22}(L) = 1$, so that both $u(t)$ and $\varepsilon(t)$ are white noises. Now within the entire class of solutions given by (7), there is a singular solution which is of exponential order π_1. This particular solution emerges when $(d_{01}, d_{02}, d_{03}, J_2)$ are selected so as to deactivate the π_2 mode of this system. This is accomplished by setting $J_2 = 0$, $d_{03} = 0$, and by selecting d_{01} and d_{02} so that a multiplicative factor of $(1 - \pi_2 L)$ appears in each of the numerator terms in the moving average polynomials operating on $w_1(t)$ and $w_2(t)$, respectively. The values of d_{01}, and d_{02} that accomplish this are given by

$$d_{01} = 1/\lambda\pi_2$$

$$d_{02} = \frac{-\gamma(1+n)}{\lambda(1-\pi_2(1+n))}$$

$$d_{03} = 0$$

$$J_2 = 0. \tag{9}$$

When $(d_{01}, d_{02}, d_{03}, J_2)$ are set at the values given by (9), the solution (7) simplifies to

$$\begin{bmatrix} p(t) \\ h(t) \end{bmatrix} = \frac{\lambda^{-1}}{(1-\pi_1 L)} \begin{bmatrix} \left(1 - \frac{1}{1+n}L\right)\frac{1}{\pi_2}, & -\gamma(1+n)/(1-\pi_2(1+n)) \\ \xi/\pi_2, & \lambda - (\xi\gamma(1+n))/(1-\pi_2(1+n)) \end{bmatrix}$$

$$\begin{bmatrix} w_1(t) \\ w_2(t) \end{bmatrix} + \begin{pmatrix} \frac{J_1\gamma}{1-\lambda\pi_1} \\ J_1 \end{pmatrix} \pi_1^t \tag{10}$$

In this solution, there appears no spurious indicator. Evidently, the solution is of mean exponential order π_1. Unless the parameters (d_{01}, d_{02}, d_{03}, J_2) satisfy (9), the solution is of mean exponential order π_2.

Some observations are in order about interpreting the multiplicity of solutions that we have described. One way to interpret this multiplicity of equilibria is as reflecting the incompleteness of the 'feedback law' (1b) as a description of the evolution of $h(t)$. According to (1b), the monetary authority simply prints whatever new money is required to purchase $[\xi + \varepsilon(t)/p(t)]$ goods per capita at the ruling price level $p(t)$. This is an easy rule to implement, requiring little information about the economy, only the real amount of goods to be purchased and the price level. Furthermore, following this rule assures that the budget is financed.

An alternative way to have set up the model would be as follows. We could have imagined the monetary authority as having selected a contingency plan for the per capita money supply of the form

$$h(t) = g(L)w(t) + J_1\pi_1^t + J_2\pi_2^t, \tag{11}$$

subject to the restrictions that portfolio balance prevails and that the government budget constraint be satisfied, i.e., that (1a) and (1b) hold. These restrict $h(t)$ to obey a law given by the second row of (7), namely

$$h(t) = \frac{\lambda^{-1}L}{(1-\pi_1 L)(1-\pi_2 L)}\{\xi(1-\lambda d_{01}L^{-1})w_1(t) - [\xi\lambda d_{02}L^{-1} + (1-\lambda L^{-1})]w_2(t) - \xi\lambda d_{03}L^{-1}w_3(t)\} + J_1\pi_1^t + J_2\pi_2^t. \tag{12}$$

Equation (12) represents the class of rules or strategies of class (11) among which it is feasible for the monetary authority to choose. The monetary authority's choice among such rules amounts to its choosing values of (d_{01}, d_{02}, d_{03}, and J_2). If the monetary authority has enough information, it is possible for it to select these parameters so that (9) is satisfied, thereby implementing the singular equilibrium described in (10). Notice that to formulate policy in this way, the authority has to know the parameters of the model, and to observe current and lagged $(w_1(t), w_2(t))$. To execute (1b), the authority needs much less information.

From this viewpoint, it seems that if a specification of a policy means specification of a strategy of form (11), then the equilibrium is unique. It also makes sense that uniqueness vanishes when policy is specified in the less restrictive way represented by (1b). In a way, this example illustrates a general point, namely the importance of the specification of strategy spaces in influencing matters of existence and uniqueness of equilibria.

However, the claim for uniqueness of equilibrium under a policy of the form (12) is somewhat artificial because it hinges critically on our having defined an equilibrium as a stochastic process $h(t)$, $p(t)$ that satisfies both (1a) and (1b). In particular, by requiring that (1b) be satisfied, we are insisting that the seignorage raised by money creation finance the real expenditure process $(\xi + \varepsilon(t)/p(t))$. This is a natural requirement to impose in defining equilibrium when the government's rule for creating base money is stated in the form (1b), but is one that seems artificial when the rule for creating base money is of the form of the contingency plan (12). When the rule for creating base money is of the form (12), a natural candidate for a definition of equilibrium is a stochastic process for $(p(t), h(t))$ that satisfies (1a) and (12), with the process for per capita real seignorage being given by $[h(t) - (1/1+n)h/t-1)]/p(t)$. Under this definition of equilibrium, for any choice of $h(t)$ process of the form (12), there is a single equilibrium that satisfies (1b). However, there is a continuum of additional equilibria in which the price level is eventually of mean exponential order λ^{-1}. For such equilibrium, real balances tend to disappear, and (1b) is not satisfied. Such equilibria correspond to the speculative bubble equilibria familiar from overlapping generations models (for example, see Wallace, 1980), which occur when the government sets out an exogenous sequence of nominal balances, there existing many equilibria in which real balances tend to zero with the passage of time. In the present case, the government is once and for all setting forth a contingency plan of the form (12), which involves setting $h(t)$ as a function of exogenous variables, and refusing to feed back on $p(t)$.

From these considerations, we draw the conclusion that it is not easy to devise an operating rule for the government that eliminates the multiplicity of solutions of the form (7) without making the system vulnerable to multiple equilibria, elements of which ironically are eventually even more inflationary that those associated with (7).[5]

III ECONOMETRIC IDENTIFICATION

Despite the existence of many equilibria, the view that the economy is operating along one of them turns out to restrict observations. More precisely, according to 'order conditions', the model represented by (7) is over-identified even when the parameters $(d_{01}, d_{02}, d_{03}, J_2)$ that index the multiplicity of equilibria are among the free parameters to be estimated.[6]

To discuss identification, we shall specialise (4) by setting $\mu = 1$ and assuming that

$$Ew(t)w(t)^T = \begin{pmatrix} \sigma_{11} & \sigma_{12} & 0 \\ \sigma_{21} & \sigma_{22} & 0 \\ 0 & 0 & 1 \end{pmatrix} \equiv V. \tag{13}$$

Our having set $\sigma_{33} = 1$ is merely a normalisation, since clearly only $d_{03}\sqrt{\sigma_{33}}$ is identified (see (7)). We shall consider the special case in which $a_{11}(L) = 1$, $a_{22}(L) = 1$. This is the case in which identification is least likely to occur.

When $a_{11}(L) = a_{22}(L) = a_{22}(L) = 1$, representation (7) becomes

$$\begin{pmatrix} p(t) \\ h(t) \end{pmatrix} = \frac{-\lambda^{-1}}{(1-\pi_1 L)(1-\pi_2 L)} \begin{bmatrix} \left(1 - \frac{1}{1+n}L\right)(L - \lambda d_{01}), & -\left(1 - \frac{1}{1+n}L\right)\lambda d_{02} + \gamma L, & -\lambda d_{03}\left(1 - \frac{1}{1+n}L\right) \\ \xi(L - \lambda d_{01}), & -\xi\lambda d_{02} + (L - \lambda), & -\xi\lambda d_{03} \end{bmatrix}$$

$$\begin{bmatrix} w_1(t) \\ w_2(t) \\ w_3(t) \end{bmatrix} + \pi_1^t \begin{pmatrix} \frac{\gamma J_1}{1-\lambda\pi_1} \\ J_1 \end{pmatrix} + \pi_2^t \begin{pmatrix} \frac{\gamma J_2}{1-\lambda\pi_2} \\ J_2 \end{pmatrix}. \tag{$\tilde{7}$}$$

The form of ($\tilde{7}$) and the vector white noise characterisation of $w(t)$ implies that $(1-\pi_1 L)(1-\pi_2 L)p(t)$ is a second-order moving average process, and that $(1-\pi_1 L)(1-\pi_2 L)h(t)$ is a first-order moving average process that is correlated with $(1-\pi_1 L)(1-\pi_2 L)p(t)$ lagged 0, -1, $+1$, and -2 times (here a lag of -2 refers to $(1-\pi_1 L)(1-\pi_2 L)p(t+2)$). At all other leads and lags, $(1-\pi_1 L)(1-\pi_2 L)p(t)$ is uncorrelated with $(1-\pi_1 L)(1-\pi_2 L)h(t)$. These facts imply that a uniquely identified Wold representation for $(p(t), h(t))$ exists of the form

$$\begin{pmatrix} p(t) \\ h(t) \end{pmatrix} = \frac{1}{(1-\pi_1 L)(1-\pi_2 L)}$$

$$\begin{bmatrix} c_{11}^0 + c_{11}^1 L + c_{11}^2 L^2, & c_{12}^0 + c_{12}^1 L + c_{12}^2 L^2 \\ c_{21}^1 L, & c_{22}^0 + c_{22}^1 L \end{bmatrix}$$

$$\begin{bmatrix} a_1(t) \\ a_2(t) \end{bmatrix} + \begin{pmatrix} c_{31} \\ c_{32} \end{pmatrix} \pi_1^t + \begin{pmatrix} c_{41} \\ c_{42} \end{pmatrix} \pi_2^t \qquad (14)$$

where $Ea(t)a(t)^T = I$, and where $p(t) - E_{t-1}p(t)$ and $h(t) - E_{t-1}h(t)$ can each be expressed as linear combinations of the (2×1) vector $a(t) = (a_1(t), a_2(t))^T$. (Here $E_{t-1}(\cdot)$ denotes the linear least squares forecast of $(\cdot)$ conditional on values of $p(s)$, $h(s)$ for $s \leqslant t-1$.) The identifiable parameters of the model (i.e., a minimal set of parameters in terms of which the likelihood attains its maximal value) are the π_js and the c_{ij}^ks in (14). There are 15 of these parameters.

Notice that the restriction $c_{21}^0 = 0$ is imposed in (14). This is normalisation that selects from among all Wold representations the unique one for which $a_2(t) = h(t) - E_{t-1}h(t)$.

The theoretical model ($\tilde{7}$) is a collection of restrictions on (14). The nature of the restrictions can be explored by studying the spectral factorisation identity that links the parameters of ($\tilde{7}$) and (14). The theoretical model has 12 deep free parameters (λ, γ, ξ, n, d_{01}, d_{02}, d_{03}, σ_{11}, σ_{12}, σ_{22}, J_1, J_2). These 12 parameters are linked to the 15 parameters of (14) by 15 restrictions which arise as follows. Begin by representing (7) as

$$\begin{pmatrix} p(t) \\ h(t) \end{pmatrix} = \frac{1}{(1-\pi_1 L)(1-\pi_2 L)} D(L)w(t) + \pi_1^t$$

$$\begin{pmatrix} \dfrac{\gamma J_1}{1-\lambda\pi_1} \\ J_1 \end{pmatrix} + \pi_2^t \begin{pmatrix} \dfrac{\gamma J_2}{1-\lambda\pi_2} \\ J_2 \end{pmatrix} \qquad (7')$$

where $D(L) = (1-\pi_1 L)(1-\pi_2) \begin{pmatrix} d(L) \\ g(L) \end{pmatrix}$.

Next, represent (14) as

$$\begin{pmatrix} p(t) \\ h(t) \end{pmatrix} = \frac{1}{(1-\pi_1 L)(1-\pi_2 L)} C(L)a(t) + \pi_1^t \begin{pmatrix} c_{31} \\ c_{32} \end{pmatrix} + \pi_2^t \begin{pmatrix} c_{41} \\ c_{42} \end{pmatrix} \qquad (14')$$

where $C(L)$ is the (2×2) matrix of moving average polynomials on the right-hand side of (14). The parameters of (7′) and (14′) are partially linked via the identity $D(L)w(t) = C(L)a(t)$. The implications of this identity are exhausted by the spectral factorisation identity

$$D(L)VD(L^{-1})^T = C(L)C(L^{-1})^T \tag{15}$$

where det $C(z)$ has all of its zeros on or outside the unit circle. Equation (15) supplies a total of nine equations restricting the elements of $D(L)$, V (corresponding to the nine identifiable parameters in $C(L)$).[7] We obtain four more equations by equating coefficients on π_1^t and π_2^t in (7′) and (14′), namely

$$\begin{aligned} c_{31} &= \frac{\gamma J_1}{1-\lambda\pi_1} & c_{41} &= \frac{\gamma J_2}{1-\lambda\pi_2}. \\ c_{32} &= J_1 & c_{42} &= J_2 \end{aligned} \tag{16}$$

Finally, two more restrictions are implied by equation (8), which we repeat here for convenience

$$\begin{aligned} \pi_1 &= [(\lambda^{-1} + (1+n)^{-1} - \xi\gamma/\lambda) - \sqrt{((\lambda^{-1} + (1+n)^{-1} - \xi\gamma/\lambda)^2 - 4/(1+n)\lambda)}]/2 \\ \pi_2 &= [(\lambda^{-1} + (1+n)^{-1} - \xi\gamma/\lambda) + \sqrt{((\lambda^{-1} + (1+n)^{-1} - \xi\gamma/\lambda)^2 - 4/(1+n)\lambda)}]/2. \end{aligned} \tag{8}$$

Equations (15), (16), and (8) supply a total of 15 independent restrictions on the 12 free parameters of the model $(\lambda, \gamma, \xi, n, d_{01}, d_{02}, d_{03}, \sigma_{11}, \sigma_{12}, \sigma_{22}, J_1, J_2) \equiv \theta$. According to these 'order condition' considerations, the model is over-identified.

To this point, our discussion has assumed that $a_{11}(L) = a_{22}(L) = 1$. In general, richer specifications for $a_{11}(L)$ and $a_{22}(L)$ will lead to stronger over-identification. As (7) reveals, the higher is the order of $a_{11}(L)$ or $a_{22}(L)$, the more restrictions there are on the moving average representation for $(p(t), h(t))$.

The appendix describes identification in the singular case in which (9) holds so that the solution collapses to (10). We find that over-identification vanishes, but that identification still obtains. Thus, identification is more fragile than when the π_2 root is activated. This situation reflects the intuitive notion that when the π_2 root is activated, there occurs richer behaviour of the time series, which contain more information about the parameters of the model.

IV GRANGER CAUSALITY

An advantage of the model described by Sargent and Wallace (1973) and Sargent (1977) is that it predicts that inflation Granger causes money creation, while money creation fails to Granger cause inflation. This predicted pattern of Granger causality has been found in data drawn from the hyperinflations (see Sargent and Wallace, 1973). It is useful to study what restrictions need to be imposed on the present model in order to produce such patterns of Granger causality.

First consider the special case of the model in which $a_{11}(L)=a_{22}(L)=1$, $w_{3t}=0$. Also assume that (9) holds, so that the π_2 mode of the system has been deactivated. In this special case, we saw that the solution for $p(t)$, $h(t)$ has the representation

$$\begin{pmatrix} p(t) \\ h(t) \end{pmatrix} = \frac{\lambda^{-1}}{1-\pi_1 L}\begin{bmatrix} \left(1-\frac{1}{1+n}L\right)\frac{1}{\pi_2}, -\gamma(1+n)/(1-\pi_2(1+n)) \\ \xi\pi_2,\ \lambda-(\xi\gamma(1+n))/(1-\pi_2(1+n)) \end{bmatrix} \begin{bmatrix} w_1(t) \\ w_2(t) \end{bmatrix} + \begin{pmatrix} \gamma J_1/(1-\lambda\pi_1) \\ J_1 \end{pmatrix} \pi_1^t. \quad (10)$$

Note that in the representation for $h(t)$, the polynomials in L on $w_1(t)$ and $w_2(t)$ are proportional to one another, while in the representation for $p(t)$, the polynomials in $w_1(t)$ and $w_2(t)$ are not proportional. This implies that $h(t)$ Granger causes $p(t)$, while $p(t)$ fails to Granger cause $h(t)$.

This structure of Granger causality is a special feature of the singular case in which $(1-\pi_2 L)$ has been cancelled out. In the general case, $p(t)$ and $h(t)$ Granger cause each other, which can be proved by studying the structure of the solution (7). We now seek special cases in which $p(t)$ Granger causes $h(t)$, with no Granger causality extending from $h(t)$ to $p(t)$.

We begin with a case in which there is no spurious indicator impinging on the solution, so that in (7) $d_{03}=0$. Suppose that $a_{11}(L)$ and $a_{22}(L)$ satisfy the restriction

$$a_{22}(L)=\frac{d_{02}}{\gamma d_{01}}\left(1-\frac{1}{1+n}L\right)a_{11}(L).$$

The reader can verify that under the above restriction, the polynomials on $w_1(t)$ and $w_2(t)$ in $d(L)$ are proportional to one another, while the polynomials in $g(L)$ are not proportional to one another. Under this special condition, it follows that $p(t)$ Granger causes $h(t)$, but that $h(t)$ fails to Granger cause $p(t)$.

To motivate the next special case, notice that real balances demanded at a constant expected gross return on money of unity are given by $(1-\lambda)/\gamma$. Let us reparameterise the system by setting $\gamma=(1-\lambda)\theta$, where $\theta=(p/h)(1)$, the inverse of real balances at a gross inflation rate of unity. To achieve the following special case, we shall think of holding θ fixed as we vary λ, so that as $\lambda\to 1$, $\gamma\to 0$. In the limiting case with $\lambda=1$, $\gamma=0$, (7) implies

$$(1-\pi_1 L)(1-\pi_2 L) \begin{pmatrix} d(L) \\ g(L) \end{pmatrix}$$

$$= \begin{pmatrix} \dfrac{d_{01}-L}{1-L}, & \dfrac{d_{02}}{1-L}, & \dfrac{d_{03}}{1-L} \\ \dfrac{\xi(d_{01}-L)}{(1-L)(1-\frac{1}{1+n}L)}, & \dfrac{\xi d_{02}+(1-L)}{(1-L)(1-L)\frac{1}{1+n}L)}, & \dfrac{\xi d_{03}}{(1-L)(1-\frac{1}{1+n}L)} \end{pmatrix}$$

where we are using the fact that when $\gamma=0$, $\pi_1=(1+n)^{-1}$, $\pi_2=1$. In the special case that $w_{1t}=0$, so that the portfolio balance schedule is exact, $d(L)$ is such that p_t is a martingale, so that $p(t)$ is not Granger-caused by $h(t)$. However, $p(t)$ Granger causes $h(t)$ so long as the spurious indicator is present. (The martingale characterisation of $p(t)$ under these conditions can also be deduced directly from equation (1a).)

These examples constitute singular cases in which $h(t)$ fails to Granger cause $p(t)$. They indicate the presence of a range of examples close to these in which Granger causality extends from $h(t)$ to $p(t)$, but is difficult to detect in short samples. The model thus appears to be potentially capable of accommodating Granger causality patterns such as those detected in earlier work (Sargent and Wallace, 1973).

V ESTIMATION

We shall describe two estimators which are modifications of the time domain and frequency domain estimators described by Hansen and Sargent (1981). The modifications involve properly taking account of the restrictions that exist across the initial conditions and the remaining parameters of the model.

Let us define $y(t)^T \equiv (p(t), h(t))^T$, and represent (7) as

$$y(t) = \frac{1}{(1-\pi_1 L)\,1-\pi_2 L)} D(L)w(t) + H_1\pi_1^t + H_2\pi_2^t \tag{17}$$

where

$$D(L) \equiv (1-\pi_1 L)(1-\pi_2 L) \begin{pmatrix} d(L) \\ g(L) \end{pmatrix}$$

$$H_1 = \begin{pmatrix} \dfrac{\gamma J_1}{1-\lambda\pi_1} \\ J_1 \end{pmatrix} \qquad H_2 = \begin{pmatrix} \dfrac{\gamma J_2}{1-\lambda\pi_2} \\ J_2 \end{pmatrix}$$

We assume that $Ew(t)w(t)^T = V$. It is to be understood that $D(L)$, π_1, π_2, H_1 and H_2 are all functions of the list of deep parameters of the model $\theta \equiv (\lambda, \gamma, \xi, n, d_{01}, d_{02}, d_{03}, \sigma_{11}, \sigma_{12}, \sigma_{22}, J_1, J_2)$.

The first step in constructing the time domain estimator is to replace $D(L)w(t)$ by its Wold representation $F(L)a(t)$ where

$$\underset{2\times 3}{D(L)}\ \underset{3\times 1}{w(t)} = \underset{2\times 2}{F(L)}\ \underset{2\times 1}{a(t)}$$

where

$$F(L) = I + F_1 L + F_2 L^2$$

$$\det F(z^0) = 0 => |z^0| \geqslant 1,$$

and

$$a(t) = y(t) - E(y(t)\,|\,y(t-1), \ldots, y(0)),$$

where $Ea(t)a(t)^T = \Omega$. To compute $F(L)$ we solve the spectral factorisation equation

$$D(L)VD(L^{-1})^T = F(L)\Omega F(L^{-1})^T \tag{18}$$

subject to the zeros of det $F(z)$ not being inside the unit circle. Practically, given the parameters of $D(L)$ and V, this equation can be solved for F_1, F_2, Ω in a variety of ways, for example, by use of the Kalman filter.

The white noise vector $a(t)$ is fundamental for $y(t)$ and, therefore, is in the space spanned by current and lagged $w(t)$'s. It follows from $w(s)=0$ for $s\leqslant 0$ that $a(s)=0$ for $s\leqslant 0$. We can then represent (17) as

$$y(t)=\frac{1}{(1-\pi_1 L)(1-\pi_2 L)}F(L)a(t)+H_1\pi_1^t+H_2\pi_2^t. \tag{19}$$

We propose to use this equation to calculate the $a(t)$ vector implied by a given set of parameter values θ. Suppose we have a sample on $y(t)$ for $t=1, \ldots, T$. Writing (19) for $t=0$, 1, and using $a(s)=0$ for $s\leqslant 0$, we have

$$\begin{aligned} y(0)&=H_1+H_2 \\ y(1)&=a(1)+H_1\pi_1+H_2\pi_2 \end{aligned} \tag{20}$$

Multiplying (19) by $(1-\pi_1 L)(1-\pi_2 L)$ and solving for $a(t)$ gives

$$\begin{aligned} a(t)=y(t)&-(\pi_1+\pi_2)y(t-1)+\pi_1\pi_2 y(t-2) \\ &-F_1 a(t-1)-F_2 a(t-2) \end{aligned} \tag{21}$$

We can thus solve for $a(t)$ by beginning with (19), and then using recursions on (21):

$$\begin{aligned} \hat{a}(1)&=y(1)-H_1\pi_1-H_2\pi_2 \\ \hat{a}(2)&=y(2)-(\pi_1+\pi_2)y(1)+\pi_1\pi_2[H_1+H_2]-F_1\hat{a}(1) \\ \hat{a}(3)&=y(3)-(\pi_1+\pi_2)y(2)+\pi_1\pi_2 y(1)-F_1\hat{a}(2)-F_2\hat{a}(1), \\ &\;\;\vdots \\ \hat{a}(t)&=y(t)-(\pi_1+\pi_2)y(t-1)+\pi_1\pi_2 y(t-2)-F_1\hat{a}(t-1)-F_2\hat{a}(t-2). \end{aligned} \tag{22}$$

Equation (22) is to be understood as expressing estimated innovations as functions of the deep parameters θ that determine H_1, H_2, and $F(L)$.

In estimation problems without restrictions on the (2×1) vectors of initial conditions, H_1 and H_2, it is possible to choose them so that the first two sample disturbances $\hat{a}(1)$ and $\hat{a}(2)$ of (22) are set equal to zero. In practice, this is accomplished by first setting $\hat{a}(1)$ and $\hat{a}(2)$ to zero and ignoring the first two equations of (22). All of the free parameters of the model except the initial conditions H_1 and H_2 are then estimated, conditional on $\hat{a}(1)=\hat{a}(2)=0$. As a final step, H_1 and H_2 are estimated by solving the first two equations of (22) for (H_1, H_2) with π_1 and π_2 taken at their estimated values. The restrictions across the rows of H_1 and H_2, and across H_1, H_2, and the remaining parameters, prevent this procedure from being applicable here. These restrictions, and the inapplicability of the standard procedure, reflect the information about the deep parameters carried by the initial conditions.[8]

Assuming that the $w(t)$ process is multivariate normal, the log likelihood function can be approximated by

$$L_T = -T \log 2\pi - T/2 \log \det \Omega - \frac{1}{2}\sum_{t=1}^{T} \hat{a}(t)^T \Omega^{-1} \hat{a}(t).$$

This is to be maximised with respect to the free parameters of θ subject to the $\hat{a}(t)$'s being given by (22) and $F(L)$ and Ω satisfying (18).

Alternatively, approximate maximum likelihood estimates can be obtained by minimising

$$\det T^{-1} \sum_{t=1}^{T} \hat{a}(t)\hat{a}(t)^T \tag{23}$$

with respect to the free parameter θ. The $\hat{a}(t)$s are functions of the parameters θ via (22) and (18).

The frequency domain estimator has the virtue of avoiding the need to factor the spectral density matrix $D(L)VD(L^{-1})^T$ as in (18). To employ the frequency domain method, one uses (17) for $t=0, 1$, to get

$$y(0) = H_1 + H_2$$
$$y(1) = D_0 w(1) + \pi_1 H_1 + \pi_2 H_2.$$

Solving for $D_0 w(1)$ gives

$$D_0 w(1) = y(1) - \pi_1 H_1 - \pi_2 H_2 \tag{24}$$

Then iterating on (17) gives

$$D(L)w(2) = y(2) - (\pi_1 + \pi_2)y(1) + \pi_1\pi_2[H_1 + H_2]$$
$$D(\mathrm{L})w(t) = y(t) - (\pi_1 + \pi_2)y(t-1) + \pi_1\pi_2 y(t-2) \quad \text{for } t \geqslant 3. \tag{25}$$

For a given value of the parameter vector θ and the associated $D(L)w(t)$ series generated by solving (24)–(25), the periodogram is to be formed. Letting $z(t) \equiv D(L)w(t)$, we define

$$\tilde{z}(w_j) = \sum_{j=1}^{T} z(t)\mathrm{e}^{-iw_j t}, \qquad w_j = \frac{2\pi_j}{T}, \qquad j = 1, \ldots, T.$$

The periodogram is then defined as

$$I(w_j) = T^{-1} z(w_j)\overline{z(w_j)}^T \tag{26}$$

where the bar denotes complex conjugation. It is important to note that the periodogram $I(w_j)$ of $D(L)w(t)$ is a function of the parameters of the model θ, and must be recalculated for each step in the nonlinear maximisation of the criterion function (28) below.

Next, the theoretical spectral density matrix of $D(L)w(t)$ is given by

$$S(z) = D(z)VD(z^{-1})^T \tag{27}$$

Approximate maximum likelihood estimates can be obtained by maximising with respect to θ

$$L = -\frac{1}{2}(2T) - \frac{1}{2}\sum_{j=1}^{T} \log \det S(\mathrm{e}^{-iw_j})$$

$$-\frac{1}{2}\sum_{j=1}^{T} \mathrm{tr}[S(\mathrm{e}^{-iw_j})^{-1} I(w_j)]. \tag{28}$$

It is to be emphasised that both $S(\mathrm{e}^{-iw_j})$ and $I(w_j)$ are functions of the parameter θ, and must be recomputed at each step of the maximisation. The need to recompute $I(w_j)$ at each step of the optimisation is a result of the fact that cross-equation restrictions exist on the parameters in H_1 and H_2, and that these restrictions contain information about θ. This distinguishes the current estimation problem from standard ones in which the absence of such cross-equation restrictions means that there are sufficient free parameters in H_1 and H_2 to make it appropriate to eliminate exponential terms before estimation, so that the counterpart of $I(w_j)$ need be computed only once.

VI CONCLUSIONS

This paper has described a model in which there is a four-dimensional continuum of equilibrium stochastic processes for the base money supply and price level. In many of these equilibria, there is a spurious indicator or 'sunspot' variable that affects the base money supply and price level even though it fails to influence the fundamental forcing variables, namely, the random disturbances to portfolio balance and the government's budget constraint. Technically, the existence of equilibria depending on sunspots appears to be intricately tied to the existence of multiple equilibria depending on the fundamental driving processes.

Despite the existence of a four-dimensional continuum of equilibria, the model is econometrically over-identified. In other words, the view that the economy is operating along one member of the continuum of equilibria restricts the behaviour of the time series for base money and the price level, and permits one to estimate the behavioural parameters that describe portfolio balance and the government budget constraint, and also the 'nuisance parameters' that serve to select one from among the many equilibria. That the model is over-identified in this way gives empirical content to the hypothesis that hyperinflations have been characterised by a process of sliding down the slippery side of the Laffer curve. In a sequel to this paper, we intend to use the model econometrically to study this hypothesis.

APPENDIX ON IDENTIFICATION

This appendix studies identification in the singular case in which (9) holds. In this case, the bivariate $(p(t), h(t))$ process evolves according to

$$\begin{pmatrix} p(t) \\ h(t) \end{pmatrix} = \frac{\lambda^{-1}}{1-\pi_1 L} \begin{bmatrix} (1-\frac{1}{1+n}L)\ \frac{1}{\pi_2}, & -\gamma(1+n)/(1-\pi_2(1+n)) \\ \xi/\pi_2, & \lambda-(\xi\gamma(1+n))/(1-\pi_2(1+n)) \end{bmatrix} \begin{bmatrix} w_1(t) \\ w_2(t) \end{bmatrix} + \begin{pmatrix} \gamma J_1/(1-\lambda\pi_1) \\ J_1 \end{pmatrix} \pi_1^t. \tag{10}$$

We assume that the covariance matrix of $w(t)$ is given by

$$Ew(t)w(t)^T = V$$

where V is a positive definite matrix. Let G^{-1} be a lower triangular matrix that normalises and diagonalises V, i.e., $I = G^{-1}VG^{-1T}$. Define the transformed disturbance vector

$$\eta(t) = G^{-1}w(t).$$

Thus, $E\eta(t)\eta(t)^T = I$. Now using $w(t) = G\eta(t)$, we can express (10) as

$$(1-\pi_1 L)I\begin{pmatrix} p(t) \\ h(t) \end{pmatrix} = \lambda^{-1}\begin{bmatrix} \left(1-\dfrac{1}{1+n}L\right)\dfrac{1}{\pi_2}, & \dfrac{-\gamma(1+n)}{1-\pi_2(1+n)} \\ \xi/\pi_2, & \lambda - \dfrac{\xi\gamma(1+n)}{1-\pi_2(1+n)} \end{bmatrix}$$

$$\begin{bmatrix} g_{11} & 0 \\ g_{21} & g_{22} \end{bmatrix}\begin{bmatrix} \eta_1(t) \\ \eta_2(t) \end{bmatrix} + \begin{bmatrix} \gamma J_1/(1-\lambda\pi_1) \\ J_1 \end{bmatrix}\pi_1^t$$

or

$$(1-\pi_1 L)\begin{pmatrix} p(t) \\ h(t) \end{pmatrix}$$

$$= \lambda^{-1}\begin{bmatrix} \left(1-\dfrac{1}{1+n}L\right)\dfrac{g_{11}}{\pi_2} - \dfrac{\gamma g_{21}(1+n)}{1-\pi_2(1+n)}, & -\dfrac{g_{22}\gamma(1+n)}{1-\pi_2(1+n)} \\ \xi g_{11}/\pi_2 + g_{21}\left(\lambda - \dfrac{\xi\gamma(1+n)}{1-\pi_2(1+n)}\right), & g_{22}\left(\lambda - \dfrac{\xi\gamma(1+n)}{1-\pi_2(1+n)}\right) \end{bmatrix}\begin{bmatrix} \eta_1(t) \\ \eta_2(t) \end{bmatrix}$$

$$+ \begin{pmatrix} \gamma J_1/(1-\lambda\pi_1) \\ J_1 \end{pmatrix}\pi_1^t. \tag{A1}$$

In this representation, the three parameters, g_{11}, g_{21}, g_{22} represent the covariance matrix of the original $w(t)$ process. The $\eta(t)$ process was constructed by orthonormalising the $w(t)$ process with the matrix G. The matrix G thus summarises all of the information in V.

Equation (A1) is a vector autoregressive moving average representation whose identifiable parameters can be displayed as follows. Represent (A1) as[9]

$$(1-\pi_1 L)\begin{pmatrix} p(t) \\ h(t) \end{pmatrix} = \begin{pmatrix} c_{11}^0 + c_{11}^1 L, & c_{12} \\ c_{21}, & c_{22} \end{pmatrix}\begin{pmatrix} \eta_1(t) \\ \eta_2(t) \end{pmatrix} + \begin{pmatrix} c_{13} \\ c_{23} \end{pmatrix}\pi_t^1.$$

The identifiable parameters are π_1 and the c_{ij}^ks. From (A1) and the formula (8) for π_1, π_2, these parameters are linked to the deep parameters of the model by the following equations:

$$c_{11}^0 = \lambda^{-1}\left(\frac{g_{11}}{\pi_2} - \frac{\gamma g_{21}(1+n)}{1-\pi_2(1+n)}\right) \tag{A2}$$

$$c_{11}^1 = \frac{-\lambda^{-1}g_{11}}{(1+n)\pi_2} \tag{A3}$$

$$c_{12} = \frac{-\lambda^{-1}g_{22}\gamma(1+n)}{1-\pi_2(1+n)} \tag{A4}$$

$$c_{21} = -\lambda^{-1}\left(\frac{\xi g_{11}}{\pi_2} + g_{21}\left(\lambda - \frac{\xi\gamma(1+n)}{1-\pi_2(1+n)}\right)\right) \tag{A5}$$

$$c_{22} = \lambda^{-1}g_{22}\left(\lambda - \frac{\xi\gamma(1+n)}{1-\pi_2(1+n)}\right) \tag{A6}$$

$$\pi_1, \pi_2 = \{(\lambda^{-1} + (1+n)^{-1} - \xi\gamma/\lambda) \pm [(\lambda^{-1} + (1+n)^{-1} - \xi\gamma/\lambda)^2 - 4/(1+n)\lambda]^{1/2}\}/2 \tag{A7}$$

$$c_{13} = \gamma J_1/(1-\lambda\pi_1) \tag{A8}$$

$$c_{23} = J_1. \tag{A9}$$

The known variables (identifiable parameters) in the nine equations (A2)–(A9) are π_1, c_{11}^0, c_{11}^1, c_{12}, c_{21}, c_{22}, c_{13}, c_{23}. The unknown variables to be determined are λ, ξ, γ, n, π_2, g_{11}, g_{21}, g_{22}, J_1. We thus have nine equations to be solved for nine unknowns, which is promising from the viewpoint of identification.

To highlight the role of equations (A8) and (A9) in helping to achieve identification, we shall begin by ignoring them. This amounts to considering identification in the system from which the deterministic components π_1^t (J_1, F_1) have been removed prior to estimation.[10] In this case, equations (A2)–(A7) form seven equations in the eight unknowns λ, ξ, γ, π_2, g_{11}, g_{21}, and g_{22} so that these parameters are in general under-identified. However, under the special assumption that

$g_{21}=0$, local identification obtains. The assumption that $g_{21}=0$ is equivalent with the hypothesis that $w_1(t)$ and $w_2(t)$, the disturbances to portfolio balance and to the government budget, respectively, are orthogonal.

In the case that $g_{21}=0$, identification can be thought to proceed as follows. Equations (A2) and (A3) imply that

$$(1+n) = -c_{11}^0/c_{11},$$

while equations (A5) and (A2) imply that

$$\xi = -c_{21}/c_{11}^0.$$

So n and ξ are identified.

After some algebra, (A6), (A4) and (A7) imply that

$$c_{22}/c_{12} = (1-\pi_1\lambda)/-\gamma$$

Given knowledge of n and ξ, equation (A10) together with (A7) for π_1, namely,

$$\pi_1 = \left\{\left(\lambda^{-1}+(1+n)^{-1}-\frac{\xi\gamma}{\lambda}\right) - \sqrt{\left(\left(\lambda^{-1}+(1+n^{-1})-\frac{\xi\gamma}{\lambda}\right)-4/(1+n)\lambda\right)}\right\},$$

form two equations in γ and λ which possess a locally unique solution. Given π_1, λ, ξ, and n, π_2 can be obtained from (A7). Then g_{11} can be obtained from (A2), and g_{22} from (A4). This completes the discussion of identification in the special case in which $g_{21}=0$ and $J_2=0$.

With $J_1=0$ and g_{21} an unknown to be identified, the parameters of the model become under-identified. In this case, we are one restriction short of having an identified system. When $J_1 \neq 0$, equations (A8) and (A9) add two equations but only one unknown to the system. This leaves us with a system of nine equations in the nine unknown parameters to be identified.

The preceding analysis shows that in the singular case in which the root π_2 has been eliminated from the system, identification is delicate. Identification hinges either on including the deterministic component (π_1^t) explicitly in the estimation process, or by *a priori* imposing orthogonality between $w_1(t)$ and $w_2(t)$.

ACKNOWLEDGEMENTS

Helpful comments on this paper were made by Danny Quah, Peter Garber, Lars Hansen, Lawrence Christiano, Kenneth Singleton, Christopher Sims, and Mark Watson.

NOTES

1. This was thus an application of the same method that John Muth (1960) used to discover a univariate stochastic process for income that made Friedman's (1957) geometric lag formulation for forming permanent income consistent with rational expectations.
2. John Taylor (1977) has studied rational expectations models in which solutions exist that depend on a spurious indicator.
3. This is the solution strategy used by Whiteman (1983) and Saracoglu and Sargent (1978).
4. There are tight links between the dimensionality of solutions depending on the spurious indicators, the dimensionality of the multiplicity of solutions depending on the 'fundamental' noises $w_1(t)$ and $w_2(t)$, and the fact that solution (7) is a second-order system in which two roots are being solved backwards and none forwards. It is no coincidence that the number of 'extra' roots solved backwards (one) equals the dimensionality both of the multiplicity of solutions dependent on each of the fundamental noises (one), and the dimensionality of solutions depending on the spurious indicator. It is our conjecture that these links reflect the workings of an as yet unproved theorem that would extend Whiteman's theorem (1983, Ch. 5) to permit spurious indicators to impinge on the solution.
5. They are more inflationary because $\lambda^{-1} > \pi_2$.
6. The order conditions described in the text and appendix are suggestive, but are not sufficient for identification. In econometric practice, local identification can be checked numerically by inspecting the condition of the information matrix.
7. The (2×1) vector of innovations $a(t)$ lies in the linear space spanned by current and past values of the (2×1) vector $(p(t), h(t))$. In general, even if $d_{03} = 0$, the (3×1) vector $w(t)$ does not lie in the linear space spanned by current and past values of $(p(t), h(t)$. The likelihood function is most readily viewed as a funtion of the $a(t)$'s (see Box and Jenkins (1970) or Hansen and Sargent (1981) for examples). The identity $F(L)a(t) = D(L)w(t)$ and (15) are used to present the model in a form that exposes parameters that appear in the likelihood function. Note that $a(t)$ may span a smaller space than $w(t)$ for two reasons. A first occurs when $d_{03} \neq 0$. A second occurs when $d_{03} = 0$, and in which det $D(z)$ has one or more zeros inside the unit circle.
8. However, note in (22), that as t grows large, the dependence of $\hat{a}(t)$ on (H_1, H_2) becomes attenuated. The reason is that the zeros of det $F(z)$ in general lie outside the unit circle. This observation suggests that it will not be possible to estimate J_1 and J_2 consistently.

9. The off-diagonal parameters c_{12} and c_{21} are both uniquely identified because $c_{12}(L)$ as a polynomial has been restricted to be zero order. It is possible to obtain an alternative representation in which $c_{21}(L)=c_{21}=0$. However, in such an alternative representation, it is necessary to make $c_{12}(L)$ a first-order polynomial $(c_{12}^0+c_{12}^1L)$ with $c_{12}^1\neq 0$. (In the section on identification in the text, such a representation setting $c_{21}^0=0$ was used.)
10. The structure of identification in this case is closely related to that which characterises the model described by Sargent (1977).

REFERENCES

Box, C. E. P. and G. M. Jenkins (1970) 'Time Series Analysis, Forecasting, and Control' (San Francisco: Holden-Day).

Cagan, P. (1956) 'The Monetary Dynamics of Hyperinflation', in Milton Friedman (ed), *Studies in the Quantity Theory of Money* (University of Chicago Press, Chicago).

Fischer, S. (1983) 'The Economy of Israel', National Bureau of Economic Research, Working Paper No. 1190, August 1983.

Friedman, M. (1957) *A Theory of the Consumption Function* (Princeton: Princeton University Press).

Granger, C. W. J. (1969) 'Investigating Causal Relations by Econometric Models and Cross-Spectral Methods', *Econometrica*, vol. 37, no. 3.

Hansen, L. P. and T. J. Sargent (1981) 'Formulating and Estimating Dynamic Linear Rational Expectations Models', in R. E. Lucas, Jr. and Thomas J. Sargent (eds), *Rational Expectations and Econometric Practice* (University of Minnesota Press).

Jacobs, R. (1975) 'A Difficulty with Monetarist Models of Hyperinflation', *Economic Inquiry*, 13, September.

Keynes, J. M. (1971) *A Tract on Monetary Reform*, vol. IV of the *Collected Writings of John Maynard Keynes* (Macmillan, 1971 edition).

Muth, J. F. (1960) 'Optimal Properties of Exponentially Weighted Forecasts', *Journal of the American Statistical Association*, vol. 55, no. 290.

Saracoglu, R. and T. J. Sargent (1978) 'Seasonality and Portfolio Balance Under Rational Expectations', *Journal of Monetary Economics*, 4, pp. 435–58.

Sargent, T. J. (1976) 'Econometric Exogeneity and Alternative Estimators of Portfolio Balance Schedules for Hyperinflations', *Journal of Monetary Economics*, 2, pp. 511–21.

Sargent, T. J. (1977) 'The Demand for Money During Hyperinflations Under Rational Expectations', *International Economic Review*, vol. 18, no. 1.

Sargent, T. J. and N. Wallace (1973) 'Rational Expectations and the Dynamics of Hyperinflation', *International Economic Review*, vol. 14, no. 2.

Sargent, T. J. and N. Wallace (1981) 'Some Unpleasant Monetarist Arithmetic', Federal Reserve Bank of Minneapolis *Quarterly Review*, Fall 1981.

Sims, C. A. (1972) 'Money, Income, and Causality', *American Economic Review*, vol. 62, no. 4.

Taylor, J. B. (1977) 'Conditions for Unique Solutions in Stochastic Macroeconomic Models with Rational Expectations', *Econometrica*, 45 (September), 1377–85.

Wallace, N. (1980) 'The Overlapping Generations Model of Fiat Money', in John H. Kareken and Neil Wallace (eds), *Models of Monetary Economies* (Federal Reserve Bank of Minneapolis).

Whiteman, C. (1983) *Linear Rational Expectations Models: A User's Guide* (University of Minnesota Press: Minneapolis).

Comments on Thomas Sargent and Neil Wallace, 'Inflation and the Government Budget Constraint' by Zvi Eckstein

The Israeli economy fits very well with the main stylised facts of hyperinflations as they are described in Sargent and Wallace. Since 1973 the ratio of the money base to GNP ($h(t)$) in Israel decreased from 16 per cent to about 4 per cent or less. Inflation increased at that period from the range of 20 to 30 per cent to about 350–400 per cent today. At the same time the government deficit stayed in the range of 6 to 10 per cent of GNP. Furthermore, a study at the Bank of Israel showed that inflation Granger caused the real balances but real balances did not Granger cause inflation. All these facts are consistent with the main properties of the Sargent–Wallace model of hyperinflation.

This model suggests that the dynamic properties of the hyperinflations can be explained by one of the *many* equilibria that are derived from a simple dynamic, stochastic model that is described by two structure equations: a linear portfolio balance equation and the government budget constraint that is subject to a given real deficit that is financed by money creation. These two equations contain four parameters. λ and γ are parameters related to consumer preferences and aggregation, n is the constant growth rate of the economy and ξ is the constant deficit. The two steady states inflation rates are functions of these four parameters. However, whether the economy would converge to the low inflation level (the 'good' equilibrium) or to the high inflation level depends on the initial levels of prices (P) and the real money base per capita (h).

In the stochastic version of the model the main result is that the stochastic properties of the model (e.g. direction of Granger causality) and the mean of inflation at the stochastic steady states, depends on the parameters that relate agents expectations on prices and real balances to the random effects. In particular, the existence of random variables that are unrelated to the structural equations ('sunspots'), may affect critically the properties of the equilibrium. Three parameters are related to the relation between the random variables and the expectations and are related to the initial conditions. The other parameters of the model are related to the stochastic forcing variables of the economy.

The two novel results of the paper are:

(1) Optimal policy is a choice of a feedback rule on money creation, $h(t)$, that force the economy to be at the unique optimal equilibrium. This policy is a mapping from the parameters of the model to the government feedback rule. It is surprising that in order to implement this policy the government has to know not only the four parameters of the structural equation (λ, γ, n, ξ) but also the three parameters that are related to the expectations.

(2) The optimal policy can be identified by an econometric model, i.e. although there are many equilibria, the structural parameters of the model can be estimated from a finite sample of observations.

The observational equivalence property of this and other models certainly suggest that the only way to test theory and to analyse policy is by estimating the deep parameters of the model. Information from a simple linear regression estimation seems to shed *no* light on the main debates in theory and practice.

It should be noted that in most of the existing dynamic models economists ignore the implications due to the existence of bad equilibria. In this paper most of the analysis is devoted to the properties of these neglected equilibria. For example, if the budget deficit is zero the equilibrium that is mostly discussed here is non-monetary in the steady state, i.e. there is no valued fiat money in the economy in the long run. Is hyperinflation a phenomenon that is closely related to equilibria where fiat money is worthless at the steady state? The answer can be given by the results of the econometric estimation.

Comments on Thomas Sargent and Neil Wallace, 'Inflation and the Government Budget Constraint' by Stanley Fischer

This paper develops the econometrics that might be used to study multiple equilibria occurring in a standard model of hyperinflation. It thus returns to the fundamental question raised by Cagan in his classical study of the hyperinflations, whether the hyperinflations were a result of errant government behaviour, or on the contrary could be attributed to destabilising behaviour by the public in its attempts to rid itself of the rapidly depreciating money. Cagan's answer was that typically the government was to blame, in that the public's expectations adjusted sufficiently slowly that the model he developed to analyse hyperinflation would have produced stable inflation rates if the government had not printed money at increasing rates.

Rather than pretend to discuss the econometrics developed in the paper, I will concentrate on explaining the underlying model and the two types of multiple equilibria with which it is concerned. It remains to be seen whether the relatively short time series available for the hyperinflations will allow Sargent and Wallace to produce useful empirical results with the heavy artillery they put on show in the paper.

The basic Sargent–Wallace model used in this paper consists of equations (1a) and (1b). I use a virtually identical model, developed in joint research with Michael Bruno, to demonstrate the multiple equilibria that can arise in such a model. There is, first, a problem of multiple equilibria in a rational expectations model even without sunspots. There is an additional 'sunspots' problem that can arise when extraneous (to the fundamentals of the model) beliefs about the behaviour of prices become self-fulfilling prophecies. Sargent and Wallace are concerned with both these possibilities.

Suppose the demand for high-powered money has the Cagan form:

$$H/P = h = \exp(-a.pe) \tag{1}$$

where P is the price level, a is a parameter, and pe is the expected rate of inflation. The government finances fixed real expenditures, d, by printing high-powered money:

$$\dot{H}/P = d. \tag{2}$$

Equation (2) is the government budget constraint. For ease of exposition, assume there is no real growth.

Figure 1 is used to analyse the behaviour of the system. With g as the growth rate of high-powered money, (2) can be rewritten:

$$g.\exp(-a.pe) = d. \tag{2'}$$

This is the government budget constraint, *BB*, in Figure 1, showing the relationship between the growth rate of the monetary base and the expected rate of inflation that enables the government to raise the required amount of revenue, d, from the printing of H.

The dynamics of the inflation rate are obtained by combining (1) with the rational expectations (in this case perfect foresight) assumption: differentiating (1) we obtain

$$g - p = -a.\dot{pe} = -a.\dot{p} \tag{1}$$

where p is the actual inflation rate, and we have equated the rates of change of the expected and actual inflation rates. The 45° line in Figure 1 is the locus on which the rate of inflation is not changing.

In Figure 1 the economy is always on the *BB* locus, since the government budget constraint has to be honoured. The directions of motion on that locus follow from (1). Note that as drawn, there are two steady state equilibria, the low inflation steady state at *A* and a high inflation equilibrium at *B*. At *A* an increase in the inflation rate *along the 45° line* increases the government's inflation revenue; at *B* an increase in the inflation rate along the 45° line reduces inflation revenue. Equivalently, at *A* the inflation elasticity of the demand for high-powered money is less than one whereas at *B* it is greater than one.

The existence of two steady state equilibria is itself interesting, suggesting that a government that depends on the inflation tax may find itself at a higher than necessary inflation rate over long periods. But the specific multiple equilibrium problem to which Sargent and Wallace first address themselves can be seen by noting that the steady state at *B* is stable. Starting from any position to the right of *A*, the economy will converge to point *B*, if expectations are rational and, so far, excluding sunspots.

This means, in particular, that the assumption of rational expectations together with an additional assumption that eventually the economy reaches a steady state is not sufficient to tie down the short

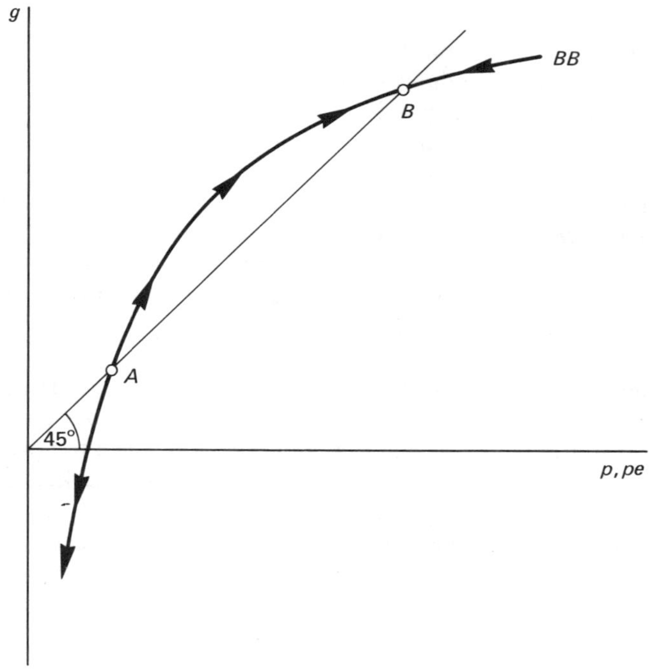

FIGURE 1 *Inflation dynamics with the government budget constraint.*

run equilibrium of the economy. An economist visiting this economy could expect to find it anywhere at or to the right of point A, unless he knew the history of the economy. Any change in the equilibrium, for instance an increase in the amount of resources required by the government (an increase in d) that was unexpected could instantaneously take the economy to a new equilibrium far removed from the existing one.

Until recently such multiple equilibrium problems were not taken seriously by rational expectations theorists. Most likely it would have been explained that a maximising government together with maximising consumers looking infinitely far ahead would get the economy to point A by a suitable choice of initial conditions – and that in the absence of maximising assumptions, it was not surprising that multiple equilibria could arise. Now, the Sargent–Wallace approach seems to be more empirical, in that the possibility of multiple equilibria is not ruled out, but rather a set of tests is devised to try to search for such equilibria. Such a development is to be welcomed, especially in light of the many examples of multiple equilibria in maximising models in which individuals do not have infinite horizons.

At the same time, the possibility of multiple equilibria of this type raises interesting theoretical questions. Confronted with an actual economy, most economists would be reluctant to believe that the system is not causal, in that *given the policies followed to that date and expected for the future, and given the disturbances that have affected the economy*, the inflation rate could be at any of a continuum of points. Relatively mundane possibilities – like stickiness of prices that prevent price level jumps – might be sufficient to remove these multiple equilibria.

In the empirical part of the paper, Sargent and Wallace introduce another possible indeterminacy, that of sunspots. The disturbance $w_3(t)$ is not 'fundamental' but may none the less affect the price level. The possibility of such bubbles in a variety of assets markets has been investigated by Leroy and Porter (1981), Blanchard and Watson (1982), and others. There is as yet no verdict on their existence, though there is a verdict that establishing their existence is very difficult.

How successful is the Sargent–Wallace model in meeting the three criteria set out at the beginning of the paper? First, it offers an explanation of the increasing rates of inflation and falling real balances during hyperinflations as arising from initial conditions between points *A* and *B* in Figure 1. It is not entirely obvious that this is the dynamics that would have been observed in practice, since the economy could have started out to the right of *B* or the left of *A*. Further, since an increase in the government's need for revenue through the printing of money would produce a reduction in the steady state rate of inflation if the economy were at *B*, it is not obvious that increasing government pressures on resources (which likely occurred during hyperinflations) would have produced the observed dynamic patterns. Perhaps the simple rational expectations assumption is at fault here, for it is difficult to believe that economic agents in the hyperinflations understood the dynamic processes in which they were participating without undergoing some learning process that would be the equivalent of adaptive expectations.

The model explains the claim that inflation eventually exceeded the revenue maximising rate by pointing to *B* as the position to which the economy tended. It thus meets the second requirement Sargent and Wallace set. The third requirement is that the model have a sound economic motivation. Budget constraints indeed provide economic motivation to those suffering from them, but the model leaves two questions open, that of the structure of the demand function for money in a hyperinflation when alternative assets may begin serving as medium of exchange and store of value, and that of alternative sources of finance for the government. In particular, if the efficiency of the tax system is reduced as the inflation rate rises, reliance on the inflation tax may have to rise more rapidly than the simple inflation tax analysis suggests.

Readers of the paper will look forward to seeing whether it is an empirical success.

REFERENCES

Blanchard, O. and M. Watson (1982), 'Bubbles, Rational Expectations and Financial Markets', in P. Wachtel (ed.) *Crisis in Economic and Financial Structure*. Lexington Books, Lexington, Massachusetts.

Leroy, S. and R. Porter (1981), 'The Present-Value Relation: Tests Based on Implied Variance Bounds', *Econometrica* 49, pp: 555–574.

Part Three
The World Debt Problem

6 International Capital Flows and the World Debt Problem[1]

Rudiger Dornbusch and Stanley Fischer

In 1983 the debt problems of developing countries, especially Latin America's problems, appeared on the way to a solution. Despite the strains following first the Polish and then major Latin American borrower difficulties, the international financial system did not collapse. Moratoria quickly gave way to IMF adjustment programmes and debt rescheduling that provided the debtors with a way of avoiding default and meeting debt service liabilities by borrowing fresh money from the banking system.

However, the 'muddling through' strategy is becoming increasingly doubtful as high world interest rates force massive additional transfers from debtors to creditors, at the cost of deep recession in the adjusting countries. There is much discussion of whether the debt crisis is a liquidity or a solvency problem. But the definition of solvency for a nation is not as clear-cut as that for a corporation: given the existing sizes of debts, living standards in debtor countries could be depressed to levels so low as to make it possible to pay off the debts. The real issue is whether their political systems and citizens can and should be made to stand the strain.

A broad front of opinion has called for change. Martin Feldstein (1984) has made the case for a new approach as follows:

> But the time has surely come to go beyond high-risk crisis management. The debtor nations need new longer-term financial arrangements that embody explicit safeguards against destabilising changes in world financial markets. Within such a financial framework, the debtor nations and their industrial trading partners can take the steps necessary to promote the increased exports that can provide the basis for long-term growth and financial independence.

This paper reviews the debt problem and, briefly, the already extensive literature on the subject. After setting out an analytical framework we present an historical analysis of the present debt crisis. From there we proceed to our evaluation of the sustainability of the 'muddling through' process. The paper concludes with an evaluation of alternative proposals, in particular the idea of interest rate caps and interest rate capitalisation.

I DEBT DYNAMICS

In this section we set out a framework for the discussion of debt history and proposed solutions. The dynamics of the debt problem are analysed starting from the debt accumulation equation:[2]

$$D_t = (1+i_t)D_{t-1} - NX_t \qquad (1)$$

where D is the dollar value of outstanding debt, i is the nominal interest rate on the outstanding debt and NX is the non-interest component (measured in dollars) of the current account; $(-NX)$ is the 'resource gap'.

The ratio of debt to exports is the most widely used indicator of a country's external debt position. Transforming (1) into an equation for the debt–export ratio, d (with exports measured in dollars):

$$d_t = K_t d_{t-1} - nx_t$$
$$K_t \equiv (1+i_t)/(1+gx_t) \qquad (2)$$

where gx is the nominal (dollar) growth rate of exports and nx is the ratio of NX to exports, or the negative of the resource gap measured as a fraction of exports.

The debt–export ratio is analogous to the debt–income ratio used as a measure of debt-capacity for individuals, or the debt–GNP ratio used in discussing fiscal policy. It suffers obvious shortcomings as an indicator of a country's foreign debt situation: as a measure of debt burden it would be preferable to have the real interest bill, perhaps relative to GNP; as a measure of liquidity needs, the debt-service-to export ratio might be preferable; as a measure of the vulnerability of an economy to a cutoff of lending, it would be preferable to have in the denominator a variable representing the economy's potential *net* earnings of foreign currency – for a cutoff of foreign capital would by reducing imports, reduce exports as well; as a measure at a moment of time it neglects future developments that would affect a country's ability to pay its debts.[3] But the debt–export ratio serves well as an indicator of the viability of projected paths of the balance of payments, in the sense that any forecast with an ever-increasing debt–export ratio describes a situation that is not viable.

Of course, in some instances a transitorily rising debt–export ratio may be consistent with an improvement of a country's ability to service its external debt. For instance, to the extent that debt accumulation has as a counterpart investment and future export earnings, rising debt–export ratios are a leading indicator of prosperity, not catastrophe. Unfortunately, it cannot be argued that debt accumulation in the debtor countries has in fact been predominantly financing investment that was productive by the test of net dollar earnings (as opposed to useful, desirable, socially justified etc.), at least in the late 1970s.

Equation (2) points to the four key determinants of the debt–export ratio. Assuming a positive outstanding stock of debt, the debt–export ratio at the end of period t is higher the higher the nominal interest rate, and the higher the inherited debt–export ratio; a high growth rate of the value of exports, or a positive non-interest current account, tend to reduce the ratio. The analysis of the history of the debt problem of the 1980s to be presented in Section II is summarised by equation (2). Borrowing during the 1970s had made accumulated debt, d_{t-1} large. The second oil shock and overvalued exchange rates made net exports, nx, negative. The increase in the interest rate, followed by a world recession that reduced the growth rate of exports and further worsened the non-interest current account, complete the story.

Equation (3) extends (2) to distinguish real from nominal interest rates:

$$K_t \equiv \frac{(1+r_t)(1+gp_t)}{(1+gvx_t)(1+gpx_t)} \tag{3}$$

where r is the real interest rate, gp is the US inflation rate, gvx is the growth rate of the volume of exports and gpx is the rate of increase of the dollar price of exports.

Equation (3) focuses on interest rates, inflation and growth. The real interest rate that the developing country borrowers will have to pay depends in part on the real rate of interest in the capital markets of the industrialised world. The real rate of interest in turn is a function of the fiscal/monetary mix and the level of capacity utilisation in the developed economies.

The growth rate of exports from the developing countries will depend on the growth rate of output in the OECD, on the path of the real exchange rate, and on OECD countries' tariffs and other trade barriers impeding exports from the developing countries. Increases in the relative prices of exports of the developing countries, reflected in the ratio $(1+gpx)/(1+gp)$, in effect reduce the real interest rate that has to be paid by the developing countries (DCs). Commodity prices are typically highly cyclical, so that the relative price of commodity exports will rise with OECD expansion. Depending on trade elasticities, such changes in the terms of trade will affect debt dynamics in addition through the *nx* term. The non-interest current account, *nx*, improves with OECD growth and deteriorates with DC growth; it improves as the DCs produce real devaluation, and it improves with the willingness of the OECD to accept imports from the DCs.

Examination of equation (3) thus shows that real devaluation, contractionary domestic policy in the DCs to reduce imports, and a change in the OECD fiscal/monetary mix that reduces the real interest rate, will all unambiguously reduce the debt–export ratio of the DCs. The effects of OECD expansion appear, however, to be ambiguous: OECD growth will increase DC exports, but likely also increase the real interest rate. Which of these effects dominates has to be determined empirically: indeed, this is a key issue in evaluating future debt developments.

We have already noted the importance of distinguishing the real interest rates in the main industrial countries and the real interest rates relevant for debtor countries. The two will differ to the extent that the terms of trade are changing as captured by the term $(1+gp)/(1+gpx)$ in (3) above. But there are other important differences, arising first from the spread between list rates (prime, Libor) and rates including fees and commissions that are actually paid by borrowers, and second, from the proportion of concessional financing obtained by the DCs. The spread above Libor charged the DCs by commercial lenders may be substantial, as high as 2.5 percentage points, and varies across borrowers.[4] To the extent that the debt problem is handled by commercial bank lending, this above-Libor rate will be the subject of bargaining between lenders and borrowers in trouble.

To summarise our discussion we present an expression for the growth of the debt–export ratio, d_t/d_{t-1}, in terms of two variables:

$$\text{debt growth} = K_t + \text{Gap}_t \quad (4)$$

The first term summarises the opposing influences of interest rates and the growth of export revenue in dollars. The second term is the ratio of the resource gap or non-interest current account deficit to the stock of debt: in the terminology of (2), $\text{Gap}_t = (-nx_t)/d_{t-1}$. Neither of these two terms (K and Gap) is entirely exogenous to the policies of a debtor country and neither is entirely or even primarily under the control of debtor countries. It is therefore necessary in a historical analysis to disentangle shocks and policy responses in their respective influences on the growth of external debt.

This conceptual framework will now be used to interpret the accumulation of debt in the 1970s, focusing on the relative roles of the world macroeconomic environment and individual countries' policies.

II HISTORY

Debt difficulties for isolated countries are common. Debt reschedulings in the post-war period have been frequent (see IMF, 1983, 1984), but the debt difficulties of the early 1980s are on a different scale. The World Bank (1985) in a survey of debt relief agreements records 84 separate multilateral reschedulings in the 1975–83 period: more than three-quarters occurred in the last three years. Of the nearly $90 billion rescheduled in the 1975–83 period, 85 per cent was in the last three years. The pervasiveness of the debt problem resembles the 1930s when most LDCs incurred debt service difficulties and many defaulted, at least partially, on their external debt. Every country in Latin America, except Argentina, failed to service the debt on the terms contracted. The magnitude of the debt problem, as measured by the debt–export ratio of Latin America, was much the same as today, as Table 6.1 shows.[5]

But even the 1930s were not the first occasion of large scale debt difficulties as the following quote from the period suggests:

> The experience of European lending to South America has from the beginning been marked by numerous disasters. Waves of intense optimism, during which almost any properly engraved certificate could be sold at a high price, have alternated with troughs of profound pessimism, in which export of capital stopped completely.

Table 6.1 Debt–export ratio of Latin America (debt as percent of exports)

1929	*1935*	*1955*	*1973*	*1978*	*1983*
149	224	60	176	212	243

SOURCE: United Nations (1964) and IMF (1983, 1984).

Every South American state has been in default at least twice and it still has always, after a greater or lesser delay, been possible for these states to secure funds. (C. Griffin, *American Economic Review*, March 1935, p. 79.)

As a further reflection on the 1930s it is worth remembering that debt service disruption and actual default occurred in Europe and in Latin America, but not in Asia or Africa.

Overview and Analysis

We start the discussion of debt history in the 1970s by looking at the influence of the external environment. Table 6.2 and Figures 6.1 and 6.2 show details on developments in the world macroeconomy over the period. In Table 6.2 the real price of oil and real commodity prices are measured in terms of the world price level as given by the dollar export prices of industrial countries. Real interest rates are shown for both the US and for developing countries. By using the dollar price of DC exports to measure the US prime rate we show how the development of export prices affected the effective cost of borrowing for the DCs. Real commodity prices show substantial variation, from a peak of 130 in 1974 to a low of 81 in 1982; despite dropping in 1983, real oil prices at the end of the period were nearly seven times their 1970 level.

In Figure 6.1 we show the constituent elements of the real DC prime rate. The early 1970s were a debtor's paradise with large negative real interest rates. But by the late 1970s, and especially in the early 1980s, the real interest rate was large and positive. The shaded areas identify the periods of positive real interest rates. The measure of real interest rates is certainly very sensitive to the inflation rate used to define it. We use the rate of inflation of DC export prices because dollar export prices reflect the effects of world economic develop-

Table 6.2 World macroeconomic variables (indices 1980 = 100)

	GDP growth (%)	*Real oil price*	*Real commodity price*	*US prime rate*	*Real prime rate, US (%)*	*Real prime rate DCs (%)*
1970	2.8	17	107	7.9	2.9	10.3
1971	3.6	19	96	5.7	1.5	0.5
1972	5.4	19	100	5.2	−0.5	−27.1
1973	6.0	22	127	8.0	−0.8	−27.4
1974	0.7	62	130	10.8	1.5	12.3
1975	−0.4	60	94	7.9	2.7	2.3
1976	5.0	63	108	6.8	1.0	−8.3
1977	3.9	63	121	6.8	−0.6	3.0
1978	4.0	57	102	9.1	0.4	−7.6
1979	3.2	66	103	12.7	3.5	2.1
1980	1.3	100	100	15.3	5.6	20.3
1981	1.5	117	87	18.9	12.8	25.5
1982	−0.5	126	81	14.9	11.0	18.7
1983	2.3	113	89	10.8	7.0	9.3

Notes
1. The first column is the growth rate of industrial countries' GDP.
2. The real oil price is the price of oil deflated by the export unit value of industrialised countries.
3. The real commodity price is the index of 'all commodities' in IFS (excluding oil) deflated by industrialised countries' export unit value.
4. The real prime rate, US, is the US prime rate minus the US GNP deflator inflation of the subsequent year.
5. The real prime rate, DCs, is the US prime rate minus the rate of increase of the dollar price of non-oil DC exports over the subsequent year.

SOURCE IMF

ments on the DCs ability to pay off loans without any change in the volume of exports.

In Figure 6.2 we show the link between the real price of commodities and industrial production in the major OECD countries. In the early 1970s there was sustained, strong growth and a major boom in commodity prices. In the late 1970s and early 1980s growth of industrial production vanishes and real commodity prices fall to low levels. At the end of the period, commodity prices and industrial production both turn up, but prices are still well below the average levels of the 1970s.

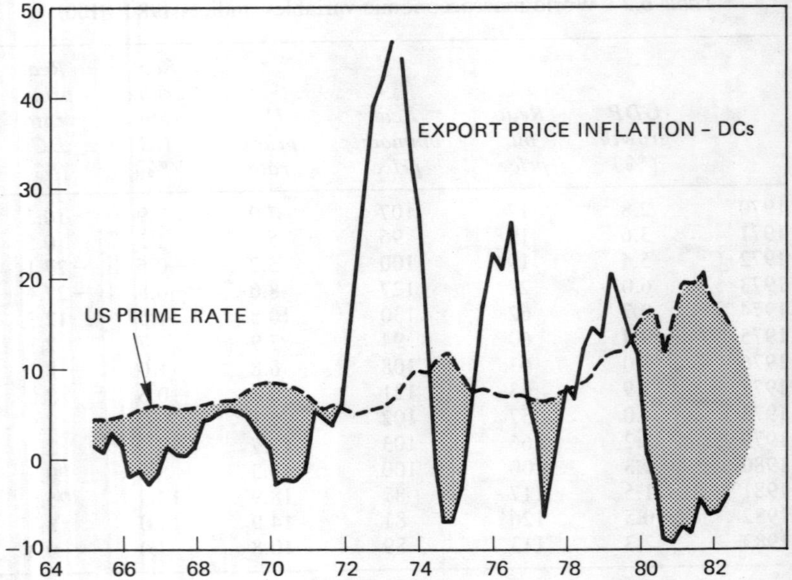

FIGURE 6.1 *Inflation and interest rates.*

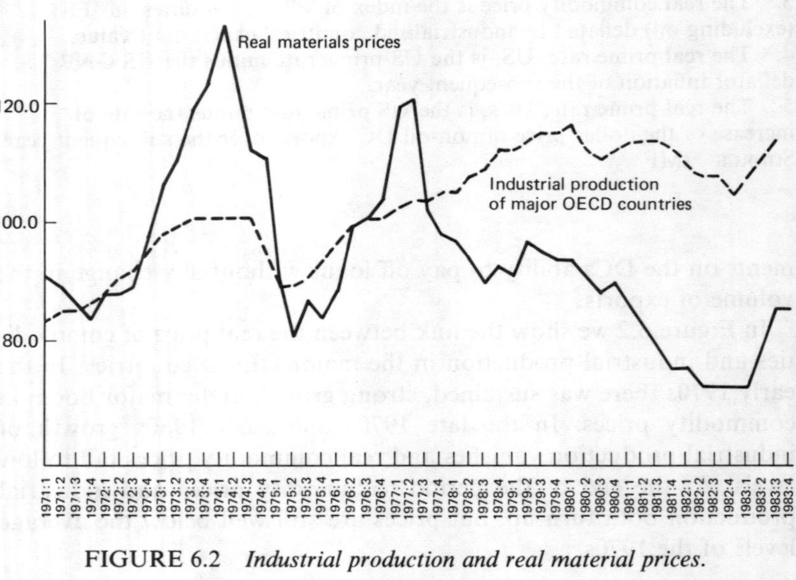

FIGURE 6.2 *Industrial production and real material prices.*

Debt statistics

A broad overview of gross external debt developments is given in Table 6.3. The table shows the very large increase in external debt over the 1973–83 period. It also places that increase in perspective by showing the debt data in constant 1980 dollars. Again we use the industrial countries' export unit value as a measure of the price level in world trade.[6] While the debt increased in nominal terms by 446 per cent, the increase in real terms was only 165 per cent. This amounted to an average annual growth rate of the real debt of 9.3 per cent; that growth rate, of course, exceeded the average real income growth of these countries and hence external debt increased relative to GDP. Table 6.3 also shows the debt–GDP ratio, which rose by 67 per cent over the period.

The second point to note in Table 6.3 is the significant differences in the external debt position of different regional groups. Asia shows very small debt–export ratios while the Western hemisphere leads in size.

A counterfactual exercise

We now place in perspective the relative roles of external factors and domestic policies in the debt build-up. We do this by asking what part of the debt increase would have occurred if the debtor countries, starting from some base year, had in each year pursued policies that ensured a zero non-interest current account. They would accordingly have borrowed only the interest on their existing debt, but no more. Under that assumption would debt–export ratios in the 1970s have increased as sharply as they did?

Figure 6.3 shows the result of the following simple exercise: suppose a hypothetical country at the end of 1969 had a debt–export ratio of 150. Throughout the 1970–83 period the country is assumed to have a non-interest current account that is balanced, or Gap = 0 in terms of (4) above. Interest is paid at the actual prime rate. Export earnings in dollars are assumed to grow at the rate at which non-oil developing countries' exports actually grew. The exercise in effect shows what share of the current debt is due to (non-interest) current account deficits over the 1970–83 period.

Figure 6.3 shows that starting from an initial level of 150 per cent in 1969 the debt–export ratio in 1969 would have ended by 1983 at a level of 79 per cent. The most striking features of Figure 6.3 are: the

Table 6.3 Developing countries: external debt outstanding (in billions of US dollars)

	1973	*1977*	*1978*	*1979*	*1980*	*1981*	*1982*	*1983*	*1984*
Non-oil developing countries	130.1	280.3	334.3	395.3	475.2	559.6	633.3	668.6	710.9
Debt in 1980 dollars*	290.1	413.4	435.3	445.0	475.2	581.7	681.7	744.1	768.5
Long-term and short-term debt by area									
Africa (excluding South Africa)	NA	30.8	36.9	45.3	50.9	55.5	62.5	66.3	70.7
Asia	30.0	68.7	78.7	92.8	114.6	131.2	152.6	165.0	179.3
Europe	14.5	37.6	47.0	55.0	67.2	71.1	72.3	74.8	76.6
Middle East	8.7	21.9	26.7	32.0	36.3	40.6	45.6	50.7	56.2
Western hemisphere	44.4	109.1	132.4	157.8	192.6	246.0	283.1	294.4	310.5
Ratio of external debt to exports of goods and services (%)									
Non-oil developing countries	115.4	126.1	127.7	117.2	111.2	122.5	144.1	149.5	144.7
Africa (excluding South Africa)	NA	135.8	151.1	149.7	143.2	168.6	204.5	223.5	215.8
Asia	92.9	80.7	75.4	68.4	67.5	69.1	79.8	81.4	79.9
Europe	102.4	114.9	123.6	115.8	117.7	110.8	119.4	126.0	121.0
Middle East	145.4	138.9	140.7	134.0	110.7	120.9	136.2	157.2	161.8
Western hemisphere	176.2	202.9	217.4	198.2	187.0	219.7	274.4	288.5	273.3
Ratio of external debt to GDP (%)									
Non-oil developing countries	22.4	23.7	24.1	23.3	23.9	27.1	32.5	36.7	37.5
Africa (excluding South Africa)	NA	35.8	36.6	38.0	35.7	41.5	49.5	59.6	61.8
Asia	19.7	15.7	14.8	14.7	15.9	17.8	20.7	21.4	21.3
Europe	24.5	21.2	23.1	20.9	25.0	28.3	29.2	34.3	37.6
Middle East	36.2	45.0	47.9	56.1	51.7	52.2	52.9	50.6	49.2
Western hemisphere	23.0	27.9	29.4	27.9	27.3	31.6	42.1	54.8	57.6

*Deflated by index of export unit values for developed countries.

IMF (1983), (1984)

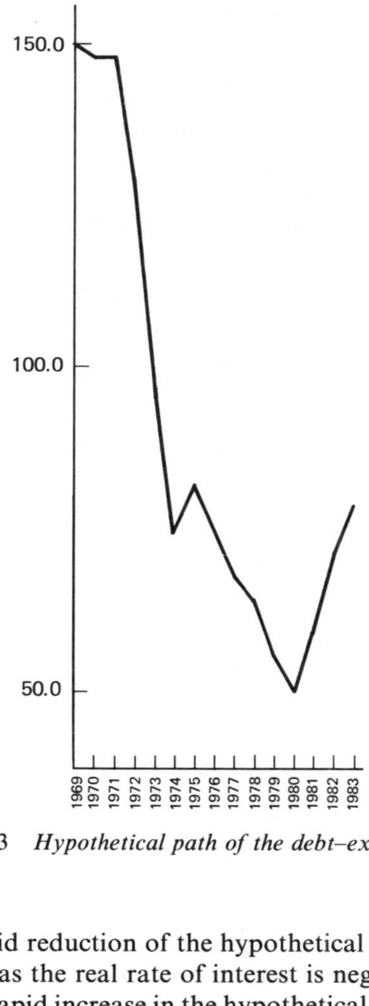

FIGURE 6.3 *Hypothetical path of the debt–export ratio.*

extraordinarily rapid reduction of the hypothetical debt–export ratio from 1969 to 1974 as the real rate of interest is negative and exports grow fast; and the rapid increase in the hypothetical debt–export ratio from 1980 to 1983 under the influence of large positive real rates and weak export performance.

Figure 6.3 tells us, as a first approximation, that external circumstances – interest rates and export growth – cannot by themselves account for the severe increase in debt problems over the 1970–83 period. Over the 1973–83 period the debt–export ratio would have remained unchanged if the non-interest current-account had been balanced. Instead it increased 64 per cent. Non-interest current-account imbalances are clearly an essential part of the debt problem. These non-interest current account imbalances in turn are linked to short-run and long-term macroeconomic developments: investment trends, budget deficits, private sector saving, disequilibrium exchange rates, and to the manner in which some of these domestic variables responded to external shocks.

Figure 6.4 focuses further on the influence of the external environment in terms of interest rates and growth of dollar export earnings. The figure shows the ratio K_t of equation (4) for the period 1950–83 using the US prime interest rate and the actual growth of non-oil DCs exports. The interesting point to note is the relation between Figures 6.3 and 6.4. The peaks and troughs in the debt–export ratio of Figure 6.3 are related to successive realisations of K above or below unity. Thus the runs of 1971–3 and 1975–80 lead to a cumulative decline in indebtedness. On the other side a sequence of high values of K in 1980–83 leads to a build-up of indebtedness.

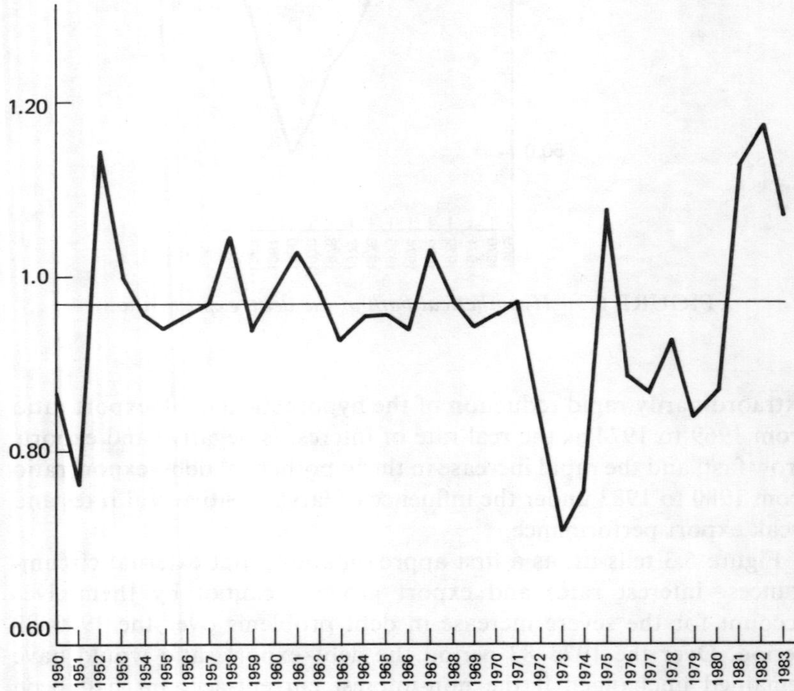

FIGURE 6.4 *The coefficient K_t.*

A further point to note about Figure 6.4 is the much larger volatility in the 1970–83 period than in the period from the end of the Korean War (1954) to 1970. Table 6.4 shows data for different subperiods that bring out this fact.

Table 6.4 shows important differences in the subperiods. The most recent period features more adverse conditions for debtors since the average value of *K* significantly exceeds unity. A country that had followed in this recent period a policy of rolling over a given initial debt, borrowing the capital to finance interest charges, would have experienced debt growth, relative to exports, at an average rate of nearly 3 per cent per year.

Table 6.4 The debt growth coefficient *K*

	1950–70	*1954–70*	*1970–83*	*1978–83*
Average	0.99	1.00	0.96	1.03
Standard deviation	0.07	0.03	0.13	0.13

The relative role of the world environment and domestic policies is brought out by considering the period dominated by unfavourable external shocks, 1980–83. Table 6.5 shows for different groups of non-oil DCs the actual percentage increase in the debt–export ratio and the percentage increase associated with a balanced non-interest current account, debt service at prime rate, and the actual export growth of the region. Except for Latin America the actual percentage increase in the debt–export ratio matched or fell short of what would be implied by the hypothetical path. In these cases countries were reducing their debt relative to exports by running current account surpluses.

Table 6.5 The external shock of 1980–83

	Actual % rise in debt–export ratio	*Hypothetical % rise*
Non-oil DCs	23.0	25.5
Africa	36.6	65.4
Asia	16.7	16.5
Middle East	1.6	18.2
Latin America	38.4	24.4

The evidence in Table 6.5 points to the common external shock as one force that greatly increased external indebtedness. But the differences between regions are significant. The large increase in Latin American debt–income ratios represents both non-interest current account deficits and differences in effective interest rates that are not captured in our hypothetical scenario.

Up to this point we have used the US prime rate to represent the average DC borrowing rate. But, as Table 6.6 shows, effective interest costs vary substantially. The effective interest rate (total interest as a fraction of total debt) depends on the terms at which external debt was acquired: at concessional or market rates, at fixed or floating rates, whether public or private, whether short- or long-term. Given the recent history of rising interest rates, the effective interest rate will be higher the larger the share of private, floating-rate debt. This effect is further reinforced by the fees and commissions associated with rescheduling of private debts and, of course, with the spreads over Libor on private debt. Table 6.6 shows that part of the differences in Table 6.5 between Latin America and the other groups reflects these differences in effective interest rates.

Table 6.6 shows that effective interest costs are below Libor or the prime rate, though by 1983 they are equal to Libor in the case of Latin America.[7] This is the case even though front-end fees, commitment

Table 6.6 Effective interest cost (per cent)

	1979	*1980*	*1981*	*1982*	*1983*
US prime rate	12.7	15.3	18.9	14.9	10.8
Libor	12.1	14.2	16.8	13.2	9.6
Total DC debt*	7.7	9.0	9.7	10.0	8.7
Fixed interest	5.8	6.0	6.0	6.3	6.7
Floating rate	12.3	15.5	17.4	17.1	12.7
Lower income countries*	3.8	3.8	3.8	4.0	3.7
Lower-middle income countries*	7.3	8.7	9.0	9.8	8.3
Upper-middle income countries	9.3	11.0	12.1	12.2	10.6
Major Developing borrowers†	7.6	9.2	11.1	11.5	9.4
Major Latin borrowers†	8.4	10.1	12.4	13.4	10.8
Major Asian borrowers†	6.8	8.7	10.1	9.8	8.0
Major Mid-East and African borrowers†	6.5	7.7	8.7	8.3	7.3

*OECD, †Morgan Guaranty.
SOURCES OECD (1984), Morgan Guaranty, DRI and IMF.

fees and spreads significantly increase the cost of debt obtained from banks. The World Bank (1985) reports that average spreads on new credits to oil-importing countries were 1.86 percentage points, up from 1.11 percentage points in 1982. Brau *et al.* (1983) report details on fees in recent reschedulings and show that they fall in the range of 2 to 3 percentage points. These facts along with the level of Libor and the US Prime rate must be borne in mind in interpreting the effective interest cost in Table 6.6. The inference is that poor countries have borrowed predominantly at fixed and concessional rates. By contrast major Latin borrowers have so significant a component of bank debt that spreads and fees nearly offset the low-interest part of their debt.

We return to the interest rate issue later in the paper where we discuss the impact of current interest rate developments on the sustainability of the 'muddling-through' approach to the debt problem. The difference between borrowers already noted here becomes important at that point.

Some Econometric Evidence

The behaviour of interest rates and of aggregate DC dollar export growth is of course governed predominantly by the macroeconomic conditions of industrial countries. Policies in DCs – particularly exchange rate policies – do affect individual country experiences, but for the present we assume that there is sufficient independence of their policies so that *aggregate* non-oil DC export performance is largely determined by the macroeconomics of the industrial countries.

Consider now the determinants of the growth in export volume of non-oil DCs. Considering the period 1954–82, using annual data, we explain export volume growth in an OLS regression on the current growth rate of industrial countries' real GDP. The constant term is allowed to differ in the 1971–82 period from the earlier period by using a dummy that assumes a value of unity in these years and zero elsewhere.

$$\text{Export volume growth} = \underset{(-0.13)}{-0.19} + \underset{+(3.73)}{4.49\text{DUM}} + \underset{(3.85)}{1.15\text{INDGrowth}} \quad R^{-2} = 0.41 \ \text{DW} = 2.0$$

In the 1970s export volume grew at an annual rate of 4.5 per cent higher than in other years, given the growth rate of the developed countries. In addition every extra point of OECD growth raises export volume growth by 1.15 percentage points. There is thus a significant effect of growth in industrial countries on the export performance of non-oil DCs. Note that although the equation explains only 40 per cent of the variation in export growth, the impact of industrial countries' growth is highly significant, as suggested by the high *t*-ratio, and there is no indication of serial correlation pointing to systematic omitted variables.

We also examined the determinants of the real price of commodities. We measured the real price by deflating the IMF dollar price index of all commodities (excluding oil) by the dollar index of industrial countries' exports prices. The growth in the real commodity price in the period 1958–83 is explained by industrial countries' growth:

$$\begin{array}{lll} \text{Real commodity} = -10.6 + 2.67\ \text{INDGrowth} & & R^{-2} = 0.24\ \ \text{DW} = 2.02 \\ \text{price growth} \qquad\quad (-2.7)\ \ (3.0) & & \end{array}$$

Once again the equation explains only a small part of the variation in the dependent variable. But industrial countries growth appears as a significant determinant. An extra percentage point of growth raises the real commodity price by nearly three percentage points. In the absence of growth there is a steep downward trend at a rate of 10.5 per cent per year. This trend effect is largely offset during the sample period, by an average growth of developed countries at a rate of 3.7 per cent. In combination with the elasticity of about 2.7 this is sufficient to keep the real price of commodities approximately constant.

We have not had much success in pinning down the determinants of the real price of non-oil developing countries' exports. The variable we tried to explain is the non-oil DCs export unit value index deflated by industrial countries unit value of exports. Current growth in industrial countries, or changes in growth do not appear significant. Lagged growth *changes*, however, are significant and remain so in different subperiods. We must add though that there is no theoretical basis for the claimed relationship between growth in real export price and the *change* in *lagged* growth rates.[8]

The results we have obtained show that a one percentage point increase in industrial countries' growth raises the real commodity prices by 1.3 percentage points. This is a one time only increase associated with a change to a higher growth rate. Thus the effect is quantitatively small and, as already noted, theoretically hard to defend. We give it attention because in some debt scenarios, specifically Cline's (1984), the cyclical recovery of real commodity prices plays a quantitatively large role.

Figure 6.5, which shows the real commodity price series, also suggests why it is difficult to explain. The series is dominated by two periods of extreme change, 1970–75 and 1977–8. Any attempt at sorting out the role of oil, industrial countries' growth, and the dollar in these price movements fails because there are simply not enough episodes to do so in a robust way. This point is reinforced by differences between country groups and by supply-side factors that are neglected in equations that focus uniquely on cyclical effects.

The empirical evidence on the growth in export earnings and its relation to OECD growth is broadly summarised by equation (4). Here we look at growth in export earnings of non-oil DCs. They are

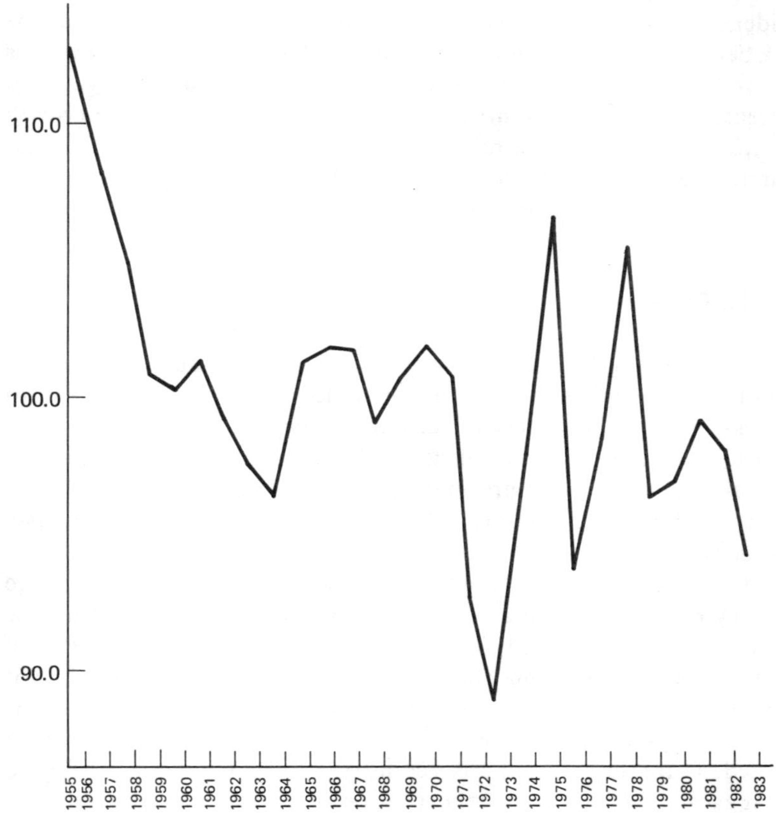

FIGURE 6.5 *The real price of non-oil DC exports (index 1980 = 100).*

explained by inflation in world trade as measured by the growth rate of the unit export values of industrial countries, INF, and by real growth, INDGrowth, already discussed above and a 1970s dummy, DUM. The last term INF3 is introduced to capture an apparent non-linearity in the response to inflation and is the cube of INF.

$$\underset{\text{growth}}{\text{Export revenue}} = \underset{(-2.1)}{-6.7} + \underset{(2.7)}{0.76\text{INF}} + \underset{(3.9)}{2.4\text{INDGrowth}} + \underset{(2.6)}{0.0015\text{INF3}} + \underset{(2.1(4)}{5.8\text{DUM}}$$

$R^{-2} = 0.83 \qquad DW = 1.92$

The equation shows that export earnings grow approximately one-for-one with world inflation. Industrial country growth translates with a coefficient of 2.5 into earnings growth. Finally, for the post-1970 period there is roughly no trend growth. Taking into account evidence from further work not reported here, we conclude that the link between export revenue growth and industrial countries growth is about 2:1. To give a range one might say that a one percentage point increase in industrial countries' growth raises export revenue growth by 1.5 to 2.5 percentage points. But as a working number 2:1 best summarises all the available evidence.[9] We return to this relationship in examining alternative debt scenarios.

Special Cases

Following the global overview we now examine data for specific countries, to emphasise the large differences among countries and to discuss, briefly, the variety of reasons for debt difficulties. Table 6.7 shows the behaviour of total debt and the debt-to-export ratio for several countries. They are mainly the big Latin American debtor countries, but also an oil-producing country and examples from Asia and Africa.

The comparison is made between 1975 and 1983 because there are no very reliable debt data for the earlier part of the 1970s. But it is worth commenting briefly on the earlier debt positions. The 1970 data, imperfect as they may be, show that Mexico and the Republic of Korea had debt–export ratios of 347.0 and 331.2 respectively. This is of interest because the ratios were as high then, if the numbers can be trusted, as are the ratios of crisis countries today. Of course, as Figure 6.1 suggests, the high debt–export ratios of 1970 were sharply reduced by the negative real interest rates up to 1973; no such relief is in sight currently.

Table 6.7 External debt and debt–export ratios

	1975		*1983*	
	Debt ($US)	*Debt/exports (%)*	*Debt ($US)*	*Debt/exports (%)*
Non-oil DCs	116.0	92.7	710.0	144.7
Argentina	7.9	171.3	45.3	452.0
Brazil	26.0	236.6	93.1	364.9
Chile	5.4	282.3	18.6	374.9
Mexico	22.5	263.8	89.8	315.3
Venezuela	5.5	44.1	44.9	200.5
Nigeria	1.3	14.3	17.0	126.0
Indonesia	9.7	131.4	29.5	136.1
Republic of Korea	11.6	171.9	40.1	125.0

Note The debt/export ratio is calculated by averaging current and past year-end debt and dividing by current year exports of goods and services.
SOURCE Morgan Guaranty.

Table 6.7 makes it clear that the Latin American debt situation is quite different from that of other large borrowers, in particular the Republic of Korea. The debt–export ratios are much higher and, indeed, started off higher in 1975 than they are today for the other countries shown. Both the absolute size of the debts and the magnitude of the debts relative to exports stand out.

The second point to note in Table 6.7 is that the debt–export ratios did not uniformly increase. On the contrary, the Republic of Korea is an interesting example because here a significant increase in external debt was matched by even larger export growth. This difference, as we will note below, reflects in part a different pattern of adjustment to external shocks between Korea and Latin American countries, and in part it reflects a different economic structure. Specifically, Korea is a material importer and as such benefits from a collapse of commodity prices whereas other DCs are net exporters of commodities and therefore are hurt.

The reasons for debt accumulation vary across countries. In some cases they include, perhaps even predominantly, investment booms. In other cases they represent lack of adjustment to external interest rate or terms of trade shocks, the financing of capital flight, or the flight into importables under the incentive of currency overvaluation. The experience of several Latin American countries points to the interaction of domestic policy mistakes and world macroeconomic developments. Domestic expansionary policies financed by external debt accumulation were pursued on a very large scale. A course that could have been corrected with reasonable difficulty then became extraordinarily difficult and costly to correct once world interest rates escalated in world markets and commodity prices plummeted. The interaction lies in the fact that the domestic policies led to an overexposure in terms of external debt which then was vastly magnified by the world macroeconomic shocks.[10]

We also discuss in more detail the cases of Mexico and the Republic of Korea, to examine both domestic DC causes of the debt problem and alternative strategies for declining with it. Mexico's debt problem arose from three domestic causes, as well as the external developments studied earlier. The three domestic causes were capital flight, flight into importables, and extremely large public sector investment, deficits and imports. While the oil discoveries helped reduce the large external indebtedness (relative to exports) of the early 1970s, poor policies in 1980–82 together with a softening of oil prices more than compensated and ultimately led to the 1982 suspension of debt service.[11]

Table 6.8 shows the key Mexican indicators in the period 1978 to 1982. The table shows the sharply rising budget deficit and a matching external debt increase. The large public sector deficit spilled directly over into imports and a trade deficit. But it also gave rise to inflation and overvaluation and therefore to capital flight in anticipation of depreciation. The real exchange rate, measured by Mexican relative to US consumer prices, *appreciated* by more than 30 per cent in the

Table 6.8 Mexican macroeconomic indicators

	1978	*1979*	*1980*	*1981*	*1982*
Budget deficit (% of GDP)	5.5	6.0	6.9	13.6	16.3
Inflation (Dec. to Dec.)	17.5	18.2	26.4	27.9	58.9
Real exchange rate (index 1980 = 100)	117	113.5	100.0	90.6	137.9
External debt ($US billions)	34.0	40.4	52.5	78.9	84.6

SOURCE *Informe Hacendario Mensual*, November 1983, IFS and Morgan Guaranty.

1978–81 period thus creating the firm expectation of depreciation. Maintenance of fixed rates and an open capital account meant that there was no means to stop the capital outflow. The corrective devaluation, however, occurred only in late 1982 once the large external debt had already been incurred.

It is important to distinguish gross from net external debt in the Mexican case.[12] Significant private capital outflows meant that the government was in effect borrowing abroad using the proceeds to finance private acquisition of foreign assets. This acquisition of private assets abroad is to a limited extent reflected in the non-bank Mexican claims on the banking system of the major industrial countries. Data reported by the Federal Reserve show an increase of deposits with US banks by residents of Mexico between 1980 and 1982 of $4 billion.[13] This does not take into account deposits in other countries or purchases of dollar currency, securities and real estate.

There is an interesting difference between the Latin American debtors and the Republic of Korea. The Republic of Korea is a major oil importer, and is also a major debtor. She is therefore subject to the same shocks as many other DCs. But the response and the outcome in terms of external debt has been very different from the average as Table 6.9 shows.

Perhaps the most interesting aspect of the Republic of Korea experience is that there is no simple story. The budget was in increasing deficit over the period, and the debt did increase rapidly. The major difference is in the behaviour of the real exchange rate. In the case of the Republic of Korea unit labour costs in dollars have declined, securing a strong gain in external competitiveness and

Table 6.9 Republic of Korea macroeconomic indicators

	1978	*1979*	*1980*	*1981*	*1982*
Growth	11.6	6.4	−6.2	6.4	5.4
Budget deficit (% of GDP)	2.7	1.6	3.6	4.3	4.5
Unit labour cost (in $US, 1978 = 100)	100	111	98	90.8	92.6
External debt ($US billions)	17.8	21.5	26.7	32.3	37.2

Source Morgan Guaranty, *Republic of Korea Economic Indicators*, Park (1984).

therefore a reduction in the non-interest current account deficit. This happened despite continued high growth, after 1980, and despite the oil price increase. The strategy of using the real exchange rate as a means of sustaining growth, particularly in the case of adverse shocks is apparent from the rise in the ratio of exports to GDP. In 1978 that ratio was 33.4 per cent. By 1982 the export share had increased to 38.9 per cent. We shall return to this point in the context of adjustment programmes.

The Republic of Korea and Latin American borrowers also differ in respect to the economic structure. The former imports materials and exports manufactures. Brazil, Chile or Argentina, by contrast are, substantially commodity exporters even though manufacturing has become important. This explains the very different behaviour of the terms of trade for these countries. For Brazil the terms of trade deteriorated nearly 50 per cent in the 1978–82 period, but for the Republic of Korea they deteriorated by only 16 per cent. The smaller terms of trade deterioration of course eases the adjustment process and, indeed, dispenses with the need for severe adjustment at least until the terms of trade move adversely during the cyclical recovery.

III AN EVALUATION OF THE OUTLOOK

Debt scenarios abound. Several authors and/or teams, using the basic debt accumulation equation (1) and assumptions about growth and interest rates in the OECD countries have constructed projections of the debt situation of individual debtor countries over the next few years.[14] The projections typically show the debt–export ratio of the debtor countries falling over the period, and are optimistic that the debt problem can be handled without future disasters. Perhaps the best known of these scenarios is that of William Cline (1984), who sees the debt–export ratio for the largest 18 debtor countries dropping from 187 per cent in 1982 to 162 per cent by 1986. Some pessimism emerges from authors[15] who find that the developing countries will be able to grow only slowly over the next three years if they are to meet their debt obligations.

Rather than evaluate these forecasts,[16] we present in this section our own assessment of where the debt problem is leading and what it implies for the debtor countries. In doing so, we bring together outside forecasts of OECD performance with the empirical relationships presented in Section II above.

Forecasts of Developed Country trends

The critical external variables in debt projections are industrial countries' growth, inflation and nominal interest rates. A number of short-term forecasts dated May to July 1984 are available from official institutions and commercial forecasting firms. Table 6.10 shows three of these forecasts. The forecasts show average real growth of about 3 per cent for the 1983–5 period. They coincide in predicting a significant slowdown of growth in 1985, following the strong expansion that has been underway particularly in the first part of 1984. Available forecasts also coincide in predicting the persistence of low inflation rates in 1984–5 of around 5 to 6 per cent. Given the high nominal interest rates that means high real rates.

Table 6.10 Forecasts for industrial country growth

	1983	*1984*	*1985*
European Communities			
OECD Growth	2.4	4.4	2.6
OECD			
OECD Growth	2.4	4.3	2.8
Data Resources Inc.			
World GNP Growth	2.1	4.0	2.6

SOURCES OECD (1984) DRI.

Market expectations of the future path of interest rates can be inferred from the term structure of interest. On 21 June, 1984, the following rates were quoted for US treasury securities: 3-month T-bills at 9.93 per cent, 6-month T-bills at 10.49 per cent, 1-year Treasury securities at 10.87 per cent and 5-year Treasury securities at 13.3 per cent. The term structure is thus clearly upward sloping, reflecting the expectation that future interest rates will exceed current rates. With inflation expectations of about 5 per cent to 6 per cent, the real interest rate is thus 5 to 7 per cent, a rate that is exceptionally high by historical standards.

The reason for the high real interest rates remains uncertain. But the most plausible hypothesis is the combination in the US of tight monetary policy and expansionary fiscal policy, both current and expected. The discussion focuses on the US economy because the course of US policy will set the tone for the world economy.

To get a clearer idea of the possibilities we therefore look at the likely evolution of the US economy. Table 6.11 shows the detailed July forecast of Data Resources Inc. for the US economy under two alternative scenarios. Scenario A is the base case which is assigned a probability of 55 per cent. It assumes some fiscal correction and no outright clash between real growth and monetary tightness. In scenario B the lack of fiscal correction leads to an overly strong 1984 expansion and, with money unaccommodating, to an escalation of interest rates and 1986 recession. This scenario has a probability of 30 per cent.[17]

The difference between the two scenarios in Table 6.11 points to the critical importance for the developing countries of a move towards fiscal contraction in the United States as the economy reaches full employment. In the recovery from the end of 1982 to 1984, rising interest rates were associated with high growth: DC losses from higher interest rates were to an extent offset by gains from increasing exports. But the difference between scenarios A and B in Table 6.11 has serious implications for the DCs, for in scenario B US (and world) growth is *lower* and interest rates higher than in scenario A. Scenario B does not even provide the consolation of a depreciating dollar, as high interest rates and low income growth in the US maintain the exchange rate.

Scenario A shows an average US growth rate of 3.7 per cent over the years to 1986, compared with 2.2 per cent under scenario B. The Libor interest rate averages 11.2 per cent in scenario A and 14.2 per

Table 6.11 The DRI forecast for the US economy (average annual rates)

	1984		*1985*		*1986*	
	A	B	A	B	A	B
Growth	6.5	7.0	2.1	2.3	2.5	−2.6
Inflation	3.7	3.8	4.5	6.3	5.4	6.0
Libor	11.2	12.0	12.0	16.1	10.6	14.6
Dollar*	107	108	103	109	96	106

*Index of the effective nominal exchange rate, 1982 = 100. An increase in the index represents a strengthening of the dollar.

SOURCE DRI 28 June, 1984 forecast.

cent in scenario B. We use these ranges of interest rates and growth rates to evaluate the range of outlooks for the DCs.

Implications for DCs

We draw attention to three assumptions we make in evaluating the international debt problem. First, the problem is largely one for the big debtors, primarily but not entirely in Latin America. The rationale for this view was developed in Tables 6.5, 6.6, and 6.7. Further evidence is presented in Table 6.12, which shows the ratio of debt service, and of the interest component, relative to income and GDP for different groups of borrowers. Both in terms of size and in terms of changes the debt burden appears to be very much the problem of large debtors and specifically of Western hemisphere countries. This matches the evidence we saw earlier in looking at effective interest rates in Table 6.6. We saw there that low income countries enjoy low effective rates reflecting a significant share of concessional and fixed interest debt. In Table 6.12 the counterpart is a low and relatively unchanged share of debt service and of interest payments as a fraction of GDP. By contrast the major borrowers show a massive increase in debt service and interest charges relative to their exports of goods and services and relative to their incomes.

Our second assumption is that the problem is one of bank loans, a result of the rapid expansion of commercial bank lending to the DCs in the 1970s and early 1980s. The crisis if there is one will involve both

Table 6.12 The debt burden

	Low income countries		*Major borrowers*		*W. hemisphere*	
	1977	*1983*	*1977*	*1983*	*1977*	*1983*
Debt service						
% of exports	12.1	13.3	19.1	29.9	28.2	44.0
% of GDP	1.0	0.7	3.4	6.5	3.9	8.4
Interest payments						
% of exports	4.7	5.4	7.2	18.6	10.0	32.2
% of GDP	0.4	0.5	1.3	4.1	1.4	6.1

Note 'Major borrowers' is a Group of 25 DCs defined in IMF *World Economic Outlook*, 1984, p. 159.
SOURCE Calculated from IMF (1984), Tables 36 and 47.

the commercial banks of developed countries and the large DC debtors. Third, there is no strict economic criterion by which the issue of 'solvency' of the debtors can be determined. The issue is much more one of the political ability to depress living standards enough to handle the problem – and of the desirability of depressing developing countries living standards.

We now use the forecasts together with our earlier discussion of empirical growth-export links and of effective interest rates to assess the macro implications for DC countries. Our procedure assumes that external financing constraints limit import volumes and hence growth potential. The IMF (1984, p. 160) follows the same procedures and assumes that imports remain the relevant constraint:

> In the present scenario exercise, imports are treated as principally determined by export earnings and the availability of financing. During 1981–83 the growth rate of imports was constrained by the weak export performance of most developing countries and the shrinking of available financing from international banks. This constraint, although somewhat eased, will to some extent remain in effect during 1985–87, so that exports plus bank financing were felt to be a better indicator of import growth than developing country GDP . . .

This neglects the potential from DC adjustment policies which we discuss in the next section.

To arrive at the available level of imports we use the basic debt equation, (1), noting that NX is exports less imports of non-interest goods and services. We thus have:

$$\text{Imports} = \text{exports} + \text{increase in exposure} - \text{interest payments} \quad (5)$$

In symbols:

$$M_t = X_t + (D_t - D_{t-1}) - i_t D_{t-1} \quad (6)$$

where M_t is imports, X_t is exports, D_{t-1} is the debt at the end of period $(t-1)$, and i_t is the *effective* interest rate paid on the external debt. The effective rate, as discussed above is the weighted average of the rates applying to different kinds of debt. From (6) we can go to imports in constant prices by simply dividing by the price level. Equation (6) together with assumptions about inflation, real export growth and the effective interest rate will supply values for real imports. The import numbers in turn can be used to assess the room for growth in output in debtor countries.

Letting m_t and x_t denote real imports and exports, and assuming an inflation rate of 6 per cent, we then have:[18]

$$m_t = x_t + RD(0.06 - i_t)/(1.06) \tag{7}$$

where RD is the real value of the debt in the base year which by assumption is to remain constant.

Consider now an application to a hypothetical country that has an initial debt of $100 billion and exports of goods and services equal to $25 billion. In accordance with our emphasis on large scale debtors, the debt to export ratio is 400 per cent. Base year imports are assumed to be $21 billion. To assess the outlook we look at four possible combinations of export growth rates and effective interest rates, based on Table 6.11. Table 6.13 shows the possible scenarios. Using a basic 2:1 relationship between DC real exports and industrialised country growth, and assuming a range of industrialised country growth of 2 to 3 per cent over the 1983–6 period, we examine the consequences of real export growth rates of 4 per cent and 6 per cent. For effective interest rates we assume a low 9 per cent and a high of 12 per cent.

The numbers in the body of Table 6.13 represent the average growth rates of real imports in the 1984–6 period implied by equation (7) and the specified growth and interest rate combinations. The trade-offs are highly significant: an extra point on the interest rate or a percentage point decline in export growth will cost 1.1 to 1.5 percentage points of average import growth. The interesting combination, of course, is a shift from a stable interest rates and growth scenario in the upper right-hand corner to high interest rates and lower growth of exports. Here the cost is more than 6 percentage points of reduced import growth.

Table 6.13 Import growth under alternative assumptions

	Real export growth	
	4%	6%
Effective interest rate:		
9%	6.4%	8.7%
12%	2.0%	5.2%

The final step is to consider the effects of different rates of import growth on DC GNP growth. The IMF (1984, p. 221) estimates that a forced 2 percentage point reduction in import growth reduces DC GNP by 1 percentage point. Accordingly the implied range of growth rates for our hypothetical debtor is 1 per cent per annum to 4.3 per cent per annum.

A growth rate of output of 4.3 per cent is likely to make it possible for our hypothetical debtor country to meet its balance of payments goals without reducing living standards to levels that would force a change in policy. But a growth rate of GNP of 1 per cent per annum will not be sustainable. For countries where imports are already depressed relative to output, and where unemployment is high, so low a rate of growth leaves no room for a recovery. There would certainly be no room to absorb a strongly growing labour force. Something would have to give.

The low import and real growth scenario becomes more plausible the more world interest rates rise, and the longer US fiscal correction is delayed. Failing US fiscal corrections, there are two ways out. One is the extra efforts debtor countries can make toward achieving growth within the external parameters set by the world economy. The other is to look for debt relief. The remainder of the paper addresses these questions.

Before we leave this section three remarks are in order. First we have not considered optimistic scenarios – sustained 8 per cent average real export growth and a 5 per cent effective interest rate. If the world turns that way there is no debt problem. But the macroeconomic forecasts that are available give no evidence that such an outlook is plausible.

Second, we have looked at the case where banks are willing to finance a constant real debt. But what would happen if for the case of countries with severe debt problems (Mexico, Brazil, etc.) banks would seek a reduction in real debt? As equation (7) makes clear the outlook for import growth would be much more confined since now imports must be compressed to retire debt in real terms. More adjustment by debtors or debt relief and freer market access would become even more urgent.

Third, optimism is difficult to sustain. There is a serious possibility that the large debtors will be unable to continue to service their debt without further concessions.

IV THE ADJUSTMENT EFFORT IN DEBTOR COUNTRIES

The sustainability of the international lending process depends on how long the present adjustment programmes can be continued. Until the recovery of the world economy leads to strong export growth, the debtor countries have to contain domestic demand and employment in an effort to reduce imports and free foreign exchange for debt service. This curtailment in demand coincides and overlaps with the adjustment of public sectors toward budget balance or even surplus. The results so far have been dramatic. Trade surpluses have in most cases come out well within the targets of the IMF adjustment programmes; in this sense adjustment has taken place and has been successful. But it is also the case that the trade surpluses have been generated primarily by demand compression and depression, rather than by export growth. The question therefore arises whether these programmes can reasonably be expected to continue and, whether they will in the long-run, contribute to a solution of the debt problem.

The rationing of finance, in conjunction with the 1981–3 world recession and steeply increased interest rates, has visited a depression on developing countries and in particular on Latin America. The depression of economic activity in that region is already worse than it was in the 1930s. For the Western hemisphere the decline in per capita income since 1981 amounts to 12.6 per cent. In Africa, where income was lower to start with, per capita income has fallen by at least 2.5 per cent. To restore the 1980 level of per capita consumption by 1990, growth would need to be significantly faster than the scenarios of the previous sections would lead us to expect. Attention therefore must turn to the way the debt problem tends to depress growth and what kind of adjustment, on the part of the debtors, can improve things.

The debtor countries problems can be analysed in terms of the ideas of the classical transfer problem. In these terms there are three stages of the transfer problem: the problem of raising fiscal revenue for external debt service; the problem of translating these fiscal resources into potential dollar earnings via import substitution or increased exports under conditions of full employment; and last, securing the foreign exchange earnings or savings. We now comment on each of these stages in more detail.

The fiscal problem

Consider the case where all external debt is public and hence falls within the government's general fiscal responsibility. The need to service the external debt means that the government budget deficit is thereby increased. Extra taxes must be raised, spending must be curtailed or money creation must finance the deficit.

It is difficult to cope with the domestic fiscal policy aspect of debt in a country where the budget, not counting external debt service, is already in a large deficit. Restrictive policies will be highly controversial because in many instances the debt has been incurred for the benefit of the middle and upper classes whereas the adjustment and servicing costs are borne by the public at large. For example, the debt service might be assured by a cut in public sector wages or in food subsidies. The situation is particularly serious when the debt, as in the case of Argentina for example, has largely been incurred to finance capital flight.

In judging the fiscal effort required to service the debt we have to look at the ratio of debt service to GDP. In the period 1981–4, according to IMF (1984) data, the ratio of debt service to GDP for non-oil debtor countries was 5.4 per cent. This includes interest and amortisation payments. Interest payments alone in that period amounted to 3.3 per cent of GDP. Raising that fraction of GDP in extra taxes or through programme cuts is an enormous task. Total tax collection typically account for say 20 per cent of GDP in a DC, and thus this requirement is to cut government spending by 15 per cent or raise revenue by that amount. The difficulty is increased when we consider that the tax structure in many developing countries remains rudimentary and relies strongly on withholding taxes. Taxation of income from capital is often negligible. Financing the debt service then involves in all likelihood yet another severe worsening of income distribution. This is certainly the case when withholding taxes and subsidy cuts are the chief way for the government to secure revenue for debt service.

The full-employment problem

Suppose the government could in fact achieve the fiscal task of raising the revenue for debt service, or could accept the inflationary consequence of deficit finance. The next question is whether the fiscal adjustment can readily be translated into increased export earnings under conditions of full employment. Here the question is how to transfer the resources that are freed by the fiscal correction into increased exports or into replacement of previous imports.

Unless the country is 'small' and has the ability to switch resources it will be necessary to change relative prices. Profitability of the traded goods sector must be enhanced, thus creating incentives for the transfer of productive resources in that direction. On the demand side the fiscal tightening directly reduces demand for traded goods thus freeing foreign exchange. But that effect must be reinforced by an increase in the relative price of tradeables that discourages domestic demand. In the terminology of balance of payments theory, the expenditure cutting effect of the fiscal correction must be accompanied by switching policies that move resources and demand into the right place.

The question that inevitably arises is whether these adjustments can be achieved while maintaining employment. More specifically, what are sensible short-run policies that support the fiscal part of the transfer? The conventional argument calls for a real depreciation in order to maintain full employment in the face of higher taxes, reduced subsidies or reduced government demand. But a real depreciation runs into three snags. First depreciation will be inflationary, second perhaps it will not be effective, and third it will cut real wages and with it, in the short run, employment. We will comment on each of these objections.

The inflation is unavoidable. But unless there are indexation linkages, the inflation shock will be transitory and thus will ultimately represent a minor cost. The cost is only extreme if the corrective devaluation follows after a sequence of already unsuccessful devaluations, or budget corrections, that have produced inflation without a gain in competitiveness. We add that inflation is not the ultimate evil and that reluctance to have a real depreciation may be much more destabilising for real activity and financial markets than the extra inflation impact of a devaluation. Certainly the uniformly unsuccessful experiences of countries that have tried to stop inflation through overvaluation bears this out very strongly.

The ultimate effectiveness of real depreciation in providing export growth and import substitution is firmly established. One piece of evidence is the devastating effect of overvaluation on the trade balance that we discussed earlier. But we need not go that far. All available evidence from trade equations supports the view that with a sufficient adjustment time (one year or perhaps as much as 18 months) trade patterns respond strongly to real exchange rates.

There remains the question of how large a contribution devaluation can make to the maintenance of employment. In the Republic of Korea, for example, matters are decidedly favourable. The export sector accounts for 40 per cent of GDP, and trade is strongly responsive to the real exchange rate. In these conditions devaluation provides both relief on the external balance and, at the same time, a direct and substantial boost to output and employment. By contrast, in countries where the export sector is much smaller, devaluation mainly serves as a means of removing the external balance constraint on growth. Supplementary domestic policies are required to bring about a significant expansion of employment.

Real exchange rate adjustment raises the problem of the short-run deflationary effects on output and employment. Before the export expansion and import substitution get under way there is already a cut in real wages. The real wage cut translates into a reduction in spending, a large part of which will fall on domestic goods and services. In the short run a devaluation is likely to create unemployment. This view is firmly established in theory, but there is also supporting empirical evidence. The implication for policy purposes surely is not that devaluation must be avoided. It is rather that devaluation should if possible be accompanied by transitory fiscal policies that sustain employment. One way would be to create public sector projects that have a minimal import content and are labour intensive, i.e. construction. These programmes would be in effect until the output and employment responses are underway to increase demand and employment.

The trade problem

The third aspect of the transfer problem is to assure the effectiveness of the switching policies, translating potential export supply into actual earnings. Here is the problem posed by developed countries' protectionism and by competition among DCs. There is no reason to believe that a much more liberal world trading system is around the corner. Nor is it reasonable to overlook the fact that DCs will be competing with each other in all markets.

There may be limited scope for discriminatory trading arrangements between DCs, such as a Latin American common market. But by and large the assumption must be that the broader-based the export effort the more likely that it can circumvent commercial policy obstacles in the developed countries and avoid ruinous competition between DCs. A devaluation policy, as opposed to say subsidies for isolated products, thus stands a much better chance of making for an effective export policy.

The recommendation that DCs seek export-led growth raises the system-wide issue of what happens if many DCs try at the same time to capture markets in the developed countries that are already being increasingly protected. Should we not expect further trade restrictions and would DC terms of trade not deteriorate? The answer to both questions is quite possibly yes. But there are few other ways of maintaining employment. The scope for import substitution, other than in the form of regional arrangements, has been largely exhausted and therefore growth must come from exports. These exports might go to other DCs because increased competitiveness and export orientation makes their products preferable to those of industrial countries. The primary attention has still to centre on developed countries' markets. The Asian countries have certainly demonstrated that market penetration is possible even when protection is fierce.

The long-run outlook also suggests the need for real depreciation. Looking beyond the immediate debt service difficulties we have to ask how DCs expect to achieve growth in the future. In any plausible scenario, the banks do not increase their exposure by lending more than the interest bill. The international bond market is unlikely to open up for DCs, and there will be no grand aid schemes because the developed countries perceive that they themselves have serious fiscal problems. That leaves foreign direct investment as the only form of external capital. This may be an important supplement to domestic saving, but experience suggests that it will be a very limited one. Accordingly, to provide for growth the export sectors will have to develop much more strongly and much more broadly than has been so far the case. Significant, sustained real depreciation is the best way to bring about such an adjustment.

V DEBT RELIEF AND OTHER PROPOSALS

A variety of proposals have been offered over the last eighteen months for the solution of the debt problem. These proposals differ widely from grand to cosmetic. They also differ in that some propose to lighten the debt service burdens on DCs at the expense of banks or the taxpayer, while others are merely concerned to assure with greater certainty that the debts will ultimately be serviced in full. We will review some of these proposals briefly to ask whether by themselves they can make a significant contribution to solving the debt problem. We are thus not questioning desirability.

We will not spend any time on grand schemes. It appears a foregone conclusion that the industrial countries have no inclination whatsoever to create institutions that assume the service of DC debts, for a number of reasons. First tax dollars are thought of as particularly scarce, too scarce to give either to DCs or to the banks. But there is the additional argument that a bail-out of big debtor DCs would send the wrong signals. It would send the message that overborrowing can be rewarded. Even proposals as modest as the IMF quota increase have had a very hard time getting accepted.

Defining Debt Problems

In evaluating debt problems it is important to ask whether we are addressing liquidity problems, solvency or equity issues. Liquidity problems involve an inability to service and amortise debts *now* on the time schedule initially contracted. There is no question there is a liquidity problem. Equity problems involve the question of how the burden of large, unanticipated increases in the costs of debt service should be borne between lenders and borrowers. Finally solvency involves the question whether the value of a country's liabilities exceeds the ability to pay. The ability to pay is, as we have argued above, in large measure a political question involving the extent to which activity and standards of living can be depressed to service the debt.

We have already argued above that the debt problem is mainly one of the major borrowers. Thus with the evidence in Table 6.12 above and the definitions of debt problems arrived at earlier we take the debt problem to be one of liquidity and equity, not solvency, and we take it to be primarily an issue for major borrowing countries.

Some Proposals

Having given the debt problem operational definition, we can now look at alternative proposals. Some debt proposals are insignificant in that they involve minor points of debt management that do not address the multi-billion dollar debt service problem of the DCs. Specific examples are the diversification of the currency denomination of new debts to avoid the concentration of the US dollar that has so far characterised borrowing and has proven a costly mistake in the 1979–83 dollar appreciation. Another proposal along the same lines draws attention to interest-rate swaps that would allow DCs a departure from floating rates. Of course, the swaps will be done implicitly at the anticipated future rates and therefore do not get away from the chief problem, namely that interest rates are high and expected to rise. Yet another proposal addresses the difficulties of rescheduling debts by suggesting that small banks be bought out. It is hoped that with fewer and larger banks involved in the rescheduling there is more scope for differentiation between borrowers and in particular more room for using both the carrot and the stick.

Three specific proposals merit attention. The first of these is a new SDR allocation proposed some time ago by the Group of Twenty-Four. The case for a new SDR allocation rests on the fact that international reserves are low relative to world trade and that therefore the perception of reserve shortage leads to unnecessarily restrictive policies. The case is strengthened by taking into account the effect of increased variability of the value of trade in goods and services. A new SDR allocation is clearly a desirable measure. But it must also be clear that it is not a solution to the debt problem, neither for large nor for small debtors. If the SDR's are used to pay off debts, the reserve inadequacy problem remains. If they are not used, the debt problem remains. This is none the less an opportune time to present a case that clearly stands on its own merits.

A quantitatively more important proposal is to extend in a big way the role of the World Bank. World Bank ability to borrow in world markets would be increased. The World Bank would use the increased resources to provide DCs with leverage in borrowing. The good experience with World Bank lending in this respect makes this one of the important long-run steps.

The third measure is a call for an IMF interest rate facility. (See Dornbusch (1983).) Currently the IMF provides financial accommodation to countries that experience a temporary decline in export earnings. It is natural to extend this shock absorber facility to interest rate rises, which can be as much of an external shock for some debtor countries as are the commodity price fluctuations for primary commodity exporters. Organised as a revolving fund such a facility would play an important role in helping debtor countries withstand interest rate shocks.

How far can such an interest rate facility (IRF) go in coping with debt service difficulties? At present a one percentage point increase in interest rates increases debt service by all DCs by approximately \$US5 billion. But interest rate increases have in the latter half of 1984 already been larger than $1\frac{1}{2}$ per cent and are expected to last for two or even three years. As a shock absorber the facility can thus cope at best with part of the liquidity problems posed by interest rate escalation unless the fund is of the order of \$10 billion or even more. Whatever the quantitative contribution the IRF can make, there is no doubt that on analytical grounds such a facility has the same justification and merit as compensatory facility for export fluctuations.

Another direction in which institutional change should be pressed concerns external assets of the nationals of debtor countries. It is a well-established fact that a significant part of the external debt of Mexico or Argentina, for example, has as a counterpart holdings of assets by nationals of these countries in the industrialised world. These holdings may be real estate, securities or bank accounts. The fact that they are not available to help finance debt service severely aggravates external and fiscal adjustment problems. It is natural to go from there to recommend that industrial countries offer assistance to debtor DCs in gaining information on those assets and on the incomes they yield. This is a routine procedure among the Revenue Services of many industrial countries and it is entirely appropriate that it should be extended to debtor DCs. Viewed in this perspective the US proposal for the abolition of withholding taxes on non-residents appears an open invitation for more capital flight from debtor DCs rather than a step in the direction of supporting DCs in marshalling *equitably* resources to service their debts.

The Cap

The central proposal in coping with the liquidity and equity problems posed by present levels of interest rates is the idea of an interest rate cap. The cap idea comes in three variants. An outright concessional cap (con-cap) would place a ceiling at say 7 per cent and forgive any excess of market interest rates over that ceiling indefinitely. A second form, at the other extreme, would also set a ceiling but, rather than forgiving the difference between market rates and the ceiling, would add the difference to the principal of the debt. This is a liquidity-cap since it copes chiefly with the liquidity problems posed by interest rate increases. The third kind, which we advocate and develop in more detail below, involves both concessional and liquidity aspects and thus is an intermediate variant.

The con-cap amounts to a dramatic rewriting of debts that implies a massive capital loss for the banks. Taking only the loans to DCs by financial institutions and assuming that over the next seven years interest rates decline from 14 per cent to the 7 per cent level of the cap, the total reduction in the present value of these debts would be about $100 billion or close to 30 per cent. If the loss were not absorbed by taxpayers it would imply the bankruptcy of major banks in the US and in other countries. Because the proposal goes beyond taking losses to the almost certain bankruptcy of some major US banks, it is unreasonable to assume that banks should choose to accept such a proposal or that governments should find it attractive to legislate it. This is all the more the case in that it involves a redistribution from creditors to many countries who experience debt service difficulties that are by no means extreme.

As the outcome of a negotiation a 7 per cent cap seems implausible. But, of course, if debtors were well organised this might well represent a unilateral proposal that some particular group might advance. As such it is not out of line. It is often argued that any unilateral move to rewrite the debt would have dramatic implications for that country's future access to the lending by banks. But fresh lending of more than a part of the interest bill is in any case unlikely over the next few years. Banks are reducing exposure or the relative proposition of DC debts in their portfolios and hence the prospect of ample future financing as a counterpart of current faithful debt service is in no way assured.

At the other extreme of the con-cap is the liquidity cap proposal. This proposal envisages stretching maturities and *capitalising* all interest payments above a cap level of say 10 per cent. It starts from the realistic recognition that DC borrowing in the past was based on the presumption of rolling over the principal and capitalising interest by fresh loans. The credit rationing that has taken place since 1982–3 has changed these rules, but with enough adjustment having been achieved and/or initiated it is time now to return to this former pattern. Accordingly, it is argued that the amortisation component of debt service should automatically be rescheduled in a long-term fashion. Debts maturing now would be renewed to become due ten years hence. This first part of the proposal copes with the problem of a debt service *hump*, a bunching of debt service due to simultaneously high interest and amortisation payments.

The proposal goes further to argue that because real interest rates are transitorily high, there should be an arrangement that copes with the resulting liquidity problem. Rather than forcing debtors into unreasonably steep depression of activity to marshal debt service dollars, part of the increased interest bill would be *automatically* lent and added to the principal. For banks the proposal is of interest because it removes the debtors' liquidity problems as a potential source of default temptation. It has the further advantage that it precludes the bank free-rider problem in the rescheduling process. At present when loans are rescheduled some banks do not participate which implies that they reduce their exposure to the debtor country, with other banks having correspondingly to increase their exposures. If the liquidity cap were automatic with respect to amortisation and interest, all initial lenders would be participating in the capitalisation of above cap interest and in the stretching of maturities.

From the debtor point of view the liquidity cap proposal offers little attraction beyond the current rescheduling process. The rescheduling process would become more automatic and some of the crisis features would be removed, but there would be no real gains. Specifically interest not paid today would be paid, with interest, tomorrow or the day after tomorrow. It is primarily a proposal to make the creditor cartel more operational. The problem for debtor countries is apparent when we look at a high interest period. Suppose, as discussed above that over the next three years the effective interest rate averages 13 per cent and the growth of export earnings is only 10 per cent. Over a three-year period, with a balanced non-interest current account, the debt–export ratio would rise by 8.4 per cent. The liquidity problem would be solved but the debt burden would rise. The liquidity-cap thus amounts to giving DC debtors a credit card, not debt relief.

Our own proposal deals with rescheduling of principal and with the problems posed by presently high interest rates. With respect to the problem posed by a bunching of amortisation, we see a need for an automatic stretching of debts to a much longer maturity, at least ten years. The fact that debtors have run into an unanticipated problem of record interest rates and poor export earnings should not lead to an extra burden of the amortisation of debts that normally would have been rolled over automatically. On the contrary, the extra burden of debtors needs to be avoided by requiring lenders to maintain their exposure in respect to principal.

But there also needs to be an arrangement to cope with the difficulties posed for *some* countries by *temporarily* high interest rates. We recommend a 9–10 per cent ceiling on interest rates, the difference between market rates and the ceiling entirely forgiven (rather than capitalised), during a three-year grace period. Clearly this cap amounts to a transfer from the creditor banks to the debtor DCs. The capital loss on outstanding loans would be 9–11 per cent. The loss is significant but falls short of creating conditions of bankruptcy.

However, we do not believe that the interest ceiling should be available unconditionally to all debtors, DC debtors, non-oil DC debtors or any broadly defined group. Rather we believe it should be rationed to those countries genuinely in need *and undergoing adjustment*. For that reason we recommend that access to the cap be limited to countries that are accepting an IMF standby agreement. Specifically we recommend that to make the proposal directly operational and remove it from the discretion of banks, member countries should instruct the IMF not to sign agreements unless a prior cap agreement has been secured from the banks. This procedure forces the IMF to change its procedures in two respects. The IMF will have to require limited debt relief rather than merely manage the liquidity feature of the debt problem. Second, the IMF will have to give much more emphasis to making countries, in the medium term, look toward growth and debt servicing. This represents an important change from the current concentration on inflation and budget cutting.

Our proposal appears very limited: temporary, limited debt relief for a selected group of countries in sufficient trouble that they must seek an IMF standby agreement. But the proposal has the advantage of being completely operational. There is no direct call on taxpayers money, there is no need for banks to agree and there is no recommendation that would imply wiping out the ten major banks in the world. The emphasis is on keeping countries in severe difficulties sheltered from the extra damage that comes from the currently high rates. But the principal advantage of the proposal is to get around the present deadlock between banks and debtors. Governments of industrialised countries have quite explicitly taken a liquidity view of the problem. They have, directly or through the IMF, supported the integrity of existing debts at market rates plus fees and spreads, by creating facilities for rolling, bridging and capitalising. It is time now to recognise that there is also an equity issue. Governments, via instructions to the IMF should throw their weight more in the direction of borrowers by seeking a limited, responsible debt relief for countries particularly burdened by debt service at current rates.

There is an extra feature worth pointing out. Our scheme for debt relief invokes a transfer from banks to debtors. It involves only a limited and indirect participation of the taxpayer. We see that as an essential feature. The contribution is limited to the reduction in income taxes, corporate and personal, arising from reduced earnings of banks. The fact that the taxpayer contribution is indirect and limited implies that there is no direct threat to concessional resource flows to countries that are not beneficiaries of debt relief because they never acquired significant bank debt in the first place. A proposal that would go much further than the one we advance would inevitably draw in tax dollars in a major, overt way and therefore almost certainly lead to some and perhaps even large offsetting reductions in concessional lending or other forms of resources made available to the lower income DCs. Our proposal therefore does recognise that the debt problem is not a generalised DC problem and that an imprudent solution worsens the distribution within the DC countries.

A word of caution is needed. Our proposal for limited debt relief is based on the assumption that interest rate problems are strictly temporary. Specifically, we assume that over a ten-year period growth of export earnings will comfortably exceed the effective rate of interest. That does assume a more reasonable monetary-fiscal policy mix and growth in industrial countries, and it assumes no further restrictions on the exports and debtor countries. If either assumption is incorrect, debtor countries will have to take a dramatically different view of their debts.

This point has been put in a particularly forceful manner by Simonsen (1984b, p. 41):

> To keep developing debtor countries cooperating with the international financial community, a basic question should be addressed: under what conditions rational policy makers in debtor nations would prefer cooperation to retaliation? While precise rupture points are difficult to locate, a general principle remains valid: a growing economy with expanding exports hardly would seek confrontation with its creditors. In the same line, solvency at the expense of prolonged recession may be politically unsustainable.

VI POSTSCRIPT

The international debt problem is very far from the clean analytic world examined in many of the other papers in this volume. What if any analytic questions does such a problem pose? The main point is that major efforts are being devoted to solving a problem that arose out of circumstances that were certainly not regarded as likely – or perhaps even possible – when the contracts that embody the problem were entered into. The current levels of real interest rates, and the world recession of 1981–3, were not anticipated by either bankers or economists in the heady days of the late 1970s, when loans were being extended quite freely, and the prospects for the newly industrialising economies looked so good.

The analytic problem is one of how to handle optimally the current situation, given the possibility that similar situations will arise in future, and given institutional constraints (for example bankruptcy laws) that rule out solutions such as forgiving the debts. But it is also necessary to recognise that there is no single optimal solution, for there is undoubtedly a trade-off between the well-being of the debtors and that of the creditors.

Notes

1. We are indebted to Zvi Eckstein for comments, Patricia Mosser for research assistance, and the National Science Foundation for financial support.
2. See Dragoslav Avramovic *et al.* (1964) and Bahram Nowzad and Richard Williams, 'External Indebtedness of Developing Countries', Occasional Paper no. 3 (International Monetary Fund, 1981).
3. Such summary measures are bound to be needed when the complex question of debt capacity, for which the theory is still extremely rudimentary and the financial stakes large, is at issue. For analysis of optimal borrowing, see Pranab K. Bardhan, 'Optimum Foreign Borrowing', in Karl Shell (ed.), *Essays on the Theory of Optimal Economic Growth* (MIT Press, 1967), and Olivier J. Blanchard, 'Debt and the Current Account Deficit in Brazil', in Pedro Aspe Armella *et al.* (eds), *Financial Policies and the World Capital Market: The Problem of Latin American Countries* (University of Chicago Press, 1983).
4. For details of interest rates charged DCs, see E. Brau and R. C. Williams *et al.*, 'Recent Multilateral Debt Restructurings with Official and Bank Creditors', IMF Occasional Paper 25 (December 1983).
5. Of course, the debt data of the 1920s and 1930s might be no better than those we have today.

6. The real debt is larger than the nominal debt after 1980 because the export unit values of industrialised countries *fell* from 1980 to 1983.
7. The interest cost measures in Table 6.6 give some guidance to the differences in debt service costs between countries. But the data must be interpreted with caution for two reasons. First the 1982–3 estimates may be distorted by arrears. Second, estimates of the stocks of debt outstanding remain very tentative even today.
8. Although we consider the question wide open we show here the typical result for the 1958–82 period. DINDGrowth here represents the one period lagged change in industrial countries' real growth.

$$\text{Growth of real export price} = \underset{(-0.015)}{-0.012} + \underset{(3.27)}{1.3}\ \text{DINDGrowth} \qquad R^{-2}=0.29,\ \text{DW}=2.14$$

Unlike Cline (1984) we did not find a significant impact of the current change in growth.
9. On this point see, too, Goldstein and Khan (1983). The IMF (1984) *World Economic Outlook* uses a relation between export revenue growth and industrial country growth of 1.7.
10. The examples of Argentina, Chile, Brazil and Mexico are examined in detail in Dornbusch (1984a).
11. The Mexican case is particularly well documented in studies by Solis and Zedillo (1984) and Aspe and Cordoba (1984).
12. Dornbusch (1984a) shows that the same distinction is important in the Argentinian case.
13. See *Federal Reserve Bulletin* (March 1984), Table 3.17 and Bank for International Settlements, *International Banking Developments*, Fourth Quarter 1983 and *International Banking Statistics, 1973–83*.
14. Among the scenarios are those by: Cline (1983), Dooley *et al.* (1983), Enders and Mattione (1983) and the IMF, in its 1984 *World Economic Outlook* (Ch. 4), and Morgan Guaranty Trust Co. (1983a,b).
15. For example, Enders and Mattione (1983) predict negative per capita growth rates in much of Latin America over the period to 1987.
16. An evaluation of the leading forecasts, as of July 1984, is available from us on request. Our conclusion is that the leading forecasts, particularly that of Cline, are too optimistic, largely because their assumptions about the effects of OECD growth on DC exports are on the high end, and because their forecasts of OECD interest rates are too low. In some cases we have the benefit of an extra year's data in making the evaluations.
17. There is a further scenario that involves optimism.
18. To derive (7), divide in (6) by P_t, obtaining

$$\frac{M_t}{P_t}=\frac{X_t}{P_t}+\frac{D_t}{P_t}-\frac{D_{t-1}}{P_t}-\frac{i_tD_{t-1}}{P_t}.$$

Then $m_t=x_t+\frac{D_t}{P_t}-\frac{D_{t-1}}{P_{t-1}}(1+i_t)(\frac{P_{t-1}}{P_t})$

With the real debt constant at *RD*, and $P_t/P_{t-1}=1.06$, we obtain (7).

REFERENCES

Aspe, P. and J. Cordoba (1984) 'Stabilisation Policies in Mexico (1983–84)' (Institute of Statistics and Secretariat of Programming and Budget: Mexico DF).

Avramovic, D. *et al.* (1964) *Economic Growth and External Debt* (Johns Hopkins University Press).

Brau, E., Williams, R. C., Keller, P. M., and Nowak, M. (1983) 'Recent Multilateral Debt Restructuring with Official and Bank Creditors', Occasional Papers of the International Monetary Fund, No. 25.

Central Bank of Brazil (1984) *Internal and External Adjustment*, Vol. 3 (May).

Cline, W. (1983) *International Debt and the Stability of the World Economy*, Institute for International Economics (September).

Cline, W. (1984) *International Debt: Systemic Risk and Policy Response* (MIT Press).

Cohen, D. (1984) 'A Note on the Value of LDC Debt', unpublished manuscript (CEPREMAP).

Dale, R. and R. Mattione (1983) *Managing Global Debt* (Brookings).

de Grauwe, P. and M. Fratianni (1984) 'The Political Economy of International Lending', (Catholic University of Louvain).

de Vries, B. (1984) 'Dealing with External Debt. Longterm Financing for Restructuring the Debtor Economies', unpublished manuscript (World Bank).

Dooley, M. *et al.* (1983) 'An Analysis of External Debt Positions of Eight Developing Countries Through 1990', Board of Governors of the Federal Reserve, Discussion Paper No. 227.

Dornbusch, R. (1983) 'Adjustment in Brazil: Comment', in J. Williamson (ed.), *Prospects for Adjustment* (Institute for International Economics and MIT Press).

Dornbusch, R. (1984a) 'The International Debt Problem', forthcoming in *The World Economy*.

Dornbusch, R. (1984b) 'External Debt, Budget Deficits, and Disequilibrium Exchange Rates', unpublished manuscript (MIT).

Enders, T. and R. Mattione (1983) 'Latin America: The Crisis of Debt and Growth', unpublished manuscript (Brookings).

Feldstein, M. (1984) 'International Debt Policy: The Next Steps', Remarks before the Council of Americas, Washington, DC, May 8th.

Goldstein, M. and M. Khan (1982) 'Effects of A Slowdown in Industrial Countries on Growth in Non-Oil Developing Countries', Occasional Paper No. 12 (IMF).

Guttentag, J. and R. Herring (1983) 'The Current Crisis in International Banking', unpublished manuscript (University of Pennsylvania).

Guttentag, J. and R. Herring (1983b) 'Uncertainty and Insolvency Exposure by International Banks', unpublished manuscript (University of Pennsylvania).

Harberger, A. (1984). 'Lessons for Debtor Country Managers and Policy Makers', unpublished manuscript (University of Chicago).

Inter-American Development Bank (1984) *External Debt and Economic Development in Latin America* (Washington, DC).

International Monetary Fund (1983) 'World Economic Outlook', Occasional Paper No. 21, April.
International Monetary Fund (1984) 'World Economic Outlook', Occasional Paper No. 27.
Khan, M. and M. Knight (1983) 'Determinants of Current Account Imbalances of Non-Oil Developing Countries in the 1970s: An Empirical Analysis', IMF Staff Papers (December).
Krugman, P. (1984). 'International Debt Strategy in an Uncertain World', unpublished manuscript (MIT).
Lewis, C. (1938) *America's Stake in International Investment* (Brookings).
McFadden, D., R. Eckaus, G. Feder, V. Hajivassiliou and S. O'Connell (1984) 'Is There Life After Debt? An Econometric Analysis of Creditworthiness of Developing Countries', unpublished (MIT).
Morgan Guaranty Trust Company of New York (1983a) 'International Debt: Progress Report and the Task Ahead', *World Financial Markets* (September).
Morgan Guaranty Trust Company of New York (1983b) 'Global Debt: Assessment and Longterm Strategy', *World Financial Markets* (June).
OECD (1984) *Economic Outlook* (July).
Park, Y. C. (1984) 'Korea's Experience with External Debt Management', unpublished manuscript (Korea University).
Sachs, J. (1982) 'LDC Debt in the 1980s. Risk and Reforms', in P. Wachtel (ed.), *Crises in the Economic And Financial Structure* Lexington Books, Lexington, Massachusetts.
Simonsen, M. (1984a) 'The Debt Crisis', unpublished manuscript (Fundacao Getulio Vargas).
Simonsen, M. (1984b) 'The Developing Country Debt Problem', unpublished manuscript (Fundacao Getulio Vargas).
Sjaastad, L. (1983) 'Failure of Economic Liberalism in the Cone of Latin America', *The World Economy* (March).
Solis, L. and E. Zedillo (1984) 'Stabilisation Policies in Mexico (1983–84)' (Banco de Mexico, Mexico DF).
Tejeiro, M. (1984) 'Southern Cone: The Time Machine Experiment', unpublished manuscript (International Monetary Fund).
United Nations (1961) *International Flows of Long-term Capital and Official Donations, 1951–59*.
United Nations (1964) *El Financiamento Externo de America Latina* (Cepal).
World Bank (1985) *World Development Report*.

7 Aspects of Capital Flows Between Developing and Developed Countries

Anne O. Krueger[1]

After the Mexican problems of mid-1982, a large number of other developing countries found themselves in deep difficulty with respect to their debt-servicing obligations. Some of these countries were middle-income, Latin American countries with relatively high debt–service ratios; others were low-income African countries where debt–service ratios were low; some were oil importers and some oil exporters, some had a record of rapid growth while others had grown slowly, if at all. The fact that the countries affected seemed to have little in common other than their debt-servicing difficulties led most observers to focus upon the 'debt problem' as the phenomenon for analysis, although not all countries experienced debt-servicing difficulties and there had been earlier instances of these problems.

Explanations abounded: the worldwide recession had cut debtor countries' export earnings and thereby their ability to pay; the sharp increase in interest rates had made previously sustainable levels of debt unsustainable; countries had borrowed foolishly and were finally paying the penalty; there had been too great a shift from reliance on official capital flows to the private markets and especially to debt financing. Forecasts of future prospects likewise varied: some asserted that private banks had been so badly burned that they would not voluntarily resume lending, while others viewed the abrupt reduction in new lending as a temporary phenomenon likely to be reversed as soon as debt–service ratios attained more reasonable levels. As to developing countries' prospects, some observers thought that, without some extraordinary measures, many countries would be unable to service their debt and would be forced to default, some regarded the difficulties as likely to reduce prospective growth rates but manageable, and still others regarded future prospects for growth as only temporarily impaired.

These analyses were widely at variance with earlier held conclusions. During the 1970s, most economists observing the international economy had viewed the emergence of the middle-income countries as borrowers in the private international capital market as a sign of success in the development effort. Prior to that decade, most capital flows to developing countries had originated from official sources as those countries were not regarded as creditworthy in private markets. As more and more developing countries attained economic structures and levels of income that rendered them creditworthy, the increased importance of private capital flows seemed to mark progress in the international economy. Indeed, it appeared that more and more developing countries would attain levels of development at which they could access private markets. That increased access, in turn, was regarded as signifying progress in raising living standards and making economies more productive. Although individual countries occasionally had debt-servicing difficulties in the 1960s and 1970s, these were viewed as temporary and emanating out of the particular circumstances of the country. Recent developments, however, have called that view into question, and observers have questioned whether the issue is not more systemic.

A Conference on Economic Policy in Theory and Practice seems an appropriate occasion for attempting to set forth a simple framework for understanding capital flows and debt, and to use that framework to assess the often conflicting assertions made with respect to the origins and consequences of the 'debt problem', and the policy prescriptions that emerge. A natural way to proceed is to review the simple theory of capital flows in a world with efficient resource allocation, and then to examine the consequences of various phenomena that might impair efficiency. This permits a typography of 'debt problems' with different countries falling into different categories with respect to causation of difficulties. It also provides a framework within which the policy lessons arising from the experience of the past decade can be assessed.

The first part sets forth the simplest possible framework, in which the international capital market functions efficiently and resource allocation in the borrowing country is efficient. Within that framework, ways in which international lending might differ from national lending are discussed, and the analysis is extended to cover more than one kind of financial instrument. The second part then considers ways in which, in the context of a well-functioning international market, domestic economic conditions might lead to difficulties with respect to debt servicing. A third part contains an assessment of the effects of various inefficiencies in the international capital market.[2] The fourth part then addresses the debt difficulties of the developing countries in light of the analysis and the available empirical evidence. A final part draws some tentative conclusions, both with respect to policy and with respect to further needed research.

I CAPITAL FLOWS IN A WELL-FUNCTIONING INTERNATIONAL ECONOMY

It is simplest to start by assuming that international lending is the only means by which savings in one country can finance investment in another.[3] Recall that we start with the assumption that both domestic markets and international capital markets function smoothly. In a static framework, theory is then straightforward: at a uniform real rate of interest there will be more savings than investment opportunities in some countries and more investment opportunities than savings in others. Capital flows will be from countries with an excess of savings over investment at the prevailing world real rate of interest to those with an excess of profitable investment opportunities over domestic savings. It is natural to suppose that in reality, labour-abundant, capital-poor developing countries would be net capital importers from labour-scarce, capital-abundant developed countries.

A number of complications to this simple proposition immediately arise that need not be dealt with here: in a dynamic setting, a theory of the determinants of investment would be required; there might be 'corner solutions' in which some countries had higher rates of return than others even after capital flows if there was no new investment in the low-return countries; and so on.

I.1 Differences between Foreign and Domestic Lending in the Simple Case

For present purposes, the questions at issue pertain to why international lending might differ from domestic lending. It is widely recognised that investors might demand a premium for investing abroad as contrasted with acquiring domestic assets because of sovereign risk. This risk arises because investors are protected within their own countries by laws which may not protect foreigners. In the literature, this has been taken to mean that a government might find it in its self-interest to fail to honour the overseas obligations of its citizens simply in the sense that the present value of future repayment streams would outweigh the present value of expected future net inflows of capital (Eaton and Gersowitz, 1981). In practice, it is doubtful whether any country which has achieved a state of development sufficient to be creditworthy to any major degree would ever find it in its self-interest to default: the gains from trade and normal financing (as contrasted with the loss of trade credits and costs of restoring to barter that would arise as a consequence of deliberate default) and the willingness of lenders to 'reschedule' are probably sufficiently large to preclude the default option. Rescheduling itself is a continuum, in that the present value of repayment obligations can be reduced; because of this the extreme case of 'no rescheduling and no payment' seems unlikely.

If 'wilful' default, in the sense of deciding not to pay when the present value of the future flow of capital and interest will be negative, is ruled out, the question arises as to whether there are differences between domestic and international lending under the simple assumptions made so far. At first glance, it would at first sight appear that if laws protecting creditors are enforced equally for foreigners as for domestic residents, then any project yielding an income stream which the creditor can attach, which is sufficient to service the debt, will be viewed equally by potential lenders regardless of the location of the project or the financial condition of the debtor. That this is overly simplistic can immediately be seen by noting two interrelated propositions: (1) even within countries, borrowers with greater earning ability and assets are more likely to repay in the event a specific investment goes sour and, therefore, typically receive more favourable terms than the small investor whose assets and other sources of income are limited; and (2) even if a project in a foreign country generates the anticipated income stream, the borrower must convert the domestic currency earnings into foreign exchange in order to service the debt.

Turning to the first proposition, the fact that large firms can use their generalised earning and asset position to permit them to borrow on more favourable terms suggests that even within domestic markets, lenders may prefer to have the borrower share the risk associated with his activities (for moral hazard, possibly, as well as other reasons). Internationally, small investors are probably even more disadvantaged due to the lenders' lack of information, costs of evaluating projects, and related reasons than they are in domestic markets. This implies that international lending is likely to take place largely through financial intermediaries, known to foreign borrowers, whose role may be largely that of knowing local conditions, and presenting an asset and earnings position that provides foreign lenders the same sorts of assurances that larger size may provide domestically. For present purposes, the important point is that, when lending is to intermediaries (or, more generally when claims are backed by earnings stream other than the individual project financed), it is not only the prospective rate of return on potential new investments that will be relevant to the lender, but also the existing asset and income position of the borrowing entity. Thus, the volume of outstanding debt and debt service obligations, as well as the prospective earnings stream from past investments, will be relevant to determinations of creditworthiness. As will be seen below, creditworthiness may then be impaired when earnings streams from existing assets decline.

The second proposition is that there is need for additional assurance about convertibility of a repayments stream into foreign exchange. In all cases where there is any question whatever about the government's commitments to full convertibility of its currency, there is an additional risk associated with foreign lending that is absent within a unified currency area: even if the realised earnings stream from a project was satisfactory, the lenders might be unable to purchase foreign exchange. Hence, for countries where there is some degree of exchange control, lenders might be well advised to seek government guarantees of convertibility, or otherwise attempt to reduce this risk.

As will be discussed below, these two propositions would in any event lead lenders to distinguish risks between lending to domestic residents and lending to foreigners even under conditions of efficient resource allocation. If, for whatever set of reasons, a series of past investments had yielded lower rates of return than anticipated, the debt-servicing obligations already existing would necessarily be a factor of some importance in lenders' willingness to extend new credit. When, however, there are also domestic inefficiencies, the situation would be substantially confounded.

I.2 Role of Uncertainties

The complications described thus far pertain to the degree to which there are risks inherent in lending abroad that exceed the risks associated with generating the same earnings stream in the lender's home country. A second type of risk arises because the phenomena described in Section I.1 can interact with floating interest rate obligations.

This can be most easily seen by assuming a very simple world in which the earnings streams from future investments are known with certainty. If the income stream from a given investment project is known with certainty and the investment can be financed by fixed-rate lending, the income stream from the project can finance the loan when the investment constitutes the sole activity of the borrower. The lender would not need to concern himself with any broader aspects of macroeconomic policy, the likely generation of foreign exchange earnings, or other phenomena within the borrowing country provided only that he had assurances that his claim against the earnings stream would be honoured.

With variable-rate lending (or with unexpected fluctuations in earnings streams due, for example, to terms of trade changes), the situation could differ significantly. In particular, with an increase in the real interest rate, the yield on past investment might not adequately finance the debt-service obligation. In so far as default on past lending would affect the borrower's ability to finance future investments, it could be rational to honour the obligation. Clearly, however, part of some other income streams would need to be diverted to financing the obligation. If new income streams are among those against which the claim is exercised, then additional borrowing which just equated the rate of return on investment with the real cost of the borrowing would not be warranted.[4]

Once the possibility of variable rate borrowing (or fluctuations in terms of trade) is taken into account, it is immediately apparent that the economically efficient capital inflow does not depend only on the real interest rate. It is also a function of: (1) the prospective earnings stream in the economy that is potentially capturable to service debt in the event of a rise in interest obligations, (2) the outstanding stock of variable rate debt, (3) and the expected variability in earnings streams and interest rates.

I.3 Relevance for the Debt Problem

The potential relevance of the above considerations for analysis of the debt difficulties of the developing countries should be immediately apparent. First and foremost, both because expected earnings streams dropped and because the cost of servicing the outstanding volume of debt rose, countries became less creditworthy than they had been. Even when a country had followed a 'prudent' borrowing strategy, it is quite possible that higher real interest rates and reduced export earnings might have rendered it 'uncreditworthy' as a reduced income stream was available to finance a larger debt-service burden.

Secondly, as will be elaborated further below, the additional step of converting a domestic income stream into foreign exchange could cause difficulties with a sharp and unexpected deterioration in the terms of trade, even if the domestic income stream itself was of the expected magnitude. The ease of substitution in production between non-tradeables and tradeables therefore becomes a critical issue in examining creditworthiness.

II IMPERFECT DOMESTIC MARKETS

To this point, discussion has been couched in terms of an efficiently functioning domestic economy in which private incentives appropriately reflect the relevant trade-offs and in which levels of saving and investment are optimal. Since the optimal rate of capital inflow is really the optimal rate of investment less the optimal rate of savings, evaluation of actual flows can be undertaken only by assessing the overall macroeconomic policy stance within a country. This in itself raises a host of difficulties which must be briefly analysed here (issue 1). Secondly, other inappropriate domestic signals (exchange rate, interest rate, non-uniformity of incentives for imports and exports) may create a major wedge between rates of return in domestic currency and those in foreign currency (issue 2). Thirdly, and closely related to the second, when markets are imperfect, there are questions, additional to those already raised in Section I.2, about the ease with which returns denominated in domestic currency can be transformed into foreign exchange (issue 3). Finally (issue 4), it is widely recognised that markets do not always adjust instantaneously. This may be particularly important when there are large shifts. In this section, these four issues are discussed in turn.

II.1 Optimality of Domestic Savings and Investment

In Part I, it was assumed that domestic savings and investment were both at appropriate levels. Since the optimal amount of foreign borrowing (or, more generally, capital inflow) is the difference between domestic savings and investment at the prevailing world real interest rate, it is apparent that anything which makes either of those aggregates inappropriate will affect the amount of foreign borrowing.

There are two sets of interrelated, but distinct, reasons why these domestic aggregates might be inappropriate. One, discussed here, concerns the interaction between the public sector budget and private expenditure decisions. The other, discussed in Section II.2, concerns the extent to which inappropriate incentives to the private sector may influence investment and savings decisions in ways that make foreign borrowing privately profitable but economically unwarranted when the true trade-offs are recognised.

Turning, then, to the overall stance of macroeconomic policy, it is widely recognised that a public sector deficit can be financed either through 'crowding out' of private investment or through some combination of increased private and foreign savings. Since governmental borrowing is usually backed by its ability to tax the individual, activities financed by additional borrowing (even if one could identify the marginal activities) need not necessarily be productive. It is the entire array of activities encompassed within the government budget that needs to be reasonably economic if a capital inflow financing a public sector deficit is to generate the earnings stream to finance it.

A rational consumer, confronted with an unexpected downward shift in his expected future earnings stream, may gradually adjust his consumption pattern downward, borrowing or drawing down assets in the short run in full knowledge that future consumption will be even lower on that account. An irrational consumer, by contrast, might choose to run down all his assets or borrow until no further credit was available, failing to adjust until various sanctions forced it upon him. There is, however, nothing in economic theory that explains apparently irrational individual behaviour.[5]

For countries, however, individuals may behave rationally while the outcome is none the less analogous to the irrational consumer: after 1973 and 1979, for example, some oil importing countries failed to alter domestic energy prices, incurring larger public sector deficits to finance the additional costs of imports or incurring larger current account deficits when the exchange rate was maintained at its earlier level in altered circumstances. Consumers, behaving rationally (given the incentives with which they were confronted), continued their earlier expenditure patterns.[6] For the country as a whole, however, this continuation resulted in dissaving (or a reduction in saving) contrasted with the earlier situation. The resulting current account deficits, financed by borrowing abroad, would have been smaller had appropriate trade-offs been reflected to domestic residents.

Borrowing of this type – to avoid ajusting to altered circumstances – is clearly very different from borrowing to finance investments in new income streams. While a consumer could, in principle, rationally decide that given his time preference, he would consume more than his income now, it is hard to believe that decisions taken in the 1970s to maintain oil imports and pre-1973 energy price levels were based on rational consideration of alternate future time paths of consumption. While even those countries that did alter their internal relative prices in 1973 and 1979 none the less incurred current account deficits in 1974 and 1980, those deficits appear to have been of proportionately smaller magnitude and were diminishing almost from the outset (see Table 7.2 below).

In summary, one way in which the model of efficient borrowing set forth in Part I might be violated is through the incurring of public sector deficits financed by borrowing abroad. Such a capital inflow, if used to finance current consumption expenditures (or, for that matter, investment expenditures with rates of return lower than the real interest rate), could clearly fail to generate the additional income stream that would service the debt. If repeated for a sufficient period of time (presumably because it is the totality of governmental receipts that back any borrowing), debt-servicing problems might well arise. In addition, adjustment would be required simply in order to reduce capital inflows, the topic of Section 2.4 below.

II.2 Domestic Distortions

Given the large existing literature on the effects of domestic distortions on resource allocation, little analysis is required here. Suffice it to say that in many developing countries, credit is rationed at artificially low interest rates, scarce foreign exchange is allocated by licence to the fortunate recipients at far less than its scarcity value, and automatically prohibitive protection is granted to new industries which produce import substitutes for the domestic market. In these circumstances, it is readily demonstrable that some capital inflows that finance privately profitable investments may none the less have a much lower or even negative 'true' rate of return (see Bhagwati and

Brecher (1979) and Bhagwati and Srinivasan (1978) for demonstration of this result).

Moreover, there is some presumption that policies that encourage substitution of domestic production for imports without due regard to cost may result in increasing divergences between economic and private rates of return over time. If that happens, mounting debt service obligations with ever smaller average actual returns could lead to debt-servicing difficulties. In the absence of a reversal of underlying economic policies, one would anticipate that a 'debt problem' would ultimately arise.

Another source of difficulty might arise in circumstances in which rates of return were adequate but were non-capturable. Suppose, for example, that a government borrowed to finance elementary education. It could recapture only that fraction of the additional earnings stream that was reflected in its tax structure. In this case, the 'distortion' is in the financing of the investment. For developing countries where transport, education, agricultural extension, and related activities are a major part of total investment, this 'distortion' may be quantitatively significant.

II.3 Transforming Domestic Currency into Foreign Exchange

Many highly profitable investments in developing countries are in 'home goods' – education, transport, power generation, communications, and so on. These investments typically have a very long payout period and could, on that account alone, result in debt-servicing difficulties under some conditions (see Section III.2) if financed by foreign borrowing of shorter maturity structure.

Otherwise, assuming that capital markets are sufficiently flexible, there is no reason in principle why problems should arise if domestic markets are reasonably efficient: the real exchange rate would appropriately reflect the marginal rate of transformation of home goods into tradeables and hence the relevant costs and returns to investment in home goods would be adequately reflected via the price mechanism.

When exchange rates are overvalued, there is a major market distortion: the overvaluation of the exchange rate penalises export activities. This raises the possibility that, while rates of return to investments in home goods activities might be at or above the rate of interest on foreign borrowing, there would be no commensurate increase in foreign exchange earnings. Under these conditions, rates of return (on some investments in home goods) might yield at least the international borrowing rate in domestic currency, yet the foreign exchange to service the debt which financed the investments might simply not be available.

II.4 Speed of Adjustment

It is often assumed that adjustments can be undertaken instantaneously and costlessly. In reality, it is widely recognised that adjustments take time and that large shifts in macroeconomic variables in short periods of time may entail high economic, as well as social and political costs.

Since a net capital inflow permits an increase in expenditure relative to income, a change in the size of the capital inflow requires an adjustment of commensurate size in other macroeconomic aggregates. If, for example, the warranted capital inflow fell to zero, the required shift in domestic aggregates would be the magnitude of the earlier inflow as a percentage of GNP. When this percentage becomes sizeable (as it has in many countries, as will be seen in Part IV), the macroeconomic magnitudes of potential shifts will also be large. This is more likely to be the case, the more that activities financed by inflows employ both home goods and traded goods. If, for example, half the cost of a new investment project typically consists of imports, then the cutback of such a project will entail the reallocation of half the (home goods) resources employed in the project to the production of other tradeables (since the capital inflow would presumably have freed the home goods from other activities).

It is readily apparent that, when capital inflows drop, domestic adjustment will be warranted. Combining this proposition with the theory set forth in Part I, two questions arise: (1) what is the magnitude of the shift in the warranted inflow when the real interest rate rises?; and (2) given that there are costs of adjustment, is not the rate of inflow itself a variable to be monitored?

With respect to the first, it is arguable that the higher real interest rate confronting borrowers with variable rate debt probably implied that the outstanding level of indebtedness, although economically desirable at a real rate of interest of 3 per cent, was not justified or sustainable at real rates of interest of 6, 8, or 10 per cent. In those circumstances, economically justified borrowing (even when domestic policies were sound) may well have shifted from positive to negative as some repayment may have become warranted (because of overall creditworthiness considerations, discussed above). The magnitude of the required shift in the domestic economy may well have been sizeable, especially when the required additional interest payments on existing debt added to the magnitude of the necessary adjustment.

With respect to the second question, one suspects that the appropriate policy response to potential vulnerability induced by wide swings in the current account may well be to hold additional reserves, rather than to restrain current flows. When, in reality, there are adjustment costs, that is clearly reason to moderate fluctuations in the current account balance that might otherwise be required. (See Harberger on this question with respect to Chile.) It will be seen in Section IV.3 that the required shifts on the part of some developing countries have been large enough to raise question as to their manageability.

III IMPERFECTIONS IN INTERNATIONAL CAPITAL MARKETS

In part I, the simple theory of capital flows was examined with respect to developing countries' debt problems on the assumption that the international capital market and the economy of the borrowing country were efficient. In part II, the assumption that the domestic economy functioned efficiently was relaxed, to examine the sorts of problems that might arise with borrowing in a perfectly functioning international capital market when the domestic economy is, in one way or another, distorted.

In this section, it is assumed that the borrowing country's economy functions efficiently, but that there may be distortions in the international capital market. No effort is made to examine the possible sources of those distortions (bank regulations, political uncertainties, etc.). Rather, focus is on the potential effect of these features on the borrowing country's economy and its ability to service its debt.

Two major sources of 'distortion' come to mind: once it is recognised that there are other financing mechanisms than bank lending, the composition of a capital inflow might be inappropriate; and the maturity structure of the debt or the payback schedule may not match that of the earnings stream financed by the loan. Each of these is considered in turn.

III.1 Lending and Other Capital Flows

The discussion of Part I for the most part implicitly assumed certainty about future earnings streams, and paid little attention to uncertainty. In reality, the presence of uncertainty alters the analysis in an important way: unless asset markets and flow markets all function well, the portfolio composition of finance of a new project makes a difference. When the stream of returns is uncertain (whether because of project-specific features or because of uncertainty about the environment in which the project will operate), lending and equity finance have different implications for the sharing of risk. Should an investment be financed by an entrepreneur in a developing country through foreign borrowing only, the foreigners have a future claim regardless of what happens to the income stream. In that case, the proportionate variance in the entrepreneur's return will exceed that of the project itself. By contrast, should an investment be undertaken by foreign entrepreneurs, the nationals of a country (ignoring the possibility of distorted incentives discussed in Section II.3) have smaller obligations in the event of an unfavourable outcome on the investment.

As these considerations suggest, an 'optimal' capital inflow undoubtedly has an 'optimal' composition, given the availability and terms of equity and debt financing on the international market. To the extent that the portfolio of the capital inflow diverges from that composition, the warranted size of the inflow will be smaller. Moreover, to the extent the portfolio is unbalanced (toward debt, and especially short-term debt, to be empirically relevant), the likelihood of debt-servicing difficulties arising under outcomes with low probabilities (prolonged and severe recession, high real interest rates, etc.) increases.

The reluctance of the developing countries to accept equity finance in the 1970s may have intensified their debt-servicing difficulties in the worldwide recession of 1980–83. Whether this is regarded as an imperfection of the international capital market, as an imperfection in the domestic economy, or as a case of inappropriate expectations about future conditions in the international economy hardly matters: the combination of adverse events which took place concurrently in the early 1980s had even more impact on the developing countries than it would have had their capital inflows been financed by a higher proportion of equity investment.[7] It may be noted, too, that equity finance implies a different time path and structure of the servicing stream than does debt financing (and is equivalent to the use of consols in that principal as such is never repaid). How much of the apparent disproportionate use of borrowing led to difficulties because of inappropriate distribution of risk and how much because the maturity structure of obligations was shorter with a higher proportion of debt-to-equity finance is difficult to judge.

For very low-income countries, the unavailability of concessional assistance (which can in large part be regarded as compensating for a market failure in that available maturities are insufficiently long – see Section 3.2 below) in the 1970s led to resort to private capital flows to a greater extent than may have been warranted by the state of development and ability to withstand cyclical fluctuations. Further discussion of that issue must, however, await consideration of factors pertaining to the maturity structure of outstanding debt.

III.2 Maturity Structure of Debt

It is widely recognised that unless there is to be refinancing, the time profile of debt repayment must match, or at least not be substantially shorter than, the payout period of a project. And, the greater the mismatch between the time structure of debt-service obligations and that of the project, the greater is the likelihood of difficulty.

There are two distinct ways in which mismatches probably occurred in the 1970s: the term of much private lending fell short of the structure of expected returns; and nominal interest rates rose with inflation to increase the disparity. The first, the shorter term structure of outstanding debt, is probably more important for low-income countries, for which many of the appropriate investments have payout periods of decades rather than years. The average maturity of outstanding private medium- and long-term debt never exceeded eleven years, and fell to less than ten after 1973. As this happened, maturities became increasingly disconnected from expected cash flows.

Even for middle-income countries, however, the fact that nominal interest rates rose sharply in the late 1970s implicitly shortened the real maturity structure. Consider two loans, on each of which a fixed sum annual repayment stream will service the loan over n years. In one case the rate of inflation is zero, and the real and nominal rate of interest 3 per cent. In the other case the rate of inflation is 10 per cent per year, so the nominal rate of interest is 13 per cent. In the latter case, 10 per cent of the real debt is repaid in the first year of the loan, as the higher nominal interest rate implicitly compensates for the reduced real value of the outstanding principal balance. I shall argue in Part IV that a significant factor in the debt difficulties of the developing countries was the sharp shift in implicit maturity structure from the mid-1970s (when negative real rates of interest in effect lengthened maturity structures and the cost of debt) and the 1980s when the inflation-induced premium over the real rate of interest implicitly shortened the term structure of the debt.

It seems evident that a project could realise a satisfactory rate of return, but that servicing might be difficult or impossible if the maturity structure of the debt is shorter than that of the project. Given the sorts of projects that constitute a large part of investment in developing countries, the explicit and implicit shortening of the maturity structure of the debt resulting from inflation has surely resulted in an increased imperfection of the international capital market over the past decade.

IV THE DEBT PROBLEM IN ANALYTICAL PERSPECTIVE

The foregoing review of possible market imperfections, and their implications for analysis of the current debt situation, is far from exhaustive: it would require at a minimum further analysis of the possible interactions of domestic market imperfections and international capital market imperfections, and then the construction of a model within which the relative magnitudes of various contributory factors might be quantified. Such a quantification of the various phenomena and the extent that they may have contributed to the current problem is well beyond the scope of this paper, and may not be possible at all given the current state of knowledge. Moreover, as the previous discussion indicates, debt-servicing difficulties can originate in a variety of different situations. While some factors, such as rising real interest rates, were common to all countries, others (such as macroeconomic policies) differed significantly across countries.

None the less, it is worthwhile to pull together some suggestive pieces of evidence to shed light on the current situation. To anticipate the argument and help the reader, it may be useful to summarise tentative conclusions at this stage. They are:

(1) External shocks, inappropriate domestic economic policies, and the shift in the optimal level of borrowing all contributed to the 'debt problem', but the relative importance of each component differed vastly among countries;
(2) The warranted shift in the size of the current account, with the consequent large implied shift in flows of national product and expenditure, which resulted from the change in the real interest rate, was probably the major reason why developing countries found the adjustment so very difficult;
(3) The shortened term structure of the debt, and other 'distortions' arising from international inflation have intensified the problems that would anyway have arisen.

Before turning to the implications for policy, it will be useful to examine each of these in turn.

IV.1 Causes of the Debt Problem

It seems unarguable that both the worldwide recession and the inappropriate macroeconomic policies of some developing countries contributed to bringing about the virtually simultaneous difficulties many developing countries faced. One set of estimates of the relative importance of these two sets of factors has been presented by Enders and Mattione (1984). They have quantified the magnitude of external shocks and the degree to which domestic policies responded for a number of developing countries.[8]

Their results are reproduced in Table 7.1 for a group of Latin American debtors. The first row estimates the magnitude of the external shock facing each country, defined as the deterioration in the current account balance brought about by increased interest payments and worsened terms of trade. It should be noted that Latin America had a high fraction of variable-rate debt, thus exacerbating the interest-rate shock. As can be seen, some countries (e.g. Mexico because of oil) experienced an improved external environment.

The second row gives the actual change in the current account. When that change is larger in magnitude than the external shock, Enders and Mattione attribute the additional deterioration to poor domestic macroeconomic policies; when it is smaller, they attribute the difference as resulting from macroeconomic policies designed to bring about adjustment. Thus, they interpret the Brazilian macroeco-

Table 7.1 Enders' and Mattione's calculations of over-all adjustment/disadjustment to external shocks (Billions of dollars)

Country	*Results of shock*	*1979*	*1980*	*1981*	*1982*	*Cumulative*[a]
Colombia	Shock	−0.8	−1.2	−2.1	−2.8	−6.8
	Current account change[b]	*	−1.1	−2.5	−3.0	−6.6
	Capital export[c]	−0.1	0.3	0.5	*	0.7
Brazil	Shock	−3.3	−9.4	−16.5	−19.3	−48.5
	Current account change[b]	−4.1	−6.0	−4.7	−8.8	−23.6
	Capital export[c]	1.3	1.6	−0.3	−0.7	2.0
Chile	Shock	0.4	*	−2.6	−2.6	−4.8
	Current account change[b]	−0.7	−1.5	−4.3	−1.9	−8.5
	Capital export[c]	0.4	0.5	0.9	−0.8	1.0
Argentina	Shock	*	−3.5	−4.6	−5.4	−13.4
	Current account change[b]	−2.1	−6.5	−5.9	−4.4	−18.9
	Capital export[c]	1.7	−2.3	−8.7	−5.0	−14.3
Peru	Shock	0.3	0.5	*	−0.5	0.4
	Current account change[b]	1.5	0.9	−0.6	−0.5	1.3
	Capital export[c]	*	0.2	0.5	0.6	1.3
Mexico	Shock	0.3	3.3	3.9	4.2	11.7
	Current account change[b]	−2.8	−4.8	−10.1	−1.0	−18.7
	Capital export[c]	−0.8	−1.1	−4.9	−8.3	−15.2
Venezuela	Shock	2.6	5.9	6.7	3.9	19.1
	Current account change[b]	3.6	8.3	7.9	−0.2	19.5
	Capital export[c]	2.4	−3.1	−4.9	−7.4	−13.0

*Between −$0.05 billion and $0.05 billion.
[a]Figures may not add because of rounding.
[b]Adjusted for inflation.
[c]A minus sign denotes capital flight, that is, an unfavourable movement in the relevant items of the capital account.
SOURCE Thomas O. Enders and Richard P. Mattione, *Latin America The Crisis of Debt and Growth*, Studies in International Economics (The Brookings Institution: Washington DC, 1984).

nomic adjustments to have resulted in an improvement in current account of about $25 billion compared with what it would have been with 'neutral' macroeconomic policies, while they regard Argentine economic policies as having led to a current account over $5 billion more negative than it would have been with 'neutral' policies. The third row for each country gives the Enders–Mattione estimate of the order of magnitude of capital flight from each country, which clearly exacerbated the problems of Argentine, Mexico and Venezuela substantially.

There are a large number of qualifications that must be made to any interpretation of the Enders–Mattione results. An important assumption is that, once terms of trade and interest rate changes are accounted for, the current account would remain unchanged in the absence of deliberate policy changes. Despite the necessary qualifications, however, the estimates give an idea of both the relative orders of magnitude for that particular group of countries. Enders and Mattione interpret their results to show that:

> for this group of Latin American countries as a whole, internal causes of the crisis predominated over external. The net total shock was $42.3 billion for the seven countries. But the total incremental financing requirement came to $96.9 billion, $55.7 billion in increased current account deficits after correcting for inflation, and $41.2 billion in increased capital export. (Enders and Mattione, p. 33)

While this general conclusion holds when summing over the seven countries, perhaps the most striking aspect of their findings as they themselves note is the major differences between countries. At one extreme, Mexico experienced a favourable external environment and yet experienced a sharp deterioration in her current account; the explanation must lie largely in domestic macroeconomic policies. At the other extreme (of this group) Brazil adopted policies which offset some of the negative external shock.

As one would expect, the countries that were most adversely affected were those whose domestic policies were initially inappropriate and for whom the external environment turned most sharply unfavourable. The apparent coincidence of timing of debt difficulties probably arose at least as much because a worldwide recession would be expected to impact most heavily on those with underlying economic problems as because of the incidence of the recession itself.

IV.2 Extreme Adjustment Difficulties

It is self-evident that higher interest rates, all else equal, intensify the difficulties of the developing countries. In fact, about three-quarters of the middle-income countries' outstanding medium- and long-term debt to private lenders has been at variable interest rates so that debt-servicing obligations on existing loans have increased. And the average interest rate paid on all LDC medium- and long-term debt to private lenders rose from 9.7 per cent in 1978 to a peak of 14.6 in 1981, falling to 13.1 per cent in 1982 and probably a little further in 1983.

Obviously, increased interest payments combined with reduced prices for exports and shrinking international markets made developing countries' situations more difficult than they would otherwise have been. Some countries would in any event have been unable to continue on their existing paths – Turkey is an example of a country which, before the effects of higher real interest rates or worldwide recession anyway was confronted with an impossible situation due largely to earlier failures to adjust. Even without the oil price increase of 1979, Turkish economic policy would have required major reforms during 1980. The question arises, however, as to whether the orders of magnitude so obtained even begin to capture the nature of the problem. If one takes $500 billion as the total outstanding debt of developing countries in 1980, the increase in interest rates from 9.7 per cent to 14.6 per cent would have accounted for about $25 billion. While this is certainly a sizeable amount, it cannot be the major reason for difficulty.

A more plausible interpretation has to do with the magnitude of the shift in the optimal size of outstanding debt and desirable amount of capital inflows. A shift in the real interest rate of the order of magnitude experienced between 1978 (when export unit values were rising at a rate almost equal to the interest rate) and 1981, when export unit values fell 5 per cent, is enormous. Warranted borrowing in 1981 and 1982, along the lines of reasoning of Section 2.4, must have been negligible, if not negative, abstracting from the question of an optimal speed of adjustment. However, many developing countries had been running net current account deficits ranging from 2 to 10 per cent of GNP (see Table 7.2 below), delaying the needed adjustment to

Table 7.2 Current account deficits less interest payments as percentage of GNP for selected countries, 1970–82

	1970	*1971*	*1972*	*1973*	*1974*	*1975*	*1976*	*1977*	*1978*	*1979*	*1980*	*1981*	*1982*	*1983*
Brazil	1.4	2.6	2.1	1.7	5.6	3.9	3.1	1.8	1.9	2.5	2.7	1.4	2.5	−0.5
Chile	−0.1	0.9	3.6	2.2	1.7	4.4	−4.0	2.3	4.9	3.1	4.1	10.9	2.2	−1.7
Colombia	4.0	5.6	1.6	−0.3	2.0	−0.1	−2.3	−3.1	−2.1	−2.7	−0.4	3.6	4.1	5.5
Korea	7.3	8.6	2.6	0.7	10.2	8.0	0.2	−1.2	0.9	5.5	7.2	4.9	1.3	−0.4
Mexico	2.3	1.4	1.3	1.7	2.9	3.4	2.4	0.3	1.1	1.7	2.1	3.5	−2.9	−2.6
Philippines	1.2	0.4	0.3	−4.0	1.7	6.1	5.9	3.4	4.0	4.1	4.8	4.4	6.2	4.7
Venezuela	0.4	−0.5	0.1	−6.2	−23.3	−8.4	−1.4	7.9	13.2	−2.5	−10.5	−9.0	2.2	−8.1

Notes
(1) Current account deficits exclude official transfers.
(2) Interest payments are for public and private guaranteed and non-guaranteed long-term debt.
(3) GNP data are derived from local currency estimates converted to US dollars at official exchange rates.
(4) Data for 1983 are estimates.
SOURCE World Bank, Economic Analysis and Projections Department; *Balance of Payments Handbook*; World Bank, *World Debt Tables, 1983/84*.

the changes of the 1970s. When the oil price rose in 1979 and the real interest rate rose sharply, the required shift in domestic expenditure and resources was too massive, both because debt was already sizeable and because adjustment to earlier changes had been too long delayed.

Table 7.2 gives the net capital inflow less interest payments for seven large debtor countries as a percentage of GNP. As can be seen, the swings in these inflows was massive. For Chile, the shift amounted to 8 per cent of GNP in one year, and for Mexico over 6 per cent. For Venezuela, a shift of more than 23 per cent took place over two years. Moreover, the recorded shifts are those that countries were able to effect: clearly in some cases, the adjustment (in the absence of adjustment costs) simply could not be made as quickly as would have been desirable.

Seen in this light, much of the pain arising from the debt situation from the perspective of the developing countries may be interpreted as emanating not from the height of interest payments *per se*, but from the difficulties associated with adjusting to any large change in the current account balance. If decisions were based on the expectation that real interest rates would remain negative or barely positive, then the warranted shift when the real rate was in excess of 10 per cent was massive. Such a shift entailed not only a real reduction in growth prospects (for those countries that were adopting policies that permitted efficient use of capital inflows) but also a massive adjustment in macroeconomic aggregates. And, given the height of real interest rates, countries could not quickly begin to work down their variable-rate debt so that total real debt was rising while the serviceable level of outstanding debt was falling.

Given the unobservability of the magnitude of the warranted outstanding debt of developing countries, there is no way of verifying this interpretation of the debt problem. Some more inferential evidence is available, however, and presented in Table 7.3. Column 1 gives the medium- and long-term debt of all developing countries as of the end of each year. Column 2 gives net medium- and long-term borrowing (i.e., the difference between years in Column 1 adjusted for valuation changes in outstanding debt). Column 3 then gives the real debt outstanding at the end of each year, calculated by deflating nominal debt by the index of export unit values of non-oil developing countries. As can be seen, during the burst of borrowing after the 1973 oil price increase, worldwide inflation implied that real debt was falling in 1974. By contrast, after the 1979 oil price increase, total real

Table 7.3 Change in developing countries' real inflows and liabilities, 1972–83

	Debt ($b)	Net borrowing ($b)	Real debt (Constant 1980 prices) ($b)	Net borrowing less interest ($b)	Real transfer (Constant 1980 prices) ($b)	Debt/GNP (*)	Index of export unit value (1980 = 100)	GNP ($b)
	(1)	(2)	(3)	(4)	(5)	(6)		
1970	66.3	7.8	203.4	5.2	16.0	17.3	32.6	382.3
1971	77.4	8.8	243.4	5.9	18.6	18.3	31.8	422.7
1972	90.8	12.8	271.0	9.4	28.1	19.3	33.5	469.3
1973	109.2	15.7	246.5	10.8	24.4	18.6	44.3	587.0
1974	135.6	23.4	226.0	16.8	28.0	18.0	60.0	753.5
1975	161.5	29.0	272.8	20.8	35.1	19.2	59.2	839.8
1976	194.9	32.8	311.8	23.8	38.1	20.4	62.5	955.0
1977	239.5	39.4	333.1	28.4	39.5	22.2	71.9	1079.7
1978	299.9	48.2	402.0	32.8	44.0	23.9	74.6	1254.9
1979	353.0	53.7	405.3	31.2	35.8	23.2	87.1	1521.8
1980	406.5	55.5	406.5	24.9	24.9	22.3	100.0	1825.9
1981	464.6	69.4	489.6	30.4	32.0	24.1	94.9	1924.0
1982	517.8	52.9	583.8	6.6	7.4	29.0	88.7	1783.8
1983	575.0	35.0	672.5	−11.0	−12.9	n.a.	85.5	n.a.

Notes The debt figures for 1983 are preliminary and subject to revision. The index of export unit value for 1983 is an average of the first two quarters only. GNP data are derived from local currency estimates, and then converted at official exchange rates. Debt is public and private, medium and long term; short term is excluded.

SOURCE World Bank, *World Debt Tables*, 1983/84 (and related data files); International Monetary Fund, *International Financial Statistics* (various issues).

medium- and long-term debt outstanding rose sharply. Column 4 gives the net borrowing of each year less interest paid on the debt during that interval (it may be noted that interest payments as a percentage of debt are less than the average interest rate on outstanding private borrowing because of concessional assistance and grace periods on longer term loans).

Column 5 gives the 'real transfer', that is net borrowing less interest payments. This number most closely reflects the additional resources available for domestic utilisation over and above domestic production. As can be seen, the real values of these net transfers were smaller in the early 1980s than ten years earlier. The final column gives debt outstanding relative to all developing countries' GNPs.

Several observations are in order. First, in the 1970s, there was a significant positive transfer of resources *and* the real value of outstanding debt was falling, thus in effect providing resources as a pure transfer from the viewpoint of the borrowing country. By contrast, in the 1980s, a smaller real transfer was accompanied by a much larger increase in real debt outstanding (at a higher real interest rate). Second, debt as a percentage of developing countries' GNP was no higher in 1980 than it had been in 1970. By contrast, the percentage rose sharply in 1981 and 1982.

All economic considerations therefore suggests that borrowing in the 1970s was economically warranted from the viewpoint of those developing countries that had adjusted to altered international conditions; their outstanding indebtedness was not increasing relative to their incomes; their cost of borrowing was low if not negative; and the real outstanding debt was growing relatively slowly. In the early 1980s, the cost of new borrowing was much higher, and the ratio of debt to GNP was rising. It is not unreasonable to interpret the developing countries' anguish as a consequence of their inability to shift expenditures relative to income sharply enough. They, therefore, had to borrow more, thereby increasing outstanding debt when the sustainable level of outstanding debt was in fact falling.

I conclude, therefore, that if one calculates only the increased interest payments on outstanding variable-rate debt, the orders of magnitude do not appear overwhelming. But if, instead, the shift in the warranted size of the current account less interest payments is examined relative to real income in developing countries, the implied orders of magnitude of needed adjustments in the domestic economy in many developing countries are truly staggering.

IV.3 Shortened Term Structure of Debt

As discussed in Part III, when the nominal rate of interest increases at a constant real interest rate, the economic time profile of scheduled repayments of principal is shortened. The premium of the nominal over the real interest rate implicitly is a payment of principal.

The rise in nominal interest rates in the late 1970s may therefore be interpreted as having increased a distortion in international capital markets due to developing countries' inability to match the schedule of repayments against the payout period for investment projects. Because worldwide inflation resulted in a greater implicit principal repayment in early years of loans, more debt rollover was needed.

That this problem is not inconsequential for the debt difficulties of the developing countries is evidenced by two statistics: the ratio of debt-servicing obligations to principal payments and the maturity structure of currently outstanding debt. With respect to the first, interest payments are estimated to have been $46 billion in 1983, contrasted with scheduled principal repayments on medium- and long-term debt of $50 billion. Since no interest payments are supposed to roll over during debt rescheduling, it is actually rescheduling of principal payments that have been in the headlines (although new credits have been extended partially or entirely covering interest payments in some cases). The second statistic even more vividly illustrates the nature of the problem: over 70 per cent of all medium- and long-term debt of developing countries outstanding at the end of 1983 was repayable in the years 1985–7. Clearly, if developing countries were to repay according to that schedule, the magnitude of the shift in macroeconomic aggregates would be beyond the reasonable adjustment range of either developed or developing countries.

V POLICY IMPLICATIONS AND CONCLUSIONS

Perhaps the biggest single question confronting policy-makers in developing countries is the likely future path of the real interest rate in international private capital markets. Should the real rate of interest remain at or above its range of 1982–3, it is questionable whether many developing countries would find it in their rational economic self-interest to borrow very much to finance new investments, once the current readjustment phase was over. The outstanding level of real debt, which may have been comfortable at the levels of real interest rates prevailing in the late 1970s, clearly caused servicing difficulties in the early 1980s.

Should high real interest rates continue, and if there is no other change in the international economy that makes debt-service less onerous than it now is, policy-makers might continue to undertake measures to increase their current account surpluses and hence reduce outstanding debt. This would, naturally, mean that resources available for new domestic investment would be reduced relative to what they would otherwise be, although the considerable scope for increased efficiency in resource allocation (via improvement in domestic economic policy regimes) may provide an offset.

However, given the difficulties associated with adjustments of the magnitude called for in reversing the direction of capital flows (and the consequently lessened prospects for growth that result), there will be high costs for continuing those adjustments should the real interest rate return to more historical levels. For, at real rates of interest at 3–5 per cent, there is little question but that those developing countries whose internal incentive structure is appropriate and whose macroeconomic policies are conducive to growth can benefit substantially from augmenting their domestic savings with foreign savings.

From the viewpoint of policy-makers in developing countries, this conclusion is somewhat uncomfortable: there will be high costs entailed in failing to adjust further should the real interest rate remain very high, and there will be high costs of adjusting further should the real interest rate return to more usual levels in the near future. If wide variability in real interest rates is likely to persist, that in itself would require flexible economic policies capable of adapting to fluctuations.

Whatever the future, however, the cries of anguish from developing countries' politicians over high interest rates may be heard much more sympathetically when seen in light of the role of the real interest rate in affecting their long-term development path and the appropriate role of international capital flows in it.

Regardless of the level of the real interest rate, however, three major lessons emerge from the experience of the past decade. One is the importance of domestic economic policies in affecting rates of return on all investments. As the analysis of Part II indicated, this may be especially important in the context of countries relying on the international capital market, as the costs of inappropriate economic policies may be magnified in so far as foreign financing is employed. If there is a lesson from the experience of the 1970s and early 1980s, it is the overriding importance of the overall macroeconomic policy framework including the trade and payments regime and the efficiency of public sector investment, that is important in determining ability to device debt. The second, which is closely related to the first, is that the marginal-average distinction in rates of return is important. Even if a particular investment project is sound, it is the average rate of return on all investments that will influence a country's ability to finance its outstanding debt. This is especially important for countries at very low levels of income. For them, the fact that gestation periods of investment are very long, combined with the length of available private lending, strongly suggests that the world was too quick to reduce concessional assistance to low-income countries. The third lesson relates to the role of foreign equity financing in development. The tradeoff between borrowing and equity may have been appropriately perceived in the 1970s when the real rate of interest was very low. For the foreseeable future, however, it seems unlikely that that regime will return. In the presence of positive real interest rates (whether of the 3–5 per cent range or 10 per cent or more), developing countries' policy-makers might be wise to reevaluate their policies with respect to equity investment. While there are clearly trade-offs, and hence political judgements to be made, greater reliance on equity-financed capital inflows in the 1970s would have eased some of the difficulties encountered in the early 1980s.

For the medium term, there seems little doubt that the pressing policy issue pertains to finding ways to restructure the scheduled principal payments on developing countries' debts. The implausibility of the currently scheduled principal repayments in itself suggests the crucial importance of finding ways to reschedule without year-to-year efforts. For new borrowing, putting a cap on nominal interest payments with any excess added to the outstanding principal balance regardless of the nominal interest rate, would stretch out the maturity structure of the debt. For debt currently outstanding, however, other mechanisms will have to be found.

A final policy lesson of some importance will be relevant if real interest rates resume more normal levels. Under those circumstances, many developing countries might find that the economically warranted level of borrowing rose sharply. They might do well to consider mechanisms to smooth the swings in the size of capital inflows, to avoid the need in future for abrupt shifts in the current account balance. If, indeed, there are sizeable costs of adjustment, and especially if those costs increase with the magnitude of the required adjustment, policies that damp those swings may be economically warranted. Clearly, larger holdings of international reserves might serve this function.

Notes

1. In writing this paper, I benefited greatly from reading papers by Harberger and Swoboda on the subject of international debt, and from the discussion at the Conference on International Debt held at the World Bank in April 1984. Comments on the conference draft by Francis Colaco, Constantine Michalopoulos, Ernest Stern, and T. N. Srinivasan are gratefully acknowledged. Nicholas Hope not only provided valuable comments, but also suggested far better data than had been used in the earlier version, and David McMurray assisted with data preparation.
2. Focus is on capital flows entirely from the viewpoint of borrowing countries. Therefore, only difficulties in the international capital market that affect the borrowers are discussed here. That rules out consideration of ways in which bank regulation, taxation, and other policies in lender countries may affect the supply of capital in ways detrimental to efficient resource allocation in the international economy. For purposes of analysing the origins of the debt problems and the policy lessons that arise, this limitation is probably not important. There are two ways in which supply-side phenomena may affect the ease of ameliorating the situation, however: regulations on lending institutions clearly inhibit the development of a secondary market in debt and also may affect banks' willingness to resume lending and their portfolio choices. Those issues are not discussed here, as they take the analysis into an entirely different field.
3. The simple theory of capital flows essentially addresses the issue of net flows. In the evolution of the debt difficulties of the developing countries, two aspects of gross flows have been relevant: first, countries have simultaneously borrowed to augment reserves; and, second, there have been a number of situations in which private capital outflows, motivated by concern over monetary stability, have been offset by public borrowing. The public-indebtedness, private-asset problem is discussed in Part II below, and both issues are dealt with in assessing the origins of the debt problem. Reviewing the theory underlying the demand for reserves would take the analysis far from the main theme of the paper and is not attempted here.
4. The capturability of income streams to finance obligations has several other aspects, discussed below. One pertains to the situation where private capital flight has been financed by public borrowing. The inability of the authorities to tax earnings of the private assets may in itself present a major debt-service problem. Another pertains to the situation in which the government has financed high-yielding investments but cannot capture a sufficient portion of the return, e.g. with investments in primary education in rural areas.
5. Of course, even that behaviour could be rational if the consumer expected never to have to repay his obligations, but as stated in section I, that seems unlikely in the case considered here.

6. If consumers know that government price and borrowing policies are unsustainable, that will affect their behaviour but not in the same way as would alternative macroeconomic policies.
7. This statement assumes that profits would have fallen during the recession. In circumstances where equity financing is devoted to highly protected domestic industries, high profitability may not have any counterpart in real rates of return, and difficulties in financing profit repatriation could be severe.
8. Capital flight is separately estimated as a third factor because this made gross borrowing larger than net borrowing. Capital flight is normally symptomatic of underlying difficulties in macroeconomic policy.

REFERENCES

Bhagwati, J. and R. Brecher (1979) 'National Welfare in an Open Economy in the Presence of Foreign-Owned Factors of Production', *Journal of International Economics*.

Bhagwati, J. and T. N. Srinivasan (1978) 'Shadow Prices for Project Selection in the Presence of Distortions: Effective Rates of Protection and Domestic Resources Costs'. *Journal of Political Economy*, vol. 86, no. 1 (February) pp. 97–116.

Cline, William R. (1983) *International Debt and the Stability of the World Economy*, Institute for International Economics, September.

Eaton, Jonathan and Mark Gersowitz (1981) 'Debt with Potential Repudiation: Theoretical and Empirical Analysis', *Review of Economic Studies*, vol. 48, pp. 289–309.

Enders, Thomas O. and Richard P. Mattione (1984) *Latin America: The Crisis of Debt and Growth* (Brookings Studies in International Economics).

Harberger, Arnold C. (1984) 'Lessons for Debtor Country Managers and Policymakers', paper presented at Conference on International Debt, World Bank, Washington DC, April.

Simonsen, Mario Henrique (1984) 'The Developing Country Debt Problem', paper presented at the Conference on International Debt, World Bank, Washington, DC, April.

Swoboda, Alexander K. (1984) 'Debt and the Efficiency and Stability of the International Financial System', paper presented at Conference on International Debt, World Bank, Washington, DC, April.

Comments on Anne O. Krueger, 'Aspects of Capital Flows Between Developing and Developed Countries' by Zvi Eckstein

The current 'debt crisis' attracts attention by economists who try to understand its causes and suggest solutions. Krueger's paper provides us with a very good survey of many aspects of the problems we face today. The paper starts with a review of the theory and leads us toward the analysis of the current events as they are summarised by aggregate data for the developing countries from 1970 to 1982.

Krueger arrives at the conclusion that the fact that many countries face the same type of liquidity crisis at the same time is due to two changes in the world economy; (a) increase in real interest rates; (b) reduction in exports owing to 'world recession'. The fact that this is a severe problem to some countries and not to others is due to the particular country's policies with respect to the current account deficits and real exchange rate appreciation.

Krueger argues that if real interest rates stay at their current level it is desirable for developing countries to reduce their outstanding stock of debt. Hence, they should have a *negative* flow of capital. Given the high current accounts deficits and the compounding interest payments the adjustment to this new situation is not pleasant.

Therefore, she suggests three main policy lines in order to smooth the transition.

(1) Reduction in current accounts deficits by proper real exchange rate policies.
(2) Replacement of debt with direct foreign investment (DFI).
(3) Long term rescheduling of the payments in order to match the timing of the projects expected returns with the loan payments.

Krueger arrives at these conclusions after she surveys different aspects of the theory of capital flows, the impact of the imperfection in markets in the borrowing countries and imperfections in the international capital markets. She then summarises the data on the debt by looking on some aggregate indicators of different countries and all of the developing countries.

Krueger suggests that we have to consider simultaneously the optimal level of external debt and the level of borrowing (the adjustment path). Diamond (1965) analyses a neoclassical growth model (Solow, 1956) which addresses the issues of optimal public debt. In his framework free capital flows equate the internal interest rates to the international interest rates and then it is shown that foreign public debt is not desirable if the economy growth rate is smaller than the interest rate. If the economy growth rate is higher than the interest rate, it may be true that a positive public debt is desirable. Although his analysis is conducted for the steady state, one can easily get results with respect to the equilibrium path from any initial conditions. In any case, Diamond's model proves the obvious result that says that as the international real rate increases, the optimal public and private debt abroad decreases.

Diamond's analysis is conducted in a model with no default risk. Eaton and Gesowitz (1981) discuss the issues of default within a neoclassical growth model that are closely related to that of Diamond. They arrive at the conclusion that at some point, when real interest rates are high, it may be desirable for the borrowing country to default and to enjoy the existing capital stock that has been invested by foreigners.

It is important to be aware of the two different ways that real capital flows into the country – public debt, private debt and direct foreign investment (DFI). Diamond considered the first aspect and Eaton and Gesowitz considered the last aspect of capital flows.

I support Krueger's view that one should look at these categories of debt differently. Theoretically the developing countries can sell local real assets to foreigners in order to replace short term public debt with long term DFI. In this way the liquidity problem of the current situation might be resolved without default, reschedulings and the implementation of other policies that would distort the internal capital market.

Although I agree that the 'debt crisis' is a real problem that requires real changes in the borrowing country, I would like to point out how the monetary system may be closely related to the *causes* of the crisis. There are at least two points:

(1) Governments borrow abroad partly, at least, in order to finance their expenditures. Hence, foreign capital flow reduce the need to tax and to print money in order to finance the same *real* expenditures. Hence, the government costs and benefits from taking foreign debt depends on the real interest rates it has to pay.
(2) The magnitude and structure of the private debt is affected critically by the central bank regulations and guarantees to the local banking system.

I found this paper interesting and important since it lays out many issues that are important for the understanding of the reasons and the alternative solutions for the current 'debt crisis'.

REFERENCES

Diamond, P. (1965) 'National Debt in a Neoclassical Growth Model', *American Economic Review* 55, no. 5 (December), pp. 1126–1150.

Eaton, J. and M. Gersowitz (1981) 'Debt with Potential Repudiation: Theoretical and Empirical Analysis', *Review of Economic Studies*, 68, pp. 289–309.

Solow, R. M. (1956) 'A Contribution to the Theory of Economic Growth', *Quarterly Journal of Economics* 70, pp. 65–94.

Part Four
Political Economy

8 The Political Economy of Leviathan*

Ronald Findlay and John D. Wilson

The theory of the state is something that most economists have been content to leave to the political scientists. When the state does appear in economic analysis it usually does so in one or the other of the following roles. One is as a benign and omniscient authority that obligingly imposes taxes, bounties or other measures at just the right level to offset some 'distortion' in the price mechanism, owing say to externalities of one sort or another, so as to assure Pareto-efficiency of market outcomes. This aspect of the state in economics is particularly pronounced in what may be called the Pigou–Meade tradition in welfare economics, which has dominated the modern developments of public finance and international trade. The other, dramatically opposed role of the state in standard economic analysis, is as the culpable or innocent tool of malevolent special interests, that instead of correcting distortions à la Pigou and Meade is the very source of them, e.g. minimum wage or usury laws, rent control, tariffs and so on. Conservative economists denounce these interventions on both equity and efficiency grounds, while liberals are apt to be apologetic, sympathising with real or alleged distributional objectives but usually pointing out that alternative (not always feasible) measures could be used that would achieve these goals at a lower cost in efficiency.

The analysis of special interests and pressure groups has recently become quite a popular pastime among economists, as for instance, Becker (1983) and Findlay and Wellisz (1982), following the lead of pioneers such as Anthony Downs (1957), Mancur Olson (1965) and Gordon Tullock (1967). The 'rent-seeking' model of Krueger (1974) fits into this framework and has indeed provided an umbrella term to cover all of this sort of analysis, as in the recent volume edited by Buchanan *et al.* (1980). Another earlier term denoting this approach is of course 'public choice', the name of a distinguished journal that has been appearing since the late 1960s. Much of the substance of this

*Findlay's work on this paper was mostly done while visiting the Institute for International Economic Studies in Stockholm. We would like to thank participants in seminars at Stockholm and the University of Maryland for very helpful comments.

analysis has been expounded in a lucid and balanced way by Mueller (1979), while Frey (1978) represents a merging of this approach with some independent European traditions and concerns.

The 'predatory' view of the nature of the state has perhaps received its fullest expression to date in a recent work by Brennan and Buchanan (1980). For them the state is a leviathan that preys on its citizens, with an insatiable appetite for revenues that it consumes for its own sake. The authors devote much ingenious analysis to the 'taming' of the revenue-gobbling monster by means of 'fiscal constitutions' that limit the powers of the state to tax, spend and issue debt.

The economic historian Douglass North has protested vigorously against the tendency by writers in the 'public choice' tradition to ignore the 'productive' view of the state, which of course has a long and distinguished tradition in the economic literature going back at least to the *staatsbildung* of the Mercantilists. Adam Smith himself, in his famous 'duties of the sovereign', compiled a rather extensive list of necessary and desirable public functions, ranging from defence and law and order to education and canals. No one other than an anarchist or extreme libertarian would contest that there is an essential productive role for the state, without which the price mechanism itself could not work effectively. The trouble is that we take law and order, enforcement of contracts and so on for granted and do not acknowledge the necessity of government at the outset. The standard neoclassical approach has been to consider the private economy exclusively to begin with, assuming away the necessity of resources to be allocated for the 'organisation' of the market system itself, and then only introducing the government to take care of particular public goods by a diversion of production from a 'private' sector, the maximal level of productivity of which is quite independent of any public goods at all.

Our intention in this paper is to present a simple minimal model of 'productive' government, in which the allocation of resources between the public and private sectors is determined endogenously in a system that includes behavioural hypotheses about the agents exercising the power of the state to tax and spend. At the same time as we allow a 'productive' role for the state we also examine the possibilities of 'predatory' behaviour as well. In our view the state as an institution is intrinsically both 'productive' and potentially 'predatory' in character, and our intention is to try to capture this dual character in a simple general equilibrium model. Hobbes' *Leviathan* was a monster, but he did say that before the rule of the *Leviathan*, in the state of nature, life was 'solitary, poor, nasty, brutish and short'. Economists, of all people, should not forget that there are no free lunches, and the price for relief from the state of nature may often be high. How rapacious the *Leviathan* is depends on what he is trying to maximise and as we shall see there is no commanding unique answer to that question.

I

Thomas Carlyle, who hated the economists of his day, derided their theory of the state as 'anarchy plus the constable'. The economists of our day, for the most part, have even left out the constable from formal models of general equilibrium, of whatever level of mathematical sophistication. The very *raison d'être* of the theory is to determine resource allocation between competing uses *endogenously*. Thus the state can only be accommodated in the usual framework by assuming that it requires either negligible resources, or that the required resources are 'subtracted' from the available pool before the analysis of markets begins, which is entirely contradictory to the spirit of general equilibrium analysis.

We propose the following simple model. Let 'real national income', conceived as a Hicksian composite commodity Y, be

$$Y = A(L_g)F(L_p, \bar{K}) \qquad (1)$$

with

$$L_g + L_p = \bar{L} \qquad (2)$$

where L_g and L_p are labour employed in the government and private sectors respectively, $\bar{L}$ is the fixed total of available labour and $\bar{K}$ is the fixed capital of the private sector. We assume that

$$A'(L_g) > 0,\ A''(L_g) < 0,\ A(0) = 1 \qquad (3)$$

while the function F is homogeneous of the first degree in L_p and K. When L_g is zero, i.e. there is no government at all, we are in the Hobbesian state of nature and the 'life of man' is described by his famous string of adjectives. Thus $F(L_p, \bar{K})$ is the level of real output achievable under anarchy. Once there are 'constables', i.e. L_g is positive, real output can be higher since $A(L_g)$ with $L_g > 0$ will be greater than unity. This can only be achieved, however, by reducing L_p, so that $F(L_p, \bar{K})$ itself is lower. Thus it is possible to determine the distribution of the fixed labour force $\bar{L}$ between L_g and L_p that maximises Y. This is easily done by maximising (1) subject to (2) and obtaining as the necessary first order condition that

$$FA'(L_g^*) = A(L_g^*)F_L(L_p^*) \tag{4}$$

where the asterisks indicate the optimal levels of L_g and L_p and F_L the partial derivative of F with respect to L_p. It is natural to interpret the left-hand side of (4) as the marginal productivity of a government worker and the right-hand side as the marginal productivity of a worker in the private sector. The requirement for optimality is that these two marginal productivities be equated.

Denoting the left- and right-hand sides of (4) by x and y respectively we have

$$\frac{dx}{dL_g} = FA''(L_g) - A'(L_g)F_L < 0 \tag{5}$$

$$\frac{dy}{dL_p} = A(L_g)F_{LL} - A'(L_g)F_L < 0 \tag{6}$$

In Figure 8.1 the horizontal axis represents the fixed labour force $\bar{L}$, with L_g measured from 0 and L_p from 0′. The negatively sloped curves depict x and y as functions of L_g and L_p respectively, the reasons for the negative slopes being established by (5) and (6). The intersection of the two curves at G determines L_g^* as OH and L_p^* as $O'H$.

With perfect mobility of the homogeneous labour pool between employment in government and the private sector, and perfect competition in the markets for labour and the fixed factor $\bar{K}$ in the private sector, the real wage corresponding to the maximal level of Y and hence to the 'optimal' division of $\bar{L}$ between L_g and L_p, is indicated by the equal distances OW and $O'W'$ on the vertical axes. The curve showing $y(L_p)$ with $L_p = \bar{L} - L_g$ that is depicted in the diagram is an 'envelope' of particular marginal productivity of labour curves, each drawn for a particular value of L_g. The curve GG' that we have drawn is the marginal productivity of labour curve for the private sector with $L_g = L_g^*$, which is tangential to the envelope curve at the 'optimal' point G. The wage-bill in the government sector,

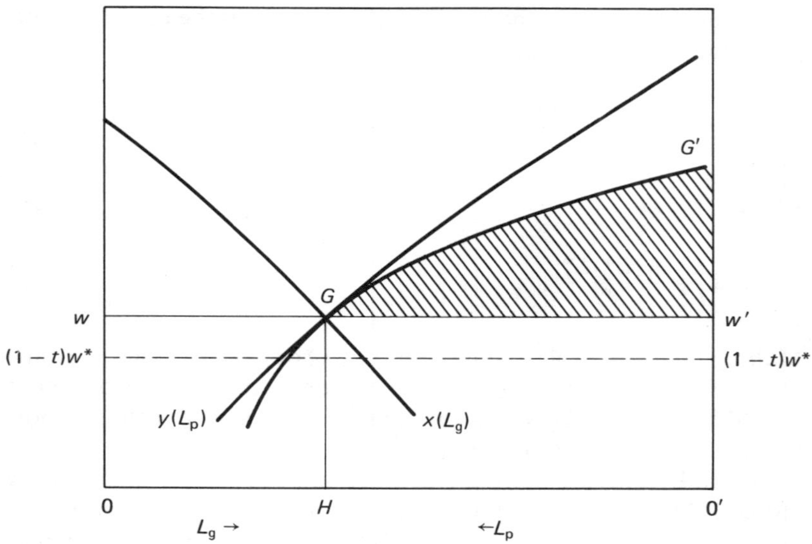

FIGURE 8.1

which is also total government expenditure, is equal to $0WGH$. The wage-bill in the private sector is $0'W'GH$, while the shaded area under GG' and above GW' represents the 'profits' or 'rents' in the private sector, that is the competitively imputed returns on the 'fixed' factor $\bar{K}$. By Euler's Theorem the area $GG'HO'$ is equal to Y, the total output of the private sector. National income, as conventionally measured, is equal to Y plus the 'output' of the government sector, which is again by convention taken as the wagebill in that sector $OWGH$.

Since there is no market for government 'output' it of course has to be financed by taxation. One possible scheme is by a simple proportional tax t on the output of the private sector, Y. The real wage in the private sector after tax then becomes the real wage that the government has to pay. The tax rate necessary to exactly finance the optimal employment L_g^* in government can easily be computed from the condition that

$$(1 - t^*)AF_L L_g^* = t^* Y^* \tag{7}$$

i.e. government employment times the competitive wage equals the yield from t^* levied on the maximum output Y^* in the private sector. From this it follows that

$$t^* = \frac{\lambda}{(1+\lambda)} \tag{8}$$

where

$$\lambda \equiv \frac{L_g^*}{L_p^*} \cdot \frac{F_L(L_p^*)L_p^*}{Y^*} \tag{9}$$

Making the reasonable assumption that $L_g^* < L_p^*$, λ is a fraction of the share of labour in the output of the private sector. The tax burden is shared between workers and 'capitalists' in the private sector proportionally to their shares in output.

In terms of Figure 8.1 the real wage in both sectors is uniformly reduced from w^* to $(1-t^*)w^*$, with L_g^* and L_p^*, and therefore Y^*, unchanged. In Figure 8.2 we plot government revenue and expendi-

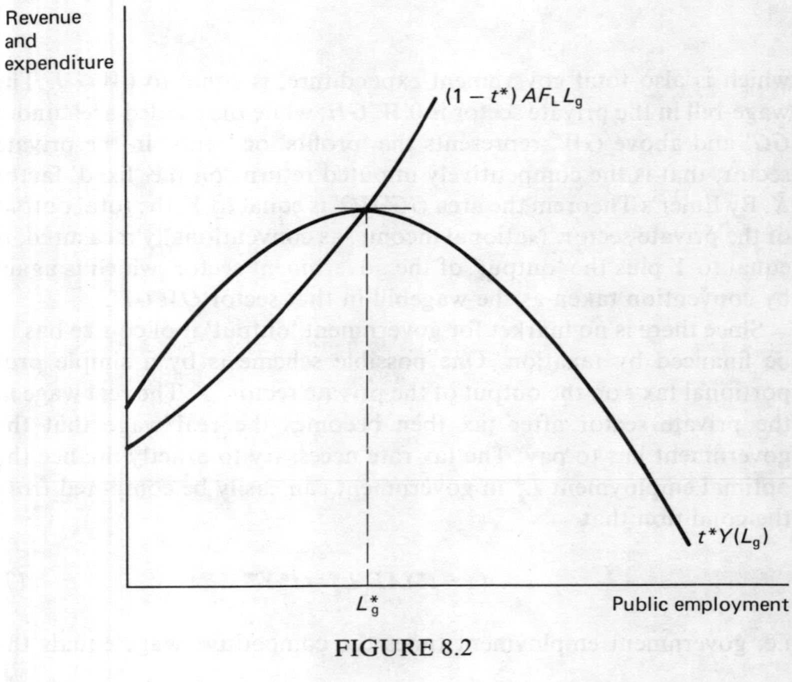

FIGURE 8.2

ture as functions of L_g, with the tax rate as t^*. The revenue function reaches a maximum when $L_g = L_g^*$ while the expenditure function is monotonically increasing, as can be seen by differentiating the left-hand side of (7) with respect to L_g, and cuts the revenue function from below at the point where it reaches a maximum at $L_g = L_g^*$. Thus the optimal solution is achieved by setting the tax rate at t^* and having the government hire labour competitively until the budget is exactly balanced. Government employment in excess of L_g will result in deficits and less than L_g in surpluses so the balanced budget 'rule' at tax rate t^* generates the optimal solution as the only possible one for the government.

Note that the output tax is *not* distortionary in our simple model since it is simply shifted back on to the two factors, both of which are in perfectly inelastic supply.

II

In the previous section we have identified the 'optimal' level of government for our simple model and a possible method for its financing. We now turn to the basic problem with which we started which is the behaviour of a purely self-interested 'Leviathan'. We must now identify the creature in some way, since merely to say that it maximises its own 'utility' in some sense is vacuous without the specification of the appropriate utility function. We do not believe that there is a unique answer to this question in view of the extreme variety of historical state systems. Our procedure will be to consider two major alternatives that appear to be of interest.

As the first case let us consider an absolute ruler or sovereign, who might be conceived as a king or sultan as in earlier times, or a contemporary dictator. We assume that the sovereign is constrained by a historically given tax rate on the output of the private sector that he cannot alter. Subject to this tax rate, however, he has full powers to decide the level of employment in the public sector and hence, indirectly, the national income. He is also constrained to pay the public employees at least the same wage as they can earn in the private sector, i.e. there is no *corvée* or conscription permitted.

Under the circumstances it would be 'rational' for the sovereign to maximise the 'surplus' which we define as

$$S \equiv tY(L_g) - (1-t)AF_L L_g \tag{10}$$

The sovereign will thus set L_g at such a level as to maximise the difference between the revenue and the expenditure, taking into account the interdependence between the two, due to the labour constraint (2). Differentiating (10) with respect to L_g and taking account of (2) we obtain as a necessary condition for maximising S

$$FA'(L_g) = AF_L + \frac{(1-t)}{t}(A'F_L - AF_{LL}) \tag{11}$$

Since the second term on the right-hand side is positive we obtain the result that the sovereign will employ *less* government workers than the socially optimal level L_g^* determined by (4).

The reason for this result is clear. The sovereign being interested in the surplus of revenue $tY(L_g)$ over expenditure $(1-t)AF_L L_g$ he equates marginal revenue to the marginal cost of hiring more government workers, which is exactly what (11) says. He has no incentive to achieve the 'optimal' level of public employment for society, L_g^*, since this would yield him less than the maximum surplus obtainable.

In Figure 8.3 we plot the revenue and expenditure of the government as functions of public employment L_g, with L_p being equal to $\bar{L} - L_g$ and the wage in the public sector being equal to $(1-t)AF_L$. The tax rate t for which Figure 8.3 is drawn is arbitrary, including t^* of the previous section as a possibility. The surplus-maximising leviathan will choose public employment as $\tilde{L}_g$, in keeping with (11), which is less than L_g^* the point at which Y^* and tY^* are maximised. $\tilde{Y}$ is the level of output corresponding to $\tilde{L}_g$.

If we denote the maximised surplus that the Leviathan swallows as $\tilde{S}$ the citizens can then consume $(\tilde{Y} - \tilde{S})$. By citizens we mean owners in the private sector and workers in both public and private employment. It is of course true that

$$(\tilde{Y} - \tilde{S}) < Y^* \tag{12}$$

the level of consumption that the citizens could enjoy if the Leviathan were to altruistically provide optimal government at zero cost. But Hobbes would say that the Leviathan is *not* bound by the social contract to do this. All that the citizens have a right to expect is that

$$(\tilde{Y} - \tilde{S}) > Y_0 \tag{13}$$

where Y_0 is the level of output in the 'state of nature'. So long as (13) is

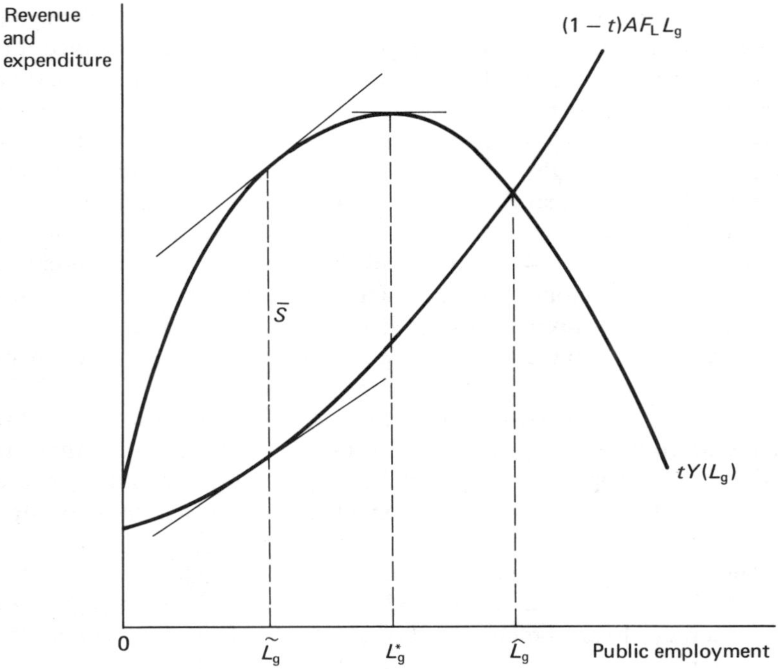

FIGURE 8.3

satisfied the citizens are benefited by the rule of the leviathan and have a corresponding obligation to obey.

It is apparent from (11) that how close $\tilde{Y}$ is to Y^* depends on the level of the parameter t, with $\tilde{Y}$ approaching Y^* as t approaches unity. This does not mean, of course, that the interest of the citizens is better served the *higher* is the tax rate, since they only consume $(\tilde{Y} - \tilde{S})$ and not $\tilde{Y}$, and $\tilde{S}$ also will be an increasing function of the tax rate. Thus there will be some 'optimum' tax rate for the citizens, between zero which is the 'state of nature' and unity that attains Y^* but at the price of too high a surplus for the Leviathan. This problem will not be investigated here though it is one of considerable interest.

The fact that the Leviathan is constrained by a given tax rate is realistic, since even the absolute monarchs of early modern Europe generally could not raise tax rates without the consent of parliaments and other representative assemblies of the nobility and the people. Modern dictators are no less constrained by fears of riots and revolts.

In the Hobbesian view, which is the one that we have taken, the state is a 'natural monopoly' and the 'surplus' as we have defined it is a sort of monopoly 'rent' that the sovereign can enjoy. The alternative Lockean view sees the exercise of governmental power as being a more conditional or 'competitive' process, in which the citizens as it were 'auction' the right to rule over them to the lowest bidder. In spite of the criticism of historians of political thought, it is difficult not to identify Hobbes' view with someone who lived through the English Civil War of the 1640s, and Locke's with that of the so-called 'Glorious Revolution' of 1688 in which the English people deposed James II, with his pretensions to 'divine right', and replaced him with the 'limited' or 'constitutional' monarchy of Mary and William of Orange.

In 1984, of all years, it is difficult to consider the problem of the leviathan to be that it provides too little government. Surely the fear today is the opposite, that civil liberty and private initiative are threatened by an excess of government. How can this be accounted for in our model?

The link between the surplus-maximising Leviathan and the obtrusive Orwellian leviathan of today is provided by the growth of bureaucracy. From being the obedient tools of absolute monarchs bureaucracies have evolved into monolithic institutions in their own right, Frankenstein monsters that have somehow got out of control. The 'rent-seeking' hypothesis of Anne Krueger (1974) provides a convenient framework into which to place our discussion, though it is much wider in scope than her original paper which only considered the limited problem of import quotas in less developed countries.

The $\tilde{S}$ that the sovereign enjoys, as we have said, is a kind of monopoly rent that he can spend on palaces, mistresses and other luxuries. The actual administration of government, however, is likely to be, and historically generally was, in the hands of professional specialists, originally colourful figures such as Wolsey and Richelieu but increasingly the grey, faceless tribe of today. We thus postulate, in the fashion of Krueger, that the rent $\tilde{S}$ originally enjoyed purely by the sovereign attracts a horde of office-seekers anxious to get their hands on some of it. The heads of the bureaucracies, for empire-building reasons made familiar by the writings of Parkinson, Niskanen (1971) and others, would not be averse to this. In keeping with these ideas we propose the following Parkinson–Niskanen Law:

'Government expenditure expands to absorb all the revenue available to finance it.'

Application of the Law to Figure 8.3 indicates that equilibrium will be attained at the level of public employment corresponding to $\hat{L}_g$, with revenue $t\hat{Y}$ entirely absorbed in the wages (at competitive rates) of the $\hat{L}_g$ workers, with employment in the private sector at $(\bar{L}-\hat{L}_g)$. We assume that the exogenous tax rate t is sufficiently high so that $\hat{Y} < Y^*$ in spite of the fact that $\hat{L} > L^*_g$, i.e. the public sector is too large relative to the optimal levels associated with L^*_g and Y^*. If t were sufficiently lower, the dissipation of the surplus $\tilde{S}$ could have brought the economy closer to Y^*, with the expenditure function crossing the revenue function to the left of L^*_g and tY^*. The case that we have chosen, of t greater than t^*, is what corresponds to the '1984' image of an overly bloated bureaucratic Leviathan. The citizens no longer have a sovereign who enjoys a glittering court, financed by $\tilde{S}$, at their expense. It is still, however, entirely possible for

$$(\tilde{Y}-\tilde{S}) > \hat{Y} \tag{14}$$

for the same parameters t, $\bar{K}$ and $\bar{L}$. A faceless bureaucracy, without any conspicuous 'privileged' consumption, can nevertheless result in a lower level of welfare for the citizens than an absolute monarchy with all its trappings.

Unlike the monarchical leviathan, however, the bureaucratic leviathan can in principle be tamed. If the exogenous tax rate parameter were to be set at t^*, the 'optimal' level of the previous section, then the Parkinson–Niskanen process will lead to exactly L^*_g workers in government service and output of Y. The bureaucracy is permitted just that amount of revenue as will lead to the optimal level of government employment and expenditure, at competitive wage-rates with the private sector. This is the 'proposition 13' approach.

If the bureaucracy could manipulate the tax rate itself, however, then it is easy to see that government expenditure would be carried beyond the social optimum. In Figure 8.4 we show the level of output Y in the private sector as a function of the tax rate t, with the distribution of employment for each tax rate, and hence Y, being determined by the Parkinson–Niskanen process at that tax rate. Y reaches a maximum Y^* at t^* and thereafter declines for higher values of t. The budget-maximising bureaucracy would be best off at the maximum revenue point, where $tY(t)$ is at a maximum. This will clearly be on the negative side of the 'Laffer Curve', where its elasticity is equal to minus unity. The collective self-interest of the bureaucracy therefore always results in tax rates, public employment

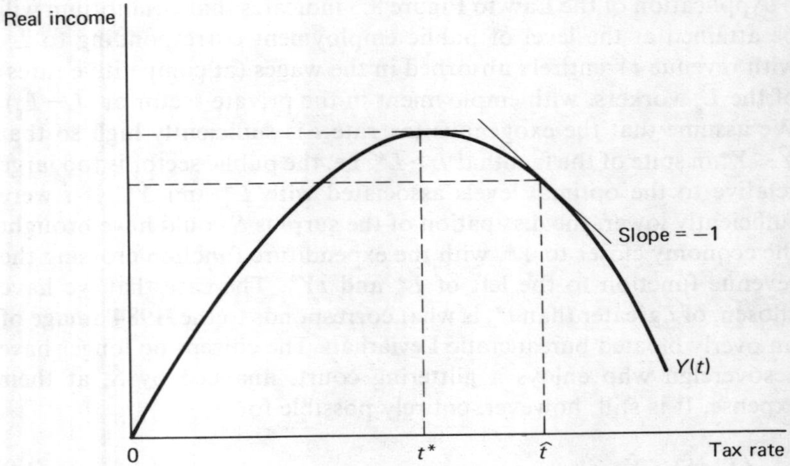

FIGURE 8.4

and competitive wage-rates that are above the socially optimal levels.

Though we have discussed the surplus-maximising and bureaucratic leviathans as alternative cases they can also be regarded as the limiting cases of a continuous spectrum. Intermediate cases correspond to some positive but less than maximum surplus being enjoyed by some elements in the society. In addition to the royal 'Court' that we have considered it could be benefits for the sick and aged and other handicapped groups, as in the modern 'welfare state'. Another possibility is salaries for the bureaucracy at higher than competitive levels, with entry restricted by some device such as the famous examination system for Chinese mandarins or the modern British Oxbridge variant. Ironically, such 'rent-keeping' devices can be socially beneficial in our model, since they prevent the 'rent-seeking' entry of workers from the private sector where their social productivity is higher though their private earnings are less.

One of the problems with 'welfare state' dispositions of the 'surplus' is that they tend to lend themselves to bureaucratic proliferation in administration, that swallows up the surplus itself while reducing output in the private sector. 'Feudal' rather than 'democratic' ways of disposing of the surplus are probably more of a bulwark against Parkinsonian encroachments.

Finally, we may note that 'property' in our model will favour limited government, while 'labour' will be in favour of any expansion of the public sector that is feasible. The latter proposition follows simply from the fact that diverting workers from private to public employment at competitive wage-rates always increases the wage-rate and hence the wage-bill since total employment is fixed. The wage-rate w is $(1-t)(A(L_g)F_L$ and

$$\frac{dw}{dL_g}=(1-t)[A'F_L-AF_{LL}]>0 \tag{15}$$

The qualification to this statement that 'labour' will always favour expansion of the public sector is that part of the 'surplus' may be enjoyed by labour as a whole or by some segments of it. In this case there may be resistance to an expansion of the public sector that dissipates this disposition of the surplus.

The result that 'property' will favour only a limited extent of government is also easy to establish. Total profits after tax, denoted R, are $(1-t)A(L_g)F_K\bar{K}$ and

$$\frac{dR}{dL_g}=(1+t)\bar{K}[A'F_K-AF_{KL}]=0 \tag{16}$$

defines the optimal extent of the public sector for 'property' as the point where the additional profit generated by public employment at the margin $(1-t)A'F_K\bar{K}$ is equal to the loss due to the contraction of employment in the private sector which is $(1-t)\ AF_{KL}\bar{K}$.

Thus we have a natural coalition between government bureaucracy and 'labour' to expand the public sector and between the owners of real 'property' and 'rights' to the disposition of the surplus to limit it. The changing social balance of power between these groups could be a significant hypothesis in accounting for the 'growth of government' in modern society that many observers have noted. Peltzman (1980) and Meltzer and Richard (1981) put forward interesting models to account for this phenomenon in terms of voting on redistributive transfers. Our approach here in terms of an over-expansion of a productive government sector may be complementary to these contributions.

III

The ideas behind the simple model that we have examined in this paper have an ancient lineage but at the moment are perhaps most closely associated by economists with two major recent works, by Brennan and Buchanan (1980) and North (1981). In this final section we make a brief attempt to relate our model to their work and that of some others. We of course have no intention to try to provide a detailed examination and critique of their very rich and diverse views, a task that would be extremely rewarding but quite beyond the scope of this paper.

Brennan and Buchanan consistently adopt a 'constitutional' perspective throughout their book. Their view is that the basic fiscal structure of a state should be elevated above the messy arena of interest group politics in a pluralist democracy, since for all the reasons that have been extensively investigated in the public choice literature the outcomes of such processes are likely to be extremely inefficient. They also have no faith in the benign and omniscient intervention of a Bergson–Samuelson or Pigou–Meade planner. Their view is the classical liberal one that it is only prudent for a citizen to *assume* that he will be governed by rascals rather than saints, and that he should consequently choose to live under a system of rules that will oblige the rascals in power to act in the citizens' interest rather than their own, wherever that is possible. Hence they adopt the hypothesis that the state is a Leviathan in a 'minimax' spirit, i.e. minimise the maximum damage that a malevolent state can do to you.

Throughout most of their book the authors adopt the hypothesis that the leviathan maximises *revenue*. They say that this is equivalent to maximising the surplus if public expenditure is fixed and the level of revenue is independent of the level of expenditure. The one exception is in chapter 7, where they consider a problem in which the Leviathan's ability to obtain revenue is made conditional by the citizens on the provision of public goods. It is thus only in this chapter that they consider surplus maximisation proper, in the manner of our investigation here. While Niskanen and other writers on bureaucracy are frequently referred to by the authors, they do not distinguish sharply as we have done between the divergent analytical consequences of the surplus-maximising and budget-maximising hypotheses about the behaviour of the Leviathan. Their model in chapter 7 is strictly partial equilibrium in character and does not consider the interdependence between the public and private sectors explicitly as we have done. Furthermore, the state in our model raises the productivity of the private sector itself, through the provision of the indispensable framework of law and order without which the enforcement of contracts and so on would be difficult if not impossible. While they are presumably not anarchists, the reader does get the impression that the state in their view is a pure predator on the body politic, like the Mongols or the Mafia.

Douglass North, on the other hand, has stressed the fact that the state is an indispensable institution for the very possibility of civilisation and economic progress, in spite of the fact that ruling groups have undoubtedly been motivated in their actions to generate and preserve the rents associated with their control of this particular natural monopoly. The very insightful and suggestive sketch of 'A Neoclassical Theory of the State' in chapter 3 of North's book has been an important source of inspiration for our work. Our contribution has been to incorporate very similar ideas into a simple but explicit general equilibrium model.

Our model also links up with the work on the expansive tendencies of bureaucracies by Niskanen (1971), Borcherding (1977) and others and represents a start in linking the more specific concerns of that literature to an analysis of their interaction with the economy as a whole. The well known study by Bacon and Eltis (1976) on Britain's economic problem as being one of 'too few producers' is related to our discussion of how the Parkinson–Niskanen process can take the economy to the 'right of the Laffer Curve', or beyond the 'optimal' level of public employment. Bacon and Eltis appeal to the Classical–Physiocratic distinction between 'productive' and 'unproductive' labour in their distinction between 'marketed' and 'non-marketed' output sectors. This terminology is somewhat misleading and unnecessary. It is not that public servants or 'non-marketed' output suppliers are 'unproductive' in any absolute sense, according to our model, but that this sector, for the reasons given, has expanded excessively at the expense of the other.

To conclude, we may note that the analysis is capable of extension in a number of directions. The production technology can be made considerably more general, for instance by introducing capital as well as labour into government activities, leading to a model with many of the features of the Heckscher–Ohlin–Samuelson model in the theory of international trade. Nationalisation, or the 'public provision of private goods' can also be introduced. Government borrowing and public debt, money and seigniorage are other possibilities. Most interesting of all, perhaps, would be to endogenise the tax rate by an explicit modelling of the various pressure groups identified in the paper, along the lines of Findlay–Wellisz (1982) and other work in that area. We hope to accomplish some of these extensions in future work.

REFERENCES

Bacon, R. and W. Eltis (1976) *Britain's Economic Problem: Too Few Producers* (Macmillan).

Becker, G. S. (1983) 'A Theory of Competition Among Pressure Groups for Political Influence', *Quarterly Journal of Economics* (August).

Borcherding, T. E. (ed.) (1977) *Budgets and Bureaucrats: the Sources of Government Growth* (Duke University Press).

Brennan, G. and J. M. Buchanan (1980) *The Power to Tax* (Cambridge University Press).

Buchanan, J. M. *et al.* (eds) (1980) *Towards a Theory of the Rent-Seeking Society* (Texas A & M University Press).

Downs, A. (1957) *An Economic Theory of Democracy* (Harper).

Findlay, R. and S. Wellisz (1982) 'Endogenous Tariffs, the Political Economy of Trade Restrictions and Welfare', in J. N. Bhagwati (ed.), *Import Competition and Response* (University of Chicago Press).

Frey, B. (1978) *Modern Political Economy* (Wiley).

Krueger, A. O. (1974) 'The Political Economy of the Rent-Seeking Society', *American Economic Review* (June).

Meltzer, A. and S. Richard (1981) 'A Rational Theory of the Size of Government', *Journal of Political Economy* (October).

Mueller, D. (1979) *Public Choice* (Cambridge University Press).

Niskanen, W. (1971) *Bureaucracy and Representative Government* (Aldine).

North, D. (1981) *Structure and Change in Economic History* (Norton).

Olson, M. (1965) *The Logic of Collective Action* (Harvard University Press).

Peltzman, S. (1980) 'The Growth of Government', *Journal of Law and Economics*.

Tullock, G. (1967) 'The Welfare Costs of Tariffs, Monopolies and Theft', *Western Economic Journal* (June).

Comments on Ronald Findlay and John D. Wilson, 'The Political Economy of Leviathan' by M. June Flanders

I wish to open the discussion with an examination of the name of the paper. 'Leviathan' is a common Israeli surname (including that of at least two economists); it means a whale, including the specific whale who swallowed (and subsequently released) the prophet Jonah; and it is also 'a fabulous sea animal, reserved as food for the righteous in the hereafter' – so if we are but patient, the day of reckoning will come, and we will eat the monster!

The paper is both interesting and thought provoking; having said that, there is little left to do but to carp at some details and criticise the authors for not having written a different paper.

First the 'model' is a framework, not in itself an analysis. Its very generality, which is part of its charm, is also its weakness. Like the theory of evolution, and like much of the paradigm of neoclassical economics, it is both irrefutable and useless as a predictor.

Second, the game of armchair historicism is a dangerous one – and everybody can play it. Thus, it is difficult to imagine the despots of history, either the Mongolian potentates or the French Bourbons, being characterised as generating 'too small' a government sector. And while the trappings of royalty and imperial splendour *may* yield greater social utility than a 'faceless, grey, bureaucracy' (whom admittedly nobody gets much pleasure from as they torture honest, hard-working citizens), the generality of the phenomenon probably depends heavily on the fact that the model ignores the disutility of envy (like all other neoclassical models, of course). Thus the British today seem to enjoy and even love their royalty and its trappings. The French at the end of the eighteenth century had apparently reached satiation. It would be more convincing if this difference could be made endogenous in the model.

Third, the literature on social choice and equity versus efficiency assumes that redistribution is always carried out by means of lump sum taxes and grants. I have never seen a recipe for computing these, or read or heard any statement that took this seriously as a practical device for redistributing wealth. One way of bringing about redistribution, even with proportional taxes, is hinted at here, with the provision of various benefits and welfare expenditures for the aged, the handicapped and even the 'undeserving poor' (see *Pygmalion*, by G. B. Shaw). The issue of how to determine the optimum size of the whale which would yield the desired quantity of blubber for this purpose might be dealt with in an extension of this model. I am not certain that is possible, technically, but it might merit some thought. Probably easier, conceptually, would be to incorporate the provision of public consumption goods into the model – presumably one could add the total utility accruing from these to the utility of the model's *Y*.

The difficulty of carping about this paper is that the authors have done much of it for us – and in the last paragraph they offer us a multitude of future goodies in the form of extensions. At least one of these may be fundamental: the switch (not the extension) to a Heckscher–Ohlin production model. I am fairly convinced that the difference between the Ricardian model and the Heckscher–Ohlin model in this case is significant. In addition, the exogeneity of factor supplies is crucial. The tone of the model and of the paper is classical rather than neoclassical, more a discussion of long-term historical trends than about statics. In a Heckscher–Ohlin model, the sectoral gains and losses from an expansion of the whale depend, of course, on the intensities of factor use in the two production functions. In the model as it stands, labour gains and 'capital' loses from an increase in government; in a Heckscher–Ohlin world, this is no longer necessarily the case. Factor incomes depend on the government-private sector mix; if factor supplies depend on factor prices, then growth becomes endogenous. So do the structure of the economy and the pattern of comparative advantage.

Finally, in case Findlay and Wilson are looking for additional hard work they might think of extending their model to encompass something like the Scandinavian model of the international transmission of inflation, since there is generally believed to be a close correspondence between the government sector and the non-traded goods sector in most countries.

Part Five
Resource Allocation and Taxation

9 Notes on the Effect of Capital Gain Taxation on Non-Austrian Assets

Daniel J. Kovenock and
Michael Rothschild

I INTRODUCTION

Capital gains taxes are different from most other taxes on capital. Because they are levied on a realisation basis, how much capital gains tax is paid depends on when an asset is sold not when the capital gain actually occurred. If you buy an asset for price $P(t_0)$ at time t_0 and you sell it at T, your tax (payable at T) is $\tau\,[P(T)-P(t_0)]$, where τ is the statutory rate of capital gains tax. This is true regardless of when the increase in value took place. That is, the tax depends only on $P(t_0)$ and $P(T)$; it is independent of the rest of the price path $P(t)$. If assets appreciate, the longer you hold an asset the lower the discounted value of taxes paid on increases in value which took place just after you acquired the asset. In the United States, if sale of an asset can be put off until death no capital gains taxes need be paid. Accrual taxation of capital gains would tax capital gains as they accrue. If capital gains are taxed on an accrual basis, the effect is to lower the after tax rate of return by a factor equal to the tax rate. That is, if an asset grows according to

$$P(t)=P(t_0)\exp\int_{t0}^{t}\alpha(s)\,ds,$$

under accrual taxation at rate λ, its rate of return at time s will be $\alpha(s)(1-\lambda)$. Since tax obligations are incurred as capital gains are earned, if investors pay tax at the same rate, tax burdens are independent of changes in ownership.

As compared with taxation on an accrual basis, the capital gains tax discourages sales of appreciated assets. This is called the 'lock-in' effect. Investors who hold assets which have increased in value are locked into these assets. They can sell them only on pain of paying taxes which could be deferred or avoided.

Economists have documented that the lock-in effect is real. Feldstein and Yitzhaki (1978), Feldstein and Slemrod (1978), and Feldstein *et al.* (1980) have demonstrated that the holding period for assets subject to the capital gains tax is sensitive to tax considerations. Bailey (1969) and more recently Protopapadakis (1983) have found, after examining tax returns, that on average assets on which capital gains taxes are levied are held for a long time. Protopapadakis estimates that the average holding period is between 24 and 31 years.

In a previous paper (Kovenock and Rothschild, 1983) we analysed the effect of capital gains taxation on 'Austrian' assets, that is, on assets whose real value depends on when they are harvested or consumed. The standard examples are wine and trees. We discussed the impact of capital gains taxation on the harvest time of Austrian assets and on the allocation of investment between Austrian and non-Austrian assets. In our model, capital gains taxation decreased the harvest times of some Austrian assets and left unchanged the harvest times of other Austrian assets. We did, however, find a financial lock-in effect. The owner of an Austrian asset would never find it profitable to sell the asset to another investor before the asset was harvested or consumed.

Most assets subject to capital gains taxation are not of the Austrian type. They represent claims to the profits of continuing enterprises. For such assets the economic consequences of capital gains taxation are different and less apparent. In general, taxes on capital can have two kinds of effects on economic efficiency. First, by reducing the attractiveness of investing, the capital gains tax can distort the savings consumption decision. Second, by making some investments more attractive than others or by interfering with the efficient operation of the capital market, taxes on capital can cause an inefficient allocation of the funds which are available for investment.[1]

Conventional wisdom suggests the first effect is small. Because appreciated assets are held for a long time, the effective rate of the capital gains tax is held to be quite low. Protopapadakis puts the effective rate of capital gains taxation between 3.4 and 6.6 per cent in the period from 1960 to 1978. This is much less than the statutory rate. For the same period Protopapadakis reports that the statutory rate which the average dollar of reported capital gains income faced varied from 18.1 to 27.1 per cent. We will reexamine this assumption in the next section. There, we contend that conventional estimates could seriously underestimate the effective rate of capital gains taxation because they ignore uncertainty.

In the remainder of this section we will discuss the consequences of the lock-in effect on the efficient allocation of capital. We conclude that there are ways in which the lock-in effect can lead to an inefficient allocation of capital. However, we believe, without knowing how we would document our belief, that these effects are small if not insignificant.

We find this problem easiest to think about within the following framework: suppose that society has a number of potential investment projects, projects which can be ranked in terms of their social desirability. Ignoring uncertainty and capital market imperfections, this ranking is equivalent to an ordering in terms of the rate of return of each project. Capital market misallocations occur when projects with a high return are deferred while projects with a low return are undertaken. Thus, our questions are: can the capital gains tax cause such mistakes and are they likely to be large?

The capital gains tax *can* cause such misallocations. The tax may make a project with high social returns unattractive to the person who will decide whether the project will be undertaken. Consider, for example, a company which is largely owned by its founder. Suppose that most of the founder's wealth is in the stock of the company which shows large (unrealised) capital gains. As an investor, the founder is anxious to diversify his holdings. He can do this by selling shares of the company's stock, paying capital gains taxes, and using the proceeds to buy a diversified portfolio. He can avoid the capital gains tax by having his company buy the same diversified portfolio. In an extreme case he can turn his company into a mutual fund. In a less extreme case he can choose to have his company undertake projects which diminish the risk of his own portfolio. If there are investment projects which this company alone can pursue, then there is a potential social loss if this company does not develop them. Society can diversify the risk; the company's founder cannot. For this reason, valuable projects are shelved. It is clear that this problem, which we have labelled the 'Steve Jobs problem', probably does occur. We doubt that it is very significant. However, we have no idea how we would demonstrate this.

We note another possible effect of the capital gains tax on market efficiency. Since the capital gains tax is a transactions tax, it diminishes trading. If investors get information from asset prices, reduced trading may entail investors getting less information and thus making less good decisions. We have worked out an example (not reported here) which illustrates this point. It is difficult to assess the importance of this aspect of the lock-in effect but we doubt it is very significant.

Other theories of how the capital gains tax can distort the allocation of investment are less credible. Most stories of how the tax system distorts investment allocation depend on the favourable (relative to dividends) tax treatment of retained earnings rather than the lock-in effect. Because capital gains are taxed at a lower rate than dividends, companies have an incentive to retain earnings rather than to pay dividends. The difficulty this causes is that companies must do something with their retained earnings. If they invest them in their own projects, and if their own projects have lower rates of return than the projects of companies which have no retained earnings, then it may happen that worthy projects go begging while relatively unprofitable projects receive funding. Again, for this mechanism to cause misallocations of investment it is necessary that projects be tied specifically to firms. If all firms can invest in all projects then the financing of investments by retained earnings cannot by itself cause harm.

Even with this assumption, it is difficult to understand how financing projects out of retained earnings can lead firms to invest in projects with below market rates of return. Suppose there is a competitive bond market which provides funds to companies for investment at a constant cost. If the rate of interest on bonds is B, then all companies will undertake investments which promise a rate of return of B or more. Furthermore, if all companies finance some projects with bonds then the market will operate efficiently. Marginal projects are financed out of bonds; if all companies are in the bond market then all are using the same cutoff rate to determine the marginal investment project. A company with so much retained earnings that the marginal project can be financed out of retained earnings has a rate of return of B. To obtain this rate of return, it is not necessary to invest in the bonds of other companies. An alternative is to buy its own bonds on the open market or to call outstanding bonds. Thus a competitive bond market ensures that rational companies will, even when using retained earnings as a primary source of financing, invest in projects which earn B or more and not invest in projects which earn B or less. While the capital gains tax may encourage companies to retain earnings rather than to pay dividends, this should not lead to inefficient allocations of investment.

This model is oversimplified. Companies do not all pay the same price for bonds. Differences in interest rates charged companies have many causes. An important one is the debt–equity ratio. The extent to which companies use the bond market may increase the rate of interest which they must pay to raise new funds. The lock-in effect of the capital gains tax may exacerbate differences in interest rates charged to different companies. The lock-in effect reduces the incentive to sell the shares of companies with retained earnings. This may keep the prices of their shares artificially high relative to what they would be in a world of accrual taxation. That is, the lock-in effect may cause share prices to reflect past earnings as well as future expected earnings. This will raise the value of equity of firms with past (retained) earnings and lower the cost of bond capital to them. Again, it is hard to know how important are such deviations from the perfectly competitive model (of the bond market); we doubt they are significant.

II THE EFFECTIVE RATE OF CAPITAL GAINS TAXATION

Suppose you had a million dollars which you did not need and you decided to give it to your children on your death which you knew would be in T years. Rather than letting the money lie idle, you decide to invest it. Mindful of the tax law, you invest only in assets which pay neither dividends nor interest but instead reward their owners with capital gains when they are sold. You do not plan to sell any of the assets which you have put in the portfolio to be turned over to your children. On your death, the portfolio will be liquidated and its proceeds will be distributed to your children. In the United States at least, the capital gains in the portfolio will escape taxation. What then is the effective rate of capital gains tax which you will pay on the investments you have undertaken on behalf of your children?

At first glance the answer to this question seems clearly to be: 'Zero'. This is certainly the answer which is consistent with the method which most economists use to calculate the effective rate of capital gains taxation. The standard source for such calculations is Bailey (1969) whose procedure is described below.

'Zero' seems a perfectly reasonable answer if capital gains accrue with certainty. However, the values of most assets which produce capital gains evolve in a manner which is highly uncertain. For such assets the effective rate of capital gains taxation is not zero. Here is why. Consider again the million dollars you plan to invest to leave to your children. To avoid paying capital gains taxes, you must not sell any assets which have increased in value. Suppose, to take an extreme case, that because of inflation all assets always show a paper gain. Then to avoid paying capital gains taxes, you must never sell any asset; in other words, you must follow a buy and hold policy. If there were no capital gains tax (and no other transaction costs) then you would not follow a buy and hold policy. You would continually rebalance your portfolio to maintain the optimal composition of assets. If assets followed a stationary distribution, you would often want to keep the share of each asset in the entire portfolio constant. To do this you would have to sell the assets which had increased in value (relative to the average) and buy those which had decreased in value. This is the opposite of the rule: 'sell losers and hold winners' which those who wish to avoid the capital gains tax are urged to follow. To avoid the capital gains tax, you must give up the privilege of managing your portfolio. Tax avoidance has a price and this price should be calculated as part of the effective rate of taxation. With strong assumptions we can calculate this price and thus the effective rate of capital gains taxation.

In the remainder of this section we build a model which will allow us to calculate the value of being able to manage a portfolio actively. We then use this model to calculate the effective rate of capital gains taxation. We find that for some parameter values the effective rate is quite high – much higher than the statutory rate. For others it is very low. The parameters that seem to matter most are those which describe the level of diversifiable risk. However, the degree of risk aversion is also important.

Not all economists will find the model and the assumptions we have used to calculate the effective rate of taxation compelling. We discuss some of the more serious objections to our procedure in the final part of this section.

1 A Model for Calculating the value of Portfolio Management

Suppose an investor has the opportunity of dividing his wealth among N assets. Asset returns are correlated; each asset's value grows according to

$$\mathrm{d}P_i = P_i(\alpha \mathrm{d}t + \delta \mathrm{d}Z_i + \sigma \mathrm{d}Z_0) \qquad i = 1, \ldots, N. \tag{1}$$

Where $Z_0, Z_1, \ldots, Z_N$ are independent Wiener processes. As we will see σ^2 represents a common component of undiversifiable variance and δ^2 represents uncertainty which can be diversified away. A risk averse investor facing investment opportunities given by (1) will split his wealth evenly among the N assets. Suppose he follows a buy and hold policy. After T years his wealth will be $W(T)$, a random variable whose distribution we now calculate. Let $b_i(T) = \log P_i(T)$ and $b(T) = (b_1(T), \ldots, b_N(T))$. It is straightforward (for details see Arnold, 1974, 141–4) to show that $b(T)$ has a multivariate normal distribution with mean

$$\mu(T) = T(\alpha - (\sigma^2 + \delta^2)/2)\iota \tag{2}$$

where ι is a vector of N ones, and variance covariance matrix

$$\Sigma(T) = T \begin{pmatrix} \delta^2+\sigma^2 & \sigma^2 & \sigma^2 \ldots \sigma^2 \\ \sigma^2 & \delta^2+\sigma^2 & \sigma^2 \ldots \sigma^2 \\ \cdot & \cdot & \cdot \\ \cdot & \cdot & \cdot \\ \cdot & \cdot & \cdot \\ \sigma^2 & \sigma^2 \ldots & \delta^2+\sigma^2 \end{pmatrix} \tag{3}$$

It follows that $P(T) = (P_1(T), \ldots, P_N(T))$ has a multivariate log-normal distribution (Johnson and Kotz, 1972, 20) with mean vector

$$E(P(T)) = e^{\alpha T}\iota \tag{4}$$

and variance covariance matrix $\Omega(T)$ with elements

$$\Omega(T)_{ij} = \begin{cases} e^{2\alpha T} & (e^{T(\delta^2+\sigma^2)}_{-1}) & i=j \\ e^{2\alpha T} & (e^{T\sigma^2} - 1) & i \neq j \end{cases} \tag{5}$$

Suppose $W(0) = 1$ is the amount initially invested in the portfolio (under the assumption, soon to be made, of constant relative risk aversion this is a normalisation). Then $W(T) = N^{-1} \sum_{i=1}^{N} P_i(T)$, and the mean and variance of a buy and hold portfolio are

$$E[W(T)] = e^{\alpha T} \tag{6}$$

and

$$V[W(T)] = e^{2\alpha T}[N^{-1}e^{T(\delta^2+\sigma^2)} + (1 - N^{-1})e^{T\sigma^2} - 1].$$

If the proceeds of this portfolio are taxed on a realisation basis at rate τ, after tax returns are

$$W(T, \tau) = W(T)(1-\tau) + \tau \tag{8}$$

with mean and variance

$$E[W(T, \tau)] = \mathrm{e}^{\alpha T}(1-\tau) + \tau \tag{9}$$

and

$$V[W(T, \tau)] = (1-\tau)^2\, \mathrm{e}^{2sT}[N^{-1}\, \mathrm{e}^{T(\delta^2+\sigma^2)} + (1-N^{-1})\, \mathrm{e}^{T\sigma^2} - 1]. \tag{10}$$

Now consider how the wealth of the same investor evolves if before tax asset returns continue to evolve according to (1) but (i) the investor continually rebalances his portfolio and (ii) assets are taxed on an accrual basis at rate λ. Let $Y(T,\lambda)$ be the value of such a portfolio. Let $S_i(t)$ denote the number of shares which the investor holds in asset i; then

$$Y(T, \lambda) = \sum_{i=1}^{N} S_i(T)P_i(T)$$

and, as Merton (1971, 378–9) shows,

$$\mathrm{d}Y = \textstyle\sum_i S_i \mathrm{d}P_i \tag{11}$$

describes the evolution of the portfolio's value. If the investor is risk averse, then he will manage his portfolio so as to keep an equal share of his wealth invested in each asset. Let

$$w_i(t) = \frac{S_i(t)P_i(t)}{Y(t,\lambda)}.$$

In the optimal portfolio $w_i(t) = N^{-1}$. Thus, (11) becomes

$$\mathrm{d}Y = \textstyle\sum_i Y w_i P_i^{-1}\, \mathrm{d}P_i = Y N^{-1} \sum_i P_i^{-1} \mathrm{d}P_i. \tag{12}$$

Accrual taxation changes asset dynamics from (1) to

$$\mathrm{d}P_i = (1-\lambda)P_i(\alpha \mathrm{d}t + \delta \mathrm{d}Z_i + \sigma \mathrm{d}Z_0). \tag{13}$$

To see this suppose that at t, the vector of holdings of assets is $P(t)$. Let $\rho(t, t+h) = P(t+h) - P(t)$; $\rho(t, t+h)$ is a random vector which depends on t, h, and the events which have occurred up to, and including, time t. The meaning of (1) is essentially that for h small the expected value of $\rho(t, t+h)$ is approximately equal to $\alpha h P(T)$ and the variance covariance matrix of $\rho(t, t+h)$ is approximately equal to $h\hat{P}(T)\sum\hat{P}(T)$, where $\hat{P}(T)$ is a diagonal matrix with $P(T)$ on the diagonal and $\sum$ is a matrix with $\sigma^2 + \delta^2$ on the diagonal and σ^2 elsewhere.

Now suppose there is accrual taxation at rate λ; we can approximate the effect of accrual taxation by considering realisation taxation over short time intervals. If there is a before tax gain of $\rho(t, t+h)$, then after tax gains have means approximately equal to $P(T)\alpha(1-\lambda)h$ and variance covariance matrix approximately equal to $h(1-\lambda)^2\hat{P}(T)\sum\hat{P}(T)$. But this is the meaning of (13).

Substituting (13) in (12) we see that

$$dY = Y(1-\lambda)\,(\alpha dt + \sigma dZ_0 + N^{-1}\delta\textstyle\sum_i dZ_i). \tag{14}$$

Assuming that $Y(0, \lambda) = 1$, the solution to this stochastic differential equation is (Arnold, 1974, 138)

$$Y(T, \lambda) = \exp[(\alpha(1-\lambda) - \left(\frac{\delta^2}{2N} + \frac{\sigma^2}{2}\right)(1-\lambda)^2)T + (1-\lambda)\left(\frac{\delta^2}{N} + \sigma^2\right)^{\frac{1}{2}} T^{\frac{1}{2}} X] \tag{15}$$

where X is a standard normal random variable; that is $T(T, \lambda)$ is lognormally distributed with mean

$$E[Y(T,\lambda)] = e^{\alpha(1-\lambda)T} \tag{16}$$

and variance

$$V[Y(T, \lambda)] = e^{2\alpha(1-\lambda)T}[\exp((T)\,(1-\lambda)^2(\sigma^2 + \delta^2/N)) - 1]. \tag{17}$$

As is clear from the formulae (9), (10), (16), and (17) taxation changes the distribution of returns of the two portfolios we have examined. Taxes reduce both the mean and variance of returns; however, the relative effects of taxation on the two portfolios are different. Specifically, suppose $\lambda = \tau$ and compare $E[W(T, \tau)]$ with $E[Y(T, \tau)]$. It is straightforward to calculate that $E[W(T, \tau)] \geqslant E[Y(T, \tau)]$ for all $\tau \in [0, 1]$ with equality holding only if $\tau = 0$ or $\tau = 1$. Similarly, $V(W(T, \tau)) \geqslant V(Y(T, \tau))$ for $\tau \in [0, 1]$ equality holding if $\tau = 1$ or if $N = 1$ and $\tau = 0$. Figures 9.1, 9.2 and 9.3 show the mean and variance of these portfolios as the level of taxation varies for various values of the parameters. In all the figures $\alpha = 0.1$, $\sigma^2 = 0.039$, and $N = T = 10$; in Figure 9.2, $\delta^2 = 0.038$ and in Figure 9.3, $\delta^2 = 0.39$. The reasons for choosing these parameter values are discussed in subsection 3 below. As is clear from the figures, taxes reduce mean and variance in each case. Figure 9.4 shows the parametric curves giving the means and standard deviations of the two portfolios as τ varies from 0 to 1. In both Figure 9.4(a) and 9.4(b), $T = 10$, $\alpha = 0.1$, $\sigma^2 = 0.039$, and $\delta^2 = 0.39$; in Figure 9.4(a), $N = 1$ while in Figure 9.4(b), $N = 10$. Realisation taxation induces a linear trade-off between mean and standard deviation; as τ increases the decrease in the standard deviation is proportional to the decrease in the mean. Under accrual taxation the standard deviation decreases with the mean at a decreasing rate; standard deviation is a convex function of the mean.[2] For $N = 1$ the endpoints of both curves coincide. At low levels of τ accrual taxation

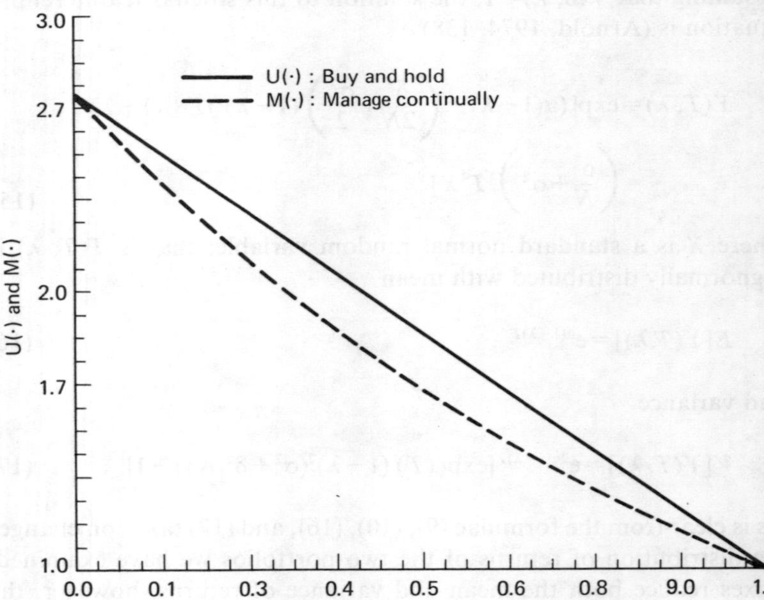

FIGURE 9.1 *Mean returns of portfolios.*
Parameters: $\alpha = 0.1$, $N = 10$, $T = 10$

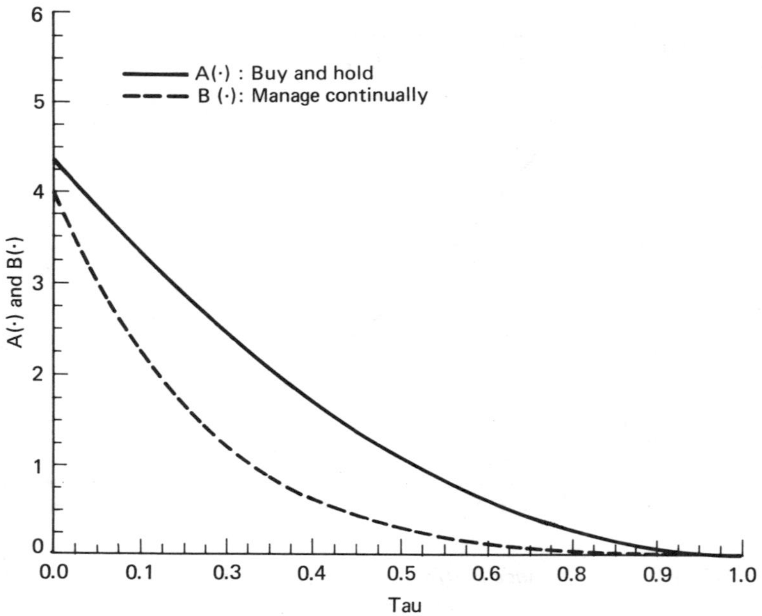

FIGURE 9.2 *Variance portfolio return,* $N = 10$, $\delta^2 = 0.038$
Parameters: $\alpha = 0.1$, $\sigma^2 = 0.039$, $T = 10$

provides a more favourable trade-off of mean for decreases in standard deviation, while at high rates of taxation accrual taxation provides a less favourable trade-off of mean for decreases in standard deviation. For $N = 10$ the right endpoint of the curve for accrual taxation is below the right endpoint for realisation taxation. This reflects the fact that with a zero tax rate both portfolios have the same mean, while the continually managed portfolio is less risky.

2 The Effective Rate of Taxation

In the context of certainty, Bailey (1969) defined the effective rate of capital gains taxation as the rate of accrual taxation, λ, which would ensure equality between the following two things: The after tax profits on an investment subject to capital gains tax on a realisation basis at rate τ and the after tax profits on the same investment taxed on an

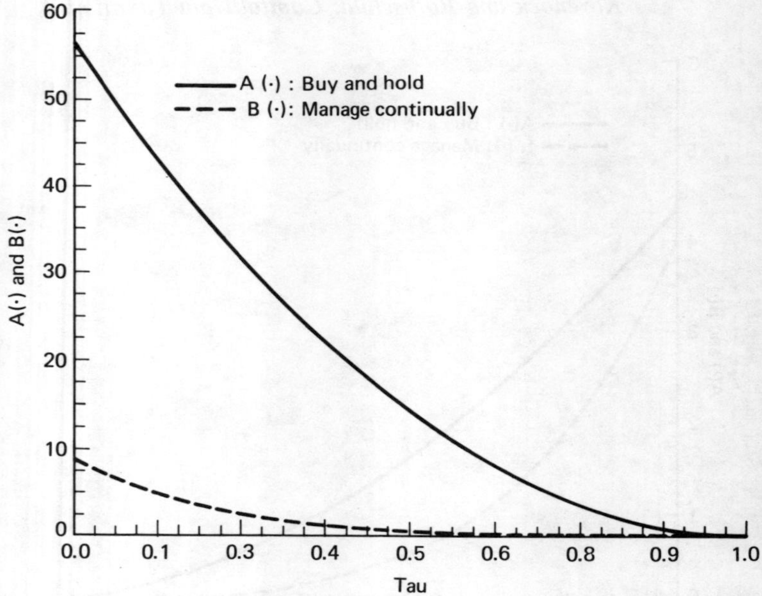

FIGURE 9.3 *Variance portfolio return,* $N=10$, $\delta^2=0.39$
Parameters: $\alpha=0.1$, $\sigma^2=0.039$, $T=10$

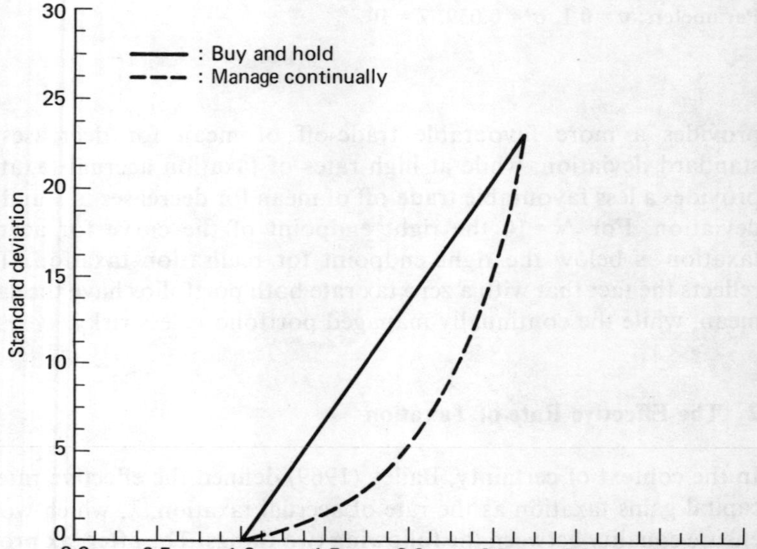

FIGURE 9.4(a) *Standard deviation vs mean,* $N=1$, $\delta^2=0.39$.
Parameters: $\alpha=0.1$, $\sigma^2=0.039$, $T=10$

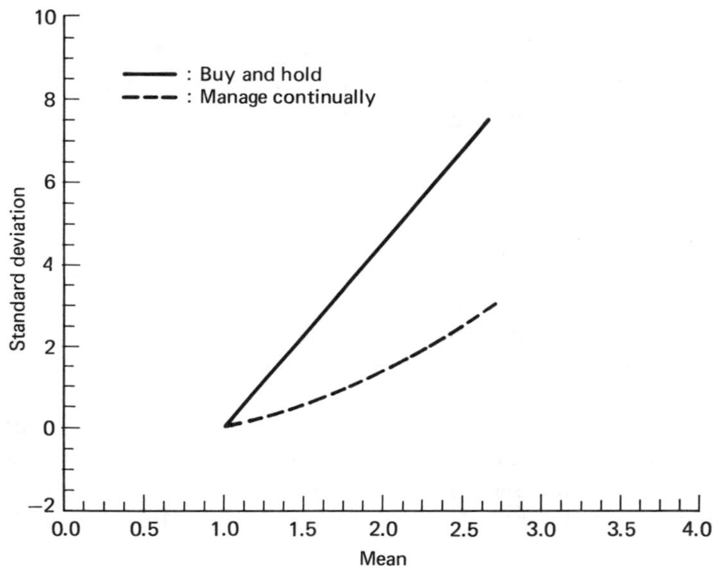

FIGURE 9.4(b) *Standard deviation vs. mean,* $N=10$, $\delta^2=0.39$.
Parameters: $\alpha=0.1$, $\sigma^2=0.039$, $T=10$

accrual basis at rate λ. With this definition, the effective rate of taxation depends on the characteristics of the investment, the rate of capital gains taxation and the length of time the investment is held. If an investment has an instantaneous rate of return of $\alpha(s)$ and it is held T years, its after tax return is

$$C=[\exp\int_0^T\alpha(s)\mathrm{d}s](1-\tau)+\mathrm{T}. \qquad 18)$$

Taxes levied on an accrual basis reduce the rate of return from $\alpha(s)$ to $\alpha(s)(1-\lambda)$. Thus the equivalent accrual rate is the solution to the equation

$$C=\exp\int_0^T\alpha(s)(1-\lambda)\,\mathrm{d}s. \qquad (19)$$

Therefore,

$$\lambda(\tau,T)=1-\frac{\log[(\exp\int_0^T\alpha(s)\mathrm{d}s)(1-\tau)+\tau]}{\int_0^T\alpha(s)\mathrm{d}s} \qquad (20)$$

is the formula for the effective rate of taxation as a function of τ and T. Clearly, $\lambda(0,T)=0$ and a simple application of L'Hospital's rule gives $\lambda(\tau, 0)=\tau$. It is also straightforward to show that $\lambda_\tau>0$. The effective rate of capital gains taxation declines with the holding period. To see that this is so, note that sign $\lambda_T = -\,\text{sign}\, f\,(\int_0^T \alpha(s)\,ds)$ where

$$f(x)=\frac{xe^x(1-\tau)}{e^x(1-\tau)+\tau}-\log\,(e^x(1-\tau)+\tau).$$

Note that $f(0)=0$ and calculate that $f'(x)>0$ to conclude that $\lambda_T<0$. Figure 9.5 graphs the effective rate of taxation as a function of the holding period T under the assumption that $\alpha(s)=\alpha=0.1$ and $\tau=0.2$.

We extend this definition in a straightforward way to uncertainty: the effective rate of taxation is that rate of actual taxation which makes an investor indifferent between holding a buy and hold portfolio which is taxed at rate τ and holding a continually managed portfolio which is taxed at accrual rate λ. A definition in terms of indifference is a definition which depends on preferences. If the

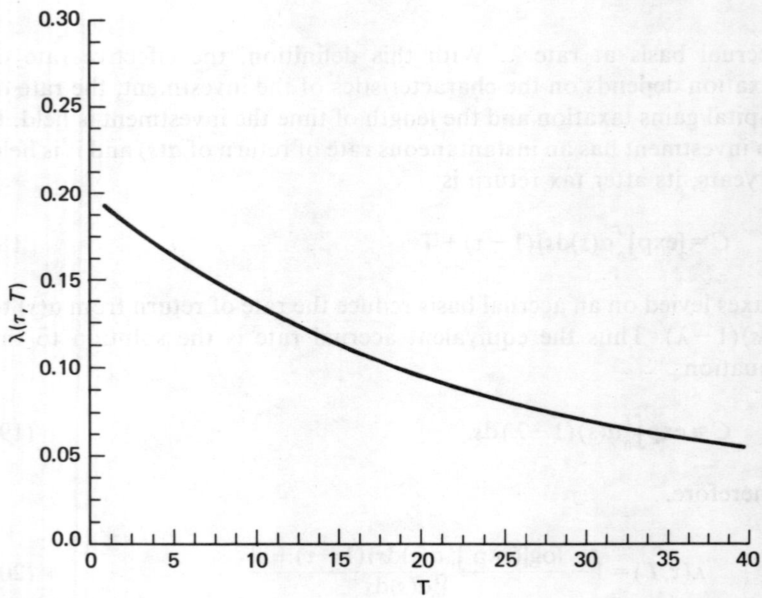

FIGURE 9.5 *Effective rate of taxation.*

investor maximises expected utility and has utility function $U(\cdot)$ then the effective rate of taxation is the solution, $\lambda(\tau, T)$, to

$$E[U(W(T,\tau))] = E[U(Y(T,\lambda))]. \tag{21}$$

Having the effective rate of taxation depend on the utility function is unfortunate but unavoidable. No rate of accrual taxation can make the distributions of the two random variables $W(T, \tau)$ and $Y(T, \lambda)$ equal in any sense. For our calculations we choose a constant relative risk aversion utility function. We do this both because it makes some calculations tractable and because it makes the effective rate of taxation independent of the amount invested.

Let $(1-\gamma)$ be the coefficient of relative risk aversion. Then $U(X) = \gamma^{-1}X^{\gamma}$. Let $A(T, \lambda) = E[U(Y(T, \lambda))] = E\gamma^{-1}Y(T, \lambda)^{\gamma}$. This is, because of (15), the moment generating function of a normal random variable. Thus,

$$A(T,\lambda) = \gamma^{-1} \exp\left[\gamma T\alpha(1-\lambda) - \left(\frac{\delta^2}{2N} + \frac{\sigma^2}{2}\right)(1-\lambda)^2 + \gamma^2(1-\lambda)^2\left(\frac{\delta^2}{2N} + \frac{\sigma^2}{2}\right)T\right]. \tag{22}$$

Similarly let

$$R(T, \tau) = E[U(W(T, \tau))] = \frac{1}{\gamma}E[W(T, \tau)^{\gamma}].$$

Unfortunately, $R(T, \tau)$ does not have such a neat closed form expression. However, the value of $R(T, \tau)$ for given parameters can be approximated using Monte Carlo methods. That is let

$$S(T, \tau; Q) = Q^{-1}\gamma^{-1}\sum_{q=1}^{Q}(N^{-1}\sum_{i=1}^{N}(\exp b_{iq}(T))(1-\tau)+\tau))^{\gamma}$$

where the $b_q(T) = (b_{1q}(T), \ldots, b_{Nq}(T))$ are independent realisations of a random vector with mean $\mu(T)$ and variance matrix $\sum(T)$ as given in equations (2) and (3). Then

$$\lim_{Q\to\infty} S(T, \tau; Q) = R(T, \tau)$$

and we can estimate λ by $\hat{\lambda}(T, \tau; Q)$ the solution of

$$S(T, \tau; Q) = A(T, \hat{\lambda}(T, \tau; Q)). \tag{23}$$

Because $S(T, \tau; Q)$ is a sample mean, the central limit theorem states that it is approximately normal for large values of Q. We estimate the variance of $S(T, \tau; Q)$ by

$$\hat{\sigma}(Q) = \frac{\left[\sum_{q=1}^{Q} [\gamma^{-1}(N^{-1} \sum_{i=1}^{N} \exp(b_{iq}(T))(1-\tau)+\tau)^{\gamma} - S(T, \tau, Q)]^2 \right]}{Q^2} \tag{24}$$

Thus, we can compute an asymptotic 95 per cent confidence interval for λ as $[\underline{\lambda}, \bar{\lambda}]$ where $\underline{\lambda}$ and $\bar{\lambda}$ are the solution of

$$R(T, \tau) + 2\hat{\sigma}(Q) = A(T, \underline{\lambda})$$
$$R(T, \tau) - 2\hat{\sigma}(Q) = A(T, \bar{\lambda})$$

respectively.

3 Parameters

In this subsection we discuss the parameters we used to estimate the effective rate of taxation.

1. α

We set α, the mean rate of return, equal to 0.1. Ibbotson and Sinquefield (1982) report an average rate of return (from 1926 to 1981) of 0.091 for the Standard and Poor's 500 and 0.121 for stocks of small companies – the smallest (in value) fifth of the companies listed on the New York Stock Exchange.

2. σ^2

The annual variance of a portfolio which is completely diversified ($N=\infty$) is

$$V_{\infty} = e^{2\alpha}[e^{\sigma 2} - 1].$$

Arguably this is the annual variance of the market portfolio. Ibbotson and Sinquefield report $V_{\infty} = 0.048$ from 1926 to 1981. (This is actually the variance of the value weighted Standard and Poor's 500 and as such it may understate the variance of returns on a more widely diversified portfolio. Ibbotson and Sinquefield report a much higher variance (0.14) for the returns of the equities of the smallest one-fifth of the companies held on the New York Stock Exchange in the same period.) A value of $V_\infty = 0.048$ implies $\sigma^2 = 0.039$.

3. δ^2

The parameter δ^2 measures the gains from diversification. It is easiest to express this as follows. If a portfolio of 10 stocks is held for a year (and not managed), the variance of returns is,

$$V_{10} = e^{2\alpha}(0.1\ e^{\sigma^2+\delta^2} + 0.9e^{\sigma^2} - 1).$$

Let $h = (V_{10}/V_\infty)^{\frac{1}{2}} - 1$, h is a measure of the efficacy of diversification or of the rate at which the benefits of diversification are achieved as more assets are added to a portfolio; $h \times 100$ is the percentage by which the standard deviation of a 10 stock portfolio exceeds the standard deviation of the optimally diversified portfolio. If $h = 0.1$ then a 10 stock portfolio is only 10 per cent more variable than the optimally diversified portfolio. Clearly h determines δ^2. It is easy to calculate that

$$\delta^2 = \log[10[e^{-\sigma^2} - 0.9 + (h+1)^2(1 - e^{-\sigma^2})]].$$

We are unsure what value of h best describes the opportunities available to investors; setting $h = 0.05$ ($\delta^2 = 0.038$) and $0.5(\delta^2 = 0.39)$ seems to encompass the range of alternatives.[3]

4. γ

$1 - \gamma$ is the coefficient of relative risk aversion. The theoretical literature identifies $\gamma = 0$ as a pivotal case; the empirical literature produces estimates of γ ranging from 0.95 to -1000. See Choi and Menzes (1984) for a compendium of such estimates. With this guidance we felt free to choose γ to suit our purposes. Low values of γ correspond to high values of relative risk aversion. It would seem that high degrees of risk aversion would make the reduction of risk which can be achieved through active portfolio management more valuable. This should raise the effective rate of taxation as we have defined it.

However, high values of relative risk aversion have other consequences for the calculation of the effective rate of taxation. Our procedure assumes full loss offsets; the government shares in both gains and losses of investment. As Figures 9.1 to 9.4 make clear increasing taxes decreases both the mean and the variance of returns. If an investor is sufficiently risk averse then his expected utility can be an increasing function of the rate of taxation. To see this note that the sign of the effect of an increase in taxation on a continuously rebalanced portfolio is determined by

$$\text{sign } A_\lambda = \text{sign}\left[\left(\sigma^2 + \frac{\delta^2}{N}\right)(1-\lambda)(1-\gamma) - \alpha\right] \tag{25}$$

thus for high values of relative risk aversion expected utility increases as taxes increase.

Figures 9.1 to 9.4 suggest that the sign of R_τ (which cannot be calculated directly) is also likely to be positive if γ is small. While the possibility that increasing rates of taxation can increase utility raises many tantalising issues, it does confuse the meaning of the phrase 'effective rate of taxation'. Thus we have used relatively high values of γ (low values of relative risk aversion) in our calculations: In particular we have chosen $\gamma = 0.8$ and $\gamma = -0.5$; in the sequel the first case is described as a low degree of risk aversion, the second as a high degree of risk aversion.

5. *T*

We have chosen values of T ranging from 1 to 30. Protopapadakis (1983) estimates that assets on which capital gains taxes are assessed are held on the average between 24 and 31 years.

6. *N*

As explained above N and δ^2 together calibrate the gains from diversification and portfolio rebalance. The larger N is, the smaller is the variance of returns; however, for small N, as N increases so do the benefits of portfolio management. In the calculations we have chosen N sufficiently large that $A_\lambda < 0$. It is easy to calculate using (25) that this implies $N \geqslant 1$ for $\gamma = 0.8$ and $h = 0.05$. If both diversifiable risk and risk aversion are high ($\gamma = -0.5$ and $h = 0.5$), then we must have $N \geqslant 15$.

7. Q

Q determines the accuracy of $\hat{\lambda}$ as an estimate of the effective rate of taxation. However, the accuracy of the estimate is measured by the size of the interval $[\underline{\lambda}, \bar{\lambda}]$ which is reported along with $\hat{\lambda}$. For most of our estimates we set $Q = 5000$.

4 Results

The results of our attempts to estimate the effective rate of taxation are reported in Tables 9.1 to 9.8. From these we draw the following conclusions:

1. The effective rate depends on the parameters; it is increasing in diversifiable risk, risk aversion, and, by and large, the statutory rate. For low values of these variables the effective rate is negligible. The entries in Table 9.1 are not significantly different from zero.[4] The effective rates reported in Table 9.2 do not differ significantly from effective rates under certainty. For high values of these variables, the effective rate can be very high. The rates reported in Tables 9.7 and 9.8 are much higher than the statutory rate. Such very high rates indicate that a buy and hold policy is not optimal; if transaction costs other than capital gains taxes are low, then the investor always has the option of trading often. His effective rate cannot exceed the statutory rate. Still the very high rates of Tables 9.7 and 9.8 illustrate dramatically that buy and hold policies have costs when investment results are uncertain.

2. If the statutory tax rate is zero and the level of diversifiable risk is high, the effective tax rate is greater than zero for most asset portfolios held ten years or longer. This is shown in Table 9.5. The effective rate is especially high for portfolios with five assets. As Figure 9.4 demonstrates, realisation taxation offers a different, and on the whole, less favourable trade-off between risk and return than does accrual taxation. For a one asset portfolio subject to a zero statutory tax rate there is no difference between buying and holding and continually rebalancing. As the number of assets in an untaxed portfolio gets large the portfolio variance under a buy and hold policy approaches that of a policy of continuous management. This indicates that the effective rate of taxation will be greatest for portfolios only partially diversified. This is reflected in the high effective tax rates for

Table 9.1 Estimates of the effective rate of taxation. Diversifiable risk – Low; Risk aversion – Low; Statutory tax rate – 0

N/T	*1*	*3*	*5*	*10*	*15*	*20*	*25*	*30*
5	0.059	0.013	−0.018	−0.001	0.006	0.004	−0.006	0.001
	(+0.068)	(+0.040)	(+0.032)	(+0.024)	(+0.020)	(+0.019)	(+0.022)	(+0.017)
	(−0.068)	(−0.040)	(−0.031)	(−0.024)	(−0.019)	(−0.018)	(−0.021)	(−0.016)
10	0.022	−0.006	0.003	0.005	0.009	0.003	−0.003	−0.007
	(+0.066)	(+0.038)	(+0.030)	(+0.022)	(+0.019)	(+0.018)	(+0.017)	(+0.016)
	(−0.066)	(−0.038)	(−0.030)	(−0.022)	(−0.019)	(−0.018)	(0.017)	(−0.015)
15	0.036	0.020	−0.006	−0.003	−0.003	0.004	−0.008	0.005
	(+0.063)	(+0.037)	(+0.029)	(+0.022)	(+0.018)	(+0.017)	(+0.015)	(+0.014)
	(−0.063)	(−0.037)	(−0.029)	(−0.022)	(−0.018)	(−0.016)	(−0.015)	(−0.013)
20	−0.002	0.030	0.009	0.002	0.021	−0.016	0.000	−0.015
	(+0.063)	(+0.037)	(+0.029)	(+0.021)	(+0.017)	(+0.017)	(+0.015)	(+0.015)
	(−0.063)	(−0.037)	(−0.028)	(−0.021)	(−0.017)	(−0.017)	(−0.015)	(−0.015)

Confidence intervals are at the 95 per cent level.

Table 9.2 Diversifiable risk – Low; Risk aversion – Low; Statutory tax rate – 20 per cent

N/T	*1*	*3*	*5*	*10*	*15*	*20*	*25*	*30*
5	0.161 (+0.055) (−0.055)	0.175 (+0.033) (−0.033)	0.143 (+0.027) (−0.027)	0.134 (+0.022) (−0.022)	0.124 (+0.018) (−0.018)	0.110 (+0.017) (−0.017)	0.090 (+0.018) (−0.017)	0.095 (+0.016) −0.015)
10	0.201 (+0.051) (−0.051)	0.186 (+0.031) (−0.031)	0.150 (+0.025) (−0.025)	0.135 (+0.021) (−0.021)	0.124 (+0.017) (−0.017)	0.107 (+0.016) (−0.016)	0.084 (+0.016) (−0.015)	0.075 (+0.016) (−0.016)
15	0.196 (+0.051) (−0.051)	0.153 (+0.032) (−0.032)	0.181 (+0.025) (−0.025)	0.169 (+0.019) (−0.019)	0.113 (+0.017) (−0.017)	0.104 (+0.016) (−0.015)	0.086 (+0.015) (−0.014)	0.078 (+0.015) (−0.015)
20	0.221 (+0.050) (−0.050)	0.218 (+0.030) (−0.030)	0.164 (+0.024) (−0.024)	0.158 (+0.019) (−0.019)	0.131 (+0.016) (−0.016)	0.103 (+0.015) (−0.015)	0.098 (+0.014) (−0.014)	0.076 (+0.014) (−0.014)

Effective rate under certainty

	0.192	0.177	0.164	0.135	0.113	0.095	0.081	0.070

Table 9.3 Diversifiable risk – Low; Risk aversion – high; Statutory tax rate – 0

N/T	*3*	*5*	*10*	*15*	*20*	*25*	*30*
5	0.039	0.044	0.039	0.009	0.075	0.068	0.076
	(+0.099)	(+0.076)	(+0.058)	(+0.051)	(+0.040)	(+0.038)	(+0.033)
	(−0.127)	(−0.092)	(−0.067)	(−0.059)	(−0.044)	(−0.042)	(−0.036)
10	0.039	0.043	0.035	0.012	0.000	0.029	0.045
	(+0.084)	(+0.066)	(+0.049)	(+0.041)	(+0.037)	(+0.033)	(+0.029)
	(−0.099)	(−0.074)	(−0.054)	(−0.045)	(−0.040)	(−0.035)	(−0.031)
15	−0.103	0.018	0.014	0.022	0.007	0.033	0.023
	(+0.097)	(+0.064)	(+0.047)	(+0.039)	(+0.036)	(+0.031)	(+0.029)
	(−0.122)	(−0.072)	(−0.052)	(−0.042)	(−0.038)	(−0.033)	(−0.031)
20	−0.004	−0.013	−0.016	−0.006	−0.024	−0.009	0.011
	(+0.081)	(+0.065)	(+0.047)	(+0.038)	(+0.035)	(+0.031)	(+0.028)
	(−0.093)	(−0.073)	(−0.052)	(−0.041)	(−0.037)	(−0.033)	(−0.029)

large T and $N=5$ in Table 9.5. It is also evident in Table 9.3 where diversifiable risk is low but risk aversion is high. Although most entries in Table 9.3 are close to zero, for $T \geqslant 20$ and $N=5$ the effective tax rate is significantly higher.

If the statutory tax rate is 20 per cent and either the level of diversifiable risk or the level of risk aversion is high, the effective rate of taxation is higher than in the certainty case for most asset portfolios held ten years or longer. In these cases the effective rate does not decline rapidly with the holding period as it does under certainty. This is demonstrated in Tables 9.4, 9.6 and 9.8. In Table 9.4, the effective rate does not change much as the holding period changes. In Table 9.6, the same appears to be true, except perhaps for $N=5$, where the effective tax rate may increase. In Table 9.8 the effective rate increases as the holding period lengthens.

3. In some cases the effective rate of taxation can decrease as the statutory rate increases. Compare the entries for $T \geqslant 5$ in the high diversifiable risk – high risk aversion cases of Tables 9.7 and 9.8. This is again a reflection of the fact that increasing taxes may increase utility by reducing risk. The effective rate of taxation, $\lambda(\tau)$, is defined as the solution to the equation

$$R(T, \tau) - A(T, \lambda) = 0.$$

Table 9.4 Diversifiable risk – Low; Risk aversion – High; Statutory tax rate – 20 per cent

N/T	*1*	*3*	*5*	*10*	*15*	*20*	*25*	*30*
5	0.163 (+0.109) (−0.135)	0.222 (+0.061) (−0.068)	0.165 (+0.052) (−0.057)	0.199 (+0.037) (−0.039)	0.194 (+0.032) (−0.034)	0.164 (+0.030) (−0.032)	0.172 (+0.027) (−0.029)	0.168 (+0.026) (−0.028)
10	0.177 (+0.093) (−0.107)	0.179 (+0.056) (−0.060)	0.153 (+0.047) (−0.051	0.201 (+0.032) (−0.034)	0.187 (+0.028) (−0.030)	0.132 (+0.027) (−0.029)	0.172 (+0.023) (−0.024)	0.150 (+0.023) (−0.024)
15	0.177 (+0.091) (−0.103)	0.185 (+0.054) (−0.058)	0.180 (+0.044) (−0.047)	0.158 (+0.033) (−0.034)	0.146 (+0.028) (−0.029)	0.148 (+0.026) (−0.027)	0.136 (+0.023) (−0.025)	0.152 (+0.022) (−0.023)
20	0.258 (+0.081) (−0.090)	0.183 (+0.054) (−0.058)	0.163 (+0.043) (−0.045)	0.161 (+0.032) (−0.034)	0.156 (+0.028) (−0.029)	0.145 (+0.025) (−0.026)	0.142 (+0.023) (−0.024)	0.165 (+0.020) (−0.021)

Effective rate under certainty

	0.192	0.177	0.164	0.135	0.113	0.095	0.081	0.070

Table 9.5 Diversifiable risk – High; Risk aversion – Low; Statutory tax rate – 0

N/T	*1*	*3*	*5*	*10*	*15*	*20*	*25*	*30*
5	−0.041	0.150	−0.028	0.149	0.080	0.182	0.314	0.250
	(+0.137)	(+0.087)	(+0.085)	(+0.067)	(+0.124)	(+0.103)	(+0.091)	(+0.215)
	(−0.141)	(−0.088)	(−0.085)	(−0.065)	(−0.115)	(−0.094)	(−0.081)	(−0.157)
10	−0.019	0.049	0.056	0.008	0.159	0.147	0.128	0.188
	(+0.101)	(+0.068)	(+0.057)	(+0.063)	(+0.059)	(+0.081)	(+0.164)	(+0.145)
	(−0.103)	(−0.068)	(−0.056)	(−0.061)	(−0.056)	(−0.074)	(−0.131)	(−0.113)
15	0.020	−0.012	0.038	0.100	0.138	0.198	0.241	0.183
	(+0.086)	(+0.058)	(+0.051)	(+0.049)	(+0.050)	(+0.059)	(+0.067)	(+0.088)
	(−0.087)	(−0.058)	(−0.050)	(−0.048)	(−0.048)	(−0.055)	(−0.060)	(−0.075)
20	−0.022	0.016	0.036	0.073	0.112	0.108	0.185	0.202
	(+0.080)	(+0.052)	(+0.045)	(+0.043)	(+0.053)	(+0.079)	(+0.082)	(+0.091)
	(−0.081)	(−0.052)	(−0.044)	(−0.042)	(−0.051)	(−0.072)	(−0.072)	(−0.076)

Table 9.6 Diversifiable risk – High; Risk aversion – Low; Statutory tax rate – 20 per cent

N/T	*1*	*3*	*5*	*10*	*15*	*20*	*25*	*30*
5	0.155	0.143	0.262	0.202	0.236	−0.040	0.265	0.319
	(+0.104)	(+0.077)	(+0.061)	(+0.071)	(+0.082)	(+0.799)	(+0.106)	(+0.085)
	(−0.107)	(−0.077)	(−0.060)	(−0.069)	(−0.078)	(−0.452)	(−0.093)	(−0.074)
10	0.236	0.236	0.208	0.296	0.288	0.310	0.246	0.283
	(+0.077)	(+0.052)	(+0.049)	(+0.045)	(+0.059)	(+0.050)	(+0.136)	(+0.072)
	(−0.078)	(−0.052)	(−0.049)	(−0.044)	(−0.056)	(−0.047)	(−0.112)	(−0.063)
15	0.187	0.186	0.207	0.193	0.191	0.254	0.211	0.107
	(+0.070)	(+0.046)	(+0.043)	(+0.047)	(+0.096)	(+0.059)	(+0.145)	(+0.607)
	(−0.070)	(−0.046)	(−0.043)	(−0.046)	(−0.088)	(−0.055)	(−0.117)	(−0.266)
20	0.150	0.181	0.164	0.188	0.190	0.252	0.181	0.185
	(+0.066)	(+0.042)	(+0.038)	(+0.040)	(+0.050)	(+0.051)	(+0.101)	(+0.372)
	(−0.066)	(−0.042)	(−0.038)	(−0.039)	(−0.048)	(−0.048)	(−0.087)	(−0.208)

Effective rate under certainty

	0.192	0.177	0.164	0.135	0.113	0.095	0.081	0.070

Table 9.7 Diversifiable Risk – High; Risk aversion – High; Statutory tax rate – 0

N/T	*3*	*5*	*10*	*15*	*20*	*25*	*30*
15	0.436	0.571	0.814	0.971	1.062	1.123	1.189
	(+0.093)	(+0.061)	(+0.034)	(+0.026)	(+0.021)	(+0.018)	(+0.017)
	(−0.119)	(−0.069)	(−0.036)	(−0.027)	(−0.022)	(−0.019)	(−0.018)
20	0.333	0.479	0.731	0.875	0.972	1.026	1.104
	(+0.096)	(+0.064)	(+0.036)	(+0.027)	(+0.021)	(+0.019)	(+0.017)
	(−0.123)	(−0.072)	(−0.038)	(−0.028)	(−0.022)	(−0.020)	(−0.018)

Table 9.8 Diversifiable Risk – High; Risk aversion – High; Statutory tax rate – 20 per cent

N/t	*3*	*5*	*10*	*15*	*20*	*25*	*30*
15	0.453	0.521	0.745	0.817	0.913	0.969	1.000
	(+0.075)	(+0.053)	(+0.029)	(+0.021)	(+0.016)	(+0.013)	(+0.011)
	(−0.089)	(−0.059)	(−0.030)	(−0.022)	(−0.017)	(−0.013)	(−0.011)
20	0.367	0.407	0.662	0.773	0.848	0.897	0.954
	(+0.074)	(+0.056)	(+0.029)	(+0.021)	(+0.017)	(+0.014)	(+0.011)
	(−0.087)	(−0.063)	(−0.030)	(−0.022)	(−0.017)	(−0.014)	(−0.012)
Effective rate under certainty							
	0.177	0.164	0.135	0.113	0.095	0.081	0.070

Thus,

$$\frac{d\lambda}{d\tau}=\frac{R_\tau}{A_\lambda}.$$

We choose parameters so that $A_\lambda<0$. Thus,

$$\text{sign}\ \frac{d\lambda}{d\tau}=-\text{sign}\ R_\tau.$$

Thus a finding that the effective rate of taxation decreases as the statutory tax rate increases indicates that $R_\tau>0>A_\lambda$.

5 Conclusions and Caveats

The calculations reported above suggest that the effective rate of capital gains taxation under uncertainty is higher than conventional estimates which take no account of uncertainty would suggest. Three strong arguments weaken the force of the case we have made. First as Stiglitz (1983) and Constantinides (1983) have argued, only fools pay capital gains taxes.[5] If tax liabilities only are considered, the optimal portfolio policy is obviously to sell losers and keep winners. Stiglitz shows that for every transaction which violates this rule there is another transaction with the same real and financial consequences which adheres to the rule. The equivalent tax free transaction involves options, short sales, or other relatively complex transactions which we feel many investors are unwilling to engage in. We do not question the logic of the Constantinides–Stiglitz position that capital gains taxes can be avoided. We believe that many people pay capital gains taxes even if they could avoid them. The reported responsiveness of sales of appreciated assets to tax rates is evidence for this position. For people who could but do not avoid taxes the effective rate of taxation is the effective rate on the taxes they pay, not on those they could avoid. We believe that for many people the effective tax rate on capital gains is positive.

A second, and related, argument is that the buy and hold policy which we have compared with a policy of continual management in order to compute the effective rate is obviously not the optimal portfolio policy even if options and short sales are ruled out. If there are no transactions costs other than capital gains taxes, then the investor has the option of continually managing his portfolio and paying an effective rate of taxation of 20 per cent. Every entry in Tables 9.1 to 9.8 with a higher effective rate than 20 per cent reflects the return on a policy which is dominated by such a policy. However, while the buy and hold policy is not the optimal policy we have not the faintest idea what the optimal portfolio policy in the presence of capital gains taxes (and possibly other transaction costs) is. The study of optimal portfolio policy with transactions costs is in its infancy. Almost the only problem which has been studied is the simple one of dividing one's portfolio between a risky and a riskless asset in the presence of linear transaction costs. For this standard problem Constantinides (1984b) has done calculations which show that losses from transactions costs may be very small. It is not clear that the relatively few results on this problem will carry over to the different problem we have considered. One problem that we have investigated is the problem of dividing one's portfolio between a riskless asset and a mutual fund consisting of $1/N$ shares of each of N assets with returns generated by (13). We assume that the riskless asset is subject to the same accrual tax rate as the mutual fund. If P_0 is the price of the riskless asset

$$dP_0 = r(1-\lambda)P_0 dt.$$

While continuous rebalancing between the riskless asset and the mutual fund is allowed rebalancing of asset weights within the mutual fund is not allowed. Using Ibbotson and Sinquefield's (1982) estimate of the average return on short term US Treasury bills as the riskless rate of return ($r = 0.03$) we can estimate the optimal portfolio shares. With $\alpha = 0.1$, $\sigma^2 = 0.039$, $N = 10$, and $\lambda = 0.2$ three out of the four possible combinations of values for δ^2 and γ provided in Part 3 yield portfolio shares for the mutual fund which are greater than one. The exception is the case of high diversifiable risk and high risk aversion. In this case 0.75 of wealth is held in the mutual fund. If we extend our analysis and assume that rebalancing between the mutual fund and the riskless asset can only take place periodically, the results of Goldman (1979) can be used to show that, as the period between rebalancing opportunities increases, all of the portfolios examined plunge into the mutual fund of risky assets. These results seem to indicate that the problem addressed here and that analysed by Constantinides are sufficiently different that there is no reason to suppose that his unimportance result should carry over. For a sampling of recent work on the transactions costs problem see Constantinides (1979, 1984b); Kandel and Ross (1983); Taksar *et al.* (1983).

Third, we have discussed portfolio choice in a partial equilibrium context. General equilibrium considerations might make it either unnecessary or impossible for people to continually rebalance their portfolios. Suppose for example that the Capital Asset Pricing Model (CAPM) held. Then all investors would hold the same, market, portfolio. No one would ever want to revise his portfolio. An investor who followed a buy and hold policy would hold an optimally diversified portfolio. Our only response to this is that we do not believe that anything like the CAPM describes the asset markets of the United States. Investors have diverse holdings; many do not hold the market portfolio. For these investors the need to rebalance their holdings through active management is probably real. Furthermore, our findings that the effective rate was high depended on the fact that buy and hold portfolios taxed on a realisation basis are riskier than portfolios taxed on an accrual basis as well as on the advantages of portfolio management.

Thus, despite these arguments, we believe our results are at least weak evidence for the proposition that the effective rate of capital gains taxation is higher than the 3 to 7 per cent which, for example, Protopapadakis (1983) reports.

ACKNOWLEDGEMENTS

We are indebted to Mark Machina, Ross Starr and Halbert White for helpful discussions, to Ray Chou and Rodrigo Peruga for computational assistance, and to the National Science Foundation for research support. The research reported here is part of the NBER's research program in Taxation and project in Government Budget. Any opinions expressed are those of the authors and not those of the National Bureau of Economic Research.

Notes

1. Students of reswitching will note that this is an artificial distinction; it is none the less a useful one and we will adopt it.
2. The proof of this is tedious and is omitted. It involves inverting equation (16) to obtain λ as a function of the mean, inserting this function in place of λ in the square root of the right-hand side of equation (17), and twice differentiating with respect to the mean. The resulting expression gives the second derivative of the standard deviation of a portfolio with respect to the mean, and can be shown to be positive for the relevant range of values of the mean.
3. Evans and Archer (1968) examine how the variability of a portfolio of randomly selected stocks declines as the number of (equally weighted) assets held in the portfolio increases. They conclude that their results 'raise doubts concerning the economic justification of increasing portfolio sizes beyond 10 or so securities'. Since Evans and Archer's estimate of undiversifiable risk differs from ours, it is difficult to compare their measure of relative variability with the one employed here.
4. One of the entries in Table 9.1 is significantly different from zero at the 0.95 level. Our discussion here focuses on the economic significance and not the statistical significance of our results.
5. This conclusion rests on the assumption, made throughout this paper,

that short and long term capital gains are taxed at the same rate. For an analysis of optimal trading policies with differential taxation of short and long term gains and losses see Stiglitz (1983) and Constantinides (1984a).

REFERENCES

Arnold, L. (1974) *Stochastic Differential Equations* (Wiley).

Bailey, M. J. (1969) 'Capital Gains and Income Taxation', in Arnold C. Harberger and Martin J. Bailey (eds), *The Taxation of Income from Capital* (Brookings).

Choi, E. K. and C. F. Menzes (1984) 'On the Magnitude of Relative Risk Aversion', mimeo.

Constantinides, G. M. (1979) 'Multiperiod Consumption and Investment Behaviour with Convex Transactions Costs', *Management Science*, 25, 1127–37.

Constantinides, G. M. (1983) 'Capital Market Equilibrium with Personal Tax', *Econometrica*, 51, 611–36.

Constantinides, G. M. (1984a) 'Optimal Stock Trading with Personal Taxes: Implications for Prices and the Abnormal January Returns', *Journal of Financial Economics*, 13, 65–89.

Constantinides, G. M. (1984b) 'Capital Market Equilibrium with Transactions Costs', mimeo.

Evans, John L. and S. H. Archer (1968) 'Diversification and the Reduction of Dispersion: An Empirical Analysis', *Journal of Finance*, 5: 761–767.

Feldstein, M. and J. Slemrod (1978) 'The Lock-in Effect of the Capital Gains Tax: Some Time Series Evidence', *Tax Notes*, 134–5.

Feldstein, M. and S. Yitzhaki (1978) 'The Effects of the Capital Gains Tax on the Selling and Switching of Common Stock', *Journal of Public Economics*, 9, 17–36.

Feldstein, M., J. Slemrod and S. Yitzhaki (1980) 'The Effects of Taxation on the Selling of Corporate Stock and the Realization of Capital Gains', *Quarterly Journal of Economics*, 94, 777–91.

Goldman, M. B. (1979) 'Anti-Diversification or Optimal Programmes for Infrequently Revised Portfolios', *Journal of Finance*, 34, 505–516.

Ibbotson, R. G. and R. A. Sinquefield (1982) *Stocks, Bonds, Bills and Inflation: The Past and the Future* (Financial Analysts Research Foundation, Monograph No. 15, Charlottesville, VA).

Johnson, L. and S. Kotz (1972) *Distributions in Statistics: Continuous Multivariate Distributions* (Wiley: New York).

Kandel, S. and S. A. Ross (1983) 'Some Intertemporal Models of Portfolio Selection with Transactions Costs', mimeo.

Kovenock, D. J. and M. Rothschild (1983) 'Capital Gains Taxation in an Economy with an "Austrian Sector",' *Journal of Public Economics*, 21, 215–56.

Merton, R. C. (1971) 'Optimum Consumption and Portfolio Rules in a Continuous-Time Model', *Journal of Economic Theory*, 3, 373–413.

Protopapadakis, A. (1983) 'Some Indirect Evidence on Effective Capital Gains Tax Rates', *Journal of Business*, 56, 127–38.
Stiglitz, J. E. (1983) 'Some Aspects of the Taxation of Capital Gains', *Journal of Public Economics*, 21, 257–94.
Taksar, M., J. Klass and D. Assaf (1983) 'A Diffusion Model for Optimal Portfolio Selection in the Presence of Brokerage Fees', Technical Report Number 4 (Department of Operations Research, Stanford University).

Comments on the Effects of Capital Gain taxation on Non-Austrian Assets by Dagobert L. Brito and Eytan Sheshinski

'Notes on the Effect of Capital Gains taxation on Non-Austrian Assets', by Professors Kovenock and Rothschild is an interesting and ambitious paper that addresses the question of the optimality of a capital gains tax on Non Austrian assets. Kovenock and Rothschild argue that the conventional estimates of the effective rate of capital gains taxation due to Bailey are too low because they ignore uncertainty. They point out that the capital gains tax has lock in effects that can distort investment decisions and result in suboptimal portfolios. This reduces the rate of return from investing and is thus a form of an implicit tax.

The problem of determining how important this distortion is not analytically tractable, so they use Monte Carlo methods to compute the effective tax rates on portfolios for various number of assets. The effective tax rates computed by Kovenock and Rothschild, however, can not be compared directly to the tax rates computed by Bailey, since they are defined in terms of expected utility rather than expected return.

They find the effective rate is increasing in deversifiable risk, risk aversion and in most cases, the statutory rate. These calculations suggest that the effective rate of taxation under uncertainty is higher than conventional estimates that ignore the cost of not being able to optimise portfolios.

Kovenock and Rothschild report some calculations which are surprising. They find that in some cases the effective rate of taxation can decrease as the statutory rate increases. It appears that avoiding taxes increases the effective rate of taxation. One is better off paying taxes!

A few simple calculations are sufficient to see why this is a remarkable result. Adopting a notation similar to the one used in the paper, we can define:

$W(T)$ as pre-tax wealth at time T if the agent adopts a buy-and-hold policy

$R(\tau, T)$ as expected utility at time T of a portfolio that pays a capital gains tax τ at time T.

$A(\psi, T)$ as the expected utility of holding an optimised portfolio to time T when the accrual tax rate is ψ.

$\lambda(\tau, T)$ as the effective tax rate. It is the solution to the equation

$$A(\lambda, T) = R(\tau\ T) \quad (1)$$

Denote partial derivatives by subscripts, then

$$\lambda_1(\tau, t) = \frac{R_1(\lambda, T)}{A_1(\lambda, T)} \quad (2)$$

For the Kovenock and Rothschild computations to be correct we believe that it is necessary that $\lambda_1(\tau, t)$ be negative. This requires that $R_1(\tau T)$ and $A_1(\lambda, T)$ have different signs. Intuition would suggest that the signs of both of these partial derivatives are negative; we would expect that an increase in either the capital gains tax or the accrual tax would reduce expected utility for an individual. Kovenock and Rothschild state that the parameters they used in the computation were chosen such that $A_1(\lambda, T) < 0$. Thus the numerical calculations require that $R(\tau, T) > 0$ if their result is correct.

Assume that initial wealth is 1. If individuals pay capital gains taxes at the terminal time period their after tax wealth is $W(T)(l-\tau)+\tau$. Thus

$$\begin{aligned} R(\tau T) &= E[W(T)(1-\tau)+\tau]^{\varphi}/_{\varphi} \quad (3) \\ &= [(1-\tau)E[W(T)]+\tau]^{\varphi}/_{\varphi} \end{aligned}$$

Calculating $R_1(\tau, T)$ it appears that

$$R_1(\tau, T) = [(1-\tau)E[W(T)]+\tau]^{\varphi-1}[1-E[W(T)]] < 0 \quad (4)$$

if $E\ [W(T)] > 1$. Thus, if the numbers calculated by Kovenock and Rothschild are correct, there appears to be an interesting puzzle for theorists.

Finally, Kovenock and Rothschild argue in the paper that the lock in effect may cause the price of the shares of a company with retained earnings to be artificially high. This is correct if these shares were unique and necessary to hedge against some state of nature. In that case the capital gains tax would reduce the supply of the shares and agents might be willing to pay a premium in order to diversify their portfolio. However, Kovenock and Rothschild argue that the reason that the price of these shares is artificially high is that they reflect past as well as future earnings. Surely, this can not be correct. Any firm that has retained earnings has invested these earnings in income producing assets. The price of the shares reflects the expected income stream from these assets.

In their paper, Kovenock and Rothschild address some interesting and difficult questions. Their calculations illustrate the magnitude of the distortions caused by a capital gains tax. Although not flawless, this paper is valuable because it is an ambitious attempt to solve difficult questions.

10 Right of Way and Congestion Toll

Eitan Berglas, David Fresko and David Pines

I INTRODUCTION

This paper is concerned with the economics of reserved right of way, i.e. assigning separate facilities (roads or lanes within roads) to automobiles and buses in congested urban areas. The discussion of this issue appears frequently in conjunction with second-best considerations. The reserved right of way is judged as a device for changing the relative attractiveness of mass transportation *vis-à-vis* the automobile, when the warranted congestion toll is not levied (see Vickrey, 1963). We show in this paper that assigning different facilities (roads or lanes) may be optimal both when a congestion toll is charged from automobile drivers (hereafter 'first-best') and when no such toll is charged (hereafter 'second-best').

The separation result has appeared in the literature before as a variant of the theory of clubs (see Mohring (1965) and Berglas and Pines (1981)). However, in those cases it stemmed from an assumption that people have different tastes, or different cost functions. In this paper it is derived exclusively from differences in the characteristics of the modes. We distinguish two main differences between modes which are reflected in the congestion functions commonly used in the literature. First, modes differ in the contribution of a passenger trip to congestion. Second, the effect of congestion on cost, defined as aversion towards congestion, differs according to the mode. The paper elaborates on the role of these two kinds of differences between modes in justifying facility separation. A comparison is made between the characteristics of the allocations under common and separate use of transportation facilities and between first and second-best for each allocation regime.

Finally we reexamine the question of a second-best optimal pricing of buses (i.e. when the automobile driver does not pay the warranted congestion toll). Our analysis implies that, under facility separation regime, it is less likely (relative to the common use of facilities, which is extensively analysed in the literature) that the buses should be subsidised.

Section II presents the model and the concept of aversion to and creation of congestion. Section III is devoted to first-best and Section IV to second-best allocations. Some possible extensions are included in the concluding remarks of Section V.

II THE MODEL

Let the utility of a representative individual depend on a composite good, X, and number of trips made in two different modes, A (say automobiles) and B (say buses), i.e. $u(X, A, B)$. With the price of the composite good as a numeraire, and the prices of trips according to the mode, P_A, P_B, the compensated demands are:

$$X = x(P_A, P_B, u), \tag{1}$$

$$A = a(P_A, P_B, u), \text{ and} \tag{2}$$

$$B = b(P_A, P_B, u). \tag{3}$$

Each of the n individuals is endowed with I units of the composite commodity of which he consumes directly X units. The total quantity of resources used in transportation depends on the volume of traffic and its composition according to modes, on the resources used in producing the facilities which accommodate the traffic, and on the allocation of these facilities between the two modes. More specifically, we distinguished between two alternative transportation regimes:

I Common Use of the Facility

In this case the resource constraint is represented by:

$$nX + nAF^A(nA, nB, W)) + nBF^B(nA, nB, W) + \varphi(W) = nI, \tag{4-I}$$

where W is the size of the common facility (say road width), $F^i(\ )$ is the average cost (in terms of the composite good) of a trip using mode

i which depends on volume of traffic of the two modes and the size of the facility, and ($\varphi(W)$ is the cost (in terms of the composite good) of producing W.

II Separate Facilities

In this regime the resource constraint is represented by:

$$nX + nAF^{A}(nA, 0, W_{A}) + nBF^{B}(0, nB, W_{B}) + \psi(W_{A}, W_{B}) = nI, \quad \text{(4-II)}$$

where W_i is the size of the facility accommodating the traffic of mode i, ($i = A, B$).
$\psi(W_A, W_B)$ = cost (in terms of the composite good) of producing W_A and W_B.

Assumptions

Throughout the paper we shall make different assumptions concerning the trip and the infrastructure cost functions from among the following:

AS1 (*differentiability*) The cost of trip function $F^i(nA, nB, W)$, (i=A, B) is twice differentiable and the derivatives (denoted by subscripts) obey:

$$F_1^i > 0,\ F_2^i >,\ F_3^i < 0,\ F_{11}^i > 0,\ F_{22}^i > 0,\ F_{12}^i > 0,\ F_{21}^i > 0,\ F_{23}^i > 0.$$

AS2 (*separability*) The cost of trip function is weakly separable (assumed by Sherman (1971)):

$$F^i(\cdot) = g^i(h(nA, nB), W)$$

AS3 (*weighted sum*) The volume of traffic appears as a weighted sum of the number of trips in the two modes:

$$h(nA, nB) = knA + nB$$

and, therefore,

$$F^i(\cdot) = g^i(knA + nB, W)$$

where k is the number of bus passenger trips which have the same effect on congestion as one automobile passenger trip.

AS4 (*density*) The cost of a trip is a function of density, where density is defined as $D=(knA+nB)/W$. Thus

$$F^i(\cdot)=g^i(\cdot)=f^i[(knA+nB)/W]\equiv f^i(D).$$

AS5 (*constant-elasticity*) The elasticity of the congestion effect with respect to density is constant:

$$F^i(\cdot)=g^i(\cdot)=f^i(D)=\rho_0^i+\rho_1^i[(knA+nB+nB)/W]^{\rho_2^i}=\rho_0^i+\rho_1^i D^{\rho_2^i}$$
$$\rho_0^i,\ \rho_1^i>0,\ \rho_2^i>1.$$

Observe that the same restrictions on derivatives apply to all of the five assumptions and furthermore that each assumption is a special case of the earlier one. We add two assumptions that refer to the cost of the facilities functions in the two regimes.

AS6 (*constant marginal cost*) The marginal cost of capacity is constant:

$$\psi(W_A,\ W_B)=C_0+\varphi(W_A+W_B)=C_0+C_1W_A+C_1W_B$$

Assumption AS6 allows positive separation cost, C_0 (the cost of separated lanes exceeds the cost of the same number of lanes when they are used simultaneously by the two modes).

AS7 (*zero separation costs*)

$$\psi(W_A,\ W_B)=\varphi(W_A+W_B)$$

$$0<\varphi'\leqslant\varphi/W$$

The following table of derivatives where $f'^i=\mathrm{d}f^i(D)/dD$ will be helpful in the consideration of the different assumptions.

Assumptions (AS1) to (AS7) are widely used in both theoretical and empirical literature. At a later stage we shall discuss their compatibility with empirical evidence. At this stage we prefer to continue with the analysis and derive the implications for the allocation of resources of the different assumptions.

Table 10.1

	AS1	*AS2*	*AS3*	*AS4*	*AS5*
F^i_{nA}	F^i_1	$g^i_1 h_1$	kg^i_1	$\frac{k}{W} f'^i$	$\frac{k\rho^i_2}{knA+nB}(F^i-\rho^i_0)$
F^i_{nB}	F^i_2	$g^i_1 h_2$	g^i_1	$\frac{1}{W} f'^i$	$\frac{\rho_2}{knA+nB}(F-\rho^i_0)$
F^i_W	F^i_3	g^i_2	g^i_2	$-\frac{knA+nB}{W^2} f'^i$	$-\rho^i_2 \frac{knA+nB}{W^2}(F^i-\rho^i_0)$,

Before we proceed, it is useful to introduce two definitions. All definitions apply to Regime I, i.e. to the case where the two modes use a common facility.

F-1. Mode i will be said to demonstrate a greater and mode j a smaller aversion to congestion if $F^i_1 > F^j_1$ and $F^i_2 > F^j_2$ at any given combination of nA, nB, and W. (Given assumption (AS4) (density) this implies $f'^i > f'^j$ for any D.)[1]

F-2. Mode A is said to create a larger congestion effect than mode B if for any given combination n, A, B, and W:

$$F^A_1 > F^A_2 \quad \text{and} \quad F^B_1 > F^B_2.$$

Given AS4 (density) this implies $k > 1$.

In the next section we first derive the optimal allocation and prices, starting with the more general case, using AS1 (differentiability), and then turn to study the implications of the more restrictive assumptions.

III FIRST-BEST ALLOCATION

In the first-best allocation the planner can choose the prices, P_A and P_B, the size of the facility (facilities) in regime I(II), and the regime itself, in order to maximise u. Formally, the problem is to maximise u over P_A, P_B, and W, subject to (1)–(3) and (4-I), to maximise u over P_A, P_B, W_A, and W_B, subject to (1)–(3) and (4-II), and to choose the regime under which the resulting maximised utility is higher. Forming the appropriate Lagrangian using (1)–(3) and the property of compensated demand functions, the well known first order conditions can be derived (using abbreviated notation):

For Regime I:

$$P_A = F^A + nAF^A_{1+}nBF^B_1, \tag{5-I}$$

$$P_B = F^B + nAF^A_2 + nBF^B_2, \tag{6-I}$$

$$nAF^A_3 + nBF^B_3 + \varphi' = 0, \tag{7-I}$$

and for regime II:

$$P_A = F^A + nAF^A_1, \tag{5-II}$$

$$P_B = F^B + nBF^B_2, \tag{6-II}$$

$$nAF^A_3 + \psi_1(W_A, W_B) = 0, \text{ and} \tag{7-II-A}$$

$$nBF^B_3 + \psi_2(W_A, W_B) = 0. \tag{7-II-B}$$

Equations (5) and (6) imply marginal-cost pricing and equations (7) say that the marginal cost equals the marginal benefit of the facility. It is assumed that the average variable cost is paid directly by users. Thus the following congestion tolls (t^i) are to be levied on a passenger trip by the respective modes (i= A, B):

Regime I:

$$t^A_I = nAF^A_1 + nBF^B_1,$$

$$t^B_I = nAF^A_2 + nBF^B_2.$$

Regime II:

$$t^A_{II} = nAF^A_I,$$

$$t^B_{II} = nBF^B_2$$

Solving the above maximisation problem we obtain $u^*(n)$, $P^*_A(n)$,

$P^*_B(n)$, and $W^*(n)$, where stars denote optimal values, given n. These solutions vary, of course, with n. It has been shown (see Berglas and Pines (1981)) that the revenue collected from the tolls and the cost of the facility (Regime I) or facilities (Regime II) satisfy the following relation:

$$\text{Revenue} - \text{Cost} \gtreqless 0 \Leftrightarrow \mathrm{d}u^*(n)/\mathrm{d}n \lesseqgtr 0$$

If the size of the population happens to be optimal, the revenue from the toll is just sufficient to cover the cost of the facility. Furthermore, if F^A and F^B are homogeneous of degree zero in nA, nB, and W, and φ and ψ are homogeneous of degree one in W, then $\mathrm{d}u^*(n)/\mathrm{d}n = 0$ for all n and therefore the revenue is equal to the cost for any population size.

Observe that AS4 (density) implies zero homogeneity of F^i. Thus AS4(Density), AS7 (zero separation costs), and linear homogeneity of φ guarantee that the optimal revenue collected from toll exactly covers costs in both of the Regimes I and II.

Now we turn to characterise the allocations in the two regimes.

Proposition 1 If:

(a) AS4 (density)
(b) AS6 (constant marginal cost)
(c) The two modes demonstrate equal aversion to congestion, i.e. $f'^A(D) = f'^B(D) = f'(D)$ and,
(d) Mode A creates more congestion than B, i.e. $k > 1$,

Then: the optimal densities under Regime II differ from that under Regime I such that

$$D^*_A > D^*_{A+B} > D^*_B,$$

where D^*_A and D^*_B denote optimal density in separate roads for modes A and B respectively, while D^*_{A+B} is the optimal density in the common road.

Proof It follows from (7-II), (7-II-A), and (7-II-B) that under the above assumptions:

$$\text{(i)} \qquad \frac{A + B}{kA + B} = C_1,$$

(ii) $\frac{1}{k} f'(D^*_A)D^{*2}_A = C_1,$

(iii) $f'(D^*_B)D^{*2}_A = C_1,$

or

(i)′ $f'(D^*_{A+B})D^{*2}_{A+B} = C_1 \frac{kA+B}{A+B},$

(ii)′ $f'(D^*_A)D^{*2}_A = C_1 k,$

(iii)′ $f'(D^*_B)D^{*2}_B = C_1,$

Since

$$1 < \frac{kA+B}{A+B} < k,$$

and $f'(D)$ increases with D (this follows from ASI (differentiability)). Therefore

$D^*_A > D^*_{A+B} > D^*_B.$

Q.E.D.

Proposition 2. If:

(a) AS4 (density),
(b) AS6 (constant marginal cost),
(c) The two modes create the same congestion effect, i.e. $k=1$, and,
(d) Mode A and B demonstrate different aversion to congestion,

Then:

$$D, f'^A \gtreqless f'^B \Rightarrow D^*_A \lesseqgtr D^*_{A+B} \lesseqgtr D^*_B$$

Proof We provide the proof for the case $f'^A > f'^B$.

It follows from (7-I), (7-II-A), and (7-II-B) that under the above assumptions:

(i) $$\left[\frac{A}{A+B} f'^A(D^*_{A+B}) + \frac{B}{A+B} f'^B(D^*_{A+B})\right] D^{*2}_{A+B} = C_1,$$

(ii) $f'^A(D^*_A)D^{*2}_A = C_1,$

(iii) $f'^B(D^*_B)D^{*2}_B = C_1$

Since $f'^{A}(D^*_{A+B}) > f'^{B}(D^*_{A+B})$ we have

$$F'^{A}(D^*_{A+B})D^{*2}_{A+B} > C_1 = F'^{A}(D^*_{A})D^{*2}_{A}.$$

Since F'^{A} increases with D (AS1 (differentiability)), we must have

$D^*_{A+B} > D^*_{A}$. Similarly, $D^*_{A+B} < D^*_{B}$. Q.E.D.

Propositions 1 and 2 suggest that *in optimal separate roads traffic density is higher as the congestion creation is higher and the aversion to congestion is lower. In the common road the density is averaged according to some average congestion creation and congestion aversion of the two modes*. Under certain conditions this averaging can be shown to be inefficient.

Proposition 3 Under AS4 (density) and AS7 (zero separation costs), Regime I cannot be superior, and most probably is inferior, to Regime II.

Proof Suppose X^*, A^*, B^*, W^* maximise u under Regime I such that $u = u^*$. Consider an alternative allocation $(\tilde{X}, \tilde{A}, \tilde{B}, \tilde{W}_A, \tilde{W}_B)$ under Regime II

$$\tilde{X} = x^*,\ \tilde{A} = a^*,\ \tilde{B} = b^*,\ \tilde{W}_A = \frac{kA}{kA^* + B^*}W^*,$$

$$\tilde{W}_B = \frac{B^*}{kA^* + B^*}W^*.$$

It can easily be verified that the allocation $(\tilde{X}, \tilde{A}, \tilde{B}, \tilde{W}_A, \tilde{W}_B)$ which allows u^* is also feasible. But it is not optimal as long as it does not satisfy conditions (5-II), (6-II), (7-II-A), and (7-II-B).

If $f'^{A} \neq f'^{B}$ or $k \neq 1$, then by propositions 1 and 2 the density on the separate roads is not optimal and utility can be increased. The only exceptional case where the common road is not inferior is the case where $k > 1$ and $f'^{A} < f'^{B}$ in a coordinated way such that the congestion on optimally separate roads will be exactly equal to that of the common road. Given (7-II-A) and (7-II-B)

$$f'^{A}(D_A)D_A^2 = C_1 K$$

$$f'^{B}(D_B)D_2^{B} = C_1$$

For equal optimal D it is necessary that

$$f'^{A}/f'^{B}=k.$$

This is certainly a very special case.[2]

A calculation of the difference in utilities under mixed and separate roads is illustrated for specific functions and parameters in Appendix C.

Proposition 3 is analogous to the segregation theorem of the club theory (Berglas and Pines, 1981). But in that case, the segregation results from the assumption that individuals may have different tastes or private costs of congestion (e.g. different valuation of time) by the individuals (see also Mohring, 1965). In the present case, the segregation theorem results from different characteristics of different modes of transportation used by identical individuals.

It should be emphasised that separation is necessary as part of the optimal allocation and that optimal density depends on characteristics of the different modes.

The validity of propositions 1–3 hinges, of course, on the underlying assumptions. We therefore turn to consider the existing literature. AS3 (weighted sum) is common practice in measuring the volume of traffic (e.g., see Highway Research Board, 1965). AS4 (density) is most commonly used (see survey by Mohring (1976)). The more restrictive form of AS5 (constant elasticity) is used in empirical works, e.g., Vickrey (1963), (1965); US Department of Transportation (1977) and in theoretical work, e.g., Solow and Vickrey (1971) and Mills and Ferranti (1971). Vickrey (1965) states the empirical observation that ρ_2 is constant over a substantial range of density. Thus at any rate, AS4 (density) which is used in the proof of propositions 1–3 is not at odds with existing literature and the empirical evidence.

Assumption AS6 (constant marginal cost) is also widely used; see, for example, Meyer *et al.* (1965) and Mohring (1976). It is also not inconsistent with Vickrey (1963) as long as separation costs are independent of the distribution of lanes between modes (see below).

In proving Proposition 3 we used AS7 (zero separation costs). The opinions as to the validity of this assumption differ. Some researchers believe in an even stronger form of AS7, i.e.

$$\psi(W_A, W_B)=\varphi(W_A+W_B)=C_1W_A+C_1W_B$$

This is the case where road construction exhibits constant returns to scale. Mohring (1976, p. 145) mentions the inconclusive empirical evidence regarding the returns to scale in road construction. However, following Meyer *et al.* (1965), he calculates road construction cost functions that imply increasing returns to scale. But increasing returns to scale in road construction in itself does not invalidate AS7 (zero separation costs) as long as separation of lanes according to modes is costless.

The costs of lane separation are discussed by Vickrey (1965), who believes that reserving lanes for buses introduces formidable problems in dealing with intersections and pick-up points. The reserving of right-of-way for buses in many cities may indicate that separation costs are not prohibitive, or, alternatively, that the benefits from separation indicated by Proposition 3 outweigh separation costs.

Finally there is the questions of indivisibility. The number of buses may be too small to justify even one lane (or an integer number of lanes). This integer problem is discussed extensively in club theory (see Berglas and Pines, 1981). Anyhow, the importance of this consideration declines with the increase in the number of users.

When optimality requires separation a question may arise as to whether an administrative allocation of rights of way is indispensable or if certain pricing rule may be sufficient. It is straightforward that if we can charge each mode a different price on road A and road B such prices exist. In particular, it can be shown that marginal cost pricing is sufficient in this case for voluntary separation.[3]

After demonstrating that a segregation of modes may be optimal in the first-best we turn to examine its role and implication in second-best conditions where full pricing is infeasible.

IV A SECOND-BEST ALLOCATION

In this section we discuss the case in which it is not feasible to charge the warranted price of a trip by mode A, say automobiles. Thus, the price paid by the individual for a trip by A is the average variable cost, which, in turn, depends on the traffic conditions. The planner can, however, determine the price of B.

Formally, u is maximised subject to (1)–(4) and an additional constraint

$$P_A = F^A(nA, nB, W), \tag{8-I}$$

in case of Regime I, and

$$P_A = F^A(nA, 0, W_A), \tag{8-II}$$

in case of Regime II. Define:

$$\Delta \equiv a_1 b_2 - a_2 b_1 > 0. \tag{9}$$

where, as before, $a(P_A, P_B, u)$ and $b(P_A, P_B, u)$ are the compensated demand functions for A and B, and subscripts denote partial derivatives.

The inequality sign follows from the concavity, i.e. $E_{11}E_{22} - E_{12}^2 > 0$, and the derivative properties, i.e. $E_1 = a$, and $E_2 = b$ of the expenditure function, E. Then, the necessary conditions for an optimal common road are (see Appendix A):

$$P_B - F^B = nAF_2^A + n\mathrm{B}\mathrm{F}_2^B - \lambda[F_2^A + a_2/(n\Delta)], \text{ and} \tag{10-I}$$

$$nAF_3^A + nBF_3^B + \varphi' - \lambda F_3^A = 0, \tag{11-I}$$

where

$$\lambda \equiv n^2\Delta(AF_1^A + BF_1^B)/(h\Delta F_1^A - b_2). \tag{12-I}$$

λ is the shadow price of constraint (8-I) in terms of the composite good. It reflects the quantity of resources that can be saved by increasing the price of automobiles by one unit. The term in the brackets of equation (10-I) is the effect of a unit increase in B on the price of A, P_A. This effect is composed of direct component F_2^A and an indirect one $a_2/(n\Delta)$. The total effect is multiplied by λ to reflect a social gain element, resulting from an additional unit of bus traffic. It is therefore subtracted from the direct marginal social cost of a unit trip by B, $F^B + nAF_2^A + nBF_2^B$, to arrive at the net social cost of a trip by bus.

Similarly, in comparison to first-best, an additional cost element is added to the marginal cost–benefit calculation of W, λF_3^A. F_3^A reflects the reduction of F^A resulting from a marginal increase in W. But this reduction in cost is also a reduction in the price of A which increases the distortion by λ (per unit of price reduction).

In the case of Regime II, (10)–(12) become (see Appendix A)

$$P_B = F_B + nBF_2^B - \lambda a_2/(n\Delta) \tag{10-II}$$

and

$$nAF_3^A + \psi_1 - \lambda F_3^A = 0, \tag{11-II-A}$$

$$nBF_3^B + \psi_2 = 0 \tag{11-II-B}$$

where

$$\lambda \equiv n^2 \Delta A F_1^A/(n\Delta F_1^A - b_2) > 0. \tag{12-II}$$

These equations allow us to examine the applicability of Propositions 1–3 to the second-best case. The results are given below and their proofs are in Appendix B.

Proposition 1′ Under the assumptions of Proposition 1 we have:

$$D_A^* > D_B^*$$
$$D_{A+B}^* > D_B^*$$

The difference between Propositions 1 and 1′ is that in the latter we cannot determine the relation between D_{A+B}^* and D_A^*.[4]

Proposition 2 becomes:

Proposition 2′ If assumptions (a)–(c) of Proposition 2 are satisfied, and

(d) $f'^A(D) < f'^B(D)$ for all D,

then:

$$D_{A+B}^* > D_B^*$$
$$D_A^* > D_B^*$$

We cannot determine the relation between the densities if $f'^A > f'^B$; nor can we determine the relationships if $f'^A = f'^B$.

Proposition 3 becomes

Proposition 3′ Given AS4 (density), AS6 (constant marginal cost), and the second-best restriction on the pricing of mode A, it is still true that separate roads are never less efficient, and are most probably more efficient than a common road.

The proof follows the same steps as that of Proposition 3 and need not be repeated.

In the case of the first-best we have shown that appropriate pricing can guarantee the optimal segregation of roads according to mode. By definition, in the second-best the automobile pays the average cost. Therefore, if the automobile driver is left to decide which road to use he certainly would prefer the bus road, where, according to proposition 1′, the density is lower. Therefore, optimality requires an administrative exclusive right-of-way for the bus.

We now turn to a comparison between first- and second-best allocations.

Proposition 4 If:

(a) AS4 (density)
(b) AS6 (constant marginal cost)
(c) Mode A creates higher congestion effect than mode B ($k>1$), then, in Regime II:

(1) The optimal density in the facility of mode A is higher in the second- than in the first-best,
(2) The optimal density in the facility of mode B (for which optimal pricing is feasible) is the same in the first- and second-best.

Proof Denote by D_i^{**} the optimal density in facility $i(i=\mathrm{A, B})$ under second-best allocation. Then (7-II-A), (7-II-B) (11-II-A), and (11-II-B) imply:

$$\frac{nA-\lambda}{knA}f'^{\mathrm{A}}(D_{\mathrm{A}}^{**})\,D_{\mathrm{A}}^{**2}=C_1=\frac{1}{K}f'^{\mathrm{A}}(D_{\mathrm{A}}^{*})\,D_{\mathrm{A}}^{*2}.$$

It follows that $D_{\mathrm{A}}^{**}>D_{\mathrm{A}}^{*}$ (since $(nA-\lambda)/(knA)<1/k$).
Also we have

$$f'^{\mathrm{B}}(D_{\mathrm{B}}^{**})\,D_{\mathrm{B}}^{**2}=C_1=f'^{\mathrm{B}}(D_{\mathrm{B}}^{*})\,D_{\mathrm{B}}^{*2},$$

which implies

$$D_{\mathrm{B}}^{**}=D_{\mathrm{B}}^{*}$$ Q.E.D.

Proposition 4 implies also:

Proposition 5 If:

(a) AS4 (density),
(b) AS6 (constant marginal cost),

then, in Regime II, the optimal price of B in the second-best, denoted by P_B^{**} is never higher than that of the first-best, denoted by P_B^*.

Proof. The assumptions imply:

$$nBF_2^B = \frac{nB}{W} f'^B(D_B) = D_B f'^B(D_B).$$

Therefore

(i) $$F^B + nAF_2^B = f^B(D_B) + D_B f'^B(D_B).$$

In the first-best we have

(ii) $$P_B^* = F^B + nBF_2^B = f^B(D_B^*) + D_B^* f'^B D_B^*$$

In the second-best we have

(iii) $$P_B^{**} = F^B + nBF_2^B - \lambda a_2/n\Delta \leqslant F^B + nBF_2^B$$
$$= f^B(D_B^{**}) + D_B^{**} f'^B(D_B^{**}) \qquad \text{(by 12-II)}.$$

According to Proposition 4, $D_B^* = D_B^{**}$; therefore

$$P_B^* \geqslant P_B^{**}$$ Q.E.D.

It follows from (10-I) and (10-II) that the price of a trip by bus is lower than the direct marginal cost. A question immediately arises whether the price should be higher or lower than the average cost which is borne by the user. In other words, the question is whether $t_i^B = P_B - F^B (i = \text{I, II})$ is positive or negative.

The sign of t_i^B seems to be of special interest in the literature since $t_i^B > 0$ implies that buses should pay a congestion toll even in the case where automobiles do not; while the case of $t_i^B < 0$ means that buses should be subsidised. Thus our following analysis will concentrate on the sign of t_i^B.

Using (9), (10-I), (12-I), and AS2 (separability) we can derive (see Appendix A):

$$t_{\mathrm{I}}^{\mathrm{B}} = P_{\mathrm{B}} - F^{\mathrm{B}} = -\frac{nb_2(AF_1^{\mathrm{A}} + BF_1^{\mathrm{B}})}{n\Delta F_1 A - b_2}\left[\frac{\eta_{\mathrm{a}:P\mathrm{B}}}{\eta_{\mathrm{b}:P\mathrm{B}}} + \frac{\eta_{F\mathrm{B}:nB}}{\eta_{F\mathrm{B}:nA}}\right]\frac{\mathrm{A}}{\mathrm{B}} \tag{13-I}$$

where $\eta_{i:j}$ = elasticity of i with respect to j.

Thus,

$$t_{\mathrm{I}}^{\mathrm{B}} = P_{\mathrm{B}} - F^{\mathrm{B}} \gtreqless 0 \Leftrightarrow -\frac{\eta_{\mathrm{a}:P\mathrm{B}}}{\eta_{\mathrm{b}:P\mathrm{B}}} \lessgtr \frac{\eta_{F\mathrm{B}:nB}}{\eta_{F\mathrm{B}:nA}} \tag{14-I}$$

which is the condition derived by Sherman (1971). If, in addition, we assume AS3 (weighted sum), the above condition reduces to:

$$t_{\mathrm{I}}^{\mathrm{B}} = P_{\mathrm{B}} - F^{\mathrm{B}} \gtreqless 0 \Leftrightarrow ka_2 + b_2 \lesseqgtr 0, \tag{15-I}$$

It follows from (15-I) that bus passengers should pay congestion toll, i.e. $t_{\mathrm{I}}^{\mathrm{B}} > 0$ if either (1) $a_2 \leqslant 0$, or (2) the weighted volume of traffic $kA + B$ declines when the price of a bus trip increases.

So far we have considered the optimal toll when the road is commonly used (Regime I). This issue is extensively discussed in the existing literature. We now turn to consider optimal tolls under Regime II, which by proposition 3′ is more efficient than Regime I.

Under Regime II, (10-I) collapses to:

$$P_{\mathrm{B}} - F^{\mathrm{b}} = nBF_2^{\mathrm{B}} - \lambda a_2 / n\Delta \tag{10-II}$$

Comparing (10-II) with (10-I) we observe that $F_2^{\mathrm{A}} nA - \lambda F_2^{\mathrm{A}} = F_2^{\mathrm{A}}((nA - \lambda)$, of (10-I) disappears in (10-II). $F_2^{\mathrm{A}} nA$ is the additional external *negative* effect of a unit of bus traffic on automobile travellers. $-\lambda F_2^{\mathrm{A}}$ is the *favourable* effect of increasing bus traffic, and thus congestion, on resource allocation. This increased congestion is associated with an increase by F_2^{A} of the effective price for automobiles. A unit increase in the price of the automobile is associated with an increase of λ in social benefit. (λ is the shadow price of constraint (I-II).) this mean that subsidising buses in the case of a common road has an extra benefit which is missing in the case of separate roads.[5] Consequently it is shown below that under regime II it is less likely that buses should be subsidised.

Proposition 6 If:

(a) $\eta_{FA:nA} \leqslant \eta_{FB:nB}$, and,
(b) B and A and B and X are net substitutes,

then,

$$t_{\text{II}}^{\text{B}} = P_{\text{B}} - F^{\text{B}} > 0.$$

Proof The above assumptions imply:

(i) $a_2 P_{\text{A}} + b_2 P_{\text{B}} = b_1 P_{\text{A}} + b_2 P_{\text{B}} < 0,$

since the compensated demand is homogeneous of zero degree in price, and since $a_2 = b_1$. Thus:

(ii) $a_2/b_2 > -P_{\text{B}}/P_{\text{A}},$ since $b_2 < 0.$

Suppose that the proposition is false. Then,

(iii) $t_{\text{II}}^{\text{B}} = P_{\text{B}} - F^{\text{B}} < 0$, and (ii) becomes

(iv) $a_2/b_2 > F^{\text{B}}/P_{\text{A}} = -F^{\text{B}}/F^{\text{A}}$ (since $P_{\text{A}} = F^{\text{A}}$).

It follows from (10-II) and (12-II) that:

(v) $$t_{\text{II}}^{\text{B}} = P_{\text{B}} - F^{\text{B}} = nBF_2^{\text{B}} - nAF_1^{\text{A}} a_2/(nF_1^{\text{A}}\Delta - b_2)$$
$$> nBF_2^{\text{B}} + nAF_1^{\text{A}} a_2/b_2,$$

since $nAF_1^{\text{a}} a_2, nF_1^{\text{A}}\Delta$ and $-b_2$ are all positive.

Substituting (iii) into (v) yields:

(vi) $$\begin{aligned} t_{\text{II}}^{\text{B}} &> nBF_2^{\text{B}} - nAF_1^{\text{A}} P_{\text{B}}/P_{\text{A}} \\ &> nBF_2^{\text{B}} - nAF_1^{\text{A}} F^{\text{B}}/P_{\text{A}} \\ &= nBF_2^{\text{B}} - nAF_1^{\text{A}} F^{\text{B}}/F^{\text{A}} \text{ (since } P_{\text{A}} = F^{\text{A}}) \\ &= F^{\text{B}}(\eta_{FB:nB} - \eta_{FA:nA}) \geqslant 0 \end{aligned}$$

(since, by assumption (a) $\eta_{FA:nA} \leqslant \eta_{FB:nB}$). (iii) contradicts (v).

Q.E.D.

On the basis of Proposition 6, we claim that under Regime II it is likely, that buses should be taxed. First, observe that Proposition 6 remains valid if assumption (a) refers to the elasticity of the congestion-dependent portion of F^A and F^B. Thus, if AS5 (constant elasticity) is satisfied and $\rho_2^A \leqslant \rho_2^B$, then $t_{11}^B > 0$. According to the US Department of Transportation (1977), $\rho_2^A = \rho_2^B$. This is sufficient for $t_{11}^B > 0$. Furthermore, because of inferior manoeuvrability of the bus (Vickrey, 1963), it may be true that bus passengers suffer more from congestion (in terms of cost) than automobile drivers, i.e. $\rho_2^A < \rho_2^B$. If this is the case, then, *a fortiori*, $t_{\mathrm{II}}^B > 0$.

V CONCLUDING REMARKS

In this paper we have demonstrated the case for reserved rights-of-way for buses and private automobiles. Furthermore, we have proved that the case for separation arises from differences in the characteristics of the two modes. More specifically, it has been shown that differences in either aversion to congestion or in the creation of congestion are sufficient to justify separation of traffic, provided that the technology of road construction demonstrates, properly defined, zero separation cost. It was further argued that road separation, i.e., assigning exclusive right-of-way, is also required in the second-best situation where a congestion toll is being paid by buses but not by automobiles. The optimal congestion toll for this case and conditions where buses should pay tax even when automobiles do not were derived. The likelihood of these conditions was discussed. It is shown that the case for charging buses with congestion toll increases when separate lanes are allocated for the buses.

As in any study, our results follow the assumptions. It is, therefore, important to examine the implications of some changes in these assumptions. In particular, throughout the paper it is assumed that all consumers are identical. This assumption can be relaxed by introducing several alternative cases:

(1) There are different consumers, everybody using both modes, and cost functions for every individual are identical – all the results hold.

(2) There are two types of individuals having different utility functions and income. Given their tastes, in the range of the considered prices, type-one individuals use only buses while type-two only automobiles. Considering Pareto-efficient allocations, all

propositions in this paper regarding optimal densities and superiority of road separation are unchanged. There is one stronger result which is that bus travellers, provided they use separate roads, should pay first-best congestion tolls also under the second-best conditions. This strengthens the case for charging congestion tolls on exclusive roads for buses. Under these assumptions, some identify automobile drivers as the rich and bus users as the poor, and use this to recommend subsidies for buses. The analysis of this paper was restricted to the issue of efficient allocation and pricing and has abstracted from equity considerations. It is still useful for the study of excess burden associated with equity-motivated subsidies.

(3) Different people using the same mode have different cost functions, perhaps because they have different values of time (or, what is equivalent, have different utility functions while density is an argument in the utility function). In this case there is an added benefit to road separation. There should even be several roads for automobiles serving people having different values of time, provided, of course, that the demands are high enough to justify at least one lane for every type of individual. This is the case analysed by Mohring (1965), and by Berglas and Pines (1981).

APPENDIX A CALCULATION OF THE OPTIMAL SECOND-BEST TOLL

The Lagrangian of the second-best allocation under Regime II (in abbreviated notation)

$$L = u - \lambda_1(nx + naF^{A} + nbF^{B} + \varphi - nI) - \lambda_2(P_{A} - F^{A})$$

The necessary conditions are (where use is made of the property of the compensated demands):

$$x_i P_{A} a_i + P_{B} b_i = 0, \qquad i = 1, 2 \text{ and (2) and (3)):}$$

$$b_1[nAF_2^{A} + nBF_2^{B} - \lambda F_2^{A} + F^{B} - P_{B}] + a_1[nAF_1^{A} + nB_1^{B} - \lambda F_1^{A} = -\lambda/n], \tag{A-1}$$

$$b_2[nAF_2^{A} + n\mathrm{B}\mathrm{F}_2^{B} - \lambda F_2^{A} + F^{B} - P_{B}] + a_2[nAF_1^{A} + nBF_1^{B} - \lambda F_1^{A}] = 0, \tag{A-2}$$

and

$$nBF_3^{\rm A}+nAF_3^{\rm A}+\varphi'+\lambda F_3^{\rm A}=0, \tag{A-3}$$

where $\lambda=\lambda_2/\lambda_1$.

Substituting (A-1) into (A-2) yields

$$\lambda=\frac{n^2(a_1b_2-a_2b_1)(aF_1^{\rm A}+bF_1^{\rm B})}{n(a_1b_2-a_2b_1)F_1^{\rm A}-b_2}>0 \tag{A-4}$$

The inequality follows from $F_1^{\rm A}$, $F_1^{\rm B}>0$, $b_2<0$ and $a_1b_2-a_2b_1>0$ (the expenditure function is concave in the prices).

(A-1) and (A-2) constitute a system of two linear equations in two unknowns. Its solution yields:

$$P_{\rm B}-F^{\rm B}=nAF_2^{\rm A}+nBF_2^{\rm B}-\lambda\left[F_2^{\rm A}+\frac{a_2}{n(a_1b_2-a_2b_1)}\right]. \tag{A-5}$$

Substituting (A-4) into (A-5) it reduces to:

$$\begin{aligned}P_{\rm B}-F^{\rm B}=&\left[nB(a_1b_2-a_2b_1)F_1^{\rm B}F_2^{\rm B}\left(\frac{F_1^{\rm A}}{F_1^{\rm B}}-\frac{F_2^{\rm A}}{F_2^{\rm B}}\right)\right.\\&\left.-na_2F_1^{\rm B}\left(\frac{AF_1^{\rm A}}{F_1^{\rm B}}+B\right)-nb_2F_2^{\rm B}\left(A\frac{F_2^{\rm A}}{F_2^{\rm B}}+B\right)\right]\\&\left[n(a_1b_2-a_2b_1)F_1^{\rm A}-b_2\right]^{-1}.\end{aligned} \tag{A-6}$$

AS2 (separability) implies

$$F_1^{\rm A}/F_1^{\rm B}=F_2^{\rm A}/F_2^{\rm B}. \tag{A-7}$$

(A-6) and (A-7) yield:

$$\begin{aligned}P_{\rm B}-F^{\rm B}&=-\frac{nb_2(AF_1^{\rm A}+BF_1^{\rm B})}{[n(a_1b_2-a_2b_1)F_1^{\rm A}-b_2]}\left[\frac{a_2}{b_2}+\frac{F_2^{\rm B}}{F_1^{\rm B}}\right]\\&=-\frac{\text{n}b_2(AF_1^{\rm A}+BF_1^{\rm B})}{n(a_1b_2-a_2b_1)F_1^{\rm A}-b_2}\left[\frac{\eta_{a:P_{\rm B}}}{\eta_{b:P_{\rm B}}}+\frac{\eta_{F^{\rm B}:nb}}{\eta_{F^{\rm B}:nA}}\right]\frac{A}{B},\end{aligned} \tag{A-8}$$

where

$$\eta_{a:P_B} = a_2 P_B / A$$

$$\eta_{b:P_B} = b_2 P_B B$$

$$\eta_{F^B:nA} = F_1^B nA / F^B$$

$$\eta_{F^B:nB} = F_2^B nB / F^B$$

Under Regime II, (AS6) collapses to:

$$P_B - F^B = nBF_2^B - \frac{nAF_1^A a_2}{n(a_1 b_2 - a_2 b_1)F_1^A - b_2}. \qquad \text{(A-9)}$$

APPENDIX B PROOFS OF PROPROSITIONS 1′ AND 2′

(a) AS4 (density),
(b) AS6 (constant marginal costs),
(c) the two modes demonstrate equal aversion to congestion.
(d) mode A creates more congestion than B, i.e. $k > 1$,
then:

The optimal densities under Regime II differ from those under Regime I such that:

$$D_A^* > D_B^*$$

$$D_{A+B}^* > D_B^*$$

Proof:

(i) $$f'(D_{A+B}^*)D_{A+B} = C_1 \frac{knA + nB}{nA + nB - \lambda} > C_1$$

(ii) $$f'(D_A^*)D_A^2 = C_1 \frac{knA}{nA - \lambda} > kC_1 > C_1$$

(iii) $$f'(D_B^*)D_B^2 = C_1$$

The above relations imply Proposition 1′. Q.E.D.

Proposition 2′ If:

(a) AS4 (density),
(b) AS6 (constant marginal costs),
(c) The two modes create the same congestion effect, i.e. $k=1$, and
(d) $f'^{\mathrm{A}}(D)<f'^{\mathrm{B}}(D)$ for all D,

then:

$$D^*_{\mathrm{A+B}}>D^*_{\mathrm{B}}$$
$$D^*_{\mathrm{A}}>D^*_{\mathrm{B}}$$

Proof As in Proposition 2, we can derive:

(i) $$\left[\frac{nA-\lambda}{nA+nB}f'^{\mathrm{A}}(D^*_{\mathrm{A+B}})+\frac{B}{A+B}f'^{\mathrm{B}}(D^*_{\mathrm{A+B}})\right]D^{*2}_{\mathrm{A+B}}=C_1$$

(ii) $$f'^{\mathrm{A}}(D^*_{\mathrm{A}})\,\frac{nA-\lambda}{nA}\,D^{*2}_{\mathrm{A}}=C_1$$

(iii) $$f'^{\mathrm{B}}(D^*_{\mathrm{B}})\,D^{*2}_{\mathrm{B}}=C_1$$

If $f'^{\mathrm{A}}(D)<f'^{\mathrm{B}}(D)$ for all D, we have

$$f'^{\mathrm{B}}(D^*_{\mathrm{B}})D^{*2}_{\mathrm{B}}=C_1=\left[\frac{nA-\lambda}{nA+nB}f'^{\mathrm{A}}(D^*_{\mathrm{A+B}})+\frac{B}{A+B}f'^{\mathrm{B}}(D^*_{\mathrm{A+B}})\right]D^{*2}_{\mathrm{A+B}}$$
$$<f'^{\mathrm{B}}(D^*_{\mathrm{A+B}})D^{*2}_{\mathrm{A+B}}.$$

Hence:

$$D^*_{\mathrm{A+B}}>D^*_{\mathrm{B}}.$$

Also

$$f'^{\mathrm{B}}(D^*_{\mathrm{B}})D^{*2}_{\mathrm{B}}=C_1=f'^{\mathrm{A}}(D^*_{\mathrm{A}})\frac{nA-\lambda}{nA}D^{*2}_{\mathrm{A}}<f'^{B}(D^*_{\mathrm{A}})D^{*2}_{\mathrm{A}}.$$

Therefore

$$D^*_{\mathrm{A}}>D^*_{\mathrm{B}}.$$ Q.E.D.

APPENDIX C A NUMERICAL EXAMPLE OF THE OPTIMALITY OF LANE SEPARATION

B.1 First-Best Allocation without Lane Separation

We assume the following utility function

$$u = X + 0.6 \ln \mathrm{A} + 0.4 \ln \mathrm{B}.$$

The cost of road construction is given by:

$$\varphi(W) = W.$$

The direct (user's) cost of undertaking a trip in each of the two modes will be given by:

$$F^{\mathrm{A}} = F^{\mathrm{B}} = \frac{(10nA + nB)^2}{W^2}.$$

It can be seen from the above expressions that each trip by mode A is assumed to contribute to congestion 10 times as much as each trip by mode B.

We will also assume that population size, $n = 100$, and per capita income, $I = 100$.

B.2 First-Best Allocation with Lane Separation

We assume the same utility function

$$u = X + 0.6 \ln A + 0.4 \ln B.$$

The cost of constructing each of the two sections of the road is given by:

$$\varphi(W_{\mathrm{A}}) = W_{\mathrm{A}}$$
$$\varphi(W_{\mathrm{B}}) = W_{\mathrm{B}}.$$

The direct cost of undertaking a trip in each of the two modes is given by:

$$F^{A} = \left[\frac{10nA)}{W_A} \right]^2$$

$$F^{B} = \left[\frac{nB}{W_B} \right]^2.$$

Again, $n = 100$, and $I = 100$.

B.3 Second-Best Allocation with Lane Separation

We assume the same functions as in Section B.2.

B.4 Comparison of Alternative Allocation Schemes

Solving the allocation problems described in Sections B.1, B.2 and B.3 we get the following results:

		First-best without lane separation	*First-best with lane separation*	*Second-best with lane separation*
W_A	Road width allocated to mode A	—	40.00	40.00
W_B	Road width allocated to mode B		26.67	26.67
W	Total road width	66.67	66.67	66.67
X	Quantity of composite good consumed	99.00	99.00	98.60
A	Number of trips by mode A	0.06	0.07	0.10
B	Number of trips by mode B	0.18	0.21	0.21
$A+B$	Total number of trips $a+b$	0.24	0.28	0.31
F^A	Direct cost of trip by mode A	1.39	2.92	6.08
t_i^A	Congestion toll levied on mode A	8.48	5.85	0
P_A	Total cost of trip by mode A	9.87	8.77	6.08

F^B	Direct cost of trip by mode B	1.39	0.63	0.63
t_i^B	Congestion toll levied on mode B	0.85	1.26	1.26
P_B	Total cost of trip by mode B	2.24	1.89	1.89
D_{A+B}	Density in common road	1.18		—
D_A	Density in road for mode A	—	1.71	2.47
D_B	Density in road for mode B	—	0.79	0.79
u	Utility	96.62	96.77	96.56

Comparing the results obtained under the two allocations corresponding to the two alternative regimes in the first-best we derive the following conclusions:

Utility, as expected, rises when roadway separation is introduced. Total road width remains the same in the two cases,[6] as does the quantity of the composite good consumed. The number of trips in each of the two modes rises, which in fact, causes the rise in utility. This is a result of the drop in the total cost of travel in each of the two modes. In case of mode A (which is the more congestion-causing mode), the direct cost of travel rises as a result of lane separation, but the optimal congestion toll drops. In the case of mode B, the direct cost of travel drops, but the congestion toll rises. This means that as a result of lane separation, general travel conditions (travel speed, etc.) improve (density drops) for the less congestion-causing mode, while they deteriorate (density rises) for the competing mode. This provides an illustration of Proposition 1. We can see that lane-separation by itself provides the planner with an additional parameter which enables him to achieve a Pareto improvement over the optimal conditions which existed prior to the introduction of lane separation.

Comparing the results of lane-separation in the first-best and second-best we reach the following results:

Utility, obviously, is higher in the first-best than in the second-best. Road width allocated to each mode remains the same. The amount of the composite good consumed is less in the second-best than in the first-best, resulting in a drop in utility in spite of the use in the total number of trips. Travel conditions in mode B (number of trips and travel costs) where optimal congestion tolls are levied in both cases, remain the same. (This is a particular result, coming from the fact that in the particular utility function assumed, $a_2 = 0$.) The number of trips in mode A rises, even though the total cost of undertaking the trips rises. Density rises in mode A, while remaining the same in mode B (illustrating Proposition 4).

ACKNOWLEDGEMENTS

Financial assistance from the Foerder Institute for Economic Research is gratefully acknowledged. We are indebted to Richard Arnott for very helpful comments and suggestions.

Notes

1. We use the term 'aversion' in spite of the fact that in the context of this paper the congestion affects the cost rather than utility. But none of our results should be changed if we modify the model presented in this paper such that the congestion affects the utility rather than the cost.
2. The same proof can be extended to the case where D_A and D_B appear also in the utility function and therefore in the compensated demand functions. Observe that this provides an additional motive for different densities on separate roads. Different densities on separate roads can now be optimal even if $k = 1$ and $f'^A = f'^B$.
3. An indication of the proof is simple; consider the case where $f_A = f_B$. If the automobile driver was charged P_B for using facility B, he would use facility B. But, if he was charged kP_B, he would prefer to use facility A rather than B. This is because by Proposition 1, his cost minimisation requires that he use a road with higher density.
4. If, however, b is homogeneous of zero degree in P_A and P_B, Δ vanishes and so does λ. In this case Proposition 1′ and 1 are identical.
5. Note that $nA > \lambda$, as can be verified from (12-II).
6. This results from the specific form of the utility and cost functions.

REFERENCES

Berglas, E. and D. Pines (1981) 'Clubs, Local Public Goods and Transportation Models: A Synthesis', *Journal of Public Economics*, vol. 15, pp. 141–62.

Highway Research Board (1965) *Highway Capacity Manual* Special Report 87, Washington.

Meyer, J. R., J. F. Kain, and M. Wohl (1965) *The Urban Transportation Problem* (Cambridge: Harvard University Press).

Mills, E. and D. de Ferranti (1971) 'Market Choices and Optimum City Size', *American Economic Review*, vol. 61, pp. 340–45.

Mohring, H. (1976) *Transportation Economics* (Cambridge: Bellingers).
Mohring, H. (1965) 'Urban Highway Investment', in Robert Dorfman (ed.), *Measuring Benefits of Government Investments* (Washington DC: Brookings Institution) 233–41.
Sherman, R. (1971) 'Congestion Interdependence and Urban Transit Fares', *Econometrica*, vol. 39, pp. 565–76.
Solow, R. M. and W. Vickrey (1971) 'Land Use in a Long Narrow City', *Journal of Economic Theory*, vol. 3, pp. 430–47.
US Department of Transportation, Federal Highway Administration (1977) *Computer Programs for Urban Transportation Planning, General Information* (Washington DC) April.
Vickrey, W. (1963) 'Pricing in Urban and Suburban Transport', *American Economic Review*, vol. 53, pp. 452–65.
Vickrey, W. (1965) 'Pricing as a Tool in Coordination of Local Transportation', in *Transportation Economics*, National Bureau of Economic Research (New York: Columbia University Press) 275–91.

Comments on Eitan Berglas, David Fresko and David Pines, 'Right of Way and Congestion Toll' by Alan Auerbach

The paper by Berglas, Fresko and Pines (hereafter BFP) provides a useful analysis of the situation in which there are two modes of transportation (which they choose to call automobiles and buses) that may or may not be separated by route, and under conditions where it may not be possible to levy congestion tolls on one of the modes (automobiles). Their results compare optimal prices and congestion levels for the different modes under various assumptions about preference and technology, and for different cases with regard to route separation and the available automobile congestion taxes. The paper's results are clearly presented so I shall make some selective comments about how some of these results might be interpreted or extended.

My first comment concerns the specification of preference in expressions (1)–(3). It would seem that a less general utility function might be in order, given the nature of the problem. One might consider trips by automobiles and buses as intermediate inputs into a single consumption goods, transport, and see what effects this separability has. At present, all of the simplifying assumptions relate to the production side.

Before continuing, let me review the salient aspects of the model. There are two modes of transportation, automobiles and buses that may be provided with separate routes or may be forced to use the same route. The use of each mode causes congestion. A variety of assumptions are offered, and their effects analysed, concerning the technology of route provision, the technology of congestion and the sensitivity of different modes to the presence of congestion. In a competitive market it is assumed that each mode bears only the average cost of their trips, i.e. they do not internalise the congestion costs imposed on others. Under a first-best outcome, users pay Pigouvian taxes, and the planner chooses the preferred solution between pooled and separate routes.

The first results discuss how outcomes will compare under first-best allocations for the pooled and separate route regimes. The message of Proposition 3 is familiar from the literature on local public goods. Unless there are economies of scale in the provision of public goods – in this case the roads – there can be no benefits to pooling bus and automobile routes. When there are no costs in providing a given level of road services and, when the density function satisfies the homogeneity property provided, it would be possible to divide a single route into two and randomly sort buses and automobiles into two separate routes without affecting welfare. By thus sorting automobiles and buses, one can tailor the congestion levels for each route separately, thus improving welfare. This is analogous to sorting by taste in the demand for local public goods.

My last comment relates to the question of whether there should be a toll on bus traffic even when automobile traffic cannot be taxes. Here it should be emphasised that even with a toll, the traffic may be assessed at a price below its social marginal costs. Hence, it may be optimal to reduce the price on bus traffic as a response to suboptimality in the automobile market and still have a positive toll. Indeed, Proposition 5 shows that the fuel price of bus traffic is always higher under the first-best scheme than under the second-best scheme for the route separate regime. Whether the toll should be actually negative depends on various production and consumption elasticities, as described in expression (14-I) for the pooled regime and Proposition 6 for the separate regime. Here, I would argue with the authors' contention that it is more likely that buses will be subsidised under the pooled regime. Their intuition is that an increase in bus traffic is more desirable when routes are pooled, since this causes an increase in congestion suffered by automobiles, thereby raising their price towards a socially optimal level. However, let us compare condition (a) of Proposition 6 to expression (14-I), which, using the Slutsky equation may be written:

$$t_{\mathrm{I}}^{\mathrm{B}} \gtrless 0 \Leftrightarrow \frac{\eta_{a:P_{\mathrm{A}}} + \eta_{n:P_X}}{\eta_{A:P_{\mathrm{B}}}} \lesseqgtr \frac{\eta_{F\mathrm{B}:nB}}{\eta_{F\mathrm{B}:nA}} \qquad \text{(4-I}')$$

If A and X are substitutes, and A and B are substitutes as posited by Proposition 6, it is still possible for this ratio of elasticities to be less than unity, making it more likely for there to be a tax under the pooled regime.

Comment on Eitan Berglas, David Fresko, and David Pines, 'Right of Way and Congestion Toll' by Charles Wilson

This paper extends the existing literature on the problem of optimal congestion tolls to the case where the public authority can create separate lanes for different modes of transportation (e.g. cars and buses). They address the questions of how many lanes should be allocated to each mode and what toll should be levied on each mode of transportation. The model is analysed first under the assumption that a toll can be levied on both buses and cars and then under the assumption that a toll can be levied only on buses.

The analysis of the paper is clear and to the point. They go to considerable length to identify the kind of assumptions needed for each of their results, and the propositions are proved at the appropriate level of generality. They also distinguish in a neat parametric way the two relevant aspects of a transportation mode for determining the optimal congestion toll: (a) its effect on congestion; and (b) the effect of congestion on its cost (which they label 'aversion to congestion'). Presumably cars create more congestion per passenger than do buses, but buses are more averse to congestion than are cars. They also provide a specific functional form which captures each of these effects in a single parameter. These parameters could easily be estimated with appropriate data on the flow of traffic.

I have no serious criticisms of the paper. My main reservations are concerned not so much with what it contains, but with what it does not contain. I will confine my remarks, therefore, to a list of issues that might be addressed with this model.

The only real weakness of the paper is that there is no serious application of the model. Although the model is developed in a way ideally suited for empirical application, this possibility is not even discussed. Furthermore, except for one example in the appendix, there is very little discussion of which parameters of the model are likely to be significant. I would like to have seen more discussion of such questions as the sensitivity of the elasticity of congestion aversion to the form of the transportation mode and the sensitivity of the optimal toll to the different parameters of the model.

It might also be interesting to determine the conditions under which it is optimal to encourage more traffic when the possibility of taxing cars is eliminated. In the example presented in Appendix C, total capacity is the same in both cases. In that example, however, the cross price elasticities of demand are zero. Suppose that the cross price elasticities between the two modes are positive. Then the optimal toll on buses will tend to be lower to discourage car traffic. If in addition the inability to levy a toll on cars reduces the effective price of using a car, the bias would seem to be to encourage more traffic when cars cannot be taxed. In any case, these kind of results should be worked out in more detail.

Another possibility is to explicitly consider the case where the total number of lanes is fixed and the problem is simply to allocate them between the two modes. In the formal problem this amounts to simply replacing the marginal cost of capacity with the appropriate shadow price. The problem then will be to examine how the shadow price of capacity is related to the number of modes which can be taxed.

A related issue is what they briefly refer to as the integer problem. As they recognise, all of their qualitative results hinge on the ability to continuously vary the capacity of each mode. For many practical applications, this assumption may not be appropriate for all modes of transportation. In many cases, allocating even one lane to buses may provide sufficient excess capacity for buses so that the congestion costs are zero. In such cases, the bias they suggest in Proposition 6 toward taxing bus travel will be reversed. Assuming that the cross price elasticity between cars and buses is positive and there are no congestion costs for buses, their analysis implies that bus travel should be subsidised in order to reduce the use of cars. Another and perhaps even more important question to ask in this context is how much excess capacity in the bus lanes can be tolerated for the separation of lanes to be beneficial.

Finally, I think the paper could benefit by a little more discussion of the economic logic behind many of the results. For instance, the optimal density of each mode is determined by the requirement that the marginal cost of capacity be equated to the marginal reduction in congestion costs from increasing capacity. In some cases, this leads to a powerful separation property. Suppose that the cost of capacity is linear and the public authority can introduce separate lanes for cars and buses and suppose that a separate toll can be levied on both cars and buses. Then since the costs of congestion from the two modes are independent of each other, the optimal density of each mode (and hence the optimal toll) is independent of demand. Given the optimal density, demand determines only the size of the two lanes.

When only buses may be taxed, the separation property disappears. Since the marginal cost of car traffic is not equated to its marginal benefit, small changes in car traffic have first order welfare consequences. Consequently, the number of lanes devoted to car traffic must take into account not only the marginal reduction in congestion costs but also the effect on the level of car traffic. Similarly, the toll on buses must take into account both the congestion costs imposed by buses and the effect of an increase in the cost of bus travel on use of cars.

Similar arguments can be used to explain why higher congestion externalities imply higher densities and higher congestion aversion implies lower densities. A little more discussion of the logic behind these results would make the paper much more readable.

11 Corporate Taxation in the US*

Alan J. Auerbach

The US corporation income tax has been the focus of much criticism and debate during the past decade. Many hold it responsible for the low level of business investment in the US, and it has been criticised as a fundamentally unfair and illogical tax because it taxes corporations as independent entities, regardless of the tax brackets of individual shareholders. Much of the academic discussion in the 1970s about reform of the corporate tax centred on the 'integration' of corporate and individual income taxes, to make the corporate 'tax' essentially a withholding mechanism for the individual income tax.[1] More recently, the emphasis has shifted toward 'reform' by repeal, with President Reagan's call for the abolition of the corporate tax typical of this viewpoint.

Any analysis of the current economic effects of the US corporate tax should begin with the recognition of what has heppened over the years to corporate tax revenues. Put simply, the corporate tax has been disappearing. The marked drift in composition of federal revenues away from the corporate tax is illustrated in Table 11.1, which presents the revenues from the income tax, as a percentage of federal revenue and GNP, since 1953. The year 1953 is significant, for it was in 1954 that Congress passed the first of many tax acts that have successively shortened the permissible lifetimes over which tax deductions for depreciation could be taken and accelerated the pattern of depreciation deductions over such lifetimes. As of 1953, the common practice was to use straight line depreciation for tax purposes over

*This paper was presented at the Brookings Panel on Economic Activity, 15–16 September, 1983. I am grateful to Jim Hines and David Reishus for able research assistance, to Don Fullerton for providing unpublished data, to them and to Henry Aaron, William Brainard, Harvey Galper, Robert Hall, Mervyn King, George Perry, Emil Sunley, Alvin Warren and members of the Brookings panel for comments on earlier drafts, and to the Sloan Foundation for financial support through a Sloan Research Fellowship. The views expressed herein should not be attributed to any organisation with which I am associated.

Table 11.1 Sources of Federal revenues fiscal years 1953/88

	Individual income tax		*Corporate income tax*	
	% Federal Revenues	*%GNP*[b]	*% Federal Revenues*	*% GNP*[b]
1953	45.2	8.6	28.4	5.4
1954	46.0	8.3	26.3	4.7
1955	44.1	7.4	28.0	4.5
1956	44.0	8.0	28.2	5.1
1957	45.3	8.3	25.7	4.7
1958	46.5	8.1	22.9	4.0
1959	44.7	7.8	25.1	4.4
1960	44.8	8.4	23.5	4.4
1961	45.9	8.3	21.1	3.8
1962	45.4	8.4	21.8	4.0
1963	45.1	8.3	21.2	3.9
1964	43.9	8.0	22.2	4.0
1965	42.8	7.4	22.6	3.9
1966	43.3	7.6	23.2	4.1
1967	44.1	8.1	20.8	3.8
1968	44.7	8.2	20.7	3.8
1969	47.5	9.6	19.4	3.9
1970	48.3	9.5	16.9	3.3
1971	45.7	8.2	16.6	3.0
1972	47.1	8.5	16.0	2.9
1973	44.6	8.1	17.1	3.1
1974	45.2	8.6	16.0	3.0
1975	45.0	8.2	14.7	2.7
1976	43.6	8.0	16.7	3.1
1977	45.4	8.7	16.1	3.1
1978	45.0	8.6	16.2	3.1
1979	46.3	9.2	15.8	3.1
1980	47.6	9.5	13.3	2.7
1981	47.5	9.9	11.5	2.4
1982	49.0	9.9	8.1	1.6
1983[a]	47.2	8.9	6.6	1.3
1984[a]	45.1	8.4	8.5	1.6
1985[a]	44.9	8.4	9.1	1.7
1986[a]	45.0	8.3	9.6	1.8
1987[a]	45.2	8.3	10.1	1.9
1988[a]	44.6	8.3	10.0	1.8

[a]Estimated.
[b]For years 1953–82, fiscal year revenue are divided by calendar year GNP.
SOURCES 1953–7, Economic Report of the President, 1977; 1958–82, Economic Report of the President, 1983; 1983–8, Congressional Budget Office, Baseline Budget Projections for Fiscal Year 1984–8.

what were taken to be 'useful' lives for assets. In that year, the corporation income tax accounted for 28.4 per cent of federal receipts and 5.4 per cent of GNP. Of total income tax receipts, it accounted for 38.6 per cent. Throughout the late 1950s and most of the 1960s, corporate revenues provided about one-third of total income tax revenues. A familiar rule of thumb from that era was that tax cuts should be 'one-third business, two-thirds individual', perhaps reflecting this relatively stable ratio. By 1980, the year before passage of the Economic Recovery Tax Act, corporate revenues had declined to half the level that existed in 1953, relative to GNP. The experience since then, and estimates for the next five years, show important additional erosion in the corporate tax as a revenue source.

This steady downward trend stands in contrast to the stability of the individual income tax, which has ranged only between 42.8 per cent and 49.0 per cent of revenues over the same period, and between 7.4 per cent and 9.9 per cent of GNP. The corporate tax will provide revenue in 1983 equal to only a small fraction of the concurrent annual federal deficit. It is in light of this low level of receipts that many have called for the abolition of the corporate tax; though if the trend in Table 11.1 continues, little action toward this goal will be required. Yet this trend is the product of frequent changes in both tax policy and the economic environment. Changes in aggregate revenues convey only limited information about the economic impact of the corporate tax. Underlying these statistics are important distortions in the ways firms behave, with respect not only to the overall level of investment but also financial policy, asset choice, and the degree of risk-taking. The decline in corporate tax collections does not necessarily indicate a corresponding reduction in such distortions.

The purpose of this paper is to provide an economic analysis of the impact of the corporate tax in the US as it is now and has been during the post-war years. Among our findings are:

(1) Even accounting for inflation, the corporate tax wedge faced by fixed investment in the aggregate has declined steadily since the early 1950s. At its minimum, in 1981, the marginal corporate tax rate was less than one-third of its 1953 level;
(2) Despite this reduction in the average marginal tax rate, the misallocation of capital within the corporate sector that resulted from differential asset taxation, measured as a fraction of the corporate capital stock, increased over the same period, reaching an estimated peak of 3.90 per cent in 1973, and equalling 3.19 per

cent in 1981, with the passage of the Economic Recovery Tax Act.

(3) The lack of refundability for losses incurred by corporations presents firms having different earnings histories with different incentives to invest. Fully taxable firms quite possibly possess an advantage relative to those in the apparently favourable position of having previous losses to carry forward. This prospect has been increased by recent legislation accelerating depreciation schedules.

(4) The effect of inflation on the incentive to invest depends especially on the degree of corporate leverage and the gap between ordinary personal and corporate tax rates. Differences in assumptions about these parameters have led to greatly varying estimates of the impact of inflation, with the direction as well as the magnitude subject to dispute.

(5) Tax reform proposals should distinguish between tax revenues and marginal tax rates. Given the current pattern of asset taxation, much of the present value of revenues that will come from the corporate tax can be attributed to assets already in place. Hence, abolition of the corporate tax would accomplish a small reduction in the average marginal tax rate at the expense of a large, essentially lump sum transfer to the owners of existing capital. This transfer would have been approximately 427 billion dollars in 1981.

We begin with a review of the corporate tax and its provisions and how it has generated the pattern of revenues presented in Table 11.1.

THE CORPORATE TAX: 1953 TO 1981

The corporate tax is essentially a flat rate tax, with this rate currently equal to 46 per cent.[2] There has been little movement in the statutory corporate tax rate during the last three decades. As shown in the second column of Table 11.2, the rate was reduced from 52 per cent to 48 per cent by the 1964 tax cut, raised temporarily by the 10 per cent Vietnam War surcharge, and lowered again by the tax act of 1978 to its current level. Most of the 'action' in the corporate tax has come from changes in the tax base.

For a non-financial corporation investing in fixed assets, the tax base is derived by subtracting from gross sales the costs of inputs, including wages, materials and, through depreciation allowances,

Table 11.2 Average Corporate Tax Rates 1953–82

Year	*Corporate tax liability % corporate profits (w/CCA + IVA)*	*Statutory corporate rate*	*Difference*
1953	55.9	52.0	−3.9
1954	50.0	52.0	2.0
1955	48.4	52.0	3.6
1956	50.3	52.0	1.7
1957	49.4	52.0	2.6
1958	49.4	52.0	2.6
1959	47.6	52.0	4.4
1960	47.7	52.0	4.3
1961	46.9	52.0	5.1
1962	42.4	52.0	9.6
1963	42.2	52.0	9.8
1964	40.5	50.0	9.5
1965	38.6	48.0	9.4
1966	39.6	48.0	8.4
1967	39.4	48.0	8.6
1968	44.0	52.8	8.8
1969	46.4	52.8	6.4
1970	47.9	49.2	1.3
1971	45.1	48.0	2.9
1972	43.1	48.0	4.9
1973	45.2	48.0	2.8
1974	54.4	48.0	−6.4
1975	45.8	48.0	2.2
1976	46.2	48.0	1.8
1977	43.5	48.0	4.5
1978	43.2	48.0	4.8
1979	45.0	46.0	1.0
1980	46.6	46.0	−0.6
1981	42.6	46.0	3.4
1982	36.5	46.0	9.5

SOURCE *Economic Report of the President, 1983*, Table B-82.

capital costs, and interest payments. This base is effectively reduced when any of these components increases, or when tax credits are allowed against calculated tax liabilities. Through various legislation, there have been increases in levels of depreciation allowances and credits at any given level of income. Increases in the inflation rate have effected declines in depreciation allowances and measured materials costs and increases in interest payments.

Either through shortened tax lifetimes or increased speed of write-off over such lifetimes, depreciation allowances were accelerated in 1954, 1962, 1971 and 1981. All of these actions had the effect of increasing the present value of depreciation allowances received per dollar invested. The investment tax credit was introduced in 1962, briefly suspended in 1966, removed in 1969, reinstated in 1971, increased in 1975, and altered by both the 1981 and 1982 tax acts.[3] Thus, there has been a general *legislative* movement toward reduced corporate taxation, since most non-residential fixed investment is undertaken by corporations.

As has been emphasised by many authors,[4] inflation affects taxable corporate profits in three important ways. To the extent that the first-in, first-out (FIFO) inventory method is used, rising prices lead to an understatement of materials costs, and purely nominal 'inventory profits' are taxed. Because depreciation allowances are based on historic asset cost, their real value declines with price level increases. Finally, nominal interest payments include an inflation premium that is essentially a return of principal to bondholders. Yet these payments are fully deductible to the corporate borrower. This last effect works against the first two, to lower corporate tax liabilities, though there may be offsetting effects at the individual level, both with respect to the taxation of interest received and nominal capital gains on stock.[5]

The combined effect of changes in the tax law and, through changes in the inflation rate, implicit changes in the treatment of inventories and depreciation, can be seen in Table 11.2, which compares average corporate tax rates (corporate taxes as a percentage of corporate profits corrected with the capital consumption and inventory valuation adjustments) over the past thirty years with the statutory tax rates over the same period. (Since nominal interest payments are deducted from this profits measure, as well as the tax base but also tax payments.) The primary differences in the two tax rates for a given year come from investment tax credits and differences between estimated depreciation and materials costs and those actually deducted on tax returns. When the statutory rate exceeds the average rate, the effect of investment tax credits and accelerated depreciation allowances outweighs the erosion of such allowances and taxation of inventory gains caused by inflation.

The effects of both legislated and inflation-induced tax changes can be clearly seen in the table. In 1953, the average corporate tax rate exceeded the statutory rate. Since the inflation rate in that year was below 1 per cent, this must be due to the use of straight-line depreciation that was less generous than the economic depreciation estimated for the national income accounts. With the 1954 legislation, average tax rates fell below 52 per cent. The gap widened further with the introduction of the investment tax credit in 1962. As inflation increased in the late 1960s, the gap narrowed again, increasing with the additional tax incentives of 1971 and 1975, and decreasing in years of serious inflation, such as 1974. Except for the initial drop in the early 1950s, and the recent decline caused by the 1981 and 1982 legislation, there is no obvious trend in average corporate tax rates since 1953.

There are two factors that reconcile these results with the declining revenues shown in Table 11.1. First, the increase in nominal interest rates during the 1970s, combined with a relatively stable aggregate corporate debt–equity ratio,[6] decreased measured corporate profits as a fraction of GNP. Even with interest payments added back in, there is evidence that the total return to corporate capital declined during the 1970s.[7] Neither of these factors necessarily indicates a lessening of the impact of the corporate tax on behaviour, as we shall discuss below.

THE RECENT TAX ACTS

The Economic Recovery Tax acts of 1981 (ERTA) substantially reduced the corporate tax burden by replacing the system of numerous asset depreciation classes with three 'capital recovery' classes. Light equipment may be written off over three years, other equipment over five years, and business structures over fifteen years. The associated reduction in taxes was mitigated by the passage of the Tax Equity and Fiscal Responsibility Act of 1982 (TEFRA), which repealed accelerations in the write-off pattern that were to have occurred in 1985 and 1986, and instituted a 50 per cent basis adjustment for the investment tax credit. That is, investors receiving the 10 per cent investment tax credit now receive depreciation deductions on a base of 95 cents per dollar of capital purchased.[8] Another important change brought about by the 1982 act was the reduction and eventual repeal of the 'safe-harbour leasing' mechanism introduced by the 1981 act to facilitate the transfer of tax deductions and credits from one company (typically not with positive taxable income) to another. This last change is discussed in greater detail below.

The estimated net impact of ERTA and TEFRA on corporate tax revenues is evident in Tables 11.1 and 11.2. As a percentage of GNP, corporate tax collections were roughly one-third the 1953 level, while the average corporate tax rate fell to a new low in 1982.

IDENTIFYING THE APPROPRIATE MARGINAL TAX RATE

Many authors have used average tax rates such as those in Table 11.1, or related measures incorporating interest payments and personal taxes, to measure the impact of the corporate tax on the incentive to invest.[9] For many important reasons, however, such measures may fail to capture changes in the marginal tax rate on income from new capital investment.

1 Returns to Non-capital Factors

Corporations receive income from sources in excess of a competitive return to capital. The sources of such income may include but are not limited to the entrepreneurial ability of management and the exercise of market power. Since such income does not come from depreciable capital, nor does it qualify for an investment tax credit, it faces an effective tax rate equal to 46 per cent. Such taxation is not directly relevant to the incentive to invest in fixed capital, but is incorporated in measured average tax rates.

2 Returns to Old Capital

Even when the tax law is not changed over time (by legislation or inflation), assets of different vintages face different tax rates in a given year on the income they generate. This is easily illustrated by considering equipment purchased under the 1981 tax law. After five years, the equipment receives no depreciation allowances – its gross rents are fully taxed. In the year of its purchase, the equipment received not only a substantial depreciation allowance (15 per cent)[10] but also a 10 per cent investment tax credit. Because of the acceleration of depreciation allowances relative to actual depreciation, assets face higher taxes on the income they generate in later years relative to earlier years. Since each investment is made once, these tax rates must be combined in some useful way to derive the overall impact of taxation. Simple averaging over cohorts of assets in a given year is unlikely to give the correct answer. Moreover, with changes in the tax code, assets of older cohorts are currently being depreciated under tax rules that do not apply to new investment.

3 Anticipated Changes in the Tax Code

It does not require strong assumptions about rational expectations to conclude that investors may anticipate changes in the tax law: sometimes, these changes are legislated. Such was the case in 1981, when increases in the generosity of depreciation schedules were to take place in 1985 and 1986.[11] Since existing assets can generally not be converted to the new schedules, anticipated tax incentives can represent an implicit tax on current investment. This has long been recognised but is not accounted for in the computation of average annual tax rates.

4 Asymmetries in the treatment of Gains and Losses

The tax code imposes essentially two corporate tax rates: 46 per cent on positive taxable income and zero on negative taxable income. If a firm incurs a tax loss, it has two alternatives. If sufficient taxes were paid during the previous three tax years, the current tax loss may be 'carried back' and used to offset previous taxable income, with a resulting tax refund equal to 46 per cent of the current loss. To this extent, current losses do receive the same treatment as gains. If, however, the current loss exceeds the previous three years' taxable income, the excess must be 'carried forward', with the hope that future income will be sufficient to absorb it. Since losses carried forward do not accrue interest, they decline in present value at the nominal interest rate. The current limitation to carrying forward is fifteen years, increased from seven years by the 1981 act.

This feature of the tax code affects investment in two ways. First, firms currently carrying losses forward face a different pattern of expected deductions, credits and taxable income than firms currently taxable. Second, even taxable firms face the possibility of being non-taxable at some date in the future.

The law may have this feature in part as a protection against fraudulent 'losses' produced by fictitious companies, and the related problem of 'hobby' losses in which consumption expenditures are characterised by the taxpayer as business expenses. That it was perceived as a problem for legitimate businesses was evident when the Economic Recovery Tax Act included a provision making it easier for firms to transfer tax benefits to other firms through the guise of leasing. The complicated impact of this asymmetry cannot be captured by aggregate average tax rates. Different firms could face enormously different marginal tax rates on the same new investment because of differences in their current or anticipated status with regard to taxable income.

5 Risk

Average tax rates compare taxes to earnings, but these may have different risk characteristics. Corporate earnings are extremely volatile, while depreciation allowances are known with a fair amount of certainty, at least in nominal terms. The extent to which measured *ex post* tax rates accurately reflect the real burden imposed by the tax system, *ex ante*, has been the subject of much recent discussion.

In the remaining sections of this paper, we consider the impact of each of these issues. We begin by ignoring the questions of tax losses and risk and consider what has happened over the past thirty years to the incentive for corporations to make equity-financed investments in several classes of assets. The results enable us to compute not only aggregate marginal tax rates but also those faced by different industries. The differing incentives faced by different industries to invest in various assets produce a production distortion which we estimate, using the calculated tax rate series.

In succeeding sections, we analyse how these basic results are affected by a more realistic treatment of risk and the asymmetric tax treatment of gains and losses and how, in the presence of personal taxes and the corporate financial decision, inflation affects the incentive to invest. Finally, we estimate the extent to which accelerated depreciation has led to a reduction in the market value of corporate capital, relative to its replacement cost, in reflection of the deferred taxes faced by older assets. this phenomenon is important not only when interpreting trends in corporate tax receipts but also in the evaluation of tax reform proposals that would alter the relative treatment of old and new assets.

MEASURING EFFECTIVE TAX RATES ON CORPORATE CAPITAL

In this section, we focus on the problem of extracting marginal tax rates on prospective investments from observed tax collections. Our strategy is to use actual information on the composition of business-fixed investment in the US, and the tax law in each year, to derive the effective tax rates faced by individual investments in each year. These can then be aggregated to obtain overall effective tax rates. Because we focus only on fixed capital, we eliminate the problem posed by the existence on corporate returns of non-capital income. Because we consider each cohort of assets independently, the problem of aggregating vintages does not occur.

The basic formula giving rise to these calculations is the well-known Hall–Jorgenson user cost of capital:

$$c = q(r+\delta)(1-k-uz)/(1-u) \quad (1)$$

which expresses the instantaneous shadow price of a unit of capital (under the assumption that the tax law will remain fixed), where q is the relative price of capital goods, r is the real raie of return the firm must earn after corporate taxes, δ is the exponential rate at which the capital good decays, k is the investment tax credit, u is the corporate tax rate, and z is the present value of depreciation allowances, discounted at $r+\pi$, when π is the inflation rate.

Expression (1) implicitly assumes the use of equity finance, for if debt finance were used, r itself would depend on the tax rate u, because of the deductibility of interest payments. Letting b represent the fraction of its investment a firm finances with debt, with i the nominal interest rate and e the required nominal return of equity-holders before personal taxes, it can be shown that[12]

$$r = bi(1-u) + (1-b)e - \pi \quad (2)$$

Thus, by ignoring the impact of u on r, we are, essentially, calculating the effective corporate tax rate for an equity financed investment.

While interest deductibility is important, so are personal taxes on interest and equity income. The present calculations could be adjusted up or down to account for these additional taxes. Our present concern is with trends in the corporate tax itself.

At the margin, the firm will earn zero profits after tax, in present value, if it invests until the marginal product of capital equals c. We may define the effective corporate tax rate by asking what rate of tax, τ, on the corporation's true economic income would present the same incentive to invest, for a given rate r. Under an income tax, depreciation allowances would equal economic depreciation, and the investment tax credit would equal zero. Since economic depreciation per dollar of investment equals $(1-\delta)^t$, t years after the asset's purchase, the present value of such allowances would be $\delta/r+\delta$, and hence τ would be defined implicitly by the expression:

$$c=q\left(\frac{r}{1-\tau}+\delta\right) \tag{3}$$

where c is defined in (1). Combining (1) and (3) yields the solution for τ:

$$\tau=\frac{c/q-(r+\delta)}{c/q-\delta}=\frac{(r+\delta)(1-k-uz)-(r+\delta)(1-u)}{(r+\delta)(1-k-uz)-\delta(1-u)} \tag{4}$$

We apply (4) to historical data to determine the effective tax rates over time under the assumption that future tax changes were not anticipated. This has been the assumption that future tax changes were not anticipated. This has been the standard assumption in many related studies,[13] so the current calculations will facilitate a comparison of our results with those of others.

Our data come from various empirical sources and assumptions. For each asset, we assume depreciation practice followed was the most advantageous available to the investor in the year of investment. This rules out the use of straight-line depreciation in a year when, say, double-declining balance depreciation was available. Although there is evidence that not all businesses immediately switch to newly provided accelerated depreciation options,[14] modelling the causes of such behaviour is difficult without a more general model capable of explaining it. The detailed assumptions used about depreciation methods and lifetimes is presented in Appendix A. The asset classes themselves are those for non-residential investment used in national income account calculations, 34 in number. The real economic depreciation rate, δ, used for each asset class comes from calculations based on patterns of price declines in asset resale markets.[15]

The final pieces of information needed to calculate τ are the real discount rate, r, and the inflation rate π. Future values of π needed for the calculations of z are set equal in each year to those predicted from an ARIMA forecast based on lagged values of the inflation rate. Somewhat arbitrarily, we set r equal to 4 per cent.

Shown in Table 11.3 are the asset categories for which effective tax rates are calculated, along with their estimated rates of economic depreciation. Table 11.4 shows the historical series for the effective tax rates for two representative assets, in addition to the total annual rates, weighted by capital stock composition.

The table clearly shows the effects of both legislated tax changes and inflation. During the 1976–8 period, for example, there were no changes in the tax law. However, as inflation declined and then increased, so did effective tax rates. The same effect is evident between 1979 and 1980. The general results are consistent with time series estimates of the type done by Hulten and Robertson.[16] Even before 1981, the net effects of inflation and the tax law had been to keep tax rates during the 1970s, overall, at levels comparable to (or lower than) those in the mid-1960s. Adding the 1950s and the period 1981–2 leads to an overall picture of declining rates, a trend that is weaker than the decline in revenues in Table 11.1 but stronger than that of the average effective tax rates in Table 11.2. This demonstrates the importance of looking at marginal tax rates.

The overall trend in aggregate tax rates masks a very strong shift between structures and equipment that is typified by the two assets in Table 11.4. From 1953 to 1961, structures were favoured, relatively. Since then, almost all tax incentives have been aimed at equipment, with the widening gap in effective tax rates curbed somewhat in 1982, when the partial basis adjustment for the investment tax credit was introduced. This also served to remove, for the most part, the negative tax rates enjoyed by equipment in general.

Effective tax rates by industry also have varied substantially over the years. Complete time series for 44 corporate industries are shown in Appendix A. The values for 1982 are shown in Table 11.5. The rates range from a maximum of 39.4 per cent to a minimum of 6.3 per cent. The importance of such inter-industry distortions is discussed below.

Table 11.3 Asset categories and depreciation rates

	Asset category	*Depreciation rate*	*Percentage of 1978 corporate investment*
1	Furniture and fixtures	11.00	2.7
2	Fabricated metal products	9.17	1.7
3	Engines and turbines	7.86	0.7
4	Tractors	16.33	1.5
5	Agricultural machinery	9.71	0.2
6	Construction machinery	17.22	3.3
7	Mining and oilfield machinery	16.50	1.2
8	Metalworking machinery	12.25	3.5
9	Special industry machinery	10.31	2.9
10	General industrial equipment	12.25	4.1
11	Office, computing, and accounting machinery	27.29	4.7
12	Service industry machinery	16.50	1.8
13	Electrical machinery	11.79	10.4
14	Trucks, buses, and trailers	25.37	11.9
15	Autos	33.33	4.8
16	Aircraft	18.33	1.7
17	Ships and boats	7.50	0.8
18	Railroad equipment	6.60	1.7
19	Instruments	15.00	4.5
20	Other equipment	15.00	1.5
21	Industrial buildings	3.61	6.3
22	Commercial buildings	2.47	7.3
23	Religious buildings	1.88	0.0
24	Educational buildings	1.88	0.0
25	Hospital buildings	2.33	0.1
26	Other non-farm buildings	4.54	0.4
27	Railroads	1.76	0.5
28	Telephone and telegraph facilities	3.33	2.8
29	Electric light and power	3.00	7.1
30	Gas	4.50	1.1
31	Other public utilities	4.54	0.3
32	Farm	2.37	0.1
33	Mining, exploration, shafts and wells	5.63	6.1
34	Other non-building facilities	2.90	0.5

SOURCE Dale Jorgensen and Martin Sullivan, 'Inflation and Corporate Capital Recovery', in C. R. Hulten (ed.), *Depreciation, Inflation and the Taxation of Income from Capital* (Urban Institute, 1981).

Table 11.4 Effective tax rates by asset class 1953–82

	Asset class		
Year	*General industrial equipment* (10)	*Industrial buildings* (21)	*All assets*
1953	64.1	55.6	58.8
1954	61.0	52.3	55.5
1955	58.2	50.6	53.5
1956	59.3	51.3	54.3
1957	60.2	51.9	55.0
1958	60.9	52.3	55.6
1959	59.7	51.5	54.6
1960	60.4	52.0	55.1
1961	58.8	51.0	53.9
1962	40.3	49.1	43.3
1963	41.5	49.6	44.0
1964	27.4	47.1	37.2
1965	26.1	45.5	35.7
1966	27.4	45.8	36.5
1967	49.4	46.6	45.5
1968	37.0	51.5	43.5
1969	41.0	52.7	45.8
1970	53.5	52.0	49.7
1971	53.2	51.2	49.1
1972	16.4	51.2	32.9
1973	14.4	50.9	31.8
1974	18.3	51.5	33.9
1975	24.1	52.6	37.0
1976	26.4	53.1	35.1
1977	21.2	52.1	32.0
1978	23.2	52.4	33.2
1979	19.0	50.3	30.1
1980	22.0	50.8	31.9
1981	−6.8	41.7	17.7
1982	8.4	42.1	24.6

SOURCE See text.

Table 11.5 Effective tax rates by industry 1982

*Industry no.**	*Rate*
1	27.0
2	24.3
3	22.8
4	25.3
5	18.3
6	28.1
7	20.1
8	33.2
9	19.8
10	27.4
11	25.3
12	28.6
13	24.6
14	26.0
15	23.3
16	24.6
17	24.7
18	30.4
19	21.3
20	27.0
21	25.8
22	16.8
23	14.7
24	34.3
25	19.1
26	32.2
27	15.6
28	13.1
29	21.4
30	10.0
31	14.7
32	6.3
33	11.5
34	22.9
35	17.1
36	19.7
37	25.8
38	25.0
39	20.0
40	39.4
41	18.7
42	27.5
43	37.3
44	23.9

SOURCE Table 11.A1 in Appendix A.
*Industries by number are listed in Table 11.A2 in Appendix A.

THE DISTORTIONARY IMPACT OF DIFFERENTIAL CORPORATE TAXATION

One of the impressive facts about the effective tax rates in Tables 11.4 and 11.A1, is how much, in any given year, they vary across investments. Since the seminal work of Harberger,[17] there has been much concern about the distortion caused by the misallocation of capital between the corporate and non-corporate sectors, particularly housing. There has been relatively less emphasis until recently on the massive distortions among investments within the corporate sector, and within any given industry in the corporate sector. In part because of the complex way in which personal taxes interact with corporate taxes (discussed below), it is not clear that corporate investment faces a substantially higher overall tax rate than non-corporate investment. Thus, one of the strongest arguments for reforming the corporate tax would come from evidence that tax induced distortions within the corporate sector are important.

Little empirical work has been done on this topic. This is not surprising, given that it would require knowledge of elasticities of substitution among different types of capital and labour in production in each corporate industry, about which there is very little evidence. To provide some insight into this question therefore, we consider the distortion imposed by the corporate tax under what has come to be a fairly standard 'baseline' assumption: that each industry has a production function that is Cobb–Douglas in each type of capital used, and labour. Under this assumption, it is possible to compute a measure that answers the following question: given the vector of outputs being produced by the corporate sector, how much of the existing capital stock could be disposed of with no change in production, if the remaining capital were allocated optimally.

This measure of the welfare cost of differential corporate taxation is derived in Appendix B. It contains two components, each of which is non-negative. The first, which expresses the distortion due to differential taxation *within* industries, is zero only when there is uniform taxation within each industry. The second, which expresses the distortion due to differential taxation *between* industries, is zero only when the weighted geometric means of the before-tax rates of return in each industry are the same. The measure we derive is related to that obtained by Gravelle,[18] who also used the Cobb–Douglas assumption but aggregated the corporate sector into a single industry.

Application of this technique to the asset-specific effective tax rates yields the series in Table 11.6 for the fraction of the capital stock effectively wasted under the long-run allocation of capital according to the effective tax rates prevailing in that year.

These distortions show no downward trend, despite the steady decline in corporate tax collections. On the contrary, the overall loss has exceeded 1.54 per cent since 1972, whereas it was never as high before. The two components of the total distortion have generally moved together, with the 'within' component accounting for about

Table 11.6 The welfare cost of differential corporate taxation (per cent of capital stock)

	'Within' distortion	*'Between' distortion*	*Total distortion*
1953	0.59	0.13	0.72
1954	0.53	0.11	0.64
1955	0.37	0.07	0.45
1956	0.43	0.09	0.52
1957	0.48	0.10	0.58
1958	0.51	0.11	0.62
1959	0.45	0.09	0.54
1960	0.49	0.10	0.59
1961	0.40	0.08	0.48
1962	0.45	0.12	0.57
1963	0.41	0.11	0.52
1964	1.11	0.29	1.40
1965	1.01	0.26	1.27
1966	0.94	0.24	1.18
1967	0.25	0.04	0.29
1968	0.82	0.21	1.03
1969	0.62	0.16	0.78
1970	0.27	0.05	0.33
1971	0.27	0.05	0.32
1972	2.95	0.69	3.64
1973	3.17	0.74	3.90
1974	2.74	0.64	3.38
1975	2.18	0.50	2.69
1976	2.13	0.57	2.70
1977	2.69	0.71	3.40
1978	2.40	0.64	3.04
1979	2.52	0.67	3.19
1980	2.23	0.59	2.83
1981	2.64	0.55	3.19
1982	1.29	0.25	1.54

SOURCE See Appendix B

four-fifths of the distortion. Major increases in the degree of distortion occurred in 1964, with the repeal of the Long Amendment, and 1972, with the introduction of the Asset Depreciation Range. A smaller increase was associated with the 1981 legislation, while the basis adjustment instituted in 1982 substantially lowered the estimated distortion. To get a sense of the magnitude of the 1981 distortion, it implies that 3.19 per cent of the 1981 corporate capital stock of 2.05 trillion dollars[19] was being wasted. At a before-tax return of 8 per cent, this would imply a loss of over 5 billiion dollars in 1981. Moreover, it should be emphasised that this measure does not account for the additional distortions to the *mix* of outputs within the corporate sector and the relative levels of productions in the corporate and non-corporate sectors. One would expect these additional distortions to increase the estimated efficiency loss imposed by the corporate tax, perhaps substantially.

TAX LOSSES UNDER THE CORPORATE TAX

Over the years, as depreciation schedules have become more and more accelerated, the problem of firms without taxable income has become more important. This is easy to understand. Under the current tax law, an investor purchasing an asset in the five-year capital recovery class receives an immediate deduction of 15 per cent, a deduction of 22 per cent after one year (both on a basis equal to 95 per cent of purchase price) and an immediate investment tax credit. Gross receipts in the first year of at least 56.9 cents per invested dollar $((15+22)\times 0.95+10/0.46)$ would be required to absorb these tax benefits, even without accounting for the fact that investment credits cannot be used to offset all taxable income. Firms without substantial existing sources of income, or fast-growing firms, are likely to have to carry losses back or forward. Carrying losses forward, however, essentially reverses the benefits of accelerated depreciation. This problem provided an impetus for the introduction of 'safe-harbour' leasing under ERTA. To understand why this process was structured as it was and also why it was so unpopular, it helps to review why the current tax system discriminates against tax losses.

Aside from the administrative problems mentioned above, the lack of a loss offset in the tax system possibly derives in part from a perception among policymakers that losing firms are just that: 'losers'. For some reasons, the stockholders of such firms are unable to replace poor management or, for some other reason, the helping hand of government is necessary to discourage such firms. The benefit of having carryback and carryforward provisions, so this argument would continue, is that successful, risk-taking firms with an occasional 'bad draw' would lose little or nothing, while those with more permanent problems would benefit less from these provisions.

Aside from the questionable economic merit in discriminating among firms by the state of their income, there are at least two additional problems with this approach. First, even if 'losers' are initially discouraged from investing because of the prospect of non-refundable losses, once these losses have occurred, the desire to use them up through carrying forward may offer an increased incentive to invest in the future, to generate higher expected taxable income. Second, under a tax system which does not have economic income as its base, there need be no systematic relationship between a firm's taxable income and its underlying profitability. Indeed, under a system with accelerated depreciation, it is the firms whose capital stocks are growing fast that face the severest problem.[20]

'Safe Harbour' Leasing as a Solution

For years before 1981, leasing was recognised as a method for transferring tax benefits among firms. That many airlines leased some or all of their planes from financial institutions was well known. By making payments to the lessor over the period of the lease timed to coincide better with the income from the project, the lessee could obtain a greater part of the value of the tax benefits, which would be transferred by the lessor in the form of reduced lease payments.

But leasing could only be used for certain assets, essentially those which could be used by a firm other than the lessee at the expiration of the lease: planes, but not casts used to make cars of a particular model. Moreover, there were other provisions prohibiting lessee finance or a fixed repurchase price option, and requiring a 'reasonable' profit for the lessor before tax, which made leases imperfect as a transfer mechanism.

Most of these hindrances were removed in 1981, and the result was a spate of 'wash leases' under which cash changed hands only at the initiation of a lease, and title to the asset in question never left the possession of the user. In essence, the purchaser of the tax benefits (the lessor) received the investment tax credit and depreciation deductions in exchange for this initial 'down payment', plus a stream of future increases in tax liability resulting from the paper lease payments received exceeding paper interest payments made to the lessee by the amount of principal repayments on the paper loan made to the lessor initially to make up the difference between the down payment and the asset's full price. In addition to the down payment, the lessee received a stream of future decreases in tax liability mirroring those of the lessor.[21]

Safe-harbour leasing was criticised and scheduled under TEFRA for repeal after 1983, to be replaced by yet another type of leasing, referred to in the legislation as 'finance leasing'. From initial inspection, finance leasing appears to be a hybrid of safe-harbour leasing and the pre-1981 leasing, often referred to as leveraged leasing.[22] Much of the criticism took the form of declamations against 'welfare for corporations' and news stories relating the success of companies like General Electric in using leases to offset its current income tax liability as well as those of *previous* years (via a carry back) and Occidental Petroleum's use of leasing to enable it to use foreign tax credits that otherwise would have expired. Perhaps a more fundamental problem with leasing was that it was available to all investors.

In considering this problem, it is helpful to consider three extreme types of investor: the company with taxable profits now and for the foreseeable future (the 'taxable' company), the company with a substantial current tax loss being carried forward and little prospect for being taxable in the future (the 'tax-exempt' company), and the company undertaking large initial investments that generate large current deductions and credits that cannot be used, but with the prospect of taxable income in the near future (the 'start-up' company).[23] First, consider the case where no deductions are generated by the use of debt finance.

Under ACRS, the taxable investor purchasing an asset in the five-year capital recovery class in 1981 obtained a negative tax rate. As shown in Table 11.4, the present value of the investment tax credit and ACRS depreciation allowances slightly exceeded those that would have been proferred under a cash flow tax. For the start-up firm, however, this was not the case. By having to carry unused credits and deductions forward, the benefits of acceleration were lost. By engaging in a lease, the start-up company could get the full benefits, through the immediate downpayment and the future tax deductions, timed to occur after the company had become taxable. But 'tax-exempt' firms could engage in leases, too, and did so. Since such firms were already roughly in the same tax position as the taxable firms (concerning new investments), the receipt of the initial downpayment appeared to provide them with a substantial advantage. Given down payments under five year leases in the neighbourhood of 20 cents per dollar of investment, this was an important issue.

Once one considers the existence of debt finance, however, these results are altered. In particular, the tax-exempt firms face the additional disadvantage of not being able to deduct interest payments. Calculations by Warren and Auerbach[24] suggest that, for firms using all debt finance at the margin, leasing as structured under the 1981 act would have been inadequate to reduce the user cost of capital to that of the taxable corporation.

The Impact of Losses on the Incentive to Invest

'Taxable', 'start-up' and 'tax-exempt' companies are extreme cases that exist only in papers such as this. In reality, each firm has a finite probability of being taxable in a particular year in the future, given its current and past experience. In this section, we seek to determine how large an effect this has on incentive to invest. The question bears some similarity to those that arise in the literature on labour turnover, and the methodology is related, too. The basic approach involves observing individual firms over time, optimising subject to a particular tax system, and estimating the probabilities of a firm being taxable or not taxable in one year based on the experience of previous years. With such estimates, one can obtain the expected present value of taxes the firm will pay in connection with a new investment project, by translating the accrued tax lability (positive or negative) that the project generates in each year into a distribution of dates over which those taxes actually will be paid. Since we limit our consideration to marginal projects that do not affect the firm's probabilities, this is a straightforward calculation. Our calculations will be based on observations of the tax loss carryforwards of individual firms over time (data on annual accured tax liabilities are not available).

Under the tax law, a firm with a current tax loss may get a refund for this loss and hence may be viewed as taxable at the margin, if the nominal value of its previous three years' taxable income is at least as large. Such losses are said to be 'carried back' against previous income. A firm that has insufficient potential for carrying back must carry excess current losses forward, in the hope that their nominal value can be offset against future taxable income. Losses can now be carried forward for up to fifteen years. Before 1981, they expired after seven years.

One may think of current taxable profits in a symmetric way. If, for example, the firm has a larger loss carried forward from previous years, the profits are set against the loss carryforward; the firm pays no taxes and carries forward any excess to the next year. If the firm has a potential carryback in the form of previous taxable income, it pays taxes on its current income and adds it to the potential carryback that it has available in the following year.

Thus, we may summarise the firm's current tax status by a continuous variable y_t, equal to the value of its tax loss carryforward at the end of year t, when positive, and, in absolute value, the firm's potential carryback, when negative. Whether increments to a given year's tax liabilities are paid in year t or some later year depends on the sign of y_t. If y_t is negative, whatever additional taxes positive or negative) the firm owes are paid in year t. If y_t is positive, the firm can neither receive additional benefits nor pay incremental taxes at the margin in year t. The additional liability (perhaps negative) is added to the pre-existing loss carryforward and is ultimately paid (in fixed nominal terms) in the first subsequent year when y_t is negative. Thus, to calculate the expected present value of a particular dated tax liability, we must know the joint distribution of y_t and its past and future values.

The modelling of y_t is complicated, because its relation to past values depends both on the tax law and the characteristics of the firm. One would expect substantial serial correlation in y_t, since the current year's taxable income or loss may be small relative to the stock of losses carried forward or gains available for a potential carryback. However, y would decay even with a zero current tax liability, for two reasons. First, since an unused carryforward (or carryback) accrues without interest, there is a natural decay rate at the rate of inflation if y is measured in real terms. Moreover, the expiration of carryforwards and potential carrybacks imparts a further, vintage-related decay to y.

To the extent that a firm would normally expect taxable income in a given year, this will lead to decreases in y_t, whatever its value. The rate of this decrease, and its variance, would depend not only on the tax law (with respect to depreciation allowances, etc.) but also on the firm's overall level of profitability and the stochastic process generating its annual returns. Moreover, firms facing a loss carryforward may alter their behaviour to influence y, since the accrual of losses over time without interest provides an incentive to 'use them up'.[25]

Because even a simple specification of the evolution of y leads to fairly complicated procedure for the derivation of the conditional probabilities needed for our calculations, we summarise all the effects just mentioned by the first-order process:

$$y_t = \alpha + \beta y_{t-1} + \varepsilon_t \tag{5}$$

where the tax loss carryforward y_t is divided by a measure of the firm's assets to correct for potential heteroscedasticity. We use the estimated variance of ε_t along with the estimates of α and β to generate conditional distributions for y_t, conditional on its past value, under the assumption of normality. Using the estimated distribution of y_t conditional on y_{t-1}, that of t_{t-1} on y_{t-2}, and so forth, we generate the conditional probability that y_t exceeds zero, given information on whether each of y_{t-1}, y_{t-2}, ... exceeded zero. The distribution of actual tax payments deriving from a tax liability T_t dated year t then equals ${}_tp_0 \times T_t$ in year t, ${}_{t+1}p_{10} \times T_t(1-\pi_{t+1})$ in year $t+1$, ${}_{t+2}p_{110} \times T_t(1-\pi_{t+1})(1-\pi_{t+2})$ in year $t+2$, and so on, where π_t is the inflation rate in year t, and ${}_{t+i}p_{1,\ldots,10}$ is the probability that $y_{t+i} < 0$, conditional on $y_t, y_{t+1,\ldots,}y_{t+i-1} > 0$. With a perfect loss offset, p_0 (the unconditional probability of being taxable in year t) would equal 1, and the remaining probabilities would equal zero. The time it takes for the probabilities p_0,p_{10}, ... to converge to zero give us an estimate of how long a firm with a loss takes to become taxable.

To estimate equation (5), we used the Compustat data file, a panel of large American corporations. Our version of Compustat contains data from 1959 to 1978. The variable y, which we have defined to be the tax loss carryforward when positive and the potential carryback when negative is observed only when positive. That is, Compustat contains an annual observation for each firm on the tax loss carryforward but nothing on the potential carryback. Construction of such a number would require information on the previous three years' taxable income, which is unavailable. Thus, for many observations, we are missing either y_t, y_{t-1}, or both.

To obtain consistent estimates of α and β, we use the following technique. We first select all observations for which y_{t-1} is observed and, using a standard Tobit procedure, estimate (5). From this, we obtain predicted values of y_t for all these observations, including those for which the actual value is censored. Adding observations for which a predicted value of y_{t-1} is now available, we re-estimate (5).[26] For the first stage of the estimation we had available 1750 observations over the years 1959–77, with most of the observations occurring in the latter part of the sample. By the method just described for adding observations, an additional 317 observations were added to the original 1750 for the second stage of the estimation. The resulting equation is[27]

$$\underset{(0.009)}{y_t = -0.063} + \underset{(0.023)}{0.729\, y_{t-1}} \qquad \text{Standard error of estimate} = 0.348 \tag{6}$$

where standard errors are in parentheses, and y_t (when positive and observed) equals the firm's tax loss carryforward divided by a corrected measure of its net capital stock.[28] The coefficients α and β conform to prior expectations that the former should be negative and the latter between zero and one. This combination yields a long-run value of y_t that is negative and the decay to this long-run value of shocks away from it. The long-run value of y_t implied by (6) is -0.232; the typical firm would have available a potential carryback equal to 23.2 per cent of its net capital stock. Given typically observed before-tax rates of return, this represents approximately two years of profits, a reasonable figure.

This long-run value, however, is simply the mean of a long run distribution of y_t. It is the value to which y_t converges with no shocks of above average losses or gains. More generally, there will be a long-run probability distribution for y_t that depends on the magnitude of these shocks. By assuming that the annual random shock to y_t is normally distributed, with a standard deviation equal to the standard error of estimate in (6), we can calculate the long-run probability distribution for y_t. Using this long-run distribution, we can then calculate (using a numerical integration technique) the probabilities P_0, P_{10}, P_{110}, etc., as defined above: the unconditional probability of a gain in a given year, the probability of a gain following a loss, following two losses, and so forth, where 'gain' and 'loss' are defined in terms of the sign y_t. These probabilities are presented in Table 11.7. Even though the *expected* long-run value of y_t is negative, over 30 per cent of the long-run distribution of y_t is positive. One way to summarise the distribution is that it predicts that a tax payment accrued immediately would be paid, on average, 1.055 years later.

With these probabilities, we can estimate the effect of the asymmetric treatment of losses on the incentive to invest. This is done by first

Table 11.7 Estimated long-run transition probabilities

Number of years	*Probability that $y_t > 0$ for exactly this many years*
0	0.6926
1	0.1041
2	0.0599
3	0.0397
4	0.0277
5	0.0199
6	0.0144
7	0.0105
8	0.0077
9	0.0058
10	0.0044
11	0.0033
12	0.0025
13	0.0019
14	0.0014
15	0.0011
16	0.0008
17	0.0006
18	0.0005
19	0.0003
20	0.0010

SOURCE See text. The last probability equals the sum of all remaining values. It is assumed in our calculations that losses cannot occur for more than twenty years in a row.

positing a certain before-tax internal rate of return on an asset and an economic depreciation rate. With these, we generate a time pattern of marginal products for the asset. We assume that these returns are certain. Then, with an hypothesised pattern of depreciation allowances and investment tax credits, we calculate the pattern of accrued tax liabilities generated by the asset over time. These are then converted into an *expected* tax payment pattern using the probabilities in Table 11.7 and an assumed inflation rate. The latter is necessary since tax liabilities are carried forward in nominal terms, decaying in real terms through inflation. Finally, we calculate the internal rate of return for the firm's expected after-tax flows. Comparing this with the assumed before-tax return using equation (4) yields, as before, a value for τ, the effective tax rate.[29]

These rates are presented in Table 11.8 for two representative

Table 11.8 Effective tax rates: the impact of losses

	Asset			
	General industrial equipment		*Industrial buildings*	
Inflation rate	$P_0 = 1$	*Actual*	$P_0 = 1$	*Actual*
1965 tax law:				
0	13%	22%	38%	37%
0.04	33	37	52	47
0.08	48	47	58	52
1972 tax law:				
0	8	18	40	38
0.04	27	33	55	50
0.08	42	43	62	55
1982 tax law:				
0	−13	10	27	27
0.04	0	18	38	37
0.08	12	25	45	42

Tax rates labelled '$P_0 = 1$' assume tax payment occurs when liability is accrued. Those labelled 'actual' are based on Table 11.7, using the method described in the text.

assets, industrial buildings and general industrial equipment. A before-tax return of 6 per cent, is assumed, and the economic depreciation rates listed in Table 11.3 (0.0361 and 0.1225, respectively) are used. Estimates of τ for the tax laws of the mid-1960s, early 1970s and at present, and for inflation rates of 0, 4 per cent and 8 per cent are given. For comparison, we also present effective tax rates, comparable to those in Table 11.4, based on the assumption that taxes are paid when the liability is accrued.

It should be kept in mind, of course, that the estimates on which the probabilities are based come from a reduced form equation that would not necessarily be stable over changes in tax regime or economic environment. The value of P_0, for example, will undoubtedly be lower in the 1980s because of the tax changes enacted in 1981. Thus, estimates of the impact of losses for 1982 probably understate their actual importance. However, one can view the results as illustrations of the general magnitude of the effect that losses may have.

Table 11.8 has many interesting results. First, it shows the tax rates, including tax deferral, to be less sensitive to the inflation rate.

Moreover, tax rates are generally lower, once tax losses are accounted for, for structures, but higher for equipment. To understand this, it helps to consider the tax liabilities generated by gross rents and the benefits generated by depreciation deductions separately. The deferral of tax payments and receipts through losses may benefit or hurt the taxpayer, depending on the sign of the tax liability being deferred. It is possible that either effect can dominate the bigger the depreciation allowances, the more likely their deferral will lead to a net increase in tax rates. In general, then, the lower the effective tax rate, the more likely deferral will raise it. This is evident at zero inflation from a comparison of the values for the representative equipment and structure and is reinforced by the relative impact of inflation, which lowers the value of depreciation allowances an asset receives.

These calculations indicate how, in the long-run, the representative firm will be affected by the tax law. In any year, however, each firm will have a different tax history and, in our terminology, a different value of y_t. That firms face the same incentives in the long run should not be confused with the fact that a firm with a large loss carryfor-

Table 11.9 Effective tax rates: the impact of losses (by taxable status)

	Asset			
	General industrial equipment		*Industrial buildings*	
Inflation rate	*Low tax*	*High tax*	*Low tax*	*High tax*
1965 tax law:				
0	17%	12%	37%	37%
0.04	33	30	48	48
0.08	47	43	53	53
1972 tax law:				
0	12	7	40	38
0.04	28	23	52	52
0.08	40	35	57	57
1982 tax law:				
0	−3	−15	27	25
0.04	10	−3	37	35
0.08	20	5	42	42

Tax rates labelled 'high tax' assume initial value of y_t is one standard deviation below long-run mean. Those labelled 'low tax' assume initial value of y_t is one standard deviation above mean.

ward faces very different incentives than one with a large potential carryback. To evaluate this issue, we generated the matrices of annual loss probability distributions, one for a firm with an initial value of y_t one standard deviation below its long run mean (a 'high tax' firm), and one with an initial value of y_t one standard deviation above its long run mean (a 'low tax' firm). After several years, the entries in each matrix converge to the steady state probabilities listed in Table 11.7. In the short run, however, actual history is very important.

Effective tax rates for these firms, comparable to the columns labelled 'actual' in Table 11.8, are shown in Table 11.9. The striking result in this table is that the firms more likely to be taxable in the future (the 'high tax' firms) face *lower* effective tax rates. This is because, in the early years when the firm differences are greatest, accelerated depreciation allowances generate tax losses, especially for equipment. Being 'tax exempt' in these years, is a hindrance, not a help.

Thus, the asymmetric treatment of gains and losses under the corporate tax may lower or raise taxes for the average firm and is, under recent and current tax law, most helpful for firms with a history of taxable profits.

THE CORPORATE TAX AND RISK-TAKING

One of the fundamental reasons for the existence of public corporations is to allow risks to be efficiently diversified through the stock market. Various aspects of the corporate tax influence the extent to which the tax influences risk-taking. In addition to the discrimination against tax losses, which we have already discussed, there is the fact that uncertain inflation makes the value of depreciation deductions and nominal inventory profits uncertain. Uncertainty about future changes in the law themselves affect current decisions. However, much of the recent discussion has focused on the role of the corporate tax in sharing the private risks of corporations by collecting more revenue when profits are high and less when they are low.

In a provocative paper, Gordon[30] argued that the corporate tax, though collecting revenues, has roughly no real effects on behaviour. The argument is intuitively simple, and follows from the results of Tobin concerning the effects of taxation on risk-taking.[31] Tobin showed that a proportional income tax would exert no effect on the welfare of investors choosing between risky assets yielding an expected positive return and safe assets yielding a zero return, but would cause the undertaking of more private risk to compensate for the risk absorbed by the government through tax collections. Gordon pointed out that assuming these tax collections could not be made less risky through additional government risk-pooling, the need for them to be borne ultimately by households would just offset the induced desire to bear more risk, still without any change in individual welfare. In essence, under this view corporate tax revenues represent risky claims with exactly zero value that when taken away from households and then returned, exert no net impact on behaviour.

A corollary of this result is that to the extent that the safe return exceeds zero, a proportional tax affects investors only to the extent that it reduces that return. For example, suppose the expected return on risky assets is 12 per cent and the safe return is 2 per cent. An income tax at a rate of 50 per cent would reduce these to 6 per cent and 1 per cent, respectively. In risk-adjusted terms, however, the investor's loss would be a 1 per cent return.

This argument was criticised by Bulow and Summers,[32] who pointed out that the corporate income tax differs from the hypothetical one in Gordon's analysis in that it does not permit depreciation allowances to vary with *ex post* depreciation. The extent of the risk-sharing is confined to gross return. If the anticipated change in an asset's value is uncertain, none of this risk is borne through the provision of depreciation allowances that vary in real terms only because of inflation.

This issue can be analysed, in the context of effective tax rates. In Appendix C we show that the effective tax rate on a risky investment, defined as before to be the rate of tax on economic income that would yield the same incentive to invest as the current tax system, is:

$$\tau = \frac{(y+\bar{\delta}+\alpha_\delta)(1-k-uz)-(y)\bar{\delta}(\alpha_\delta)(1-u)}{(y+\bar{\delta}(\alpha_\delta)(1-k-uz)-(\delta+\alpha_\delta)(1-u)} \quad (7)$$

here the real, after-tax return, *r*, has been replaced by the safe return, *y*; δ, is now calculated using this rate plus the inflation rate; $\bar{\delta}$ is *expected* depreciation, and α_δ is the component of the risk premium required by investors because of the riskiness of asset value. Increases in the riskiness of depreciation, through increases in α_δ, have the same effect on the firm's decisions as increases in the expected depreciation rate itself. Hence, two assets with the same overall risk premium, expected rate of depreciation and depreciation allowance will normally face different effective tax rates, with the asset whose depreciation provides more of the overall asset risk being at a disadvantage. For this asset, the proportional tax on gross returns is of less value in the sharing of risks, because the returns are not as risky.

Unfortunately, while there is much evidence on the risk-free rate of return, little is known about the stochastic processes generating the returns from individual assets. Bulow and Summers pointed out that the annual volatility of the stock market was many times as great as that in gross corporate earnings, suggesting that the riskiness of asset values is the dominant risk facing investors. However, this does not imply that the individual assets owned by firms are as risky. For example, an airline that owns its fleet of planes may have a very volatile share price without the depreciated value of the planes themselves varying very much. More empirical work is needed on this issue for conclusions to be drawn.

None the less, it is useful to observe how the introduction of risk alters conclusions about effective tax rates, for a range of reasonable parameter values. Table 11.10 shows the values of τ under the 1982 law for an inflation rate of $\pi=0.06$, an assumed after-tax, risk-free return of $y=0.02$, and a range of values of α_δ from 0 to 0.06. The effective tax rate is calculated for two representative assets, where δ is set equal to the previously used values of δ in Table 11.3. We set the after-tax return lower to account for the fact that this is now meant to be a risk-free rate, and assume that depreciation allowances themselves are riskless, so that z is calculated using $y+\pi$ as the

Table 11.10 Taxation and risk.
The impact of stochastic returns on effective rates
(1982 tax law)
asset

δ	*General industrial equipment*	*Industrial buildings*
0.00	−21.8%	45.6%
0.02	−25.6	53.2
0.04	−29.7	59.0
0.06	−34.1	63.5

SOURCE Equation (10), with $y=0.02$, $\pi=0.06$ and δ taken from Table 11.3. Comparable values to Table 11.4 (with $y=0.04$ and $\alpha_\delta=0$) are −0.3 per cent and 39.7 per cent, respectively.

discount rate. The range of values for α_δ is meant to provide bounds for movements in τ. An asset for which $\alpha_\delta = 0.06$ has depreciation so risky that an additional *after-tax* return of 6 per cent is required over the risk-free rate (in addition to the risk premium associated with the variability of gross flows).

Looking at Table 11.10, we see that the use of a lower after-tax return, in itself, has an ambiguous effect on the estimated effective tax rate. For industrial structures, the decrease in the discount rate causes the effective tax rate, for $\alpha_\delta = 0$, to rise from 39.7 per cent to 45.6 per cent. For equipment, the rate declines from -0.3 per cent to -21.8 per cent. As with the impact of losses, there are several effects at work here. Moreover, as α_δ rises, the effective tax rates diverge.

In general, it may be shown that tax rates will increase with α_δ unless they are negative, in which case they will decline. Thus, the general expectation that effective tax rates increase with capital risk is valid, if we rule out negative tax rates (which would require a nominal discount rate of at least 11 per cent, for equipment).

INTEREST DEDUCTIBILITY AND PERSONAL TAXATION

One of the reasons why the corporation tax receipts have declined over time has been the increase in nominal interest rates, which combined with the deductibility of interest payments and the relative stability of the aggregate corporate debt–equity ratio led to an increase in interest deductions. We have generally ignored both interest deductibility and personal taxes until now, focusing primarily on tax issues related to the 'real' rather than the 'financial' side of corporate investment.

For many questions, however, these additional components of the income tax are crucial. Most obviously, the actual collections from the corporate tax decline with increase in corporate borrowing. Whatever the ultimate tax consequences at the individual level, this has implications about the probability of individual corporations failing to have taxable income, as well as concerning the viability of the corporate tax as an independent vehicle for raising revenues.

With respect to the overall incentive to invest in capital, it is important to know what the total tax wedge is between the return to corporations before tax and the return to holders of debt and equity after tax. Under competitive assumptions the identity of the entity remitting the actual tax payment is of little consequence.

Most discussions in this area require an understanding of how taxes influence the corporate decision between debt and equity finance for their investments. The stability of the aggregate debt–equity ratio at about one to three[33] requires some explanation, given the apparent tax advantage to debt finance. Since payments to stockholders in the form of dividends are not tax deductible but interest payments are, there appears to be a strong incentive to finance with debt. Reasons often given for the relatively limited use of debt involve both tax and nontax factors.[34]

Bankruptcy costs are often cited as a reason why corporations do not borrow more. A related argument concerns the increasing social cost that occurs with leverage by the ability of a firm to lower the value of their existing long-term debt through investment decisions making the firm riskier than had been anticipated.

On the tax side, there is a personal tax advantage to equity and a potential corporate tax disadvantage to debt that act to offset debt's apparent tax advantage. For any taxable investor, long-term capital gains receive favourable tax treatment via a 60 per cent exclusion and the advantage of deferral until the gains are actually realised. Moreover, the customary approach of weighting dividends and capital gains taxes to derive some overall personal tax rate on equity income has no justification, to the extent that marginal equity funds come through retentions, as the majority presently do.[35]

When investment is financed through foregone dividends, stockholders avoid paying dividend taxes. When the retentions and the additional earnings they generate are ultimately distributed, the dividends are taxed. In this manner, the dividend tax acts like a consumption tax, allowing deductions for saving via the corporation and taxing withdrawals. The net impact of such taxation is zero on new investment through retentions. The positive present value of dividend tax receipts comes from the fact the capital currently inside the corporation will be taxed upon distribution and that some equity funds will come from the sale of new shares, for which there is no corresponding personal tax deduction.

Even with the relatively small capital gains tax serving as the only effective individual tax on equity income, it remains difficult to argue that very many investors would have a tax preference for equity, given that the maximum personal tax rate on interest income is 50 per cent, only 4 points higher than the corporate rate at which interest payments are deducted. Moreover, evidence from bond markets suggests that individuals in tax brackets substantially below the top marginal rate can limit their tax liability by holding tax exempt municipal debt.[36] Hence the potential individual tax gain from holding equity versus debt would appear to be substantially below the corporate tax rate.

Even if increased leverage does not lead to a serious threat of bankruptcy, however, it does increase the probability that the full value of interest deductions will not be received. One recent study[37] using actual corporate tax returns for 1978 estimated that under 1983 tax law the average marginal tax rate at which interest payments would be deductible is 0.31 per cent, not accounting for the possibility of carrying these deductions back, nor the expected value from carrying them forward. Thus, assuming an individual tax rate on debt of below 30 per cent, there remains a small advantage to debt that can only be explained by non-tax factors such as those mentioned above.

One implication of this result is that firms or individual assets for which non-tax leverage costs are lower can take fuller advantage of borrowing and face a lower total effective tax rate. It has often been supposed that this is the case for structures, versus equipment.[38] This would be an important offset to the apparent distortion against structures imposed by the corporate tax. However, while highly leveraged purchase of apartment buildings and shopping centres by doctors and other professionals may be common, there has yet to be any convincing empirical evidence in favour of this argument for corporate level investment.[39] Thus, there is no evidence that the results derived above about differential taxation of assets would be qualitatively affected by the incorporation of interest deductibility and personal taxes in the calculations.

INFLATION AND THE EFFECTIVE TAX RATE

The primary reason why effective corporate tax rates did not fall appreciably during the 1970s was the steady increase in inflation over the period that decreased the value of depreciation allowances received, and led to the taxation of nominal inventory profits. For capital purchased by corporations, however, the overall incentive to invest is affected by inflation in three additional ways: through the increase in inflation premia on debt that are tax deductible, through the increased individual taxation of such premia, and through the taxation of capital gains of shareholders that are purely nominal in character. The aggregate impact of inflation has been the subject of several studies. Two major ones reached quite different conclusions about the sensitivity of the tax wedge on corporate source income to inflation.

Feldstein and Summers[40] estimated the total tax wedge by combining weighted average of estimated marginal tax rates of holders of corporate securities with average tax rates at the corporate level, and found the total tax rate to be very sensitive to inflation. For example, in 1970, they estimated a total effective tax rate on corporate source income of 76.8 per cent at an inflation rate of 5.5 per cent, with 26.6 per cent of the taxes collected due to inflation. This translates into a 3.3 percentage point increase in the total effective tax rate per percentage point increase in the inflation rate.

Using a cost of capital methodology such as that used in this paper to account for both corporate and individual taxes, King and Fullerton,[41] found both a lower tax wedge and a smaller sensitivity to the inflation rate. Under the same 1970 tax law, they estimated that a rise in the inflation rate from zero to $6\frac{2}{3}$ per cent would have raised the estimated effective tax rate by 3.5 percentage points, from 43.7 to 47.2 per cent, or 0.5 percentage points per percentage point increase in the inflation rate.

There are many methodological reasons why these estimates differ. Estimates of the impact of inflation are particularly sensitive to assumptions about the marginal tax rate faced by recipients of corporate interest payments. As shown in Appendix D, the total effective tax rate, accounting for interest deductibility and the taxes paid by the holders of corporate securities, can be written:

$$\tau=\frac{(r+\delta)(1-k-uz)-(n+\delta)(1-u)}{(r+\delta)(1-k-uz)-\delta(1-u)} \tag{8}$$

where

$$r=n\left[b\frac{1-u}{1-\theta}+(1-b)\frac{1}{1-c}\right]+\pi\left[b\frac{\theta-u}{1-\theta}+(1-b)\frac{c}{1-c}\right] \tag{9}$$

is the real, after corporate tax return, as before, and n is the net return to investors, after all taxes.

Using expressions (8) and (9), we can estimate the marginal impact of inflation on τ for different assets and tax parameters. This is done in Table 11.11 for two representative assets under the current tax system. In all calculations, we set $r=0.04$, $c=0.05$, and $u=0.46$, and

Table 11.11 The sensitivity of taxes to inflation effective tax rates

	General industrial equipment			Industrial buildings		
Inflation rate	*Low*	*Intermediate*	*High*	*Low*	*Intermediate*	*High*
0.00	−70.9	−54.0	−45.5	13.5	22.1	26.4
0.04	−46.5	−21.1	−7.5	16.2	30.7	38.5
0.8	−35.3	−3.8	13.2	15.0	34.7	45.5

SOURCE See text; 'low' estimates set $b=0.5$ and $r=0.2$; 'medium' estimates set $b=0.25$ and $r=0.2$; 'high' estimates set $b=0.25$ and $r=0.4$.

estimate effective tax rates at different inflation rates under different assumptions about the parameters θ and b.

As can be seen, the introduction of interest deductibility and personal taxes has the effect of lowering the overall effective tax rate on both equipment and structures. At low levels of inflation, the different assumptions lead to relatively similar results. However, as inflation increases, the size of b and the wedge between u and θ is crucial. For the intermediate case in which the debt–assets ratio is set at 0.25 and the personal tax rate at 0.2, the effective tax rate on equipment rises from −54.0 per cent to −3.8 per cent, while that on structures rises from 22.1 per cent to 34.7 per cent. The general result that the tax rates faced by short-lived assets more sensitive to inflation has been documented before.[42] Raising the assumed personal tax rate on interest income from 0.2 to 0.4, in line with Feldstein and Summers, makes both tax rates rise more rapidly. On the other hand, setting $b=0.5$ instead of 0.25 essentially removes the effect of inflation on the structures tax rate. Since it has been argued that observed debt–assets ratios may understate *marginal* leverage,[43] this, too, could be a reasonable assumption to make. Hence, it appears difficult to measure with any degree of certainty the impact that inflation has on the effective tax rates facing fixed investment.

ASSET VALUATION AND DEFERRED TAXES

Just as aggregate revenues from the corporate tax are often cited as evidence of the tax's overall impact, it is customary to measure the effects of investment incentives in terms of associated reductions in annual tax receipts. The error involved in doing so can be quite severe.

For example, suppose there were a change in the timing of depreciation allowances that accelerated their rate of receipt but compensated for this with a lower base on which the allowances were calculated, with the net impact on the present value of these depreciation allowances being nil. There would be no impact on the incentive to invest, nor would there be any obvious reason why the shortfall in government revenue caused by the earlier deduction of depreciation allowance would have an effect on saving: owners of assets receiving these 'tax cuts' would also receive the promise of having to repay them in the future, with interest. By assumption, the government has not given them a *net* increase in resources.

This argument might seem to carry over directly to the case of all taxes: if the government, in the long run, repays its debt, lower taxes today must be compensated for by higher ones in the future. The difference here is that with capital assets future taxes are immediately capitalised. One does not have to believe in Barro's altruistic families[44] to conclude that a pure change in the timing of tax payments will be neutral. It is not even necessary that the owners of such assets look beyond the present. This neutrality is the result of simple arbitrage. Assets that already have received a tax benefit but now are liable for future 'deferred taxes' are less attractive to the investor than comparable new assets that have yet to receive the initial benefits.

Consider, for example, a five year old piece of equipment under current law which has no remaining depreciation deductions or investment tax credits. For it, the value of $k+uz$, in the terminology used above, is zero. The cash flows that it generates in the future will be fully taxable. A comparable new asset is more attractive (*after* adjustment for differences in real productivity), because for it the value of $k(uz$ is non-zero. Hence, its price will be higher, by the ratio $1/(1-k-uz)$.

A second source of old assets carrying a discount is the general practice of introducing investment incentives that apply only to new assets. It has often been suggested that investment tax credit increases or the acceleration of depreciation allowances provide more 'bang for the buck' in terms of reductions in the cost of capital per dollar of revenue lost. This is not surprising, given that such incentives do not lower the effective tax rate on existing capital goods, while such changes as corporate rate reductions would. The increased gap between the taxation of old and new assets caused by such investment incentives leads to a further discount in the value of old assets, relative to new ones.[45] A corollary is that when there is inflation, old assets will be discounted because their depreciation allowances are based on a lower price index than those of new assets.[46]

When older assets face higher effective tax rates than new ones, we may think of the resulting discount in their price as being caused by an implicit obligation to the government to pay taxes in excess of those due on comparable new assets. Such a convention is useful in thinking about how accelerated depreciation works. Moreover, it is the case that an investor purchasing such an asset could offset this 'loan' by committing the difference in the price of two assets to government debt, using the interest payments to cover the extra taxes due in the future. Hence, any tax system is equivalent to a tax on true economic income that imposes the same effective rate on new assets as the current system and extends this rate to old assets as well, combined with a liability of asset owners to the government equal to the total discount in old assets under the current system.

Making such a correction is important, because tax revenues in a given year can change for many reasons: a change in the corporate tax burden in general, a change in the relative tax burdens on old and new assets, or a change in the timing of the collections. These have very different 'substitution' effects via the cost of capital, and very different 'income' effects through changes in the value of existing assets. It is impossible to draw any general conclusion from a drop in current corporate revenues, about whether the incentive for corporations to invest has increased or whether potential crowding out has been increased through an increase in private wealth.

For example, an increase in the statutory corporate tax rate, combined with a further acceleration of depreciation allowances aimed at maintaining the same incentive to invest in new capital, would increase the present value of corporate tax receipts, essentially via a lump-sum tax on existing capital. This may be thought of as the owners of such capital being forced to assume an additional debt to the government. The real effects of such a policy would be equivalent to that of a one-time tax used to retire government debt, a scheme without direct substitution effects that would reduce crowding out. Yet, as measured, this policy would quite possibly appear to increase the current deficit, due to the acceleration of depreciation allowances on new capital.[47] It would clearly be desirable to adjust annual corporate revenues to include changes in the value of the deferred tax liability of asset holders to the government. Such an adjustment requires an estimate of the size of the discount on existing capital due to the tax system.

To estimate the value of an existing unit of capital, note that at any time the value of the after-tax flows from a new unit of capital equals its purchase price. Normalising this price to 1, we have:

$$1=(1-u)F+k+uz \tag{10}$$

where F is the present value of the asset's before-tax flows and u, k and z are as defined in expression (1). For an existing capital good of age t, which under the assumption of geometric decay is equipment in terms of productivity to $(1-\delta)^t$ units of new capital, the value is:

$$v^t=(1-u)F(1-\delta)^t+uz^t \tag{11}$$

where z^t is the present value of depreciation allowances that remain for the asset. The ratio of value to replacement cost of such an asset, its 'q' value, is:

$$q^t=\frac{v^t}{(1-\delta)^t}=(1-k-uz)+\frac{uz^t}{(1-\delta)^t} \tag{12}$$

This value equals one when $z^t=(1-\delta)^t(k+uz)$: assets receive tax benefits proportional to their productivity or physical value. This would be true under a tax on economic income, for then $k+uz$ would equal $\delta/r+\delta$ and z^t would equal $[\delta/(r+\delta)]/(1-\delta)^t$. Generally, however, q^t is below one. Even without the intentional acceleration of depreciation allowances, inflation causes the present value of old allowances based on original asset purchase prices to fall well short of the value of allowances new assets receive.

Using equation (12), we estimated the values for q^t for all vintages of each of the 34 asset classes from 1953 to 1982, ignoring tax law changes before 1953. These vintage-specific values of q were aggregated into yearly, asset-specific average of q under the assumption that each net asset stock grew over the period at a growth rate of 4 per cent.[48] Using the capital stock weights described in Appendix A, these were then aggregated to form a single series for the overall value of average q, shown in the first column of Table 12. The series is characterised by a downward trend. In the 1950s, average q values actually exceeded unity for some assets. With the investment tax

Table 11.12 Average values of '*q*' implied by the corporate tax law

Year	*Average* *q*	*Implied Revenue Adjustment (in billions of 72$)*
1953	0.921	—
1954	0.898	7.6
1955	0.908	−2.6
1956	0.924	−4.7
1957	0.935	−3.4
1958	0.940	−1.9
1959	0.940	0.1
1960	0.946	−2.1
1961	0.945	0.5
1962	0.894	21.0
1963	0.900	−2.0
1964	0.893	4.0
1965	0.898	−0.4
1966	0.899	1.9
1967	0.927	−12.9
1968	0.889	22.6
1969	0.890	1.8
1970	0.928	−21.8
1971	0.926	1.9
1972	0.867	40.1
1973	0.864	5.1
1974	0.865	1.9
1975	0.867	−1.2
1976	0.845	17.3
1977	0.834	10.2
1978	0.835	1.6
1979	0.838	0.7
1980	0.838	2.6
1981	0.781	60.8
1982	0.792	NA

SOURCE See text.

credit, accelerated depreciation and inflation, these values fell. Large reductions occurred with the tax changes of 1962, 1972 and 1981. The corporate rate reductions in the mid-1960s and late 1970s had no observable impact, since they applied uniformly to old and new capital. Note also that q increased in years when the treatment of new capital goods was made less favourable, as with the removal of the investment tax credit in 1967 and again in 1970.

As suggested above, this divergence of average 'q' from one is essentially a deferred tax liability of holders of existing assets. The second column of Table 11.12 shows the adjustments to annual revenue that would be made if such debt were explicitly accounted for. The numbers equal each year's change in the value of the implicit debt,[49] less real, after-tax interest payments on the stock of such debt, based on a return of 2 per cent. By this measure, corporate tax revenues were really 134.6 billion (current) dollars higher than reported in 1981, because of the substantial increase in the implicit debt held by owners of existing capital.

THE FUTURE OF THE CORPORATE TAX

As a fraction of GNP, the corporate tax now raises less than a third of what it did three decades ago. While effective marginal tax rates on investment have declined accordingly, the distortions of the corporate tax structure have not. The calculations in Table 11.6 suggest a steadily worsening allocation of fixed capital with the US corporate sector.

Many other problems remain, too. The use of accelerated depreciation and the investment tax credit to reduce effective tax rates have made the problem of tax losses more acute. Any resemblance between economic income and taxable income that existed thirty years ago has vanished, and many profitable companies, particularly those that are growing, cannot use all their tax benefits. Though effective tax rates are lower than they were in the 1970s, they still are sensitive to the inflation rate, because of the use of nominal magnitudes in calculating the tax base. Moreover, the choice between debt and equity finance remains distorted by the presence of two levels of taxation of corporate source income.

Given the low level of corporate revenues at present, abolition of the corporate tax has its appeal. Such a move would certainly alleviate some of the problems just alluded to. At the same time, however, it would be a singularly ineffective way of stimulating investment, providing reductions in average tax rates much more than in marginal tax rates.

As shown in Table 11.4, the effective corporate tax rate on new, equity financed fixed capital is now below 25 per cent. Removal of the corporate tax would bring this rate to zero but also eliminate the substantial benefit of interest deductibility and thus would probably result in a very small net reduction in taxation for new investments. At the same time, repeal of the corporate tax would result in the forgiving of the implicit debt owed the government in deferred taxes, currently in excess of 20 per cent of the fixed corporate capital stock. Given the capital stock's 1981 replacement cost of 2.05 trillion dollars,[50] this amounts to a strictly inframarginal transfer of 427 billion dollars.

The continued interest in the consumption tax as an alternative to the individual income tax and, indeed, the recent move towards such a tax via the sheltering of individual capital income also provide an argument for removing the corporate tax, for capital income would not be taxed under a consumption tax. An alternative scheme that would have the same marginal impact without the windfalls is a cash flow tax, discussed in detail by the Meade Committee in the United Kingdom[51] as a companion for a personal consumption tax. Like a consumption tax, it would amount to a tax on the difference between initial assets plus income and final assets in each tax period, in this case at the corporate level. The most straightforward method of accomplishing this would be through the immediate expensing of gross investment (real plus financial) in conjunction with the continued taxation of gross income, before depreciation. The chief drawback of the cash flow tax, however, is that it does not solve the problem of tax losses in the way that repeal of the corporate tax would. Otherwise, the two alternatives differ only in the size of the wealth transfer to owners of corporations.

If any alternative to outright repeal of the corporate tax is to be adopted, some solution to the problem of tax losses appears needed. Straightforward economic solutions exist: allowing unlimited carrying forward with interest for example, would maintain the protection against fraudulent loss claims while at the same time preserving the value of tax deductions for viable enterprises. But one should be educated by the recent legislative fiasco involving safe-harbour leasing. This is an area of tax policy where common perceptions seem particularly resistant to economic evidence.

APPENDIX A

In this appendix, we discuss the methodology used to calculate effective tax rates in the text and present time series for each of the 44 industries for which 1982 tax rates are presented in Table 11.5.

The first step in these calculations is to estimate each asset's effective tax rate according to equation (4) in the text. As already stated, we assumed investors all used accelerated methods where available. Investments are assumed to take place midway through the year, with the investment credit and (before 1981) half the first full year's depreciation allowances received immediately. Marginal products and remaining depreciation allowances are assumed to come at subsequent one year intervals.

The major changes in the tax code taken account of, in chronological order, are:

1954 Introduction of accelerated methods; all assets assumed to use double-declining balance with a switchover to straight-line, instead of straight-line previously assumed.
1962 Introduction of a 7 per cent investment tax credit (with full basis adjustment) and shortened Treasury 'guideline' lifetime, instead of Bulletin F lifetime previously assumed.
1964 Repeal of basis adjustment for investment tax credit. Cut in corporate tax rate from 52 per cent to 50 per cent.
1965 Cut in corporate tax rate from 50 per cent to 48 per cent.
1967 Suspension of investment tax credit.
1968 Introduction of 10 percentage surcharge on income tax.
1969 Reinstatement of investment tax credit.
1970 Removal of investment tax credit; reduction of surcharge; reduction of structures write-off to 150 per cent declining balance, with switchover to straight-line.
1971 Removal of surcharge.
1972 Shortening of asset lives through the asset depreciation range system; reintroduction of investment tax credit.
1975 Increase of investment tax credit to 10 per cent.
1979 Reduction in corporate tax rate from 48 per cent to 46 per cent.
1981 Economic Recovery Tax Act, as described in text.
1982 Tax Equity and Fiscal Responsibility Act, as described in text.

The years listed are the first for which the changes are included. Generally, we counted any change in the year enacted if it was effective before July 1 of that year. Otherwise, it was deferred to the following year.

Special tax rules apply to public utility structures and oil drilling equipment. The latter category is problematic, since there are various depletion and write-off provisions that are difficult to capture in the current framework. Here, we followed the assumptions used in King and Fullerton,[52] to which the reader is referred for further discussion.

Table 11.A1 Industry by industry number

Industry IDs
1. Food and kindred products
2. Tobacco manufacturers
3. Textile mill products
4. Apparel and other fabricated textile products
5. Paper and allied products
6. Printing, publishing, and allied industries
7. Chemicals and allied products
8. Petroleum and coal products
9. Rubber and miscellaneous plastic products
10. Leather and leather products
11. Lumber and wood products, except furniture
12. Furniture and fixtures
13. Stone, clay and glass products
14. Primary metal industries
15. Fabricated metal industries
16. Machinery except electrical
17. Electrical machinery, equipment and supplies
18. Transportation equipment, except motor vehicles, and ordnance
19. Motor vehicles, and motor vehicle equipment
20. Professional photographic equipment and watches
21. Miscellaneous manufacturing industries
22. Agricultural production
23. Agricultural services, horticultural services, forestry and fisheries
24. Metal mining
25. Coal mining
26. Crude petroleum and natural gas extraction
27. Non-metallic mining and quarrying, except fuel
28. Construction
29. Railroads and railway express service
30. Street railway, bus lines and taxicab service
31. Trucking service, warehousing and storage
32. Water transportation
33. Air transportation
34. Pipelines, except natural gas
35. Services incidental to transportation
36. Telephone, telegraph, and miscellaneous communication services
37. Radio broadcasting and television
38. Electric utilities
39. Gas utilities
40. Water supply, sanitary services, and other utilities
41. Wholesale trade
42. Retail trade
43. Finance, insurance and real estate
44. Services

To convert these asset-specific rates into industry rates, we used the capital stock matrix also used by King and Fullerton. This 44 by 34 matrix has entries equal to the estimates of the net stock of each type of the 34 assets present in each of the 44 industries, for 1977. This matrix is converted to a corporate version using estimates for each industry of the fractions of equipment and structure in the industry which are held by corporations. The capital stocks themselves were derived by Fraumeni and Jorgenson,[53] using data on capital flows and annual levels of industry by industry investment. Further details are provided by King and Fullerton.

Using this fixed-weight matrix, we derived the industry tax rates for each year, which are shown in Table 11.A1.

APPENDIX B MEASURING THE DEADWEIGHT LOSS FROM DIFFERENTIAL CORPORATE TAXATION

Suppose that value added in industry i can be represented by the Cobb–Douglas production function:

$$Y_i = a_i \prod_j K_{ji}^{\alpha_{ji}} X_i^{1-\beta_i} \left(\beta_i = \sum_j \alpha_{ji} \right) \tag{B1}$$

where K_{ji} is the capital stock of class j used in industry i and X_i is labour used in industry i. With no loss of generality, we can define capital stock units so that the relative price of each capital good, q_j, equals one.

Consider first the case where capital is allocated according to the actual costs of capital imposed by the market. By the normalisation that $q_j = 1$, the cost of capital type i is

$$c_j = \frac{r-\pi}{1-\tau_j} + \delta_j = \rho_j + \delta_j \tag{B2}$$

where τ_j is the effective tax rate, $r-\pi$ is the real, after-tax return (assumed to be 4 per cent) and δ_j is the asset's depreciation rate. We may think of corporate sector allocation as being made by a single, competitive firm seeking to maximise profits, which equal gross output (including depreciation) less the cost of capital, subject to the constraint that the vector of actual outputs, $Y = (Y_1, \ldots)$, be produced and the economy's actual stock of labour, $\bar{X}$, be used. This yields a Lagrangian expression for the actual capital stock, K^a:

$$K^a = \max \sum_i (a_i \Pi K_{ji}{}^{\alpha_{ji}} x_i{}^{1-\beta_l} + \sum_j \delta_j K_{ji} - \sum_j c_j K_{ji})$$

$$- \sum_i \theta_i (a_i \Pi K_{ji}{}^{\alpha_{ji}} X_i{}^{1-\beta_i} - \bar{Y}_i) + \varphi(\sum_i X_i - \bar{X}) \tag{B3}$$

the first-order conditions from (B3) may be combined to yield:

$$K^a = \sum_i \left(\frac{\varphi^{(1-\beta_i)} \tilde{\rho}_i^{\beta_i} \tilde{Y}_i}{\nu_i} . \sum_j \frac{a_j}{r_j} \right) \tag{B4}$$

where

$$\sum \left(\frac{\varphi^{-\beta_i}(1-\beta_i)\tilde{\rho}^{\beta_i} \bar{Y}_i}{\nu_i} \right) = \bar{X} \tag{B5}$$

$$\nu_i = a_i \pi_j \alpha_{ji}{}^{\alpha_{ji}} (1-\beta_i)^{(1-\beta_i)} \tag{B6}$$

and

$$\tilde{\rho}_i = \prod_j \rho_j{}^{(\alpha_{ji}/\beta_i)} \tag{B7}$$

is the weighted geometric mean of the required, before-tax rates of return in industry i.

Expressions (B4) and (B5) can be simplified. Note that, under competitive conditions, the total supply of labour, $\bar{X}$, satisfies:

$$\bar{X} = \frac{1}{w} \sum_i (1-\beta_i) Y_i \tag{B8}$$

(where w is the competitive wage) and the technological term ν_i also equals:

$$\nu_i = \tilde{\rho}_i^{\beta_i} w^{1-\beta_i} \tag{B9}$$

We may choose, the units of labour so that $w = 1$, with no loss of generality, and use (B8) and (B9) to re-express (B4) and (B5):

$$K^a = \sum_i \varphi^{(1-\beta_i)} \bar{Y}_i \cdot \sum_j \frac{\alpha_j}{\rho_j} \tag{B10}$$

where

$$\sum_i (\varphi^{-\beta_i} - 1)(1-\beta_i)\tilde{Y}_i = 0.$$

The solution to (B11) is $\varphi = 1$. This is not surprising, since (see (B3)) φ is the shadow price of labour, i.e., the market wage.

The minimum capital stock necessary to produce $\bar{Y}$, holding $\bar{X}$ fixed, is found by solving the Lagrangian:

$$K^* = \min \sum_i \sum_j K_{ji} - \sum_i \lambda_i \left(a_i \prod_j K_{ji}^{\alpha_{ji}} X_i^{1-\beta_i} - \bar{Y}_i \right) + \gamma \left(\sum_i X_i - \bar{X} \right) \tag{B12}$$

Using the same solution technique as before, we obtain:

$$K^* = \sum_i \frac{\gamma^{(1-\beta_i)} \beta_i \bar{Y}_i}{\nu_i} \tag{B13}$$

where

$$\sum_i \left(\frac{\gamma^{-\beta_i}(1-\beta_i)\bar{Y}_i}{\nu_i} \right) = \bar{X} \tag{B14}$$

Again using (B8) and (B9), we may rewrite (B13) and (B14) as:

$$K^* = \sum_i \gamma^{(1-\beta_i)} \tilde{\rho}_i^{-\beta_i} \beta_i \bar{Y}_i \tag{B15}$$

where

$$\sum_i ((\gamma\tilde{\rho}_i)^{-\beta_i} - 1)(1-\beta_i)\bar{Y}_i = 0 \tag{B16}$$

The term γ may be thought of as the inverse of a weighted average aggregate cost of capital term. Were $\tilde{\rho}_i$ constant across i, it would equal $1/\gamma$. For purposes of exposition, we define $\bar{\rho} = 1/\gamma$. Subtracting the expression for K^* from that for K^a yields an expression for the 'wasted' capital stock:

$$\Delta K = \sum_i Q_i \sum_j \left(\frac{\alpha_{ji}}{\beta_i} \right) \left(\frac{\tilde{\rho}_i}{\rho_j} - 1 \right) + \sum_i Q_i \left[1 - \left(\frac{\tilde{\rho}_i}{\bar{\rho}} \right)^{(1-\beta_i)} \right] \tag{B17}$$

where

$$Q_i = \bar{Y}_i \beta_i \tilde{\rho}_i^{-1} \tag{B18}$$

It may be shown that the first sum on the right-hand side of (B17) achieves a minimum of zero when $\tilde{\rho}_i = \rho_j \forall_{i,j}$, and that the second term achieves a minimum of zero when $\tilde{\rho}_i$ is constant over *i* and (by (B16)) equal to $\bar{\rho}$. Hence, it is natural to interpret these terms as the wastage due to variation in effective tax rates within industries, between them, respectively. Dividing (B17) by (B10) gives an estimate of the *fraction* of the capital stock that is wasted:

$$L = \frac{\Delta K}{K} = \frac{\sum_i Q_i \sum_j \left(\frac{\alpha_{ji}}{\beta_j}\right)\left(\frac{\tilde{\rho}_i}{\rho_j} - 1\right) + \sum_i Q_i \left[1 - \left(\frac{\tilde{\rho}_i}{\bar{\rho}}\right)^{(1-\beta i)}\right]}{\sum_i Q_i \sum_j \left(\frac{\alpha_{ji}}{\beta_i}\right)\left(\frac{\tilde{\rho}_i}{\rho_j}\right)} \tag{B19}$$

To solve (B19), we set β_i equal to the share of capital in value added in industry *i* taken from the 1972 Census of Manufacturers. Y_i equal to that value added, and use the 1977 capital stock weights described in Appendix A for (α_{ij}/β_i). Because three of our 44 industries (38–40) are combined in the Census (which has 42 industry categories), we combine these three industries' capital stocks in doing the calculations. The terms ρ_j come from each year's estimated effective tax rates by asset category.

APPENDIX C ESTIMATING THE EFFECTIVE TAX RATE ON RISKY ASSETS

The analysis in this section uses the methodology presented in Alan J. Auerbach, 'Evaluating the Taxation of Risky Assets', NBER Working Paper no. 806, November 1981.

Suppose capital of a certain type is homogeneous and depreciates each year at some stochastic rate, $\tilde{\delta}$, yielding a risky cash flow, $\tilde{f}$, per unit of capital. Assume for simplicity that $\tilde{\delta}$ and $\tilde{f}$ are each independently and identically distributed over time with means δ and $\bar{f}$, respectively.

Let *i* be the discount rate that, when applied to the mean $\bar{f}$, yields the risk-adjusted present value of $\bar{f}$. Define *x* similarly for δ, and let *y* denote the risk-free rate.

For ease of notation, observe that any system of depreciation allowances and investment tax credits has the same value to the investor, *ex ante*, as a scheme that allows fractional economic depreciation at rate ψ. With this simplification, and because of stationarity and independence of $\tilde{f}$ and $\tilde{\delta}$, we may consider the firm as facing a series of identical one-period decisions. The condition for equilibrium is that the risk-adjusted one period holding yield equals the interest rate, or

$$\frac{\tilde{f}(1-u)}{1+i}-\frac{\tilde{\delta}}{1+x}+\frac{u\psi\tilde{\delta}}{1+x}=\frac{y}{1+y} \tag{C1}$$

where, as before, u is the statutory tax rate.

To solve for ψ, we must know the present value of economic depreciation. The value of this period's depreciation is $\delta/1+x$. Next period's value is the value seen from next period per dollar of capital, also $\delta/1+x$, times the present value of capital at the beginning of next period,

$$\left(\frac{1}{1+r}-\frac{\delta}{1+x}\right).$$

Continuing in this way, we obtain the present value of economic depreciation:

$$z_E=\frac{\tilde{\delta}}{1+x}+\left(\frac{1}{1+y}-\frac{\tilde{\delta}}{1+x}\right)\frac{\tilde{\delta}}{1+x}+\ \cdots\ \left(\frac{1}{1+y}-\frac{\tilde{\delta}}{1+x}\right)^{t}\frac{\tilde{\delta}}{1+x}+$$

$$\cdots=\frac{\delta}{\delta+y\left(\dfrac{1+x}{1+y}\right)} \tag{C2}$$

Thus, if actual depreciation allowances provide value z, and there is an investment tax credit at rate k, we obtain:

$$\psi=\frac{k+uz}{u\tilde{\delta}}\left[\delta+y\left(\frac{1-x}{1+y}\right)\right] \tag{C3}$$

which, substituted into (C1), yields:

$$\frac{\left[\dfrac{\tilde{f}(1-u)}{1-k-uz}\right]}{1+i}-\frac{\delta}{1+x}=\frac{y}{1+y} \tag{C4}$$

which can also be written:

$$\left(\frac{\bar{f}(1-u)}{1-k-uz}-\bar{\delta}\right)=y+\alpha_f\left(\frac{1-u}{1-k-uz}\right)+\alpha_\delta \tag{C5}$$

where

$$\alpha_f=\bar{f}\left(\frac{i-y}{1+i}\right) \tag{C6.a}$$

$$\alpha_\delta=\bar{\delta}\left(\frac{y-x}{1+x}\right) \tag{C6.b}$$

The terms α_f and α_δ are the risk premia associated with the riskiness of $\bar{f}$ and $\bar{\delta}$, respectively. At one extreme, where only f is risky, the asset's annual returns are independent. At the other extreme, with only δ risky, the asset's annual return follows a random walk with a drift of $-\bar{\delta}$.

We once again define the effective tax rate as that particular rate that would provide the same incentive to invest as the current system. Since under an income tax at rate τ the equilibrium condition for holding period yield is:

$$\frac{\bar{f}(1-\tau)}{1+i}-\frac{\bar{\delta}(1-\tau)}{1+x}=\frac{y}{1+y} \tag{C6}$$

we can combine (C5) and (C6) to solve for the effective tax rate analogous to equation (4) in the text:

$$\tau=\frac{(\bar{f}-\alpha_f)-(y+\bar{\delta}+\alpha_\delta)}{(\bar{f}-\alpha_\delta)-(\bar{\delta}+\alpha_\delta)}$$

$$=\frac{(\bar{y}+\delta+\alpha_\delta)(1-k-uz)-(\bar{y}+\delta+\alpha_\delta)(1-u)}{(y+\bar{\delta}+\alpha_\delta)(1-k-uz)-(\bar{\delta}+\alpha_\delta)(1-u)} \tag{C7}$$

The effective tax rate is precisely that which would apply in the absence of risk for a risk-free rate y and an economic depreciation rate $\bar{\delta}+\alpha_\delta$. Hence, there are two corrections in order for the effective tax rates calculated above: replace the return r with a risk-free return and, as suggested by Bulow and Summers,[54] consider economic depreciation to be at rate $\bar{\delta}+\alpha_\delta$.

APPENDIX D INFLATION AND THE COST OF CAPITAL

As used in the text, the corporation's cost of capital is

$$c = q(r+\delta)(1-k-uz)/(1-u) \tag{D1}$$

where the real discount rate, r, is based on a weighted average of the nominal returns to debt and equity, i and e:

$$r = bi(1-u) + (1-b)e - \pi \tag{D2}$$

We assume all equity finance comes through retentions. In the current context of measuring the marginal sensitivity of taxes to inflation, this is not an important issue.

As shown in Auerbach, 'Wealth Maximization and the Cost of Capital', when marginal equity finance is through retentions, the effective tax rate on equity is c, the accrual-equivalent rate of tax on capital gains. Letting θ be the personal tax rate on interest income, and assuming, for simplicity, that equity and debt yield the same real after-tax return, n, then (D2) may be written (see Auerbach, 'Inflation and the Tax Treatment of Firm Behavior')

$$r = bn\left(\frac{1-u}{1-\theta}\right) + (1-b)\frac{n}{1-c} + \pi\left[b\frac{\theta-u}{1-\theta} + (1-b)\frac{c}{1-c}\right] \tag{D3}$$

the second term accounts for the change in the corporation's after-tax cost of funds, r, as the result of the taxation of nominal interest payments and nominal capital gains at the individual level and the deductibility of nominal interest payments by corporations.

Using n rather than r as the base for our calculations, we can compute the total effective tax rate, including corporate and personal taxes, using expression (4) in the text.

Notes

1. See Charles McLure, *Must Corporate Income Be Taxed Twice?* (Brookings Institution, 1979), and Martin Feldstein and Daniel Frisch, 'Corporate Tax Integration: The Estimated Effects on Capital Accumulation and Tax Distribution of Two Integration Proposals', *National Tax Journal*, vol. 30 (March 1977), pp. 37–52.
2. Under current law the first $100,000 of a corporation's income is taxed at rates below the maximum rate of 46 per cent. The only important class

of corporation taxpayers without most income in the top bracket are companies with negative taxable income that face a tax rate of zero. This is discussed further below.

3. For a historical review of these changes, see Alan J. Auerbach, 'The New Economics of Accelerated Depreciation', *Boston College Law Review*, vol. 23 (September 1982), pp. 1327–55.
4. See, for example, John B. Shoven and Jeremy I. Bulow, 'Inflation Accounting and Nonfinancial Corporate Profits: Physical Assets', *BPEA 3:1975*, pp. 557–98. T. Nicholaus Tideman and Donald P. Tucker, 'The Tax Treatment of Business Profits Under Inflationary Conditions', in Henry J. Aaron, ed., *Inflation and the Income Tax* (Brookings Institution, 1976), pp. 33–77; Martin S. Feldstein and Lawrence Summers, 'Inflation and the Taxation of Capital Income in the Corporate Sector', *National Tax Journal*, vol. 32 (December 1979), pp. 445–70, and Alan J. Auerbach, 'Inflation and the Tax Treatment of Firm Behavior', *American Economic Review*, vol. 71 (May 1981, *Papers and Proceedings, 1980*), pp. 419–23.
5. Estimates of the inflation-induced tax payments at the individual level are presented in Feldstein and Summers, 'Inflation and the Taxation of Capital Income in the Corporate Sector.'
6. For more detail on this debt-equity ratio see Roger H. Gordon and Burton G. Malkiel, 'Corporation Finance', in Henry J. Aaron and Joseph A. Pechman, eds, *How Taxes Affect Economic Behavior* (Brookings Institution, 1981), pp. 131–96.
7. This point is the subject of some dispute. Although Martin Feldstein and Lawrence Summers, 'Is the Rate of Profit Falling?' *BPEA, I:1977*, pp. 211–28, argue that observed declines were primarily cyclical, recent evidence presented in Barry Bosworth, 'Capital Formations and Economic Policy', *BPEA, 2:1982*, pp. 273–317, makes a compelling case for a secular decline in the rate of return to capital.
8. These changes are described in more detail in Auerbach, 'The New Economics of Accelerated Depreciation'.
9. See, for example, Feldstein and Summers, 'Inflation and the Taxation of Capital Income in the Corporate Sector'.
10. The 15 per cent allowance corresponds to half of the first year of depreciation permitted a five-year asset under the 150 per cent declining balance formula. The so-called half-year convention built into the 1981 formulas gives assets a half year of allowances during the first year, irrespective of purchase date.
11. Because such changes were repealed in 1982, fully rational investors might have anticipated this in 1981 and expected no change to occur in 1985 and 1986.
12. Studies that have calculated effective tax rates using this methodology include Charles Hulten and James Robertson, 'Corporate Tax Policy and Economic Growth: An Analysis of the 1981 and 1982 Tax Acts' (Washington, DC: Urban Institute, 1982), and Mervyn King and Don Fullerton, eds, *The Taxation of Income from Capital: A Comparative Study of the US, UK, Sweden and West Germany* (National Bureau of Economic Research, 1984). The first of these studies, like this one, looks

only at taxes at the corporate level, while the second also includes the effects of corporate interest deductibility and personal taxes.

13. Studies that have calculated effective tax rates using this methodology include Charles Hulten and James Robertson, 'Corporate Tax Policy and Economic Growth: An analysis of the 1981 and 1982 Tax Acts' (Urban Institute, 1982), and Mervyn King and Don Fullerton (eds), *The Taxation of Income from Capital: A Comparative Study of the U.S., U.K., Sweden and West Germany* (NBER, 1984). The first of these studies, like the current one, looks only at taxes at the corporate level, while the second also includes the effects of corporate interest deductibility and personal taxes.
14. See Terence Wales, 'Estimation of an Accelerated Depreciation Learning Function', *Journal of American Statistical Association*, 61 (December 1968) pp. 995–1009, and Thomas Vasquez, 'The Effects of the Asset Depreciation Range System on Depreciation Practices', US Treasury, Office of Tax Analysis Paper, no. 1, May 1974.
15. These depreciation rates are presented in Dale Jorgenson and Martin Sullivan, 'Inflation and Corporate Capital Recovery', in C. R. Hulten (ed.), *Depreciation, Inflation and the Taxation of Income from Capital* (Urban Institute, 1981). Most of the depreciation rates were originally calculated and presented by Charles Hulten and Frank Wykoff, 'The Measurement of Economic Depreciation', in C. R. Hulten (ed.), *Depreciation, Inflation and the Taxation of Income from Capital.*
16. Charles Hulten and James Robertson, 'Corporate Tax Policy and Economic Growth: Analysis of the 1981 and 1982 Tax Acts' (Washington, D.C.: Urban Institute, 1982).
17. Arnold C. Harberger, 'Efficiency Effects of Taxes on Income from Capital', in M. Krzyzaniak (ed.), *Effects of the Corporation Tax* (Wayne State University Press, 1968).
18. Jane G. Gravelle, 'The Social Cost of Nonneutral Taxation: Estimates for Nonresidential Capital', in C. R. Hulten (ed.), *Depreciation, Inflation and the Taxation of Income from Capital.* Her measure also differed in the use of a Cobb–Douglas function for gross rather than net output. While the former approach may be conceptually more appealing, only the latter allows a closed form solution in the multi-industry case. This difference helps explain why our estimate of excess burden is somewhat higher for 1981, since the elasticity of substitution is higher when the net Cobb–Douglas function is used.
19. John C. Musgrave, 'Fixed Reproducible Tangible Wealth in the United States', *Survey of Current Business*, October 1982.
20. These issues are explored more fully in Alan J. Auerbach, 'The Dynamic Effects of Tax Law Asymmetries', *Review of Economic Studies*, 53(2) (April 1986) pp. 205–225.
21. Leasing is described more fully and a sample wash lease worked out, in Auerbach, 'The New Economics of Accelerated Depreciation'.
22. The 1982 changes are discussed and analysed in Alvin C. Warren and Alan J. Auerbach, 'Tax Policy and Equipment Leasing after TEFRA', *Harvard Law Review*, 96(7) (May 1983) pp. 1579–98.
23. The following discussion draws on the arguments in Alvin C. Warren

and Alan J. Auerbach, 'Transferability of Tax Incentives and the Fiction of Safe-Harbor Leasing', *Harvard Law Review* 95(8) (June 1982) pp. 1752–86.

24. Warren and Auerbach, 'Transferability of Tax Incentives and the Fiction of Safe Harbor Leasing'.
25. This is discussed in Auerbach, 'The Dynamic Effects of Tax Law Asymmetries'.
26. The argument for doing so is that otherwise α and β will be derived only from observations for which y_{t-1} is negative. Any asymmetry in the equation connected with the sign of y_{t-1} would not be discernible. In fact, this two-stage procedure, in principle, allows estimation of individual values of α and β depending on the sign of y_{t-1}. Unfortunately, such an experiment proved unsuccessful, as the coefficient for negative values of y_{t-1} was estimated with insufficient precision.
27. Since the two stages were estimated separately, these standard errors lack the adjustment necessary to account for the fact that some values of y_{t-1} are estimated. However, given that such observations are a small part of the sample, and that the standard errors are so small relative to the coefficients, we did not attempt such a correction for the current draft.
28. This capital stock measure was calculated for the Compustat firms and is described by Clint Cummins, Bronwyn Hall and Elizabeth Laderman, 'The R&D Master File: Documentation', mimeo, August 1982.
29. These calculations are based on a fixed before-tax return, rather than those above, which started with the after-tax return and generated a before-tax return. The difference lies only in that the overall levels at which the two rates are compared will normally differ.
    A second point about τ is that it implicitly assumes risk neutrality with respect to the risky tax payments. This makes sense if the risk is entirely diversifiable. Otherwise, additional corrections of the type discussed in the next section will be necessary.
30. Roger H. Gordon, 'Taxation of Capital Income: Tax Revenues versus Tax Distortions' (Bell Labs, 1981).
31. James Tobin, 'Liquidity Preference as Behavior Towards Risk', *Review of Economic Studies* 25(1) (February 1958) pp. 65–86.
32. Jeremy Bulow and Lawrence Summers, 'The Taxation of Risky Assets', NBER Working Paper no. 897, June 1982.
33. See Gordon and Malkiel, 'Corporation Finance', and Robert Taggart, 'Secular Patterns in the Financing of U.S.', in B. Freidman (ed.), *Corporate Capital Structure in the United States* (NBER, forthcoming).
34. See Roger Gordon, 'Interest Rates, Inflation and Corporate Financial Policy', *Brookings Papers on Economic Activity* (1982(2), pp. 461–88, for a review of these theories.
35. This point is developed in the literature in Mervyn King, 'Taxation and the Cost of Capital', *Review of Economic Studies*, 41(1) (January 1974) pp. 21–35, Alan J. Auerbach, 'Share Valuation and Corporate Equity Policy', *Journal of Public Economics*, 11(3) (June 1979) pp. 291–305, and David Bradford, 'The Incidence and Allocation Effects of a Tax on

Corporate Distributions', *Journal of Public Economics*, 15 (April 1981) pp. 1–22. For a detailed discussion of its implications, see Alan J. Auerbach, 'Taxation, Corporate Financial Policy and the Cost of Capital', *Journal of Economic Literature* (September 1983) pp. 905–40.

36. The estimates in Gordon and Malkiel, 'Corporation Finance', put the marginal tax rate implicit in municipal debt at between 20 per cent and 30 per cent, before the tax reduction of 1981.
37. Joseph Cordes and Steven Sheffrin, 'Estimating the Tax Advantage to Debt', *Journal of Finance* 38(1) (March 1983) pp. 95–105.
38. This point of view is stated, for example, in Robert E. Hall, 'Tax Treatment of Depreciation, Capital Gains and Interest in an Inflationary Economy', in G. R. Hulten (ed.), *Depreciation, Inflation and the Taxation of Income from Capital* (Urban Institute, 1981).
39. In Alan J. Auerbach, 'Real Determinants of Corporate Leverage', in B. Friedman (ed.), *Corporate Capital Structure in the United States* (NBER, forthcoming), I found no evidence using firm panel data (which included information on asset composition) that structures were financed more heavily with debt than equipment. I did find, however, that the presence of a tax loss carryforward exerted a negative impact on leverage, as would be expected.
40. Martin Feldstein and Lawrence Summers, 'Inflation and the Taxation of Capital Income in the Corporate Sector'.
41. Mervyn King and Don Fullerton (eds), *The Taxation of Income from Capital: A Comparative Study of the U.S., U.K., Sweden and West Germany*.
42. See Alan J. Auerbach, 'Inflation and the Choice of Asset Life', *Journal of Political Economy*, 87(3) (June 1979) pp. 621–38.
43. See Joseph Stiglitz, 'Taxation, Corporate Financial Policy and the Cost of Capital', *Journal of Public Economics*, February 1973.
44. Robert Barro, 'Are Government Bonds Net Wealth?' *Journal of Political Economy* (November/December 1974) pp. 1095–1117.
45. This presumes old assets are not sold to take advantage of the new provisions. Even ignoring transaction costs, such behaviour would only yield a net reduction in taxes for a small fraction of the capital stock, because of the tax treatment of the sale and the limited availability of the investment tax credit for used assets. See Auerbach, 'The New Economics of Accelerated Depreciation', and Alan J. Auerbach and Laurence Kotlikoff, 'Investment versus Savings Incentives: The Size of the Bang for the Buck and the Potential for Self-Financing Business Tax Cuts', in L. H. Meyer (ed.), *The Economic Consequences of Government Deficits*, 1983.
46. See Auerbach, 'Inflation and the Choice of Asset Life'.
47. An example of this problem of confusing changes in timing and changes in the tax burden came in the discussion of my proposal with Dale Jorgenson (Alan J. Auerbach and Dale Jorgenson, 'Inflation-Proof Depreciation of Assets', *Harvard Business Review*, September/October 1980), to give investors the discounted value of economic depreciation allowance in the year of an asset's purchase. While our original proposal

would not have lowered effective tax rates on capital in the aggregate, some viewed it as infeasible because of the large 'deficits' it would have produced in the initial years of its application.

48. This is the annual growth rate of the net corporate stock of fixed non-residential capital from 1952 to 1981, based on numbers presented in John C. Musgrave, 'Fixed Capital Stock in the United States: Revised Estimates', *Survey of Current Business* (February 1981), and Musgrave, 'Fixed Reproducible Tangible Wealth in the United States'.
49. The value of the implicit debt for each year equals $(1-q)$ multiplied by the aggregate net stock of fixed corporate capital taken from Musgrave. 'Fixed Capital Stock in the United States: Revised Estimates' and 'Fixed Reproducible Tangible Wealth in the United States'.
50. See Musgrave, 'Fixed Reproducible Tangible Wealth in the United States'.
51. Institute for Fiscal Studies, *The Structure and Reform of Direct Taxation* (London: Allen and Unwin, 1978).
52. King and Fullerton, eds., *The Taxation of Income from Capital*.
53. See Barbara M. Fraumeni and Dale W. Jorgenson, 'Capital Formation and U.S. Productivity Growth, 1948–1976', in Ali Dogramaci (ed.), *Productivity Analysis: A Range of Perspectives* (Martinus Nijhoff Publishing, 1981), pp. 49–70.
54. Bulow and Summers, 'The Taxation of Risky Assets'.

Comments on Alan J. Auerbach, 'Corporate Taxation in the US' by Rafael Eldor

Alan has presented briefly a very interesting and ambitious paper on an important issue: the US corporate taxation.

This paper successfully shows how distortionary the US system is, especially in the area of structure and equipment earnings. The tax system taxes the earnings of structure and subsidised equipment. In Table 11.6, Alan calculates the welfare loss due to the differential corporate taxation. The results indicate that the same output could have been produced with about 1 per cent less capital before 1972, and 2–3 per cent less capital after 1972.

More importantly, this wastage of capital shows no downward trend despite the steady decline in corporate tax collection and corporate average taxes. On the contrary, it shows an upward trend.

I have only two points to make.

As many of us often do, Alan assumes Cobb–Douglas production, probably because of its tractability, in order to compute the welfare cost of the distortions. The C–D production function implies a unitary elasticity of substitution. Nobody knows what the elasticity of substitution really is; hence, before these numbers could be brought before a policymaker, a sensitivity analysis with elasticity of substitution less than one should be carried out. These cases should, of course, be solved numerically.

Alan's study focuses on the misallocation of capital within the corporate sector, due to the US corporate tax law. But this tax law also causes other distortions that should be looked at, such as misallocation of resources between the corporate and non-corporate sectors.

Finally, let me say that the evidence presented here strongly suggests that the US corporate tax law needs a reform.

Part Six
Market Organisation

12 The Effect of Labour Unions on Investment in Training: a Dynamic Model

Yoram Weiss[1]

I INTRODUCTION

Control over the amount of training required of new entrants is a potentially important tool available to many craft unions. This is often exercised through licensing based on schooling and apprenticeship requirements, and on passing special examinations. The standards are to a large extent determined and monitored by the incumbent practitioners. Thus physicians are required to train in various forms of schooling, internship, and residence for up to eight years. Architects need five years of schooling and three years of apprenticeship. Accountants require four years of college and one year of apprenticeship. Less widely known are the schooling and apprenticeship requirements of barbers, plumbers, and mine foremen, which require up to five or six years of investment. Finally, most craft unions require apprenticeship periods of two to four years (see Kolberg, 1976).

Two questions arise: Would such long periods of training be observed also under competitive conditions, where each worker is free to choose his own level of training? what prevents the senior workers from imposing very severe entry standards? the conventional view is summarised by S. Rottenberg (1980, pp. 9).

> Practitioners in licensed occupations are given an advantage if the standards and costs of entry are made higher than they were when current practitioners entered the relevant occupation. Practitioners have an incentive to promote *continuously* higher standards and costs of entry into licensed occupations.

In this paper I show that the impact of labour unions training depends on the organisation of the union and its power to control other variables in addition to training. In the first section of this paper I consider a union consisting of two overlapping generations, young and old. The old workers have the power to control training and to impose entry fees. It is shown that in the long run unions will select the *efficient* (i.e., competitive) level of training. The short run impact of unionisation is, however, to increase training beyond the efficient level. In the second section of the paper I assign some power to the junior workers in setting the training standards allowing them to enjoy positive rents. It is assumed that the distribution of rents between two overlapping generations is resolved by Nash bargaining. It is then shown that the steady state outcome is over-investment in training. In the last section of the paper, I consider the case in which direct transfers are replaced by an exchange of productive services which occurs during the training period. Again it is shown that the steady state outcome is over-investment in training.

The general conclusion which emerges from the analysis is that overtraining is not a necessary consequence of the fact that training standards are set by the senior workers, but it is a likely outcome in second-best situations. Overtraining can be avoided if effective inter-generational transfers exist in which case the effects of training are internalised by the senior workers. The evidence on direct transfers is not clear. While in most unions entry fees are small[2] there is a substantial contribution into pension funds which are not immediately vested.[3] There are various other benefits which are related to seniority (e.g., paid vacations) and thus serve as a tool to impose intergenerational transfers. These fringe benefits are generally more important in unionised industries. (Freeman and Medoff, 1981; Mincer, 1981).[4] In some licensed occupations such as medicine or accounting there seems to exist no direct mechanism for intergenerational transfers. Instead, during the training period (residence, internship) junior workers produce services from which senior workers benefit. The distinguishing aspect of this arrangement is the dependence of the transfer on the amount of training. A testable implication of our analysis is that such unions or professional organisations will require overtraining.

The available evidence on the effects of unions on training is scant. In recent papers Mincer (1981) and Duncan and Stafford (1980) provide evidence that union members learn fewer skills on the job 'which would lead to a better job or to a promotion'. However, these studies do not exclude the possibility that new entrants are selected on basis of prior training (see Mincer (1981), p. 42) suggesting higher training requirements. Indeed, there are several studies which indicate that 'other things equal workers in unionised industries tend to have more human capital' (see Freeman and Medoff, 1981). To the best of my knowledge the interaction between training requirements, pension funds and entrance fees has not been studied.

Despite the lack of clear evidence supporting the use of prices in regulating entry into the craft unions I entertain this working hypothesis throughout most of the paper. Nor do I make a sharp distinction with regard to the form that these transfers take, except in the last section where an explicit dependence on the amount of training is introduced. Clearly, various forms of intergenerational transfers may differ in their implications. Pension funds and seniority fringes are not as flexible as initiation fees, nor are seniority wages equivalent to direct transfers because of the interactions with effort. My justification is the usual one. Hopefully, a firm understanding of the relatively simple cases discussed in the paper will prove useful in the analysis of more complex, and realistic, situations.

II A DYNAMIC MODEL OF THE LABOUR UNION

Consider an economy in discrete time in which workers live two periods. Let there be a labour union consisting in each period of old and young workers. Assume that the old workers can impose a training requirement for young workers and charge an entry fee. Young workers can decide whether to join the union under these conditions.

Each young worker enters with one efficiency unit. Training affects the number of efficiency units the worker will have in the second period of his life. Let λ_t denote the portion of time spent in training by a worker in period t, $0 \leqslant \lambda_t \leqslant 1$, then the worker will have $P(\lambda_t)$ efficiency units in period $t+1$. The learning function $P(\ )$ is assumed to be twice differentiable monotone increasing and strictly concave. Thus $P'(\ )>0$, $P''(\ )<0$, also $P(0)=1$.

The number of young workers entering at period t is denoted by N_t, an integer, $N_t \geqslant 0$. The number of senior workers actually employed is L_t, an integer, where $L_t \leqslant N_{t-1}$. We assume that quits do not occur.[5]

Old and young workers are perfect substitutes in production[6] and the amount of efficiency units available to the industry is:

$$E_t = P(\lambda_{t-1})\,L_t + (1-\lambda_t)\,N_t. \tag{1}$$

The union determines the *total* supplies of young and old workers. The industry is competitive and firms compete for the available supplies. Wages are determined so as to clear the markets in each period. The relative wages of young and old are fully determined by their relative efficiency, and the wage per efficiency unit, W_t is equated to the value of the marginal productivity of workers.[7] Thus

$$W_t = F(E_t), \tag{2}$$

where $F(\ )$, is the inverse, industry-wide, demand function for labour and is assumed to be positive, decreasing and twice differentiable. We further assume that the wage bill $R(E_t) = E_t F(E_t)$ is bounded above and concave, and that labour is essential to the industry (i.e. $\lim_{E\to 0} F(E) = \infty$).

The supply of young workers to the union is perfectly elastic at the level of life time earnings y_0.[8] The lifetime earnings that a new entrant expects if he enters the union, depends on the entry conditions imposed by the current senior workers, and on the option value of becoming a senior worker next period. In each period the income of senior workers consists of their wage fund $L_t P(\lambda_{t-1}) W_t$ and the taxes collected from new entrants $T_t N_t$. For $N_{t-1} > 0$, let $V(\lambda_{t-1}, N_{t-1})$ denote the *maximal* collective income of the current senior workers assuming that all future generations choose their controls optimally. It is assumed that the option for unionisation extends indefinitely into the future. For $N_t > 0$ we can define the expected net earnings of each junior to be

$$y_t = -T_t + (1-\lambda_t) W_t + \frac{1}{1+r} V(\lambda_t, N_t) \frac{1}{N_t}, \tag{3}$$

where r is the market rate of interest.

We can now specify the supply constraint facing the senior workers as:

$$y_t \geqslant y_0 \qquad \text{for all } N_t > 0. \tag{4}$$

For $N_{t-1} > 0$, $V(\lambda_{t-1}, N_{t-1})$ is defined recursively by:

$$V(\lambda_{t-1}, N_{t-1}) = \max_{\lambda_t, T_t, L_t, N_t} \{L_t P(\lambda_{t-1}) W_t + T_t N_t\} \tag{5}$$

subject to (1), (2), (3), (4) and the side constraints:

$$0 \leqslant \lambda_t \leqslant 1, \ L_t \leqslant N_{t-1}.$$

The statement of the problem can be simplified substantially if one can assure that senior workers always allow in some junior workers. The sufficient condition is provided in Proposition 1.

Proposition 1 If

$$\frac{R(P(1))}{1+r} > y_0,$$

then the optimal policy of the senior workers is to allow in at least one junior worker.

Proof Suppose $N_{t-1} > 0$ and $N_t = 0$ for some t. In this case the income of the current seniors is

$$\underset{L_t \leqslant N_{t-1}}{\text{Max}} \{L_t P(\lambda_{t-1}) F(P(\lambda_{t-1}) L_{t-1})\}.$$

Now consider an alternative feasible programme of setting $\lambda_t = 1$ and $N_t = 1$. This policy provides the same current income *and* tax revenue to the senior workers. By (3) and (4) the maximal tax revenue is

$$T_t = \frac{1}{1+r} V(1, 1) - y_0.$$

From the recursive definition (5), it is clear that $V(1, 1) \geqslant P(1) F(P(1))$. Hence given the hypothesis of the theorem the tax revenue will be positive, and the assumed policy with $N_t = 0$ cannot be optimal.

Given our assumption that labour is essential to the industry, the required condition that a *single* worker with the maximal number of efficiency units can enjoy positive rent is rather mild. The result in Proposition 1 can be easily explained. From the point of view of senior workers the admission of junior workers yields two opposing effects; it reduces the wages of senior workers and broadens the tax base. By allowing young workers in but forcing them to train at the highest possible rate, $\lambda = 1$, the negative effect on wages can be eliminated while the taxing power over future generations is retained. As long as a positive tax can be collected some junior workers will be allowed in. Thus despite the assumption that junior workers are not essential for the production process in any given period the generational chain continues.

Clearly, senior workers will choose the highest feasible tax, and the constraint (4) is, therefore satisfied as an equality. That is, senior workers obtain all the rents and junior workers are strictly on their supply function. Using Proposition (1) we can eliminate the tax variable from (5), (3) and (4) and restate the maximisation as:

$$V(\lambda_{t-1}, N_{t-1}) = \underset{\lambda_t, N_t, L_t}{\mathrm{Max}} \{E_t W_t - N_t y_0 + \frac{1}{1+r} V(\lambda_t, N_t)\}. \tag{7}$$

Subject to the demand constraints (1) and (2), the side constraints (6), and the additional constraint:

$$N_t \geqslant 1. \tag{8}$$

If we also impose the boundary condition

$$\lim_{t \to \infty} \frac{1}{(1+r)^t} V(\lambda_t, N_t) = 0, \tag{9}$$

then (7) is equivalent to the maximisation:

$$\underset{\{\lambda_t, N_t, L_t\}}{\mathrm{Max}} \sum_{t=0}^{\infty} \left(\frac{1}{1+r}\right)^t (E_t W_t - N_t y_0), \tag{10}$$

subject to (1), (2), (6), (8), and initial conditions λ_{-1} and N_{-1}.

We thus obtain:

Proposition 2 The maximisation of incomes by each generation of senior workers leads to an outcome which is identical with the joint maximisation of the present value of rents (wage bills minus opportunity costs), under the constraint that at least one young worker is hired each period.

Since we have modelled the entrance fees as direct transfers, the result of Proposition 2 is to be expected. It simply states that, when the continuation of the generational chain is guaranteed, and if transfers across generations can be imposed, then each generation of senior workers will internalise all the future impacts of his choices. Note the second-best nature of this result. Depending upon initial conditions the unrestricted maximisation of (10) may require to set $N_t = 0$ for some t. However, no generation of senior workers will be willing (according to Proposition 1) to follow such a policy. In other words an outside planner who can impose transfers across generations which do *not* overlap may attain a higher present value of rents.

The behaviour of the sequences λ_t, N_t, L_t, for given initial conditions N_{-1}, λ_{-1} can be determined from the solution of the optimal growth problem (10). In deriving this solution, it will be convenient to pretend that N_t, L_t are real numbers. Correspondingly we shall replace (8) by $N_t \geqslant \underline{N}$ where $\underline{N}$ is a positive number.[9]

The first-order conditions for the solution of (10) are:

$$MR_t \geqslant 0 \text{ with equality if } L_t < N_{t-1}, \tag{11}$$

$$-N_t MR_t + \frac{P'(\lambda_t)}{1+r} L_{t+1} MR_{t+1} \quad \begin{matrix} \leqslant 0 & \text{if } \lambda_t = 0, \\ = 0 & \text{if } 0 < \lambda_t < 1, \\ \geqslant 0 & \text{if } \lambda_t = 1, \end{matrix} \tag{12}$$

$$(1-\lambda_t) MR_t + \frac{P(\lambda_t)}{1+r} MR_{t+1} \leqslant y_0$$

with equality if $N_t > \underline{N}$, where we denote

$$MR_t = \frac{\delta}{\delta E_t}(F(E_t)E_t).$$

The interpretation of the first-order conditions is transparent. Condition (11) states that the senior workers may lay-off some of their members if they can increase the wage bill by so doing. Condition (12) states that training will be determined so as to equate the marginal cost to the current generation, in terms of foregone wage bill, to the marginal benefit, in terms of the future increase in the wage bill. Because of the power to tax future generations all future gains accrue to the current generation of senior workers. For the same reason the loss of current earnings by the trainees is accounted as a cost. Condition (13) states that new workers will be allowed to enter as long as their contribution to current and future earnings exceeds their opportunity costs. The senior workers 'purchase' young workers at a supply price y_0 and appropriate all the potential benefits via the entry fee. Note that the marginal revenues at each period play the role of prices in this problem.

In Appendix A we show that the necessary conditions (11), (12) and (13) are also sufficient. That is, any path satisfying them will provide a value for (10) which is at least as high as the one attained from any other feasible path.

There is a unique (interior) steady state which satisfies equations (11), (12) and (13). This solution is given by:

$$P'(\lambda^*) = 1 + r \tag{14}$$

$$MR(E^*)\left(1 - \lambda^* + \frac{P(\lambda^*)}{1+r}\right) = y_0. \tag{15}$$

Using equations (14) and (15) we can solve for the implied values of N^* and T^*, that is,

$$N^* = \frac{E^*}{1 - \lambda^* + P(\lambda^*)}, \tag{16}$$

$$T^* = \frac{1+r}{r} y_0 \left(\frac{F(E^*)}{MR(E^*)} - 1\right). \tag{17}$$

The comparable competitive steady state solution is given by:

$$P'(\lambda^c) = 1 + r, \tag{18}$$

$$F(E^c)\left(1 - \lambda^c + \frac{P(\lambda^c)}{1+r}\right) = y_0. \tag{19}$$

The two solutions are compared in Figure 12.1 and Proposition 3.

Proposition 3 The steady-state level of training chosen by the union is the competitive one, and no senior worker is laid off at the steady state.

Proposition 3 states that the only lasting effect of the union on the allocation of resources is the restriction in the output of the unionised industry. In particular, a tax is imposed on junior workers such that entry is reduced to the level at which the marginal revenue is equated to the competitive wage. Given this output, inputs are used efficiently. Specifically, the amount of training acquired by each worker maximises the present value of lifetime output and all workers in the industry are employed.

The absence of union effects on the amount of training at the steady state arises from the fact that, with a union arrangement, training requirements are determined by the *ratio* MR_{t+1}/MR_t. Under compe-

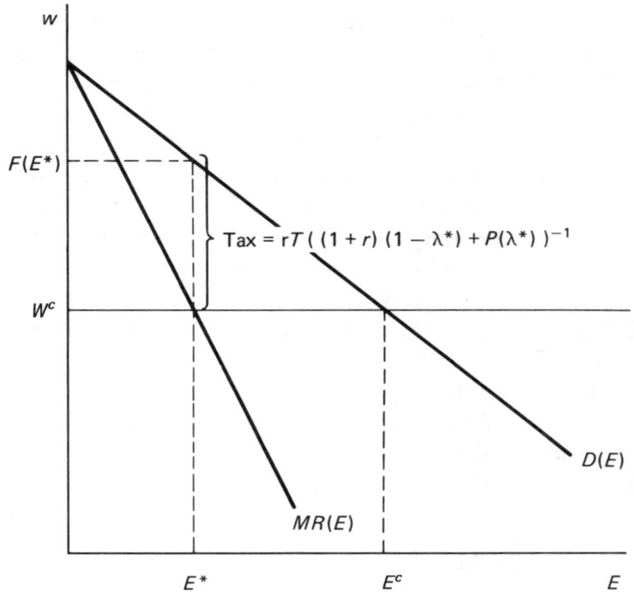

FIGURE 12.1 *Comparison of the monopoly and competitive solutions.*

tition the relevant ratio is W_{t+1}/W_t. At the respective steady states these ratios are both equal to 1, and there is thus no union effect. This neutrality need not hold outside the steady state since the respective price ratios, W_{t+1}/W_t and MR_{t+1}/MR_t may follow different time paths under competitive and monopoly situations. While it is difficult to compare the whole time paths of training under competition and monopoly one may compare the first element of the two sequences. Consider the case in which a competitive industry (in steady state) becomes unionised at time 0, then the immediate impact is to increase the amount of trainings above the competitive (and long run) level. (That is λ_0 is set by the newly formed union above λ^*.) This result is related to a more general proposition on the effects of initial conditions on the choice of the optimal programme:

Proposition 4 If the value function is strictly concave then any increase in the number or efficiency of senior workers has an immediate positive impact on the training requirements, and an immediate negative impact on the number of junior workers.

A formal proof of Proposition 4 is given in Appendix A, but the intuitive argument is easily stated. When a competitive industry becomes unionised, the initial state is such that there are too many senior workers (that is $N^c > N^*$). By laying-off some of the senior workers it is feasible to adopt immediately the union's steady-state policy $\lambda_t = \lambda^*$, $N_t = N^*$, $L_t = N^*$ for $t = 0, 1, 2 \ldots$. We know, however, that for such policy $MR_0 = MR^* > 0$. Hence the union can definitely gain by increasing L_0, holding all other variables the same. But such an adjustment will reduce MR_0 and call for further adjustments, and in particular since MR_0 is below the future values of MR investment in training at period 0 is encouraged.

An interesting aspect of the behaviour of the system outside steady state is that prices and quantities move in *cycles*. A period with relatively stringent standards is followed by a more relaxed one. This process may or may not converge to a steady state depending upon a stability condition, which we shall now derive.

For the stability analysis it will be convenient to define the function:

$$G(MR_t, MR_{t+1}) = \underset{\lambda_t}{\text{Max}} \left[(1-\lambda_t)MR_t + \frac{P(\lambda_t)}{1+r} MR_{t+1} \right]. \tag{20}$$

The function $G(,)$ may be interpreted as the marginal value of a junior worker to the current union of senior workers, while y_0 can be interpreted as the marginal cost of a junior worker. The first order conditions (11), (12), and (13) imply that for $N_t > \underline{N}$

$$G(MR_t, MR_{t+1}) = y_0. \tag{21}$$

In Figure 12.2 we plot the combinations of MR_t, MR_{t+1} which satisfy the above equality. The slope of this locus is

$$-\frac{1-\lambda_t}{P(\lambda_t)}(1+r)$$

implying a *negative* relation between MR_t and MR_{t+1}. This means that the adjustment process requires *cycles* in the 'prices' MR_t, MR_{t+1} and in the quantities E_t, E_{t+1} which correspond to them. These cycles arise because each junior worker is retained for two periods and is paid a fixed amount in present-value terms, y_0. Thus any change which leads to a reduction in the current value of MR_t must be offset by a corresponding increase in MR_{t+1}. As seen from Figure 12.2, local stability of the price path is guaranteed if the slope of the locus $G(MR_t,$

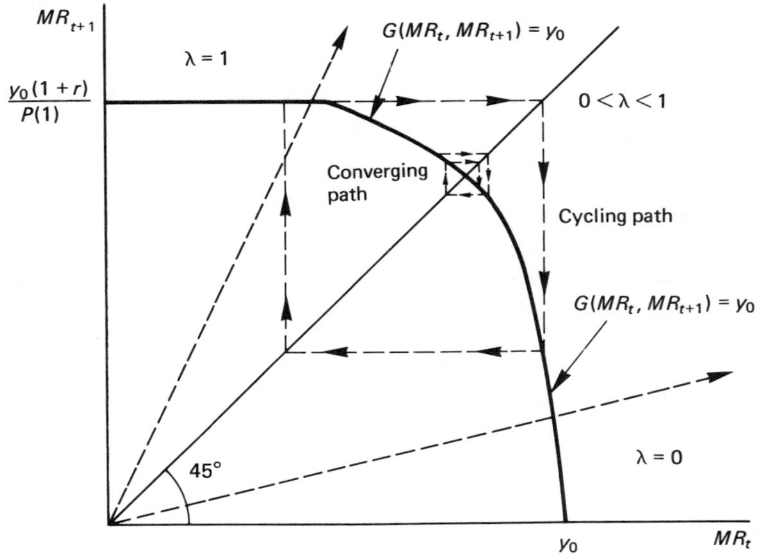

FIGURE 12.2 *Dynamics of MR_t.*

$MR_{t+1}) = y_0$ is less than unity, in absolute value, at the intersection with the 45° line. That is:

$$\frac{P(\lambda^*)}{1-\lambda^*} > 1+r. \tag{22}$$

The stability condition (22) has the interesting implication that the lifetime earnings of each worker, at the steady state, increases at a rate which exceeds the interest rate. The tilt in productivity towards the second period of the worker's life allows for smaller adjustment in the future 'price' MR_{t+1} as MR_t changes.

If the stability condition (22) is not satisfied the solution may converge to a limit *cycle* in which a period with $\lambda = 1$ is followed by a period with $\lambda = \lambda_0$ where, $0 < \lambda_0 < \lambda^*$, and this pattern repeats indefinitely (see Figure 12.2). Depending upon the initial conditions the solution may settle on such a cycle even if *local* stability is guaranteed (see Appendix B).

Another distinction between long-run and short-run impacts may be made on the basis of the expected duration of the union arrangement. In the model described here there is no reason for any of the parties to break away from the union arrangement (except for possible strategical attempts by the young to increase their share of the rents). But we may consider an exogenous limit, say τ, on the duration of the union arrangement. In this case the most natural specification of the end conditions is to assume that the union is replaced at time $\tau+1$ by a *competitive* industry. With this end condition the first-order conditions (11), (12) and (13) continue to hold, except for the last period τ where we define $MT_{\tau+1} \equiv W^c$ and allow N_τ to be strictly zero. Proposition 1 is still valid for $t=0, 1, 2, \ldots, \tau-1$. In the last period, τ, the senior workers will choose a policy such that

$$N_\tau = 0,\ \lambda_t \quad \text{undefined} \qquad \text{if } X_{\tau-1} \geqslant E^*, \tag{23}$$

$$N_\tau = \frac{E^* - X_{\tau-1}}{1-\lambda^*},\ \lambda_t = \lambda^* \qquad \text{if } X_{\tau-1} < E^*,$$

where $X_t \equiv P(\lambda_t) N_t$.

That is, young workers are hired only if their entry increases the wage bill and the training requirement is set at the *efficient* level. The reason for the failure of Proposition 1 is that the last generation of junior workers has no further taxing power and is therefore of no use to the current senior workers, unless the seniors' endowment of efficiency units is too small to fully exploit the union power.

At period $\tau-1$ the optimal policy for the senior workers is to set

$$N_{\tau-1} = \underline{N}, \qquad 1 \geqslant \lambda_{\tau-1} \geqslant \lambda^* \qquad \text{if } X_{\tau-2} \geqslant E^*,$$

$$N_{\tau-1} = \frac{E^* - X_{\tau-2}}{1-\lambda^*}, \qquad \lambda_{\tau-1} = \lambda^*$$
$$\text{if } P(\lambda^*)N^* - (N^* - \underline{N})\frac{(1-\lambda^*)^2}{P(\lambda^*)} \leqslant X_{\tau-2} < E^*,$$

$$N_{\tau-1} > \frac{E^* - X_{\tau-2}}{1-\lambda^*}, \qquad \lambda_{\tau-1} < \lambda^* \text{ if } X_{\tau-2} < P(\lambda^*)N^* - (N^* - \underline{N})\frac{(1-\lambda)^2}{P(\lambda^*)}. \tag{24}$$

That is, it now becomes optimal to select levels of training above λ^* if the number of senior workers (or their efficiency) is large, and levels of training below λ^* if the number of senior workers (or their efficiency) is small. As in the one-period case, there exists an intermediate range of initial conditions in which it is optimal to select λ^* *immediately*. More generally:

Proposition 5 If the duration of the union arrangement is finite, then there exists a non-empty set of initial conditions at which it is optimal to select the long run efficient level of training, λ^*, immediately. As the horizon lengthens this set shrinks to the single point $\lambda_{-1}=\lambda^*$, $N_1=N^*$.

Proof It is optimal to select λ^* immediately only if it is optimal and feasible to sustain E^*. In order to sustain E^* one must satisfy the equation:

$$N_{t-1}P(\lambda^*)+(1-\lambda^*)N_t=E^* \qquad \text{for } t=1,2,\ldots,\tau$$

which may also be written:

$$(N_t-N^*)=-\frac{P(\lambda^*)}{1-\lambda^*}(N_{t-1}-N^*) \qquad \text{for } t=1,2,\ldots,\tau.$$

Since $P(\lambda^*)>1>\lambda^*$ this difference equation defines a *diverging* sequence. For a finite τ and N_0 sufficiently close to N^* it is feasible to sustain E^* but if τ is increased indefinitely then, unless $N_0=N^*$, for a sufficiently large t the lower bound $\underline{N}$ must be hit, at which point E^* will not be sustained. (It may be feasible to lay-off some workers to sustain E^* but this cannot be optimal at a point at which MR is strictly positive.)

The discussion above explains why in the infinite horizon case it is generally not optimal to select λ^* immediately and to adjust only N(and L) so as to sustain E^*. If there are currently many old workers such a policy is not feasible without laying-off some of the senior workers, which, in turn, is suboptimal as long as $MR>0$. In this case it is more profitable to let in N young workers and require from them high level of training $\lambda>\lambda^*$. Conversely, if there are only few senior workers then to sustain E^* the union would allow in many young workers, and thus in the *subsequent* period there will be too many old and MR will be pushed below $MR(E^*)$. But since this change in relative prices is fully anticipated it is more profitable to currently require $\lambda<\lambda^*$.

Before I move on to extensions of this simple model I wish to comment on the empirical relevance of some of its implications.

One implication which seems counterfactual is that all generations except for the first one enjoy no rent. In principle, in a world with unexpected changes in demand, *every* generation behaves as if it is the first generation and *ex-post* rents may be either positive or negative. Most of the available literature on union wage effects does not bear directly on the impact of unionisation on *lifetime* earnings. The only sustained research effect, of which I am aware, is the attempt to estimate rents in medicine. A recent review of these attempts concludes 'Physicians received only small rents during equilibrium periods' (see Leffler, 1978).

The simple model implies that the direction of transfers within labour unions is from the young towards the senior workers. This seems to be consistent with the observed patterns of seniority related fringe benefits (pensions and paid vacations) and lay-offs, but inconsistent with the apparent tendency of unions to flatten the wage profile. A question may be raised concerning the implied size of the tax. Using equation (17), setting the intergenerational interest rate at 1 (a real rate of 2 per cent per annum over a 35-year generation) and the relative wage effect of the union

$$\frac{F(E^*)}{MR(E^*)} - 1 = \frac{W^*}{W^c} - 1$$

to 10 or 15 per cent, as indicated by most studies, one gets that T^* is 20 to 30 per cent of the lifetime earnings in the alternative occupation, y_0. This is a substantial transfer and it is doubtful whether the net seniority premium (in wages and in fringes combined) is sufficient to impose such a transfer.

Another implication of interest is the positive short-run impact of unionisation on the training standards. Friedman and Kuznetz (1945, ch. 1) document the sharp increase in standards and the reduction in the number of schools and medical students following the establishment of the A.M.A. in 1904. The number of admissions has later increased stabilising the system at a lower number of physicians per capita (see Lewis, 1963, pp. 114–35). The admission standards have also stabilised but at higher than the initial level. Contrary to the predictions of the simple model it appears that the A.M.A. had a lasting impact on the required level of training.

III BARGAINING BETWEEN YOUNG AND OLD

In the previous section it was assumed that old workers dominate the union's decisions while young workers are 'purchased' at their supply price and enjoy no rent. If the young workers organise they can bargain with the current senior workers in an attempt to obtain part of the rents. In this section I assume that, each period, senior workers in the unionised industry and the *potential* entrants agree on a *binding contract* which determines L_t, N_t, λ_t, T_t. The role of the contract is to prevent entry of some of the young workers who are willing to enter at the selected values of L_t, λ_t, T_t from doing so, thus enabling potential entrants to obtain higher *expected* income.

The expected income of a young worker is:

$$u_t = \frac{M - N_t}{M} y_0 + \frac{N_t}{M} y_t = y_0 + \frac{N_t}{M}(y_t - y_0), \tag{25}$$

where y_t is the expected income conditioned on joining the union, and it is assumed that a random mechanism is used to select the N_t junior workers employed in the union from the available pool, M.

The income of a senior worker from the current contract is:

$$v_t = \frac{1}{N_{t-1}}(L_t P(\lambda_{t-1}) W_t + N_t T_t) \tag{26}$$

and hence,

$$y_t = (1 - \lambda_t) W_t - T_t + \frac{1}{1+r} v_{t+1}. \tag{27}$$

Thus the expected utility of a junior worker depends also on the subsequent contract.

For $N_t > 0$ we can multiply (27) by N_t to obtain the basic trade-off between the incomes of the two overlapping generations:

$$M(u_t - y_0) + N_{t-1} v_t = W_t E_t - y_0 N_t + \frac{1}{1+r} N_t v_{t+1}. \tag{28}$$

Assuming some stable rule of behaviour, the income for seniors in the subsequent contract can be written as $N_t v_{t+1} = V(\lambda_t, N_t)$, where $V(\ ,\ )$

is a function to be determined. The problem facing the current pair of overlapping generations can now be solved in two stages. First the right-hand side of (28) is maximised with respect to the 'basic' variables λ_t, L_t and N_t. Then, a fee, T_t, is chosen to determine the allocation of the resulting income. The second stage is a standard bargaining problem, and we assume that the outcome is determined by a Nash bargaining model. The threat available to the young is to refuse entry, in which case their income per member will be y_0. The threat available to the old is to prevent entry, in which case their income per member will be

$$\frac{C(\lambda_{t-1}, N_{t-1})}{N_{t-1}} \equiv \frac{1}{N_{t-1}} \underset{L_t \leqslant N_{t-1}}{\text{Max}} \left\{ L_t P(\lambda_{t-1}) F(L_t P(\lambda_{t-1})) \right\}. \tag{29}$$

The Nash bargaining model predicts that the available income will be divided so as to maximise $M(u_t - y_0)(N_{t-1}\, v_t - C(\lambda_{t-1}, N_{t-1}))$.[10] Hence,

$$M(u_t - y_0) = N_{t-1} v_t - C(\lambda_{t-1}, N_{t-1}). \tag{30}$$

This rule will generally imply $u_t > y_0$ and thus $N_t > 0$. That is, some young workers are allowed in as long as there are potential gains from taxing the future generations. In contrast to the model of Section II where new entry was motivated solely by the potential gains from taxes which accrue to senior workers, in this model the rate of entry also reflects the bargaining power of the young. Using (30) to eliminate $M(u_t - y_0)$ from (28), we can derive the recursive relation

$$V(\lambda_{t-1}, N_{t-1}) = \frac{1}{2} \underset{L_t, \lambda_t, N_t}{\text{Max}} \{ W_t E_t - y_0 N_t + C(\lambda_{t-1}, N_{t-1}) + \frac{1}{1+r} V(\lambda_t, N_t) \} \tag{31}$$

subject to

$$L_t \leqslant N_{t-1}, \quad 0 \leqslant \lambda_t \leqslant 1, \quad N_t \geqslant 0,$$

which can be compared to (7) in the previous section.

The first-order conditions for maximisation are:

$$MR_t \geqslant 0, \text{ with equality} \qquad \leqslant 0 \qquad \text{if } L_t < N_{t-1}. \tag{32}$$

$$-N_tMR_t+\frac{1}{1+r}\frac{\delta V}{\delta\lambda_t}(\lambda_t,N_t)\quad \begin{array}{ll}\leqslant 0 & \text{if } \lambda_t=0\\ =0 & \text{if } 0<\lambda_t<1,\\ \geqslant 0 & \text{if } \lambda_t=1,\end{array} \tag{33}$$

$$(1-\lambda_t)MR_t+\frac{1}{1+r}\frac{\delta V}{\delta N_t}(\lambda_t,N_t)\leqslant y_0, \text{ with equality if } N_t>0. \tag{34}$$

Differentiating (31) with respect to the initial state variable, using definition (29), we obtain

$$\frac{\delta V}{\delta\lambda_{t-1}}=\frac{1}{2}L_tP'(\lambda_{t-1})\,[MR(E_t)+MR(E_t-(1-\lambda_t)N_t)], \tag{35}$$

$$\frac{\delta V}{\delta N_{t-1}}=\frac{1}{2}P(\lambda_{t-1})\,[MR(E_t)+MR(E_t-(1-\lambda_t)N_t)]. \tag{36}$$

We can use these relations to eliminate $\delta V/\delta\lambda_t$ and $\delta V/\delta N_t$ to obtain recursive relations comparable with (11), (12) and (13). The basic difference is that the future value of a unit of training to the current pair of overlapping generations reflects the rule of allocation between young and old next period.

Owing to the strict concavity of $R(E_t)$ it is clear that, for $\lambda_t<31$ and $N_t>0$, $MR(E_t)<MR(E_t-(1-\lambda_t)N_t)$. Hence, in contrast to (11), (12) and (13) in the previous section, we now have at an interior solution:

$$-MR_tN_t+\frac{P'(\lambda_t)}{1+r}MR_{t+1}L_{t+1}<0, \tag{37}$$

$$(1-\lambda_t)MR_t+\frac{1}{1+r}P(\lambda_t)MR_{t+1}<y_0. \tag{38}$$

In particular, at the steady state, the level of training λ is such that:

$$P'(\lambda)<1+r. \tag{39}$$

We therefore conclude:

Proposition 6 For the dynamic Nash bargaining model there is over-investment in training at the steady state.

It should be emphasised that over-investment is not a necessary outcome of allowing binding contracts but depends on the actual bargaining procedure and outcome. If, for instance, the bargaining outcome is such that the young always receive the *same* expected lifetime earnings (the model in Section II is a special case with $u_t = y_0$) then the steady state level of training will be efficient. The result obtained here arises from the fact that an increase in the level of training improves the future bargaining position (i.e. threat point) of the current young. Thus the current old and current young together can benefit from raising the level of training somewhat above the income maximising level. The inefficiency reflects the absence of bargaining amongst generations which do not coexist.[11]

IV SENIOR WORKERS AS PART TIME EMPLOYERS

A crucial assumption in the preceding sections was that unions can impose effective intergenerational transfers. In practice these transfers take the form of entrance fees, payments into non-vested pension funds and seniority related benefits. In looser professional associations such as the A.M.A. the transfers are less explicit. In this section I analyse the case in which direct transfers are replaced by productive services performed by the junior workers and from which senior workers benefit. I thus introduce a source of complementarity between the two age groups during the training period. This is in contrast to the previous analysis in which the two groups were strictly competitive. The training process is now viewed as if junior workers at period t spend a portion λ_t of their first period in life acquiring training *and* working for the senior workers. A portion $1-\lambda_t$ is spent working for the firm. During the training period junior workers produce services at a constant rate γ for which they are paid an apprenticeship wage W^y_t. Working for the firms they receive the value of their marginal product $F(E_t)$.[12]

The total income of senior workers is:

$$N_{t-1}v_t = L_t P(\lambda_{t-1})W_t + \lambda_t N_t(\gamma - W^y_t). \tag{40}$$

In contrast to the formulation in Sections II and III the 'tax' collected by the old depends on the duration of the training period. Moreover, in the absence of direct transfers we impose $W^y_t \geqslant 0$. (In practice the apprenticeship wage must be above the minimum wage.) Hence there is an upper bound on the per capita tax which can be imposed. For $N_{t-1} > 0$ let $V(\lambda_{t-1}, N_{t-1})$ be the maximal collective income of the senior workers then the following recursive relation holds:

$$V(\lambda_{t-1}, N_{t-1}) = \underset{L_t, \lambda_t, N_c^y,}{\text{Max}} \; W_t^y\{L_t P(\lambda_{t-1}) W_t + \lambda_t N_t(\gamma - W_t^y)\} \tag{41}$$

subject to

$$\lambda_t W_t^y + (1-\lambda_t) W_t + \frac{1}{1+r}\,\frac{V(\lambda_t, N_t)}{N_t} \geqslant y_0 \qquad \text{for } N_t > 0, \tag{42}$$

$$N_t \geqslant 0,\ L_t \leqslant N_{t-1},\ 0 \leqslant \lambda_t \leqslant 1,\ W_t^y \geqslant 0. \tag{43}$$

I will only discuss the steady state properties of this system. Suppose first that the constraint $W_t^y \geqslant 0$ is not effective. In this case, as in Section II, intergenerational transfers, represented by the gap $\gamma - W_t^y$, are not constrained. However, due to the assumed complementarity between young and old workers the analysis differs somewhat from that of Section II. The difference is immediately seen if we consider the competitive (and efficient) solution in steady state. It is characterised by equations:

$$F(E)\left(-1 + \frac{P'(\lambda)}{1+r}\right) + \gamma = 0 \tag{44}$$

$$F(E)\left(1 - \lambda + \frac{P(\lambda)}{1+r}\right) + \gamma\lambda = y_0 \tag{45}$$

When intergenerational transfers are not constrained, the monopolistic solution is determined by analogous equations (see Appendix C) where $MR(E)$ replaces $F(E)$. Therefore, Proposition 3 of Section II still holds. That is, the steady state level of training required by the union is the *same* as the competitive one. It is not true, however, that the competitive level of training is efficient *given* the choice of wages by the union. In contrast to the analysis of Section II the efficient level of training is not independent of the steady state level of wages.[13] The union will assign a relative price to the services performed by the young, $1/MR$ which is too high (relative to the true value $1/W$) and will therefore require training standards which exceed the efficient level given its (inefficient) choice of wages (or employment).

A new situation arises when the constraint $W_t^y \geqslant 0$ becomes effective and the tax per new entrant is therefore bound by γ. It can be shown that the effect of such a constraint is to increase training requirements further *above* the competitive level. This is stated in Proposition 7.

Proposition 7 If direct transfers are effectively constrained then the steady state solution for the level of training will be above the competitive level. There will be no laid-off workers at the steady state.

Proof See Appendix C.

The reason for overtraining in the absence of direct transfers is quite clear. The transfers to the senior workers depend on the duration of the training period and there is therefore an incentive to require a longer training period.

It is also straightforward to prove that:

Proposition 8 The steady-state apprenticeship wage is below the value of services provided to the old, $W^y < \gamma$, thus establishing an implicit tax on the young.

Proof See Appendix C.

If the provision of training is decentralised then Proposition 8 implies that senior workers will wish to 'hire' more junior workers than the number who choose to enter given the policy of the union. There will be an apparent 'shortage' of apprentices (e.g. medical residents).[14]

V CONCLUSIONS

The paradigm of overlapping generations seems to provide a flexible tool for the analysis of dynamic models of union behaviour. The basic insight of this approach is that the conflict between senior and junior workers which arises from their substitutability in production cannot be resolved without some expectations about the future in which *different* agents will also be involved. Thus, requiring high training standards may be beneficial to the incumbents, but they must also concern themselves with the *future* impact on the earnings of the trainees, since this will affect the rents which they can extract from the young. The future impact is partially dependent on the training of junior workers, controlled by the current union, and partially on the decisions of the future generation of senior workers. Assuming that expectations are formed rationally, that is, that each generation takes into account the correct mode of behaviour for future generations, the analysis can be reduced to a dynamic programming problem. In particular, the case in which transfers can be effectively imposed was reduced to an almost standard optimal growth model. The solution thus presents itself in the form of time sequences of the key variables, namely, the number of workers which enter each period and their level of training.

In describing the solutions a sharp distinction was made between long and short-run effects. The basic qualitative result is that in the long run the training requirements set by the unions will be efficient if direct transfers can be imposed. In other words training requirements will not be used to regulate entry if a more efficient tool such as an entry fee is available. In the short run, on the other hand, this neutrality result will not hold. If, for instance, senior workers first unionise at time 0 and (as one would assume) their number at time 0 exceeds the eventual size of the union membership at the steady state, then the *initial* impact would be to raise the training standards above the efficient level. This initial impact is followed by a series of cyclical adjustments in which training standards are raised and reduced alternately.

Two reasons were provided for possible overtraining in the long run. One is that young workers can use their bargaining power to induce higher training standards. It may seem curious that such an outcome is in the interest of the junior workers, but the reason is that they are willing to trade off lower entry fees for more training because their *future* bargaining position is enhanced. The other reason for overtraining in the long run is that transfers may be limited to the training period when senior workers have an actual 'hold' on junior workers. In this situation there is a clear incentive to extend the training period.

The real life manifestations of overtraining are varied; heavy, and apparently irrelevant, schooling requirements, long waiting times for board examinations with inexplicably high failure rates and long apprenticeship periods. It is important to realise that even though training time is not completely wasted, that is, workers do indeed improve, overtraining reduces the efficiency of human capital. The point being, that over a whole lifetime a worker is not used in the best possible way. While much attention has been given to the possible adverse effects of unions on the use of technology and capital, their impact on *human* capital is often ignored. It is not inconceivable that empirical evidence will show the union effects on investment in human capital to be quite important.

APPENDIX A

In this appendix we prove the sufficiency of the first-order conditions, and Proposition 4 in the text.

Let $\{N_t, \lambda_t, L_t\}$ be a path satisfying conditions (11), (12) and (13) and let $\{\tilde{N}_t, \tilde{\lambda}_t, \tilde{L}_t\}$ be any other feasible path starting from the same initial conditions λ_{-1} and N_{-1}. The difference between the value of the two paths is:

$$D=\sum_{t=0}^{\infty}(R(E_t)-y_0N_t)\left(\frac{1}{1+r}\right)^t-\sum_{t=0}^{\infty}(R(\tilde{E}_t)-y_0\tilde{N}_t)\left(\frac{1}{1+r}\right)^t.$$

Owing to the strict concavity of $R(E_t)\equiv F(E_t)E_t$,

$$D>\sum_{t=0}^{\infty}\{R'(E_t)(E_t-\tilde{E}_t)-y_0(N_t-\tilde{N}_t)\}\left(\frac{1}{1+r}\right)^t$$

$$=MR_0P(\lambda_{-1})(L_0-\tilde{L}_0)+\sum_{t=0}^{\infty}MR_t[N_t(1-\lambda_t)-\tilde{N}_t(1-\tilde{\lambda}_t)]\left(\frac{1}{1+r}\right)$$

$$+\sum_{t=0}^{\infty}\frac{1}{1+r}MR_{t+1}(L_{t+1}P(\lambda_t)-\tilde{L}_{t+1}P(\tilde{\lambda}_t))\left(\frac{1}{1+r}\right)^t$$

$$-\sum_{t=0}^{\infty}y_0(N_t-\tilde{N}_t)\left(\frac{1}{1+r}\right)^t,$$

where $MR_t\equiv R'(E_t)$. We first note that

$$-\sum_{t=0}^{\infty}y_0(N_t-\tilde{N}_t)\left(\frac{1}{1+r}\right)^t\geqslant\sum_{t=0}^{\infty}(MR_t(1-\lambda_t)$$

$$+\frac{P(\lambda_t)}{1+r}MR_{t+1})(\tilde{N}_t-N_t)\left(\frac{1}{1+r}\right)^t.$$

This follows from the first order condition (13) which implies that if

$$N_t>\underline{N}\text{ then }y_0=MR_t(1-\lambda_t)+\frac{P(\lambda_t)}{1+r}MR_{t+1},$$

and if $N_t = \underline{N}$ then $\tilde{N}_t \geqslant N_t$ and $y_0 \geqslant MR_t(1-\lambda_t) + P(\lambda_t)/(1+r)/MR_{t+1}$. We next note that $MR_0 P(\lambda_{-1})(L_0 - \tilde{L}_0) \geqslant 0$. This is certainly true when $MR_0 = 0$, while if $MR_0 > 0$ then by (11) and by feasibility $L_0 = N_{-1} \geqslant \tilde{L}_0$. We finally note that:

$$\sum_{t=0}^{\infty} \frac{MR_{t+1}}{1+r}(L_{t+1}P(\lambda_t) - \tilde{L}_{t+1}P(\tilde{\lambda}_t)) \left(\frac{1}{1+r}\right)^t \geqslant \sum_{t=0}^{\infty} \frac{MR_{t+1}}{1+r}(N_t P(\lambda_t) - \tilde{N}_t P(\tilde{\lambda}_t)) \left(\frac{1}{1+r}\right)^t.$$

Comparing the sums term by term we see the inequality certainly holds for $MR_{t+1} = 0$, while if $MR_{t+1} > 0$ we have $L_{t+1} = N_t$ and by feasibility $\tilde{N}_t \geqslant \tilde{L}_{t+1}$. Combining all these inequalities we obtain:

$$D > \sum_{t=0}^{\infty} \tilde{N}_t \left\{ MR_t[(1-\lambda_t) - (1-\tilde{\lambda}_t)] + \frac{MR_{t+1}}{1+r} [P(\lambda_t) - P(\tilde{\lambda}_t)] \right. \left(\frac{1}{1+r}\right)^t.$$

From the first-order condition (11) λ_t *maximises*

$$(1-\lambda_t) MR_t + \frac{P(\lambda_t)}{1+r} MR_{t+1}$$

hence each term in the above sum is non-negative. We conclude that $D > 0$.

We remark that the maximand in (10) is *not* concave in λ_t, N_t, L_t λ_{t-1} due to the appearance of products of these variables in the definition of E_t.

We next prove Proposition 4 in the text:

Proof of Proposition 4 Suppose that at time 0, there is an interior solution for λ_0 and N_0 (this implies also $L_0 = L_{-1}$ and $L_1 = N_0$). Then we can rewrite the first-order conditions as:

$$-N_0 MR_0 + \frac{1}{1+r}\frac{\partial V}{\partial \lambda_0}(\lambda_0, N_0) = 0$$

$$(1-\lambda_0) MR_0 + \frac{1}{1+r}\frac{\partial V}{\partial N_0}(\lambda_0, N_0) = y_0$$

Define $X_{-1}=P(\lambda_{-1})N_{-1}$ and differentiate totally with respect to X_{-1}, to obtain the system:

$$\begin{pmatrix} N_0^2 MR_0' + \dfrac{1}{1+r}\dfrac{\partial^2 V}{\partial \lambda_0^2} & d \\ d & (1-\lambda_0)^2 MR'_0 + \dfrac{1}{1+r}\dfrac{\partial^2 V}{\partial N_0^2} \end{pmatrix} \begin{pmatrix} \dfrac{d\lambda_0}{dX_{-1}} \\ \dfrac{dN_0}{dX_{-1}} \end{pmatrix}$$

$$= \begin{pmatrix} N_0 MR'_0 \\ -(1-\lambda_0)MR'_0 \end{pmatrix}$$

where $d \equiv -MR_0 - N_0(1-\lambda_0)MR'_0 + \dfrac{1}{1+r}\dfrac{\partial^2 V}{\partial \lambda_0 \partial N_0}$ and MR' denotes the second derivative of $EF(E)$, w.r.t. E.

Using the first-order conditions

$$d = -N_0(1-\lambda_0)MR_0' + \frac{1}{1+r}N_0\frac{P'(\lambda_0)}{P(\lambda_0)}\frac{\partial^2 V}{\partial N_0^2}.$$

Using this expression for d and the concavity of $V(\ ,\ )$, Proposition 4′, that is,

$$\frac{d\lambda_0}{dX_{-1}} > 0 \quad \text{and} \quad \frac{dN_0}{dX_{-1}} < 0$$

follows by direct calculation.

We now turn to examine the conditions under which $V(\lambda_{t-1}, N_{t-1})$ is concave. By definition:

$$V(\lambda_{t-1}, N_{t-1}) = \underset{\{L_i, \lambda_i, N_i\}}{\text{Max}} \sum_{i=1}^{\infty} (R(E_i) - y_0 N_i)\left(\frac{1}{1+r}\right)^{i-t}$$

Subject to the constraints (1), (2) and (6).

It is well known that if the summand $R(E_i) - y_0 N_i$ is concave in L_i, N_i, λ_i and λ_{i-1} for all $i \geq t$ then $V(\lambda_{t-1}, N_{t-1})$ must be concave (see Lau, 1976). For the case in which $\lambda_i = \lambda_{i-1}$ is constant, such concavity follows directly from the assumed concavity of $R(E)$ and the definition of E

which implies that E_i is linear in L_i and N_i. However, when λ_i is endogenous the concavity of E_i in its arguments is destroyed due to the appearance of the products $(1-\lambda_i)N_i$ and $P(\lambda_{i-1})L_i$. To assure concavity one needs to strengthen the assumptions that $R(E)$ and $P(\lambda)$ are concave in their arguments and impose *joint* restrictions on these functions. In some cases the restrictions may hold only locally, say around the steady state. In this case, Proposition 4 will be applicable only around the steady state (i.e. $\lambda_{-1}=\lambda^*$ and $N_{-1}=N^*$) and only if the solution is locally stable.

APPENDIX B DYNAMICS

In this appendix we establish some dynamic properties of the system (11), (12) and (13) in the text.

Consider first the issue of local stability around the steady state values (λ^*, N^*). Linearising equations (12) and (13) around the steady state values, we obtain:

$$-R''(E^*)(E_t-E^*)+R''(E^*)\,(E_{t+1}-E^*)+\frac{P''(\lambda^*)}{1+r}(\lambda_t-\lambda^*)=0,$$

$$(1-\lambda^*)R''(E^*)\,(E_t-E^*)+\frac{P(\lambda^*)}{1+r}(E_{t+1}-E^*)=0,$$

where it is assumed that in the neighbourhood of the steady state $MR_t>0$ and $L_t=N_{t-1}$. The equations imply:

$$(E_t-E^*)=(E_0-E^*)A^t,$$

$$(\lambda_t-\lambda^*)=B(E_0-E^*)A^t,$$

where

$$A=\frac{-(1-\lambda^*)}{P(\lambda^*)}(1+r)<0 \quad \text{and} \quad B=(1-A)\,\frac{R''(E^*)}{R'(E^*)}\frac{P'(\lambda^*)}{R''(\lambda^*)}>0.$$

It follows that $|A|<1$ is a necessary and sufficient condition for *local* stability of the sequence λ_t. To find the stability conditions for N_t we expand E_t using definition (2). Again we assume that around the steady state $L_t=N_{t-1}$. We obtain:

$$E_t - E^* = P(\lambda^*)(N_{t-1} - N^*) + N^* P'(\lambda^*)(\lambda_{t-1} - \lambda^*) + (1 - \lambda^*)(N_t - N^*) - N^*(\lambda_t - \lambda^*).$$

Using the solutions for $E_t - E^*$ and $\lambda_t - \lambda^*$ we have:

$$N_t - N^* = c_1 A^t + c_2 D^t,$$

where $D = -P(\lambda^*)/1 - \lambda^*$ and c_1, c_2 some constants.

As one would expect $N_t - N^*$ displays the usual *saddle-point* property with the roots satisfying $AD = 1 + r$ (see Levhari and Leviatan, 1972; Scheinkman, 1976. The root D is necessarily explosive hence $c_2 = 0$ is required for stability. We can now solve for c_1,

$$c_1 = \frac{A(1 + N^*B) - N^*P'(\lambda^*)B}{P(\lambda^*) + (1 - \lambda^*)A}(E_0 - E^*)$$

Again $|A| < 1$ is necessary for the stability of the sequence $N_t - N^*$. We conclude that condition (22) in the text (i.e. $|A| < 1$) and the condition that $N_t - N^*$ is proportional to $E_t - E^*$ (i.e. $c_2 = 0$) are necessary and sufficient for *local* stability.

We now consider the possibility that a limit cycle of the form:

$$\{L_t, \lambda_t, N_t\} = (N^2, \lambda^1, N^1) \qquad \text{for } t = 1, 3, 5, \ldots$$

$$\{L_t, \lambda_t, N_t\} = (N^1, \lambda^2, N^2) \qquad \text{for } t = 0, 2, 4, \ldots$$

satisfies the first-order conditions (11), (12) and (13).

Suppose first $0 < \lambda^1, \lambda^2 < 1$. If such a solution exists then (12) implies:

$$P'(\lambda^1)P'(\lambda^2) = (1 + r)^2,$$

and (13) and (12) imply:

$$g(\lambda^1) = g(\lambda^2)\frac{P'(\lambda^2)}{1 + r},$$

where, $g(\lambda) \equiv 1 - \lambda + \dfrac{P(\lambda)}{P'(\lambda)}$, $g'(\lambda) > 0$.

We thus obtain two equations with two unknowns (λ^1, λ^2). It is easy to verify that the first equation implies a negative relation between λ^1 and λ^2 while the second implies a positive relation. There is therefore a *unique* solution (λ^1, λ^2) satisying both equations. Since the steady state solution, $\lambda^1 = \lambda^2 = \lambda^*$, solves these equations there is no other solution and a limit cycle of the suggested form cannot exist.

Now suppose $\lambda^2 = 1$ and $0 < \lambda^1 < 1$. In this case equation (12) holds as inequality and we have

$$P'(\lambda^1)P'(1) > (1+r)^2.$$

Equation (13) implies

$$\frac{P(1)}{1+r} = g(\lambda^1).$$

Assuming $g(0) < p(1)/1+r$ and $P'(1) < 1+r$ we have a unique solution $\lambda^1 > 0$. Owing to the concavity of $P(\lambda)$,

$$P(1) < P'(\lambda^1)(1-\lambda^1) + P(\lambda^1) = g(\lambda^1)P(\lambda^1).$$

Therefore, the solution for λ^1 which solves $P(1)/1+r = g(\lambda^1)$ must be such that $\lambda^1 < \lambda^*$. This is also consistent with the inequalities $P'(\lambda^1)P'(1) > (1+r)^2$ and $P'(1) < 1+\text{r}$. It remains to show that the solution can be made consistent with $N^1 > 0$ and $N^2 > 0$. Denote $E^1 = (1-\lambda^1)N^1 + P(1)N^2$ and $E^2 = P(\lambda^1)N^2$. Since we assume $P'(1) < 1+r$, (12) implies that $R'(E^2) > R'(E^1)$ which implies $N^1 > 0$. To make sure that $N^2 > 0$ we only need to find a specification of $R(E)$ such that

$$\frac{P(1)}{1+r}R'(E) = y_0$$

is satisfied for a positive E.

We thus conclude that for admissible functions $P(\lambda)$ and $R(E)$ there exists a limit cycle with $\lambda^2 = 1$ and $0 < \lambda^1 < \lambda^*$. If it so happens that $\lambda_{-1} = \lambda^1$ and $N_{-1} = N^1$ then it will be optimal to select $\lambda_0 = 1$ and $N_0 = N^2$ and then stay in the cycle indefinitely.

As a special case consider an example in which the only feasible level of training is $\lambda = \lambda_0$ and lay-offs are not feasible so that $E_t = \alpha N_{t-1} + \beta N_t$ where $\alpha > 1$, $1 > \beta > 0$. In this case the stability condition is $\alpha/\beta > 1+r$. If the stability condition is reversed then the maximisation of

$$\sum_{t=0}^{\infty} (R(\alpha N_{t-1} + \beta N_t) - y_0 N_t)\left(\frac{1}{1+r}\right)^t$$

subject to $N_t \geqslant \underline{N}$ and given $N_{-1} = \underline{N}$ yields:

$$N_t = N^1 \qquad \text{for } t = 0, 2, 4, \ldots$$

$$N_t = \underline{N} \qquad \text{for } t = 1, 3, 5, \ldots$$

where N^1 solves

$$\beta MR(\alpha\underline{N} + \beta N^1) + \frac{\alpha}{1+r} MR(\alpha N^1 + \beta\underline{N}) = y_0.$$

For any initial conditions (except $N_{-1} = N^*$) the optimal path will converge to such a pattern.

APPENDIX C

The purpose of this appendix is to prove Propositions 7 and 8 in the text.

The first-order conditions for the maximisation of (41) are:

$$P(\lambda_{t-1})W_t + L_t P(\lambda_{t-1})^2 F'(E_t) + \psi_t(1-\lambda_t)P(\lambda_{t-1})F'(E_t) - \mu_t = 0, \tag{c1}$$

$$\psi_t \geqslant 0, \text{ with equality if } \lambda_t W_t^y + (1-\lambda_t)W_t + \frac{1}{1+r}\frac{V(\lambda_t, N_t)}{N_t} > y_0. \tag{c2}$$

$$\mu_t \geqslant 0, \text{ with equality if } L_t < N_{t-1}. \tag{c3}$$

$$\begin{aligned}&-N_t L_t P(\lambda_{t-1})F'(E_t) + N_t(\gamma - W_t^y) + \psi_t[(W_t^y - W_t) - N_t F'(E_t)(1-\lambda_t) \\ &+ \frac{1}{(1+r)}\frac{1}{N_t}\frac{\partial V(\lambda_t, N_t)}{\partial \lambda_t} \quad \begin{cases} \leqslant 0 & \text{if } \lambda_t = 0, \\ = 0 & \text{if } 0 < \lambda_t < 1, \\ \geqslant 0 & \text{if } \lambda_t = 1, \end{cases}\end{aligned} \tag{c4}$$

$$\begin{aligned}&L_t P(\lambda_{t-1})(1-\lambda_t)F'(E_t) + \lambda_t(\gamma - W_t^y) + \psi_t\Bigg[(1-\lambda_t)^2 F'(E_t) \\ &- \frac{1}{1+r}\frac{V(\lambda_t, N_t)}{N_t^2} + \frac{1}{1+r}\frac{1}{N_t}\frac{\partial V(\lambda_t, N_t)}{\partial N_t}\Bigg] \leqslant 0,\end{aligned} \tag{c5}$$

with equality if $N_t > 0$.

$$-\lambda_t N_t + \psi_t \lambda_t \leqslant 0, \text{ with equality if } W_t^y > 0. \tag{c6}$$

Differentiating (41) with respect to the initial state variables, using the envelope relation, we also have:

$$\frac{\partial V(\lambda_{t-1}, N_{t-1})}{\partial \lambda_{t-1}} = L_t P'(\lambda_{t-1}) \, [W_t + L_t P(\lambda_{t-1}) F'(E_t) + \psi_t (1-\lambda_t) F'(E_t)], \tag{c7}$$

$$\frac{\partial V(\lambda_{t-1}, N_{t-1})}{\partial N_{t-1}} = \mu_t. \tag{c8}$$

Shifting the time index in (c7) and (c8), we can eliminate the value function $V(\lambda_t, N_t)$ and its derivatives from (c2), (c3) and (c4) to obtain a system of difference equations which is comparable to (11), (12) and (13). In particular an interior solution for λ_t and N_t, respectively, implies:

$$\frac{-\mu_t}{P(\lambda_{t-1})} + \frac{L_t}{N_t} \frac{P'(\lambda_t)}{1+r} \frac{\mu_{t+1}}{P(\lambda_t)} \frac{\psi_t}{N_t} + \gamma + (W_t - W_t^y)\left(1 - \frac{\psi_t}{N_t}\right) = 0, \tag{c9}$$

$$(1-\lambda_t)\frac{\mu_t}{P(\lambda_{t-1})} + \frac{\psi_t}{N_t} \frac{P(\lambda_t)}{1+r} \frac{\mu_{t+1}}{P(\lambda_t)} + \lambda_t \gamma + ((1-\lambda_t) W_t + \lambda_t W_t^y)(-1 + \frac{\psi_t}{N_t}) = \frac{\psi_t}{N_t} y_0. \tag{c10}$$

We are now ready to prove Propositions 7 and 8 in the text.

Proof of Proposition 7 We begin by proving that $\mu_t > 0$ at the steady state. Suppose $\mu_t = \mu_{t+1} = 0$ then (c9) and (c10) imply that

$$W\left(-1 + \frac{\psi}{N}\right) = \frac{\psi}{N} y_0$$

from (c6) we also have $\psi/N \leqslant 1$ and therefore we reach a contradiction. Thus at the steady state $\mu > 0$ and $L_t = N_{t-1} = N_t = N$. If the solution is such that $W^y > 0$ then from (c6) $\psi_t = N_t$ and equations (c9) and (c10), evaluated at the steady state, are reduced to

$$-MR+\frac{P'(\lambda)}{1+r}MR+\gamma=0$$

$$(1-\lambda)MR+\frac{P(\lambda)}{1+r}MR+\gamma\lambda=y_0$$

which together imply that the level of training is the same as the competitive level determined by equations (44) and (45) in the text. If the constraint $W^y \geqslant 0$ is effective then from (c6) $\psi < N$ and we proceed as follows.

First, note that the competitive steady state level of training is given from (44) and (45), by the condition:

$$h(\lambda)\equiv y_0\left(-1+\frac{P'(\lambda)}{1+r}\right)+\gamma\left(1-\frac{\lambda P'(\lambda)}{1+r}+\frac{P(\lambda)}{1+r}\right)=0.$$

Note also that

$$h'(\lambda)=(y_0-\gamma\lambda)\frac{P''(\lambda)}{1+r}\leqslant 0.$$

Suppose $\psi > 0$, then eliminating μ/P from equation (c10), substituting into (c9) and using (c2) we obtain

$$h(\lambda)+\left(1-\frac{\psi}{N}\right)\left[\gamma\frac{N}{\psi}-\frac{P'(\lambda)}{1+r}\lambda\gamma+W\frac{P(\lambda))}{1+r}\left(1-\frac{P'(\lambda)}{1+r}\right)\right]=0 \tag{c11}$$

For $\psi < N$ equation (c9) also implies that

$$\frac{P'(\lambda)}{1+r}<1.$$

It follows that the term in the square brackets in (c11) is positive and therefore $h(\lambda)<0$.

Suppose next that $\psi = 0$, then (c9) (or (c4)) cannot hold as equality and $\lambda = 1$. In both cases the solution to equations (c9) and (c10) implies a higher level of training than under competitive conditions.

Proof of Proposition 8 The proposition is obviously correct for $W^y=0$. For the case $W^y>0$ we have from (c6) $\psi = N$. Hence, from (c1) $N=P(\lambda)MR(E)$. We can therefore rewrite equation (c10) as

$$(1-\lambda)MR(E)+\frac{P(\lambda)}{1+r}MR(E)+\lambda\gamma=y_0.$$

From the constraint (42) we have at the steady state:

$$(1-\lambda)F(E)+\lambda W^{y}+\frac{1}{1+r}[p(\lambda)F(E)+\lambda(\gamma-W^{y})]=y_{0}$$

Since $MR(E)<F(E)$ these two equations are consistent only if $W^{y}<\gamma$.

Notes

1. Support was provided by the Stanford Workshop on the Microeconomics of Factor Markets. Other research support was provided by the Center for Economic Policy Research, Stanford University, Stanford, California 94305, USA.

   Helpful discussion with K. Arrow, G. Becker, P. Hammond, J. Pencavel, A. Robson, S. Rosen, J. Scheinkman, D. Starrett, Y. Tauman, R. Willis and C. Wilson is gratefully acknowledged. A shortened version of this work, using slightly different assumptions, appeared in Weiss (1985).
2. 'A survey in 1974 shows that: "Of the 89 unions with initiation fees, 45, representing 74 per cent of the membership charged less than 40 dollars. Major unions charging between 20 and 39 dollars include the auto workers, State County and Municipal employees, clothing workers and paperworkers. The 29 unions (20 per cent of membership) requiring payments of 100 dollars or more tended to represent a small number of specialised professional workers or craftworkers such as the elevator contractors, directors guild, football players and radio association (which charged 2000 dollars). A few large unions such as mine workers also charged some new members 100 dollars or more' (Hickman, 1977). These small fees puzzled economists, e.g. Becker (1959). Martin (1980) suggests that 'the non proprietary status of union membership precludes personal claims to revenues generated from the sale of new membership' and therefore direct transfers are replaced by various seniority related wages, hours, layoff, regressive dues and discriminatory benefit programmes.
3. Lazear (1983) suggests that pension funds may also be used by senior workers to control the work performance of junior workers.
4. During the period 1967–72 unionised firms in manufacturing allocated 3.3 per cent of total compensation per man-hour into pension funds (excluding social security). In non-unions establishments the percentage was 1.7. Paid vacations which are strictly seniority related accounted for 4.1 and 2.7 per cent respectively, see Freeman (1981). Alpert (1982) finds that the fringe benefit–wage *ratio* is increasing with age and with a *positive* interaction with union status. This holds for each of the components; health and life insurance, pensions, vacations. Thus suggests intergenerational transfers within unions.
5. If the income per senior member exceeds the alternative productive use of the senior workers' time, there will be no desire to quit. One can imagine, however, initial conditions in which there are so many senior workers that quitting became attractive. To make the model strictly correct I have to assume either that such a situation does not arise or that the net productivity outside the industry (including moving costs) is zero. The latter assumption will also guarantee that the union does not

'send' some of its senior workers into other industries when it wants to restrict their supply.

6. This simplifying assumption is maintained in order to sharpen the question raised in the introduction why are the young workers admitted into the union. Clearly, a cheap answer would be to *assume* that both young and old are required for the production process. I intentionally avoid this assumption, emphasising instead, the financial motive on the part of the senior workers.
7. The assumption that the union can only select points on the demand function implies the absence of bargaining between the union and the employers. In a more general model one could allow a more active role for the employers.
8. There is no difficulty in modifying this assumption to the case of increasing supply function. Such a modification may be required if some pretraining or specific skills are required in order to work in the unionised industry.
9. If N_t is truly a real number then even a fraction of a worker may be a tax base. Since the senior workers are seeking to increase *total* tax receipts it may be the case within some range that $T_t N_t$ is independent of N_t. That is, as N_t is reduced towards zero t_t is increased towards infinity. Still Proposition 1 implies $N_t > 0$. In this case there may be no optimal policy. One must therefore set either an upper bound on T_t (see Weiss, 1985) or a lower bound on N_t. I choose here the second alternative assuming $N_t \geqslant \underline{N}$. Since, for simplicity, the time spent by the senior workers in training the young is not accounted as cost (presumably the young learn by watching and imitating), $\underline{N}$ can be interpreted as the minimal number of workers required for training the young, and for tax collection.
10. Somewhat more generally one can consider a 'union leadership' that maximises a union's 'welfare function' which depends on the rents of the two age groups constituting the union. I assume that each age group acts as a single unit ignoring possible subcoalitions within age groups.
11. Phelps and Pollak (1968) and Kohlberg (1975) consider a non-cooperative Nash–Cournot equilibrium in the one-sector growth model. Each generation chooses its savings assuming all subsequent generations save at a fixed rate. The consistency requirement is that for all generations the optimal choices under these prescribed values will coincide with the prescribed values. This type of equilibrium results in undersaving.
12. In practice apprenticeship requirement and wage are often determined by collective bargaining between employers and the union. Generally the firm may compete with the senior workers in the provision of training. In both cases one would allow a departure of the wage paid by the firms from the marginal product.
13. Separability can be retained if one assumes that the services performed by the junior workers are valued at the going wage rate (i.e. the transfer is $\lambda\gamma W_t$ instead of $\lambda\gamma$). The interpretation of such an assumption is that the young transfer to the old efficiency units which they can then sell to the firms.
14. In 1979 the 'tax' per year on residents (i.e. the resident's assessment of value of annual services to hospital minus salary) was estimated at 20.542 dollars per annum. At the same time there was an excess demand (i.e. unfilled budgeted residency positions) of 7.27 per cent (see Marder and Hough, 1983).

REFERENCES

Alpert, W. (1982) 'Unions and Private Wage Supplement', *Journal of Labor Research*, vol. 3 (Spring) pp. 179–200.

Becker, G. (1959) 'Union Restrictions on Entry', in P. D. Braely (ed.) *The Public State In Union Power* (University of Virginia Press).

Duncan, G. and F. Stafford (1980) 'Do Union Members Receive Compensating Wage Differentials', *American Economic Review*, vol. 70 (June) pp. 355–341.

Freeman, R. (1981) 'The Effects of Unionism on Fringe Benefits', *Industrial and Labor Relations Review*, vol. 34, pp. 489–509 (July).

Freeman, R. and J. Medoff (1981) 'The Impact of Collective Bargaining Illusion or Reality', in J. Steiber, R. B. McKersie and D. Q. Mills (eds), *Industrial Relations 1950–1980: A Critical Assessment* (Industrial Relations Research Association) pp. 47–97.

Friedman, M. and S. Kuznets, (1945) *Income from Independent Professional Practice* (National Bureau of Economic Research, New York).

Hickman, C. W. (1977) 'Labor Organizations: Fees and Dues', *Monthly Labor Review*, vol. 100, pp. 19–24 (May).

Kohlberg, E. (1976) 'A Model of Economic Growth with Altruism Between Generations', *Journal of Economic Theory*, vol. 13, pp. 1–13 (August).

Kolberg, W. (1976) *The National Apprenticeship Program* (US Department of Labor Employment and Training Administration).

Leffler, K. (1978) 'Physician Licensure Competition and Monopoly in American Medicine', *Journal of Law and Economics*, vol. 21, pp. 165–86 (April).

Lazear, E. (1983) 'A Competitive Theory of Monopoly Unionism', *American Economic Review*, vol. 85, pp. 631–93 (September).

Lau, L. (1976) 'A Characterization of Normalized Restricted Profit Functions', *Journal of Economic Theory*, vol. 12, pp. 131–63 (February).

Levhari, D. and Leviatan, N. (1972) 'On Stability in the Saddle Point Sense', *Journal of Economic Theory*, vol. 4, pp. 88–93 (February).

Lewis, G. (1963) *Unionism and Relative Wages in the United States* (University of Chicago Press).

Marder, W. and D. Hough (1983) 'Medical Residency as Investment in Human Capital', *Journal of Human Resources*, vol. 18, pp. 50–64 (Winter).

Martin, D. (1980) *An Ownership Theory of the Trade Union* (University of California Press).

Mincer, J. (1981) 'Wages Turnover and Job Training', NBER Working Paper No 808 (November).

Phelps, E. and R. Pollak (1968) 'On Second Best National Savings and Game Equilibrium Growth', *Review of Economic Studies*, vol. 35, pp. 185–99 (April).

Rottenberg, S. (ed.) (1980) *Occupational Licensing and Regulation* (American Enterprise Institute, Washington).

Scheinkman, J. (1976) 'Stability of Optimal Steady States in N sector Growth Models When Utility is Discounted', *Journal of Economic Theory*, vol. 12, pp. 11–30 (February).

Weiss, Y. (1985) 'The Effect of Labor Unions on Investment in Training: a Dynamic Model', *Journal of Political Economy*, vol. 85, pp. 994–1007.

Comments on Yoram Weiss, 'The Effect of Labour Unions on Investment in Training: a Dynamic Model' by Charles Wilson

According to conventional wisdom training requirements, particularly in guild industries, are used to impose a cost on new workers, restricting entry and consequently increasing the return to existing workers. As Weiss notes in the introduction to his paper, this argument, carried to its logical extreme, suggests that existing workers should try to make the cost of training prohibitive. In rejecting this point of view, Weiss seems to be arguing that training standards should be viewed as one of a more comprehensive set of tools available to senior workers for extracting rent from incoming workers. This ability to extract rent essentially gives the senior workers monopsony power in buying the services of the new workers and monopoly power in selling the services of the new workers to firms.

The paper is concerned with two kinds of issues. The first is an analysis of the stationary state level of training under various assumptions about the tools available to senior workers for extracting rent. The other is an analysis of how training requirements will change over time when the economy is not in a stationary state. I will make a few remarks about the dynamics of this model later; however, most of my discussion will focus on the determinants of the stationary state level of training. The main point of my remarks is that the tendency to require overtraining will depend upon whether or not the ability to extract rent from new workers is tied to the *level* of training. A much more pervasive result seems to be that the monopoly power of senior workers tends to lead to a total employment level which is less than socially efficient.

Although Weiss develops his analysis in the context of a two period overlapping generations model, many of the ideas can be illustrated more simply in the context of a static model. Consequently, I will begin by outlining a simple one period model and then show how the results of the overlapping generations model be interpreted in this framework.

The basic model is illustrated in Figure 1. There are two kinds of workers, senior workers and new workers. Following Weiss, I suppose that the employers act competitively and hire labour to the point where the marginal product of labour is equal to the wage. Let N be the number of new workers hired. Then assuming that there is a fixed supply $\bar{N}$ of senior workers, $D(N+\bar{N})$ represents the inverse demand

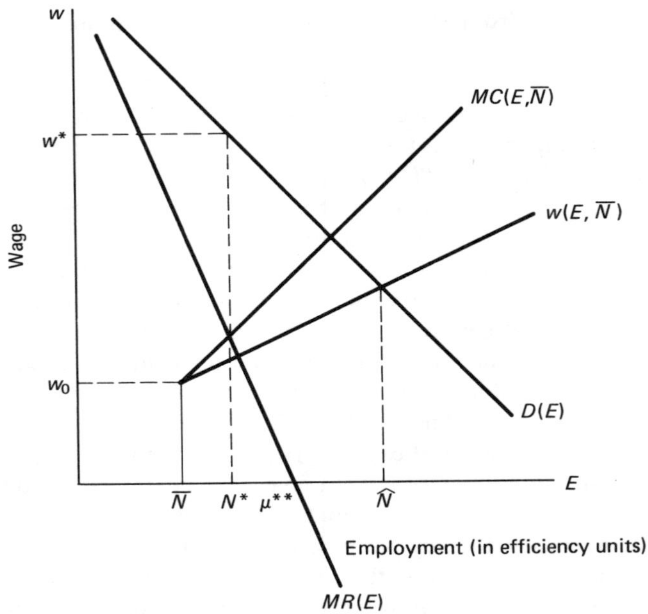

FIGURE 1

curve for labour and $MR(N+\bar{N})$ represents the corresponding marginal revenue to employees. In order to illustrate the monopsonistic power of the senior workers, I will also suppose that the supply curve of incoming workers is an increasing function. Then since the supply curve represents the average cost of hiring a new worker, the marginal cost to senior workers of obtaining new workers will lie above the wage. To facilitate a comparison with what follows, it is useful to suppose that no new workers can be employed at a wage less than w_0. Then assuming that senior workers have a reservation wage of 0, we obtain a total supply curve and marginal cost curve (to senior workers) of labour such as the one illustrated in Figure 1.

Suppose now that senior workers may levy an initiation fee on incoming workers. Then assuming that the number of senior workers is less than N^*, they will set an initiation fee of T^* per new worker, employing new workers up to the point where marginal revenue is equal to marginal cost at a wage of w^*.[1] This maximises the total revenue to senior workers, which is composed of their wage bill, $w^*\bar{N}$, plus the revenue from the initiation fee from incoming workers, $T(N^* - \bar{N})$.

Now consider the problem facing senior workers when the level of training can be made endogenous. Suppose that devoting λ units of labour to training increases the efficiency of the remaining $(i - \lambda)$ units of labour by a factor of $P(\lambda)$. Reinterpret N to represent efficiency units of labour and let $w(N, \lambda)$ be the inverse supply function of new workers per efficiency unit of labour when λ units of labour are devoted to training. Then for a given value of λ, the analysis of the optimal initiation fee remains unchanged. It will be set to equate the marginal revenue of new workers to their marginal cost. The role of training is to determine the location of the supply curve. Suppose that $\bar{w}(N)$ is the reservation wage of the marginal worker when N new workers are employed. Then $w(N, \lambda)$ is equal to $\bar{w}(N)/[(i - \lambda)P(\lambda)]$. Clearly it is in the interest of older workers to make $w(N, \lambda)$ as low as possible at the optimal employment level N^*. Therefore the optimal level of training is the value λ^* which maximises $(i - \lambda)P(\lambda)$.

For our purposes, the key point to note about this analysis is that λ^* is also the level of training that would be chosen in a competitive market. The reason is that whether the market is competitive or monopolistic, agents will always do best by using inputs efficiently. The more significant distortion seems to be in the reduction of total employment. For social efficiency, new workers should be employed to the point where the demand and supply functions intersect ($\hat{N}$ in Figure 1) rather than the intersection of the marginal revenue and marginal cost curves.

When we consider Weiss's overlapping generations model, we still obtain similar results in the stationary state, but the analysis is a little more subtle. Because workers work for two periods, the supply function of new workers in their first period must be derived from a lifetime utility function. Following Weiss, I will suppose that each new worker has a reservation value of discounted lifetime income equal to y_0.[2] Then to derive the first period supply function of new workers, we need to determine the revenue the workers can expect to earn in the second period of their lives.

Weiss assumes that a new worker with λ units of training supplies $(1 - \lambda)$ units of labour in his first period and $P(\lambda)$ units of labour in his second period. Let $v(\lambda, N)$ be the total revenue per older worker earned in his second period, discounted back to his first period, when λ units of labour are devoted to training in his first period and N efficiency units of labour (i.e. $N/(1 - \lambda)$ workers) in his cohort are employed, assuming that his generation imposes the optimal initiation fee and training requirements from the next generation. Then the first period inverse supply function of new workers per efficiency unit of labour can be expressed as

$$w(\lambda, N) = [y_0 - v(\lambda, N)]/(1-\lambda). \tag{1}$$

It is easy to show that $v(\lambda, N)$ is decreasing in N; consequently, as in the static model, the inverse supply function of new workers, $w(N, \lambda)$, is again an increasing function of N. Assuming that $y_0 - v(\lambda, 0) > 0$, the problem facing senior workers is then exactly the same as in the static model outlined above. An initiation fee is set to equate the marginal cost of new workers to their marginal revenue, and the level of training is set to minimise the first period wage required by young workers at the optimal level of employment.

Consider now how the resulting levels of employment and training compare with the efficient level. First of all, as Weiss notes, the level of training which minimises $w(N, \lambda)$ is not necessarily the same as the level of training which maximises the discounted value of a worker's lifetime marginal product. Since senior workers are able to adjust the initiation fee to extract any rent from the new workers, they can reduce the discounted lifetime income of new workers to y_0, whatever training requirements they establish. Consequently, the senior workers will set the training level to maximise the discounted value of the *marginal revenue* of new workers.

Letting E_0 represent the number of efficiency units of labour employed when the new workers are young and E_1 the number of efficiency units of labour employed in their second period, the first order condition with respect to λ for maximising marginal revenue implies.

$$-MR(E_0) + \delta P'(\lambda) MR(E_1) = 0. \tag{2}$$

where δ is the one period discount factor. The efficient level of training, however, is set to maximise the value of the marginal product. This yields a first order condition

$$D(E_0) + \delta P'(\lambda) D(E_1) = 0. \tag{3}$$

In the stationary state, E_0 is equal to E_1 so that both the ratio of marginal products and marginal revenues in the two periods will be equal to one. Consequently, in both cases, λ will be chosen to satisfy $\delta P'(\lambda)=1$. Out of equilibrium, this equality will not necessarily hold, but there is no clear bias toward either over- or under-investment in training, given the employment policy of the senior workers.

A comparison of the rent maximising level of employment with the socially efficient level is similar to the static model. Social efficiency requires that the discounted value of each worker's lifetime marginal product be equated to his reservation value y_0, which in this context yields the equation

$$(1-\lambda)D(E_0)+\delta P(\lambda)D(E_1)=y_0. \tag{4}$$

Revenue maximisation, on the other hand, requires that the discounted value of the marginal revenue be equal to y_0:

$$(1-\lambda)MR(E_0)+\delta P(\lambda)MR(E_1)=y_0. \tag{5}$$

In the stationary state, E_0 is equal to E_1 so that senior workers will employ new workers to the point where $MR(E)=y_0/[(1-\lambda)+\delta P(\lambda)]$ as compared with the efficient level where $D(E)=y_0/[(1-\lambda)+\delta P(\lambda)]$. Since $MR(E)<D(E)$, it follows that in the stationary state, a union of senior workers will underemploy new workers relative to the efficient level.

The employment distortion can also be viewed in a different way. As stated in equation (4), social efficiency requires that the discounted marginal product of workers be equal to their reservation income level. Similarly, rent maximisation by senior workers implies that the lifetime earnings of workers will also equal y_0. The difference is that each generation of workers must pay a tax to senior workers during the first period of their lives. If in the stationary state a tax of T is paid in each period, an employment level E^* will be attained which satisfies the equation:

$$(1-\lambda)D(E^*)-T+\delta[P(\lambda)D(E^*)+T)]=y_0. \tag{6}$$

Any distortion in the stationary state level of employment from the efficient level, therefore, must be a result of the fact that the pattern of income is different. Because some of the marginal product of new workers is deferred until the second period of their lives when they impose a tax on the next generation, the discounted value of their income is lowered. Consequently, a stationary state lifetime income of

y_0 can only be maintained by reducing the stationary state level of employment and increasing the wage. In fact, if $\hat{E}$ is the efficient level of employment in the stationary state and each generation of workers imposes a tax of T on incoming workers, manipulation of equation (6) reveals that the resulting marginal product of labour $D(E^*)$ must be higher than the efficient level $D(\hat{E})$ by an amount $T(1-\delta)$.

All of this analysis is based on the assumption that senior workers can use instruments other than training to extract the rent from new workers. In the analysis above, I have assumed an explicit initiation fee. As Weiss argues in his paper, however, this can be interpreted broadly to include such features as discriminatory fringe benefits, seniority lay-off provisions, etc. Nevertheless, in many industries where training represents a substantial investment of labour, there may be a relatively severe limit on the size of the tax that senior workers may levy on incoming workers by these means. I have in mind here skilled trades with substantial self-employment or professions with very small firms and considerable mobility of workers. In these industries, the primary means of extracting rent from young workers may be to use 'training' as a way of directly employing new workers at a wage below the market wage.

Even in this case, however, so long as there is no effective restriction on the wage that can be paid to trainees, the essentials of the analysis remain unchanged. Suppose that in addition to enhancing the efficiency of second period labour, training also provides a direct marginal product equal to a fraction γ times the marginal product of current labour. In order to be trained, a new worker must be employed by a senior worker at a wage w set by the senior workers. Then for any level of training which is required, the appropriate tax can be levied by adjusting the wage w.[3] The level of training will again be set to maximise the discounted marginal revenue of the worker's labour. Since training has direct value, the revenue maximising level of training will tend to be higher than before, but it will still be socially efficient in the stationary state.[4]

In obtaining our results thus far, we have relied heavily on the assumption that there is a non-distortionary way for the senior workers to extract all of the rent from incoming workers. Despite some evidence to the contrary which Weiss notes in his paper, there seems to be a common presumption that generally not all of the rent can be extracted or at least not efficiently. To account for this possibility Weiss considers a modification of his original model where the initiation fee and training level is determined as an outcome of bargaining between the new workers and the senior workers. Although I think the analysis is of some interest, I am not sure how appropriate it is for this kind of problem. Coalitions surely form within unions, but it seems unlikely that incoming workers could effectively organise before they are even trained. For this reason, I want to focus on a different line of analysis which Weiss treats only briefly at the end of his paper.

Suppose we maintain the assumption that senior workers can only extract rent by hiring incoming workers as trainees, but that now there is an effective lower bound on the wage that can be paid to trainees. Suppose also that the lower bound is sufficiently high so that senior workers are not effectively constrained in the level of training they can require in the first period or in the number of workers they can hire. If λ units of training are required from each new worker, then each new worker supplies $[(1-\lambda)+\gamma\lambda]$ efficiency units of labour of which $\gamma\lambda$ are purchased by the senior workers at a wage λw. Consequently, new workers will be employed to the point where the marginal revenue is equal to the marginal cost:

$$(\bar{N}[(1-\lambda)+\lambda\gamma]+N\lambda\gamma)D'(\bar{N}+N)+\lambda(\gamma D(N+\bar{N})-w)=0. \tag{7}$$

where again $\bar{N}$ and N measure the number of *efficiency* units of labour supplied by old and new workers respecitively in the current period. Since the inverse demand function is downward sloping ($D'<0$), equation (7) implies that the market wage must lie above the cost of a trainee to senior workers, i.e. $gD(\bar{N}+N)>w$.

Now consider the level of training that senior workers will require. An additional unit of training reduces the effective labour force per new worker by $(1-\gamma)$, resulting in an increase in the wage income of senior workers. In addition, it increases their return to training new workers by at least $\gamma D(\bar{N}+N)-w$. Consequently, the optimal policy is to require that all first period labour of new workers be devoted to training. This extreme bias towards overtraining is a result of the fact that the amount of rent that can be extracted from each new worker is directly related to the amount of training he is required to undertake.

Finally, given the level of training senior workers will require, we may examine how the resulting level of employment they will choose compares with the efficient level. Since all first period employment is devoted to training, equation (7) reduces to

$$(\bar{N}+N)D(\bar{N}+N)+D(\bar{N}+N)-\mathrm{w}/\gamma=0, \tag{7a}$$

which simply states that senior workers will employ new workers to the point where the marginal revenue of new workers in the first period is equal to their wage. It is not immediately obvious whether this implies more or less employment than is socially efficient. Nevertheless, by looking again at the intertemporal pattern of compensation, we can discern a definite bias toward underemployment relative to the socially efficient level, given that all first period employment of new workers is devoted to training.

As before, social efficiency requires that the discounted value of the marginal product be equal to the reservation level of income, which in the stationary state requires that the total level of employment be adjusted to satisfy

$$\gamma D(\hat{N}) + \delta P(1)D(\hat{N}) = y_0. \tag{8}$$

When the senior workers exploit their monopolistic power, equation (8) changes in two ways. First, since trainees are paid a wage less than their marginal product, some of the first period return is transferred to the second period. Second, since I have assumed that older workers are not constrained by the supply of trainees, it follows that the discounted return to workers may exceed y_0. Consequently, the total employment N^* must satisfy:

$$w + \delta[P(1)D(N^*) + (\gamma D(N^*) - w)] \geqq y_0. \tag{9}$$

Subtracting equation (8) from equation (9) and rearranging terms implies that

$$D(N^*) - D(\hat{N}) \geqq (1-\delta)[(\gamma D(N^*) - w)/(\gamma + \delta P(1))]. \tag{10}$$

Both the fact that some of their first period compensation is deferred until the second period and the possibility that the discounted value of the compensation can exceed y_0 tends to increase the marginal product of labour, thus reducing employment.

This extreme bias toward overtraining depends upon the assumption that regardless of the level of training required, senior workers are unable to extract all of the rent to incoming workers. This result must be modified somewhat if we assume that there is a limit to how much training can be required at the same wage and employment level before the discounted lifetime income of incoming workers falls below y_0. Nevertheless, because the marginal return to senior workers from increasing the training requirement is positive and the marginal return to increasing employment is zero, the initial effect of raising the minimum trainee wage to a point where it constrains the level of employment and training will be to lower employment rather than training.

Weiss also provides a detailed analysis of the dynamics of the model. Perhaps the most striking feature is the tendency for the level of training and employment to oscillate out of the stationary state. Although the details depend on the specific model being analysed, I expect that the tendency for training requirements and employment to oscillate will be a feature of almost any model which is based on the assumption that senior workers are trying to extract rent from junior workers. The reason is that an increase in the effective supply of senior workers implies a lower marginal revenue for new workers. Thus in the face of an increase in the effective supply senior labour, there will be a tendency to reduce the supply of junior labour. If the senior workers always require the maximum allowable level of training, then all of the adjustment must come in the level of employment. Otherwise, some of the reduction in the current supply of labour will be obtained by increasing the time in training.

Weiss also suggests that the adjustment process might be unstable. That is, starting out of the stationary state, the employment and training levels may tend to diverge to some limit cycle. The tendency towards instability, however, must be sensitive to the details of the model. Consider, for example, two possible versions of Weiss's basic model. Weiss assumes that training is not productive in the first period of a worker's life. In the stationary state this assumption implies that the level of training will be determined by the condition $\delta P'(\lambda)=1$. He then shows that the system is locally stable if and only if $\delta P(\lambda)>1-\lambda$. Alternatively, we might have supposed that training is productive in the first period. That is, λ units of training produces $(1-\lambda)P(\lambda)$ efficiency units of labour in the first period. In that case, rent maximisation by senior workers imply the following first order conditions for N_t, total effective employment in period t and λ_t, training of new workers at time t:

$$(1-\lambda_t)P(\lambda_t)MR(E_t)+\delta P(\lambda_t)MR(E_{t-1})=y_0. \tag{11}$$

$$[(1-\lambda_t)P'(\lambda_t)-P(\lambda_t)]MR(E_t)+\delta P'(\lambda_t)MR(E_{t+1})=0. \tag{12}$$

Differentiating (11) with respect to E_t, E_{t+1}, and λ_t and using equation (12), we can solve for the change in E_{t+1} with respect to E_t. In the stationary state this reduces to

$$dE_{t+1}/dE_t = -(1-\lambda)/\delta \tag{13}$$

with the level of training λ determined from (12) by

$$(1-\lambda+\delta)P'(\lambda) = P(\lambda). \tag{14}$$

Whether or not equation (14) implies more or less training than in Weiss's model depends on the specific form of $P(\lambda)$. However, the condition for stability in this model definitely requires more training in the first period, since now the system is locally stable if and only if $(1-\lambda) < \delta$.

Let me conclude with a few speculative remarks about how the implications of this model might compare with a model where the lifetime of each generation of workers spans three periods or more. From a conceptual perspective, probably the most important element that is introduced by such an extension is a potential conflict among senior workers of different ages. Since older workers are less concerned with future competition from new workers, my conjecture is that the older are the workers who make the employment and training decisions, the greater will be the levels of employment and training which are chosen. Since Weiss's model does not allow for training to affect the efficiency of workers in the first period, it should probably best be interpreted as a model where the employment and training decisions are made by the very old workers. A detailed analysis of the stationary state of a multi-period overlapping generations model might produce some interesting implications for this issue.

It might also be useful to explore the dynamics of a multi-period overlapping generations model. In allowing only a one period overlap in the lifetime of adjacent generations, we are allowing for only two employment and training decisions during the lifetime of a worker. Thus the model would seem to be most appropriate for those cases where changes in the employment and training policies of an industry are changed relatively infrequently. If the decision to adjust employment and training standards were made more frequently, I suspect that there will still be a tendency for employment and training levels to cycle out of the stationary state but the analysis of stability looks to be considerably more complicated.

Notes

1. If $\bar{N}$ exceeds N^*, then no new workers will be employed. Assuming that the reservation wage of existing workers is zero, Weiss supposes that if $\bar{N}$ exceeds N^{**}, then existing workers are laid off in order to maximise the total revenue to existing workers. Particularly in the context of a guild, it may be more realistic to assume that older workers will never be laid-off.
2. He could have assumed that the supply of new workers to be an increasing function of their discounted lifetime income without introducing any serious complications.
3. Note that implicit in this analysis is that senior workers can collude is setting both the training standards and the wage. If either the wage or the level or training standards are open to competition the results will change.
4. In the stationary state, the first order conditions for the revenue maximising value of λ imply

$$\delta P'(\lambda) = (1 - \gamma).$$

This is not exactly the same result that Weiss would obtain since he assumes that the marginal product of a trainee, γ, is independent of labour in the industry. Consequently, the corresponding first order condition for the optimal level of training is

$$\gamma - MR(E_0) + \delta P'(\lambda) MR(E_1) = 0;$$

whereas the first order condition for the socially efficient level of training is

$$\gamma - D(E_0) + \delta P'(\lambda) D(E_1).$$

In this case, because the marginal revenue of second period labour is less than its marginal product while the marginal product of trainee labour is equal to its marginal product, senior workers will require even *less* training than is socially efficient (in contrast to the assertion in Proposition 7 of the text).

Comments on Y. Weiss, 'The Effect of Labour Unions on Investment in Training' by Abba Schwartz

This paper is motivated by the observation that in a few professional associations (unions) such as that of medical doctors, lawyers, accountants, etc., very long periods of training are required by new entrants. The paper goes on to analyse whether the seemingly long periods of training constitute an over-investment (relative to what would have been the length of training under a competitive setup) because of monopoly power that seniors in the professions have over the entry and the required investment by juniors.

Professor Weiss analyses three variants of intergenerational union behaviour where training is required only to increase output. In one variant (where the first generation receives all of the monopoly rents) he obtains no over-investment in steady state (provided you start in a steady state) and in the other two, over-investment is the outcome. Professor Weiss does not recommend the adoption of any of his models as the correct description of reality. His introduction, however, implies that he prefers those that generate over-investment.

Once the assumptions are made Professor Weiss's results neatly follow. Therefore, in my comment I will only suggest what I consider to be a more realistic approach to the problem, i.e. I will discuss and criticise some of Professor Weiss's assumptions.

The professional associations (unions) which Professor Weiss reviews in his introduction are composed of many individuals scattered in many locations, therefore the unions by themselves are powerless to prevent entry. It is the threat of legal punishment, by the government, of those who practise without a 'proper' licence that effectively prevent entry of 'untrained' individuals.

The analysis in this paper ignores the role of the government in providing the legal backing of the power vested in the hands of the senior professionals to control the entry, the level of investment and the licensing of practitioners.

Further, in this paper training serves only to increase efficiency in that it causes more output to be generated per worker. If this is the sole purpose of training why should the government impose it and punish those who practise without first getting the 'required' training. Governments have no social justification to interfere in order to set the rates (per practitioner) of the services he provides.

Governments have a social justification to set the standards of the qualities of services provided by professionals if socially unaccepted damages are caused to members of society when these standards are not met and if the proper quality is not immediately identifiable by those who obtain the services. In this case members of society may be maltreated by individuals who pretend to provide services that they cannot deliver *without first learning*.

It is true that governments vest the power of setting the quality standards in the hands of the senior practitioners who thus decide on the required length of training and administer the tests that 'initiate' the juniors into the profession.

While the government's purpose is to shield society against malpractice, the seniors in each profession, once granted the monopoly power, *may* have an additional objective, that of increasing their own welfare by restricting entry. It is this possible conflict of interest which leads Professor Weiss in the introduction to his paper to speculate about over-investment.

To provide the relevant answer to his question he should alter the assumption that training increases output (that can be provided without it only at a lower rate) to one where without proper training a service cannot be provided at a predetermined quality standard. He should also introduce the government into the model and analyse how it sets the standards and if, why and how the professional associations overdo the social targets.

13 Corporate Governance and Market Structure

Robert D. Willig

I INTRODUCTION

It is an element of the conventional wisdom that product market competition disciplines firms into efficiency of operation, while market power fosters managerial sloth and x-inefficiency. In this view, movements in the market away from monopoly towards competition are doubly advantageous to social welfare. They decrease deadweight social losses in the product market while, at the same time, eliminating wasted resources and unnecessary costs internal to the firms.

Another viewpoint holds that the nature of the output market is irrelevant to internal efficiency so long as the market for managerial services, either within a firm, or across firms, is competitive enough to induce efficiency on its own. In addition, it might be argued that the market for corporate acquisitions, through raiding for example, exercises the discipline that eliminates x-inefficiency and suboptimal profit performance.

However, more careful analyses of the incentives and interactions between owners and managers (e.g., Jensen and Meckling (1976) or Fama (1980)) suggest that monitoring difficulties and asymmetries in information render inevitable internal inefficiencies in an environment where ownership and management are separated. Based on this precept, it might be argued that output market competition cannot discipline internal operations to the extent that all competitors face the same difficulties of indirect and imperfect control over managerial discretion.

The innovative work by Hart (1983) lends some support to this argument. He shows that competition among managerial firms will not significantly reduce managerial slack unless there is significant correlation among the firms' costs. Where correlation is strongly positive, the competitive output market essentially puts the managers of the various firms in competition with one another, and their slack is consequently reduced.

The purpose of this paper is to focus on the impact of the product market on *x*-inefficiency within a managerial firm, in a setting that eliminates any source of competition among managers. Instead, the paper explores the possibility that increased competitive pressure in the output market raises the sensitivity of firm profits to managerial behaviour. If so, then it might be expected that adjustments in the optimal mechanism of indirect control of managers would induce them to behave more efficiently. Thus, more competition would render internal efficiency more critical, and rational owners would be willing to spend more to motivate managers to achieve it.

To pursue the investigation of this possibility, it is necessary to work with a principal–agent model that is amenable to comparative statics analysis. For this purpose, I adapt the simple mathematical structure of the model recently developed by Baron and Myerson (1982) for a different application. This model has also been utilised in recent work by Krishna (1984).

My main finding is that increases in competition that raise the sensitivity of profit to managerial behaviour, without diminishing profit, do reduce *x*-inefficiency. Such increases in competition add to social welfare both in the product market and in the internal operations of the firm. Moreover, they result in greater compensation paid to the manager and to greater managerial utility. On the other hand, if the increase in competition principally contracts firm profit, even with some heightening of its sensitivity to behaviour, then these conclusions are reversed. Radial contraction of the profit function raises *x*-inefficiency, reduces social welfare, and reduces managerial compensation.

II THE OWNER–MANAGER MODEL

This section details the principal–agent interaction between the owner and the manager of the firm. The owner and the manager are assumed to be risk neutral. The owner's expected profit from the operations of the firm are given by $V(c,b)$, where b is a shift parameter that will be suppressed until relevant, and c is an observable measure of some aspect of the firm's costs. The measure c is determined by the labour effort, L, of the manager and by the resolution θ, of a positive random variable with interval support $D=[\Theta_0, \theta_1]$, differentiable distribution

$f(\theta)$, and cumulative $F(\theta)$. Both θ and L are observable by the manager, and neither is observable by the owner. To facilitate the analysis, a simple functional form is assumed for the relationship among L, θ, and c:

$$c = \frac{\theta}{L} \tag{1}$$

The manager's utility, as a function of his financial compensation from the firm, R, and his labour effort is simply,

$$U(R, L) = R - \alpha L, \tag{2}$$

where α is a positive parameter. Both (1) and (2) are assumed to be common knowledge, as is $f(\theta)$.

After observing θ, the manager reports to the owner a value for this random variable, $\hat{\theta}$, on the basis of his own incentives. He does so with knowledge of the schedules $R(\hat{\theta})$, $c(\hat{\theta})$, and $\varphi(\hat{\theta})$ which have been established and committed to by the owner. $c(\hat{\theta})$ is the cost target that the manager must achieve, in order to receive any compensation, given the report $\hat{\theta}$. $\varphi(\hat{\theta})$ is the probability that the owner will choose to operate the firm at all. $R(\hat{\theta})$ is the compensation that will be paid to the manager, provided that $\hat{\theta}$ is reported, that the firm will be in operation, and that the cost target is met. Note that there is no uncertainty about whether the cost target is satisfied. The owner can observe c after θ has been observed by the manager and after the manager has subsequently effected his chosen level of effort. The manager knows that to achieve $c(\hat{\theta})$, due to common knowledge about (1), he must supply effort at the level

$$L = \theta / c(\hat{\theta}).$$

Consequently, if the manager observes θ, and provided that he expects to meet his cost target (as he will be motivated to do), his expected utility from reporting $\hat{\theta}$ is

$$S(\hat{\theta} \mid \theta) = \left[R(\hat{\theta}) - \frac{\alpha\theta}{c(\hat{\theta})} \right] \varphi(\hat{\theta}). \tag{3}$$

He will choose his report to maximise (3), thereby attaining

$$S(\theta) = \max_{\hat{\theta}} S(\hat{\theta} \mid \theta).$$

Assume that the manager cannot be bound to the firm *ex ante*, that his opportunities elsewhere, after observing θ, would yield him $U=0$, and that his services are essential to the operation of the firm. Then, the owner must set $R(\hat{\theta})$ and $c(\hat{\theta})$ to ensure that

$$S(\theta) \geqslant 0, \qquad \theta \in D. \tag{4}$$

It follows that the manager will elect to meet the cost target, because otherwise his payment will be zero and his utility cannot be positive.

The problem facing the owner is to choose $R(\hat{\theta})$, $c(\hat{\theta})$, and $\varphi(\hat{\theta})$ to maximise his expected profit, net of compensation paid to the manager:

$$\int_D [V[c(\hat{\theta}^*(\theta))] - R(\hat{\theta}^*(\theta))]\varphi[\hat{\theta}^*(\theta)]f(\theta)\,d\theta. \tag{5}$$

Here, $\hat{\theta}^*(\theta)$ is the manager's report given his observation of θ. Of course, the schedules chosen by the owner will determine $\hat{\theta}^*(\theta)$.

The owner's problem is much simplified by the application of the revelation principle (see Myerson (1979); Dasgupta *et al.* (1979); Baron and Myerson (1982); or Krishna (1984) for useful presentations). This shows that any outcome of the principal–agent interaction specified here can be attained as the solution to the maximisation of (5) with respect to $R(\cdot)$, $c(\cdot)$, and $\varphi(\cdot)$, subject to the incentive compatibility constraints that $\hat{\theta}^*(\theta) = \theta$, $\theta \in D$; i.e., subject to rational truthful revelation of the private information. This constraint can be written

$$S(\theta \mid \theta) = \max_{\hat{\theta}} S(\hat{\theta} \mid \theta) = S(\theta), \qquad \theta \in D. \tag{6}$$

The problem is further simplified by the followeing lemma, which is adapted from similar results in Baron and Myerson (1982) and in Krishna (1984).

Lemma 1: $R(\cdot)$, $c(\cdot)$, and $\varphi(\cdot)$ are feasibly incentive compatible in that they satisfy (4), (6), and

$$0 \leqslant \varphi(\theta) \leqslant 1,\ \theta \in D, \tag{7}$$

if and only if (7), (4),

$$S(\theta) = S(\theta_1) + \int_{\theta}^{\theta_1} \frac{\alpha\varphi(\tilde{\theta})}{c(\tilde{\theta})}\,d\tilde{\theta}, \tag{8}$$

and

$$\frac{\varphi(\theta)}{c(\theta)} \geqslant \frac{\varphi(\tilde{\theta})}{c(\tilde{\theta})} \qquad \text{for } \theta < \tilde{\theta}. \tag{9}$$

The proof is a straightforward application of the material presented in Baron and Meyerson. Continuing to follow the methods employed by Baron and Meyerson and by Krishna,

Lemma 2 For feasibly incentive compatible $R(\cdot)$, $c(\cdot)$, and $\varphi(\cdot)$, the expected profit of the firm's owner can be written

$$EV = \int_{\theta_0}^{\theta_1} \left[V(c(\theta)) - \frac{\alpha}{c(\theta)} z(\theta) \right] \varphi(\theta) f(\theta) \mathrm{d}\theta - S(\theta_1) \tag{10}$$

where

$$z(\theta) \equiv \theta + \frac{F(\theta)}{f(\theta)}.$$

This result follows from Lemma 1 by first expressing

$$EV = \int_{\theta_0}^{\theta_1} [V(c(\theta)) - R(\theta)] \varphi(\theta) f(\theta) \, \mathrm{d}\theta. \tag{11}$$

Then, note that by the definitions of $S(\theta)$ and $S(\theta|\theta)$, and by the fact that $\hat{\theta}^*(\theta) = \theta$,

$$S(\theta)\varphi(\theta) = \left[R(\theta) \frac{\alpha\theta}{c(\theta)} \right] \varphi(\theta). \tag{12}$$

Rearranging (12) to isolate $R(\theta)\varphi(\theta)$, substituting from (8), substituting into (11), and integrating by parts yields (10).

Now, since the incentive compatibility constraints have been largely incorporated into (10), the owner's problem can be solved by simply maximising (10) with respect to $c(\theta)$ and $\varphi(\theta)$ on a point-wise basis. The result of this process, taking into account (9), is:

Proposition 1 Assume that

$$z'(\theta) \geqslant 0 \qquad \text{for } \theta \varepsilon D, \tag{13}$$

and that this second-order condition holds (subscripts denoting derivatives):

$$Vcc(c(\theta)) - \frac{2\alpha z(\theta)}{c^3(\theta)} < 0. \tag{14}$$

Then the solution to the owner's problem is $c(\theta)$, $\varphi(\theta)$, and $R(\theta)$ such that

$$Vc(c(\theta)) + \frac{\alpha z(\theta)}{c^2(\theta)} = 0, \qquad \text{for } \theta_0 \leqslant \theta \leqslant \theta^* \leqslant \theta_1; \tag{15}$$

$$V(c(\theta^*)) - \frac{\alpha z(\theta^*)}{c(\theta^*)} = 0, \qquad \text{or } \theta^* = \theta_1; \tag{16}$$

$$\varphi(\theta) = 1 \qquad \text{for } \theta_0 \leqslant \theta \leqslant \theta^*, \quad \text{and} \quad \varphi(\theta) = 0 \text{ otherwise}; \tag{17}$$

$$R(\theta) = \frac{\alpha\theta}{c(\theta)} + \int_{\theta}^{\theta^*} \frac{a}{c(\tilde{\theta})} d\tilde{\theta} \qquad \text{for } \theta_0 \leqslant \theta \leqslant \theta^*. \tag{18}$$

To understand this result, note that (15) and (14) are the first- and second-order conditions for the point-wise maximisation of (10) with respect to c. With $c(\theta)$ so chosen, the envelope theorem shows that the derivative with respect to θ of the part of the integrand of (19),

$$V(c(\theta)) - \frac{\alpha z(\theta)}{c(\theta)}, \tag{19}$$

is $-\alpha z'/c$, which is non-positive by (13). Thus, as expressed in (16), if (19) is zero at $\theta^* < \theta_1$, then it will be non-negative for smaller values of θ and non-positive for larger values. The optimal rules for φ given in (17) follow. It does not pay to operate the firm for reports greater than θ^*, and it does pay otherwise. If (19) is never zero, then it always pays to operate, and $\theta^* = \theta_1$. Maximisation requires setting $S(\theta_1)$ at its smallest feasible value, namely zero. Then (18) follows from (12) and (8). Finally, (9) must be checked. Note first that φ is non-increasing, as has just been shown. Second, comparative statics analysis of (15), making use of (14), shows that $dc(\theta)/d\theta \geqslant 0$, provided that (13) holds. Then (9) follows.

It should be noted that Baron and Myerson (1982) present a solution technique to an analogous problem that permits (13) to be violated. In the interests of simplicity, I shall not pursue this generalisation.

III INFORMATION ASYMMETRY AND X-INEFFICIENCY

In the setting just described, even though it is in the interests of the owner to experience low values of the cost measure c, it does not pay him to induce by means of $R(\cdot)$ sufficient effort to experience full cost efficiency. The resulting excessive levels of cost might be said to arise from x-inefficiency. More precisely, in this model they are the inevitable consequence of information asymmetry – for it is the owner's inability to directly monitor effort and to observe θ that force him to induce effort indirectly by means of the expensive $R(\cdot)$ mechanism.

Before studying the influence of the product market on x-inefficiency, it is useful to characterise it by contrast with the behaviour of the same firm in the event it were run efficiently. The direct way to analyse this case is by positing that the manager also owns the firm. (This case was termed by Hart the entrepreneurial firm.) Then the owner's problem becomes

$$\max_{\varphi(\theta),c(\theta)} \int_{\theta_0}^{\theta_1} \left(V(c(\theta)) - \frac{\alpha\theta}{c(\theta)} \right) \varphi(\theta) f(\theta) \mathrm{d}\theta.$$

Point-wise maximisation yields

$$Vc(c(\theta)) + \frac{\alpha\theta}{c^2(\theta)} = 0, \tag{20}$$

and

$$Vcc(c(\theta)) - \frac{2\alpha\theta}{c^3(\theta)} < 0, \tag{21}$$

as the first- and second-order conditions. Substitution of (15) into (14) and (20) into (21) indicate that the problems of both the managerial and the entrepreneurial firms have the same second-order conditions on $V(\cdot)$:

$$Vcc + \frac{2Vc}{c} < 0. \tag{22}$$

Henceforth, (22) along with the condition $z' \geqslant 0$ shall be assumed. The first-order conditions, (15) and (20), systematically differ because $z(\theta)=\theta+F(\theta)/f(\theta)>\theta$ for $\theta>\theta_0$. Of course, $z(\theta_0)=\theta_0$, so that the conditions coincide there.

Proposition 2 Under the best cost conditions (e.g. $\theta=\theta_0$), the managerial firm operates efficiently. Otherwise, the costs of the managerial firm exceed those that would be incurred if there were no informational asymmetry or if the manager owned the firm. Further, some of the cost conditions that would drive the managerial firm out of operation would not deter it from operating if it were run efficiently.

Proof Let $g(c)\equiv c^2Vc(c)$. $g'(c)=2cVc+c^2Vcc<0$, given (22). For the managerial firm, (15) implies that $g(c(\theta))=-\alpha z(\theta)$, while for the efficiently run firm, (21) indicates that $g(c(\theta))=-\alpha\theta$. Since $z(\theta)>\theta$ for $\theta>\theta_0$, $c(\theta)$ is larger in the managerial case. If the managerial firm shuts down for

$$\theta>\theta^*>\theta_0,\ V(c(\theta^*))-\frac{\alpha z(\theta^*)}{c(\theta^*)}=0.$$

At these cost conditions, the owner-manager of the entrepreneurial firm could gain positive utility from operating. This is so because he chooses c to maximise $V(c)-(\alpha\theta^*)/c$, and it has already been shown that his choice is distinct from that of the managerial firm.

Finally, to see that common knowledge of θ would eliminate the x-inefficiency of the managerial firm, note that then the owner could hold the manager to zero utility in all states by setting

$$R(\theta)=\alpha\theta/c(\theta).$$

In this scenario, the owner would simply choose $c(\theta)$ to maximise $V(c(\theta))-\alpha\theta/c(\theta)$, like the entrepreneurial firm.

Another way to view the relationship between the information structure and the x-inefficiency is to recognise that the wedge between the managerial and efficient levels of c arises from the difference between $z(\theta)$ and θ in (15) and (21). This difference is $F(\theta)/f(\theta)$. Thus, at a given level of θ, the managerial firm will experience more x-inefficiency the greater the *ex ante* likelihood that cost conditions could be better.

IV COMPARATIVE STATICS

As a prelude to considering the influence of the product market on x-inefficiency, this section details some necessary comparative-static analytics. Because product market effects enter the problem through $V(c)$, I consider the influences of changes in a parameter, b, that affects $V(c)$. Hence, I now write this function as $V(c, b)$.

I first consider effects on welfare, measured narrowly for now as the sum of the expected real incomes of the firm's owner and manager:

$$EW=\int_{\theta_0}^{\theta^*}\left[V(c(\theta),b)-\frac{\alpha\theta}{c(\theta)}\right]f(\theta)\,\mathrm{d}\theta. \tag{23}$$

Differentiating (23), and making use of (15) and (16) demonstrates that

$$\frac{\mathrm{d}EW}{\mathrm{d}b}=\int_{\theta_0}^{\theta^*}V_b(c(\theta),b)f(\theta)\,\mathrm{d}\theta-\int_{\theta_0}^{\theta^*}\frac{\partial c(\theta)}{\partial b}\frac{\alpha F}{c^2(\theta)}\mathrm{d}\theta+\frac{\alpha F(\theta^*)}{c(\theta^*)}\frac{\partial\theta^*}{\partial b} \tag{24}$$

The first term reflects the direct impact of b on the income of the firm's owner, and this term would arise for an efficiently run firm as well. The second term reflects the impact of b on the degree of x-inefficiency. Changes in b raise welfare in this regard to the extent that they induce the owner to alter his compensation and target schedules in a manner that motivates the manager to expend greater effort. This behavioural effect is summarised by $\partial c(\theta)/\partial b$.

Analysis of the impact of b on costs is a straightforward comparative statics calculation from (14) and (15). This shows that

$$\text{sign}\left(\frac{\partial c(\theta)}{\partial b}\right)=\text{sign } Vcb\ (c(\theta),b); \tag{25}$$

i.e., the more steeply decreasing is V in c, the lower will be the level of c that the owner chooses to induce.

The impact of b on θ^*, where $\theta^*<\theta_1$, can be derived by totally differentiating (16) and using (15):

$$\frac{\partial\theta^*}{\partial b}=\frac{cVb}{\alpha z'} \tag{26}$$

Hence, an increase in b that is directly beneficial ($V_b>0$), and that reduces x-inefficiency ($c_b<0$), will have the additional effect of inducing operation in more states of nature ($\theta_b^*>0$).

The effects of b on expected managerial compensation can be derived from (18):

$$\frac{dER}{db}=\int_{\theta_0}^{\theta^*}\left[\frac{-\alpha\theta}{c^2}\frac{\partial c(\theta)}{\partial b}-\int_{\theta}^{\theta^*}\frac{\alpha}{c^2}\frac{\partial c(\theta)}{\partial b}\,d\theta\right]f(\theta)\,d\theta$$

$$+\frac{\partial\theta^*}{\partial b}\left[\frac{\alpha F(\theta^*)}{c(\theta^*)}+\frac{\alpha\theta^* f(\theta^*)}{c(\theta^*)}\right] \tag{27}$$

Thus, an increase in b that lowers costs and that increases the range of operating conditions also has the effect of raising average payments to the manager. Expected managerial utility is given by

$$ES=\int_{\theta_0}^{\theta^*}\int_{\theta}^{\theta^*}\frac{\alpha}{c(\theta)}f(\theta)^*d\theta d\theta. \tag{28}$$

Consequently

$$\frac{dES}{db}=F(\theta^*)\frac{\alpha}{c(\theta^*)}\frac{\partial\theta^*}{\partial b}-\int_{\theta_0}^{\theta^*}\int_{\theta}^{\theta^*}\frac{\alpha}{c^2(\theta)}\frac{\partial c(\theta)}{\partial b}f(\theta)\,d\theta d\theta. \tag{29}$$

Thus, even though the additional effort induced in response to a change in b causes disutility, the change raises expected managerial utility provided that it does not too drastically curtail the firm's operations.

V X-INEFFICIENCY AND THE PRODUCT MARKET

Now we are finally equipped to address the principal question set forth in the introduction: Does added competitive pressure on firms in their product markets reduce x-inefficiency and thereby make a contribution to social welfare over and above the reduction of deadweight loss in the firms' supply of output?

As a first approach, I consider the following representation of the product market activities of the firm: Let the firm's demand be $Q(p,b)$, where p is the output price it sets. The firm's smooth production cost function is $M(Q, c)$, where c is the measure of the level of costs that is subject to managerial influence, so that $M_c>0$. In addition, assume that added costs are concomitant with increased marginal costs, so that $M_{Qc}>0$. We can define

$$V(c, b) = \max_p [pQ(p,b) - M(Q(p,b),c)] \equiv \max_p \pi(p,b,c). \tag{30}$$

Application of the envelope theorem gives

$$V_c = -M_c(Q(p^*, b), c), \tag{31}$$

where p^* is the profit maximising price. Also,

$$V_b = Q_b(p^* - M_Q). \tag{32}$$

Differentiating (31) with respect to the shift parameter b,

$$V_{cb} = -M_{Qc}\left(Q_p \frac{\partial p^*}{\partial b} + Q_b \right). \tag{33}$$

Let us suppose, for the moment, that the effect of b is to pivot the demand curve, leaving the current equilibrium point unchanged, and rendering the curve more elastic at the current point. Then, since

$$\text{sign}\ (\partial p^*/\partial b) = \text{sign}\ (Q_b + Q_{pb}(p^* - M_Q)), \tag{34}$$

with $Q_b(p^*,b) = 0$ it follows that $\partial p^*/\partial b < 0$. This exogenous increase in b can be properly interpreted as an increase in competitive pressure, because it increases the price sensitivity of the firm's demand and thereby motivates it to lower price closer to marginal cost, M_Q. Here, (33) and (32) show that $V_{cb} < 0$, while $V_b = 0$ so that the product market profits of the firm at its equilibrium are not directly affected by the shift. The following conclusions are immediate from (24) and (25).

In response to this increase in competitive pressure, the owner induces the manager to expend more effort, thereby reducing welfare loss from x-inefficiency. This welfare gain is an addition to the gains in consumer surplus resulting from the concomitant reduction in price. In fact, price falls as a result of the increase in demand elasticity, and, in addition, it falls as a result of the decrease in marginal cost caused by the increased managerial effort.

Further, reference to (27) and (29), or to (18) and (28), shows that if there is no effect on θ^*, then managerial compensation and utility are raised by the increase in b. *Hence, this form of increased competitive pressure in the product market benefits management.*

Now, consider relaxing the temporary assumption that $Q_b = 0$. If increased competition lowers demand, and hence, by (32), lowers product market profit, while it raises the price sensitivity of demand, then (33) shows that V_{cb} may be positive. In such cases, the just emphasised conclusions would be *reversed.* To isolate this effect, let demand now be $aQ(p,b)$, where a is a new parameter that radially shifts the demand curve. Calculation shows that

$$V_a = Q(p^*, b)[p^* - M_Q(aQ(p^*, b), c)]. \tag{35}$$

$$V_{ca} = -M_{Qc}[Q + aQ_p \partial p^*/\partial a]. \tag{36}$$

It is easy to check that if M has constant returns to scale, then $\partial p^*/\partial a = 0$ and $V_{ca} < 0$.

Hence, a profitable radial increase in demand would, by (24)–(26), induce greater managerial effort, less x-inefficiency, downward movement in price as a result of lowered marginal cost, and increased managerial compensation and utility. Here, profitability breeds efficiency.

Of course, the opposite applies as well: If the effect of added competition is to radially shrink demand, then added x-inefficiency would result. Typically, increased competition will both shrink demand and render it more elastic. Then, there are two opposing forces on x-inefficiency. The shrinkage of profits due to the shrinkage in demand is a force against operational efficiency, while the enlarged elasticity favours efficiency. In general, the balance can swing either way.

The final result pinpoints a decomposition of these forces that isolates the positive impact of competitive pressure on internal efficiency.

Proposition 3 Let $\pi(p, a, b, c) = aQ(p, b)p - M[aQ(p, b), c]$ and let $V(a, b, c) = \max_p \pi(p, a, b, c)$. For a given value of $\theta < \theta^*$, define a direction of perturbation of a and b, da/db, such that the elasticity of demand is increased and V is stationary; i.e., the change in a compensates V for the change in b that raises the elasticity of demand. Then, at θ, small perturbations in this direction lower V_c, reduce x-inefficiency, reduce output price, raise welfare in both the product market and in the operations of the firm, and increase the compensation and utility of the manager.

Proof $\frac{da}{db}=\frac{-V_b}{V_a}=\frac{-aQ_b}{Q}$

$$V_c=-M_c[aQ, c]$$

$$dV_c=\left[V_{cb}+V_{ca}\frac{da}{db}\right]db=\left[-M_{cQ}\left(aQ_b+aQ_p\frac{p^*}{\delta b}\right)\right.$$

$$\left.+\frac{aQ_b}{Q}M_{cQ}\left(Q+aQ_p\frac{p^*}{a}\right)\right]db$$

$$\frac{\partial p^*}{\partial a}=\frac{aQ_pQM_{cQ}}{\pi_{pp}}$$

$$\frac{\partial p^*}{\partial b}=\frac{aQ_b+aQ_{pb}(-Q/Q_p)}{-\pi_{pp}},$$

having substituted from $\pi_p=0$. Then,

$$dV_c=\frac{M_{Qc}a^2}{-p\pi_{pp}}\frac{d(Q_pp/Q)}{db}db$$

and

$$\text{sign }(dV_c)=\text{sign }(d(Q_pp/Q)).$$

Thus, if the perturbations raise the elasticity of demand, then $dV_c<0$, and the rest follows by the arguments earlier in the text.

VI CONCLUDING REMARKS

This paper is only the second shot, following Hart, at elucidating the connections between corporate governance and the nature of the firm's product market. It has become clear that this is a rich area for study and, the other side of the same coin, that not very much is currently known. The most obvious enrichments of the models to consider include oligopoly among managerial firms, whose managers' private information may be somewhat correlated (see Hart (1983) on this issue); a more or less competitive market for the services of managers; and dimensions of managerial decisions for which best inferences require analysis of profits as well as intermediate measures such as costs.

REFERENCES

Amihud, Y. and B. Lev (1981) 'Risk Reduction as a Managerial Motive for Conglomerate Mergers', *Bell Journal*, vol. 12, no. 2, pp. 605–17.

Baron, D. and R. Myerson (1982) 'Regulating a Monopolist with Unknown Costs', *Econometrica*, vol. 50, no. 4, pp. 911–30.

Dasgupta, P., P. Hammond and E. Maskin (1979) 'The Implementation of Social Choice Rules: Some Results on Incentive Compatability', *Review of Economic Studies*, vol. 46, pp. 185–216.

Fama, E. (1980) 'Agency Problems and The Theory of The Firm', *Journal of Political Economy*, vol. 88, no. 2, pp. 288–307.

Hart, O. (1983) 'The Market Mechanism as an Incentive Scheme', *Bell Journal*, vol. 14, no. 2, pp. 366–82.

Jensen, M. and W. Meckling (1976) 'Theory of The Firm: Managerial Behavior, Agency Costs and Ownership Structure', *Journal of Financial Economics*, vol. 3, pp. 305–60.

Krishna, Kala (1984) 'Protection, Product Lines and Welfare,' xerox.

Myerson, R. (1979) 'Incentive Compatibility and the Bargaining Problem', *Econometrica*, vol. 47, pp. 61–74.

Comments on Robert D. Willig, 'Corporate Governance and Product Market Structure', by Avishay Braverman*

Robert Willig provides us in this interesting paper with an important application of the 'moral hazard' principle in the context of an owner (principal) and a manager (agent) of a firm. He addresses in this context a major question, namely, what is the role of product market competition in enforcing *x*-efficiency.

I have two short comments on this paper. One refers to the main proposition of the paper and its validity; the other is concerned with general issues of the new 'imperfect information' literature.

Willig's main proposition is the following: increased product market competition will increase or decrease the degree of the firm's *x*-inefficiency (i.e. managers' effort in effectively reducing cost) depending upon the specification of the demand shift implied by increased competition, the functional forms of demand and cost, and other model specifications, particularly those characterising risk. Increased product market competition is modelled in terms of a downward, elasticity increasing shift of the demand function.

The two effects of (i) shrinking demand and (ii) rendering it more elastic, work, according to Willig, on opposite directions. While enlarged demand elasticity induces the manager on the margin to *increase* effort, the decline in the firm's profits due to demand shrinkage *decreases* the manager's effort in cutting cost. Hence, the sum of these two effects is ambiguous in sign.

I am not fully convinced of this ambiguity. That the enlarged elasticity effect (such that the product market profits of the firm at its equilibrium are not directly affected by the slope change) implies the increase in the manager's effort, is intuitively clear. However, that the decline in profits due to demand shrinkage implies reduction in manager's effort, is not as clear to me. From my intuition in the area of owner–manager conflict generated by the study of sharecropping contracts in the modern theory of rural organisation,[1] would like to discuss this result under the following two assumptions: (i) that in the initial equilibrium the utility taking constraint of the manager's utility is not binding, that is, managers obtain rent in their current job beyond their opportunity cost elsewhere, (ii) that the utility taking constraint is always binding.

*The author is a Senior Economist at the World Bank. The views expressed here are those of the author, and do not necessarily reflect the official views of the World Bank.

(a) The Non-binding Case

A possible outcome in markets for heterogeneous abilities under imperfect information is that managers accrue rent in their current job beyond their opportunity cost elsewhere. For my point here, though, it is sufficient to assume that even if managers obtain exactly their opportunity cost, the shift in product demand reduces their opportunity wages in addition to reducing their firm's profits. This may be the case when the shift in demand is due to foreign competition which affects the whole industry. If one of those two cases prevail, then the case for competition as an incentive scheme for managers seems stronger than that argued by Willig.

For simplicity, assume a manager endowed with a concave utility function in two goods: consumption, c, which equals income, I, and leisure, which in efficiency units is defined as $-e$, where e denotes effort; i.e. $U=U(I, -e)$. Assume further a proportional payment scheme for managers; i.e. $I=a\pi$, where α denotes the manager's share of profits, π. A decline in demand which reduces profits will therefore reduce the manager's income. First let us hold α constant. Then, if leisure is assumed to be a normal good,[2] the reduction in income will induce a reduction in leisure, that is an *increase* in effort. Clearly, in general the optimal share contract, α, will be revised by the owner following the new conditions. If under the old share, the decline in profits pushes the manager income below his reservation utility, the owner will adjust α by *increasing* it. As long as the manager's new income is lower than his income in the initial equilibrium, both the overall income effect, and the increase in α will further motivate the manager *to increase his effort*.

(b) A Utility Binding Contract

Assume the same structure as in (a) but with a utility binding constraint for the manager's expected utility. Now a decline in demand which reduces the firm's profits and hence the manager's income, has to be adjusted by increasing the manager's profit share, α. Following the sharecropping literature, the increase in α will increase the manager's effort if the elasticity of substitution between effort and the other factor is bigger than one. In the case here, this production function has to be modified, but I conjecture that the case for increased manager's effort will still be stronger than that argued by

Willig. Furthermore, allowing owners to possess broader payment schemes than a proportional share will increase their control in devising better effort inducing schemes for managers.

Clearly my conjectures require a rigorous demonstration by taking the proper compensated derivatives in the uncertainty framework. This will be done in a separate paper. What I have attempted here is to lay the ground for a more decisive case in favour of product market competition as an incentive mechanism for reducing managers' *x*-inefficiency.

My second comment does not relate to Bobby's paper, I just use here the opportunity to share with you a general observation concerning the state of research in the field of imperfect information. This remark is appropriate here since the title of the conference is 'Public policy in theory and in *practice*' (my italics). On a personal note, I might add that being currently involved in policy analysis myself, I may now judge research work on a different yardstick than I did as a theoretician. Whatever my excuse is, I shall address a condition which, I think, may become a danger to the real vitality of the important field of the economics of information.

For more than a decade, we have been applying mostly the two principles of 'moral hazard' and 'adverse selection' in different contexts. This literature has generated many insights and has been probably the main force in pushing the theoretical frontier. However, by now we are experiencing a flood of examples, a taxonomy of cases, which empirically cannot be verified, and therefore on a *real* scientific basis, and for policy analysis, provide few insights. My request to the leaders of this field is to move forward in identifying the key prototype results and policy lessons emerging from this extensive literature, and spare us a period which may resemble a second phase of the once booming, 'optimal growth' literature.

Notes

1. The first proper contractual equilibrium framework for the study of rural organisation was set by Stiglitz's sharecropping article in 1974. Braverman and Srinivasan (1981) and Braverman and Stiglitz (1982) derived comparative statics results, assuming both utility binding (taking) and non-binding (taking) equilibria in the market for sharecroppers (managers). Their results may have some relevance to the analysis of comparative statics analysed by Willig.
2. Under uncertainty slightly stronger sufficient conditions are needed.

REFERENCES

Braverman, A. and T. N. Srinivasan (1981) 'Credit and Sharecropping in Agrarian Societies', *Journal of Development Economics*, 9 (December) pp. 289–312.

Braverman, A. and E. Stiglitz (1982) 'Sharecropping and the Interlinking of Agrarian Markets', *American Economic Review* (September) pp. 695–715.

Stiglitz, J. E. (1974) 'Incentives and Risk Sharing in Sharecropping', *Review of Economic Studies*, 61 (April) pp. 219–56.

Comments on Robert D. Willig, 'Corporate Governance and Product Market Structure' by Oliver Hart

In the last few years, a great deal of work has been done in the general area of incentive theory. Among other things, this work has been very useful in clarifying the incentive problems that exist between the manager of a firm (or group of managers) and the owner (or owners) on whose behalf the firm is operated. It has long been argued, at least by some theorists of the firm, that a manager is likely to have, and to pursue, interests different from those of an owner. That is, there will be managerial slack or x-inefficiency in a manager-run firm. It has been recognised, however, that the owner can use an incentive scheme to reduce such slack. The recent incentives literature allows us to examine precisely the limits of such incentive schemes.

Almost all of the work in this area has been concerned with a firm, or possibly a group of firms, in isolation from the rest of the economy. That is, the influence of *market* pressure on managerial behaviour has received scant attention. Bobby Willig's paper, which is concerned with the impact of the product market on managerial slack, is therefore very welcome.

Willig studies a single managerial firm, which is a monopolist in its product market. The assumption that the firm is alone in this market is quite restrictive and I shall have more to say about it later. Willig's main interest is in how the position of the monopolist's demand curve affects the amount of managerial slack. He is also concerned with the question of whether an 'increase in competitive pressure', by reducing managerial slack, leads to a welfare gain *over and above* that resulting from the normal effect on consumer surplus of a price reduction.

In my comments, I shall concentrate on this welfare question. In order to understand Willig's results about this, I shall find it useful to employ a slightly different (and, I think simpler) model of a managerial firm. The two models are very much in the same spirit, however. Consider a firm which can produce either one unit or zero units of output. The cost of producing one unit is given by the random variable, $\tilde{c}$, which has the continuous distribution function F. Neither the manager nor the owner knows c when the incentive contract is signed. The manager finds out c, however, before he makes the firm's production decision, while the owner never learns c (the idea is that c is a personal cost borne by the manager). The distribution function F is common knowledge.

Since the only publicly observable variable is the level of output, q, an incentive scheme is simply a function $I = I(q)$, which relates the compensation I that the manager receives to the level of output q that he produces. Under our additional assumption that $q = 0$ or 1, the incentive scheme consists of just two numbers, I_0, I_1. Given this scheme and a particular realisation of $\tilde{c}$, c, the manager will choose to set $q = 1$ if and only if $I_1 - c > I_0$. (We ignore the zero probability event $I_1 - C = I_0$.)

In order to simplify the analysis, I shall make the strong assumption that the monopolist faces a *perfectly elastic* demand curve at price $\bar{p}$. This is a departure from Willig, but it allows me to focus on the incentive effects of changes in demand and abstract from ordinary monopoly distortions. I do not believe that this assumption is crucial.

Under the assumption of perfectly elastic demand, the owner's revenues are given by $\bar{p}q$. In order to analyse the incentive problem that exists between the owner and the manager, we must specify the manager's attitudes towards risk (the owner will be assumed to be risk neutral). For the moment, let me follow Willig in supposing that the manager is risk neutral, but cannot be bound to the firm after he observes c. Then the owner's problem is to choose (I_0, I_1) to

$$\text{Maximise } (\bar{p} - I_1 + I_0) \text{ prob}[\tilde{c} < I_1 - I_0] - I_0 \qquad (1)$$

$$\text{S.T. } I_0 \geqslant 0.$$

To understand this, note that the owner's net revenue is $(\bar{p} - I_1)$ if production occurs and $-I_0$ otherwise. The constraint reflects the inability of the owner to bind the manager; if I_0 is negative, the manager can always quit and avoid this 'exit fee'. There may also be a second constraint which says that the manager's expected net income cannot fall short of his opportunity cost, $\bar{u}$, at the time he signs the incentive contract ($\bar{u}$ can be imagined to be determined in a competitive market for managers). Following Willig, we ignore this constraint (we suppose that $\hat{u} = 0$), although we return to it below.

Note that, if the constraint $I_0 \geqslant 0$ were absent, the first-best could be achieved by setting $(I_1 - I_0) = \bar{p}$ (this ensures that production occurs whenever marginal revenue, $\bar{p}$, exceeds marginal cost, c).

In the second-best, the constraint $I_0 \geqslant 0$ will obviously be binding since the owner wants to reduce managerial compensation as much as possible. Setting $I_0 = 0$ in (1), we can write the owner's problem as

$$\text{Maximise } (\bar{p} - I_1) \text{ prob } [\tilde{c} < I_1], \qquad (2)$$

the solution to which we denote by $\hat{I}_1$ (assumed unique). Note that $c_{\min} < \hat{I}_1 < \bar{p}$, and so we obtain a version of Willig's Proposition 2: production occurs too little of the time relative to the first-best (but it does occur in the lowest cost states).

It is obvious that $\hat{I}_1$ depends on $\bar{p}$: we write $\hat{I}_1 = \hat{I}_1(\bar{p})$. It is also not difficult to see from a revealed preference argument that $\hat{I}_1$ is increasing in $\bar{p}$. We have therefore established another of Willig's results: an increase in demand increases the probability of production, prob $[\tilde{c} < \hat{I}_1]$ (note that the first-best probability of production, prob $[\tilde{c} < \bar{p}]$, also rises, and so I am not sure that it is correct to say that managerial slack has fallen).

We can also study welfare in this example. Since consumer surplus is zero with perfectly elastic demand, total (expected) surplus equals owner surplus plus manager surplus, i.e.

$$(\bar{p} - \hat{I}(\bar{p}))\ \text{prob}\ [\tilde{c} < \hat{I}(\bar{p})] + E[\hat{I}(\bar{p}) - \tilde{c}\tilde{c} < \hat{I}(\bar{p})]\ \text{prob}\ [\tilde{c} < \hat{I}(\bar{p})]$$

$$= E[\bar{p} - \tilde{c} \mid \tilde{c} < \hat{I}(\bar{p})]\ \text{prob}\ [\tilde{c} < \hat{I}(\bar{p})]. \qquad (3)$$

As we have noted, Willig is interested in the effect of a 'change in competitive pressure', or more generally a change in demand, on managerial slack and welfare. Rather than looking at this directly, we will consider a related question: can a planner manipulate demand to increase welfare?

Suppose that a planner subsidises output by offering to purchase it at a price $p^* > \bar{p}$. Then total surplus, including offsetting lump-sum subsidies or taxes, equals

$$(p^* - \hat{I}(p^*))\ \text{prob}\ [\tilde{c} < \hat{I}(p^*)] + E[\hat{I}(p^*) - \tilde{c} \mid \tilde{c} < \hat{I}(p^*)]\ \text{prob}\ [\tilde{c} < \hat{I}(p^*)] + (\bar{p} - p^*)\ \text{prob}\ [\tilde{c} < \hat{I}(p^*)] = E[\bar{p} - \tilde{c} \mid \tilde{c} < \hat{I}(p^*)]\ \text{prob}\ [\tilde{c} < \hat{I}(p^*)]. \qquad (4)$$

Now we know that $\hat{I}(p^*) > \hat{I}(\bar{p})$. It follows that for p^* close to and bigger than $\bar{p}$, the expression in (4) exceeds that in (3), since production occurs in a larger number of efficient states. In other words, the subsidy leads to an increase in welfare.

I think that this is the effect Willig is referring to when he talks about 'an increase in competitive pressure' leading to a welfare gain *over and above* that resulting from the normal effect on consumer surplus of a price reduction (note that the normal effect is absent in our model since, with perfectly elastic demand, there is no monopoly distortion). I now want to consider how robust this 'externality' effect is.

Basically, I will argue that it is very sensitive to Willig's assumptions about managerial preferences. The externality arises because the owner chooses the optimal incentive scheme to maximise his own payoff and does not take into account the manager's surplus, $E[\hat{I}-\tilde{c}\tilde{c}<\hat{I}]$ prob $[\tilde{c}<\hat{I}]$. This problem disappears, however, if the owner can tax away the manager's surplus. There are several ways in which to do this. One is to charge an exit fee, i.e. set $I_0<0$, a possibility Willig simply rules out. A second way is to charge an entry fee. Willig does not discuss this, but it is clear that, if $\bar{U}=0$, a manager would be prepared to pay $E[\hat{I}-\tilde{c}\,|\,\tilde{c}<\hat{I}]$ prob $[\tilde{c}<\hat{I}]$ up front for the privilege of working in the firm. If there is a competitive market for managers, the owner can presumably extract this amount, which turns his total payoff into the social objective, (3). He will then choose a socially incentive scheme, i.e. the externality disappears.

Of course, it can be argued that a manager may not have the funds to pay either an entry fee or an exit fee. More generally, a manager may dislike the prospect of low income levels in any state. A general way to capture this is to suppose that the manager is risk-averse. Let $U(\cdot)$ be the manager's von Neumann–Morgenstern utility function. Then an optimal incentive scheme will maximise (1) subject to

$$E[U(I_1-\tilde{c})\,|\,\tilde{c}<I_1-I_0]\ \text{prob}\ [\tilde{c}<I_1-I_0]+U(I_0)\ \text{prob}\ [\tilde{c}\geqslant I_1-I_0]\geqslant\bar{U}. \qquad (5)$$

If we assume that I_0, I_1 are otherwise unrestricted (in particular, there is no $I_0\geqslant 0$ constraint), the owner will reduce I_0, I_1 until (5) holds with equality. Since the manager gets no surplus over and above $\bar{U}$ from working in the firm, social welfare is measured by the owner's payoff, (1). The owner will choose (I_0, I_1) to maximise this and the externality again disappears.

My conclusion, then, is that the 'competitive pressure' effect on managerial slack is only present in Willig's model because the manager obtains surplus that the owner cannot get his hands on. If the owner can keep the manager down to his reservation utility level, this effect disappears.

It is important to emphasise that this conclusion would no longer be valid in a more complicated setting where several managerial firms with correlated costs operate in a competitive product market. In my *Bell Journal* (1983), vol. 14) paper, I have considered such a case and shown that, under certain assumptions, 'well-run' (entrepreneurial) firms impose a positive externality on 'badly-run' (managerial) firms. As a result of this externality, a market economy will support too few 'well-run' firms, and there is role for planner intervention in the form of a subsidy for entrepreneurs (if these can be identified).

My general feeling, then, is that, the structure of Willig's model is too simple to capture the full richness of the product market discipline effect. The model is, however, fully adequate to generate a number of very interesting comparative statics results, concerning the effect of changes in demand on the level of slack. These are very useful and it is only due to shortage of space that I have not given them the attention they deserve. Let me conclude by saying that I agree with Willig's assessment that this is a rich area for study and that not much is currently known. I look forward to future contributions by him on this topic, particularly those that introduce competing managerial firms.

14 Vertical Integration and the Distribution of Property Rights

Sanford J. Grossman and Oliver Hart

I GENERAL INTRODUCTION

What is a firm? What are the determinants of how vertically integrated are the activities of the firm? This paper builds on the foundations laid by Coase (1937), Williamson (1979) and Klein *et al.* (1978) which emphasise the benefits of 'control' in response to situations where there are difficulties in writing or enforcing complete contracts.[1] We define the firm as being composed of the assets (e.g. machines, inventories) which it owns. We present a theory of costly contracts which emphasises that contractual rights can be of two types: specific rights and residual rights. When it is too costly for one party to specify a long list of the particular rights it desires over another party's assets, it may be optimal to purchase all the rights except those specifically mentioned in the contract. Ownership is the purchase of these residual rights of control. We show that there can be harmful effects associated with the wrong allocation of residual rights. In particular a firm which purchases its supplier, thereby removing residual rights of control from the manager of the supplying company, can distort the manager's incentives sufficiently to make common ownership harmful. We develop a theory of integration based upon the attempt of parties in writing a contract to allocate efficiently the residual rights of control between themselves.

We begin by reviewing some transactions cost based arguments for integration. Coase (1937) suggested that transactions will be organised in the firm when the cost of using the market for transactions is larger than the costs of organising the transactions within the firm. He added some content to this idea by suggesting that the costs of constant recontracting with an outside firm or manager can be high relative to those of signing a long-term contract with an employee in which the employee agrees to carry out the commands of the employer. Williamson and Klein *et al.* added further content to this theory by arguing that a contractual relationship between a separately owned buyer and seller will be plagued by opportunistic and inefficient behaviour in situations where there are large amounts of surplus to be divided *ex-post*, and where, because of the impossibility of writing a complete, contingent contract, the *ex-ante* contract does not specify a clear division of this surplus. Such situations in turn are likely to arise when either the buyer or seller must make investments which have a smaller value in a use outside their own relationship than within the relationship (i.e. there exist 'asset specificities').

While these statements help us understand when the costs of contracting between separately owned firms may be high, they do not elucidate what the benefits are of 'organising the transaction within the firm'.[2] In particular, the transactions cost-based arguments for integration do not explain how, given that it is difficult to write a complete contract between a buyer and seller and this creates room for opportunistic behaviour, the scope for such behaviour changes when one of the self-interested owners becomes an equally self-interested employee of the other owner. Furthermore, if vertical integration always reduces transaction costs, any buyer A and seller B which have a contractual relationship should be able to make themselves better off as follows: (i) A buys B and makes the previous owner of B the manager of a new subsidiary; (ii) A sets a transfer price between the subsidiary and itself equal to the contract price which existed when the firms were separate enterprises, and (iii) A gives the manager of B a compensation package equal to the profit of the subsidiary. Given this, however, how can integration ever be strictly worse than non-integration, i.e. what limits the size of the firm?[3,4]

A second question raised by the transactions cost-based arguments concerns the definition of integration itself. In particular, what does it mean for one firm to be more integrated than another? For example, is a firm which calls its retail force 'employees' more integrated than one which calls its retail force 'independent but exclusive sales agents'?

Existing theories cannot answer these questions because they do not give a sufficiently clear definition of integration for its costs and benefits to be assessed. By defining integration to be the ownership of assets, not of people, we are able to evaluate the benefits and costs of integration. We will argue that if one party gets rights of control then this diminishes the rights of the other party to have control. To the extent that there are benefits of control, there will always be potential costs associated with removing control (i.e. ownership) from those who manage productive activities.

I(a) What is Integration?

We define a firm to consist of those assets which it owns or over which it has control – we do not distinguish between ownership and control and virtually define ownership as the power to exercise control. Of course, control or ownership is never absolute. For example, a firm which owns a machine may not be able to sell it without the permission of the lenders for which the machine serves as collateral; more generally, a firm may give another firm specific authority over its machines. However, ownership gives the owner all rights to use the machine which she has not voluntarily given away or which the government or some other party has not taken by force. We believe that this is roughly consistent with common usage.[5]

We do not distinguish between employees and outside contractors in the case where the firm provides all the tools and other assets used by the contractor. For example in insurance retailing a firm may use its own employees as commissioned agents, or use independent agents. The important difference between the two forms of retailing is that the employee-agent does not own the list of her clients, while the independent agent does own the list. If the firm owned the list and all the other important assets of the independent agents, then we would say that such a company had the same degree of integration as a company in which the retail sales force was composed of 'employees'. As another example, consider vertical integration in shoe manufacturing. In the eighteenth century much of the manufacturing of shoes switched from the 'putting out' system where the worker sewed the upper and lower halves of the shoe at home, to factory work where the factory owner's machines were used by the worker to put the shoes together.[6] Even if workers are paid by the piece in both cases, the firm is more integrated in the latter case because it owns more of the machines used in production.

The above examples illustrate that the issue of ownership can be separated from the issue of contractual compensation. A firm may pay another firm or person by the piece or a fixed amount (salary), irrespective of the ownership of the machines. As Coase points out, the benefits of integration must surely be more than the ability to choose a new payment method. We assume that a payment method, whether it be salary compensation to an employee in the integrated company, or a price for goods to be delivered between companies, is some function of the observable states of nature and the observable performance of the parties to the contract. We further assume that integration in itself does not make any new variable observable to both parties. Any audits which an employer can have done of her subsidiary are also feasible when the subsidiary is a separate company.[7]

It may be extremely costly to write a contract which specifies unambiguously the payments and actions of all parties in every observable state of nature. We assume that vertical integration in itself does not change the cost of writing down a particular contractual provision.[8] What it does change is who has control over those provisions not included in the contract. Consider, for example, a contract between a publisher and a printer for a particular number of copies of a book. If the contract has no provision for an additional print run, but the publisher receives some new information which makes it profitable for another run, then it is obvious that the right to decide whether or not to have the run belongs to the owner of the printing press. This is the simplest possible example of our assumption that the benefit of ownership is the residual right of control, that is the right to control all actions that have not been explicitly given away by contract. Since ownership has value because of the rights it bestows in the case of missing provisions in a contract, models of optimal contracts under asymmetric information, which determine the division of contractible income and actions between parties to a contract, would appear to have no implication for who owns what property, that is for vertical integration. We elaborate on this point below.

I(b) Introduction to Specific Models

We consider an upstream and downstream production process, with the upstream firm being the seller, and the downstream firm the buyer of some input. For expositional simplicity, we assume that there are two periods in their relationship. In the first period a contract is signed and in the second period a production decision is made. We will sometimes assume that unobservable reliance expenditures are made in the first period after the contract is signed. Let s and R represent the realisations of random variables which determine the buyer's benefit function and the seller's cost function respectively at the beginning of the second period. Let q represent a complete description of both the output that the seller delivers to the buyer and of all the inputs used to produce the output. If there are no transactions costs in writing or implementing contracts, then the two parties will write a contract which specifies three functions: $q(mb, ms)$, $Pb(mb, ms)$, and $Ps(mb, ms)$. These functions indicate the q which will be implemented and the price paid by the buyer and the price paid by the seller, as a function of messages sent by the buyer and the seller (mb, ms), to a third party who enforces their contract. These messages, which may be based on both private and public information, will be sent at the beginning of period 2 to the third party, who then monitors the implementation of the payments and production decision.[9] If Pb is not equal to $-Ps$, the third party will be putting some money into the contract, so there must be some constraint on these functions so that *ex-ante*, the third party does not expect to suffer a loss from its involvement in the contract.

The above standard mechanism design problem is not the subject of this paper. In particular, if such a contract were feasible there would be no meaning or role for ownership. Since each party's obligation to the other party is completely specified for every state of nature, there are no residual rights of control over assets to be allocated. We will study cases where a contract of this type is not feasible. In particular, we will assume that the description of the production allocation is sufficiently complex as a function of the relevant set of messages that it is infeasible to specify all aspects of q in the contract. This immediately creates the need to allocate residual rights of control, since if it is not specified in advance how q will be chosen, there must be some implicit or explicit default which allows for some party to choose particular components of q in the cuture. We assume that there is only a simply binary choice which is feasible. Each asset will have a single owner and that owner has the right to control the asset in the case of a missing provision. For example, if a contract between a printing press owner and a publisher fails to specify the extent to which the printer is obliged to change the ink used in the event that a new colour becomes popular, then the owner of the printing plant has the power to refuse to change the colour, and if possible force the publisher to pay more for a new ink colour. However, if the publisher owns the printing press she 'controls the missing provision' and can enforce the colour of her choice.

The assumption that residual rights of control are delegated to one or the other party creates the potential that ownership will be important. Nevertheless, in a particular context it may not matter who has control over aspects of q. For example, if the set of feasible contracts is sufficiently rich to allow the buyer to extract all of the seller's benefit from a particular choice of q, then the fact that the seller controls q will be irrelevant: the buyer will have enough power to induce the seller to act in her own interest. This is the case in the standard principal–agent problem if the agent and the principal are both risk neutral: the principal can find a contract which costlessly induces the agent to choose the action which would have been chosen if the principal could control the action. Thus we will be concerned with situations where $Pb(mb, ms)$ and $Ps(mb, ms)$ are such that the party without control will not be able to induce the party with control always to act in its interest. There are two ways to achieve this. One way is to consider models where all parties are risk averse so that prices must be chosen to share risk as well as induce optimal *ex-post* decisions. Under these circumstances, it will be optimal for the parties to choose $Pb(\ )$ and $Ps(\ )$ in such a way that the allocation of *ex-post* control matters. Unfortunately this leads to models which are too complicated to analyse (at least for us). Another approach is to assume the parties are risk neutral, but to exclude particular contracts on the basis of their enforcement costs. This is the route which we follow here.

We will make three assumptions which substantially restrict the class of feasible contracts. First, we will require that the price paid by the buyer equals the price received by the seller, that is, there is no third party who is willing to put a wedge *ex-post* between these two prices.[10] There are two possible justifications for this assumption. First, if the buyer and seller have information about the probability distribution of s and R which is superior to that possessed by any third party, then a third party may be deterred from participating in the contract on grounds of adverse selection. Since adverse selection problems rarely have simple solutions, however, this justification is speculative. A second justification is that the third party will be deterred from financial participation by the possibility that the buyer and seller will collude and manipulate their actions *ex post* to get the third party always to inject money into their relationship. This argument is more solidly based, and we elaborate on it in Section II.

Our second assumption is that the price the buyer pays the seller can be a function only of the amount sold. We thus rule out contracts which involve an exchange of messages or a choice by one party in period 2 of one from a number of pre-specified price schedules. This restriction seems reasonable in situations where decisions must be made very rapidly, so that an elaborate exchange of messages supervised by a third party is not economical (we continue to assume the existence of a third party, for example, a court, which enforces the contract). In particular, the third party may simply lack the ability or information to determine what messages were exchanged, and therefore whether or not the parties have fulfilled their obligations under the contract. The restriction may also be reasonable in situations where it is too costly to think about or write a contract which specifies a choice of schedules and messages, or where it is *ex-post* costly to engage in the computations involved in sending the correct message ('bounded rationality'); this, however, is much more speculative.

Thirdly, we rule out the possibility that the two parties can renegotiate the contract *ex-post* after it has become clear what the state of the world (s, R) is or what the relevant actions the parties should take are. This assumption again seems reasonable if production decisions must be made rapidly, in which cases there may be insufficient time for a new enforceable contract to be written after this information becomes available. A second justification is that, even if there is time for a new contract to be written, the parties may fail to reach agreement about how to divide up the surplus arising from this contract and hence may be left at the status quo position, that is, at the old contract.

The existence of missing provisions creates at least two potential distortions. First, the enforcement of the contract may lead to *ex-post* productive inefficiencies. For example, a contract which specifies that a seller must deliver 5 units of a product to a particular buyer at a fixed price can be *ex-post* inefficient when a state of nature occurs for which the buyer has less of a need for the product than some other customer of the seller. Second, unobservable *ex-ante* reliance investments may be distorted because one of the parties knows that it will receive only a small share of the *ex-post* surplus should a situation arise in which there are important missing provisions.

The magnitude of these distortions will depend on the form of organisation of the firms, since each form will have different residual rights associated with it. The parties to the contract can choose between separate ownership (i.e. non-integration), integration where the seller of the product owns the buyer, and integration where the buyer owns the seller. We will analyse the determinants of the distortion minimising (i.e. surplus maximising) form of organisation.

In order to do so with any concreteness, it is necessary to be more specific about the source and type of missing provisions. We will consider two general types. Section II studies the first type where it is too costly to write a contract which specifies how the quantity and the price of a product to be delivered must vary with the state of nature. The state of nature is the benefit of the buyer in dealing with another supplier, and the benefit to the seller in dealing with another buyer. Ownership gives one party the ability to restrict the outside dealings of the other party, for example, when the seller owns the buyer, the buyer can be forced to deal only with the seller in a state with missing provisions. An alternative interpretation is that the state of nature determines the cost and benefits of a special service or modification which the buyer or the seller desires. The owner has the right to determine whether this special service or modification takes place.

Section III analyses a second type of missing provision where some dimension of quality is unspecified in the initial contract. The owner has the ability to choose this aspect of quality *ex-post* to extract the surplus from the non-owner. This distorts the non-owner's benefits from *ex-ante* investments and reliance expenditures.

Section IV contains a summary and conclusions.

II THE COSTS AND BENEFITS OF OWNERSHIP WHEN THERE ARE NON-CONTRACTIBLE STATES OF NATURE

We consider the relationship between a buyer and seller of an input. The buyer is the downstream firm and the seller is the upstream firm. It is assumed that the buyer and seller gain some advantage in trading with each other (there are asset specificities), but that each also has the possibility of buying or selling elsewhere. The relative advantage of trade between the two will depend on the 'state of nature'. To simplify matters, we assume that the seller supplies the buyer with either one unit or zero units of input.

Let R be the opportunity cost per unit which the seller bears in supplying this buyer, and let s be the (monetary) benefit the buyer receives from being supplied by this seller. We shall assume that R and s are continuous random variables, and that the state of nature is represented by the pair (s, R).

For example, the buyer's best alternative source of supply might provide an item which is worth s_2 while asset specificities with the current seller yield an item worth s_1 where in most states $s_1 > s_2$. If the price of the outside supplier is p, the buyer's revenue is s_1 if supplied by this seller and $(s_2 - p)$ if not, so that

$$s = s_1 - s_2 + p. \tag{1}$$

Note that it is possible that p and R will be correlated; hence s and R may be too.

An alternative example is where there are no outside sources of supply or demand and s represents the benefit from a 'last minute' special service required by the buyer and R represents the cost of providing the special service. For example, the seller could be a transportation company which ships the buyer's final product. The buyer needs a shipment to be delivered immediately between point A and point B, with R representing the seller's cost and s the buyer's benefits.

The buyer and seller are assumed to sign a contract at some initial date 1. We shall be interested in the form of the contract in three different situations: (1) where the buyer and seller are not integrated; (2) where they are integrated and the buyer owns the seller; and (3) where they are integrated and the seller owns the buyer. We refer to these situations as NI (non-integration), BC (buyer control) and SC (seller control), respectively.[11]

It is assumed that the contract is signed before the random variables s and R have been realised; their distributions are supposed to be common knowledge at this stage, however. At date 2, s and R are realised and q units of input are exchanged, where $q = 0$ or 1. We will suppose:

(1) The realisations of s and r are observable to both buyer and seller at date 2, but not to anyone else. Hence contingent contracts which include statements of the form '$q = \hat{q}$ if $(S, R) = (\hat{s}, \hat{R})$' are not feasible since they cannot be enforced (in a court, say). Furthermore, either there exists *no* publicly observable random variable ω at date 2 which is correlated with (s, R) or, if there does, it is sufficiently complicated to describe that contingent statements of the form '$q = \hat{q}$ if $\omega = \hat{\omega}$' cannot be written into the contract.[12]

(2) The *ex-post* value of q and the payment P made by the buyer to the seller are (subject to a qualification mentioned below) publicly observable. In fact, they are the *only* publicly observable variables.[13]

Since P, q are publicly observable, the contract can make P depend on q:$P = P_q$. A contract therefore consists simply of two numbers, P_0 (the price paid by the buyer when $q=0$) and P_1 (the price paid by the buyer when $q=1$). We will be interested in an optimal contract in the three cases NI, BC and SC. To simplify matters we shall assume that the buyer and seller are *risk neutral*. We also suppose that $s > R$ with positive probability, that is, there is some reason for the buyer and seller to have a relationship.[14]

Case 1. Non-integration (NI)

Our assumption is that, if the buyer and seller are non-integrated, *ex-post* trade must be voluntary. That is, the seller will only supply one unit of input if it wants to and the buyer will only purchase one unit if it wants to. Hence $q=1$ if and only if $s - P_1 > -P_0$ and $P_1 > R + P_0$. Or letting $k \equiv P_1 - P_0$:

$$q=1 \qquad \text{if and only if } s>k \quad \text{and} \quad R<k. \tag{2}$$

The voluntary trade assumption means that we are excluding date 1 contracts which give a non-owner the right to choose the sales or purchases of an owner. For example, we do not allow a date 1 contract which states that the buyer will tell the seller at date 2 whether or not he wants the item and the seller must always comply. We have assumed that if the seller does not comply, a court cannot assign damages based upon s and R, nor can it determine whether the item was not transferred because (a) the buyer refused to accept it or (b) the seller failed to deliver. Hence, the only penalty for a failure to comply is that the seller receives P_0 (which could be negative) instead of P_1.

We also rule out contracts which create a joint venture by sharing control between the two parties. For example, the two parties might share control of, say, the seller in such a way that output can only be produced by their mutual consent. This might be achieved in two ways. First the date 1 contract might state that only if the managers of the upstream and downstream firms sign a joint statement at date 2 can production occur. Our justification for ruling out this arrangement is the same as that given in Section I(b) of the introduction for ruling out messages. Secondly, shared control might be achieved by giving the seller authority over some aspects of his firm, such as the rate at which machines are repaired, employees' salaries, etc., but giving the buyer authority over other aspects of the firm such as certain crucial machine 'dial settings'. In practice it may be very difficult to allocate such specific rights of control in advance in such a way that each party has a veto over production. Moreover, even if it is possible, inefficiencies may be introduced due to the fact that each party will be choosing different aspects of the firm's operations independently and noncooperatively. In any case, in what follows we assume that shared control is infeasible, that is control is indivisible.

Similarly, we rule out 'exclusive dealings' contracts which state, for example, that the buyer has the right to prevent the seller from selling to other purchasers. Such contracts will not be implementable when it is difficult to verify the level of third party sales. Moreover, even when third party sales are verifiable, a joint venture is created whereby the seller must get approval from the buyer to sell to a third party. And joint ventures, as we have just argued, may be difficult to organise.

We have also ruled out the possibility that the parties agree to not have an *ex-ante* contract and leave *ex-post* decisions to be the result of bargaining. Given the assumed asset specificities, this would essentially create a joint venture with no rules set *ex-ante*, and is ruled out for the same reasons we rule out other joint ventures.

Returning to (2), we see that voluntary trade implies that the production region is given by the area BCDX in Figure 14.1.

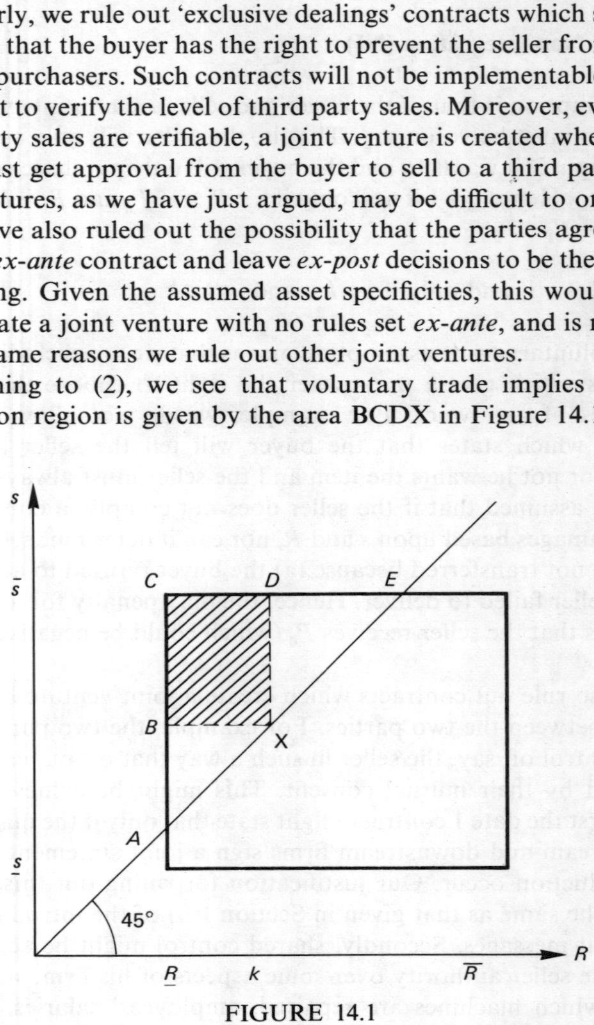

FIGURE 14.1

Here $\underline{s}$, $\bar{s}$ and $\underline{R}$, $\bar{R}$ are lower and upper bounds on s and R respectively. If a contingent contract could be written the buyer and seller would agree to set $q=1$ if and only if $s>R$, which yields the production region ACE. We see then that NI leads to less production than is desirable in efficiency terms.

Since the buyer and seller are risk neutral, they will choose k at date 1 to maximise the expected value of surplus $(s-R)$. This means that an optimal contract under NI amounts to a choice of k which solves

$$\text{Maximise } W_{\text{NI}} \equiv \iint_{R>k}^{s>k} (s-R)f(s, R)\,\mathrm{d}s\mathrm{d}R \tag{3}$$

where f is the density function of (s, R).[15] Contracts of this form have also been analysed by Hall and Lazear (1984).[16]

Case 2. Buyer Control (BC)

Suppose now that the buyer owns the seller. We assume that integration does not make it any easier to write contracts conditional on s and R than before, and so a contract again consists of two prices P_0, P_1. The interpretation is different, however. The contract is now an 'employment' one and P_0, P_1 are transfer prices which are part of the managerial compensation scheme.

The crucial difference between integration and non-integration is that, holding all residual rights, the downstream firm is now assumed to be able to insist on any level of supply, q, that it desires. The rights of ownership permit the buyer to enter his upstream subsidiary and allocate resources. Thus in the case where the seller could sell to other buyers, the owner can order plant employees and adjust the machinery in such a way that all produced items must be delivered to him. In the case where q represents a specialised good or service, the owner has the power to 'go over the head' of the subsidiary manager and force delivery if he so desires. We continue to assume that it is impossible to organise a joint venture which allocates specific rights of control over assets in such a way that the seller can veto the buyer's choice of q.

One way of understanding the power of ownership is as the ability of the owner to move first in any bargaining with his subsidiary manager. That is, the owner has the power to make decisions with regard to his property that a manager must take as given, that is, not within his legal power to alter. A manager who threatened not to pay employees who did not act in his interest could be overruled by the owner, and not conversely, since we have ruled out joint ventures where the manager is given specific legal powers. In the non-integrated situation the seller has the power to arrange his machines to produce the type of product suitable for one purchaser rather than another. The downstream firm takes this choice as given and chooses a suitable response. Conversely, when the buyer owns the seller, the buyer moves first and makes decisions within the subsidiary which the subsidiary manager does not have the legal authority to overturn.

Given that the transfer prices are fixed by the date 1 contract the buyer will choose to have the item delivered if and only if $s > P_1 - P_0 \equiv k$.

So we now have

$$q = 1 \qquad \text{if and only if } s > k. \tag{4}$$

Hence an optimal contract under BC involves a choice of k so as to

$$\text{Maximise } W_{\mathrm{BC}} \equiv \iint_{s>k} (s-R) f(s, R)\, \mathrm{d}s\, \mathrm{d}R.^{17} \tag{5}$$

The production region is illustrated by the area BCFG in Figure 14.2.

Comparing this with the non-integration case, we see that extra

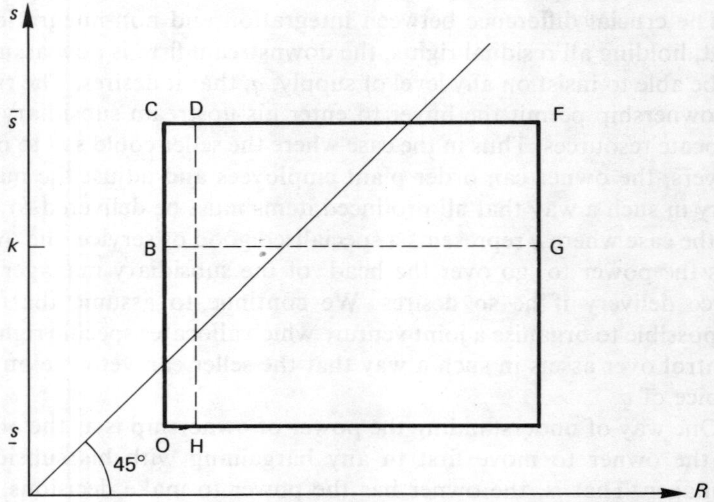

FIGURE 14.2

efficient points are introduced, but so are some inefficient ones. The latter occur because now the production rule is totally insensitive to the realisation of R.[18] Thus, buyer control leads to excessive use of the upstream subsidiary by the buyer, relative to what occurs without integration.

Case 3. Seller Control (SC)

If the seller owns the buyer, we have simply the reverse of Case 2. A contract again consists of two (transfer) prices P_0, P_1, but now ownership is assumed to give the seller *control* over the buyer's input decision, in the sense that the seller can choose allocations within the buyer's plant which make the buyer's equipment only compatible with this seller's product or enforce acceptance of a specialised good or service. Thus, the first move advantage over the buyer's assets now rests with the seller. Since the seller now controls q, the production rule will be

$$q=1 \text{ if and only if } R<k, \tag{6}$$

and an optimal contract involves a choice of k so as to

$$\text{Maximise } W_{sc} \equiv \iint_{R<k} (s-R)f(s, R)\, \mathrm{d}s\mathrm{d}R. \tag{7}$$

[19]

This production region is illustrated by the area OCDH in Figure 14.2 (with $k=k'$). Thus, there are situations where the seller is forcing the buyer to take delivery when the buyer has better alternative opportunities. Contracts of the form (4) and (7) have also been analysed by Weitzman (1981).

The Comparison Between Integration and Non-integration When s and R are Independent

We want to compare the solutions to (3), (5) and (7).[20] Note first that if the distribution of either s or R is degenerate, the solutions are the same. Suppose, for example, that $R=R^*$ with probability 1. Then the first-best (i.e. production if and only if $s>R$) can be achieved under NI and BC by setting $k=R^*$ and under SC again by setting $k=R^*$ and asking the seller (who is indifferent about q) to choose the q the buyer wants. Thus the comparison only becomes interesting when s and R are both uncertain.

The simplest case is where s and R are independent. In terms of (1), this occurs if, say, s_2 and p are non-stochastic, $R = p + \varepsilon$, and s_1 and ε are independent. That is, what varies are the specific value of the seller's input to the buyer and the specific value of the seller's input elsewhere.

We state first the following obvious proposition

Proposition 1 Suppose s and R are independent. Then if $\text{Prob}[s > R] = 1$, $W_{\text{NI}} = W_{\text{BC}} = W_{\text{SC}}$.

Proof In this case, the box in Figure 14.1 lies entirely above the 45° line. Therefore the first-best can be achieved under NI, BC and SC by setting k between $\bar{R}$ and $\underline{s}$. Q.E.D.

So if s and R are independent, the interesting case is where $0 < \text{Prob}[s > R] < 1$. We begin by calculating W_{BC} and W_{SC} for this case. Let g, h be the density function of s, R respectively (assumed to be strictly positive on the supports of s and R, which we take to be $[\underline{s}, \bar{s}]$ and $[\underline{R}, \bar{R}]$ and let $R^* = E\tilde{R}$. Then we may rewrite (5) as

$$W_{\text{BC}} = \int_{s>k} \int_{\underline{R}}^{\bar{R}} (s - R) g(s) h(R) \, \text{d}R \text{d}s$$

$$= \int_{s>k} (s - R^*) g(s) \, \text{d}s$$

$$= E[s - R^* \mid s > k] \text{Prob}[s > k]. \tag{8}$$

Since the integrand in the second expression is positive if and only if $s > R^*$, it follows that it is optimal to set $k = R^*$. Similarly, we may write

$$W_{\text{SC}} = \int_{\underline{R}<k} \int_{\underline{s}}^{\bar{s}} (s - R) g(s) h(R) \, \text{d}s \text{d}R$$

$$= \int_{R<k} (s^* - R) h(R) \, \text{d}R$$

$$= E[s^* - R \mid R < k] \text{Prob}[R < k] \tag{9}$$

where $s^* = E\tilde{s}$, and this is maximised by setting $k = s^*$. Hence we have established

Proposition 2 Suppose s and R are independent. Then

$$\hat{W}_{\text{BC}} \equiv \max_k W_{\text{BC}} = \int_{s>R^*} (s - R^*) g(s) \text{d}s$$

and

$$\hat{W}_{SC} \equiv \underset{k}{\mathrm{Max}}\ W_{SC} = \int_{R<s^*} (s^* - R)h(R)\mathrm{d}R.$$

It remains to compute $\hat{W}_{NI} \equiv \mathrm{Max}_k\ W_{NI}$. Now it is clear from Figure 14.1 that the optimal k satisfies $\underline{s} \leqslant k < \bar{s}$ and $\underline{R} < k \leqslant \bar{R}$. Hence in the independent case,

$$W_{NI} = \underset{k}{\mathrm{Max}} \left\{ \int_k^{\bar{s}} \int_{\underline{R}}^k (s-R)g(s)h(R)\ \mathrm{d}R\mathrm{d}s \right\} \tag{10}$$

This yields the first order condition

$$\frac{\mathrm{d}}{\mathrm{d}k}\hat{W}_{NI} = \int_k^{\bar{s}} (s-k)g(s)h(k)\mathrm{d}s - \int_{\underline{R}}^k (k-R)g(k)h(R)\mathrm{d}R = 0, \tag{11}$$

i.e.

$$h(k)\int_k^{\bar{s}} (s-k)g(s)\mathrm{d}s = g(k)\int_{\underline{R}}^k (k-R)h(R)\mathrm{d}R, \tag{12}$$

unless the optimum lies at a corner, $k = \bar{R}$ or $k = \underline{s}$. In general, (12) cannot be solved explicitly. An exception is where s and R are uniform, in which case we can give a complete answer to the question of whether integration is desirable or not.

Proposition 3 Suppose s is uniformly distributed on $[\underline{s}, \bar{s}]$, R is uniformly distributed on $[\underline{R}, \bar{R}]$ and s, R are independent. Suppose also that $\bar{s} > \underline{R}$ and $\underline{s} < \bar{R}$, that is $0 < \mathrm{Prob}[s > R] < 1$. Then

(A) If $\bar{s} > \bar{R} > \underline{R} > \underline{s}$, $\hat{W}_{BC} > \mathrm{Max}[\hat{W}_{SC}, \hat{W}_{NI}]$, and hence buyer control is optimal.
(B) If $\bar{R} > \bar{s} > \underline{s} > \underline{R}$, $\hat{W}_{SC} > \mathrm{Max}[\hat{W}_{BC}, \hat{W}_{NI}]$, and hence seller control is optimal.
(C) If $\bar{s} > \bar{R} > \underline{s} > \underline{R}$, $\mathrm{Max}[\hat{W}_{BC}, \hat{W}_{SC}] > \hat{W}_{SC}] > \hat{W}_{NI}$, and hence some form of integration is optimal.
(D) If $\bar{R} > \bar{s} > \underline{R} > \underline{s}$, $\hat{W}_{NI} > \mathrm{Max}[\hat{W}_{BC}, \hat{W}_{SC}]$, and hence non-integration is optimal.

(A)–(D) are mutually exclusive and exhaustive categories, if we rule out degenerate cases where $\bar{s}$ or $\underline{s}$ equals $\bar{R}$ or $\underline{R}$. The various cases in Proposition 3 are illustrated in Figure 14.3.

In case (A), let the optimal production region under non-integ-

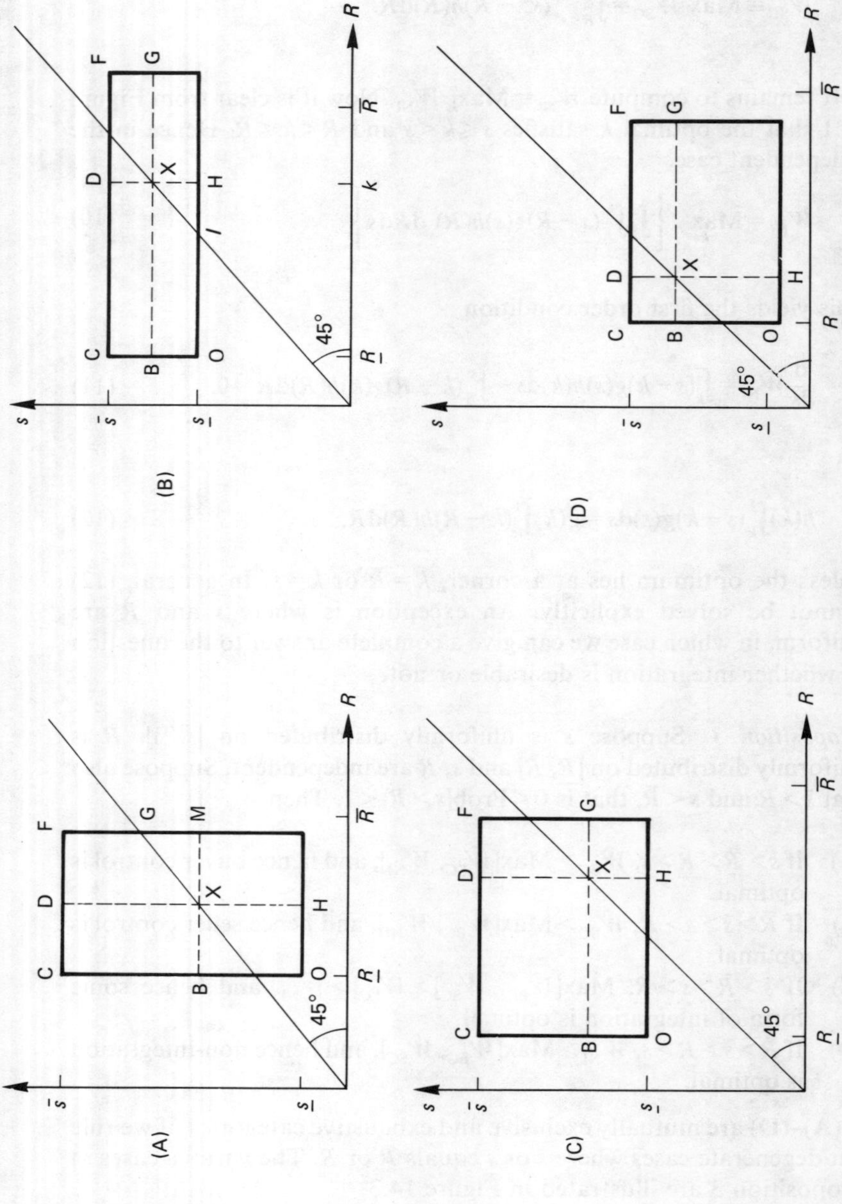

FIGURE 14.3

ration be BCDX. Now suppose the buyer is given control, with k remaining unchanged. Then the production region **P** becomes BCFM and it is clear from the diagram that $\int_{\mathbf{P}} (s-R)\, sGdH$ increases (since the inefficiency region GMX which is introduced is 'smaller'. than the extra region of efficient points XDFG). It is also clear that, if the seller were given control with k remaining unchanged, so that **P** becomes OCDH, then $\int_{\mathbf{P}}(s-R)$ would fall. The conclusion then is that buyer control is optimal in Case (A).

Exactly the opposite is the case in (B). Now OCDH is a superior production region to either BCDX or BCFG, and so seller control is optimal. In Case (C), BCFG and OCDH are both better production regions than BCDX. Hence integration is desirable, but without further information one cannot say whether buyer or seller control is preferable. Finally, in (D), BCDX is preferable to both BCFG and OCDH, and so non-integration is optimal.

A more formal proof of Proposition 3 is contained in the Appendix.

Proposition 3 has a very simple interpretation. Let us say that the buyer is decisive if production is always efficient when $s=\bar{s}$ (i.e. $\bar{s}>R$ with probability 1). Similarly, the seller is decisive if production is always efficient when $R=\underline{R}$ (i.e. $s>\underline{R}$ with probability 1). Then the buyer is decisive in Case (A) of Proposition 3; the seller in Case (B); both are decisive in Case (C); neither in Case (D). So Proposition 3 can be paraphrased as saying that control should rest in the hands of a decisive party, if one exists; and if neither party is decisive neither should have control. Unfortunately, this neat characterisation applies only to the case of uniform distributions.

It is clear from Proposition 3 that if the variation in R is small relative to that in s, buyer control is optimal (see Figure 14.3(A)), while if the variation in s is small relative to that in R, seller control is optimal (see Figure 14.3(B)). This turns out to be true for general (independent) distributions.

Proposition 4 Assume that s and R are independent and that $\bar{s}>R^*>\underline{s}$, $\underline{R}<s^*<\bar{R}$. Then:

(1) If the density function $h(R)$ is replaced by

$$h_\lambda(R)=\frac{1}{\lambda}h\left(\frac{R-(1-\lambda)R^*}{\lambda}\right),$$

defined on $[\lambda\underline{R}+(1-\lambda)R^*, \lambda\bar{R}+(1-\lambda)R^*]$, buyer control is optimal for sufficiently small values of $\lambda>0$.

(2) If the density function $g(s)$ is replaced by

$$g_\lambda(s) = \frac{1}{\lambda} g\left(\frac{s-(1-\lambda)s^*}{\lambda}\right)$$

defined on $[\lambda \underline{s} + (1-\lambda)s^*, \lambda \bar{s} + (1-\lambda)s^*]$, seller control is optimal for sufficiently small values of $\lambda > 0$.

(3) If $s^* - E[R \mid R > R^*] < 0$ and $E[s \mid s < s^*] - R^* < 0$, non-integration is optimal.

Replacing h by h_λ corresponds to a uniform contraction of R around its mean R^*, that is to replacing the random variable R with a random variable $R_\lambda \equiv R^* + \lambda(R - R^*)$. Similarly for g. It is of course very intuitive that control should reside with the firm whose payoff varies a lot relatively.[21] Part (3) gives a sufficient (but not necessary) condition for non-integration to be optimal. We know that if buyer control is optimal, k should be set equal to R^*. But if $E[s - RR > r^*] < 0$, total surplus can be increased by moving to non-integration and having $k = R^*$ (since the realisation $R > R^*$ will then be excluded). The same argument holds for seller control if $E[s - R \mid s < s^*] < 0$. Parts (1) and (2) are proved in the Appendix.

To see how Part (3) might apply, begin with some initial distributions of s and R and now start (a) moving probability mass from R's close to but greater than R^* to much higher R's, keeping the mean of R constant; (b) moving probability mass from s's close to but less than s^* to much lower s's, keeping the mean of s constant. Then eventually the conditions in (3) will hold and non-integration will be optimal. Part (3) tells us that if both s and R vary a lot in an appropriate sense, non-integration is desirable.

The Case where $\underline{s}$ and $\underline{R}$ are Correlated

Consider (1). Then it is quite likely that the price that the buyer must pay for outside input, p, is positively correlated with R, in which case s and R are also positively correlated. On the other hand, it is possible that the degree of asset specificity is stochastic, in the sense that when outside input is relatively unsuitable inside, that is s_2 is low, inside input is relatively unsuitable outside, that is, R is low. In this case, s and R are negatively correlated.

One result that is immediate is

Proposition 5 If $\text{Prob}[s > R] = 1$, then $W_{BC} = W_{SC} \geqslant W_{NI}$.

Proof Under integration, the first-best can be achieved by setting $k = \underline{s}$ if the buyer has control and $k = \bar{R}$ if the seller has control. Q.E.D.

That is, buyer and seller control are at least as good as non-integration if production should always occur. This is, of course, similar to Proposition 1 for the independent case, except that *non-integration may well be inferior*. This is illustrated in Figure 14.4, where the support of the distribution (s, R) is the shaded region. It is clear that the first-best cannot be achieved under non-integration since there is no k such that $s > k > R$ with probability one.

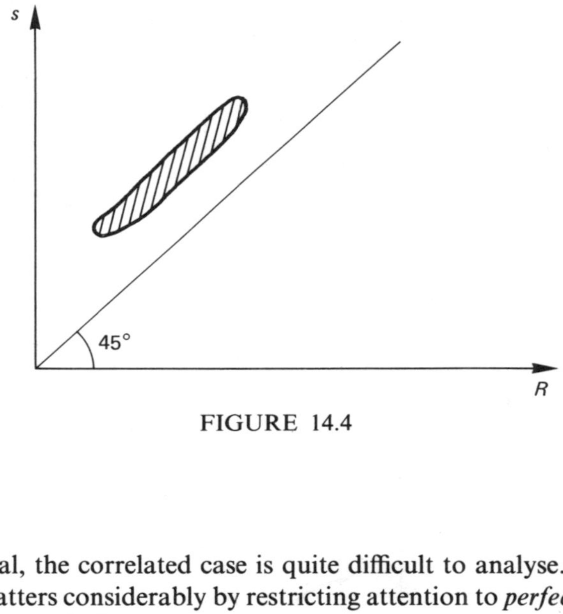

FIGURE 14.4

In general, the correlated case is quite difficult to analyse. We shall simplify matters considerably by restricting attention to *perfect* correlation, that is we shall assume:

> There is a continuous random variable t with support $[t, \bar{t}]$ and density $\varphi(t)$ such that $s = s(t)$ and $R = R(t)$ with probability one. (13)

That is, s and R are completely determined once t is.

Proposition 6 Assume (13) and that $0 < \text{Prob}[s > R] < 1$. Then:

(1) If $s(t)$, $R(t)$ and $s(t) - R(t)$ are all strictly increasing functions of t, (i.e. s, R and $(s-R)$ are perfectly positively correlated), $\hat{W}_{BC} > \text{Max}[\hat{W}_{NI}, \hat{W}_{SC}]$, and so buyer control is optimal.
(2) If $s(t)$ and $R(t)$ are strictly increasing functions of t, while $s(t) - R(t)$ is a strictly decreasing function of t, (i.e. s and R are perfectly positively correlated and each is perfectly negatively correlated with $(s-R)$), $\hat{W}_{SC} > \text{Max}[\hat{W}_{NI}, \hat{W}_{BC}]$, and so seller control is optimal.
(3) If $s(t)$ is a strictly decreasing function of t, and $R(t)$ is a strictly increasing function of t, $\hat{W}_{NI} = \hat{W}_{BC} = \hat{W}_{SC}$.

The proof of Proposition 6 is clear from Figure 14.5.

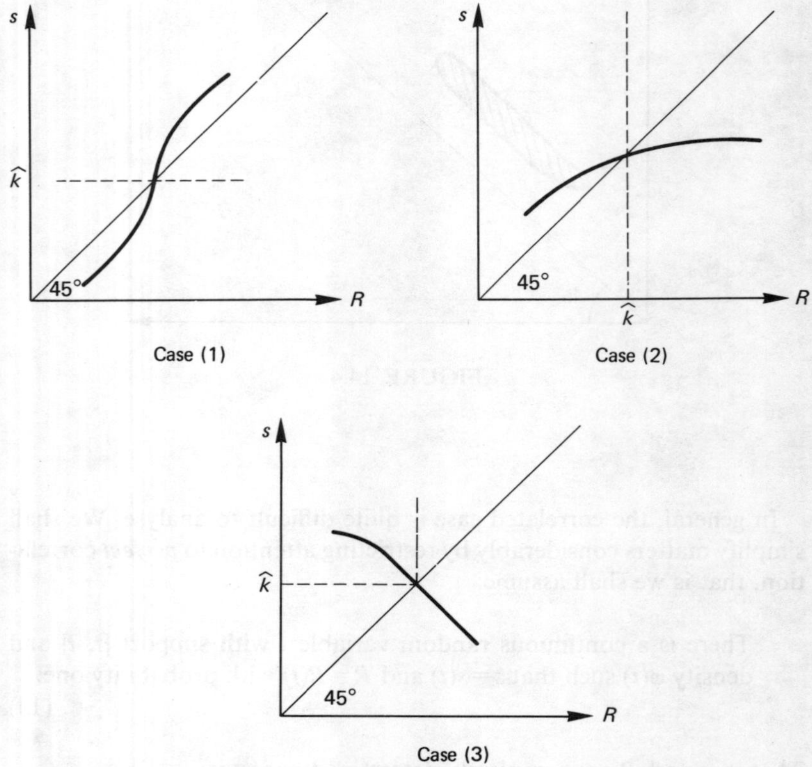

FIGURE 14.5

In Case (1), the first-best can be achieved by setting $k=\hat{k}$ and letting the buyer have control, but cannot be achieved under either seller control or non-integration. In case (2), the first-best can be achieved by letting the seller have control. In Case (3), all arrangements achieve the first-best with $k=\hat{k}$.

III NON-CONTRACTIBLE CHARACTERISTICS AND RELIANCE EXPENDITURES

In the previous section we focused on the tradeoffs in the level of *ex-post* distortions which can occur under various allocations of residual rights. However, in many situations *ex-ante* investments must be made in anticipation of delivery of the final product. If the allocation of residual rights permits a particular party to extract the *ex-post* surplus of the other party, then the latter party will have a disincentive to make *ex-ante* investments which are specific to the relationship. That is, there are potentially distorting asset specificities (see Williamson, 1979), and *ex-post* quasi-rents (see Klein *et al.*, 1979).[22]

In this section, we consider a situation where the distortion in *ex-ante* investment or reliance expenditure is caused by an unspecified dimension of product quality. An important class of examples of this type occurs when it takes time to produce an item. Assume that the buyer does not know or cannot specify what characteristics he wants the final item to have until after most of it has been produced. For example, a computer maker may need a component with characteristics that depend on what its competitors are doing as well as upon technological innovations. Suppose it takes a year to produce the component. With no contracting costs, the computer manufacturer and the component manufacturer would agree on a rule for payments as a function of the final modifications that are made say after nine months of production of the component. This complete contract would list all the characteristics that the buyer could conceivably want and specify a price for each combination of characteristics. If the characteristics are extremely complex, it may be too costly to write the above contract. Instead, some characteristics will be left unspecified.

We assume that the owner of the upstream firm has the right to choose the aspect of quality which is left unspecified in the initial contract. We will show that when the upstream firm is owner managed (non-integration) a product quality level will be chosen which reduces the downstream firm's incentives to make reliance expenditures, relative to what would occur in a complete contract. That is, the incentive for the buyer to build a plant which will *ex-post* efficiently use the seller's output is decreased. On the other hand, if the downstream firm owns the upstream firm (buyer control), the upstream firm's incentives to make reliance expenditures are reduced. That is, the incentive of the seller to build a plant which will *ex-post* efficiently produce the buyer's input is decreased. Finally, in contrast to the model of the last section, a situation where the upstream firm owns the downstream firm (seller control) turns out to be equivalent to one of non-integration.

We begin with an analysis of the contract between a pair of non-integrated upstream and downstream firms. A contract is signed at date 1. In general, the date 1 contract will specify some but not all of the product characteristics. At date 2 a final decision is made by the manager of the upstream firm as to the characteristics of the product. Let 'q' denote the characteristics that are chosen by the manager of the upstream firm. Write $q=(q_0, q_1)$, where q_0 denotes the characteristics which were included in the contract and q_1 the characteristics which were not included. We assume the buyer can accept or reject the seller's product at date 2 after he observes the final characteristics of the product. This is recognised at date 1 and a price is specified that the buyer must pay the seller if he rejects the item or if the seller does not deliver the item. (As in Section II, we assume that a court can determine whether or not the item is transferred, but cannot distinguish between rejection by the buyer and failure to deliver by the seller.) A contract at date 1 will specify payments which must be made at date 2 as a function of q_0 (assumed observable to a court) and of whether or not the item is transferred. It will simplify our exposition if we take q_0 as given, and not subject to choice in the date 1 contract. In this case, the initial contract specifies two numbers P_1 and P_0, which represent, respectively, the price that the buyer must pay if the item is transferred, and the price he must pay if the item is not transferred.[23] We shall comment below on how our results are modified if q_0 is chosen at time 1, and thus P_1 and P_0 are functions of q_0. Note that, in contrast to Section II, we rule out the possibility that the buyer or seller has an alternative source of demand or supply elsewhere in the market.

At date 1 each party must invest some resources in the setup, design and administration of this particular contractual relation. In general, only some of these costs will be publicly observable. For example, the upstream manager will devote some managerial effort to finding employees, materials, and designs for the production of the product which are cost minimising. Though the dollar expenditure on these items may be observable, the managerial effort will not be. Let 'a' denote the *ex-ante* actions that a manager takes. To simplify matters we assume that *no* part of a is publicly observable. At date 2 the buyer receives benefits and the seller incurs costs, depending on whether production occurs and the item is transferred. To simplify matters we assume that: (*) these date 2 benefits and costs are incurred if and only if transfer actually takes place. Let $B(q, a_1)$ be the benefit that the downstream firm receives when it accepts an item with characteristics q, net of costs associated with its own *ex ante* action a_1, and let $B_0(a_1)$ be the benefit the downstream firm receives if it does not take delivery of the item (which is independent of q by (*)). Similarly, let $C(q, a_2)$ be the cost to the upstream firm from producing and making delivery of the product with characteristics q, net of the cost of its own *ex-ante* action a_2, and let $C_0(a_2)$ be the cost of the upstream firm if the product is rejected or not delivered (which again is independent of q by (*)).[24] As with 'a' we assume that these benefits and costs are not publicly observable.[25]

We assume that a_1 and a_2 are chosen just after the contract is signed at date 1. Although a_1 and a_2 are not publicly observable, we suppose that they become observable to the two parties at date 2 (so that, as in Section II, there is no asymmetric information between the buyer and seller). As in Section II, however, we rule out the possibility of any messages about a_1, a_2 being sent by the buyer and seller. Finally, we assume that the functions B, B_0, C and C_0 are known to the two parties.

Let us briefly recapitulate the main features of the model. Buyer benefits and seller costs depend both on *ex-ante* actions and the *ex-post* choice of characteristics. Benefits, costs, and actions, while privately observable to the two parties, are not publicly observable, and some characteristics are too complicated to be specified in the contract. An outside party, such as a court, can observe only whether the good is transferred, and hence the price the seller pays can be conditional only on this. The difference between this model and that of the last section is that there is no randomness in the benefit and cost functions, and so, if quality were not an issue, the first-best could be achieved. However, given that it is impossible to specify quality adequately, we shall see that the outcome will be inefficient and there may be a role for integration.

The Optimal Contract Without Integration

Suppose the contract prices P_1, P_0 are such that actions a_1 and a_2 are chosen at date 1. Let $P=(P_1-P_0)$. The seller has two choices at date 2. He can either produce an item q which the buyer accepts or he cannot deliver the item (or equivalently produce an item which will be refused). The buyer will accept as long as $B(q, a_1)-B_0(a_1)\geqslant P_1-P_0=P$ and so in the first case the seller will choose q to solve

$$\text{Min } C(q, a_2) \quad \text{subject to} \quad B(q, a_1)-B_0(a_1)\geqslant P. \tag{14}$$

Let $\bar{q}^s(a_1, a_2, P)$ denote a solution to this.[26] Then the seller will deliver an acceptable item if $P_1-C(\bar{q}^s(a_1, a_2, P), a_2)\geqslant P_0-C_0(a_2)$, that is if

$$C(\bar{q}^s(a_1, a_2, P), a_2)-C_0(a_2)\leqslant P. \tag{15}$$

When a_1, a_2 are chosen, each party can use (14) and (15) to compute his date 2 payoff as a function of the expected action of the other party and the contract P_0, P_1. The seller's profit is

$$\pi_2(a_1, a_2, P_0, P_1)=\text{Max}[P_1-C(\bar{q}^s(a_1, a_2, P), a_2), P_0-C_0(a_2)] \tag{16}$$

and the buyer's profit is

$$\pi_1(a_1\, a_2, P_0, P_1)=\begin{cases} B(\bar{q}^s(a_1, a_2, P), a_1)-P_1 & \text{if (15) holds}\\ B_0(a_1)-P_0 & \text{otherwise}\end{cases} \tag{17}$$

This defines a game at date 1 with strategies a_1, a_2 and payoffs π_1, π_2. We assume that, given P_0, P_1, the value of 'a' is chosen by each party simultaneously to form a Nash equilibrium $a_1(P_0, P_1)$, $a_2(P_0, P_1)$ of this game. We will say that (P_0, P_1) implements a_1, a_2 if there is a Nash equilibrium with $a_i(P_0, P_1)=a_i$ for $i=1, 2$. Let $\bar{u}$ represent the *ex-ante* opportunity of the buyer in his relationship with other sellers. An *ex-ante* contract (P_0, P_1) will be chosen to max $\pi_2(a_1, a_2, P_0, P_1)$ subject to $\pi_1(a_1, a_2, P_0, P_1)\geqslant\bar{u}$ and subject to the requirement that (P_0, P_1) implements a_1, a_2.

It simplifies matters to assume that there is a conflict of interest between the buyer and seller regarding the *ex-post* choice of q. In particular, we assume that $B(\ \ )$ and $-C(\ \ )$ are concave in q and that

$$B(q_1, a_1) > B(q_2, a_1) \text{ if and only if } C(q_1, a_2) > C(q_2, a_2) \tag{18}$$

for any pair (a_1, a_2). We also assume that

$$\text{Min}_q\ C(q, a_2) \text{ has a unique solution } \underline{q}, \text{ which is independent of } a_2, \tag{19}$$

$$\text{Max}_q\ B(q, a_1) \text{ has a unique solution } \bar{q}, \text{ which is independent of } a_1, \tag{20}$$

$$\text{Max}_{a_1}\ B_0(a_1) \text{ has a unique solution } \underline{a}_1, \tag{21}$$

$$\text{Min}_{a_2}\ C_0(a_2) \text{ has a unique solution } \underline{a}_2. \tag{22}$$

Here $\underline{q}$ is to be interpreted as 'minimum' (non-contractible) quality, $\bar{q}$ as 'maximum' (non-contractible) quality, $\underline{a}_1$ is the optimal level of reliance expenditure by the buyer if he is not going to accept the item and $\underline{a}_2$ is the optimal level of reliance expenditure by the seller if he is not going to deliver the item.

An immediate consequence of (15) and concavity is that either the constraint

$$B(q, a_1) - B_0(a_1) \geqslant P \tag{23}$$

is binding in (14) or $q = \underline{q}$. That is, either the buyer is indifferent between accepting the item and rejecting it or the seller chooses minimum quality. Consider first the case where (23) is binding at the optimal contract. Then the buyer's payoff given by (17) is

$$\pi_1(a_1, a_2, P_0, P_1) = B_0(a_1) - P_0. \tag{24}$$

Hence the buyer will choose a_1 to maximise $B_0(a_1)$, that is, $a_1 = \underline{a}_1$ (for if $a_1 \neq \underline{a}_1$, the buyer can do better by setting $a_1 = \underline{a}_1$ and rejecting the item whatever the seller's q response is). That is, if (23) is binding, the buyer obtains no benefit from *ex-ante* investment in excess of $\underline{a}_1$ since the seller's response is simply to reduce quality to keep (23) satisfied. As a result, the buyer will always act *ex-ante* as if he is going to reject the item. Of course, this means that the buyer's choice is inefficient with respect to the actual q; an efficient choice would maximise $B(q, a_1)$.

Consider next the case where (23) is not binding at the optimum. Now $q = \underline{q}$ and so if the item is transferred, the buyer's payoff is

$$\pi_1(a_1, a_2, P_0, P_1) = B(\underline{q}, a_1) - P_1. \tag{25}$$

Hence the buyer chooses a_1 to maximise $B(\underline{q}, a_1)$.[27] Thus the buyer's choice is efficient but only with respect to the worst possible characteristics. Finally, if the item is not transferred, the buyer sets $a_1 = \underline{a}_1$.

Note that in all cases the seller's choice is efficient, i.e. cost minimising, with respect to the actual q since if the seller delivers an acceptable item his payoff is

$$\pi_2 = P_1 - C(q, a_2) \tag{26}$$

and so he chooses a_2 to minimise $C(q, a_2)$; while if the item is not delivered or is rejected his payoff is $\pi_2 = P_0 - C_0(a_2)$, and so he chooses a_2 to minimise $C_0(a_2)$.

In the case where (23) is binding, and the item is transferred, the total surplus that the buyer and seller receive from their relationship is

$$B(q, \underline{a}_1) - \underset{a_2}{\text{Min}}\ C(q, a_2), \tag{27}$$

where q satisfies $B(q, \underline{a}_1) - B_0(\underline{a}_1) = P$. Since any q can be made a solution of this last equation if P is chosen appropriately, an optimal contract for this case yields total surplus

$$\begin{aligned}\alpha &= \underset{q}{\text{Max}}\{B(q, \underline{a}_1) - \underset{a_2}{\text{Min}} C(q, a_2)\}\\ &= \underset{q,a}{\text{Max}}\{B(q, \underline{a}_1) - C(q, a_2)\} = B(q^*, \underline{a}_1) - C(q^*, \hat{a}_2),^{28}\end{aligned} \tag{28}$$

where $\hat{a}_2$ minimises $c(q^*, a_2)$.

On the other hand, if (23) is not binding and $q = \underline{q}$, total surplus is

$$\begin{aligned}\beta &= \underset{a_1}{\text{Max}}\ B(q, a_1) - \underset{a_2}{\text{Min}}\ C(q, a_2) = \underset{a_1,a_2}{\text{Max}}\{B(\underline{q}, a_1) - C(\underline{q}, a_2)\}\\ &= B(\underline{q}, a_1') - C(\underline{q}, a_2').^{29}\end{aligned} \tag{29}$$

The third (uninteresting) possibility is that the two parties agree not to deliver the item at all, and receive surplus $B_0(\underline{a}_1) - C_0(\underline{a}_2)$. We rule this out by assuming that

$$\text{Max}\ (\alpha, \beta) \geqslant B_0(\underline{a}_1) - C_0(\underline{a}_2). \tag{30}$$

We have established

Proposition 7 Let q^* solve (28). Then if $\alpha \geqslant \beta$, an optimal contract under non-integration will involve an item with characteristics q^* being delivered, the buyer choosing $a_1 = \underline{a}_1$, the seller choosing an a_2 which minimises $C(q^*, a_2)$ and $P^* = B(q^*, \underline{a}_1) - B_0(\underline{a}_1)$. On the other hand, if $\alpha < \beta$, an optimal contract under non-integration will involve an item with characteristics $\underline{q}$ being delivered, the buyer and seller choosing a_1 and a_2 respectively to maximise $B(\underline{q}, a_1)$ and minimise $C(\underline{q}, a_1)$, and $\underline{P}$ satisfying (23).

In the case where it is optimal for the parties to write a contract in which an item of above minimum quality is delivered, the effect of non-contractible characteristics is clear. When the seller has control over q he chooses the q which extracts all the surplus from the buyer. This totally destroys the incentives of the buyer to make expenditures which will increase the benefits of having $\underline{q}$.[30,31,32]

Let the first best levels of q^F, a_1^F, a_2^F be defined by the solution to

$$\gamma = \underset{q, a_1, a_2}{\text{Max}}[B(q, a_1) - C(q, a_2)]. \tag{31}$$

These are the values which would be chosen if q could be specified in the contract. It is not necessary to include a_1 and a_2 in the contract, since each party will have the incentive to choose a_1 and a_2 correctly once q is fixed. In order to emphasise that a major problem with a contract which is silent about q is that it leads the buyer to engage in a less than optimal level of reliance expenditures, we note the following corollary.

Corollary 8 If $a_1 = \underline{a}_1$ maximises $B(q, a_1)$ for all q, then the non-integrated companies will achieve the first best outcome.

This corollary says that if the optimal level of reliance expenditure is independent of both q and whether the item is delivered, the first best can be achieved. Of course, this follows immediately from the fact that $\alpha = \gamma$ if $\underline{a}_1$ maximises $B(q, a_1)$.

The Costs and Benefits of Integration

Suppose the firms now integrate with the buyer having control. We assume that the downstream firm employs a manager to run the upstream firm. We suppose that integration does not create any new opportunities to monitor inputs of effort such as a_1 and a_2, nor does it lower the cost of specifying quality characteristics in the contract. The crucial difference introduced by integration is that the buyer as owner now has all the residual rights to control machines in the upstream firm. Thus since there is a missing provision about quality, it is the buyer who now has the right to choose q in his interest at date 2.

The owner of both firms will offer the manager of the upstream firm a contract at date 1. The contract specifies an incentive scheme for the manager via transfer prices. In particular, the owner agrees to pay the manager P_1 if the item is transferred and P_0 if it is not. At date 2 the owner will choose q and the manager can then decide whether to produce the item or not. After the contract is signed, the manager chooses a level of unobservable sunk costs a_2, and the owner chooses a_1. The contract stipulates that the manager must internalise all operating costs and benefits other than those specified by the contract.

Note that whereas under non-integration the seller chooses q at date 2 and the buyer takes it or leaves it, under integration the buyer chooses q at date 2 and the seller takes it or leaves it. That is, among other things, we assume that ownership gives one the power to move first. This is the same assumption as made in Section II and a justification for it may be found there.[33]

Since the buyer control case is the mirror image of the non-integration case, it is not necessary to provide a detailed analysis. It is clear that the optimal contract can be of two types. First, the prices P_0, P_1 may be such that the seller is indifferent between delivering the item and not at date 2, that is,

$$P_1 - C(q, a_2) = P_0 - C_0(a_2). \tag{32}$$

In this case the seller obtains no benefit from production and will choose a_2 to minimise $C_0(a_2)$, that is $a_2 = \underline{a}_2$. The buyer on the other hand will choose a_1 to maximise $B_1(q, a_1)$. That is, the buyer's *ex-ante* investment is efficient, but the seller's is highly inefficient. Since q can be set arbitrarily by an appropriate choice of P, maximised total surplus in this case is

$$\delta = \underset{q, a_1}{\text{Max}}\, [B(q, a_1) - C(q, \underline{a}_2)]. \tag{33}$$

The second case is where P_0, P_1 are such that

$$P_1 - C(q, a_2) > P_0 - C_0(a_2). \tag{34}$$

In this case, the buyer will choose q to maximise $B(q, a_1)$, that is $q=\bar{q}$ (maximum quality), while a_1 and a_2 will be chosen efficiently to maximise $B(\bar{q}, a_1)$ and to minimise $C(\bar{q}, a_2)$ respectively. Total surplus is

$$\varepsilon = \underset{a_1,a_2}{\text{Max}} \{B(\bar{q}, a_1) - C(\bar{q}, a_2)\}. \tag{35}$$

Assume

$$\text{Max}(\delta,\varepsilon) \geqslant B_0(\underline{a}_1) - C_0(\underline{a}_2). \tag{36}$$

Then we have, as a parallel to Proposition 7,

Proposition 9 Let q^{**} solve (33). The if $\delta \geqslant \varepsilon$, an optimal contract under integration will involve an item with characteristics q^{**} being delivered, the buyer choosing an a_1 which maximises $B(q^{**}, a_1)$, the seller choosing $a_2 = \underline{a}_2$ and $P^{**} = C(q^{**}, \underline{a}_2) - C_0(\underline{a}_2)$. on the other hand $\delta < \varepsilon$, an optimal contract under integration will involve an item with characteristics $\bar{q}$ being delivered, the buyer and seller choosing a_1 and a_2 respectively to maximise $B(\bar{q}, a_1)$ and minimise $C(\bar{q}, a_1)$, and $\bar{P}$ satisfying (34).

We also have, as a parallel to Corollary 8,

Corollary 10 If $a_2 = \underline{a}_2$ minimises $C(q, \underline{a}_2)$ for all q, then the integrated companies will achieve the first best outcome.

Propositions 7 and 9 allow us to predict when it will be in the interest of the firms to integrate. Recall that $q = (q_0, q_1)$, where q_0 are the characteristics that can be included in the contract and q_1 are the characteristics that cannot be. Consider the case where many of the 'important' characteristics affecting both benefits and costs are contained in q_1. Then the choice of either $\underline{q}$ or $\bar{q}$ is likely to be very inefficient, that is, $\alpha > \beta$ and $\delta > \varepsilon$, and so integration should occur if and only if

$$\underset{q,a_2}{\text{Max}}\{B(q,\underline{a}_1) - C(q, a_2)\} < \underset{q,a_1}{\text{Max}} \{B(q, a_1) - C(q, \underline{a}_2)\}. \tag{37}$$

Inequality (34) states that integration is desirable when the residual rights of control are more efficiently used by the owner of the downstream firm. The tradeoff is that without integration the downstream firm gets no *ex-post* benefits from sunk expenditures which rely on the product to be delivered by the upstream firm, and this distorts its incentives to make the expenditures. On the other hand if the downstream firm owns the upstream firm then the manager of the upstream firm loses his residual rights of control and this reduces the *ex-post* benefits he can get from *ex-ante* investments which rely on the income to be received from the downstream firm. Hence integration will not occur when the reliance investments of the manager of the upstream firm are more important than the reliance expenditures of the manager of the downstream firm.

It is interesting to note that the crucial issue in this case is not the distortion in q, but rather the distortion in the a_i. There will be many cases where a particular q, say $q=q_H$, is very valuable relative to its costs. In these cases P^* and P^{**} will be chosen so that whether or not there is integration, q_H is produced. However, the costs and benefits from this q will depend on who possesses the residual rights of control. When the upstream firm has ownership of the assets which produce q, it will make large reliance expenditures so that q_H is produce at low cost, while the downstream firm will make small reliance expenditures so that q_H will be received with low benefits. The reverse occurs under integration.

Equation (37) is relevant for the case where many of the important characteristics are non-contractible. Suppose, on the other hand, that the most important aspects of quality affecting both benefits and costs are contained in q_0 and hence can be contracted for. It may still be the case that the missing characteristics q_1 are important primarily to one party. For example, q_1 can represent 'early delivery'. Early delivery may have negligible benefits for the buyer, but enormous costs for the seller. For example, assume that $B(q, a_1)=B_1(q_0, a_1)+\varepsilon B_2(q_0, q_1, a_1)$ and $C(q, a_2)=C_1(q_0, a_2)+C_2(q_0, q_1, a_2)$, where ε is small, that is the missing characteristics are relatively important to the seller. Then under non-integration an approximately first-best efficient outcome can be achieved by writing a contract which produces low non-contractible quality, but which is very cost effective:

$$P_0(q_0) = -\infty \qquad \text{if } q_0 \neq q_0^*$$

$$\begin{aligned} &P_0(q_0^*), P_1(q_0^*) \text{ satisfy } B_1(q_0^*, a_1^*) - B_0(a_1^*) \\ &\quad > P_1(q_0^*) - P_0(q_0^*) > C(q_0^*, q_1^*, a_2^*) - C_0(a_2^*), \end{aligned} \tag{38}$$

where $a_1^*, a_2^*, q_0^*, q_1^*$ solve: $\underset{a_1,a_2,q_0,q_1}{\text{Maximise}}\ B_1(q_0, q_1) - C(q_0, q_1, a_2)$.

With such a contract, the seller will choose $q_0 = q_0^*$, the item will be transferred, and both buyer and seller will select the efficient levels of reliance, a_1^*, a_2^*. The fact that the seller chooses the missing characteristics q_1^* to minimise $C_2(q_0^*, q_1, a_2^*)$, without regard to the buyer's benefits, is unimportant when ε is small.

Exactly the opposite conclusion is reached if $B = B_1(q_0, a_1) + B_2(q_0, q_1, a_1)$ and $C = C_1(q_0, a_2) + \eta C_2(q_0, q_1, a_2)$, where η is small, that is, the missing characteristics are relatively important to the buyer. Now it is efficient for the buyer to control q_1, and so integration is superior to non-integration. For example, if changing the colour of the final product has a very small cost to the seller but a very high benefit to the buyer then the existence of missing provisions about this characteristic will create benefits from integration.

IV SUMMARY AND CONCLUSIONS

When two parties enter into a relationship in which assets are going to be used to generate income, the parties can, in principle, contractually specify exactly who will have control over each dimension of each asset in each particular future contingency. We have argued that there is often a low cost alternative to contracts which allocate all specific rights of control. In particular, when it is too costly for one party to specify a long list of the particular rights it desires over another party's machines, then it may be optimal to purchase all rights except those specifically mentioned in the contract. Ownership is the purchase of these residual rights of control. Vertical integration is the purchase of the assets of a supplier (or of a purchaser), for the purpose of acquiring the residual rights of control.

The literature on transactions costs has emphasised that incomplete contracts can cause a non-integrated relationship to yield outcomes which are inferior to what would have been achieved with complete contracts. It is implicitly assumed that integration yields the outcome which would have arisen under complete contracts. We argue that the relevant comparison is not between the non-integrated outcome and the complete contract outcome, but instead between a contract which allocates residual rights to one party rather than to another. Residual rights have value to both parties so when the buyer owns the seller, the manager of the buyer's subsidiary loses residual rights relative to what he would have in the non-integrated situation. The negative efficiency consequences of the loss of residual rights by one party must be weighed against whatever benefits are generated when those rights are given to the other party.

We have presented two models which analyse the implications of different assignments of residual rights. The first model, in Section II, considered situations in which it is too costly to write a contract which specifies how the quantity and price of a product to be delivered must vary with the state of nature which determines the seller's cost function and the buyer's benefit function. All forms of organisation will lead to *ex-post* inefficient allocations, but of different kinds. Under non-integration, the level of trade between the buyer and seller will be too low. The reason is that since the seller can choose how much to deliver to the buyer, and the buyer can choose how much to accept from the seller ('voluntary trade'), there will be some trades which should take place, that is, which increase buyer and seller surplus, but which do not because they decrease one party's private surplus. This problem arises because the *ex-ante* contract does not specify price as a function of the state of nature. We assumed that integration with buyer control gives the buyer the power to choose how the seller divides his supplies between this buyer and other customers. We assumed that there is a managerial incentive scheme in the form of transfer prices, and that integration does not permit transfer prices to be any more sensitive to the state of nature than is the case without integration. The benefits of buyer control are that it gives the buyer an assured source of supply, but the costs are that the level of trade will be insensitive to the outside value of the seller's product R, since the transfer price is not conditioned on R. Seller control, on the other hand, has the advantage of giving the seller an assured source of demand, but the disadvantage that the level of trade will be insensitive to the buyer's value from purchasing elsewhere s, since the transfer price is not conditioned on s. The optimal form of organisation will depend on the probability distribution of s and R. We showed that (under the assumption that s and R are independent) if the variation in s (resp. R) is large relative to that in R (or s), buyer control (resp. seller control) is optimal, while if the variation of both s and R is large (in an appropriate sense), non-integration is optimal.

In Section III we considered a second model in which there are missing provisions about some aspect of the quality of the good to be delivered, rather than about exogenous states of nature. Examples include a contract to purchase a horse in which the seller tries to deliver a horse blind in one eye, or the purchase of specialised computer software where it is difficult to specify in advance the performance characteristics desired. When there are missing quality provisions, we argued that the principal distortion is with respect to the *ex-ante* reliance expenditures chosen by the buyer and seller. Given that the contract price or transfer price cannot be made a function of all aspects of quality, the owner has the right and power to control the missing aspects of quality so as to extract as much surplus from the non-owner as possible. This involves a choice of quality level which is best for the owner subject to the contractually given delivery prices. We showed that under non-integration the seller will choose product quality in period 2 in such a way as to reduce the buyer's incentive to make reliance expenditures in period 1, relative to the complete contracting solution. On the other hand, under integration with buyer control, the buyer chooses the quality level in period 2 in such a way as to reduce the seller's incentive to make period 1 reliance expenditures. Integration is superior to non-integration whenever the distortion associated with the seller's inappropriate reliance expenditures is less than that associated with the buyer's inappropriate reliance expenditures.

It is worthwhile to explain which of the assumptions of the 'Coase Theorem' we drop in order to get the conclusion that the distribution of ownership rights has efficiency consequences. The model in Section II did not permit *ex-post* bargaining of the type suggested in Coase (1960), so the allocation of property rights, that is, residual rights of control had efficiency consequences. However, the model of Section III is consistent with allocations which are always *ex-post* efficient, but the *ex-ante* efficiency of the relationship between the two parties will depend on how residual rights of control are allocated. The impossibility of *ex-ante* bargaining over all aspects of the product to be delivered, that is, the incompleteness of the contract, is the source of our conclusion that the distribution of property rights has efficiency consequences.

We have developed models to illustrate the idea that ownership allocates residual rights of control in situations where contracts contain missing provisions. We have emphasised the symmetry of control, namely that when residual rights are purchased by one party they are lost by a second party, and this inevitably creates distortions. That is, integration shifts the incentives for opportunistic and distortionary behaviour, it does not remove these incentives.

APPENDIX

Proof of Proposition 3 If s, R are uniform, we have

$$\hat{W}_{BC}=\int_{s>R^*}(s-R^*)g(s)\mathrm{d}s=\begin{cases}\int_{\max(R^*,\underline{s})}^{\bar{s}}(s-R^*)\dfrac{1}{(\bar{s}-\underline{s})}\mathrm{d}s & \text{if } \bar{s}>R^* \\ 0 & \text{otherwise}\end{cases}$$

$$=\begin{cases}\dfrac{1}{2}\left(\dfrac{1}{\bar{s}-\underline{s}}\right)(\bar{s}-R^*)^2 & \text{if } \bar{s}>R^*\geqslant\underline{s} \\ s^*-R^* & \text{if } \underline{s}>R^* \\ 0 & \text{otherwise.}\end{cases} \tag{1.A}$$

Similarly

$$\hat{W}_{SC}=\begin{cases}\dfrac{1}{2}\left(\dfrac{1}{\bar{R}-\underline{R}}\right)(s^*-\underline{R})^2 & \text{if } \bar{R}\geqslant s^*>\underline{R} \\ s^*-R^* & \text{if } s^*>\bar{R} \\ 0 & \text{otherwise.}\end{cases} \tag{2.A}$$

On the other hand, the first order condition (12) simplifies to

$$\int_k^{\bar{s}}(s-k)\mathrm{d}s=\int_{\underline{R}}^k(k-R)\mathrm{d}R, \tag{3.A}$$

which yields

$$k=\frac{\bar{s}+\underline{R}}{2}. \tag{4.A}$$

If, however, this exceeds (resp. falls short of) $\bar{R}$ (resp. $\underline{s}$), we have a corner solution $k=\bar{R}$ (or $k=\underline{s}$). Substituting (4.A) into (3), we obtain

$$W_{NI}=\frac{1}{(\bar{s}-\underline{s})}\cdot\frac{1}{(\bar{R}-\underline{R})}\cdot\left(\frac{\bar{s}-\underline{R}}{2}\right)^3, \tag{5.A}$$

as long as the solution is an interior one.

Consider case (B) of Proposition 3. It is not difficult to check that

$\hat{W}_{SC}$ strictly exceeds both $\hat{W}_{BC}$ and the right-hand side of (5.A). Furthermore if $(\bar{s}+\underline{R}/2)<\underline{s}$, so that we have a corner solution $k=\underline{s}$,

$$\begin{aligned}\hat{W}_{NI} &= E[\tilde{s}-\tilde{R}\,|\,R<\underline{s}]\text{Prob}[\tilde{R}<\underline{s}] < \underset{k}{\text{Max}}\ E[\tilde{s}-\tilde{R}\,|\,\tilde{R}<k]\text{Prob}[\tilde{R}<k] \\ &= E[s^*-\tilde{R}\,|\,\tilde{R}<s^*]\text{Prob}[\tilde{R}<s^*] \\ &= \hat{W}_{SC}. \end{aligned} \tag{6.A}$$

This proves that seller control is optimal in Case A. The other cases follow similarly. Q.E.D.

Proof of Proposition 4 Consider Part (1). We show first that non-integration is suboptimal. Consider the first-order condition (12). If we replace h by h_λ, this becomes

$$\frac{1}{g(k)} \int_k^{\bar{s}} (s-k)g(s)\mathrm{d}s = \frac{1}{h\left(\dfrac{k-(1-\lambda)R^*}{\lambda}\right)} \int_{\lambda \underline{R}(1-\lambda)R^*}^{k} (k-R)h\left(\frac{R-(1-\lambda)R^*}{\lambda}\right)\mathrm{d}R. \tag{7.A}$$

Let $\lambda \to 0$. Then support of R, $[\lambda\underline{R}+(1-\lambda)R^*,\ \lambda\bar{R}+(1-\lambda)R^*]$ converges to R^* and hence, since k lies in this support, $k \to R^*$. On the other hand, $(k-(1-\lambda)R^*)/\lambda$ lies in $[\underline{R}, \bar{R}]$ and so $h((k-(1-\lambda)R^*)/\lambda)$ is bounded away from zero. It follows that the right-hand side of (7.A) tends to zero. Therefore (7.A) cannot be satisfied for sufficiently small λ, and so the solution of (7.A) must be at a corner $k=\lambda\underline{R}+(1-\lambda)R^*$ or $\bar{s}$. In the first case, however, $\hat{W}_{NI}=W_{BC}(\lambda\underline{R}+(1-\lambda)R^*)<W_{BC}(R^*)$, while in the second case, $\hat{W}_{NI}=W_{SC}(\bar{s})<W_{SC}(s^*)$. So in both cases, non-integration is suboptimal.

It remains to show that buyer control is better than seller control. The former (with k chosen optimally at R^*) yields a production region $s>R^*$, while the latter (with k chosen optimally at s^*) yields a production region $R<s^*$. In the limit where $R=R^*$ with certainty, the first production region equals the first-best one, whereas the second production region is either empty or includes all points (s, R). In both cases, buyer control is superior to seller control.

Part (2) follows similarly. Q.E.D.

ACKNOWLEDGEMENTS

Research supported by the National Science Foundation, and the Alfred P. Sloan Foundation. We gratefully acknowledge helpful comments from Debra Aron, Richard Epstein, and Toni Zabalza.

NOTES

1. See also Teece (1980), Williamson (1971), Williamson (1983), Williamson *et al.* (1975).
2. Coase is quite specific about the benefit of integration: it creates a master–servant relationship out of what otherwise would have been a buyer–contractor relationship. This seems more a theory of the ownership of people than of assets. If we assume that an employee is as self-interested as an outside contractor, it is unclear what the difference between a master–servant relationship and a buyer–contractor relationship is unless some new reward structure becomes feasible.
3. See Evans and Grossman (1983) for an elaboration of the above critique of the transactions cost based arguments for integration.
4. Coase states that size of the firm is limited by the managerial capacity of the single owner to manage many activities. As noted in the text, this is unconvincing, since the owner could always hire another manager. The other authors do not give any clear statement as to what limits the size of the firm, but appear to accept Coase's view that integration transforms a hostile supplier into a docile employee, and thus the contracting problems associated with independent ownership are greatly diminished. (However, there are some references to increased bureaucracy, and its associated cost. See Keren and Levhari (1983), Rosen (1982), Williamson (1967) and Waldman (1984) for specific models of how the number of people involved in production affect the overall cost of production. None of these papers makes any distinction between the activities carried out via contract to separate owners, and the activities carried out in a single ownership unit. That is, the theories are equally valid descriptions of how a firm can use hierarchies of outside contractors, as they are theories of employment within the firm.)
5. Richard Posner, whose opinion on the legal definition of ownership we solicited, has referred us to the following statement by O. W. Holmes (1881):

   > But what are the rights of ownership? They are substantially the same as those incident to possession. Within the limits prescribed by policy, the owner is allowed to exercise his natural powers over the subject-matter uninterfered with, and is more less protected in excluding other people from such interference. The owner is allowed to exclude all, and is accountable to no one but him. O. W. Holmes, Jr., *The Common Law* 246 (1881).

6. See Chandler (1977, p. 54).
7. Arrow (1975) has analysed the benefits of vertical integration based upon the assumption that without integration it is more costly for one firm to communicate information to another than with integration. We do not see why any new method of communication becomes feasible under integration. The incentives of people to lie may change if their incentive structure changes, but Arrow does not explain how integration changes the set of feasible incentive structures.
8. Williamson (1983) gives an example (pp. 523–4) of a contract written between non-integrated firms where there is no penalty for cancellation. He assumes that under vertical integration, or via the use of hostages, it is possible to extract a penalty from the buyer when she fails to take delivery of the seller's product. To the extent that there are artificial legal barriers to cancellation penalties, the same effect can be achieved by the deposit of a large lump sum payment at the time the contract is signed which will only be partially paid back to the buyer if she refuses to take delivery.
9. That is, an optimal contract is the solution to what is now a standard mechanism design problem; see Myerson (1979).
10. Holmstrom (1982) has emphasised the importance of third parties in principal–multiagent problems. Under the assumption of risk neutrality, he shows that the presence of a third party can lead to the achievement of the first-best.
11. We model the relationship as a 'once and for all' event. To the extent that there will be a long-term relationship, the incentives for vertical integration may be different from those we have given here. See Telser (1981) and Kreps (1984) for the role of reputation in long term relationships as an enforcement device, and Williamson (1979) for arguments on the role of repetitive idiosyncratic purchases in providing a cost to non-vertical integration. None of these papers deals with the role of the ownership of assets and reputation. To the extent that reputation helps mimic the outcome of a complete contract, it would seem to have no implication for the ownership of residual rights of control.
12. This justification for the impossibility of contingent contracts may be found in Meade (1971, p. 1983). See also Weitzman (1981).
13. The assumption that s and r are not publicly observable means that these variables should be interpreted as the benefit and cost accruing to the managers of the downstream and upstream firms rather than to the shareholders in the form of (presumably observable) profit. That is, we are implicitly assuming that there is a principal–agent relationship between the owners and managers of the upstream and downstream firms. In fact, in what follows, we shall ignore the shareholders and identify firms and managers completely. Note that the assumption that s and r are not observable implies that contracts of the form 'the upstream firm's manager is paid the benefit of the downstream firm' are infeasible.
14. For reasons given in Section 1c of the introduction we are excluding contracts which involve the exchange of messages at date 2 or renegotiation of p_0, P_1 once s and R are realised. We also choose not to introduce a

(risk neutral) third party to the contract. The introduction of a third party would allow the payment made by the buyer, P_q, and the payment received by the seller P'_q to differ, with the third party making up the difference. The numbers P_0, P_1, P'_0, P'_1 must be chosen so that the third party breaks even in expected terms. Such a richer class of contracts obviously allows the buyer and seller to do better. At first sight there seems no reason why a third party should not be prepared to sign such a contract given that q is publicly observable. Suppose, however, that q is only publicly observable *if the buyer or seller want it to be*. That is, imagine that the buyer and seller together have the ability to make it look as if a different q from the true one occurred through the falsification or destruction of evidence, etc. Suppose also that the buyer and seller can make (enforceable) sidepayments unbeknown to the third party contingent on such falsification or destruction (these might take place through very complicated channels, for example, buyer and seller subsidiaries). Then a third-party contract will always be subverted, since, whatever q_j is actually chosen, the buyer and seller will agree to pretend that q_i occurred, where q_i maximises the third party's net payment $(P'_i - P_i)$. Given this, the third party will only sign the contract if $P'_j - P_j = P'_i - P_i$. In view of the zero expected profit constraint, this in turn implies that $P'_i = P_i$, $P'_j = P_j$, that is, the third party is irrelevant.

So the possibility of financial involvement by a third party can be ruled out if we assume that q is publicly observable only when the buyer or seller want it to be (this is what we meant by publicly observable subject to a qualification). Note that this does not affect the enforceability of the original two party contract as long as the buyer and seller each by itself has sufficient evidence to establish that the true q did in fact occur.

15. Throughout this section, we characterise the *ex-ante* optimal contract in terms of $k \equiv P_1 - P_0$. We assume that at the date when the contract is signed, there are competitive conditions on each side of the market which determine how the parties split the *ex-ante* surplus from the relationship, that is, which determine P_1 or P_0 from k.
16. The notion of voluntary trade at predetermined prices used here also bears a resemblance to that found in the rationing literature; see, for example, Younes (1984).
17. In the case where the owner can simply prevent the seller from selling to other buyers, we need to assume also that $k \geqslant 0$ in order to ensure that the seller prefers to supply this buyer rather than no one at all. Under our assumptions this constraint is never binding and so we ignore it.
18. We are assuming that the buyer cannot resell the seller's supply at price R. This is consistent with the idea that R is a payoff specific to the manager of the upstream firm (see note 13). One can imagine that the upstream firm's manager has invested time in finding out who the outside customers with the highest willingnesses to pay are, and this information is not available to the downstream firm.
19. In the case where the owner can simply prevent the buyer from buying from other sellers, we have to append the constraint that the buyer prefers to purchase from this seller than from no one at all, that is, in

terms of (1), $s_1 \geqslant k$. In what follows we assume this constraint is never binding.

20. A comparison of the solutions to (5) and (7) may also be found in Weitzman (1981).
21. See Weitzman for a similar result.
22. The fact that a party can get no *ex-post* surplus distorts *ex-ante* investments, or reliance expenditures, because there is some aspect of unobservability associated with them. For example, a manager's effort devoted to organising a plant, or finding the appropriate employees, machinery, etc. may not be observable. If all these expenditures were observable then each party could be reimbursed *ex-ante* for its reliance expenditures and there would be no distortions caused by the allocation of the *ex-post* rents.
23. We continue to rule out a third party to the contract.
24. It may seem odd to assume that the seller does not incur date 2 costs if the item is rejected. We have in mind a situation where the seller can select q, and the buyer can make his decision whether to accept or reject the item, before date 2 costs are sunk.
25. We assume that a_1, a_2, q lie respectively in sets A_1, A_2, φ, which are compact subsets of some finite dimensional Euclidean space, and that φ is convex. Also the functions B, B_0, C, C_0 are assumed to be non-negative and continuous in their respective arguments.
26. If a solution does not exist, we set $C = \infty$.
27. To be precise, suppose a_1 does not maximise $B(\underline{q}, a_1)$. Let the buyer switch to $\hat{a}_1$ which is a maximiser and assume that the seller responds by choosing $\hat{q}$. Then the buyer will be better off since $B(\hat{q}, \hat{a}_1) \geqslant B(\underline{q}, \hat{a}_1) > B(\underline{q}, a_1)$ where the first inequality follows from (18) and (19).
28. To sustain $(q^*, \underline{a}_1, \hat{a}_2)$ as an equilibrium, we set $P = B(q^*, \underline{a}_1) - B_0(\underline{a}_1)$. As long as α exceeds the surplus from no production, $B_0(\underline{a}_1) - C_0(\underline{a}_2)$, we have $P > C(q^*, \hat{a}_2) - C_0(\underline{a}_2)$. Hence, given $a_1 = \underline{a}_1$, the seller will find it in his interest to choose $\hat{a}_2$ and produce an item of quality q^*. Suppose the buyer chooses $a_1 \neq \underline{a}_1$. If the seller keeps the buyer indifferent between accepting and rejecting the item, the buyer's net benefit $B_0(a_1) - P_0$ cannot increase. If, on the other hand, the seller switches to minimum quality, the buyer's net benefit will not increase as long as $B(\underline{q}, a_1) \leqslant B(q^*, \underline{a}_1)$. This inequality holds for all a_1 as long as α exceeds the surplus from production of an item of minimum quality, defined as β in (26) below. This argument shows that as long as $\alpha > \text{Max}(\beta, B_0(\underline{a}_1) - C_0(\underline{a}_2))$, then $(q^*, \underline{a}_1, \hat{a}_2)$ can be sustained as an equilibrium (note that it is only under these conditions that it is desirable to sustain $(q^*, \underline{a}_1, \hat{a}_2)$ as an equilibrium).
29. To sustain (q, a_1', a_2') as an equilibrium, set $P = B(\underline{q}, a_1') - B_0(\underline{a}_1)$. Then $B(\underline{q}, a_1') - B_0(a_1') \geqslant P$ and so, given a_1', the buyer will accept an item of quality $\underline{q}$. As long as β exceeds $B_0(\underline{a}_1) - C_0(\underline{a}_2)$ (which is the only interesting case), $P \geqslant C(\underline{q}, a_2') - C_0(\underline{a}_2) \geqslant C(\underline{q}, a_2') - C_0(a_2')$ and so the seller will be prepared to deliver an item of quality $\underline{q}$ and will choose $a_2 = a_2'$. If the buyer chooses $a_1 \neq a_1'$, either he will continue to get quality $\underline{q}$, in which case his payoff $B(\underline{q}, a_1) - P_1$ falls or the seller will make him indifferent between accepting and rejecting the item in which case his payoff again falls since

it equals $B_0(a_1) - P_0 \leqslant B_0(\underline{a}_1) - P_0 = B(\underline{q}, a_1') - P_1$. This argument shows that as long as $\beta > B_0(\underline{a}_1) - C_0(\underline{a}_2)$, $(\underline{q}, a_1', a_2')$ can be sustained as an equilibrium.

30. The conclusion that it is impossible to achieve both efficient quality and efficient *ex-ante* expenditure turns out to be sensitive to our assumption that the item is indivisible. If the item is continuously divisible, it can be shown that first-best quality and investment levels can be sustained under non-integration, basically because the quantity of the item transferred can be used as an extra variable to 'screen' for appropriate q's and a's. If, however, the model is complicated to allow for the possibility that quantity itself is an important choice variable – in particular if the efficient quantity of the item varies due to some randomness in benefit or cost functions – then the first-best can no longer be achieved (quantity's screening role will now conflict with its resource allocation role). Since under these conditions our basic conclusions are unlikely to be changed substantially, we feel justified in analysing the simpler indivisible, non-random case.

31. The result that the conflict over the division of surplus at date 2 can lead to a distortion in investment at date 1 is similar to the finding of Crawford (1982) Grout (1986) and others. In Crawford's and Grout's models, however, investment expenditure is observable, there is no quality problem, and the inefficiency in *ex-ante* investment results from the assumed impossibility of writing binding contracts. Shavell (1980), in a slightly different setting, also shows that there may be a conflict between *ex-ante* and *ex-post* efficiency. As he recognises, however, in his model the result is only true when attention is restricted to a limited class of contracts.

32. We have argued that q is too complex to be included in the date 1 contract. In many situations, however, those characters of q which actually turn out to be relevant at date 2 may be simple to describe. For instance, consider the example of the computer manufacturer mentioned earlier who knows *ex-post* what characteristics some component should have, but cannot describe these *ex-ante*. Once date 2 arrives, there is an obvious reason for the two parties to renegotiate the contract, for example, the computer manufacturer can offer the component manufacturer an extra amount to produce the desired characteristics. As in Section II, we rule out such recontracting on the grounds that there may not be enough time to write a new enforceable contract between the date when the information about the relevant characteristics of q becomes available and the date when the production decision must be made.

33. In contrast to Section II, integration with seller control is not an interesting organisational form. This is because the seller already controls all the missing provisions q under non-integration, and so seller control and non-integration are the same things. Note that this equivalence no longer holds if we allow the seller to affect the buyer's willingness to pay for his input in some other way than via q, for example, as in Section II, through control of the buyer's alternative sources of supply.

REFERENCES

Arrow, K. J. (1975) 'Vertical Integration and Communication', *Bell J. of Econ.*, vol. 6, no. 1 (Spring) pp. 173–83.

Coase, R. H. (1952) 'The Nature of the Firm', *Economica* n.s. 4, (1937): 386–405; reprinted in George J. Stigler and Kenneth E. Boulding (eds), *Readings in Price Theory* (Homewood, ILL.: Richard D. Irwin, Inc.).

Coase, R. H. (1960) 'The Problem of Social Cost', *Journal of Law and Economics*, vol. 3, (October), pp. 1–44.

Chandler, A. Jr. (1977) *The Visible Hand* (Harvard University Press).

Crawford, V. (1982) 'Long-Term Relationships Governed by Short-Term Contracts', ICERD DP, LSE.

Evans, D. and S. Grossman (1983) 'Integration', in David Evans (ed.), *Breaking Up Bell, Essays in Industrial Organization and Regulation* (New York: North-Holland Publishing Co.) pp. 95–126.

Goldberg, V. P. and J. E. Erickson (1982) 'Long-Term Contracts for Petroleum Coke', Department of Economics Working Paper Series No. 206, University of California, Davis (September).

Grout, P. (1986) 'Investment and Wages in the Absence of Binding Contracts: A Nash Bargaining Approach', *Econometrica*, Forthcoming.

Hall, R. and E. Lazear (1984) 'The Excess Sensitivity of Layoffs and Quits to Demand', *J. of Labor Economics*, vol. 2, no. 2 (April).

Holmes, O. W. (1881) The Common Law 246.

Holmstrom, B. (1982) 'Moral Hazard in Teams', *Bell J. of Econ.*, vol. 13, no. 2 (Autumn).

Keren, M. and D. Levhari (1983) 'The Internal Organization of the Firm and the Shape of Average Costs', *Bell Journal of Econ.*, vol. 14, no. 2 (Autumn), pp. 474–86.

Klein, B. (1980) 'Transaction Cost Determinants of "Unfair" Contractual Determinants', *American Economic Review*, vol. 70 (May) pp. 356–62.

Klein, B., R. A. Crawford and A. A. Alchian (1978). 'Vertical Integration, Appropriable Rents, and the Competitive Contracting Process', *Journal of Law and Economics*, vol. 21 (Oct.) pp. 297–326.

Kreps, D. (1984) 'Uncertain Contingencies, Hierarchical Transactions and the Theory of the Firm', unpublished mimeo.

Meade, J. (1971) *The Controlled Economy* (London: G. Allen & Unwin). 381 pp.

Myerson, R. B. (1979) 'Incentive Compatibility and the Bargaining Problem', *Econometrica*, vol. 47, pp. 61–73.

Rosen, S. (1982) 'Authority, Control, and the Distribution of Earnings', *Bell J. of Econ.*, vol. 13, no. 2 (Autumn) pp. 311–23.

Shavell, S. (1980) 'Damage Measures for Breach of Contracts', *Bell J. of Econ.*, vol. 11 (Autumn) pp. 446–90.

Teece, D. J. (1980) 'Economics of Scope and the Scope of the Enterprise', *Journal of Economic Behaviour and Organization*, vol. 1 (September), pp. 223–45.

Telser, L. G. (1981) 'A Theory of Self-Enforcing Agreements', *Journal of Business*, vol. 53 (February) pp. 27–44.

Waldman, M. (1984) 'Worker Allocation, Hierarchies and the Wage Distribution', *Review of Economic Studies*, vol. 51 (January) pp. 95–109.
Weitzman, M. (1981) 'Toward A Theory of Contract Types', mimeo (May).
Williamson, O. E. (1967) 'Hierarchical Control and Optimum Firm Size', *Journal of Political Economy*, vol. 75 (April) pp. 123–38.
Williamson, O. E. (1971) 'The Vertical Integration of Production: Market Failure Considerations', *American Economic Review*, vol. 61 (May) pp. 112–23.
Williamson, O., M. Wachter and J. Harris (1975) 'Understanding the Employment Relation: The Analysis of Idiosyncratic Exchange', *Bell J. of Econ*. (Spring) pp. 250–80.
Williamson, O. E. (1979) 'The Transaction-Cost Economics: The Governance of Contractual Relations', *Journal of Law and Economics*, vol. 22 (October) pp. 233–61.
Williamson, O. E. (1983) 'Credible Commitments: Using Hostages to Support Exchange', *American Economic Review*, vol. 83, no. 4 (September) pp. 519–40.
Younes, Y. (1984) 'Implementation of Plans or Contracts and Equilibria with Rationing', CARESS working paper, mimeo (February).

Comments on Sanford J. Grossman and Oliver Hart, 'Vertical Integration and the Distribution of Property Rights' by Yair Tauman

The effect of integration is studied in this paper via a simple model of a buyer and a seller of an input. The advantage of a trade between the two depends on the state of nature. However, contracts which are contingent on the state of nature are either very complicated and hence very costly or cannot be verified by a third party since they are not observable. Thus binding contracts are restricted to the following form: the buyer will pay P_1 if he is delivered one unit of input ($q=1$) by the seller, or, the buyer will pay P_0 if $q=0$.

Three types of such contracts are examined. The non-integration contract assumes a voluntary trade. The Buyer Control contract offers the buyer a full control on the residual rights (which are not specified in the contract). The third contract offers the seller the full control on the residual rights.

The authors wish to characterise when each of these contracts is optimal. The state of nature is represented by the pair of random variables (R, s) where R is the opportunity cost per unit which the seller bears in supplying the buyer and s is the monetary benefit which the buyer receives from the trade.

Under the assumptions that both the buyer and the seller are risk neutral, R and s are statistically independent and (R, s) is uniformly distributed on a finite rectangular, a characterisation for the optimal contract is provided. Some study is included for the case where R and s are possibly correlated, but no characterisation is offered in this case.

I found the paper to be interesting and potentially important mainly because it supplies a simple model where costs and benefits of integration are well defined and therefore can be analysed. This allows, for example, the explanation of how integration could be strictly worse than non-integration and shed a new light on the theory of vertical integration.

On the other hand, the paper is very restrictive by its strong assumptions. Only extreme contracts are allowed in which either there is no integration at all or, otherwise, all residual rights are controlled by one party. It is much more interesting, in my view, to deal with contracts which allow a sharing of control between the buyer and the seller. This will enable the parties a strategic behaviour within the framework of cooperative games. A contract should perhaps be regarded as an agreement to restrict the strategy sets of the two players in a specific way. Sometimes these restrictions can result in a Pareto-optimal outcome. Thus, while binding agreements do exist in this game (which make it a cooperative game) a strategic game is played first to determine the exact sharing of control. It would then be interesting to see when an extreme contract, like the three suggested in the paper, results. It is true that such a game may result in some inefficiencies, but it is otherwise difficult to justify how the parties derive at an optimal contract.

Also, it is not clear to me how the buyer and the seller select the two prices P_0 and P_1 from the optimal contract k. None of them will agree to sign a contract without an agreement of the value of these two parameters. Thus, a contract should be an outcome of a bargaining procedure which selects the optimal k together with P_0 and P_1 (where $k = P_1 - P_0$). If, however, at the date when the contract is signed there exists a competitive market which determines P_0 and P_1, why is the number k not determined by the market?

To summarise, the paper offers a new approach for the assessment of costs and benefits of integration. However, the theory developed in this paper is very preliminary. Even the characterisation for the optimal contract within the narrow class of contracts is offered only in a very special case where R and s are independent and are uniformly distributed. Thus the paper provides tools but only little theory.

Author Index